Shaping Archaeological Archives

ARCHIVE ARCHAEOLOGY

General Editor
Professor Rubina Raja, *Aarhus Universitet*

Advisory Board
Professor Jennifer Baird, *Birkbeck, University of London*
Dr Olympia Bobou, *Aarhus Universitet*
Dr Lisa R. Brody, *Yale University Art Gallery*
Dr Jon Frey, *Michigan State University*
Professor Christopher Hallett, *University of California, Berkeley*
Dr Fotini Kondyli, *University of Virginia*

VOLUME 4

Previously published volumes in this series are listed at the back of the book.

Shaping Archaeological Archives

Dialogues between Fieldwork, Museum Collections, and Private Archives

Edited by
Rubina Raja

BREPOLS

British Library Cataloguing in Publication Data

A catalogue record for this book is available from the British Library.

© 2023, Brepols Publishers n.v., Turnhout, Belgium

All rights reserved. No part of this publication may be reproduced, stored in a retrieval system, or transmitted, in any form or by any means, electronic, mechanical, photocopying, recording, or otherwise, without the prior permission of the publisher.

D/2023/0095/61

ISBN: 978-2-503-60564-7
e-ISBN: 978-2-503-60565-4
DOI: 10.1484/M.ARC-EB.5.133262

Printed in the EU on acid-free paper

Contents

List of Illustrations vii

Abbreviations xxi

1. Shaping Archaeological Archives: Fieldwork, Collection, and Private Archives
  — Issues of Curation and Accessibility
  RUBINA RAJA 1

2. Who Can Access the Past? Archives, Technological Solutionism
  and Digital Colonialism in (Post-)Conflict Syria
  ZENA KAMASH 9

3. Unclassified: Structured Silences in the Archaeological Archive
  JEN A. BAIRD 19

4. Collaborative Curation of Digital Archaeological Archives:
  Promise, Prospects, and Challenges
  ANNE HUNNELL CHEN 33

5. Archiving Palmyra: Outcomes of Inquiry into Archaeological Legacy Data
  OLYMPIA BOBOU, AMY C. MIRANDA, RUBINA RAJA, and JULIA STEDING 47

6. Considerations in Archive Archaeology: Past and Present Colonialism
  in the Study of Palmyra's Archaeology and History
  AMY C. MIRANDA and RUBINA RAJA 71

7. Revisiting Harald Ingholt's Excavation Diaries: Zooming in on
  Two Graves in the South-West Necropolis of Palmyra and their Inscriptions
  RUBINA RAJA and JULIA STEDING 99

8. Pompeii as an Archive
  ERIC POEHLER 127

9. Digitizing Knossos Using the Sir Arthur Evans Archive
  JOHN POUNCETT and ANDREW SHAPLAND 143

10. Using Legacy Data to Reconstruct the University of Michigan's Early Twentieth-
  Century Excavation Methodology at Karanis
  ANDREW T. WILBURN 159

11. Placing the Container before the Content: The Cases of the 'Iron Field'
  and 'Mosaic Field' at Eski Kâhta at the Dörner Archive
  — Forschungsstelle Asia Minor, Münster
  EMANUELE E. INTAGLIATA 181

12. Excavating Time and Space: The Archive of the Hama Expedition
in the National Museum of Denmark
   ANNE HASLUND HANSEN and JOHN LUND 193

13. The Mosaics from the 1928–1929 Campaigns of the Joint British-American
Expedition to Gerasa: Drawings by Grace and Dorothy Crowfoot
   LISA BRODY and RUBINA RAJA 213

14. Digitizing the Archaeological Finds and the Photographic Archive
of the German Excavation Campaigns in Samarra (1911–1913)
at the Museum für Islamische Kunst in Berlin
   MIRIAM KÜHN 281

15. Analogue Problems through a Digital Lens: Reconsidering Underlying Issues with
Archaeological Archival Practice Using the Digitization of the Samarra Archives
   RHIANNON GARTH JONES 301

16. Digital Data and Recontextualization: The Case of South Italian Pottery
   VINNIE NØRSKOV and MARIE HÉLÈNE VAN DE VEN 311

17. From Paper to Open-Air Archive: Reconstructing Illegal Excavations and
Art-Market Circulations of Archaeological Objects in the Case of the
Archaic Sanctuary on Timpone della Motta, Southern Italy
   GLORIA MITTICA, CARMELO COLELLI, and JAN KINDBERG JACOBSEN 323

18. The History and Implications of the American Center
of Research's (ACOR) Archival Digitization
   PEARCE PAUL CREASMAN and RYDER KOUBA 343

19. From Legacy Data to Urban Experiences:
Reconstructing the Byzantine Athenian Agora
   FOTINI KONDYLI 353

20. The Future of Corinth's Archaeological Archive:
Towards an Inclusive and Interactive Heritage
   IOULIA TZONOU 371

21. The Challenge of Spatial Ambiguity in Geographic Information Systems
Using Legacy Archaeological Records
   JON M. FREY 395

22. Digitized Archives of Illicit Antiquities: Academic Research,
Dissemination, and Impact
   CHRISTOS TSIROGIANNIS 409

Indices 421

List of Illustrations

3. Unclassified: Structured Silences in the Archaeological Archive — *Jen A. Baird*

Figure 3.1.	Two sides of a card from the Dura card file, card B-29.	22
Figure 3.2.	Scan of sketch of the Dura-Europos Archive as she left it, drawn by Anne Perkins *c.* 1970.	22
Figure 3.3.	a) First page of original handwritten negative field register entry for season D, showing photograph D2, 'View of city from Triumphal arch'; b) the metadata for the digitized negative on Artstor.	24
Figure 3.4.	Scan of negative D2.	24
Figure 3.5.	Screen capture of search of fifteen thousand archival images for the subject 'workers'.	25
Figure 3.6.	Scan of 'Unclassified' photograph card. In 'Excavations and Personnel' Folder.	27
Figure 3.7.	November 1929 report, Annexe 1: workforce.	28
Figure 3.8.	Dura photograph B27, taken during Johnson's work, interior of Palmyrene Gate.	29
Figure 3.9.	Dura photograph B33, taken during Johnson's work.	30

4. Collaborative Curation of Digital Archaeological Archives — *Anne Hunnell Chen*

Figure 4.1.	Screen capture of an ArtStor record for YUAG negative number dura-d66~01.	34
Figure 4.2.	Screen capture of an ArtStor record for YUAG negative number dura-g852a~01.	34
Figure 4.3.	Author's schematic of networked data enrichment in the LOD ecosystem.	37
Figure 4.4.	Query showing the number of Dura-Europos artefact records from each IDEA partner institution currently searchable in Wikidata.	40
Figure 4.5.	Sample Wikidata item with metadata statements composed of links to additional external items.	41
Figure 4.6.	Digital surrogate for an archival document annotated with Wikidata Image Positions tool.	42
Figure 4.7.	Digital surrogate for an archival photograph annotated with Wikidata Image Positions tool.	42
Figure 4.8.	Wikidata item corresponding to the archival photograph in Figure 4.7.	44

5. Archiving Palmyra: Outcomes of Inquiry into Archaeological Legacy Data — *Olympia Bobou, Amy C. Miranda, Rubina Raja, and Julia Steding*

Figure 5.1.	A view through Palmyra's triumphal arch.	48
Figure 5.2.	Harald Ingholt standing at a Palmyrene Hypogeum in the south-west necropolis, with visitors.	48
Figure 5.3.	Harald Ingholt.	48
Figure 5.4.	Palmyrene relief portraits exhibited at the Ny Carlsberg Glyptotek in Copenhagen during the special exhibition 'The Road to Palmyra', 2019–2020.	51
Figure 5.5.	French archaeologist Maurice Dunand conducting fieldwork in Palmyra during the 1924 excavation season.	52
Figure 5.6.	Finds from Hama.	52
Figure 5.7.	Number of portraits in the database of the Palmyra Portrait Project.	53
Figure 5.8.	Loculus relief with two portrait busts, Museé du Louvre, Paris, inv. no. AO 4449.	54
Figure 5.9.	Loculus relief depicting a female, Ny Carlsberg Glyptotek, Copenhagen, inv. no. IN 1062, PS 444.	54
Figure 5.10.	Ingholt's monograph from 1928 on Palmyrene sculpture had a drawing of the rear façade of the Ny Carlsberg Glyptotek on the title page.	56
Figure 5.11.	Folders at the Ny Carlsberg Glyptotek.	58
Figure 5.12.	PS 845. A yellow archive sheet with an image of a loculus relief of a priest.	59
Figure 5.13.	PS 4. A grey archive sheet from the Ny Carlsberg Glyptotek with an image of a loculus relief of a male figure.	60
Figure 5.14.	Excerpt from diary 3 (p. 47) with the ground plan of hypogeum G.	63
Figure 5.15.	Excerpt from diary 1 (p. 104) with transcriptions and a reference to the journal *Berytus*.	64
Figure 5.16.	Ingholt and a worker with reliefs from the Tomb of Malkû.	65

6. Considerations in Archive Archaeology — *Amy C. Miranda and Rubina Raja*

Figure 6.1.	PS 8. Fragment of a banqueting relief with reclining male Figure.	83
Figure 6.2.	Harald Ingholt.	83
Figure 6.3.	PS 38. Fragment of a banqueting relief with seated female figure.	84
Figure 6.4.	Map of the region in which Palmyra is situated.	84
Figure 6.5.	View of Palmyra from the periphery of the city.	85
Figure 6.6.	View of a stretch of the colonnaded main street in Palmyra with consoles for statues.	85
Figure 6.7.	Elevation of Tower Tomb no. 71 as well as a schematic view, a section, and ground plan of a tower tomb.	86

Figure 6.8. Restored entrance to the underground Tomb of the Three Brothers in Palmyra. 86

Figure 6.9. Photograph from the Ingholt Archive showing *in situ* sarcophagi in an underground tomb, the so-called Duvaux Tomb. 86

Figure 6.10. PS 1417 showing a wall painting from a tomb. 87

Figure 6.11. Ingholt's diploma of Master of Theology, 1922. 87

Figure 6.12. Letter from the American-Scandinavian Foundation about a fellowship at Princeton University in 1921–1922. 88

Figure 6.13. French archaeologist Maurice Dunand performing fieldwork in Palmyra during the 1924 excavation season. 88

Figure 6.14. Newspaper article on Ingholt's defence of his doctoral dissertation, 1928. 88

Figure 6.15. Ingholt's monograph from 1928 on Palmyrene sculpture. 89

Figure 6.16. A letter from Yale University Library in relation to Ingholt's retirement, 1964. 89

Figure 6.17. PS 1314A. 89

Figure 6.18. PS 615. 90

Figure 6.19. PS 1430. 90

Figure 6.20. PS 1430. 90

Figure 6.21. PS 1430. 91

Figure 6.22. Letter from the director of the Ny Carlsberg Glyptotek, Copenhagen. 91

Figure 6.23. PS 845. A yellow archive sheet with an image of a loculus relief of a priest. 91

Figure 6.24. PS 410. 91

Figure 6.25. Excerpt from Ingholt's diary 2, p. 1. 92

Figure 6.26. Excerpt from Ingholt's diary 4, p. 28, with sketches and descriptions of tesserae from the Dandurin Collection. 92

Figure 6.27. The archive boxes at the Ny Carlsberg Glyptotek. 93

Figure 6.28. View of the Triumphal Arch on the main street in Palmyra with the Sanctuary of Bel visible in the background. 93

7. Revisiting Harald Ingholt's Excavation Diaries — *Rubina Raja and Julia Steding*

Figure 7.1. Photo of Harald Ingholt. 99

Figure 7.2. Palmyrene relief portraits exhibited at the Ny Carlsberg Glyptotek in Copenhagen during the special exhibition 'The Road to Palmyra', 2019–2020. 100

Figure 7.3. Title page of diary 1 from 1924. 101

Figure 7.4. Diary 1, p. 87. Transcribed inscriptions and the mention of small finds. 102

Figure 7.5.	Updated map of the south-west necropolis.	103
Figure 7.6.	A double-page spread from the diary publication, showing the scan, transcription, and translation.	104
Figure 7.7.	The Ingholt family, 1934.	104
Figure 7.8.	Workers in the grave of Malkû, discovering a sarcophagus.	105
Figure 7.9.	The Great Colonnade in Palmyra.	105
Figure 7.10.	Diary 1, p. 27.	107
Figure 7.11.	Diary 1, p. 100.	108
Figure 7.12.	Diary 1, p. 118.	109
Figure 7.13.	Diary 3, p. 82.	110
Figure 7.14.	Diary 5, p. 121a.	111
Figure 7.15.	Diary 5, p. 122b.	111
Figure 7.16.	Ground plan of Hypogeum AC.	112
Figure 7.17.	Photo of the garland sarcophagus from Hypogeum AC.	113
Figure 7.18.	Diary 1, p. 29.	115
Figure 7.19.	Diary 1, p. 121.	116
Figure 7.20.	Diary 3, p. 70.	117
Figure 7.21.	Ground plan of Hypogeum AD.	118
Figure 7.22.	Archive Sheet PS 646.	119
Figure 7.23.	Diary 1, p. 103.	120
Figure 7.24.	Diary 1, p. 130.	121
Figure 7.25.	Archive Sheet PS 58.	122
Figure 7.26.	Diary 1, p. 109.	123

8. Pompeii as an Archive — Eric Poehler

| Figure 8.1. | Pompei, 1867 | 133 |
| Figure 8.2. | Chart of nineteenth-century journals dedicated to Pompeian subjects. | 134 |

9. Digitizing Knossos Using the Sir Arthur Evans Archive — *John Pouncett and Andrew Shapland*

Figure 9.1.	Entry for 20–21 March from Arthur Evans's 1894–1899 notebook on Crete.	144
Figure 9.2.	Theodore Fyfe (1875–1945), watercolour reconstruction drawing of the Throne Room, 1901.	146
Figure 9.3.	Photograph of the Throne Room of the Palace of Knossos, 1900.	149
Figure 9.4.	Photograph of the Throne Room of the Palace of Knossos, *c.* 1930.	149
Figure 9.5.	Plan of Throne Room, including Inner Shrine and Lustral Basin	152
Figure 9.6.	Digitized version of the plan of the Throne Room Complex at ground level produced by the Ephorate of Antiquities of Heraklion.	155
Table 9.1.	Summary of rooms related to the Throne Room Complex after Hood and Taylor 1981.	153

10. Using Legacy Data to Reconstruct the University of Michigan's Early Twentieth-Century Excavation Methodology at Karanis — *Andrew T. Wilburn*

Figure 10.1.	Sketch map showing areas excavated by the University of Michigan expedition to Karanis.	162
Figure 10.2.	Plan showing excavation square F10).	164
Figure 10.3.	Sketch plan of Area G.	165
Figure 10.4.	Detail showing the Late Third (C) Layer of excavation square F10.	167
Figure 10.5.	Screenshot from <https://karanishousingproject.org>.	172
Figure 10.6.	Schematic image of the PostgreSQL database for the Karanis Housing Project.	174
Figure 10.7.	Map produced in ArcGIS 10.8, showing south-eastern part of the excavation from the Geographic Information System.	176
Table 10.1.	Table showing examples of original field numbers and converted field numbers.	175

11. Placing the Container before the Content — *Emanuele E. Intagliata*

Figure 11.1.	The area of the Iron Field ('Feld I') excavated in 1963.	182
Figure 11.2.	Still from a 1963 film showing excavators sorting and cleaning iron slag in the 'Ironfeld'	182
Figure 11.3.	Iron slag collected in 1963.	183
Figure 11.4.	One of the drawn plans of the Iron Field ('Feld II') at the Dörner Archive	186
Figure 11.5.	Selected drawings of metal artefacts from the Iron Field	187
Figure 11.6.	The Mosaic Field, 'Mosaik I' being documented.	188
Figure 11.7.	Rooms with suspensurae in the Mosaic Field.	188

12. Excavating Time and Space — *Anne Haslund Hansen and John Lund*

Figure 12.1.   Harald Ingholt and a local workman on the Citadel of Hama. 194

Figure 12.2.   Aerial photo view of the Citadel of Hama. 195

Figure 12.3.   Ejnar Fugmann A view of the Citadel behind the waterwheel el-Muhammadiya.....195

Figure 12.4.   Members of the Danish expedition, 1936. 196

Figure 12.5.   Scene from a bakery at Hama. 197

Figure 12.6.   Egyptian diggers from Quft at Hama. 197

Figure 12.7.   Fieldwork: men carrying baskets. 198

Figure 12.8.   Egyptians recognizable by their long robes, standing at some distance from the actual digging, observing and giving directions to the team. 199

Figure 12.9.   Mohammed Hussein keeps an eye on the diggers while Fugmann takes measurements. 199

Figure 12.10. The mound divided into squares with the year/s of their excavation indicated. 199

Figure 12.11. The registration card for the Hama lion, 6B601. 201

Figure 12.12. The number of specially recorded finds from each excavation campaign. 201

Figure 12.13. Registration card, *springbind*, for the Hama lion, 6B601. 202

Figure 12.14. Ejnar Fugmann, sketch of the location of the largest fragment of the Hama lion. 203

Figure 12.15. From Fugmann 1958, fig. 265. Detail. Location of the largest fragment of the Hama lion. 204

Figure 12.16. Photo of the Hama lion *in situ*. 204

Figure 12.17. One of the Syrian conservators posing with the Hama lion. 205

Figure 12.18. A 3D jigsaw: Elo at work reassembling the lion in the Ny Carlsberg Glyptotek......205

Figure 12.19. The lion being transported from the Glyptotek to the National Museum. 205

Figure 12.20. Menu card from the restaurant of the National Museum in the 'Court of the Lion'. .206

Figure 12.21. Cartoon by Fugmann from 1933 in which the members of the expedition appear downcast because the finds allegedly had not lived up to their expectations. 206

Figure 12.22. Ejnar Fugmann, Khan Rustam Pasha, watercolour. 206

Figure 12.23. Photo of the Khan Rustam Pasha from 1935. 207

Figure 12.24. Ejnar Fugmann, pencil drawing of Sunday activities in the courtyard of the headquarters of the expedition. 208

Figure 12.25. Ejnar Fugmann, pencil sketch of Ingholt overseeing the excavations at Hama in the manner of Napoleon at Wagram. 208

13. The Mosaics from the 1928–1929 Campaigns of the Joint British-American Expedition to Gerasa — *Lisa Brody and Rubina Raja*

Figure 13.1. View from the North-West Quarter towards the south. 214

Figure 13.2. Mary and James Ottaway Gallery of Ancient Dura-Europos, Yale University Art Gallery, showing installation of fragments from the Gerasa mosaic. 214

Figure 13.3. Map of Gerasa marking the churches from which the mosaic drawings stem. 215

Figure 13.4. Flag-hoisting in Gerasa in 1929. 216

Figure 13.5. Plan of the Propylaea Church. 218

Figure 13.6. Drawing of mosaic in the Propylaea Church by Dorothy Crowfoot. 219

Figure 13.7. Plan of Church of St Theodore's. 220

Figure 13.8. Photo of Church of St Theodore. 221

Figure 13.9. Drawing of mosaic in Church of St Theodore by Dorothy Crowfoot. 222

Figure 13.10. Plan of the Procopius Church. 223

Figure 13.11. Drawing of mosaic in north aisle of Procopius Church by Dorothy Crowfoot. 224

Figure 13.12. Drawing of mosaic in room 4, south-west corner of Church of St Theodore by Dorothy Crowfoot, 1928. 225

Figure 13.13. Drawing of mosaic in north-east intercolumniar pattern between columns 5 and 6 in Procopius Church by Grace M. Crowfoot, 1928. 226

Figure 13.14. Drawing of mosaic in front of south apse in Procopius Church by Grace M. Crowfoot, 1928. 227

Figure 13.15. Drawing of mosaic in north-west chapel in Procopius Church by Grace M. Crowfoot, 1928. 227

Figure 13.16. Drawing of mosaic of cypress tree in south apse in Procopius Church by Grace M. Crowfoot, 1928. 227

Figure 13.17. Procopius Church composite plan with mosaic photos incorporated. 228

Figure 13.18. Photo of Procopius Church, mosaic in north chancel. 229

Figure 13.19. Photo of Procopius Church, mosaic in south chancel. 229

Figure 13.20. Photo of Procopius Church, mosaic in north aisle, east end. 229

Figure 13.21. Photo of Procopius Church, mosaic in north aisle, centre. 229

Figure 13.22. Photo of Procopius Church, mosaic in north aisle. 230

Figure 13.23. Photo of Procopius Church, mosaic in north aisle. 230

Figure 13.24. Photo of Procopius Church, mosaic in north aisle. 230

Figure 13.25. Photo of Procopius Church, mosaic in north aisle. 230

Figure 13.26. Photo of Procopius Church, mosaic in south aisle, west end...................231

Figure 13.27. Photo of Procopius Church, mosaic in south aisle............................231

Figure 13.28. Photo of Procopius Church, mosaic in south aisle............................231

Figure 13.29. Photo of Procopius Church, mosaic in south aisle............................231

Figure 13.30. Photo of Procopius Church, mosaic in south aisle............................232

Figure 13.31. Photo of Procopius Church, mosaic in nave...................................232

Figure 13.32. Photo of Procopius Church, mosaic in nave...................................232

Figure 13.33. Photo of Procopius Church, mosaic in north chancel..........................232

Figure 13.34. Photo of Procopius Church, mosaic in chapel.................................233

Figure 13.35. Photo of Procopius Church, mosaic in south aisle............................233

Figure 13.36. Photo of Procopius Church, mosaic in north aisle............................233

Figure 13.37. Mosaic with inscription, from nave of Procopius Church, c. AD 526...............234

Figure 13.38. Mosaic with geometric design, from south aisle of Procopius Church, c. AD 526.....234

Figure 13.39. Colour scheme for drawings of mosaics..235

Figure 13.40. Pencil drawing on reverse of colour scheme showing pattern
in the north aisle of Procopius Church..235

Figure 13.41. Drawing of mosaic in chancel of north aisle in Procopius church..................236

Figure 13.42. Drawing of mosaic of two baskets from centre octagons
in north aisle in Procopius Church..237

Figure 13.43. Drawing of mosaic with of intercolumnar pattern in Procopius Church............237

Figure 13.44. Plan of Church of the Prophets, Apostles, and Martyrs........................237

Figure 13.45. Drawing of mosaic with floral scroll from Church of the
Prophets, Apostles, and Martyrs...237

Figure 13.46. Drawing of mosaic in the stable of Bakir Ibrahim.............................238

Figure 13.47. Drawing of mosaic in the house of Bakir Ibrahim..............................238

Figure 13.48. Map of Gerasa and its archaeological features................................240

Figure 13.49. Drawing of mosaic from room 26, most likely Church of St Theodore.............242

Figure 13.50. Drawing of mosaic from room 18, most likely Church of St Theodore.............242

Figure 13.51. Drawing of mosaic from room 25, most likely Church of St Theodore.............242

Figure 13.52. Drawing of mosaic from room 36, most likely Church of St Theodore.............243

Figure 13.53. Drawing of mosaic from room 37, most likely Church of St Theodore.............243

Figure 13.54. Church of St Theodore, composite plan with the mosaics located
next to the rooms in which they were found....................................244

Figure 13.55. Plan of the Churches of St George, St John, and Sts Cosmas and Damian. 245

Figure 13.56. Drawing of mosaic with peacock from Church of St George. 246

Figure 13.57. Drawing of mosaic from north aisle in Church of Sts Cosmas and Damian. 246

Figure 13.58. Drawing of mosaic from the Church of Sts Cosmas and Damian. 247

Figure 13.59. Photo of the Church of Sts Peter and Paul. 247

Figure 13.60. Plan of the Church of Sts Peter and Paul. 248

Figure 13.61. Drawing of mosaic from south aisle in Church of Sts Peter and Paul. 249

Figure 13.62. Drawing of mosaic from the Church of Sts Peter and Paul. 250

14. Digitizing the Archaeological Finds and the Photographic Archive of the German Excavation Campaigns in Samarra (1911–1913) — *Miriam Kühn*

Figure 14.1. Ernst Herzfeld: photographic list of the first campaign, 1911. 285

Figure 14.2. Ernst Herzfeld: Samarra, Haus II, stucco, room 41, south wall, east of door, 1911...286

Figure 14.3. Kurt Erdmann: list of glass negatives from Samarra
with an appendix of colour photographs, after 1927. 286

Figure 14.4. Alastair Northedge: computer-generated list of the Samarra
photographic archive, 1990. 286

Figure 14.5. Ernst Herzfeld: Samarra, excavation in congregational mosque, 1911. 287

Figure 14.6. Ernst Herzfeld: Samarra, al-Mutawakkiliyya, Abu Dulaf Mosque,
south hall, 1911, slide reproduced from a now-missing glass negative. 288

Figure 14.7. Screenshot, museum documentation system. 289

Figure 14.8. Wall painting, mud, baked; plastered, black painting, Samarra, 836–892 290

Figure 14.9. Ernst Herzfeld: Samarra, Haus XVI, 1911, glass negative. 290

Figure 14.10. Ernst Herzfeld: Samarra, marble (Ornament No. 22), 1911, glass negative.. 292

Figure 14.11. Kurt Erdmann: list of glass negatives from Samarra with an appendix
of colour photographs, after 1927. 292

Figure 14.12. Kurt Erdmann: blueprint collection, folder: Samarra, small finds after 1927. 292

Figure 14.13. Front of a fragment of a large marble panel, marble, cut,
drilled, polished, Samarra, 836–892 293

Figure 14.14. Back of a fragment of a large marble panel, cut, drilled, polished, Samarra, 836–892...293

Figure 14.15. Ernst Herzfeld: Photographic list of the first campaign, 1911. 294

Figure 14.16. Museum für Islamische Kunst, *Inventarbuch*, v. 295

Figure 14.17. Ernst Herzfeld: Samarra, Bab al-ʿAmma, 1911, plastic negative.. 296

Figure 14.18. Ernst Herzfeld: Photographic list of the first campaign, 1911. 296

Figure 14.19. Ernst Herzfeld: Man, 1911–1913, glass negative. 297

Figure 14.20. View of the exhibition 'Samarra Revisited: Excavation Photographs from the
Caliph's Palaces Revisited' at the Museum für Islamische Kunst in Berlin 297

16. Digital Data and Recontextualization: The Case of South Italian Pottery — *Vinnie Nørskov and Marie Hélène van de Ven*

Figure 16.1. British Museum database: screenshot of database entry
of an Apulian amphora by the Varrese Painter. 314

Figure 16.2. Catalogue of the Italian cultural ministry: Catalogo generale dei Beni Culturali:
screenshot of the database entry of an Apulian volute krater by the Arpi Painter,
Museo Civico di Foggia. 314

Figure 16.3. Apulian red-Figure volute krater by the Arpi Painter, RVAp 28/92,
Museo Civico di Foggia, Foggia, inv. no. 132731. 314

17. From Paper to Open-Air Archive — *Gloria Mittica, Carmelo Colelli, and Jan Kindberg Jacobsen*

Figure 17.1. Timpone della Motta seen from the west. 324

Figure 17.2. Marquis Gaetano Gallo (1822–1908) of Castrovillari. 325

Figure 17.3. Letter signed by Giuseppe Fiorelli, 21 June 1879,
instructing to safeguard archaeological objects. 325

Figure 17.4a. Archaeological stratigraphy exposed during roadworks in 1879 326

Figure 17.4b. Oinotrian-Euboean fragments from the eighth century BC
on display in the Museo Civico Archeologico di Castrovillari. 326

Figure 17.5a. Fanta cans from the second half of the 1970s 328

Figure 17.5b. Perlenbacher beer bottle from the 1980s 328

Figure 17.6. 1980s wine bottle from the Magna Grecia factory in Doria. 328

Figure 17.7. Handwritten note on the donation of Agostino De Santis
to the Museo Civico Archeologico in Castrovillari in 1957. 328

Figure 17.8a. Joining fragments from Corinthian seventh-century BC pyxis lid. 329

Figure 17.8b. Fragments from seventh-century Corinthian lekythos,
probably belonging to the same vessel. 329

Figure 17.9. Votive deposit to the south of Building Vd during excavation in 2002. 330

Figure 17.10. Photos of Corinthian vessels from the archive of Gianfranco Becchina 331

Figure 17.11. Fragments belonging to a Corinthian pyxis, seventh century BC. 332

Figure 17.12. Joining fragments from Corinthian oinochoe, later seventh century BC............333

Figure 17.13. Joining fragments from Corinthian oinochoe, middle of the seventh century BC....333

LIST OF ILLUSTRATIONS   xvii

Figure 17.14. Fragments from an East Greek plate from the Ny Carlsberg Glyptotek and the Carlos Museum in Atlanta while a third fragment was excavated on Timpone della Motta 333

Figure 17.15. Area view of the MS3 area at the central south side of the sanctuary 334

Figure 17.16. Pottery vessels repatriated from the Ny Carlsberg Glyptotek in 2016 334

Figure 17.17. Fragments from the excavations in MS3 and fragments repatriated from the Getty Museum and the Archaeological Institute, Bern 336

Figure 17.18. Laconian fragment excavated in the MS3 area on 25 July 2022 336

Figure 17.19. Fragments from a Laconian cup in the collection of the Carlos Museum, Atlanta, and joining fragment from the MS3 area 336

Figure 17.20. Complete and fragmented terracotta pinakes produced with the same mould 337

Figure 17.21. Terracotta figurines repatriated from the Getty Museum and from Area MS3, all produced with the same mould 338

18. The History and Implications of the American Center of Research's (ACOR) Archival Digitization — *Pearce Paul Creasman and Ryder Kouba*

Figure 18.1. Map of sites covered in the ACOR Digital Archive as of October 2022 345

Figure 18.2. Results of a search in the ACOR Digital Archive 346

Figure 18.3. Photographic slides with labels, potential sources of digital metadata 347

19. From Legacy Data to Urban Experiences — *Fotini Kondyli*

Figure 19.1. Example of a digitized notebook from the Agora 355

Figure 19.2. Central and west areas of the Agora in 1934 showing the extent of excavated Byzantine layers 356

Figure 19.3. Example of a cross-section in an excavation notebook of Section E, noting the stratigraphic layers of various structures 358

Figure 19.4. Architectural plan of Sections H and H' showing parts of classical, Roman, late Roman, and Byzantine structures 360

Figure 19.5. Middle Byzantine installation with vats and basins in Section MM, probably for winemaking 361

Figure 19.6. Project workflow highlighting the key steps in reanalysing and enhancing the Athenian Agora legacy data 363

Figure 19.7. 3D model of a hypothetical balcony overlooking an internal courtyard in a Middle Byzantine house in Section E 365

Figure 19.8. a) Virtual reality application of a Middle Byzantine street in Section MM blocked by a gate; b) without the gate 365

20. The Future of Corinth's Archaeological Archive — *Ioulia Tzonou*

Figure 20.1. View of Corinth with Peribolos of Apollo, Peirene Fountain, Carpenter's Folly, and Tselios's house in the foreground and with Acrocorinth in the background, from north-east, 1930. 372

Figure 20.2. Plan of central Corinth with major monuments, mostly Roman, indicated in Greek and English, Corinth Excavations Archive, James Herbst.. 373

Figure 20.3. Map of the landscape around Corinth from Acrocorinth to the south to Lechaion harbour to the north. 374

Figure 20.4. Cover of the first volume of the Management Plan for ancient Corinth. 374

Figure 20.5. Group of workmen at the Theatre, 1896. 375

Figure 20.6. Unnamed workman resting his hand on the arm of a Roman life-sized male statue, 1898. 376

Figure 20.7. George Kosmopoulos with Gaius Caesar (S 1065) in the Julian Basilica, 1914. 376

Figure 20.8. 1974 excavation group. 376

Figure 20.9. Screen capture of a search page at <http://ascsa.net>. 377

Figure 20.10. B. H. Hill notebook 86A, pp. 1–2, 1926.. 379

Figure 20.11. Drawing by Piet de Jong of C-1954-1, the so-called Pyrvias aryballos, 1954. 379

Figure 20.12. Nora Jenkins Shear documenting the wall paintings at the Theatre in 1925. 380

Figure 20.13. Terracotta votive hands from the Asklepieion, 1931.. 381

Figure 20.14. Inventory card of C-1954-1, 1954. 382

Figure 20.15. Scan of pages from Find Inventory Book of Inscriptions. 382

Figure 20.16. Coins from gold hoard of Manuel, 1938. 383

Figure 20.17. Screen capture of a search page at <http://ascsa.net> showing results of a coin search. 384

Figure 20.18. Scan of inventory card of Coin 1977–1055 in the Study Collection, Corinth Excavations Archive. 384

Figure 20.19. Scan of Notebook 143 by Gladys Davidson, pp. 43–44, 1934. 385

Figure 20.20. Scan of Notebook 922 by Leda Kostaki, pp. 42–43, 1999.. 386

Figure 20.21. Katie Petrole in action in the Corinth Museum during an educational programme on Sacred Prostitution and Aphrodite, the protecting goddess of the city, 2017. 388

Figure 20.22. Eleni Gizas in action during an Open Day session guiding a group of Ancient Corinthians at the excavation site NE of the Theatre, 2019. 388

Figure 20.23. A kindergarten student holding an aryballos during an educational session on the uses of olive oil in Antiquity in the Corinth Museum, 2019. 388

21. The Challenge of Spatial Ambiguity in Geographic Information Systems Using Legacy Archaeological Records — *Jon M. Frey*

Figure 21.1. Overall plan showing location of site and monuments in relation to the modern village of Kyras Vrysi 396

Figure 21.2. Composite plan of individually surveyed monuments showing the alignments of buildings revealed by georeferencing actual state plans.. 397

Figure 21.3. Notebook page providing specific coordinates next to a map from first pages of bound volume. 398

Figure 21.4. Orthophotomosaic of the area of the Byzantine Fortress at Isthmia showing individually georeferenced state plans with the find-spots of coins from different eras superimposed 399

Figure 21.5. Orthophotomosaic of the area of the North-East Gate of the Byzantine Fortress at Isthmia showing objects with detailed find-spots plotted as points and those with more ambiguous find-spots 401

Figure 21.6. Detail view of trenches and stratigraphic units in the Roman Bath at Isthmia showing the results of three attempts to plot ambiguous find-spots for objects...... 402

Figure 21.7. Comparison of heatmaps of random points representing three different attempts to plot ambiguous find-spots for objects 403

Figure 21.8. Plan of the Roman Bath at Isthmia showing individual trenches sorted by the number of examples of Byzantine pottery uncovered in excavation 404

Table 21.1. Confidence scores for artefacts identified in field journals. 400

Table 21.2. Roman Bath artefacts organized by 'confidence score'. 400

22. Digitized Archives of Illicit Antiquities — *Christos Tsirogiannis*

Figure 22.1. Polaroid image from the Medici archive, depicting a broken Attic black-figure kylix with a symposium scene, attributed to the style of the Lysippides Painter and to the potter Andocides, *c.* 520 BC. 412

Figure 22.2. Author's photograph of the same kylix, restored, on a loan exhibition at the New Acropolis Museum in 2008. 412

Figure 22.3. Polaroid image from the Medici archive, depicting the central part of a sculpture with two griffins attacking a hind. 413

Figure 22.4. Author's photograph of the same part, incorporated in the restored sculpture, on a loan exhibition at the New Acropolis Museum in 2008. 413

Figure 22.5. Regular-print image from the Medici archive, depicting a rare marble prehistoric idol of a female deity, broken in pieces and missing part of its head 414

Figure 22.6. The same idol, restored, was identified by the author 21 November 2014, in the Christie's, New York, 11 December 2014 antiquities auction catalogue.. 414

Figure 22.7. Regular-print image from the Medici archive, depicting an Etruscan bronze statuette of a togatus, broken in pieces and lying on a white piece of paper with a tape measure next to it.. 416

Abbreviations

CIS	*Corpus inscriptionum Semiticarum*, 5 pts (Paris: Imprimerie nationale, 1881–1950).
IGLS	*Inscriptions grecques et latines de la Syrie*, 21 vols (Paris: Geuthner, 1929–; Beirut: Institut francais du Proche-Orient, 2005–).
L.	Unpublished letters. Münster, Westfälische Wilhelms-Universität Münster, Forschungsstelle Asia Minor, Dörner Archive.
PAT	Hillers, D. R. and E. Cussini. 1996. *Palmyrene Aramaic Texts* (Baltimore: John Hopkins University Press).
P.Cair.Zen.	Edgar, C. C. 1928. *Zenon Papyri*, III, Catalogue général des antiquités égyptiennes du Músée du Caire, 85 (Cairo: Imprimerie de l'Institut français d'archéologie orientale).
P.Col.Zen.	Westermann, W. L. 1940. *Zenon Papyri: Business Papers of the Third Century B.C. Dealing with Palestine and Egypt*, Columbia Papyri. Greek Series, 4 (New York: Columbia University Press).
P.Haun.	Bülow-Jacobsen, A., C. Høeg, and T. Larsen. 1985. *Papyri Graecae Haunienses*, III: *Subliterary Texts and Byzantine Documents from Egypt* (Bonn: Habelt).
Plin., *HN.*	Plinius maior, *Naturalis historia*.
P.Mich.	Pearl, O. M., L. Amundsen, J. G. Winter, and H. C. Youtie. 1951. *Papyri and Ostraca from Karanis*, University of Michigan Studies. Humanistic Series, 50 (P.Mich. VII) (Ann Arbor: University of Michigan Press).
RES	*Répertoire d'épigraphie sémitique*, 8 vols (Paris: Imprimerie nationale, Klincksieck, 1900–1968).
RTP	Ingholt, H., H. Seyrig, and J. Starcky. 1955. *Recueil des tessères de Palmyre*, Bibliothèque archéologique et historique, 58 (Paris: Imprimerie nationale).

1. Shaping Archaeological Archives: Fieldwork, Collection, and Private Archives — Issues of Curation and Accessibility

Rubina Raja

Centre for Urban Network Evolutions (UrbNet), Aarhus University (Rubina.raja@cas.au.dk)

Shaping Archaeological Archives

Over the decades, archaeology has undergone an immense development, particularly in the field of its best practices for the handling and management of the vast amounts of data that the discipline generates. The significant amounts of data generated by archaeological fieldwork, academic research on museum collections or object provenance form vast archives of physical material. These physical resources can often go untouched for years, if not generations, despite holding critical information. Yet, past and present crises — for example the Syrian civil war, recent events in Afghanistan and Ukraine, or the COVID-19 pandemic — have alerted researchers to the fact that resources are often fragile and, in many cases, not accessible to all. Does digitization, however, offer solutions for preserving, organizing, and sharing information? Or is the digital hype a quick fix, only partly, if at all, solving much more complex issues which we should think even harder about and develop further best practices around in order to most efficiently and correctly handle such archives? Questions like these are what stands at the core of this volume.

Digital archives take shape dependent upon a variety of factors, such as the type of data they contain or the platform hosting the data. When contrasted with the issues in gaining access to physical archives (e.g. geographic location or institutional permission), the digital archive offers many opportunities and possibilities worth exploring. But is digitization a democratization of information, particularly when made open access? As scholars were denied access to physical resources due to the multiple global shutdowns caused by the COVID-19 pandemic, one might consider how digital archives allowed research to continue. Despite the benefits of digitization, scholars must also consider the affordances of digital archives and how the shift to a virtual environment changes the research dynamic. How does it affect research and insights that one might never see the objects of research in real life, but only as a digital copy or scan? What does the physicality, even of a piece of paper, mean to the research process? Furthermore, how do researchers address the ethical dilemmas of making resources openly available? Should all data be available to everyone? If not, then why? And who gets to be the gatekeeper?

Archaeology creates archives. It does so from when the first spade is stuck in the ground on fieldwork. It does so when research is done on already excavated objects — in collections or storages. It does so when researching past archaeological fieldwork through the notebooks and archives of others. Often already existing archives are not curated, not accessible, not processed in any way, and therefore they never enter academic discussions and ongoing dialogues about a site, about objects, about archaeological processes, about developing best practice. More often than not, such archives remain closed land for most, despite the fact that we know that they exist. In recent years, however, more focus has been given to archaeological archives from a range of perspectives. But most prominently the topic of digitization has been at the forefront. Digitization has taken centre stage as digital humanities have developed into something that at many research institutions now has a department of its own. These departments offer digital ways of working with humanities' sources, both primary and secondary sources, in order to digitize or visualize such material. While digital humanities have done a lot of good for humanities in general — for example unleashing information locked in paper and across many fields — digital humanities have not managed to solve all the problems we have with for example archaeological archives. It is important to have primary material in a digitized form in order to preserve it, but the digitizing does not set free the information which the material holds. In fact, whatever shape an archive might have, one often goes through complex processes both before and after digitization of the archive: the nature of the material must be assessed, and it must be decided what sort of digitization is appropriate for exactly the resource one deals with. Then there is the whole issue of databases: only what goes into a database can come out of a database. Therefore, a lot of complex issues must be decided upon if the intention is to hold archival material in a database. When all is decided upon and everything is processed and typed into the database comes the stage where it must be determined who gets access to the digitized material, in what form they get access to it, and what they can be allowed to do with it. Will it be put in the public domain, free for all to use when crediting the data owners or creators?

This edited volume addresses how scholars use, share, work with, and think about archival material in archaeology, particularly through making digital archives, but also in cases where archives are under consideration for full or partial publication. The array of papers not only showcases the depth of research on archaeological archives, but also offers reflections upon the relationship between archaeological practices and archival form. With a focus on archaeological sites in the eastern Mediterranean and the Middle East, some of which today are conflict zones, the volume offers a dialogue on best practices for the dissemination and synthetization of knowledge from digital archives. Through a variety of case studies on archaeological sites and the digital resources associated with them, the contributions explore the versatility of digital archives and new research directions being taken due to their form and accessibility. Papers also consider the multitude of forms digital information might take and bring forth problems with digital media. Finally, the volume also considers productive future avenues for archaeology after the digital turn.

The volume consists of twenty-one contributions written by scholars who work on or with archival issues in their archeologically research. Some work on publishing archives from scratch, some are curators of archives, some research topics where they need to visit archives and work on archival materials, which has made them think differently about such archives. Some work on aspects of historiography, an area where much archaeological knowledge can emerge out of forgotten papers, stored in boxes and not looked at for generations. Some research sites that have been demolished and only exist through archives or sites that cannot be visited due to armed conflicts, for example. Overall, all the contributors have first-hand knowledge of archives which contain archaeological information, and they are experts within a range of the many fields which such archive archaeology covers. They all bring to the forefront overlooked material and highlight in which way deep knowledge can be teased out of such archives.

The first contribution is written by Zena Kamash and entitled 'Who Can Access the Past? Archives, Technological Solutionism and Digital Colonialism in (Post-)Conflict Syria'. Kamash takes us through a string of considerations on the fact that as a response to recent conflicts and the concomitant cultural heritage destruction in the Middle East, numerous digital archiving projects have been generated either as part of wider reconstruction schemes or as stand-alone projects. She delves into a selection of these archives and projects, for example Iconem's 'World Heritage Database', the Institut français du Proche Orient's photographic archive, the 'Monuments of Mosul in Danger' project, and the Russian-funded project with different names ('Palmyra 3D'; 'Palmyra GIS'; 'Palmyra in Time and Space') that contains architectural plans and archival as well as recent photographs. Taking a spin on the more familiar question of 'who owns the past?', she asks: Who can access the past, specifically through digital archives? Are making available and making accessible the same things? What specific things do we need to do to make archives accessible to those who might most benefit from them? In what ways, if at all, can digital archives facilitate post-conflict healing and reparation? Or do (some) digital archives repeat colonial forms of knowledge production and control that make them damaging tools of digital colonialism? Her research on the Middle East and on healing in conflict-filled societies through engagement with the past and cultural heritage is known to many, and in this contribution she draws on knowledge from her ongoing research in Iraq contextualizing her considerations in a much wider perspective, which forces us to rethink the ways in which large-scale digital projects are often framed and published.

Jen A. Baird in her contribution 'Unclassified: Structured Silences in the Archaeological Archive' sharply addresses exactly those things which are not described in archives. These are the things on excavation and fieldwork photos that are not commented on and not brought to the forefront and therefore not part of the way we often look at the archives. Furthermore, since many things go uncommented in the original sheets or papers accompanying such photographs, many of these things are then not noted when photographs are digitized and therefore cannot be searched in the open databases either. This creates a bias in the available material and a void in the knowledge retrievable from such archival photos. Baird sets out to address the long shadows cast by archives that often are unacknowledged in contemporary reckonings with archaeological legacy data.

In the age of pandemic and big data, many institutions which hold archaeological archives are leaning harder than ever into the digital turn: in some cases, this serves to reinforce existing power dynamics.

'Collaborative Curation of Digital Archaeological Archives: Promise, Prospects, and Challenges' is the title of Anne Chen's contribution. Her contribution centres on the Yale Digital Dura-Europos Archive (YDEA)'s work in the Wikidata environment. It highlights ways that projects and institutions can harness the platform to increase the native-language discovery of collections and invite more diverse voices and perspectives into the process of knowledge creation and documentation regarding archaeological content — with all its facets of pros and cons. Chen takes her point of departure in the fact that numerous western GLAM (Galleries, Libraries, Archives, and Museums) institutions established in the eighteenth, nineteenth, and early twentieth centuries gained archaeologically related collections as a direct result of colonialist power dynamics. She goes on to explain that histories have had obvious enduring impacts on physical and intellectual access to collection holdings, as well as on collection interpretation and documentation. Numerous institutions are currently seeking to mitigate those effects, many taking the step in the last decade to create and make available digital surrogates of collection holdings in an effort to curb important barriers associated with travel to physical collections. While this is an admirable and foundational first step, the ability to visit physical collections is not the only barrier to access, nor the only past injustice in need of correction. Who gets to make the decisions about how an object, building, or document is searchable and/or discoverable in the digital realm, especially when the initial physical collection history is tied to problematic repercussions of colonialism? How do we ensure that information of significance to populations in different parts of the world, who speak different languages, and who may bring different interpretive lenses to analysis, are able to find digital GLAM content and meaningfully contribute to the shaping of knowledge related to it? The free, inherently multilingual, and editorially collaborative Wikidata digital ecosystem holds much promise in this regard according to Chen, and this is the avenue she explores in her paper on her current research project.

Olympia Bobou, Amy C. Miranda, Rubina Raja, and Julia Steding, all members of the project Archive Archaeology: Preserving and Sharing Palmyra's Cultural Heritage through Harald Ingholt's Digital Archives (the Archive Archaeology project) based at Aarhus University, tackle issues that have arisen through their work on the legacy data of the Danish archaeologist Harald Ingholt, who worked in Palmyra during the French Mandate in the 1920s. In their contribution entitled 'Archiving Palmyra: Outcomes of Inquiry into Archaeological Legacy Data', they address the fact that Ingholt did not collect his archive with the intention that it could be used by others. With its physical relocation from Yale to the Ny Carlsberg Glyptotek in Copenhagen, the Ingholt Archive became an institutional resource with access limitations (e.g. geography or institutional permission). However, the recent digitization of the archive and its online publication as open data has been one first step taken within the framework of the Archive Archaeology project to democratize the material, despite the fact that open access does not mean that everyone who in fact could benefit from the archive will get to use it since other restrictions might be in place. Considering recent attention given to digital colonialism, the question remains what more can be done to make archives truly accessible? In this contribution, the Ingholt Archive is used as a case study — from the history of its continuous development through to the present-day interventions of researchers — in order to open a discussion about how archaeologists can tackle digital colonialism. Digital archives as open data have certain benefits, for example, allowing anyone with internet to access the material. Yet, barriers such as awareness, language, or even quality of one's internet connection continue to restrict access. As archaeologists remain committed in the effort to decolonize their practices, we must reflect upon whom our research is for and to whom the data truly belongs.

Through a set of case studies in the contribution 'Considerations in Archive Archaeology: Past and Present Colonialism in the Study of Palmyra's Archaeology and History', Amy C. Miranda and Rubina Raja delve further into the material from the Ingholt Archive and the Ingholt Excavation Diaries. The relationship of archives to archaeology has traditionally been undervalued, yet thanks in part to the 'archival turn', attitudes have shifted over the past twenty years. Archaeology has increasingly utilized archives to study the inaccessible and mitigate losses due to unforeseen events, such as conflict zones or fieldwork cancelled by the COVID-19 pandemic. This attention to archives is merely a first step in fully exploiting the potential of their use for archaeological practice — in the field and beyond. Although researchers benefit from the use of archives, a discussion of whom such knowledge is for and who has access to it becomes necessary. To interrogate the future and the potential colonialist pitfalls of archive archaeology, this contribution considers the work of the Danish archaeologist Harald Ingholt, who worked, among other places, in Palmyra during the French Mandate of Syria. Through his archival materials — the Ingholt Archive and the Ingholt Excavation Diaries — and published research on Palmyra, the contribution aims at re-evaluating the relationship between colonialism and archaeological practice during the twentieth century as well as the digital colonialism of the present. This multifaceted intersecting approach facilitates a wider discussion on the history and dynamics between archival study, archaeology, and cultural heritage, including new best practices.

Staying with the Archive Archaeology project and the Ingholt Excavation Diaries, Rubina Raja and Julia Steding take us through some of the unique insights into daily life on an excavation in the early twentieth century in the Near East that we gain from Ingholt's diaries. In the contribution entitled 'Revisiting Harald Ingholt's Excavation Diaries: Zooming in on Two Graves in the South-West Necropolis of Palmyra and their Inscriptions', Raja and Steding focus on the approximately eighty hypogea that Ingholt excavated or investigated during the fieldwork campaigns in 1924, 1925, and 1928. In his excavation diaries, he noted information on the tombs' layout, interior decoration, and state of preservation, as well as the inscriptions. Ingholt also described the discovery of some smaller objects, both from the graves and found or offered to him in different contexts, such as the banqueting tesserae. Together with the extensive paper archive, the diaries are part of the Ny Carlsberg Glyptotek's collection. In 2021, the diaries were published, and scans have been made available online freely accessible to researchers and interested individuals. In this contribution, the diaries are introduced as well as the publication process, and reflections on this process, and the authors discuss the research potential that these diaries hold.

Eric Poehler's contribution entitled 'Pompeii as an Archive' focuses on the Campanian town buried by the eruption of Vesuvius in AD 79, which might well be one of the richest sites when it comes to legacy data. It is therefore also one of the most complex sites to work at and with as a scholar, both in terms of the archaeology of the site, but just as much in terms of all the data already available — or not available — to the scholars wishing to work on — but not at the site. Poehler explores a variety of aspects of studies on Pompeii, which have been and are influenced by the degree of access to legacy data and asks the question whether Pompeii itself as a site in fact can be considered an archive. In turn, this pushes the question of what the long history of studies on Pompeii has done to the way in which the site can and is studied even today. Two current digital humanities projects are the foci of the contribution serving as case studies and lenses into the large-scale infrastructures for legacy information from Pompeii: the Pompeii Bibliography and Mapping Project (PBMP) and the Pompeii Artistic Landscape Project (PALP). In Poehler's view these projects show the ways in which legacy data can be used not only to inform us about what has already been done, but can also serve as a basis for the development of new research inquiries and insights.

John Pouncett and Andrew Shapland turn to the Sir Arthur Evans Archive in their contribution 'Digitizing Knossos Using the Sir Arthur Evans Archive'. The archive was donated to the Ashmolean Museum by Sir Arthur Evans (1851–1941), who was Keeper at the museum from 1884 until 1908. He began to undertake excavations at Knossos in 1900, and these continued for more than thirty years. Over these years, an extensive archive was accumulated including over ten thousand items about Knossos. Among these items were excavation notebooks, photographs, sketches of objects, and architectural drawings. This archive is today the primary source for us to understand Evans's palace excavations and those of the surrounding buildings and tombs. As known, Evans did publish both preliminary reports and a series of volumes about the excavations and the findings, including the important *The Palace of Minos at Knossos* (1921–1935). However, the excavations, which took place in the early twentieth century with the techniques available, have not been published to modern standards. The contribution by Pouncett and Shapland considers how and whether current work on digitizing the archive can enable a different and more enlightening publication process.

Andrew T. Wilburn turns to the excavations in Karanis in Egypt in his contribution 'Using Legacy Data to Reconstruct the University of Michigan's Early Twentieth-Century Excavation Methodology at Karanis'. He draws attention to the fact that numerous large legacy datasets were produced through a type of large-scale archaeological excavations, which are rarely seen today. The legacy data produced by such missions, often over several years and even decades, now give us the opportunity to process the data in a variety of ways, but not without challenges. This contribution addresses some of these attempts and their outcomes. Wilburn addresses the translation of the legacy data into a usable, contemporary format by the Karanis Housing Project, a research group at Oberlin College.

In the contribution 'Placing the Container before the Content: The Cases of the "Iron Field" and "Mosaic Field" at Eski Kähta at the Dörner Archive — Forschungsstelle Asia Minor, Münster', Emanuele E. Intagliata addresses the historiography of part of the Dörner Archive. Often, and with good reasons, archaeologists working with legacy data focus their research on the content of an archive rather than the archive as a research object, which has also come into being through a process — more or less curated. Yet, the study of archives as a topic in itself remains crucial to understanding the quantity and quality of the datasets the archives hold. This chapter aims to raise awareness about the importance of studying the history of collections, which comes with the archives. Intagliata focuses on the creation of two batches of documents pertaining to the excavations of the 'Mosaic Field' and the 'Iron Field' by F. K. Dörner and his collaborators at Eski Kähta. Through such a study, we are forced to reflect on the types of information that are normally lost when not taking the historiography of an archive into account.

The Hama excavations in Syria funded by the Carlsberg Foundation have recently become the object of study by researchers at the National Museum of Denmark where the archives from the excavations are housed. In their contribution 'Excavating Time and Space: The Archive of the Hama Expedition in the National Museum of Denmark', Anne Haslund Hansen and John Lund address the way in which finds were registered in the Hama excavation and begin to explore in which ways such registration practice can bring new knowledge to the forefront that can even spur entirely new avenues of research. The Collection of Classical and Near Eastern Antiquities in the Danish National Museum is home to archives of several Danish archaeological expeditions to the Mediterranean, which were funded by the Carlsberg Foundation and which the museum tries to make accessible to researchers. It is the intention that the archives should be made freely accessible online, not only in order to preserve the information for posterity but also — and perhaps principally — to enable scholars to re-examine and test the data using new methodologies. However, in this contribution the authors lay open why such a strategy is easier intended than carried out, since archaeological archives were often created by numerous individuals using different methodologies and in part because archaeological fieldwork practices at the time that the archives were compiled were different from the standards of today.

Another famous but under-researched archive is that of the Gerasa Archive at Yale University Art Gallery. Recently, Lisa Brody and Rubina Raja have begun a project to fully publish the archive in a research-based manner bringing together the expertise of the curator and that of the field archaeologist who has worked at the site for more than a decade. In their contribution 'The Mosaics from the 1928–1929 Campaigns of the Joint British-American Expedition to Gerasa: Drawings by Grace and Dorothy Crowfoot', they bring to the forefront some of the unpublished material in the archives, namely the mosaic drawings done by the wife and daughter of the expedition leader J. W. Crowfoot, Grace and Dorothy Crowfoot. Brody and Raja furthermore relocate until now unknown mosaics in the churches where they were excavated and speculate on invisible knowledge hidden in such archives, which only can be unleashed in collaboration with museum experts and specialists with knowledge from the particular site at which or through which the archive was compiled.

Miriam Kühn's contribution is entitled 'Digitizing the Archaeological Finds and the Photographic Archive of the German Excavation Campaigns in Samarra (1911–1913) at the Museum für Islamische Kunst in Berlin', and it addresses the Samarra archive at the Islamic Museum in Berlin. In her contribution, Kühn focuses on two aspects of these digitization projects. Firstly, the practical constraints and limitations from the perspective of the project leader and the digitizers. Secondly, the potential of digitizing archaeological archives for scholars and the public drawing on experiences from the Berlin Museum projects.

Rhiannon Garth Jones also turns to the Samarra archive in her contribution 'Analogue Problems through a Digital Lens: Reconsidering Underlying Issues with Archaeological Archival Practice Using the Digitization of the Samarra Archives', but does so from the perspective of a researcher from outside the museum in which the archive is housed. As she argues, in line with Kühn, the digitalization of archives promises a significant opportunity to address multiple long-standing concerns of archaeological archives by opening up new sources of information for researchers, increasing and improving public access, and changing the conversation around ownership and repatriation. Some technologies, such as 3D digitization and archaeological data management systems, could be revolutionary, although the digitization of archives comes with ethical, practical, and theoretical issues of its own — many of which are also longstanding concerns of archaeology and archival practice. However, considering the problems of digitization and the ways it cannot solve those concerns — and, indeed, might replicate or reinforce them — can shed new light on the problems themselves. And through discussing the problems of digitalization, even the problems come to hold potential, as Garth Jones argues.

Vinnie Nørskov and Marie Hélène van de Ven focus on archival material with many lacunae in their contribution 'Digital Data and Recontextualization: The Case of South Italian Pottery'. They present a discussion on the current situation of the digitization of archives relevant to the study of south Italian archaeology, with a focus on ceramics. Such databases, both accessible and closed, are discussed and their potential in research evaluated. Well-known examples to us all are the established archives like the Beazley Archive and the Corpus Vasorum Antiquorum Online that allow scholars to access images, traditional vase descriptions, classifications, and, to a limited extent, information on provenance. But the contribution also turns to an evaluation of prospective projects such as the digitalization of the Trendall Archive and recent active developments such as the FEMINICON project, specifically designed to study the iconography of Apulian red-figured vases. Besides archives of Apulian material also GIS/satellite/aerial photography databases in Italy and their possible role in studies on clandestine looting and the recontextualization of illicit archaeological objects are addressed pulling together not only research issues but also the issues of illegal trade and trafficking of cultural heritage.

In the contribution by Gloria Mittica, Carmelo Colelli, and Jan Kindberg Jacobsen entitled 'From Paper to Open-Air Archive: Reconstructing Illegal Excavations and Art-Market Circulations of Archaeological Objects in the Case of the Archaic Sanctuary on Timpone della Motta, Southern Italy', the authors address issues of tracing objects and their biographies through various archival material connected to the long-standing excavations at Timpone della Motta. Mittica, Colelli, and Jacobsen piece back together how objects left the site and entered the international antiquities trade and how some of these can now be traced through a complex paper trail.

Founded in 1968, the American Center of Research (formerly the American Center of Oriental Research) is dedicated to advancing knowledge of Jordan and the interconnected region. ACOR's centre in Amman holds an extensive library and growing archive, which includes more than a hundred thousand images of archaeological sites, historic places, and modern life from across the Middle East. With content created spanning the past century, the archives provide a glimpse of the region that has changed considerably and, thus, can serve as an important resource for those studying the recent and historic past. In their contribution 'The History and Implications of the American Center of Research's (ACOR) Archival Digitization', Pearce Paul Creasman and Ryder Kouba take us through the initiative begun in 2000 with support of the U.S. Department of State, USAID, and others, in which ACOR has endeavoured to make its archives searchable and, since 2016, digitized and freely available online. With some forty thousand images and other media now accessible and searchable, the archive has seen increased use among remote researchers during the COVID-19 pandemic. The authors here introduce ACOR's efforts to assemble, care for, and provide access to its archive, with an emphasis on digitization and also discuss the implications of making such a potentially potent resource freely and widely available.

Fotini Kondyli has long worked on the legacy data connected to excavations on the Athenian Agora, and in her contribution 'From Legacy Data to Urban Experiences: Reconstructing the Byzantine Athenian Agora', she addresses new methods and technologies in archaeological practice which have played a part in changing the way in which we can work with such data and which have led to new ways to understand the data and contextualize it. She presents pivotal challenges in working with legacy data both in terms of organizing and analysing, but also in terms of synthesizing very differing data. Crucially, Kondyli also shows the ways in which such data can contribute with new knowledge and insights as has been and is the case within the framework of her project Inhabiting Byzantine Athens that pivots on legacy data from the Athenian Agora Excavations. In her contribution, it becomes clear just how much we can learn from revisiting such legacy data and embedding it within the framework of a research question.

Ioulia Tzonou's contribution 'The Future of Corinth's Archaeological Archive: Towards an Inclusive and Interactive Heritage' tackles issues arising from work with the archives from the American School in Classical Studies' Corinth Excavations. The American School of Classical Studies has been actively involved in excavations and research at ancient Corinth in Greece for the last 125 years, since 1896. The site has been continuously occupied for eight millennia, ever since the Early Neolithic period. Archaeologists have generated a vast archive recording the activities of past inhabitants that includes over 1100 excavation notebooks, tens of thousands of artefacts, coins, and drawings, and hundreds of thousands of images. Since 2007, when the digitization of the archive was initiated, a rich resource was added including over half a million records that are increasing rapidly. However, the digitization of the archive also generated problems and questions. Researchers now had access to the archive while being away from Corinth. Lacunae, mistakes, and issues of rights of access to materials were brought to the fore. At the same time that the archive was made widely accessible to academics, there has been a considerable interest from laypersons to learn and interact with it. Questions which Tzonou addresses in the contribution include: How can we accomplish the digitization of the archive in a timely manner? How can we correct problems and accommodate disparate legacy data generated by a multitude of scholars and dating back decades to our current data structures? Can we make the archive user-friendly to people other than academics creating multimedia tools for teaching archaeology locally and globally, embracing local community collaborations as well as global interactions?

Jon M. Frey's work at Isthmia stands at the core of his contribution entitled 'The Challenge of Spatial Ambiguity in Geographic Information Systems Using Legacy Archaeological Records'. The transition in ways of handling and organizing data, which the Michigan State University Excavations at Isthmia have undergone over the last years, shows just how much the prioritized study and creating open access dissemination of records documenting the progress of excavation at the site can change the ways in which both the team and other scholars can work with the data. It also shows how such an open access approach allows for accelerated results and scholarly discussions, which could not have taken place without open access.

Christos Tsirogiannis is an expert on cultural heritage trafficking. In his contribution 'Digitized Archives of Illicit Antiquities: Academic Research, Dissemination, and Impact', he reviews the discoveries, from 1995 onwards, of the dozen most important archives of illicit antiquities in the hands of notorious dealers, traffickers, and looters. Their contents, flouting the 1970 UNESCO Convention on the illicit traffic of antiquities, and the way they have been shaped for academic and other research following their digitization are summarized and discussed. Tsirogiannis addresses in detail the issues of access and publication, alongside the value of these archives and possibilities for future research and concludes with a set of case studies on the various impacts that these archives have had on academia and society.

Together, these twenty-one contributions make up a strong volume that asks important questions and adds to the field of archive archaeology on all levels — from the field to the archives in various institutions, to the archives being created now, and the role that archives play in research both on the art market and on objects and their biographies. Furthermore, this volume offers new ways of establishing best practices in the field of archive archaeology, which is rapidly developing.

Acknowledgements

The editor would like to thank the ALIPH Foundation and the Carlsberg Foundation for funding the project Archive Archaeology: Preserving and Sharing Palmyra's Cultural Heritage through Harald Ingholt's Digital Archives (grant agreement 2019-1267) and the Palmyra Portrait Project (grant agreement CF15-0493), respectively. Since the beginning of the Palmyra Portrait Project in 2012, several individuals have contributed to the digitalization and study of the material, and I wish to thank everyone involved in the different stages of the project. Furthermore, this work was supported by Centre for Urban Network Evolutions under grant 119.

Further thanks go to postdoctoral fellow Amy C. Miranda for helping with the organization of the conference Shaping Archaeological Archives, which was hosted virtually in February 2022 and from which most of the contributions in this volume stem. I also thank Jon Frey and Fotini Kondyli for letting me include four further contributions, which stem from a session they hosted at the AIA conference in 2020. I thank all the contributors for sharing their material so generously and contributing to this volume. Further thanks go to Mie E. Lind, Katarína Mokránová, and Christina Levisen (UrbNet) for their editorial help. Finally, we wish to thank Rosie Bonté, Tim Barnwell, and Martine Maguire-Weltecke at Brepols Publishers for the professional handling of this volume throughout the publication process.

2. Who Can Access the Past? Archives, Technological Solutionism and Digital Colonialism in (Post-)Conflict Syria

Zena Kamash

Royal Holloway University of London, Department of Classics (Zena.Kamash@rhul.ac.uk)

Introduction

In 1985, Isabel McBryde challenged archaeologists and cultural heritage practitioners to consider more critically who owns the past and who controls perceptions of the past. In her formulation: 'the past is the possession of those in power; the past belongs to the victor.'[1] In this chapter, I riff off that idea and ask: Who can access the past? Who controls that access? Who decides what parts of the past are made available, to whom, and in what ways? Specifically, I am interested here in who can access a past that has been destroyed in conflict, in this case during the civil war that has raged in Syria since spring 2011.

Many of us are familiar with the destruction of cultural heritage that happened in Syria during the civil war. This civil war has had many players, including but not limited to forces loyal to the President of Syria Bashar al-Assad, Russia, a US-led coalition, rebel groups, such as the Free Syrian Army and Da'esh (also known as Islamic State, IS, ISIS, and ISIL). In addition to the terrible human toll caused by this civil war, cultural heritage has been damaged in Syria in a range of ways from being caught in cross-fire to being a deliberate target for destruction. The response from the rest of the world, predominantly from western powers, media outlets, and institutions, was to shout immediately for reconstruction of this cultural heritage. This has seen a proliferation of reconstruction projects from 2015 onwards, many of which rely heavily on recent advances in digital technologies. The majority of these focus on the archaeological site of Palmyra.[2] My focus in this chapter is on the archives, data, and documentation projects that sit behind many of these reconstruction projects. These archives, data, and documentation projects are needed to generate the knowledge to plug into the reconstruction models, both real and virtual. I am aware that by looking at projects relating to Tadmor-Palmyra, I am potentially further entrenching biases towards the archaeological site of Palmyra that have been prevalent in discussions about cultural heritage destruction and reconstruction in Syria.[3] Unfortunately, those same strong biases mean that the bulk of data about such archives and documentation exists in relation to projects on the archaeological site of Palmyra, pushing my hand in that direction as well (the 'Russian project'), though I do also include projects with a wider remit (Iconem and the Institut français du Proche-Orient).[4] Given the legacies of Syria, particularly Tadmor-Palmyra and its appropriation into discourses of so-called 'western civilization', we are immediately confronted with the spectre of colonialism.[5]

The operations of colonialism and its quest for power through controlling knowledge production, including through archaeology and archaeologists, are well known and neatly summed up in this quote from Lord Curzon in his address to the House of Lords on 27 September 1909:

> Our familiarity, not merely with the languages of the peoples of the East but with their customs, their feelings, their traditions, their history and religion, our capacity to understand what may be called the genius of the East, is the sole basis upon which we are likely to be able

---

[1] McBryde 1985, 6.

[2] In a survey of these projects I conducted up to February 2019, there were *c.* twenty-five separate reconstruction projects devoted to the archaeological site of Palmyra. The analyses presented in this chapter are current up to the summer of 2021; further developments may have taken place for some of these projects after that date. I am writing a book about these reconstruction projects (Kamash (forthcoming)) and have written elsewhere about the reconstruction project by the Institute for Digital Archaeology (Kamash 2017); see also Munawar 2017 and Stobiecka 2020.

[3] A note on place names: 'Palmyra' is used here when I am making explicit reference to the archaeological site; where the wider place is being discussed that includes the modern town and its population, I use 'Tadmor-Palmyra', which reflects both the ancient and modern names for the place.

[4] In my forthcoming book, I also look at Aleppo and Mosul in an effort to redress some of that balance; see Kamash (forthcoming).

[5] On the claiming of Tadmor-Palmyra for the west, see Baird and Kamash 2019.

to maintain in future the position we have won, and no step that can be taken to strengthen that position can be considered undeserving of the attention of His Majesty's Government or of a debate in the House of Lords.[6]

In modern terms, this strengthening of position described by Lord Curzon would be termed 'data gathering' and 'knowledge production'. Critically, these data give soft power to those who control them, allowing people under the yoke of colonialism to be duped subtly (and sometimes not so subtly) into believing that decisions are being made and actions chosen that are for their benefit and in their favour. Cultural heritage and the control of knowledge production relating to cultural heritage are well-known forms of such soft power, with soft power often being held up as a virtue of cultural heritage protection and conservation.[7]

Going hand in hand with this control of knowledge production are the technologies of colonialism, i.e. the tools and machines of colonialism.[8] This is often where some of the more insidious aspects of colonialism lie, often in the guise of benevolence, but usually with the consequence of trapping people into systems of control that are hard to escape. This power of technology was clearly being deliberately harnessed in nineteenth-century colonial projects:

> We have the power in our hands, moral, physical and mechanical; the first, based on the Bible; the second, upon the wonderful adaptation of the Anglo-Saxon race to all climates, situations, and circumstances [...] the third, bequeathed to us by the immortal Watt. By his invention every river is laid open to us, time and distance are shortened. If his spirit is allowed to witness the success of his invention here on earth, I can conceive no application of it that would receive his approbation more than seeing the mighty streams of the Mississippi and the Amazon, the Niger and the Nile, the Indus and the Ganges, stemmed by hundreds of steam-vessels, carrying the glad tidings of 'peace and good will toward men' into the dark places of the earth which are now filled with cruelty.[9]

This nineteenth-century shipbuilder emphatically links technology, in this case steamships, with proselytizing and the spreading of 'peace and good will'. Here, of course, lies one of the most damaging tenets of colonialism that strips away all agency: that its technologies will make things better for people who cannot otherwise help themselves.

In the modern world, digital colonialism — the use of digital technologies to exert domination and influence over nations and their people — steps into this space of technologically controlled knowledge production and power. This is driven by a firmly held belief that technology is a salve-all. Such technological solutionism essentially posits that if we throw enough tech at a problem, it can be solved.[10] Digital technologies are, of course, not neutral and value-free, which is why digital culture has been accused of being an extension of the 'coloniality of power' that created the Global North.[11]

A technological-solutionist approach is being strongly favoured in approaches to post-conflict reconstruction in the Middle East. The reconstructions themselves have come under increasing fire for their digital colonialist approaches that further embed colonial practices in the region.[12] In addition, these reconstructions can be seen as reflecting the roles that archaeology and archaeologists have played in the Middle East from the earliest phases of the discipline, in particular through capitalizing on vacuums left in the spaces of conflict, which are then followed with 'rhetorics of rescue'.[13] In this chapter, I wish to reflect on how the data underpinning these projects are also implicated in these patterns of colonialism. Numerous institutions and states parties are manoeuvring themselves into powerful positions as data controllers through their use of digital technologies, whether that be in the acquisition of data through e.g. drone photography or in the presentation of those data in online platforms. As noted above, there is a wide potential pool of projects relating to Tadmor-Palmyra, which could be chosen for an analysis such as this. I will be focusing on three: the Institut français du Proche-Orient (IFPO) photographic archive, the Iconem 'World Heritage Database', and the 'Russian project'. These three case studies represent two of the powers who in modern history have had a strong influence on Syria and its people: Russia and France.[14] Given

---

[6] Lord Curzon, Address to the House of Lords, 27 September 1909. Quote in Bahrani 1998, 159.

[7] See, for example, the World Monuments Fund position on soft power and heritage: World Monuments Fund 2022.

[8] Kerr 1995, 91.

[9] Laird and Oldfield 1837, II, 397–98. Cited in Headrick 1979, 238.

[10] On technological solutionism, see Huggett 2004; Morozov 2013.

[11] Stingl 2016, xvii.

[12] See e.g. Stobiecka 2020.

[13] Meskell 2020, 127.

[14] The French Mandate for Syria and Lebanon lasted from 1923 to 1946. Russia has a complex history of influence in the region,

these historical entanglements, issues of digital colonialism are particularly live and pertinent. Each of these projects controls data relating to Syrian archaeology and heritage either through holding historic archives (IFPO) or through creating new data using digital technologies (the 'Russian project' and Iconem). In each case, part of their project involves making these data available via online platforms. The rhetoric accompanying these online platforms lends them a veneer of 'making accessible', which I will argue is rarely achieved when these projects are entangled, wittingly or unwittingly, in a web of digital colonialist structures. I will demonstrate that key barriers to accessibility include the choices of languages used, the levels of functionality and information provision, and digital inequalities. Sitting behind these barriers seems to be a lack of attention to the users who might feel the most benefit of being able to access these data: the people of Syria.

The Institut français du Proche Orient (IFPO) Photographic Archive

I begin with the least technologically advanced of the three projects: an online photographic archive. In 2018–2020, IFPO undertook an initiative, funded by UNESCO and the ALIPH Foundation, to digitize their photographic archive and make the archive available online through the MédiHAL portal.[15] The photographic archive comprises *c.* fifty thousand photographs of various places and archaeological sites in Syria predominantly from 1920–1977, of which *c.* fourteen thousand seem now to be available online. Photography as a practice and a technology has in itself long been recognized as a tool of colonialism.[16] The central role of photography in archaeology and by archaeologists means that archaeological photography is also implicated as a tool of colonialism. Work by Jen Baird on photographs in the archive of Dura-Europos, for example, has clearly demonstrated that such photographs were often being used to tell heavily edited and biased narratives about the past that were rooted in orientalist assumptions.[17] As the IFPO photography archive spans the period of the French Mandate in Syria and the decades immediately following it, the act of making this archive available online offered an opportunity to reflect on and perhaps even confront such colonial legacies. It is not clear from the limited description of the project available on the MédiHAL website whether this potential was recognized. They do, however, make the following claim: 'Going online is expected to improve the transparency of the Institute's mission in its regional environment and to foster a more systematic interaction with the international academic community as a whole.'[18] While the aim may be transparency and openness, the target audience is academic, which from the outset, then, limits the full potential of such a collection.

Turning now to the online platform itself and its usability, users can search the online archive through two means: a set of browse functions ('images', 'authors', 'keywords', 'latest submissions', and 'image type') and a free-text search. The 'images', 'latest submissions', and 'image type' browse functions are rather blunt instruments: 'images' gives a list of 13,911 images, 'latest submissions' a list of 13,914 images, and 'image type' links to four categories ('drawing', 'gravure', 'illustration', and 'photography'), of which 'photography' is the largest (13,887 images) — clicking on this takes you to a list of those 13,887 images. The 'authors' browse function looks, initially, to have potential, especially for understanding the histories of these photographs. Users are given a list of twenty-six 'authors'. Twenty-four of these 'authors', however, are associated with the comparatively small number of photographs in the collection from 2000 onwards. IFPO itself is given as the author of 13,636 photographs with only one person being named once within that group; this is Daniel Schlumberger who is named as the photographer of an inscription from Jebel Bal'as near Tadmor-Palmyra. Not knowing who took nearly all of the historic photographs obviously limits what can be gleaned about their historic context. Furthermore, even where 'authors' are named, we are given no further information about who these people are and their relationship to the sites and objects in the photographs; this seems like a missed opportunity to flesh out the biographies of these images. The 'keywords' browse function provides an alphabetical list of words in English

---

which includes providing support for Syrian independence in 1946 and being party to a Treaty of Friendship and Cooperation signed in 1980: see Lund 2019.

15 The platform can be accessed at MédiHAL n.d. On the funding from the ALIPH Foundation, see ALIPH n.d. Some of the photographs in the online platform seem to predate the UNESCO and ALIPH funding, but no further information is given on the platform about how it came into being.

16 See e.g. Bate 1993.

17 Baird 2011.

18 MédiHAL n.d.

and French that includes place names as well as categories such as 'archaeology' and 'animal'. Unfortunately, the list seems to be limited to the first thousand results, which covers A–Gh with no way of searching the rest of the alphabet. The free-text search function appears to be limited to searches on the preselected keywords, for example if a user searches on 'Arabic', their search returns the four images tagged with 'Arabic inscription', which has been designated as a keyword, unlike 'Arabic' which is not. This seems to mean that users are constrained by the categories deemed important and useful by the creators of the data, making those themes significantly more searchable, and by extension more findable, than others.

Using the free-text search function to understand the data being made available in more depth, I searched on 'Palmyre'. This yielded 2063 results of images, which predominantly seem to be of parts of the archaeological site and archaeological objects from the site. Each image is presented with similar information. I will use the example of 'medihal-00821433, version 1', titled 'Agora en cours de fouille, en direction de l'angle ouest (Palmyre, Syrie)', which is representative of the set up for the platform.[19] As well as the image itself, a user is provided with metadata (type, title, author, abstract/description, date, domain, keywords, licence, image type, source, credit, city, country, GPS latitude and longitude), together with a pin on a map of Syria, user metrics (e.g. number of views and number of downloads), and dates of when the entry was created and last modified. For 'medihal-00821433, version 1' this means we are told that: the date of the photograph is *c.* 1939, the building dates to the Roman period, the photograph was taken during a French mission to Palmyra, that there has been a publication, and that the name of the photographer is unknown.[20] This information is all provided in French with only a single keyword in Arabic (تَدْمُر ('Tadmor')), so the language bias of the searching functions is also present in individual entries on the platform. The information provided is very basic; there is no site plan showing where the building is in the archaeological site of Palmyra and no information about what we know about the 'agora' nor what was found during the excavation, etc.

The use of Creative Commons licensing, which has sharing and openness at its core, means that this project has actively tried to avoid the desire to control data that we will see from the 'Russian project'. There are, however, subtler forms of control and exclusion at play in the IFPO dataset. Critically, all the information is provided in French and English with Arabic only featuring in keywords in the metadata, which strongly alienates Arabic- and Kurdish-speaking users. Furthermore, the limited accompanying information means that non-expert users will find the archive of limited use and interest. Overall, then, the significant limitations of both the searching functions and of the information provided with individual images mean that this resource is tailored quite specifically, as stated in their aims, to an academic audience who have a high-level understanding both of the archaeology in the images and of French and/or English. This results in the exclusion of a wider audience, particularly non-specialists from Syria. By making this archive available, without also making it accessible, IFPO do not seem to have escaped the colonial underpinnings of the archive: knowledge is still the preserve of a privileged few from the Global North with a broader non-expert audience being unwelcome, especially those from Syria. Had IFPO considered their potential audience more broadly at the outset of the project, i.e. to include non-experts and people who do not necessarily speak English and French with ease, these pitfalls might have been avoided or at least mitigated.

The Iconem 'World Heritage Database'

Iconem is a French start-up company specializing in cultural heritage conservation projects that was launched in 2013 by French architect Yves Ubelmann. They describe their mission as follows:

> further[ing] conservation of these endangered places by digitising them for exploration and study, today and tomorrow [...]. combining the large-scale scanning capacity of drones and the photorealistic quality of 3D to create digital replicas of our most treasured places, record them for future generations, and champion them today.[21]

Technological solutionism is front and centre in this mission statement together with an uncritical view of whether digital proxies actually constitute conservation and preservation.[22] Their 'World Heritage Database' is

---

[19] The entry for 'medihal-00821433, version 1' can be accessed at: <https://medihal.archives-ouvertes.fr/IFPOIMAGES/medihal-00821433v1> [accessed 7 July 2022].

[20] The publication reference is given in the metadata as: 'L'agora de Palmyre Christiane Delplace – Jacqueline Dentzer-Feydy 2005 BAH 175.'

[21] Iconem 2018.

[22] See e.g. Conway 2010 on the distinction between 'digitization

one aspect of this technologically driven work, which they describe as being a 'global encyclopedia of knowledge' with 'photorealistic 3D models accessible to everyone'.[23] At first sight, claiming accessibility for everyone may seem promising, however the framing of 'global heritage' sets off alarm bells. The concept of 'global' heritage is now much-critiqued as it frequently serves to consolidate the interests of the Global North, downplaying the needs and claims of local communities.[24] Global heritage is, of course, the language and ethos of UNESCO, who regularly employ technocratic policies in their quest for the supposed utopia of cosmopolitan globalism.[25] We see, then, that the binds of colonialism are entwined in this mission statement.

Let us now look at what is on offer in the 'World Heritage Database' and, in particular, whether it meets the claims of accessibility for everyone, which should, of course, also include people from Syria. The 'World Heritage Database' currently contains thirty-two sites and monuments, including Tadmor-Palmyra, the Umayyad Mosque (Damascus), and the Azm Palace (Damascus) from Syria; I will look here at Tadmor-Palmyra and the Umayyad Mosque.[26] The landing page of the database takes the user to a clickable world map and to thumbnails of the thirty-two sites and monuments. Each thumbnail gives an option to view the site or monument in 3D and some, but not all, also have the option to view the data on the map. The 3D viewing option takes the user to a 3D model of the site or monument where the user can access some, but not routinely all, of the following features for each monument: 'points of interest' (which zoom into the relevant part of the model); 'media' (e.g. archive photographs and maps); and a set of 'audios' (c. four or five short one- to two-minute talks about an aspect of the monument). Where the map option exists, clicking through takes the user to the same sets of data in a slightly different interface.

Both Tadmor-Palmyra and the Umayyad Mosque were added to the database in July 2020. The Tadmor-Palmyra section comprises no 'points of interest', which seems surprising, four photographs and a map of the Roman Empire in the 'media' section, and four 'audios'.[27] The audios cover: a general introduction to the site, the Temple of Bel, the Valley of the Tombs, and the Great Colonization. Each audio is in English. The Umayyad Mosque sections gives users access to two 'points of interest', twelve images in the 'media' section, and a single five-minute 'audio'.[28] The twelve images are a combination of archival photographs and what appear to be reconstructions of parts of the building; other than the brief file names, there is no accompanying metadata, so a non-specialist user would struggle to understand the purpose, type, and content of these images. The single audio is a general overview of the building in French. Again, we see a language barrier against people from Syria gaining access. Overall, information provision for these database entries is limited in a range of ways. The models have few points of reference to help a non-specialist navigate their way around, and the images in the 'media' sections have no accompanying data to explain to a viewer what they are and how they relate to the 3D model. Although more data are given in the 'audios', these are strictly limited in their language choice and again present a barrier to speakers of Arabic or Kurdish.

One of the major accessibility issues with the database is the models themselves. I explored the database using my laptop (a MacBook Air) at home on my broadband connection, which is generally sufficient for our household needs: streaming TV, online meetings, online gaming, etc. In both cases, the models were poor quality with visibly lumpy point data. While it was technically possible for me to view the models in the tours at a higher resolution, my laptop was struggling to process the lower resolution models and was at risk of becoming unresponsive. The database was also glitchy at times; I believe that the 3D model is supposed to move and situate the user in the right place in the site and monument to accompany the audio descriptions, but the model froze in every attempt I made to listen to the audio and view the model. Furthermore, the tours were not mobile phone-friendly. When I initially undertook this research in 2021, the screen-size was too large, making it all but impossible to view on my mobile phone. As numerous changes had been made to the platform by the time of writing this chapter, I tried again in July 2022 to

---

for preservation' (where digitization creates a new digital version that needs preservation) and 'digital preservation' (where a digital object is preserved).

23 Iconem n.d., 5.

24 See e.g. Meskell 2018. And on the specific issues of 'heritage at risk', see e.g. Rico 2014; 2015.

25 On the utopian dreams and technocracy of UNESCO, see Meskell 2018, chapters 1 and 3.

26 The data on numbers of sites and monuments are current as of 8 July 2022.

27 The four photographs are: a relief from the Temple of Bel; the Temple of Bel; the monumental arch; and an aerial view of the site.

28 The 'points of interest' are: the mosaicked [sic] vaults and the dome of the treasury.

see whether the design had been made more responsive for mobile phone users: the world map and thumbnails now fit on my mobile phone screen, but neither Tadmor-Palmyra nor the Umayyad Mosque would load, so again I could not use the platform using my mobile phone. These problems immediately raise issues around digital inequalities. If we want resources to be accessible to everyone, then we need to make sure we design platforms that people can access without having recourse to the most sophisticated, and expensive, forms of technology. Given the well-documented evidence for digital inequalities in the Global South i.e. that many people around the world will not be in possession of or have access to a laptop or PC, nor a reliable, high-speed internet connection, making sure that a platform is compatible with a mobile phone is a minimum requirement.[29]

The Iconem 'World Heritage Database' is a classic case of digital colonialism expressed through technological solutionism that does not meet the needs of potential users. 'Everyone' in Iconem terms actually means people who speak English and French and have access to a high-spec laptop with a high-speed internet connection. This is not everyone. It excludes large groups of people, notably communities based in Syria, and demonstrates that access to data and information about supposedly 'global' heritage is essentially for the privileged few in the Global North.

The 'Russian Project'

The 'Russian project' goes by many names: 'Palmyra 3D'; 'Palmyra GIS'; 'Palmyra in Time and Space'.[30] These names shift over time in the press releases and available literature about the project, so for the sake of simplicity I will refer to it here as the 'Russian project'. The key Russian players in the project are: the State Hermitage Museum in St Petersburg (under the Director-General Dr Mikhael Piotrovsky) and the Institute for the History of Material Culture of the Russian Academy of Sciences (IHMC RAS; under the leadership of Natalya Solovyova). The project also operates in collaboration with the Syrian Directorate-General of Antiquities and Museums (DGAM) and at various times tries to align itself with UNESCO.[31] The project itself is complex with numerous moving parts. One of the major outputs is a 3D model of the archaeological site, generated from photographic surveys conducted in September 2016 and September 2019, as well as from a set of nineteenth-century photographs. In addition, there is a GIS with geospatial, archaeological, and historical data, a digital restoration of the Temple of Bel undertaken by Maxim Atayants Architects, and a programme to restore twenty antiquities from Palmyra. I will be focusing here on the GIS and 3D model of the archaeological site and how that model, and the data that sit behind it, are presented to the public.

Early on in the race to become the team that would be granted permission to reconstruct Palmyra, Mikhael Piotrovsky, director-general of the State Hermitage Museum, began planting flags to claim the archaeological site of Palmyra for Russia. He is quoted as saying in 2016:

> For the people of St Petersburg, the loss of Palmyra was a personal, emotional event, a tragedy. Palmyra means a great deal to us. It is not just a tourist destination but something deeply symbolic. The genius of Palmyra is like the genius of St Petersburg, where architecture flows together with nature. At around the same time that Palmyra was discovered by European travellers, Peter the Great was building St Petersburg.[32]

With this deft sleight of hand, Piotrovsky draws a comparison with St Petersburg that stakes an emotional claim over Palmyra, making any Russian involvement there culturally legitimate (supposedly). This kind of claiming makes similar moves to the concept of 'global heritage' discussed above in terms of muting local claims or making them appear at best equal to those from elsewhere. Colonial undertones also seep out here in the trope of the 'European discovery' of a place that was actively inhabited by people who had a strong cultural

---

[29] On the range of digital inequalities and their impacts in the Global South, see Ragnedda and Gladkova 2020.

[30] For the range of statements made about this project, see: Enab Baladi 2019; TASS 2019; Hermitage 2020; Press release on Palmyra 3D 2020; Russian Geographical Society 2020.

[31] An agreement was signed in Damascus on 25 November 2019 for the State Hermitage, IHMC RAS, and DGAM to work in collaboration: Hermitage 2019a. Working with the DGAM raises numerous ethical questions given that they are part of the Assad regime; as allies of that regime, Russia does not share these ethical qualms. The evidence trail relating to Russia collaborating with UNESCO is complex and at times hard to unravel. Working with UNESCO is mentioned in Stone 2019. On 8 November 2018, Piotrovsky calls for a global effort, including collaboration with UNESCO: TASS 2018. In relation to the announcement on 19 March 2019 about the nineteenth-century photographs from the Russian Geographical Society, it is reported that files will be sent to UNESCO: Enab Baladi 2019; TASS 2019. At a UNESCO meeting on the regeneration of Tadmor-Palmyra on 18 December 2019, Russia announced the collaboration agreement signed with the DGAM in November that year: Hermitage 2019b.

[32] Quoted in Polonsky 2016.

memory of the archaeological remains within which they were living.³³

The rhetoric associated with the project is equally overblown with the project being described variously as 'unique', 'highly accurate', 'the most precise', 'most detailed', and 'unparalleled anywhere in the world'.³⁴ This laser focus on accuracy does, ironically, have strong parallels with statements made by one of the early travellers to which Piotrovsky referred in his interview. Robert Wood, who travelled to the site in 1750/1751, writes in his famous book on Palmyra that his travelling companion, James Dawkins, was 'indefatigable in his attention to see every thing [sic] done accurately'.³⁵ This emphasis on accuracy was a key part of Wood's claiming of the site and knowledge about it for the west, i.e. he sets it up so that it would appear that it is only through Wood and his expert measurements that people in the west can come to know about the site. Both Wood and the 'Russian project', therefore, employ accuracy as a tool to make strong claims about the legitimacy of their knowledge and their creation of the authorized discourse about the site.

The 'Russian project' also explicitly operationalizes the other keystone of colonialism: technological superiority. In this statement, for example, we are bombarded with facts and figures about the scale of data their technologies (drones and high-tech cameras) have created:

> IHMC RAS and its partners have completed a large-scale project: total square of working area estimated at 20 sq. km, more than 55,000 high quality air photographs were made in order to produce the model comprising about 700 million polygons. Air photos were also accompanied by several thousands of ground pictures.³⁶

This leaves the reader in no doubt about the extent of Russian work and the vast amount of data, and by extension power, they now hold in relation to the archaeological site of Palmyra.

The full extent of these data will, likely, be expressed in the GIS. This has been described as being 'under development' since 2020 with no sign yet of it being made available.³⁷ We are told that it will include a 'short description, research history, description of carried-out restorations and the current condition of every monument in the ancient city'.³⁸ Such documentation does sound extremely useful and so access to it might be transformative. In the limited information that is available about the GIS on the Palmyra 3D website, we are also told that the GIS will 'provide direct access to the data for the scientific community, all organizations responsible for protection of cultural heritage, and restoration architects'.³⁹ It is not entirely clear what 'direct access' means in this case, nor how one obtains it. Furthermore, from the list given on the website (scientific community, cultural heritage organizations, and restoration architects), they do not plan to make the GIS and the data it contains available to everyone, which presents a large and seemingly insurmountable barrier to access beyond, again, this privileged few.

The part of the project currently available through the 'Palmyra 3D' website is its photogrammetric model. The website is presented in two languages: English and Russian with no provision for Arabic or Kurdish speakers. The model itself is high quality with sharp images. While I was able to view it on my phone, manipulating the model was clunky, so there are some similar problems to those seen for Iconem's 'World Heritage Database'. There is, in addition, very limited functionality. When it was originally launched in 2020 the model had no metadata, including no building tags. Building tags have now been added, in Russian only, for six parts of the site: the Temple of Bel, the Temple of Baalshamin, the theatre, the temple tomb near the Camp of Diocletian (labelled, in Russian, as 'necropolis'), Diocletian's Camp, and the Valley of the Tombs. Other than a building name, no further information is given about the date or histories of these six buildings and areas of the site. Essentially, then, a user is able only to zoom in or out of the model, making it all but inert and requiring any viewer to have pre-existing knowledge of the archaeological site, if they want to know anything more than the names of six buildings.

Further details from the website show us more about the reality of how Russia is positioning itself in relation to the data about the archaeological site of Palmyra. We are told that 'IHMC RAS presented the model to the Directorate-General for Antiquities and Museums (DGAM) of the Syrian Arab Republic and the world community'.⁴⁰ This seeming beneficence is, of course,

---

33 On tropes of 'discovery' at Tadmor-Palmyra, see Baird and Kamash 2019.

34 For instances of these uses see: Hermitage 2019b; 2020; Palmyra 3D 2020; Russian Geographical Society 2020.

35 Wood 1753, preface.

36 Palmyra 3D 2020.

37 Palmyra 3D 2020.

38 Palmyra 3D 2020.

39 Palmyra 3D 2020.

40 Palmyra 3D 2020.

an effective strategy of furthering Russia's soft power (alongside their military power) in the region and is one of the more overt examples of this kind of tactic. Yet, we are also told on the other hand that 'IHMC RAS *own* the most detailed and relevant documentation regarding the current state of Palmyra'.[41] In addition, the copyright is given as 'IHMS RAS 2020' with photo credits to Maxim Atayants, IHMC RAS, and Unmanned Systems. When it comes to the legality of ownership and copyright, then, there is no mention of the claimed collaboration with the Syrian DGAM or doing good in the world. Gertjan Plets has argued strongly that soft power is only one aspect of the Russian game with Tadmor-Palmyra.[42] He demonstrates that Russia's actions in relation to Palmyra, for example the staging of the orchestra in the theatre after Da'esh's first period in the town, set up Russia as a 'besieged fortress' that is saving 'civilization' and 'culture' not only from terrorism, but also from western destabilization.[43] In addition, Russia has used Palmyra to force its voice into the international politics of global institutions such as UNESCO.[44] We can now add an extra facet to this. What Russia has cleverly achieved here is to position itself as a powerful data controller. Russia not only has a voice, but, like all effective colonizers, it is also the gatekeeper of data potentially needed for reconstructions of the archaeological site. In this case, the lack of data accompanying the model is not an oversight in public engagement, but a deliberate and carefully crafted form of data control.

Conclusions

These three projects take up technological solutionism and digital colonialist positions to varying degrees. The 'Russian project' and the Iconem 'World Heritage Database' each have a heavy focus on using cutting-edge technologies to amass new data relating to cultural heritage in Syria. In the case of the 'Russian project', there is a clear politically motivated strategy to use these technologically sourced data as a form of control over the region, which is achieved by restricting access to data through not making it available to a general audience and by making a strong claim to ownership and copyright. In the case of the Iconem 'World Heritage Database', the stated aims of access for everyone are hindered by considerable digital inequalities, which present a barrier to access for anyone without the processing power to use their platform. Finally, a persistent problem across all these case studies was language choice, which serves to exclude people who are not proficient in English and French, and to a lesser extent Russian.

While good intentions might potentially be claimed by IFPO and Iconem, such good intentions can only hold if accompanied by sufficient preparation and thinking through of the implications of decisions made about what paths to take. It is not enough to be making data available, we also need to make them accessible. Using the languages of the country attached to this heritage should, surely, be a bare minimum. Similarly, if you want to use technological solutions, making sure that users can actually access them effectively, using what means they have available to them without incurring additional expense, seems to be an issue that should be front and centre early on in discussions. Collaboration is a central tenet of ethics and best practice in community archaeology, especially with marginalized communities.[45] It would seem that the case studies looked at here, for all their rhetoric of being accessible to everyone and for the benefit of global communities, have fallen at this crucial, and early, hurdle. In order to collaborate, we need to start with the right questions: Who are the audience? Why do they want to participate? How will they benefit?[46] As Meghan Dennis has powerfully argued, all archaeologists — including those using digital technologies — have a duty of care to people who have been marginalized and treated abusively.[47] If we exclude these groups, we mirror past colonialist practice.[48] As a consequence, if we do not get those basics right from the outset, our good intentions may well have numerous negative outcomes. Where communities have been so heavily disenfranchised from their own cultural heritage, I have shown here that even benign or naive oversights have ended up further entrenching the habits and learned assumptions of colonialism about who has the right to access the past. When such exclusionary practices are deemed acceptable and commonplace, this also leaves open a dangerous door for more sinister exploitation and political manoeuvring.

---

[41] Palmyra 3D 2020; emphasis mine.
[42] Plets 2017.
[43] Plets 2017, 22.
[44] Plets 2017, 22.
[45] See e.g. González-Ruibal 2018, 347–48.
[46] See, for example, UK Research Institute's guide to best practice in public engagement: UKRI 2022.
[47] Dennis 2020, 215.
[48] Dennis 2020, 213.

Works Cited

ALIPH. n.d. 'Documentation and Collaborative Redocumentation of Archaeological Images from Syria on Syrian Heritage' <https://www.aliph-foundation.org/en/projects/dissemination-and-collaborative-redocumentation-of-archaeological-images-from-syria> [accessed 7 July 2022].

Bahrani, Z. 1998. 'Conjuring Mesopotamia: Imaginative Geography and a World Past', in L. Meskell (ed.), *Archaeology under Fire: Nationalism, Politics and Heritage in the Eastern Mediterranean and Middle East* (London: Routledge), pp. 159–74.

Baird, J. A. 2011. 'Photographing Dura-Europos, 1928–1937: An Archaeology of the Archive', *American Journal of Archaeology*, 115.3: 427–46 <https://doi.org/10.3764/aja.115.3.0427>.

Baird, J. A. and Z. Kamash. 2019. 'Remembering Roman Syria: Valuing Tadmor-Palmyra, from "Discovery" to "Destruction"', *Bulletin of the Institute of Classical Studies*, 62.1: 1–29 <https://doi.org/10.1111/2041-5370.12090>.

Bate, D. 1993. 'Photography and the Colonial Vision', *Third Text*, 7.22: 81–91 <https://doi.org/10.1080/09528829308576403>.

Conway, P. 2010. 'Preservation in the Age of Google: Digitization, Digital Preservation, and Dilemmas', *The Library Quarterly: Information, Community, Policy*, 80.1: 61–79 <https://doi.org/10.1086/648463>.

Dennis, L. M. 2020. 'Digital Archaeological Ethics: Successes and Failures in Disciplinary Attention', *Journal of Computer Applications in Archaeology*, 3.1: 210–18 <https://doi.org/10.5334/jcaa.24>.

Enab Baladi. 2019. 'The Monuments of Palmyra in Russian Care', *Enab Baladi*, 14 October 2019 <https://english.enabbaladi.net/archives/2019/10/the-monuments-of-palmyra-in-russian-care/> [accessed 24 May 2021].

González-Ruibal, A. 2018. 'Ethics of Archaeology', *Annual Review of Anthropology*, 47: 345–60.

Headrick, D. R. 1979. 'The Tools of Imperialism: Technology and the Expansion of European Colonial Empires in the Nineteenth Century', *The Journal of Modern History*, 51.2: 231–63.

Hermitage. 2019a. 'Hermitage Statement', 26 November 2019 <https://www.hermitagemuseum.org/wps/portal/hermitage/news/newsitem/news/2019/news_357_19/?lng=en> [accessed 24 May 2021].

—— 2019b. 'Hermitage Statement', 23 December 2019 <https://www.hermitagemuseum.org/wps/portal/hermitage/news/news-item/news/2019/news_409_19/?lng=en> [accessed 24 May 2021].

—— 2020. 'Hermitage Statement', 20 August 2020 <https://www.hermitagemuseum.org/wps/portal/hermitage/news/news-item/news/2020/news_190_20/?lng=en> [accessed 24 May 2021].

Huggett, J. 2004. 'Archaeology and the New Technological Fetishism', *Archeologia e calcolatori*, 15: 81–92.

Iconem. 2018. 'Iconem Website' <https://iconem.com/en/> [accessed 8 July 2022].

—— n.d. 'Iconem World Heritage Database' <https://app.iconem.com> [accessed 8 July 2022].

Kamash, Z. 2017. '"Postcard to Palmyra": Bringing the Public into Debates over Post-Conflict Reconstruction in the Middle East', *World Archaeology*, 49.5: 608–22 <https://doi.org/10.1080/00438243.2017.1406399>.

—— (forthcoming). *Heritage and Healing in Syria and Iraq*, under contract with Manchester University Press.

Kerr, I. 1995. 'Colonialism and Technological Choice: The Case of the Railways of India', *Itinerario*, 19.2: 91–111 <https://doi.org/10.1017/S0165115300006811>.

Laird, M. and R. A. K. Oldfield. 1837. *Narrative of an Expedition into the Interior of Africa, by the River Niger, in the Steam-Vessels Quorra and Alburkah, in 1832, 1833, and 1834*, 2 vols (London: Richard Bentley).

Lund, A. 2019. 'From Cold War to Civil War: 75 Years of Russian-Syrian Relations', paper for the Swedish Institute of International Affairs <https://www.ui.se/globalassets/ui.se-eng/publications/ui-publications/2019/ui-paper-no.-7-2019.pdf> [accessed 8 July 2022].

McBryde, I. (ed.). 1985. *Who Owns the Past? Papers from the Annual Symposium of the Australian Academy of the Humanities* (Oxford: Oxford University Press).

MédiHAL. n.d. 'Archives ouvertes de l'Institut français du Proche-Orient' <https://medihal.archives-ouvertes.fr/IFPOIMAGES> [accessed 7 July 2022].

Meskell, L. M. 2018. *A Future in Ruins: UNESCO, World Heritage, and the Dream of Peace* (Oxford: Oxford University Press).

—— 2020. 'Hijacking ISIS: Digital Imperialism and Salvage Politics', *Archaeological Dialogues*, 27: 126–28 <https://doi.org/10.1017/S1380203820000252>.

Morozov, E. 2013. *To Save Everything, Click Here: The Folly of Technological Solutionism* (New York: Public Affairs).

Munawar, N. A. 2017. 'Reconstructing Cultural Heritage in Conflict Zones: Should Palmyra Be Rebuilt?', *Ex Novo Journal of Archaeology*, 2: 33–48.

Palmyra 3D. 2020. 'Palmyra 3D Website' <https://palmyra-3d.online/> [accessed 24 May 2021].

Plets, G. 2017. 'Violins and Trowels for Palmyra: Post-Conflict Heritage Politics', *Anthropology Today*, 33.4: 18–22.

Polonsky, R. 2016. 'The Russian Love Affair with Palmyra Resumes', *Standpoint*, 12 May 2016 <https://web.archive.org/web/20210118193018/https://standpointmag.co.uk/tag/mikhail-piotrovsky/> [accessed 24 March 2023].

Ragnedda, M. and A. Gladkova (eds). 2020. *Digital Inequalities in the Global South* (London: Palgrave Macmillan).

Rico, T. 2014. 'The Limits of a "Heritage at Risk" Framework: The Construction of Post-Disaster Cultural Heritage in Banda Aceh, Indonesia', *Journal of Social Archaeology*, 14.2: 157–76.

—— 2015. 'Heritage at Risk: The Authority and Autonomy of a Dominant Preservation Framework', in K. Lafrenz-Samuels and T. Rico (eds), *Heritage Keywords: Rhetoric and Redescription in Cultural Heritage* (Colorado: University Press of Colorado), pp. 147–62.

Russian Geographical Society. 2020. 'Russian Geographical Society Statement', September 2020 <https://www.rgo.ru/en/article/3d-model-ancient-palmyra-now-available-online-everyone> [accessed 24 May 2021].

Stingl, A. I. 2016. *The Digital Coloniality of Power: Epistemic Disobedience in the Social Sciences and the Legitimacy of the Digital Age* (London: Lexington).

Stobiecka, M. 2020. 'Archaeological Heritage in the Age of Digital Colonialism', *Archaeological Dialogues*, 27: 113–25 <https://doi.org/10.1017/S1380203820000239>.

Stone, L. 2019. 'Russian and Syria Announce Joint Project to Restore Ancient City of Palmyra', *The Architect's Newspaper*, 2 December 2019 <https://www.archpaper.com/2019/12/russia-syria-restore-palmyra/> [accessed 24 May 2021].

TASS. 2018. 'Hermitage Museum Director Calls for Global Effort to Reconstruct Syria's Palmyra', *TASS*, 8 November 2018 <https://tass.com/society/1029828> [accessed 24 May 2021].

—— 2019. 'Russia to Hand over Files on Restoration of Syria's Palmyra to UNESCO', *TASS*, 19 March 2019 <https://tass.com/world/1049287> [accessed 24 May 2021].

UKRI. 2022. 'UKRI Guidance on Engaging the Public with your Research' <https://www.ukri.org/what-we-offer/public-engagement/guidance-on-engaging-the-public-with-your-research/> [accessed 8 July 2022].

Wood, R. 1753. *The Ruins of Palmyra, Otherwise Tedmore, in the Desart* (London: Millar).

World Monuments Fund. 2022. 'Soft Power and Heritage' <https://wmf.org.uk/news/soft-power-and-heritage/> [accessed 1 July 2022].

3. Unclassified: Structured Silences in the Archaeological Archive

Jen A. Baird

School of Historical Studies, Birkbeck, University of London (j.baird@bbk.ac.uk)

Introduction

A well-organized archive is a dangerous place. An archive where each item has been carefully attended to, where stiff, acid-free boxes hold precisely the ordered archaeological data that a researcher might be looking for. How nice it is to be able to open a filing drawer, or click on a link, and pull out just what you need — an image of a tomb that helps you make sense of a plan, perhaps, or a list of artefacts which allows you to recreate an assemblage excavated years ago. While a cared-for and accessible archive can be a wonderful thing, the danger lies in the silences created by its seemingly comprehensive organization. The false sense of security created by systems that seem complete. The danger is in the things the system does not know where to put or how to classify, or in the metadata it does not think to write.

'Archaeological archives' are a category that has been created to deal with the mass of material collected by archaeological expeditions in support of their work, material which has often been retained as supporting documentation for collections in museums, galleries, and other institutions.[1] They are often not archives in a formal sense, and indeed some archaeological archives are held in personal collections which take on the persona of archives only when deposited in institutions.[2] It is only relatively recently that archaeological archives have been discussed as subjects of study themselves, rather than simple repositories from which archaeological information could be extracted.[3]

The archives of the 1920s–1930s excavations at Dura-Europos in Syria, held at Yale University Art Gallery in New Haven, Connecticut, are one example of an archaeological archive from which much information continues to be extracted long after it was collected.[4] While the excavations at the site were still ongoing, the records it produced were sent back to Yale, and order began to be brought to them. Like many archaeological archives, this process of bringing order has never really ceased, with a series of physical moves, restructures, different guardians and curators, conservation projects, accessions and deaccessions, and more recently, digitization projects.[5] As with many archaeological archives, its formation was not a deliberate or conscious process of creating an archive, nor has it ever been attended to by an archivist.[6] Rather, the Dura-Europos Archive existed as supporting documentation for the archaeological remains from the site: retained to support the study of the artefacts held by the art gallery and the publication of the site.

---

* I am grateful to Rubina Raja for the invitation to contribute to Shaping Archaeological Archives, and to Raja and other participants in the February 2022 workshop for their insightful questions. This contribution is a second in a series on the topic of archaeological archives, the first of which is Baird 2022. My work on the Dura-Europos archives is only possible through the generous access which has been granted to me over many years, for which I remain grateful to Susan Matheson, Molly and Walter Bareiss Curator of Ancient Art, Lisa Brody, Associate Curator of Ancient Art, and Megan Doyon, Senior Museum Assistant.

[1] I am certainly guilty myself of forcing the Dura-Europos collection into the framework of 'archaeological archive' as a means of dealing with it: Baird and McFadyen 2014.

[2] For example, the Ingholt collection, now held by the Ny Carlsberg Glyptotek, was part of Ingholt's personal papers (including field diaries and his 'archive' of images) until he deposited them in the institution. Raja, Steding, and Yon 2021; Bobou, Miranda, and Raja 2021; 2022. On personal archaeological archives, e.g. Hitchcock 2020.

[3] The Archives of European Archaeology (AREA) project was of course a key development, but focused more on the history of archaeology (and its relation to the state): Schlanger 2002; 2009.

[4] The archives of the excavations were the basis for many publications on the site, including the *Final Reports* series, and later works such as Downey 2003.

[5] Most recently, the International Dura-Europos Archive project, see Chen in this volume.

[6] This is not to say it has not been carefully stewarded, or that conservation work has not been done, only that it has not been treated as an archive *per se*, nor organized or maintained as such.

The distinction between archaeological archive as something which is supporting documentation for a collection (a collection comprising of accessioned archaeological objects) rather than as a collection itself is made clear at Yale, for instance, in the contrast with the materials from Dura-Europos held by the University Art Gallery and those held by Manuscripts and Archives Collection in the Sterling Memorial Library. The latter, including correspondence and notes of some of the key personnel at Dura (such as Mikhail Rostovtzeff and Clark Hopkins) are organized carefully and traditionally in the formal archive: by Individual, then by Series, Box, and Folder; all of whose contents are carefully inventoried in individual finding aids, and within which each document is sequentially numbered. The Dura collection held in the Art Gallery, in contrast, is much more unstable in its organization, and while the artefacts from Dura have been accessioned, the archive of plans, notebooks, correspondence, photographs, and many other items have not.[7] The Dura-Europos Archive in the Art Gallery has been very actively used by gallery staff, students, and visiting scholars as a source for research on the site and the objects excavated at Dura, but there is no stable system of numbering or nomenclature by which the documents themselves can be referred.[8]

The Dura-Europos Archive is but one example of a common phenomenon: because archaeological documentation collections did not (and often still do not) have the status of an archive, they sometimes lack stable organization, clear relationships between documents, or records of their own archival intentions. That is, they do not follow the archival principles of 'provenance' and *respect de fonds* or 'original order' in the management of the collections, principles which are core to the management and care of historical archives.[9] One outcome of such treatment of archaeological documentation is that their own accumulation and organization often goes unrecorded. For Dura, initially, the work of structuring the archive was undertaken by those who were directly involved in the excavation in some way. Some records were ordered in the field, and especially important for Dura are the field object register, made before the *partage* (the division of the finds between mandate powers on behalf of Syria and the Yale project), and the photographic negative register: both registers were made in Syria during field seasons.[10] Much of the other documentation was created and curated at Yale, initially in the Department of Classics which was the Dura collection's first home after it left Syria. Understanding the nature and shape of this early phase of the archive is thus crucial in understanding the history of the excavations at Dura and their subsequent study: Dura as we know it is a product as much of the Yale collection, its shape, and its limitations as it is a product of the Syrian earth. As Elsner has recently asserted: 'any remaining excavation *must begin in the archive* [...] that archive is crucially framed [...] by the limitations and peculiarities of the theoretical agenda which governed its assembly.'[11] It is to some of those limitations and peculiarities, to archival structures and their silences, that I now turn.

Structuring the Archive

For the Dura-Europos Archive, there is no 'finding aid' (the crucial organizational tool of archival science), because as noted above it was not considered an archive as such, but there is a summary list of its contents, made in the mid-twentieth century by one Ann Perkins. Perkins held a PhD from the University of Chicago in Middle Eastern Archaeology and was a research associate in the Department of Classics at Yale from 1949 to 1965, although she remained associated with the institution for longer. It was Perkins who appears to have conceived and implemented much of the structure of the Dura-Europos Archive, while she was a research associate in the Department of Classics, where much of her time was spent fulfilling photographic reproduction requests from the Dura collection.[12] Perkins's list summarizing the

---

[7] I am by no means implying the Dura collection at YUAG has not been carefully cared for, nor even that the lack of formal archival organization is necessarily a detriment, only a difference — it has been carefully cared for and is a model of accessibility to researchers.

[8] This does not mean they cannot be referred to — e.g. correspondence can be listed by the date, sender, and addressee. The field photographs have numbers related to the season they were taken, recorded in negative registers, and these numbers have remained stable over time, although not all photographs are included (for instance, some exist only as prints outside of the negative sequence, some have been added from personal collections such as that of the Hopkins family, etc.), and no distinction is made in the numbering system between negatives and prints (or indeed different prints).

[9] On archival principles, see e.g. Schellenberg 1961; Duchein 1983; Bettington 2008.

[10] For details on the creation of the object register, and consequences for understanding objects contextually at Dura, see Baird 2012.

[11] Elsner 2021, 5, emphasis in original. On the destruction of the site, Baird 2020.

[12] Darling and Downey 2007.

archive consists of five typewritten pages which describe the files and records from Dura. It is undated but was probably made in the early 1960s, and lists eleven items which together make up the archive, each with short descriptions: the negative catalogue, the field catalogues, the card file, the locus file, the object catalogue, the gallery accession list, the original architectural drawings, the field tracings of paintings and inscriptions, squeezes (on which she comments, 'I think the Gallery mice ate some'), the catalogue of ostraca and inscriptions, and finally the manuscripts and catalogues, followed by some 'miscellaneous material'. Perkins's list, which describes some of the earlier interventions in the archive and her own attempts in organizing it, is all that survives as a direct record of archival intentions: its shape and transformation over time are otherwise only incidentally recorded (e.g. mentioned in letters held in the archive), or evident only in the shape of the archive itself.[13] That is to say: because archaeological archives like that of Dura are considered supporting documents to archaeological objects, rather than as collections themselves, their own biographies are easily lost, despite having fundamentally shaped the discipline and our study of such sites.[14]

Even in Perkins's own time, much documentation and knowledge about the archive had already been lost. The third item she describes is the card file, a card catalogue of photographic prints, based on a parallel negative sequence. She describes it as follows:

3. The Card File. This was made at Yale, with the photograph printed on one side of the card and the negative number and pertinent information typed on the back. Apparently it was intended to have one such card for each negative, field and local alike. However, various field negatives have turned up (mostly in the E and F years) which had not previously been numbered and for which no cards exist. In the Yale series [photographs of Dura objects and records made at Yale] the later negatives also have no cards.

The 4 × 6 cards are filed by locus [area of the city] for architecture, painting, and written records, otherwise typologically. Within each category the cards are in numerical order, beginning with the field negatives, then the Yale series, finally the Damascus series.

Each of these cards usually had a contact print and gave some details, initially transcribed from the negative catalogue made in the field, but later accumulating details in the archive, often in different hands, and with different writing materials (Fig. 3.1).[15] Perkins describes her work to try to bring order to the material and the 'disheartening situation' she faced when she began: 'masses of material with no, or almost no, information, contradictory information, enigmatic notations.'

Figure 3.1 gives an example of what those cards looked like and the kind of information that was included: on one side, a print made from the negative, and on the other, the negative number (here, B-29), a short description of what is pictured, the field season (1928–1929), and the type of negative (here, glass, 2½ × 3½). Other cards have further details, including, sometimes, the photographer and precise date the photograph was taken. Notes on the cards were updated, for instance, as the site nomenclature developed; the pencil notation specifying further detail ('clearing E end of passage') is in Perkins's own handwriting. While the date when a photograph was taken is usually recorded on the negative registers, its attendant archival supports are not dated — Perkins and others intervened in the archive but did not keep a record of these interventions.[16]

---

13 Until 1975, control of the Dura collection was with the Classics Department, including what they then counted as eight thousand objects. 1978 Letter from Alan Shestack (director of the gallery) to the president of Yale, Hannah Holburn Grey, on the Dura collection (correspondence related to complaints on removal of display of Dura Christian material from the Art Gallery). Yale Manuscripts and Archives, Hannah Holburn Grey, RU581. A report which can be found in the same papers, by Harald Ingholt, Ramsay McMullen, and Jerome J. Pollitt in 1971, reviews 'all matters concerning Dura-Europos' for George Langdon (then associate provost of the university). That report notes (p. 18) that Anne Perkins had by that time already written her 'most useful, thorough five-page report on the Files and Records of Dura plus a two-page listing of the various categories used in the Object Catalogue', while also noting the 'urgent need' for 'thorough checking and possible reorganization of the Dura files'.

14 Indeed, a document recording a move of the archive from Bingham tower to Edwards Street (rooms 5 and 6), is in the correspondence drawer of the Dura-Europos Archive in a folder marked 'Misc'. Letter from Office of Buildings and Grounds planning at Yale to C. Bradford Welles on 17 May 1968.

---

15 A plan of the archive made by Perkins (Fig. 3.2) notes that the card catalogue was made by Nicholas Toll. Toll was a Russian archaeologist and director of the Kondakov Institute in Prague, and he published the volume on the necropolis at Dura, among other work on the site and nearby tombs at Baghouz: Toll 1946.

16 Perkins was never officially a curator of the material, and her position seems to have evolved from being responsible for fulfilling photographic requests to a more archival role. The letter she wrote to Bellinger from which the plans of Edwards reproduced here came also notes she was in sole charge for sixteen years (YUAG Dura-Europos Archive, Correspondence Drawer, Anne Perkins folder). The letter does not give a year, but other related letters are dated

Figure 3.1. Two sides of a card from the Dura card file, card B-29. A photograph of a group of men excavating and its typed description recording the field season (1928–1929), its classification and subject ('Architecture', 'Fortifications', 'Main Gate'), with later pencil annotations ('clearing e[ast] end of passage') and description of the negative ('glass, 2½ × 3½'). Dura-Europos Collection, Yale University Art Gallery.

Figure 3.2. Scan of sketch of the Dura-Europos Archive as she left it, drawn by Anne Perkins *c.* 1970. Preserved in correspondence with Alfred Bellinger. Correspondence Drawer, Perkins folder, Dura-Europos Collection, Yale University Art Gallery.

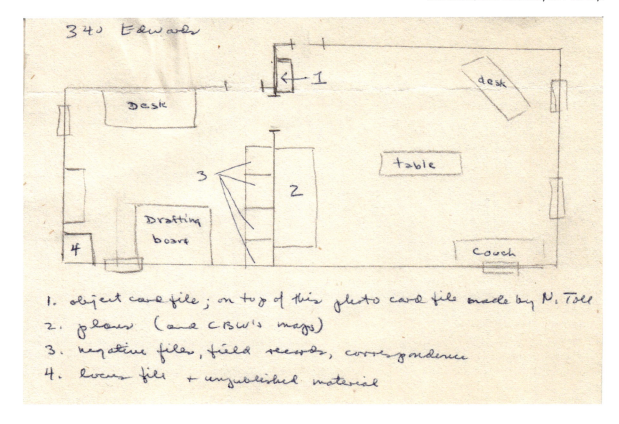

Perkins knew the material from Dura well, spending much of her time immersed in it, including fulfilling photographic requests for reproductions, and in 1973 she published her own book on the site and its art based on this familiarity.[17] Without a formal structure or archivist, however, no one else could find their way through it. After Perkins left her position at Yale, staff there could not find what they needed and continued to write to her to ask for help. Among those who sought her help was Alfred Bellinger (1893–1978), author of the Dura numismatic report and one of the editors of the publication series.[18] Preserved in Bellinger's correspondence is one such request for assistance, and Perkins's response contains her own sketch of the archive as it was when she left it, made to try and help him find what he was looking for.[19] At that time, the archive occupied some rooms in a university-owned house at 340 Edwards Street in New Haven (Fig. 3.2).[20] It is in records such as those made by Perkins that it is possible to learn something of the shifting usages and shapes of archaeological archives over time, and the complexity of understanding and using such archives. Far from being comprehensive, well organized, or methodical, like archaeological evidence itself, archaeological archives can be confusing, messy, and nibbled by mice.

One of the concerns that arises from digitization projects is the erasure of the visibility of archival supports in such projects. By this, I mean the way that physical archival documents tend to make clear, in their materiality and form, the historicity of the structures we are looking at, in the same way that recognizing Perkins's handwriting on an update to a photo card reveals the author. Another example can be seen in the attendant part of the archive which records a different photographic image, a photograph numbered D2, taken in the 1930–1931 field season (Fig. 3.3a–b). The handwritten field note records the original intention of the photograph as it was made in the field, in which it is described as 'View of City from Triumphal Arch' (Fig. 3.3a). Later, this description was appended to a scanned version of the negative for the Image AXS database which preceded the current online photographic catalogue on ArtStor. At this time, the monument in question gains a specific identification based on its inscription, the 'Arch of Trajan'. The metadata was then transferred from Image AXS to ArtStor, when a scan of the negative was made available online in 2009 (Fig. 3.3b).[21] When comparing the digital record available online and its metadata to the physical image and its records, there are clear differences. Even putting aside the issue of materiality, the digitized record loses its sense of being in a sequence, loses clarity over when nomenclature is introduced, and loses the intelligibility of being an accumulation of knowledge over time. The digital inscription of metadata gives it a sense of authority which is not in the original records.

More serious than these losses of the historicity of the archival archaeological records underlying the metadata, though, is the replication in that metadata of erasures or occlusions in the archive.[22] This single photographic record (D2) refers to this image (Fig. 3.4). Is this image really of the view of the city from the triumphal arch? In the photograph, can we only see a view of the city, along the horizon? Much more visible than the 'view of the city' supposed by the original caption or metadata is a group of local workers, some of whom are standing in a small trench and appear to be digging.[23]

1970. One of the problems with digitization projects can be the replication of descriptions, but in this instance, for whatever reason, the photograph is not included in the online catalogue at all. Further on these cards, see Baird and McFadyen 2014. The Dura photographs are online here, and as of 19 May 2022, photograph B-29 was not there, although images either side of it in the sequence were available: <https://library.artstor.org/#/collection/87730479> [accessed 30 September 2022].

[17] Perkins also contributed to the editing of Dura publications and wrote her own book on the art of the site: Perkins 1973.

[18] Bellinger's report on the coins: Bellinger 1949.

[19] Plan of 340 Edwards Street was enclosed in a letter she wrote to Bellinger (YUAG Dura-Europos Archive, Correspondence Drawer, Anne Perkins folder). This letter does not give a year, but other related letters are dated 1970.

[20] Yale Manuscripts and Archives RU 690. Scan of an image of the building in the 1970s, a Spanish revival mansion still owned by Yale, available: <https://hdl.handle.net/10079/digcoll/4340313> [accessed 30 September 2022].

[21] <https://library.artstor.org/public/SS7730479_7730479_10834525> [accessed 30 September 2022]. The scanning of the Dura negatives was undertaken with funding from the Ottoway project, which also funded the Dura gallery in the Yale University Art Gallery. The digitization first for use within the gallery and archives, and eventually online. On the Dura collection at Yale, see Brody 2016. On the 2009 deposit of the digitized photographs to ArtStor, see Brody 2011, 28.

[22] Also, by the time the images were being scanned, the negative before this in the sequence (D1) was gone. The print is still there but it does not exist in the digital archive because the scanning project worked from negatives.

[23] This photograph is also in the middle of what has recently been identified, based on satellite imagery, as a large battlefield between Roman and Sasanian forces: James 2015. The triumphal

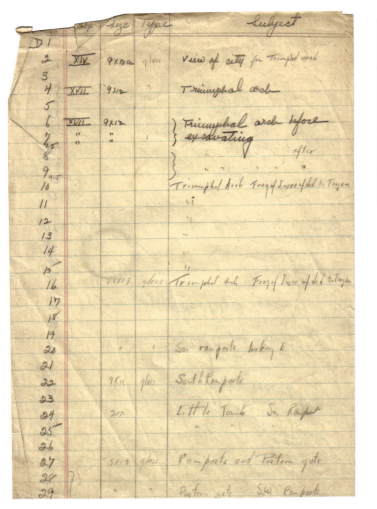

Figure 3.3. a) First page of original handwritten negative field register entry for season D, showing photograph D2, 'View of city from Triumphal arch'; b) the metadata for the digitized negative on Artstor.

Figure 3.4. Scan of negative D2. Dura-Europos Collection, Yale University Art Gallery.

Figure 3.5. Screen capture of search of fifteen thousand archival images for the subject 'workers'.

The archival supports erased from digitization projects make things seem more certain than they are, but they also replicate and embed deeply problematic institutional structures. For instance, Dura's photographs are all publicly available on ArtStor, which is a wonderful resource. But a search for 'workers' will turn up only two results, two versions of the same image, of workers gathered with Yale-French Academy archaeologists on payday (Fig. 3.5).[24] Two images of the hundreds which show labourers in this collection. Recent years have called much attention to the problematic nature of much archaeological labour, and the way those labourers' work and knowledge was unappreciated.[25] How will we ever consider seriously issues like archaeological labour and the place of archaeology in the colonial project if we do not use digitization as an opportunity to reflect on what other terms we might use here, to reflect on what else can now be seen?

The long shadows cast by archives are often unacknowledged in contemporary reckonings with archaeological legacy data. While archaeology has a responsibility to study the mass of information which it has generated but not studied or published, the form in which it is held is not necessarily a banal or benign one from which information about the past can be extracted. That is, we are limited in our ability to know the past not only by the extent of what is preserved in archaeological archives, or by the accessibility of those archives physically or online, but also by the form and structure of those archives. In the age of pandemic and big data, many institutions which hold archaeological archives are leaning harder than ever into the digital turn, and putting their archives online: in some cases, this serves to reinforce existing power dynamics within the archive while simultaneously rendering those dynamics invisible, as in the case of the photograph discussed above. In the next sections, I explore another example of an archival silence and ask how we might begin to address such silences.

---

arch was excavated under Pillet and published by members of Rostovtzeff's Yale seminar in the preliminary report Baur, Rostovtzeff, and Bellinger 1933, 3–4, 56–68.

24 <https://library.artstor.org/#/collection/87730479;page=1;size=48;term=workers> [accessed 19 May 2022].

25 Shepherd 2003; Riggs 2017; Quirke 2010.

Unclassified

Despite all this order which has been brought to archaeological archives, some things just did not fit. The title of this paper comes from a document I came across in the archive. By the time I encountered the archive (more than a decade ago), some of the photo catalogue cards had made their way into a folder marked 'Excavations and Personnel'; one of them was this one (Fig. 3.6).[26]

A small print, pasted to an index card, was annotated with the photographer's name — Jotham Johnson, and the date, the spring of 1929.[27] The photograph is of four men, standing inside the monumental western gate of the site. None are named. In the photographs at Dura, when the archaeological workers who undertook most of the labour at the site appear, they are usually invisible in such captions. This has important implications, I think, for the history of archaeology and archaeological labour.[28] But even when, as in this example, the workers push their way into view and are the undeniable subject of the photo, in crisp focus against the soft background of the ancient fortifications, the archive does not know what to do with them.[29] They are nameless and they are unclassified, in this case explicitly labelling the image with a title that reflects the fact that it does not fit: not a monument, not an object. Unclassified images, outliers in the structure, are images that evade bulk upload, and often do not get digitized at all.

As has been noted recently by Moss and Thomas in their book *Archival Silences*, silences in archives 'only exist when researchers notice them'.[30] How might we be more active in taking notice of the silences in archaeological archives — not only the things which were not recorded, but the structural absences that result from the systems and classifications we use to organize archaeological data? These archival structures have the power to determine what is a worthy object of study, and what is not.[31] Among those absences are of course the stories of local people — of local labour, knowledge, and sense of place.[32] Are there interventions we might make in the archive, which make the silences more visible, or at least address in some small way the deep structural absences of the archive? That is, to address Drake's call to attend to the production of archival dynamics, such as what is included and excluded, or the dynamic of possession versus that of dispossession.[33]

Seeing and Unseeing in the Archive: Syrian Hands and Voices

So, how do we begin to take notice of silences in the archaeological archive, to attend to the tension between what is included and what is excluded? We might think of it as a matter of a practice of archival inquiry which involves both seeing and unseeing. For some archival objects to become evident, we have to unsee the archival structure that structurally conceals them. In the case of the men in the image on the card deemed 'unclassified' (Fig. 3.6), we need to unsee the label, to look past the fact that the archive did not know what to do with this image, at the faces of the men present themselves. I say 'the men' because their names are not recorded in another archival silence. We need to attend to the people in the image, and to the fact the archive's own structure and content forces silence upon them. Shepherd has argued that attention to 'native' labour in archaeology, that 'the restoration of the dignity of a name and the lineaments of a biography is the first step in a process of redress in archaeology involving archaeology in colonial and former-colonial contexts'.[34]

While it is not always possible to have specific names or redress, how can we begin to pull at that thread, of names unrecorded, of faces staring back at us, expect-

---

26 The photograph was catalogued in the negative sequence (B178); the number is given on the card only as '178', presumably assigned before the archive was regularised by giving each season an alphabetic prefix (in the current archival sequence, there is no 'A', but 'B' starts with the second season of work and continues). The 'Excavations and Personnel' file was probably made by Perkins at the time other prints were distributed amongst 'locus' files which contained documentation for each excavation monument/city block at the site.

27 Spring 1929 was at the end of the second season of the Yale expedition; the work undertaken is summarized in Baur and Rostovtzeff 1931.

28 Baird 2011; 2019.

29 By the time the negative was scanned in the 1990s, it was torn (see image B178), and the accompanying database record lists the photographer as unknown. Johnson was later an NYU professor and first editor of *Archaeology* magazine. On his attitudes towards the local workmen at Dura, see Johnson 1929; Baird 2018, 47.

30 Moss and Thomas 2021a, 11.

31 Moss and Thomas 2021b, 10; Trouillot 1995, 99.

32 On local labour and knowledge at Middle Eastern archaeological excavations, see Mickel 2021.

33 Adapting Trouillot, Drake 2021, 14.

34 Shepherd 2003, 334. Further on photographs of archaeological workers (of Petrie in Egypt), Quirke 2010, and related to the excavation of Tutankhamun, the work of Riggs, including especially Riggs 2017; 2019.

Figure 3.6. Scan of 'Unclassified' photograph card. In 'Excavations and Personnel' Folder, Dura-Europos Collection, Yale University Art Gallery.

antly? Perhaps one way is to begin to trace, and give credit for, labour. If we look to the report of the season this photograph was taken, written by the excavation director Maurice Pillet, we can see, once again, that the 'organization', this time of the excavation itself rather than the archive, occludes most of the labour, most of the actual physical practice of archaeology, from view, although a few are named:

> The expedition was composed [...] of Mr Clark Hopkins, of Yale University, first scientific assistant and Mrs [Susan] Hopkins, of Mr Jotham Johnson, of Princeton University, scientific assistant, and Mr Serge Dairaines, secretary. In Syria [...] Victor Assal, first indigenous overseer, Abdul Messiah Taza, overseer, and Phares, foreman.[35]

The academic American staff get top billing, and while Pillet's 1929 November report gives names, or partial names, for the chauffer, cook, and foreman known only as Phares,[36] we cannot expect the details for most workers to be revealed so easily. The same happens if we go to the description in this contemporary textual report of the building in the photograph behind the men, the Palmyrene Gate (Fig. 3.6, background). In that description, objects passively are found without the need for human agency, still less local labour:

> les objets trouvés au fond de cette pièce, tels que le bouclier, deux parchemins, dont le plus grand (Ph. 12), les fragments de papyrus (Ph. 13) des cuirs et des boucliers peints et un beau swastika (Ph. 14) par exemple, sont donc antérieurs à l'an 160.[37]

---

[35] Pillet's original April 1930 French report on the campaign (Typescript in Dura-Europos Archive) was translated into English and published in the published version (both give the same names and titles). Baur and Rostovtzeff 1931, 1. In Pillet's earlier 1928 report (p. 6), he notes Assal is Armenian and was hired in Deir ez Zor. In that report, he discusses the problems (as he sees them) of hiring workers. Abdul Assiah Taza is identified in a photograph in Hopkins's popular account of the excavations, Hopkins 1979, 201.

[36] On local foremen in the nineteenth to twentieth centuries, Mairs and Muratov 2015.

[37] Pillet October 1928–April 1929 report, page 10, Yale Dura-Europos Archive. The 'Ph' abbreviations refer to photographs which were originally included with Pillet's report — the album for this year survives in the Yale Dura-Europos archive, with matching captions for the photographs in Pillet's own hand.

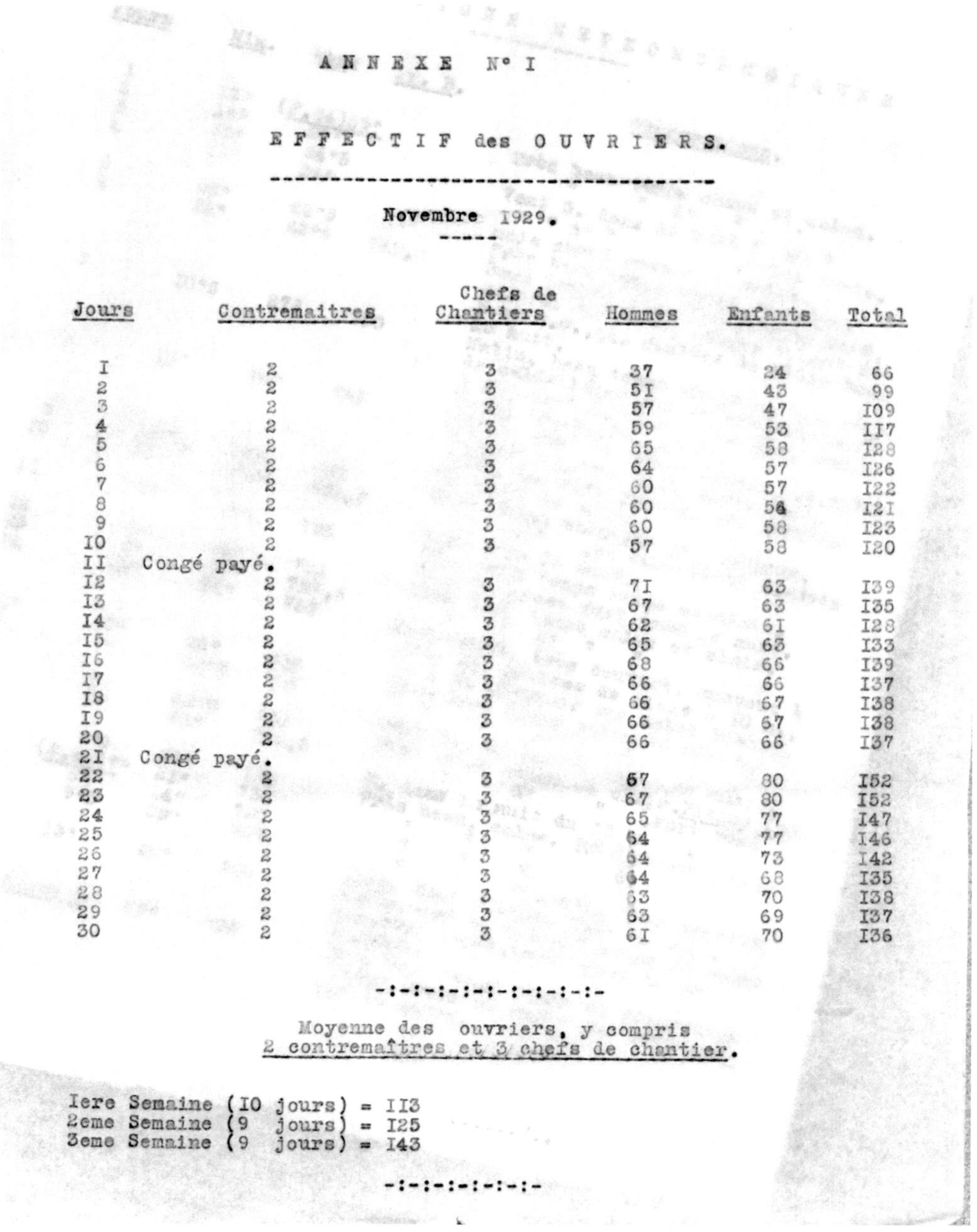

```
                    ANNEXE N° I

              EFFECTIF des OUVRIERS.
            ---------------------------------
                    Novembre 1929.
                        -----

                           Chefs de
   Jours    Contremaitres  Chantiers   Hommes   Enfants   Total

     1           2             3         37        24       66
     2           2             3         51        48       99
     3           2             3         57        47      109
     4           2             3         59        53      117
     5           2             3         65        58      128
     6           2             3         64        57      126
     7           2             3         60        57      122
     8           2             3         60        56      121
     9           2             3         60        58      123
    10           2             3         57        58      120
    11    Congé payé.
    12           2             3         71        63      139
    13           2             3         67        63      135
    14           2             3         62        61      128
    15           2             3         65        63      133
    16           2             3         68        66      139
    17           2             3         66        66      137
    18           2             3         66        67      138
    19           2             3         66        67      138
    20           2             3         66        66      137
    21    Congé payé.
    22           2             3         67        80      152
    23           2             3         67        80      152
    24           2             3         65        77      147
    25           2             3         64        77      146
    26           2             3         64        73      142
    27           2             3         64        68      135
    28           2             3         63        70      138
    29           2             3         63        69      137
    30           2             3         61        70      136

                    -:-:-:-:-:-:-:-:-
             Moyenne des ouvriers, y compris
             2 contremaîtres et 3 chefs de chantier.

   Iere Semaine (10 jours) = 113
   2eme Semaine ( 9 jours) = 125
   3eme Semaine ( 9 jours) = 143

                    -:-:-:-:-:-:-
```

Figure 3.7. November 1929 report, Annexe 1: workforce. Dura-Europos Collection, Yale University Art Gallery.

Labour is not discussed as such, but it is there nonetheless, in the movement of earth and the discovery of objects even if not named. We have to see these men, to imagine them into the story, with the movement of that earth and those archaeological objects.

Perhaps more obviously, we can follow the money — funds are usually accounted for in archaeological projects and their documentation. Labour is not only visible in the great quantity of earth moved on the ground and the monuments which were cleared, but in the budgets such as that of Pillet. The budget for this season allotted $3000 US for Pillet's salary, to which was added travel and living expenses.[38] The budget for the workers in the season our photo was taken, estimated at 110 men for

---

[38] For Dura, the institutional archives of Yale have detailed budgetary information not always contained in the archaeological archive. Detail especially from the papers of the president of Yale during the first seasons of work at Dura, James Angell. Papers are held in the Manuscripts and Archives Department of the Yale Sterling Library. For the 1928–1929 season in question I have only been able to locate budgets (not actual expenditure), but these are nonetheless a good guide. An interim report (December 1928) by Pillet also has details on pay, and similarly notes 150 average people were employed per day, including about fifty children (Pillet 1927–1930 Folder, Yale Dura-Europos Archive).

Figure 3.8. Dura photograph B27, taken during Johnson's work, interior of Palmyrene Gate. Recorded in archive as 'Main Gate (Palmyrene Gate), Springing of central arch, N. side'. Unidentified man at left. Johnson's chalked sequence visible adjacent to the inscriptions behind him on the walls of the passage. Dura-Europos Collection, Yale University Art Gallery.

150 days, was $3450. Divided into a daily wage, Pillet would earn twenty dollars a day, and each worker twenty-one cents.[39] During the season, Pillet kept detailed lists like this (Fig. 3.7) — we can see up to 150 men and boys were employed on the site on any given day. At the same time, his attention to the weather was far more detailed, and he thought the number of sandstorms was more relevant to archaeological work. So, sometimes the silences are the blind spots of the people doing the recording, for instance in Pillet's weather reports which are always more detailed than his worker lists, or even his object lists. While the weather on the Euphrates a century ago might not seem relevant to archaeological knowledge, the relative importance for those making the records makes clear that their priorities are not necessarily where ours are. Pillet's interim report of December 1928 also proudly reports when he is able to offer less pay due to an abundance of available labour: 'l'abondance de cette main d'œuvre a permis de ne payer que 12 piastres tur-

---

[39] This is the average figure: actual pay was slightly more for men and less for the boys, see further Baird 2018, 42.

Figure 3.9. Dura photograph B33, taken during Johnson's work. Recorded in archive as 'L8 House from top of Palmyrene Gate'. Dura-Europos Collection, Yale University Art Gallery.

ques argent les ouvriers nouveaux, les anciens restant au prix de 15 p.a.'[40]

As for Jotham Johnson (1905–1967), the Princeton graduate student who took our unclassified photograph, he was later president of the American Institute of Archaeology, and at the time of his death he was chair of Classics Department at New York University.[41] While at Dura, he studied the inscriptions in the passage of the Palmyra gate: he diligently recorded each and every little graffito.[42] He transcribed them, planned them, took squeezes, and made facsimiles. He wrote a number of reports, including extensive correspondence from the field back to Yale. In these reports and letters, he is a lone discover of ancient texts — he even gives them a number sequence that starts with 'J', for Johnson, to inscribe himself into the record further. And yet, if we follow the photographic sequence into the spaces he occupied, into the Palmyrene Gate, we can see that he, of course, was not alone at all (Fig. 3.8).[43] Not only does Figure 3.8 show one of the men he was working with (who looks very much like the third man from the left of the unclassified photograph and seems to be wearing the same clothes), but just visible on the walls of the gate passage behind him are Johnson's chalked series of numberings on the stone for each inscription. A few photos later in the sequence, and just a few steps away on-site (Fig. 3.9), we catch another glimpse of the man in the checked hat from the unclassified photo; his attire and facial hair is

---

[40] Pillet, *Report Sommaire sur les traveaux de l'expedition de Doura-Europos, Décembre 1928* (Pillet 1927–1930 Folder, Yale Dura-Europos Archive). Pillet also complains when, later in the season, workers are less available due to them tending to their agricultural and pastoral work. Baur and Rostovtzeff 1931, 1–2. In a letter dated Christmas Eve 1928, Clark Hopkins similarly reported that the expedition had so many applicants to work that 'we can call on them to bring their own tools'.

[41] 'Prof. Jotham Johnson, 61, Dies'; Chairman of Classics at N.Y.U.', *The New York Times*, 9 February 1967.

[42] See also Johnson's 1929 correspondence in the Yale Dura-Europos Archive: his letters to Rostovtzeff report on his finds in detail.

[43] Shepherd (2003, 346) contrasts the complete nature of the records of Goodwin's life held in the archive, compared to the lack of information on his 'co-workers'.

not like that of the local workers, but his footwear shows he is not on the Yale team, either. Is this Phares, the foreman mentioned in Pillet's notes? Perhaps, but 'perhaps' is as close as we might ever get in archives whose dynamics resolutely exclude and dispossess most of the people who conducted the work. Nonetheless, their presence and contributions can be brought into sharper focus. So, perhaps there is work we can do to take notice of silences in the archives, and a way to attend to them. We might not be able to restore names, but we can attend to our duty of care to such diasporic archives by giving notice to wages and faces and bodies and objects that do not really move themselves.

A century has now passed since the Yale excavations at Dura began, but much work remains to be done — not only in publishing the archaeology which has long waited in the archive for the attention it deserves (final reports on the paintings and the inscriptions of Dura, for example, were originally planned but never appeared). But also, for such archives, whose very collection was part of the colonial project of extraction from the Middle East, we can also now recognize a duty of care which needs to be attended to: to include the people and labour in the story, to demonstrate that places do not dig themselves, and objects do not appear, unbidden, from the earth. Redress is impossible, but we can nonetheless try to find ways to notice the silences and absences, to account for that which has been unclassified for far too long.

Works Cited

Baird, J. A. 2011. 'Photographing Dura-Europos, 1928–1937: An Archaeology of the Archive', *American Journal of Archaeology*, 115.3: 427–46.

—— 2012. 'L'habitat d'époque Romaine à Europos-Doura: replacer les artéfacts en contexte', in P. Leriche, G. Coqueugniot, and S. du Pontbriand (eds), *Europos-Doura: Varia*, I (Beirut: Institut français du Proche-Orient), pp. 231–40.

—— 2018. *Dura-Europos*, Archaeological Histories (London: Bloomsbury).

—— 2019. 'Exposing Archaeology: Time in Archaeological Photographs', in D. Hicks and L. McFadyen (eds), *Archaeological Photography* (London: Bloomsbury), pp. 73–95.

—— 2020. 'The Ruination of Dura-Europos', *Theoretical Roman Archaeology Journal*, 3.1: 1–20 <https://doi.org/10.16995/traj.421>.

—— 2022. 'The Site of the Archive: Responsibility and Rhetoric in Archival Archaeology of the Middle East', in A. Miranda and R. Raja (eds), *Archival Historiographies: The Impact of 20th-Century Legacy Data on Archaeological* (Turnhout: Brepols), pp. 161–73.

Baird, J. A. and L. McFadyen. 2014. 'Towards an Archaeology of Archaeological Archives', *Archaeological Review from Cambridge*, 29.2: 14–32.

Baur, P. V. C. and M. I. Rostovtzeff (eds). 1931. *The Excavations at Dura-Europos Conducted by Yale University and the French Academy of Inscriptions and Letters: Preliminary Report of Second Season on Work, October 1928-April 1929* (New Haven: Yale University Press).

Baur, P. V. C., M. I. Rostovtzeff, and A. R. Bellinger (eds). 1933. *The Excavations at Dura-Europos Conducted by Yale University and the French Academy of Inscriptions and Letters: Preliminary Report of Fourth Season of Work October 1930-March 1931* (New Haven: Yale University Press).

Bellinger, A. R. 1949. *The Excavations at Dura-Europos: Final Report*, VI: *The Coins* (New Haven: Yale University Press).

Bettington, J. 2008. *Keeping Archives* (Canberra: Australian Society of Archivists).

Bobou, O., A. C. Miranda, and R. Raja. 2021. 'The Ingholt Archive. Data from the Project "Archive Archaeology: Preserving and Sharing Palmyra's Cultural Heritage through Harald Ingholt's Digital Archives"', *Journal of Open Archaeology Data*, 9: 1–10 <https://doi.org/10.5334/joad.78>.

—— 2022. 'Harald Ingholt's Twentieth-Century Archive of Palmyrene Sculptures: "Unleashing" Archived Archaeological Material of Modern Conflict Zones', *Journal of Eastern Mediterranean Archaeology and Heritage Studies*, 10.1: 74–101.

Brody, L. 2011. 'Yale University and Dura-Europos: From Excavation to Installation', in L. Brody and G. Hoffman (eds), *Dura-Europos: Crossroads of Antiquity* (Chicago: University of Chicago Press), pp. 17–32.

—— 2016. 'Dura-Europos and Yale: Past, Present and Future', in T. Kaizer (ed.), *Religion, Society and Culture at Dura-Europos* (Cambridge: Cambridge University Press), pp. 206–18.

Darling, J. K. and S. B. Downey. 2007. 'Ann Perkins, 1915–2006', *American Journal of Archaeology*, 111.1: 149–50.

Downey, S. B. 2003. *Terracotta Figurines and Plaques from Dura-Europos* (Ann Arbor: University of Michigan Press).

Drake, J. M. 2021. 'Blood at the Root', *Journal of Contemporary Archival Studies*, 8: article 6.

Duchein, M. 1983. 'Theoretical Principles and Practical Problems of *respect des fonds* in Archival Science', *Archivaria*, 16: 64–82.

Elsner, J. 2021. '100 Years of Dura Europos', *Journal of Roman Archaeology*, 34.2: 764–84.

Hitchcock, M. W. 2020. 'Reflections in Shadow: Excavating the Personal Archives of Paul Jacobsthal and EM Jope', *Journal of Material Culture*, 26.1: 25–42.

Hopkins, C. 1979. *The Discovery of Dura-Europos* (New Haven: Yale University Press).

James, S. 2015. 'Of Colossal Camps and a New Roman Battlefield: Remote Sensing, Archival Archaeology and the "Conflict Landscape" of Dura-Europos, Syria', in D. J. Breeze, R. Jones, and I. A. Oltean (eds), *Understanding Roman Frontiers* (Edinburgh: John Donald), pp. 328–45.

Johnson, J. 1929. 'A Trade for Halliburton: Archaeology the Adventurous, as Viewed by One Whose Present Address is "Fouilles de Doura-Europos, Salihiyeh Euphrate, Syria"', *Princeton Alumni Weekly*, 29.24: 741.

Mairs, R. and M. Muratov. 2015. *Archaeologists, Tourists, Interpreters: Exploring Egypt and the Near East in the Late 19th–Early 20th Centuries* (London: Bloomsbury).

Mickel, A. 2021. *Why Those Who Shovel Are Silent: A History of Local Archaeological Knowledge and Labor* (Louisville: University Press of Colorado).

Moss, M. S. and D. Thomas (eds). 2021a. *Archival Silences: Missing, Lost and, Uncreated Archives* (London: Routledge).

—— 2021b. 'Theorising the Silences', in M. S. Moss and D. Thomas (eds), *Archival Silences: Missing, Lost and, Uncreated Archives* (London: Routledge), pp. 10–25.

Perkins, A. 1973. *The Art of Dura-Europos* (Oxford: Clarendon).

'Prof. Jotham Johnson, 61, Dies; Chairman of Classics at N.Y.U.', *The New York Times*, 9 February 1967.

Quirke, S. 2010. *Hidden Hands: Egyptian Workforces in Petrie Excavation Archives, 1880–1924* (London: Duckworth).

Raja, R., J. Steding, and J.-B. Yon. 2021. *Excavating Palmyra: Harald Ingholt's Excavation Diaries; A Transcript, Translation, and Commentary*, Studies in Palmyrene Archaeology and History, 4, 2 vols (Turnhout: Brepols).

Riggs, C. 2017. 'Shouldering the Past: Photography, Archaeology, and Collective Effort at the Tomb of Tutankhamun', *History of Science*, 55.3: 336–63.

—— 2019. *Photographing Tutankhamun: Archaeology, Ancient Egypt, and the Archive*, Photography, History: History, Photography (London: Bloomsbury Visual Arts).

Schellenberg, T. R. 1961. 'Archival Principles of Arrangement', *American Archivist*, 24.1: 11–24.

Schlanger, N. 2002. 'Ancestral Archives: Explorations in the History of Archaeology', *Antiquity*, 76: 127–31.

—— 2009. 'A Wrap-up of the AREA Project', *Bulletin of the History of Archaeology*, 19.1: 29–39.

Shepherd, N. 2003. '"When the Hand that Holds the Trowel Is Black…": Disciplinary Practices of Self-Representation and the Issue of "Native" Labour in Archaeology', *Journal of Social Archaeology*, 3.3: 334–52.

Toll, N. P. 1946. *The Excavations at Dura-Europos Conducted by Yale University and the French Academy of Inscriptions and Letters: Preliminary Report on the Ninth Season of Work, 1935–1936*, II: *The Necropolis*, ed. by M. I. Rostovtzeff, A. R. Bellinger, F. E. Brown, and C. B. Welles (New Haven: Yale University Press).

Trouillot, M.-R. 1995. *Silencing the Past: Power and the Production of History* (Boston: Beacon).

4. Collaborative Curation of Digital Archaeological Archives: Promise, Prospects, and Challenges

Anne Hunnell Chen
Bard College (achen@bard.edu)

Introduction

It is no secret that many Western GLAM[1] institutions, especially those established in the eighteenth, nineteenth, and early twentieth centuries, gained archaeologically related collections as a direct result of colonialist power dynamics. Such histories have had obvious enduring impacts on physical and intellectual access to collection holdings, as well as on collection interpretation and documentation. Progressively minded institutions are now seeking to mitigate those effects.[2] In the last decade, many such institutions have created and made available digital surrogates of collection holdings to curb significant barriers associated with travel to physical collections (i.e. access to international visas and prohibitive costs of long-distance travel).

While creating digital, especially open access, surrogates is an admirable and foundational first step, the ability to visit physical collections is not the only barrier to access, nor the only past injustice in need of correction. This chapter starts from the premise that metadata's inherently subjective character can impact how discoverable content is in the digital realm. This subjectivity can, in turn, shape who gets to have a voice in shaping knowledge about a given archaeological site. The chapter will demonstrate, for instance, that there are aspects of digital metadata — its silences, cataloguing language, and naming conventions, in particular — that are direct outgrowths of the colonialist dynamic that landed archaeological content in Western collections in the first place. Those outgrowths can, in turn, bias the digital discoverability — and therefore accessibility — of digital versions of that content. It is widely agreed that Western institutions that hold collections gained as a result of colonialism have an ethical imperative to curate those collections inclusively, in ways that take notice of stakeholder populations' interests and perspectives. However, such collaborative curation is hard to make good on if the material in question is neither physically accessible to the stakeholder population nor digitally discoverable in their native language. In the spirit of not just pointing to the problem but offering some thoughts on mitigating such issues, this chapter will introduce the International (Digital) Dura-Europos Archive's work in the free, multilingual, and editorially collaborative Wikidata environment. This case study will highlight ways that projects and institutions can harness the platform to increase the native-language discovery of collections and invite more diverse voices and perspectives into the process of knowledge creation and documentation regarding archaeological content. The chapter will close by sketching some of the still-outstanding issues raised by this approach and gesture toward nascent solutions currently in development.

Subjectivity of Metadata and Discoverability

Before launching into the issue at hand, a brief clarification is necessary to frame the discussion that follows. Many of the examples referenced in this chapter are drawn from the Yale University Art Gallery's collection. However, I want to be clear that the points made here are in no way meant to chastise the efforts of the excellent staff at that institution. Much to the contrary, the Yale University Art Gallery (YUAG) and its staff have been remarkably forward-thinking with respect to open access availability of digital surrogates for their collections to improve accessibility. For instance, in the early 2000s, long before many collections were thinking in such terms, YUAG digitized thousands of archival photographs, negatives, and plans from the excavation of Dura-Europos in the 1920s and 1930s. They then con-

---

[1] GLAM = Galleries, Libraries, Archives, and Museums.

[2] For the American Alliance of Museums' (AAM) policy on diversity and inclusion in museums, including the need to work 'collaboratively with key stakeholders locally, statewide, nationally and internationally to strengthen the integrity, impact and relevance of museums', see American Alliance of Museums 2014 and the associated toolkit of information and reference materials devoted to fostering greater diversity, equity, access, and inclusion in museums.

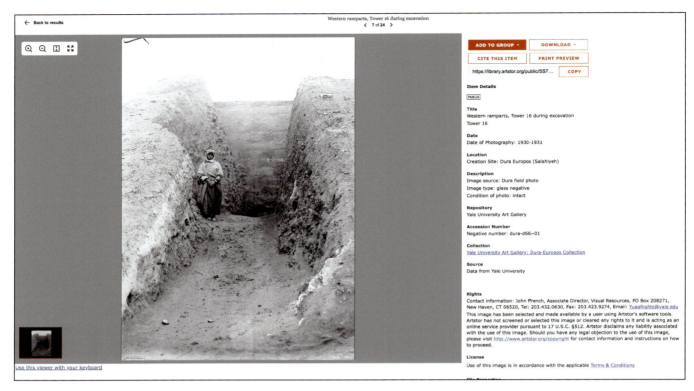

Figure 4.1. Screen capture of an ArtStor record for YUAG negative number dura-d66~01.

Figure 4.2. Screen capture of an ArtStor record for YUAG negative number dura-g852a~01.

tributed these digital surrogates to the public collections in the ArtStor image database.³ YUAG also made all of its object collections available for search, online viewing, and image download via its public collection database already in the 2010s. The problems referenced here concerning archival materials related to Dura-Europos are shared with many legacy archaeological collections. They are the product of inheritances from the past that are only now recognized as problematic. These remarks are intended to offer some practical suggestions that can help our discipline as a whole work toward undoing past colonialism's enduring impacts on the accessibility of digital archival content.

In case the term is not familiar, 'metadata' is 'information about data that promotes discovery, structures data objects, and supports the administration and preservation of records'.⁴ In the context of a discussion about digital surrogates that stand in for physical collection holdings, metadata refers to the data connected with the digital image, file, or record that stands in for a physical object. Such physical collection objects could include artefacts excavated on-site and removed to a museum collection as well as archival documents (often paper) connected with the excavation of a site and residing in a physical archival collection. Metadata can be thought of as the digital equivalent of a museum label's so-called 'tombstone data', including things like title, maker, provenance, culture, date, and the like. In fields concerned with identity formation and knowledge production, metadata are never neutral. It has been thoughtfully and succinctly summarized that 'the information that becomes data are collected because someone had a question to answer. Data serves a purpose, and people determine what those purposes are, which means that data cannot be separated from the subjective processes by which it is selected and used.'⁵

For example, consider Figure 4.1, a digitized version of an original negative taken between 1930 and 1931.⁶ Baird's important work on Dura-Europos's photographic archive has drawn attention to the ways in which legacy archaeological archives often make the gruelling conditions and physical labourers of 'Big-Dig' era excavations invisible.⁷ In the digital realm, the mechanism by which such archival silences function is, in fact, via object metadata. Note here, for instance, how the figure on the left side of the image is dehumanized and treated as a glorified archaeological scale in the photograph. For the excavators, this photograph was presumably meant to capture something of the size of an immovable archaeological feature. Hence, perhaps unsurprisingly, the digital metadata contains no mention of the human figure prominently featured in the photograph. The metadata for Figure 4.2 (from the same collection), where the scientific directors Franz Cumont and Michael Rostovtzeff are identified while the Mithraeum they stand in and the artefacts visible therein go unremarked upon, offers a stark contrast.⁸ The contrast offered by these two examples illustrates the subjectivity of decisions regarding what a photograph is 'about' as reflected in metadata created by a Western/White 'authoritative' institution. Metadata statements like these ultimately define how archival documents are searchable in the digital realm. Figure 4.1 could be cast just as validly as a record of early twentieth-century dress in eastern Syria or part of a testament to the working relationship between local populations and Western foreign overseers. However, nothing in the current digital metadata (modelled on the metadata for the physical negative) would help someone surface this photograph for such purposes. With the creation of digital surrogates, it is imperative to pause for a moment before translating institutional or non-digital format records into the public (often online) realm. To make good on postcolonial intentions, we must consider how digitization may reify the silences of physical archives and what we can do to counteract such eventualities.

Archaeological literature has at least highlighted the possibility of archival silences such that there is a possibility that subjectivities of the sort are on the radar of collection-managing staff.⁹ Other kinds of subjectivities in digital metadata — like the cataloguing language and variability in naming practices that can make it difficult for certain groups to surface archival content online — are not nearly as widely discussed. In many cases, such

---

3 ArtStor n.d: <https://library.artstor.org/#/collection/87730479> [accessed 22 September 2022].

4 Dictionary of Archival Terminology: <https://dictionary.archivists.org/entry/metadata.html> [accessed 22 September 2022].

5 Teel 2020.

6 YUAG negative number dura-d66~01. For details of the fourth season (October 1930–March 1931) of controlled scientific excavations at Dura-Europos under the joint auspices of Yale University and the French Academy of Inscriptions and Letters, see Baur, Rostovtzeff, and Bellinger 1933.

7 Baird 2011; 2018, 41–44; Baird and McFadyen 2014.

8 YUAG negative number dura-g852a~01.

9 Baird 2011; Baird and McFadyen 2014; Mickel 2021, 138–53.

subjectivities exclude the very groups that digital surrogates are envisioned to serve.

To clarify this point, let us turn to a brief thought experiment. Many readers will have had the experience of searching a collection's database for content related to a place name, returning zero results, re-searching with another language's variation on the spelling of the place name, and returning hits on the second search. That is the problem of discoverability; how easy is it for someone to find content related to their topic of inquiry? Imagine now that an institution holds archives related to a topic of interest to you or a non-academic friend. This fictional institution has just made digital surrogates of all their archival content available open access online. In this scenario, however, all the metadata for those archival materials is not only in a language you do not understand but also in a wholly different script than the one in which you normally communicate. How likely is it that a member of the educated but non-specialist general public, or even a specialized scholar would surface the fictional institution's digital content while searching about a topic of interest online? How likely would they be to surface the hypothetical collection material while searching for the rendering of the place name in their respective native languages?

For Dura-Europos, some fifteen thousand artefacts and the paper archives connected to the large-scale excavation of the site are physically located in Western countries, with YUAG holding the largest proportion of those.[10] The rest of the artefacts that the joint French-American excavations uncovered in the early twentieth century reside in Damascus as agreed under the terms of the partage at the time of excavation.[11] As mentioned, recognizing inequalities in access to travel, YUAG has been in the vanguard among GLAM collections in making its collection of Durene artefacts and archival documents available via open access databases online with high-quality imagery. Other Western collections that hold smaller numbers of Durene content have followed suit. While an admirable foundational step, these online resources must be searched independently and are usually catalogued in the language of the host institution, meaning that much of the material related to Dura-Europos is searchable only in English, with some in French. Much of the digitized content that would allow one to draw on the site of Dura-Europos for one's research, whether that be for research on the ancient or more recent periods to which the site bears witness, has not been discoverable in Arabic.

Without any capacity for searchability in Arabic, or even the inclusion of the Arabic script equivalent of the site name as part of the metadata, is this content really accessible to academic and non-academic Syrians who have an interest and/or stake in their country's cultural heritage? If the answer to the previous question is no, there is an additional and all-too-often overlooked downstream issue. If content is not easily discoverable for non-French or -English speakers, the very same folks who have not had a voice in the shaping of knowledge related to the site thanks to the physical removal of content to the West and the traditional curator-as-authority dynamic in its cataloguing, are the same populations that continue to be largely boxed-out of the possibility to bring different interpretive lenses to bear on the site, its excavation, and finds.[12]

The discoverability implications of the global diversity of place-name expressions point toward an analogous issue in the place-name variation driven by interpretational differences among scholars. Consider, for instance, a single structure that, in the hundred years since its excavation, has been referenced in the scholarly literature with identifying phrases as varied as 'temple of the Palmyrene gods', 'temple of the Oriental gods', and 'temple of Jupiter'. Following on from the previous point, remember that each interpretationally distinct naming convention can result in a corresponding variation in every global language in which one might hope to make content discoverable. As such, in the current digital landscape, instability and variability of naming practices can impede the true accessibility of digital surrogates. At present, an individual seeking to surface digital content faces the enormous burden of being familiar with an exhaustive list of place-name variations in order to perform a comprehensive search. Such a burden makes it challenging for anyone (regardless of language) to surface all the relevant digital content related to a particular archaeological site.

---

[10] Apart from YUAG, individual institutions in the West whose collections include artefacts from Dura-Europos include: Beinecke Rare Book and Manuscript Library, Yale Peabody Museum of Natural History, the Royal Ontario Museum, Harvard Art Museums, Princeton University Art Museum, the Kelsey Museum of Archaeology, Bibliothèque nationale de France, and the Louvre.

[11] Baird 2018, 1–16.

[12] On museums as sites of 'negotiated authority' and the changing relationships between curators and the public, see Longair 2015; Plumley 2022.

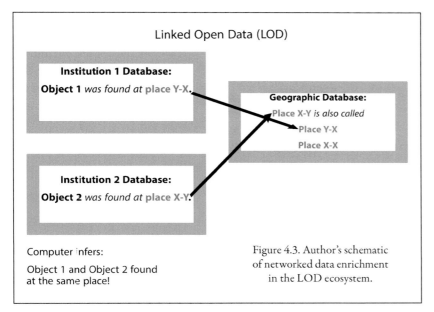

Figure 4.3. Author's schematic of networked data enrichment in the LOD ecosystem.

Dura-Europos is an effective site for illustrating the potential breadth of the problem since it contains examples caused by all three of the major factors that result in place-name inconsistency: name changes over time, variations due to linguistic differences, and interpretational differences among scholars. The site was known as both 'Dura' and 'Europos' at different points in Antiquity, leading modern scholars to invent the dual name 'Dura-Europos' to capture the complexity of the ancient naming tradition.[13] In the modern expression of the dual name, it is common to see the site's name expressed with and without a hyphen, and computers have not historically been able to infer that the two different ways of expressing the name refer to the same place. Add to this the fact that several Western European languages express the name with the addition of an 'O' in the spelling of Dura, and the problem expands. To complicate the issue even further, the most recent team to excavate at Dura-Europos has taken an intellectual stand, advocating that 'Europos' should come first in the modern amalgamated name since that was presumably the way the Hellenistic founders referred to the town.[14] The problem exponentially expands when you remember that each building within the site can have analogous complexity with regard to its own naming traditions. Each institution or database with content relevant to a given place or specific feature within an archaeological site may use different versions of a place name in their own cataloguing practices. Inconsistency of naming tradition across different databases makes it difficult for speakers of any language to be sure they have located all the content relevant to their area of inquiry, to confidently identify where an object was found according to object metadata, or to be sure which building an archival photograph or drawing references. Cataloguing language and choices regarding what name to call a site by are critical subjectivities in metadata that can bias content's digital discoverability, and therefore, its accessibility. Even with legacy archaeological content online, it is still not necessarily readily discoverable and easy to understand for all stakeholder audiences.

The problems described here around naming traditions will likely sound familiar to others who have worked with sites rich in legacy data. Complexity around naming traditions and the associated discoverability challenges is one area where the growing move toward Linked Open Data (LOD) has been particularly effective. As such, let us turn now to a brief introduction of the concept of LOD and then a more extended discussion of ways the Wikidata LOD platform, in particular, may be key in breaking the cycle of the unwitting perpetuation of archival metadata that keeps materials inaccessible to specific groups.

LOD and Digital Gazetteers

Tim Berners-Lee coined the phrase 'Linked Open Data' (LOD) in 2006.[15] The very simplified idea of LOD is that structuring metadata according to shared principles that allow for flexibility in implementation can ideally allow for data to speak the same computer-based language behind the scenes, regardless of the human language used in cataloguing. Structuring data according to LOD principles ideally allows computers to understand complex information and infer relationships between various topics, people, contexts, publications, datasets,

---

13 On the name(s) of the site in Antiquity, see Brody 2011, 17; Baird 2018, 17–19; James 2019, xli.

14 Under the direction of Pierre Leriche and Assad Al Mahmoud, the joint Mission Franco-Syrienne de Doura-Europos carried out excavations on the site from 1984 until the outbreak of the Syrian conflict in 2011. On the excavation history at Dura-Europos, see Brody 2011; Baird 2018, 1–16; James 2019, 1–10. On the rechristening of the site as 'Europos-Dura', see Baird 2018, 16; James 2019, xli.

15 Berners-Lee 2006. For a recent, concise summary of the mechanics of LOD, see Vitale and others 2021, 5–10.

and the like, more like humans. Enabling computers to make better inferences ultimately allows them to answer more complex questions in much more accurate ways than has traditionally been possible in the digital realm. Figure 4.3 schematizes the concept: imagine three separately catalogued and curated sets of digital information, managed by three different entities. The two institutions on the left have records for items associated in their metadata with specific places. LOD would allow these two databases to talk to one another and talk to the geographic database on the right, which in turn allows the computer to infer that the objects in the separate institutional databases are associated with the same place.

The vision of LOD would ultimately create a Web of Data where data points behave less like isolated islands in an online sea and more like a dynamic map charting evolving trade route connections between landmasses across the world.[16] This Web of Data maps interconnections among different ideas, people, places, things, events, publications, and datasets, such that both a human and a computer can crawl through the web to understand how data managed by different institutions or entities may have points of overlap. Within this ecosystem, data from separately conceived but tangentially related projects can be easily reused to enrich both original datasets mutually.

Entities known as 'digital gazetteers' are a vital part of the LOD ecosystem that archaeology and cultural heritage fields can productively harness to improve data accessibility challenges of the sort discussed previously.[17] The primary and secondary source material around which these disciplines revolve very often mentions, or is otherwise attributable to, places with a fixed geographic location. Archaeology/cultural heritage source material includes texts, artefacts, and features discovered during excavations, archival documents attesting to excavation and research practices, and modern books and articles. It is here that the naming tradition issue comes into play. Digital surrogates for each primary or secondary source relevant to the archaeology of Dura-Europos can be catalogued in various languages and refer in their object metadata to Dura-Europos and/or specific on-site buildings with a variety of spellings or naming traditions. It is unrealistic and inappropriate to expect speakers of languages worldwide to agree to a single definitive spelling and expression of all cultural heritage place names. Likewise, it is essential to maintain differences in name expressions that reflect intellectual and interpretive differences. This is where digital gazetteers within the LOD environment become extraordinarily helpful.[18]

Linked Open Data gazetteers gather up all the known name variants for a place, associate those names with a particular set of geographic coordinates, and assign that place a stable non-linguistic identifier. Within the LOD environment, therefore, data managers of various online databases can essentially tag entities in their online collection with the relevant stable identifier defined for the place with which the resource is associated; doing so thereby enriches the metadata for the tagged entity with all the various naming traditions known to the gazetteer.[19] This means that no matter the preferred way of referring to Dura-Europos's Temple of Bel that is chosen in a particular collection's metadata — be that Temple of Bel, Temple of the Palmyrene Gods, or a name in Arabic script — as long as data managers tag a digital record with the appropriate gazetteer ID, that record becomes linked to other digital entities associated with the same physical location no matter how they call that physical location. In this way, places defined within a digital LOD gazetteer can serve as a virtual-reassembly node for objects and archival materials potentially kept in different physical locations, catalogued in different languages, and possibly following any number of different naming conventions.

On an abstract level, it should be clearer now how archival archaeological collections' commitment to not just make their content available online via high-quality digital surrogates but also to integrate those surrogates into the growing LOD ecosystem can have important implications for more equitable access. Commitment to LOD integration is essential where the colonial dynamics of earlier eras factor into collection history and often unwittingly endure in collection metadata practices. Methods of integrating a collection's content into the

---

[16] A dynamic visualization of the cloud of LOD is available at <https://lod-cloud.net/#> [accessed 20 September 2022].

[17] Southall, Mostern, and Berman 2011; Vitale and de Beer 2019; Vitale and others 2021.

[18] On the development of digital geography applied in the field of classics, see Elliott and Gillies 2009. On the benefits of data annotation using digital gazetteers, see Vitale and others 2021. Among the most robust LOD gazetteers for ancient places are the World Historical Gazetteer (<https://whgazetteer.org/> [accessed 22 September 2022]), Pleiades (<https://pleiades.stoa.org/> [accessed 22 September 2022]), and the Getty Thesaurus of Geographic Names (<https://www.getty.edu/research/tools/vocabularies/tgn/index.html> [accessed 22 September 2022]).

[19] For detail on the mechanics and benefits of so-called Linked Open Geodata (LOG), see Vitale and others 2021.

LOD ecosystem can take many paths; in fact that flexibility is one of the LOD concept's strengths. There are, however, some distinct advantages — especially where there are issues of postcolonial equity at stake — of accomplishing LOD integration with the free, inherently multilingual, and editorially collaborative Wikidata platform. As a case study to illustrate the potential of Wikidata integration for digital archaeological archives, let us turn now to the introduction of the International (Digital) Dura-Europos Archive (IDEA), a project currently in development at Yale University and Bard College.

IDEA Case Study

The International (Digital) Dura-Europos Archive (IDEA) was founded in 2020 to use the power of LOD to (1) digitally reassemble materials related to the site but physically kept in separate collections worldwide; (2) provide context by more clearly tethering objects to their find-spots and the archival materials that attest to their discovery; and (3) accomplish those tasks while recognizing and working to improve the inequalities in access that have limited the ability of local Syrian stakeholder audiences to engage in debates relevant to the site and the materials found therein.[20] As one of the first tasks to bring about this work, in partnership with Pleiades, IDEA has systematically defined gazetteer entities for Dura-Europos and its various component parts.

Determined primarily by the commitment to develop a project that could serve multilinguistic users, open up Dura data held in Western collections for collaborative curation with stakeholder audiences that have not previously had easy access to it, and allow for the integration of the Damascus Dura collections at a later date, IDEA has opted to build its project backend in Wikidata.[21] Wikidata is a free, lower-barrier-to-entry LOD platform used by a growing number of GLAM institutions.[22]

The Wikimedia Foundation sponsors Wikipedia and other related projects like Wikidata and Wikimedia Commons, but one can think of Wikidata as essentially the 'wiki'-backed way to translate metadata into computer-readable statements that allow an institution's object metadata to integrate into the LOD ecosystem.

Importantly, from the perspective of institutional resources and sustainability, an institution that commits its data to Wikidata does not need to host its own triplestore separately. Triplestores are specially built databases that store semantic triples, the datatype that drives the LOD ecosphere. Removing the triplestore barrier is significant with regard to equity. Well-resourced institutions may be able to shoulder the burden of the specialist knowledge and the price tag for annual upkeep that accompanies such work. However, not all institutions have access to such possibilities. There is a distinct threat with the development of any potentially revolutionizing method that its uptake further entrenches existing marginalizations, so the benefits of removing the hosting impediment should not be passed over lightly.

Furthermore, Wikidata allows users — and this is key — to access data and contribute edits in some six hundred world languages, including Arabic.[23] This means that by integrating the Dura-Europos artefacts and archival documents held in the West into Wikidata, IDEA has made this content not only discoverable for the first time in many languages but has also opened it up to collaborative curation from users all over the world — including those in the Middle East — for the first time in their own native languages.

How exactly the Wikidata platform enables multilinguistic search and metadata enrichment may still seem somewhat abstract. In the spirit that concrete examples often make the conceptually complex easier to grasp, we will consider some examples drawn from IDEA's data interventions. IDEA started its data aggregation efforts with the integration of digital surrogates for artefacts excavated at Dura-Europos and physically held in Western collections. It is, therefore, the records for Dura artefacts in Western collections that are most fully theorized within the Wikidata integration. For this reason,

---

[20] <https://www.duraeuroposarchive.org> [accessed 22 September 2022].

[21] <https://www.wikidata.org> [accessed 22 September 2022]; Vrandečić and Krötzsch 2014.

[22] WikiProject Cultural Heritage, for instance, states among its chief aims to establish Wikidata as 'a central hub that interlinks GLAM collections around the world and provides links to bibliographic, genealogical, scientific and other collections of information and thereby functions as the ultimate authority file providing mapping information between these different collections', and includes among its participants a host of GLAM professionals. For GLAM community work in the Wikimedia environment (including Wikidata, Wikipedia, Wikimedia Commons), resources, and case studies, see Wikimedia Outreach: GLAM Wiki, n.d. For a systematic study of libraries' use of Wikidata for sharing and exchanging metadata, see Tharani 2021.

[23] For a list of languages currently available for use in Wikimedia projects, see <https://www.wikidata.org/wiki/Help:Wikimedia_language_codes/lists/all> [accessed 22 September 2022].

collectionLabel	count
Bibliothèque nationale de France	11
Beinecke Rare Book & Manuscript Library	154
Yale University Art Gallery	14447
Department of Near Eastern Antiquities of the Louvre	185
Yale Peabody Museum of Natural History	5
Kelsey Museum of Archaeology	64
Princeton University Art Museum	2
Royal Ontario Museum	44

Figure 4.4. Query showing the number of Dura-Europos artefact records from each IDEA partner institution currently searchable in Wikidata. Link to dynamic query: <https://w.wiki/3MFr>.

the discussion that follows opens with a close look at a record for a digital surrogate of a YUAG artefact to illustrate the discoverability benefits the Wikidata platform provides. However, keep in mind that what is demonstrated here for an ancient artefact's digital surrogate record is ultimately applicable to a digital surrogate for a more recently created entity like an archival photograph. IDEA is currently planning a large-scale Wikidata integration of digital surrogates for Yale University Art Gallery's archival holdings relevant to the Dura excavations, including photographs, negatives, plans, and the like. Therefore, the discussion that follows will preview some of the ways IDEA envisions using Wikidata's suite of tools to counter enduring colonialist silences in the context of such materials.

As captured by the query featured in Figure 4.4, in partnership with the eight different American and international host collections, IDEA has facilitated the creation of records for all the Durene artefacts in Western collections. The left portion of Figure 4.5 provides an example of such a record. Creating records for these artefacts in the Wikidata environment now means that these items are searchable together for the first time and discoverable in hundreds of languages at a basic level — and this is key — without the IDEA team performing any translation work. Let us look closer at how Wikidata makes this possible.

The sample Wikidata item record on the left of Figure 4.5 is for a YUAG relief that depicts Heracles wearing the Nemean Lion skin.[24] Not every metadata statement for this specific object has (as yet) been translated into every world language. However, thanks to the global Wikidata editorial community, widely shared concepts relevant to records from Dura-Europos, like the place name associated with the site (Fig. 4.5A) and the concept of an archaeological artefact (Fig. 4.5B), have been translated into various world languages. The concept associated with the god known as Heracles has also been translated into an impressive list of world languages (Fig. 4.5C). By translating a traditional non-LOD metadata statement into one that parses the Dura relief's critical information into links that point out to additional contextualizing information, the object's metadata statements become exponentially more tractable for people searching outside of the original cataloguing language, in this case, English. In practice, this means an Arabic or Japanese speaker, for instance, would be able to search in their native language for the equivalent of 'archaeological artefact depicting Heracles from Dura-Europos' and turn up the same results as someone searching in English.

Further, as already hinted, Wikidata offers several tools that can be harnessed to productive effect specifically for digital archaeological archival purposes. Especially important is how researchers and collection data managers can utilize such tools to begin counteracting or at least acknowledging archival silences of the type that Jen Baird's work has highlighted. The 'Wikidata Image Positions' tool, for instance, allows users to assert information contained within an image but not necessarily expressed by its original metadata.[25] In effect, this tool makes information that might be implicit to a human viewer apparent to computers.

For illustrative purposes, consider two examples. In Figure 4.6, for instance, notice that one portion of the archival document corresponds to a drawing of a figu-

---

[24] YUAG ID: 1938.5302; Wikidata QID: Q60847119.

[25] <https://wd-image-positions.toolforge.org> [accessed 22 September 2022].

4. COLLABORATIVE CURATION OF DIGITAL ARCHAEOLOGICAL ARCHIVES

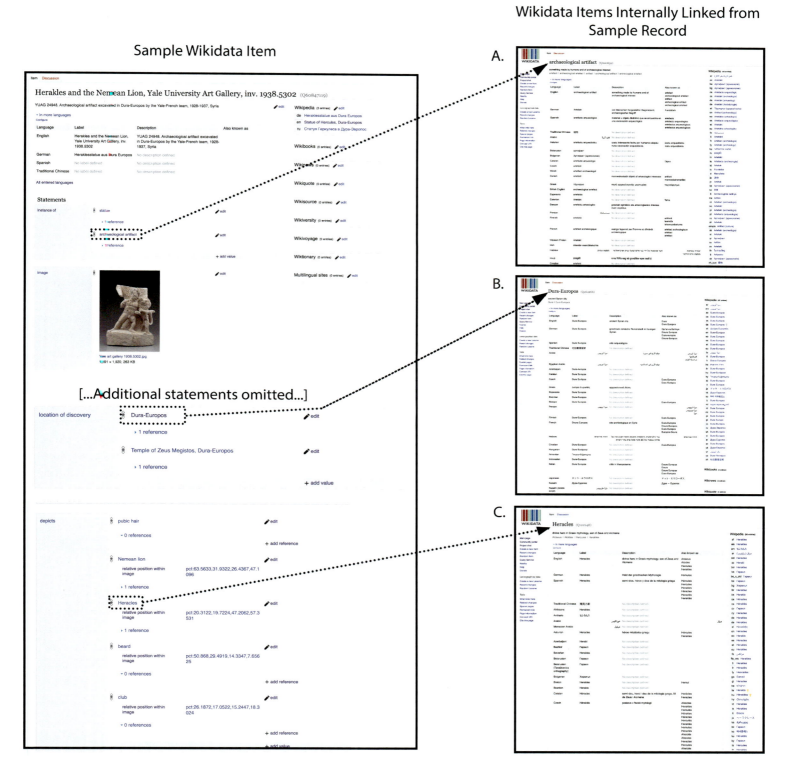

Figure 4.5. Sample Wikidata item with metadata statements composed of links to additional external items (each with its own multilinguistic labels; Arabic label highlighted).

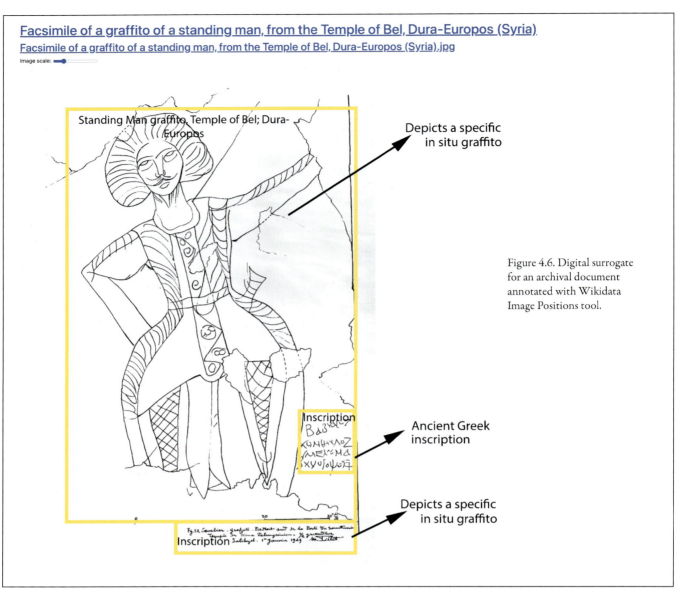

Figure 4.6. Digital surrogate for an archival document annotated with Wikidata Image Positions tool.

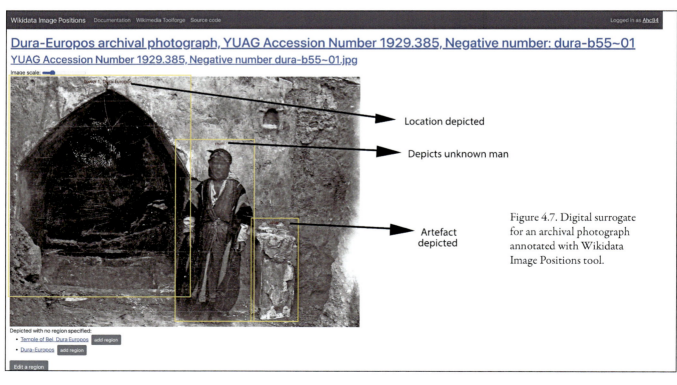

Figure 4.7. Digital surrogate for an archival photograph annotated with Wikidata Image Positions tool.

ral graffito of a man, a feature presumably still *in situ* at Dura-Europos.[26] Another portion relates to ancient inscriptional content, and a third component captures the excavator's notes at the time of recording. A human viewer would likely be able to intuit those distinctions, but without additional information making those relationships explicit, such complexity would be lost on a computer.

Archival photographs can likewise hold layers of information that are not readily apparent to computers. Image annotation tools like the 'Wikidata Image Positions' tool can be used to make evident to both humans and computers that the archival photograph in Figure 4.7 includes a human figure (whose name is currently unknown), was taken directly at the entrance to a tower on Dura-Europos's north-western corner, and includes an artefact.[27] Perhaps someone with a different knowledge base than the IDEA editors would be able to add additional annotations about, say, the aspects of early twentieth-century dress to which this image bears witness. Using this 'image positions tool' in the Wikidata context — either by a subject-area specialist or a member of the global lay public, thereby adds human- and computer-readable metadata statements to the digital surrogate in question (Fig. 4.8). Increasing the number of metadata statements on any visual resource multiplies the number of paths to discover the resource in question. The Wikidata platform's multilingualism, global reach, open editorial policy welcoming all registrants, and built-in tools to aid the creation of new metadata statements present a powerful suite for meaningful collection decolonization and stakeholder-empowerment purposes. Since the platform is inherently set up to allow users to make annotations and other editorial interventions in one's native language, Wikidata is ready-made to facilitate local stakeholder pushback on the Eurocentric narratives that have predominated in connection with sites excavated under colonialist duress.

Lingering Challenges

As bright as the prospects are for the use of Wikidata for postcolonial approaches to digital archaeological archives, like any new methodological frontier, this one does not come without its points of caution. Perhaps the most pressing is the uncertainty about how best to balance completely open global editorial input and concerns about data security. Sceptics would caution that cultural-heritage stewards must control an 'authoritative' record for objects in their collections/purview to preserve some hold on what is 'known' about a given historical entity, especially as that entity is represented in the growingly influential virtual realm.[28] While this concern is not to be dismissed out of hand, it must be borne in mind that such impulses may well be grounded in inherited judgements that privilege colonialist frameworks.

Regarding IDEA's work in Wikidata, our team was cautioned that opening the data under the IDEA aegis for entirely open editorial input could incur vandalism from ill-intended opportunists. However, the IDEA content has been online via Wikidata for two years and counting, and happily, there has not been a single incident of such intervention. This is not to say that such concerns are unfounded, especially over the long term; they are just untested. Fortunately, however, the Wikidata platform has built-in features that can act as safeguards in the event of disingenuous metadata manipulation. For instance, it is possible for the digital content manager for a particular institution to place Wikidata records for objects held in that institution's collection on a 'watchlist'. Users with a particular item placed on their 'watchlist' are alerted whenever a new edit is registered on the item in question.[29] In the event of a problematic intervention into the metadata of a digital surrogate, Wikidata provides a quick and easy intervention by which someone (actually, anyone — which is a crucial postcolonialist point) can register disagreement with an interpretive claim regarding the digital item's metadata (statements). Users can even fully roll back problematic edits, and users who are not acting in good faith can face suspension from the platform.[30]

Even more importantly, from the perspective of posterity, the Wikidata platform automatically makes a digi-

---

[26] YUAG Negative number y492; Wikidata QID: Q109673604.

[27] YUAG Negative number dura-b55~01; Wikidata QID: Q110873191.

[28] For instance, artificial intelligence-powered virtual assistants like Siri and Alexa rely upon structured knowledge bases like Wikidata to perform their functions; see Urs and Minhaj 2021.

[29] <https://www.wikidata.org/wiki/Help:Watchlist> [accessed 22 September 2022].

[30] On rollbacks in the Wikidata community, see <https://www.wikidata.org/wiki/Wikidata:Rollbackers> [accessed 22 September 2022]. On Wikidata community standards see <https://www.wikidata.org/wiki/Wikidata:List_of_policies_and_guidelines> [accessed 22 September 2022]. For policies and procedures for dealing with vandalism in the Wikidata community, see <https://www.wikidata.org/wiki/Wikidata:Vandalism> [accessed 22 September 2022].

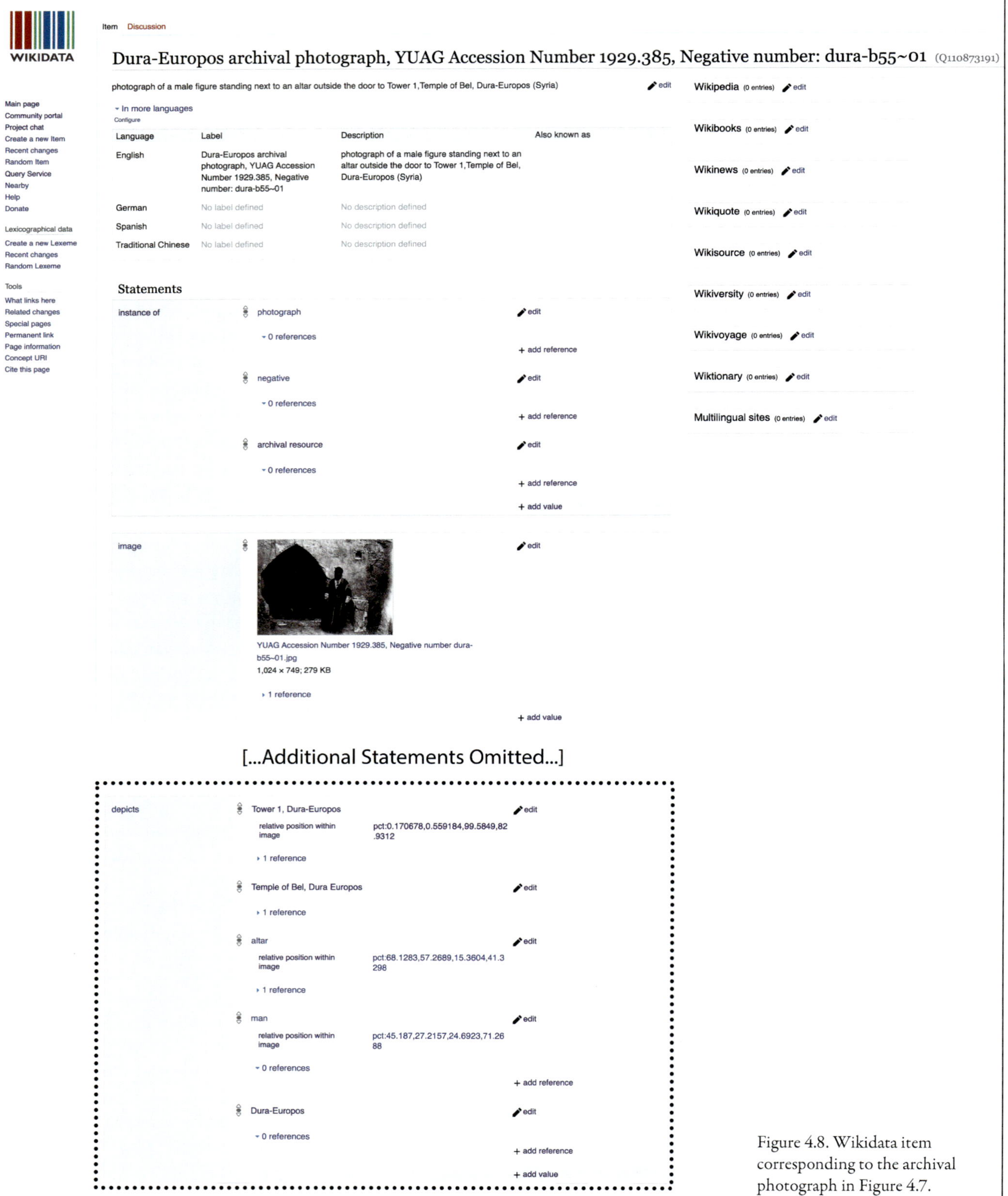

Figure 4.8. Wikidata item corresponding to the archival photograph in Figure 4.7. 'Depicts' metadata statements added with the Wikidata Image Positions tool are highlighted.

tal record of the hypothetical back-and-forth editorial exchange between the collection representative and the external editor. In this way, we can think of Wikidata as providing perhaps a valuable avenue for documenting the editorial disagreement of this contemporary moment's back-and-forth between interested parties across the world regarding the interpretation of a particular artefact or document.

There is one final challenge that requires flagging. At present, many institutions — for good reasons — keep closed, private internal records for objects and documents in their collections. Suppose such an institution creates Wikidata records (or any other LOD record that shares object metadata separate from the internal institutional record) for items in their collections. In that case, there is a well-founded concern that such LOD copies of institutional metadata may fall out of alignment with internal institutional records in important regards. Imagine, for instance, that a group of objects was accessioned into a collection without assigning individual accession numbers to each component of the group. If the collecting institution later gives each object in the original group an individual accession number, it would be essential to reflect such a change in external LOD records for the hypothetical objects in question. Conversely, it could be helpful for collections to be able to reabsorb into their internal records certain kinds of statements added to Wikidata by the broader public. This process of pushing out edits from the holding collection's record-keeping system and reabsorbing specific external edits from Wikidata (subject to institutional vetting) is called 'data roundtripping' and is already possible to partially automate.[31] However, it remains a question of how to make the automated process efficient and easy enough that it can be performed without abundant specialist technical help and how (given the demands that already exist on the time and attention of curators and archivists) to most efficiently vet the information that collections might want to reabsorb into their closed institutional records. One of the strengths of the Wikidata concept and its growing uptake by GLAM institutions worldwide is that the 'data roundtripping' and vetting questions are mutual, and solutions are already being documented, openly shared, and debated.

This chapter has drawn attention to the fact that cataloguing language and choice of place name by which to label data are both significantly loaded decisions that impact who has access to the content in question. Such subjectivities and our blind spots for the inequalities in intellectual access that they perpetuate are significant inheritances from colonialism that we are ethically obligated to continue trying to dislodge. LOD in general, and the Wikidata ecosystem more specifically, hold great promise toward this urgent end.

---

[31] Fauconnier 2019. The evolving shared space for exchange of information regarding GLAM data-roundtripping and model workflows is <https://meta.wikimedia.org/wiki/Structured_data_for_GLAM-Wiki/Roundtripping> [accessed 22 September 2022].

Works Cited

American Alliance of Museums. 2014. 'AAM Diversity and Inclusion Policy' <https://www.aam-us.org/programs/diversity-equity-accessibility-and-inclusion/> [accessed 28 May 2022].

ArtStor. n.d. 'Yale University Art Gallery: Dura-Europos Collection' <https://library.artstor.org/#/collection/87730479> [accessed 28 May 2022].

Baird, J. A. 2011. 'Photographing Dura-Europos, 1928–1937: An Archaeology of the Archive', *American Journal of Archaeology*, 115.3: 427–46 <https://doi.org/10.3764/aja.115.3.0427>.

—— 2018. *Dura-Europos* (London: Bloomsbury).

Baird, J. A. and L. McFadyen. 2014. 'Towards an Archaeology of Archaeological Archives', *Archaeological Review from Cambridge*, 29.2: 14–32.

Baur, P. V. C., M. Rostovtzeff, and A. Bellinger (eds). 1933. *The Excavations at Dura-Europos Conducted by Yale University and the French Academy of Inscriptions and Letters: Preliminary Report of Fourth Season of Work, Oct. 1930-March 1931* (New Haven: Yale University Press).

Berners-Lee, T. 2006. 'Linked Data: Design Issues' <https://www.w3.org/DesignIssues/LinkedData.html> [accessed 22 September 2022].

Brody, L. 2011. 'Yale University and Dura-Europos: From Excavation to Installation', in L. Brody and G. L. Hoffman (eds), *Dura-Europos: Crossroads of Antiquity* (Chicago: University of Chicago Press), pp. 17–32.

Dictionary of Archive Terminology. n.d. 'Metadata' <https://dictionary.archivists.org/entry/metadata.html> [accessed 25 May 2022].

Elliott, T. and S. Gillies. 2009. 'Digital Geography and Classics', *Digital Humanities Quarterly*, 3.1 <http://www.digitalhumanities.org/dhq/vol/3/1/000031/000031.html> [accessed 12 February 2023].

Fauconnier, S. 2019. 'Data Roundtripping: A New Frontier for GLAM-Wiki Collaborations', *Diff* (blog), 13 December 2019 <https://diff.wikimedia.org/2019/12/13/data-roundtripping-a-new-frontier-for-glam-wiki-collaborations/> [accessed 22 September 2022].

James, S. 2019. *The Roman Military Base at Dura-Europos, Syria: An Archaeological Visualisation* (Oxford: Oxford University Press).

Longair, S. 2015. 'Cultures of Curating: The Limits of Authority', *Museum History Journal*, 8.1: 1–7 <https://doi.org/10.1179/1936981614Z.00000000043>.

Mickel, A. 2021. *Why Those Who Shovel Are Silent: A History of Local Archaeological Knowledge and Labor* (Baltimore: Project MUSE).

Plumley, A. 2022. 'Meeting the Moment', *Museum Magazine*, 14 January 2022 <https://www.aam-us.org/2022/01/14/meeting-the-moment/> [accessed 22 September 2022].

Southall, H., R. Mostern, and M. L. Berman. 2011. 'On Historical Gazetteers', *International Journal of Humanities and Arts Computing*, 5.2: 127–45. <https://doi.org/10.3366/ijhac.2011.0028>.

Teel, J. 2020. 'Data for Religious Studies and Digital Humanities' <https://web.archive.org/web/20210512023411/https://www.jadeteel.com/academic/data-for-religious-studies-and-digital-humanities/> [accessed 22 September 2022].

Tharani, K. 2021. 'Much More than a Mere Technology: A Systematic Review of Wikidata in Libraries', *The Journal of Academic Librarianship*, 47.2: 102326 <https://doi.org/10.1016/j.acalib.2021.102326>.

Urs, S. and M. Minhaj. 2021. 'Wikipedia Infoboxes: The Big Data Source for Knowledge Bases behind Alexa and Siri Virtual Assistants', *Information Matters*, 1.11 <https://r7q.22f.myftpupload.com/2021/11/wikipedia-infoboxes-the-big-data-source-for-knowledge-bases-behind-alexa-and-siri-virtual-assistants/> [accessed 12 February 2023].

Vitale, V. and S. de Beer. 2019. 'Final Report: Urban Gazetteers', *Pelagios* (blog), 7 June 2019 <https://medium.com/pelagios/final-report-urban-gazetteers-35ba6b75f243> [accessed 22 September 2022].

Vitale, V., P. de Soto, R. Simon, E. Barker, L. Isaksen, and R. Kahn. 2021. 'Pelagios – Connecting Histories of Place. Part I: Methods and Tools', *International Journal of Humanities and Arts Computing*, 15.1–2: 5–32 <https://doi.org/10.3366/ijhac.2021.0260>.

Vrandečić, D. and M. Krötzsch. 2014. 'Wikidata: A Free Collaborative Knowledgebase', *Association for Computing Machinery*, 57.10: 78–85 <https://doi.org/10.1145/2629489>.

Wikimedia Outreach: GLAM Wiki. n.d. <https://outreach.wikimedia.org/wiki/GLAM> [accessed 28 May 2022].

5. Archiving Palmyra: Outcomes of Inquiry into Archaeological Legacy Data

Olympia Bobou, Amy C. Miranda, Rubina Raja, and Julia Steding

Centre for Urban Network Evolutions (UrbNet), Aarhus University
(Olympia.bobou@cas.au.dk, acm351@gmail.com, Rubina.raja@cas.au.dk, j.steding@cas.au.dk)

Introduction

Palmyra is a city famous for its situation, for the richness of its soil, and for its agreeable springs; its fields are surrounded on every side by a vast circuit of sand, and it is as it were isolated by nature from the world, having a destiny of its own between the two mighty empires of Rome and Parthia, and at the first moment of a quarrel between them always attracting the attention of both sides.[1]

This, perhaps the most well-known quote about Palmyra, immediately transfers one's imagination to the oasis city in the Syrian Steppe Desert, which has attracted the attention of scholars and travellers alike since it was rediscovered by European travellers in the seventeenth century.[2] In the late eighteenth century, when western travel in the region took off — both for scholarship and culture tourism — followed by a surging interest in the culture of the Near East, the export of and trade in antiquities also spiked. Numerous sites in the Near East became 'magazines' from which objects were drawn and pulled into European and later American collections — private and public. From the 1890s onwards, the earliest European collections of Palmyrene artefacts can be traced, such as the collection in the Ny Carlsberg Glyptotek in Copenhagen, the collection in the Musée de Louvre in Paris, and the collection today in the National Museum in Istanbul.[3] Today, we know of Palmyrene sculptural material spread across thirty-three countries and housed by 235 collections.[4] This underlines that trade with these artefacts has been intense and still is ongoing. We do, however, not have an overview of the looting situation, nor of the situation on the illegal art market, but often objects with a Palmyrene provenance pop up at various art dealers and in auction house catalogues. Today, most of these will not have an accepted collection history, contrary to the art dealers' claim. Most often the objects have not been published before and are said to belong to old private collections stemming from before 1970, which is one clear indication that they might not have a clean provenance history. This contribution will focus exclusively on the research done within the Palmyra projects based at Aarhus University and on what the research on the Palmyrene portraits since 2012 and the archival material compiled by the Danish archaeologist Harald Ingholt has added to our knowledge about Palmyrene archaeology and history and the collection history of Palmyrene art in general.

Already at the end of the nineteenth century, some excavations took place. However, they were not documented in any detail, since such ventures aimed to remove specific monuments from the site and transfer them to collections — such as the famous Tax Tariff from AD 137 that was excavated by the Russian Prince Abamelek-Lazarev and taken to St Petersburg.[5]

From the 1880s, the Danish brewer Carl Jacobsen began collecting pieces that would present a comprehensive picture of Palmyrene portraiture types. Through his contacts in Beirut, he managed to acquire a collection that was unparalleled in other museums outside the Ottoman Empire, of which Syria then formed part.[6]

---

[1] Plin., *HN*. v.

[2] Sartre-Fauriat 2019. The city had fallen into obscurity after the fall of the Umayyad dynasty, under whose control it had been in the Early Islamic period, and had become a small village centred in the Sanctuary of Bel: Intagliata 2018, 107–08.

[3] Raja 2018; 2019b.

[4] All known funerary portraits were collected in a database by the Palmyra Portrait Project [accessed October 2022].

[5] For the research history, see Shifman 2014, 37–46.

[6] The British Museum, the Louvre, and the Metropolitan Museum of Art have similarly large collections created in roughly the same period as Jacobsen's collection, but they do not have either the

Figure 5.1. A view through Palmyra's triumphal arch. © Palmyra Portrait Project, Ingholt Archive at Ny Carlsberg Glyptotek, and Rubina Raja.

Figure 5.3. Harald Ingholt. © Rubina Raja and Palmyra Portrait Project, courtesy of Philip Underdown.

Figure 5.2. Harald Ingholt standing at a Palmyrene Hypogeum in the south-west necropolis, with visitors. © Rubina Raja and Palmyra Portrait Project, courtesy of Philip Underdown.

Jacobsen, in a letter to his agent in Beirut, the Danish consul Julius Løytved, expressed interest in financing an archaeological expedition to the site, which, however, never was realized.[7] Another Dane, Johannes Elith Østrup, spent time in Palmyra in the 1890s and described the active scene in dealing with antiquities situated between random looting and systematic removal of objects for art dealers.[8] The late nineteenth century seems to have been a time in which one did not find oneself alone in Palmyra when visiting the site, and it was already at this point renowned for its sculpture. In the early twentieth century, after the dissolution of

---

number or the range of objects of the Ny Carlsberg Glyptotek. Only the Istanbul Archaeological Museum's collection can be compared in numbers; however, the core of its collection was formed when Syria was part of the Ottoman Empire, and several of the pieces whose provenance can be determined were products of illicit excavations that had been confiscated at the borders and then transported to Istanbul for safe keeping in the absence of an archaeological museum in Syria. See Bobou and Thomsen 2021; Dentzer-Feydy and Teixidor 1993; Musée Imperial Ottoman 1895. For Jacobsen and his collection of Palmyrene antiquities, see Raja 2019a; 2019b; 2021a; 2021b.

[7] Nielsen 2019.

[8] Østrup 1894; 1895. See also Spencer 2022 for a translation and commentary of Østrup's *Skiftende Horisonter* into English.

the Ottoman Empire and the institution of the French Mandate in Syria, archaeological missions were soon undertaken in Palmyra.[9] These focused on exploring the Roman-period monuments of the city, with a focus on the monumental religious architecture (Fig. 5.1) as well as the city's necropoleis (Fig. 5.2).[10] Much research has been undertaken since then, much of it focusing on the architecture and art of the city as well as on the city's role in the global trade network in the first three centuries AD.[11] Since the civil war broke out in 2011, there has been a surge in the research interest of the city and its cultural heritage, ranging from projects focusing on documenting the destruction of monuments in the city, on the looting of cultural goods, as well as on recreating monuments in virtual reality or physical shape to attract attention to the situation in Syria and the massive destruction of the country's cultural heritage.[12]

Palmyra is most well known for its art and architecture, almost exclusively made from the local limestone coming from quarries around the city.[13] Hundreds of publications have seen daylight since the monumental publication by Robert Wood was published in 1753, which became a famous standard work even in its own time, featuring drawings of numerous of the monuments which Dawkins and Wood studied when they visited the city in 1751.[14] Thereafter a string of publications with etchings, drawings, and descriptions of the site followed, including the work by Louis-Francois Cassas.[15]

Large-scale archaeological missions began with the institutionalizing of the French Mandate. In collaboration with a French team, the Danish archaeologist and theologian Kai Harald Ingholt, called Harald, undertook his fieldwork in Palmyra (Figs 5.2 and 5.3).[16] As knowledge about the city, its monuments, and art increased, scholars interested in this particular region of the world began to write more broadly on the site and its importance. Some of the standard works remain the books published by Ingholt in 1928 and Malcolm Colledge in 1976.[17] Numerous other overview works addressing the cities and the history of the Near East also address Palmyra, such as Kevin Butcher's *Roman Syria* as well as the works by Fergus Miller and Maurice Sartre.[18]

Despite the fact that the city is so rich in portrait material — richer than any other site in the Near East and the classical world outside of Rome — the portraits, most of them from funerary contexts, have never been collected in one corpus. Ingholt, who published his higher doctoral dissertation containing 545 funerary portraits, laid a foundation for a corpus.[19] Ingholt's work provided a first more comprehensive overview of Palmyra as a centre for portrait sculptural tradition across the first three centuries AD. This laid the foundation for our interest in the city's archaeology and history and was the foundation for undertaking the first Palmyra project based at Aarhus University, initiated in 2012.

The Palmyra Projects at Aarhus University and their Aims

Since December 2011, when funding was obtained from the Carlsberg Foundation for a project focusing on Palmyrene portrait sculpture,[20] Aarhus University has been a hub for Palmyra research.[21] In January 2012, the Palmyra Portrait Project was initiated, taking its point of departure in the collection of Palmyrene funerary limestone portraits in the Ny Carlsberg Glyptotek as well as the paper archive of Ingholt and his fieldwork diaries.[22]

---

[9] Stucky 2008.

[10] Stucky 2008 as well as the work done and published by Harald Ingholt (see throughout this contribution). Furthermore, see Bobou and others (forthcoming), with a comprehensive bibliographic overview of Ingholt's publications.

[11] Seland 2015; 2016; 2019. For new comprehensive overviews of the archaeology and history of the city, see Gawlikowski 2021 as well as Raja 2022. Also see Sommer 2018; Sartre 2005; Sartre and Sartre-Fauriat 2016.

[12] The American Society of Overseas Research (ASOR) monitors the situation in Palmyra as part of their cultural heritage initiative and documented the destruction in the city, see e.g. Ali 2015; Cuneo, Penacho, and Barnes Gordon 2015; Cuneo and others 2015. A 3D model of the city has been developed by the German Archaeological Institut (DAI), see <https://www.archernet.org/en/2019/05/17/palmyra-gis-digital-cultural-heritage> [accessed 7 March 2022]. For another project by the Vorderasiatisches Museum, see <https://www.smb.museum/en/whats-new/detail/experience-ancient-palmyra-in-360-and-in-3d/> [accessed 8 March 2022]. For a 3D model of the Tomb of Ḥairan, see Bobou and others 2020.

[13] Schmidt-Colinet 1995; 2017; Bessac 2021.

[14] Wood 1753.

[15] Cassas 1799.

[16] Raja and Sørensen 2015a; 2015b; Raja 2019a; 2021b.

[17] Ingholt 1928; Colledge 1976.

[18] Millar 1993; Sartre 2001; Butcher 2003.

[19] Ingholt 1928.

[20] Kropp and Raja 2014, 393.

[21] Raja 2013, 168.

[22] Kropp and Raja 2014; 2015; Mortensen and Raja 2021; also see these three publications, which pull together the overall results of the project: Bobou, Raja, and Romanowska 2021; Raja, Bobou, and Romanowska 2021; Romanowska, Bobou, and Raja 2021.

From this project, which compiles a complete overview of the existing funerary sculpture from the city, other projects have developed over time, as it became clear that the field diaries and the archival material held their own potential far beyond the sculptures themselves. The archival material which the Palmyra projects in Aarhus have had access to is not in any way comprehensive but was directly related to the fieldwork undertaken by Ingholt in the 1920s and 1930s as well as related to his lifelong research interest in the Palmyrene sculpture. Still it has revealed immense amounts of information about the site, its archaeology, and the way in which archaeological research was conducted in the 1920s and 1930s. It needs to be underlined that we have not worked with other Palmyra archives, apart from those we could access in relation to doing research on the sculptural material in numerous collections around the world. In this way, our archival knowledge and resources are limited to Ingholt's material. This includes the information about funerary sculpture he kept in his archive, the field diaries, and some further archival materials of Ingholt's, which are still at Yale University and with descendants of Ingholt in the US.[23]

The Palmyra Portrait Project aimed at collecting all known funerary portraiture from the city to study these as a corpus and situate them both in their local context as an expression of a strong commemorative funerary tradition and in a Roman context as expression of the ties to the Roman cultural koine. Furthermore, the project also wanted to explore the influences on the portraiture coming from the East. In the course of the project, a series of conferences and workshops were organized on themes that were central to understanding the sculptural habit in a much broader sense within its historical setting. These events led to the publication of several edited volumes. Within the project, numerous publications dealing with a variety of aspects of the city's life and its art have been produced.[24] Currently, the corpus is being prepared for publication and will be published in 2023 — eleven years after the initiation of the project.[25]

Three further projects have grown from the Palmyra Portrait Project: a project focusing on the field diaries of Harald Ingholt; a project focusing on the so-called Ingholt Archive; and the project Circular Economy and Urban Sustainability in Antiquity: The Case of Palmyra, which capitalizes on the data collected within the other projects. The diaries contain an overview of the fieldwork done by Ingholt in the 1920s and 1930s in Palmyra. The Ingholt Archive contains several thousand sheets with images of mostly Palmyrene sculpture and was used as the basis of his 1928 publication, but kept up thereafter until at least some time in the 1970s. The Circular Economy and Urban Sustainability project focuses on pulling together data from the projects as well as collecting other groups of sources, which can help us better understand the development of the city and the problems we are facing when working with archaeological and historical source materials full of lacunae.[26] Different foundations have supported the various projects. A strong focus has been on bringing results to the publication stage in order to make the legacy data accessible to non-project members to allow for further research outside the projects — also in open access and open data form whenever possible.[27]

Harald Ingholt's Life and Career

Harald Ingholt (Fig. 5.3) was an influential figure in the archaeology of the ancient Near East, heading excavations in the Syrian sites of Palmyra and Hama during the 1920s and 1930s. However, his interest in Palmyra began well before he initiated fieldwork and became an interest that would last a lifetime.

As a student at the University of Copenhagen, Ingholt was awarded the gold medal in Semitic and Oriental philology for a paper he wrote in 1918. In 1922, he graduated from the university with a Master in Theology (cand. Theol.).[28] The year 1922 was pivotal for Ingholt, as the American-Scandinavia Foundation awarded him the opportunity to study at Princeton University (New Jersey) in the United States. It is during his stay at Princeton that Ingholt seems to have furthered his interest in Palmyra: he writes that there he 'conceived the plan to make a comprehensive presentation of the Palmyrene portrait busts'.[29] He would successfully defend his higher doctoral dissertation and publish these portraits in 1928, and during those six years of work on

---

23 Raja 2021c.

24 For a full list of publications see <https://doi.org/10.6084/m9.figshare.14259707.v1>.

25 Raja, Bobou, and Yon (forthcoming).

26 Romanowska and others 2021.

27 Bobou and others 2020; Raja and Steding 2021; Miranda and Raja 2021.

28 Raja and Sørensen 2015a, 18; 2015b, 18; Raja 2019a, 57; 2021b, 29–31.

29 Ingholt 1928, 5. For an English translation, see Bobou and others 2021, 39.

Figure 5.4. Palmyrene relief portraits exhibited at the Ny Carlsberg Glyptotek in Copenhagen during the special exhibition 'The Road to Palmyra', 2019–2020.
© Courtesy of Ny Carlsberg Glyptotek, photographer Anders Sune Berg.

the project, Ingholt's engagement with Palmyra would only deepen.[30]

After spending 1923 as a research fellow at the Sorbonne in Paris, Ingholt moved to the American School of Oriental Research in Jerusalem from 1924 to 1925.[31] It is during this time that Ingholt would conduct his first excavations in Palmyra with the 1924 and 1925 field seasons.[32] Also, in 1925, Ingholt began his tenure as the deputy director of the Ny Carlsberg Glyptotek in Copenhagen, Denmark. He held this position until 1930.[33]

The Ny Carlsberg Glyptotek holds the world's largest collection of Palmyrene funerary sculpture outside of Syria (Fig. 5.4).[34] The earliest catalogue of the Palmyra collection was published in 1889 in Danish and French by Rabbi David Simonsen, and it would continue to grow over the coming decades.[35] In 1910, the archaeologist Frederik Poulsen was employed at the Ny Carlsberg Glyptotek and later served as its director from 1926 to 1943. Poulsen was also interested in Palmyra, publishing the article 'De Palmyrenske Skulpturer' (the Palmyrene sculptures) in the Swedish journal *Tidskrift för Konstvetenskap*.[36] Thus, the Ny Carlsberg Glyptotek provided a firm foundation for Ingholt to develop his interest in Palmyra and provide material for the doctoral thesis.

In parallel with the composition of his thesis and work at the Ny Carlsberg Glyptotek, Ingholt conducted three field seasons in Palmyra: 1924, 1925, and 1928. Ingholt's focus was on the city's south-west necropolis, where he worked in around eighty tombs.[37] The first season in 1924 was funded by the Rask-Ørsted Foundation. It

---

30 Ingholt 1928; Bobou and others 2021; Raja 2021a, 32.

31 Raja and Sørensen 2015a, 18; 2015b, 18; Raja 2019a, 57; 2021b, 31.

32 For Ingholt's fieldwork in Palmyra during 1924 and 1925, see Raja, Steding, and Yon 2021.

33 Raja and Sørensen 2015a 18; 2015b, 18; Raja 2019a, 58; 2021b, 31.

34 Raja and Sørensen 2015a, 12; 2015b, 12. On the history of the collection, see Raja 2019b.

35 Simonsen 1889a; 1889b.

36 Poulsen 1921; Raja 2021a, 26.

37 Raja and Sørensen 2015a, 26; 2015b, 26; Raja, Steding, and Yon 2021.

Figure 5.5. French archaeologist Maurice Dunand conducting fieldwork in Palmyra during the 1924 excavation season. © Palmyra Portrait Project, Ingholt Archive at Ny Carlsberg Glyptotek, and Rubina Raja.

was in collaboration with the French archaeologist Maurice Dunand (Fig. 5.5), a specialist of the ancient Near East. The second campaign in 1925 had the permission of the French High Commissioner and was in collaboration with the French architect Albert Gabriel.[38] Ingholt collected a wealth of material during these campaigns, and he published widely on his findings.[39]

Ingholt stepped away from his research in Palmyra for a spell in the 1930s, but he maintained a foothold in the archaeology of the ancient Near East. He returned to Palmyra in the 1930s for the excavation of the Hypogeum of Malkû. From 1930 to 1938, Ingholt led excavations at Hama, funded by the Carlsberg Foundation (Fig. 5.6).[40] The American University of Beirut employed him during this period, where he also served as the university museum's curator and worked on its large collection of Palmyrene funerary portraits, some of which Ingholt helped to acquire.[41] Ingholt founded the now renowned international journal *Berytus* in 1934, which focuses on the publication of the archaeology and history of Lebanon, Syria, Jordan, and Palestine. Ingholt would publish his own work in the journal alongside leading scholars in the field of ancient Near Eastern archaeology.[42]

Ingholt returned to Denmark in 1939, at the beginning of World War II, when he began his employment at Aarhus University as a docent in Semitic philology.[43] His tenure in Aarhus was short-lived given the impact of the war, and he fled to the United States in 1940 to join his family and

Figure 5.6. Finds from Hama. © Rubina Raja and Palmyra Portrait Project, courtesy of Mary Ebba Underdown.

---

[38] Raja and Sørensen 2015a, 18; 2015b, 18; Raja 2019a, 57. Bobou and others (forthcoming).

[39] For Ingholt's full bibliography, see Bobou and others (forthcoming).

[40] Raja and Sørensen 2015a, 18; 2015b, 18; Raja 2019a, 58.

[41] Raja 2019a, 58; Bobou and others (forthcoming).

[42] Raja 2019a, 58; Bobou and others (forthcoming).

[43] Raja 2019a, 58; Bobou and others (forthcoming).

began his appointment as an associate professor at Yale University in New Haven, Connecticut.[44] At Yale, Ingholt worked with art from the Gandhara region (present-day Afghanistan), which he published in 1957.[45] Ingholt was promoted to professor in 1960 and retired from his position in 1964, but continued to publish on Palmyra and other aspects of the ancient world.[46] In 1981, Ingholt made an agreement with the Ny Carlsberg Glyptotek to donate his archive of Palmyrene funerary sculpture, and the materials arrived in Copenhagen in 1983.[47] Shortly after that, in 1985, Harald Ingholt passed away at the age of eighty-nine, leaving behind a legacy of rich scholarship on the ancient world.

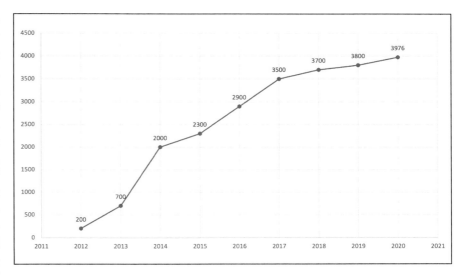

Figure 5.6. Number of portraits in the database of the Palmyra Portrait Project (© Palmyra Portrait Project).

Ingholt's Legacy Data within the Palmyra Projects

As stated in the introduction, the legacy data by Ingholt was a major part of the different projects' work. The former and ongoing projects have produced a large number of publications over the last decade, focusing on the funerary portraiture of Palmyra at first, before studying the archive as an archive in itself and extending the focus beyond the funerary portraits. From the very beginning it was intended to make the data collected by the projects accessible to everyone interested in Palmyra, and in this section we focus on the various ways in which the legacy data of Harald Ingholt and the data collected by the projects was and will be made available.

The Palmyra Portrait Database

The Ingholt Archive, a large paper archive that we will discuss in more detail below, and the collection of the Ny Carlsberg Glyptotek formed the core of the Palmyra Portrait Project. The digitization of the archive and the creation of a database for registering information on all the known Palmyrene portraits, one of the main aims of the project, were among the first activities conducted by the project members (Fig. 5.7).

After the collection of Palmyrene portraits in the Ny Carlsberg Glyptotek was studied by the project in 2012, the collections of Louvre, Yale University Art Gallery, Metropolitan Museum of Art, and Ashmolean Museum were added to the database. In 2014, the Palmyrene portraits in the Danish National Museum, the Fitzwilliam Museum, and the British Museum were registered. The Palmyrene portraits in the Vatican Museums and the Museo di Scultura Antica Giovanni Barracco were studied in 2017.[48] Some museums and private individuals reached out to the Palmyra Portrait Project to inform about Palmyrene portraits in their collection or possession. With the help of a registration form, these objects were then added to the database as well. However, the largest number of objects have been added to the database through the publications in which they occur. All objects from Ingholt's 1928 publication were added, as well as all objects from the paper archive.

Examples of single objects with multiple portraits are double loculus reliefs and sarcophagi, as they depict two or more individuals next to one another (often family members, Fig. 5.8). The total number of portraits exceeded the expectations from the very beginning of the project. In 2013, when Raja described the aims of the Palmyra Portrait Project in an article in the journal *Sfinx*, the number of Palmyrene objects was reported to be 'more than 1000 pieces'.[49] In 2014, this number had risen

---

44 Raja 2019a, 58; Bobou and others (forthcoming).
45 Ingholt 1957.
46 For example, Ingholt 1966; 1970–1971; 1974; 1976.
47 Bobou and others 2022.

48 On the database, see Kropp and Raja 2014; Raja and Sørensen 2015a, 12; 2015b, 12.
49 Raja 2013, 168.

Figure 5.8. Loculus relief with two portrait busts, Museé du Louvre, Paris, inv. no. AO 4449. © Musée du Louvre/Maurice et Pierre Chuzeville.

Figure 5.9. Loculus relief depicting a female, Ny Carlsberg Glyptotek, Copenhagen, inv. no. IN 1062, PS 444. © Palmyra Portrait Project, Ingholt Archive at Ny Carlsberg Glyptotek, and Rubina Raja.

to 'over 2000',[50] and at present, the database holds 3976 portraits that are part of 2909 objects.[51]

The database is organized by collection, meaning that every object was assigned a database number that relates to the museum name, auction house name, or name of the private collector or art dealer. The numbers are then consecutive, following the order the objects have been added. If an object has multiple portraits, these have been assigned a small letter, starting with the portrait to the left.

The database provides very detailed information on each object. In the first part of the entry, covering the object as a whole, the present location (country, collection, inv. no.), acquisition history, context (necropolis, grave), description (material, design, state of preservation), inscription, and references are provided. In the second part of the entry, the portrait is described in detail. Information on the gender, head and face, headdress, torso, arms and hands, dress, jewellery, and attributes is provided. It is thus possible to search for one or multiple specific feature(s) (e.g. males with a beard; females with a particular type of earrings; children holding a certain attribute) within the whole corpus. Based

---

[50] Kropp and Raja 2014, 393.
[51] As of March 2022.

on these pieces of information, detailed studies can be conducted, and as the Palmyrene portraits form the largest Roman portrait corpus outside of Rome, its publication has a great significance for the studies of portraits in the Roman Near East.

The database is hosted by Aarhus University. It has been accessible for project members to conduct their research (see also below), and a team has worked on creating the entries for the portraits over the years, moving objects around when they changed location or their current location got clarified, and adding the most recent references. Furthermore, project members are also responsible for checking objects that are being sent to the project or appear in new publications and, if these are unknown, adding them to the database. Once the database is online, all the portraits will be searchable, allowing other researchers to benefit from the project's work. The publication does not mean the 'end' of the database; there is flexibility to add to it after publication.

The Corpus of Palmyrene Portraits

As a result of the activities described above and based on the portraits that have been added to the database, it was possible to create the corpus of Palmyrene portraits, which was born out of a convergence of three main factors: the presence of an extraordinary number of Palmyrene artefacts in a single museum, the location of the Ingholt Archive in the same museum, and the research interests of the director of the Palmyra Portrait Project.

Every object has also been catalogued for the publication of the corpus, which will be independent of the database. Two decisions were taken that took the catalogue entries away from the database ones: the first was about the format and the second about standardization. The format decided for the entries is typical for archaeological catalogues: a short section giving the various information known from the literature or autopsy by team members, a section with the inscription and its translation, whenever applicable, and a section describing the object and the portraits. Every effort was made to avoid interpretations and to describe what was visible. Because the team members changed throughout the project's life, the decision was taken to create guidelines that would standardize the various terms and expressions used in the entries and make them as homogeneous as possible. This has resulted in entries that are streamlined to a large extent and reflect the work of a unified team rather than individual scholars.

The creation of the corpus has allowed for the study and research of the Palmyrene material in a way that was not possible before and has resulted in over a hundred publications disseminating the results of studies on aspects as varied as questions of iconography,[52] either broad, such as the study of female portraiture in Palmyra undertaken by Signe Krag as part of her PhD thesis and published in 2018,[53] or narrow, as the *dorsalium* or the brooches worn by priests.[54] In addition to the already published books and papers and the works that are currently in progress, the corpus catalogue will be accompanied by an overview of the results of the ten-year-long study of Palmyrene sculpture (Fig. 5.9).

Perhaps one of the most important outcomes of having collected the corpus of portraits and having information on their contexts is the refinement of the stylistic development of Palmyrene art over time. Ingholt's methodology of stylistic and iconographic traits that appeared on the dated reliefs and could be understood as 'period traits' led to his dividing of Palmyrene art into three chronological periods that were largely followed by other scholars.[55] The collection of another fifty objects that were dated to a specific year thanks to their inscriptions and that were published after 1928, showed that Ingholt had identified the main traits associated with specific periods. However, together with the evaluation of the collected material from inscriptions, burials, and sculptures, it was possible to refine the Palmyrene chronology further and define seven periods of production that also reflected phases of economic growth and decline of the city.[56] In consequence, all the objects in the corpus have been re-evaluated and, whenever necessary, redated.

The collection of almost four thousand portraits means that it is now possible to have better statistical data for Palmyra and its sculptural production. In some cases, the results of the inquiry may seem unsurprising

---

[52] For a list of these publications, see <https://projects.au.dk/palmyraportrait/publications-presentations-and-press/publications> and <https://doi.org/10.6084/m9.figshare.12272714.v1> [both accessed 5 March 2022].

[53] Krag 2018.

[54] Raja 2019c; 2021a.

[55] Ingholt (1928) had divided Palmyrene sculpture in three groups: (1) AD 1–150, (2) AD 150–200, and (3) AD 200–250. This division was largely followed by Colledge 1976, who wrote the only study on Palmyrene art as a whole, and as recently as Krag 2018.

[56] See Raja, Bobou, and Romanowska 2021; Romanowska, Bobou, and Raja 2021; Bobou, Raja, and Romanowska 2021.

Figure 5.10. Ingholt's monograph from 1928 on Palmyrene sculpture had a drawing of the rear façade of the Ny Carlsberg Glyptotek on the title page (after Ingholt 1928).

for a city that seems to have been trying to showcase its participation in the Graeco-Roman koine, as evidenced by the presence of the agora, the theatre, and other structures typically associated with Graeco-Roman culture, as well as the mosaics and images with mythological representations in houses and tombs.[57] For example, there are 288 honorific inscriptions from the whole of the city, some found reused, and some found in their original location, and in these, only five women are mentioned as receiving honours from the city: one empress, Iulia Maesa, one local queen, Zenobia, and three local benefactresses, Thomallachis, Hagge, and Aushai. Even if one assumes that the fourteen statues of women that have survived represented completely different women whose names have not survived, that would mean that we only have a record of nineteen females being honoured in Palmyra in comparison to over three hundred men. That is a mere 5 per cent, which is lower compared to that documented in other cities of the Roman East, but within the ranges that one would expect from a small city.[58] When one examines the evidence from the funerary sphere, however, one sees that 54 per cent of all portraits are of males, and 33 per cent are of females. When one examines different types of funerary commemorative media, one sees that the ratio gap may be even smaller: so, in loculus reliefs, 51 per cent of all portraits are males and 40 per cent are of females.[59] This highlights the differentiation in representation that existed between the public and the private/funerary sphere, and that can be explained with further investigation into the types of public inscriptions, their dates, and locations, but also comparisons with other corpora of sculpture from other cities of the Roman world and within the same period.

The publication of the corpus also considers objects that were not included in the database and were not within the project's original scope: these include undecorated sarcophagi or sarcophagi with mythological representations, wall paintings from houses or tombs without portraits, and religious reliefs. This is to present the Palmyrene sculptural figural production that has survived within its broader context. After all, it was not created in isolation, and even if the workshops producing votives or architectural decorations, for example, were separate from those producing loculus reliefs or sarcophagi, they all lived in the same city and were exposed to similar trends and ideas.

---

[57] For the agora of Palmyra, see Delplace and Dentzer-Feydy 2005. See also Gawlikowski 2021, 29–32.

[58] See Dillon 2010.

[59] The other portraits are of children or in such a fragmentary state that their gender cannot be determined.

Translation of 1928 *Studier over Palmyrensk Skulptur* (Studies on Palmyrene Sculpture)

One of the spin-offs emerging out of the Ingholt Archive was the acknowledgement that Ingholt's seminal 1928 publication *Studier over Palmyrensk Skulptur* (Studies on Palmyrene Sculptures) was still relevant. However, because it is in Danish, it has not been fully utilized by other scholars.[60] Thus, the decision was taken to translate the publication into English to place it within the framework of current research as well as update the information on the objects that Ingholt had studied.[61]

Studier over Palmyrensk Skulptur (Fig. 5.10), of course, takes pride of place and occupies the centre of the translated book. The original is located on the left-hand side of the book, and the translation on the right, so that the viewer can see and examine them both. Every effort was taken so that visually, the translation would replicate Ingholt's publication: the same layout, pagination, use of capitals for proper names, and reference system were used throughout. One thing that is apparent to Danish readers is that Ingholt's vocabulary and phrases were particular and strange — not simply dated because of the time they were written but revealing something of the thought processes and ways that Ingholt viewed the world. This feature of the 1928 book would be lost in a loose translation that would be more intelligible to and readable for an English-speaking audience, so it was decided to translate Ingholt's work as closely to the Danish original as possible — even verbatim at some points — in order to preserve his idiosyncratic figures of writing. Proper names, toponyms, and museum names were also kept the way that Ingholt had written them, as well as his index, his list of errata, and the sixteen plates that illustrated his volume.

Only three changes were made in relation to the 1928 publication. The first was in the rendering of Palmyrene Aramaic: in Ingholt's time, the epigraphic convention was to transcribe it using characters in Hebrew, but after 1940, the convention is that Latin characters are used in the transcriptions. The second is the number of illustrations. Ingholt had illustrated only the first fifty-four sculptures that were dated by inscription and that he used as the basis for establishing his chronological system of arranging the Palmyrene sculptures. Since all the images that Ingholt had used to prepare his monograph had been digitized, it was decided to publish the images of all the pieces for which there were illustrations in the archive.[62] Thus, the translation offers a complete overview of all the material that Ingholt had studied collected in one single volume for the first time. The last change was the addition of comments: in order to separate them from the footnotes in Ingholt's text, it was decided that they would be placed in endnotes. Among other things, they highlight changes in names, toponyms, and museum names, clarify points in the translation, as well as offer a few corrections on factual errors.[63]

The translation also includes an updated concordance of the location of objects. This was necessary since the location of several pieces had changed since the time that Ingholt was writing. The affected objects were mostly those in private collections, rather than in European museums or the Istanbul Archaeology Museum. A second addition was the concordance of inscriptions that appeared in the book, giving the references to the corpus of Palmyrene Aramaic inscriptions collected by Delbert R. Hillers and Eleonora Cussini in 1996, as well as to other important publications, in particular the addendum to the corpus published by Jean-Baptiste Yon in 2013.[64]

Just as important to the editors were the presentation of Ingholt, the man behind the archaeologist, the contextualization of the work, and the update on the knowledge gained on the particular pieces studied by Ingholt in 1928. For this reason, Harold Underdown, Ingholt's oldest grandchild, wrote a small preface about his family's memories of Ingholt.[65] Prehistoric archaeologist Peder Mortensen, Ingholt's associate in the excavations of Tell Shimshara, Iraq, wrote a small piece about Ingholt as a colleague and friend.[66]

The paper 'Harald Ingholt and Palmyrene Sculpture: Continuing a Lifelong Relationship a Century Later' places Ingholt's involvement in Palmyrene sculpture first within the framework of Danish antiquarian interest, collectionism, and scholarly research about the city that

---

60 For example, Colledge (1976) is using Ingholt mostly for referring to the busts, while only one of his contributions is used in Sartre 2005, and his work is not discussed, even though those of other scholars who wrote in English, Italian, and, of course, French are discussed in the text.

61 Bobou and others 2021.

62 Ingholt refers to 545 objects in his monograph; however, it was not possible to locate images of some of the last fifteen objects in his archive.

63 See for example, Bobou and others 2021, 368.

64 Hillers and Cussini 1996; Yon 2013.

65 Underdown 2021.

66 Mortensen 2021.

had begun in the second half of the nineteenth century. Then, Ingholt's own excavations, studies, and achievements are presented — among which was the discovery of one of the most elaborate and rich Palmyrene sculptures known until now, the 'Beauty of Palmyra'. The last section of the piece is a short biography.

The first of the three appendices came out of the research on the acquisition histories of the pieces discussed in Ingholt's book, and that formed the second appendix. The authors noticed that there were three main types of collectors acquiring Palmyrene artworks, as well as the different ways that the museums acquired objects: through excavations, donations or confiscations in Syria and modern Turkey, through donations or purchases through dealers, agents, or auction houses in the rest of the world. While European museums stopped acquiring objects after World War II, the collections of museums in the United States and those of private collectors were more dynamic, usually selling and less often buying Palmyrene antiquities. The last appendix is a list of the dated objects that were known to the editors at the time of the preparation of the volume.

Archive Archaeology: Preserving and Sharing Palmyra's Cultural Heritage through Harald Ingholt's Digital Archives

After several years of working with the Ingholt Archive as part of the Palmyra Portrait Project, the archive itself became the focus of another project in 2020: Archive Archaeology: Preserving and Sharing Palmyra's Cultural Heritage through Harald Ingholt's Digital Archives (funded by the ALIPH Foundation).[67] This project utilizes the Ingholt Archive in a different manner: rather than a source of information on the Palmyrene sculpture, the project treats the archive as the object of inquiry. Although the projects share data and have the common goal of preserving Syrian heritage, the Archive Archaeology project is different in its approach in that its research outcomes are focused on such issues as the archive's creation and afterlives and how such knowledge contributes to Palmyra's rich history (ancient and modern). The project works in parallel to the Palmyra Portrait Project and has three main objectives: (1) to publish and make the digital archive accessible online to the public in a searchable form and to publish the excavation diaries including a full assessment of the graves

Figure 5.11. Folders at the Ny Carlsberg Glyptotek. © Rubina Raja.

documented in these; (2) to assess damages and losses of Palmyrene cultural heritage based on the primary evidence collected in the unpublished archive and the diaries; and (3) to reconstruct lost and damaged contexts based on the evidence collected in the archive.[68]

With its foundation in 2020, the project thus embarked on its first objective: the publication of the Ingholt Archive both in print and as an e-publication, and in an online format as open data.

The first step in preparing the archive for publication was to assess the structure of the archive as it had been received from the Ny Carlsberg Glyptotek (Fig. 5.11). The Palmyra Portrait Project digitized the archive in 2012, maintaining the order of the material as it arrived in Aarhus. It is impossible to know how Ingholt organized the archive during his lifetime and if that order was kept during the long journey from New Haven to Copenhagen. The archive likely took a different shape in the 1990s, when archaeologist Gunhild Ploug worked on it. Ploug's interventions often come in the form of small, yellow post-it notes, but on occasion she does write directly on the archive sheets in black pen. The question as to how and whether she reorganized the material in Copenhagen remains open; however, when the material arrived at Aarhus University, it

---

[67] <https://projects.au.dk/archivearchaeology/> [accessed 7 March 2022].

[68] <https://projects.au.dk/archivearchaeology/about> [accessed 5 March 2022].

Figure 5.12. PS 845. A yellow archive sheet with an image of a loculus relief of a priest. The sheet shows the so-called Ingholt PS number preceded by the abbreviation 'PS'. © Palmyra Portrait Project, Ingholt Archive at Ny Carlsberg Glyptotek, and Rubina Raja.

Figure 5.13. PS 4. A grey archive sheet from the Ny Carlsberg Glyptotek with an image of a loculus relief of a male figure. © Palmyra Portrait Project, Ingholt Archive at Ny Carlsberg Glyptotek, and Rubina Raja.

was organized into nineteen dark blue folders. The first eleven folders are arranged chronologically from the first century AD to AD 250.[69] However, the exceptions in this group are folders three and four, which are simply labelled 'Palmyra'. Also, folders five and six, chronologically labelled AD 135–150, are separated into 'men' and 'women', respectively. Folder twelve is blank, while thirteen through sixteen are sorted into typologies: grave stelai, sarcophagi and funerary reliefs, votive reliefs, and other sculptures. Folders seventeen through nineteen contain images of sculptures in the collection of the Ny Carlsberg Glyptotek. However, given the inconsistencies within the folders, it may be that the organization of the archive into the blue folders was a work in progress.[70]

Another factor pointing to the restructuring of the archive after Ingholt is the so-called PS numbering system utilized on each archive sheet. 'PS', short for 'Palmyrensk Skulptur' (Palmyrene Sculpture), is an abbreviation used by Ingholt to number each sculpture, and the number appears in the upper right corner of the sheets (Fig. 5.12). However, there is a second PS number in quotation marks centred at the top of the sheet. Ploug presumably assigned the second number. The numbers for the first sculptures, through PS 527, match and correspond to Ingholt's 1928 publication, *Studier over Palmyrensk Skulptur*.[71] Those sculptures with a PS number higher than 527 have two different PS numbers, but within the blue folders, these numbers had no organizational role. Thus, the decision was made by the project to publish the archive sheets sorted by PS number. With certain sheets missing, the archive begins with PS 8 and ends with PS 1506.

One reason for some of these gaps (besides sheets going missing over the years) is that many of the objects from the Ny Carlsberg Glyptotek are not included in the print and e-publication editions of the archive. This decision reflects an earlier moment in which the objects in the museum's collection were removed from their original brown or yellow sheet and remounted on a grey sheet labelled 'NCG' (Fig. 5.13). A more mysterious and larger gap occurs between PS 1168 and PS 1261: the location of these sheets is unknown.[72]

Once the structure of the publication had been determined, the project was then able to transcribe and comment upon each archive sheet. Each sheet is given a title: the sheet's PS number and a short description of the object featured on the sheet. The commentary for each sheet then has five components: description, commentary, inscription, archive sheet bibliography, and additions to the bibliography. The description is a simple description of the sheet, whereas the commentary section includes a transcription of the annotations and the authors' comments. The inscription section identifies the script, often Palmyrene Aramaic, and describes the location of the inscription on the object. The section also provides a transcription and translation of the text into English. Some inscriptions have additional explanatory comments by Jean-Baptiste Yon. The final two components of the commentary are the bibliographies. First, the archive sheet bibliography is the works referenced by Ingholt and Ploug on the sheets, while the additions to the bibliography provide an up-to-date bibliography for each object.

After the commentary for all the PS sheets through 1506, there are four appendices. These are 260 unnumbered sheets that were scanned in 2016. The appendices are: (1) sheets without a PS number; (2) additional portraits; (3) views of architecture; and (4) miscellaneous. There are then thirteen concordances that accompany the sheets:

1. *In situ* contexts
2. Locations
3. Unknown collections
4. Objects with unknown locations
5. Unpublished portraits
6. Inscriptions
7. Unpublished inscriptions
8. Greek and Latin names
9. Object dates
10. Typologies
11. Folders at the Ny Carlsberg Glyptotek
12. Ingholt PS numbers and Ny Carlsberg Glyptotek PS numbers
13. Database numbers

These concordances aim to make information easily discoverable for interested readers, for example in focus areas such as the art and archaeology of the ancient Near East, ancient epigraphy, archival practices, and cultural heritage preservation.

---

69 For a list of the folders, see Bobou and others 2022.

70 Bobou and others 2022.

71 Bobou and others 2022.

72 Bobou and others 2022.

As the print and e-publication took shape, so did the online archive as open data. In October 2021, the Ingholt Archive went online through the repository figshare under a CC-BY 4.0 license and was published in the *Journal of Open Archaeology Data*.[73] In this publication, the archive is organized into twenty-one PDF files across four collections: (1) the numbered PS sheets; (2) sheets with no PS number; (3) Ny Carlsberg Glyptotek sheets; and (4) archive additions. Within the numbered PS sheets, the sheets are further organized into sixteen PDF files in numerical order by PS number. The archive additions are also subdivided into three PDF files: architecture, miscellaneous, and portraits. The publication online as open data provides these files to anyone with an internet connection and they are free to download. Moreover, the publication of the archive online provides context for the archive, briefly introducing Ingholt and the archive's formation for approximately fifty years and the methods used by the project to bring the archive to publication.[74] The online publication also highlights the archive's strong reuse potential. The Archive Archaeology project has taken what was once one scholar's personal research resource and transformed it into open data, meaning that it is freely available. Institutional restrictions no longer apply to this material so long as it is properly cited.

The project Archive Archaeology: Preserving and Sharing Palmyra's Cultural Heritage through Harald Ingholt's Digital Archives works to disseminate information about Palmyra's heritage and aid restitution efforts. Although the systematic looting and destruction of Palmyra mean that some objects are no more, the record of such objects lives on through the Ingholt Archive. The archive can assist scholars in tracing object biographies, in some instances charting their movements across collections. As Ingholt returned to his archive, again and again updating his records, the recent publications of the Ingholt Archive will be a resource for scholars to reference in research and the production of new scholarship. Moreover, as open data, the Ingholt Archive democratizes archaeological data and is a first step in bringing such material to a broader audience.

The Excavation Diaries

In addition to the work on the portraiture and the paper archive, the excavation diaries of Ingholt were included in the Palmyra Portrait Project. They stem from Ingholt's excavations in Palmyra in 1924, 1925, and 1928 in the south-west necropolis. In total, six diaries were donated to the Ny Carlsberg Glyptotek, most likely together with the paper archive.[75] One of the diaries turned out to be a draft diary that Ingholt used for writing diary 1, covering the field campaign in 1924. Diary 2 mainly focuses on the fieldwork from 1925. The last pages, however, he filled during the campaign in 1928. Diary 4 documents the continuation of the same campaign. Diary 3 was used as an inventory in which Ingholt sketched ground plans of several hypogea (Fig. 5.13). The title page suggests that he wrote this diary in 1925, but it cannot be excluded that he worked on this diary over multiple years. Diary 5 serves as the concordance of all excavated tombs, repeating information from the earlier diaries by collecting the inscriptions, findings, and descriptions of the hypogea in one place.[76] Ingholt returned to Palmyra in the late 1930s to excavate the Tomb of Malkû, but no diaries relating to this campaign have been found.[77]

When the diaries became part of the Palmyra Portrait Project in 2012, they were transferred from the Ny Carlsberg Glyptotek to Aarhus University. Each diary page was scanned in 1200 dpi and saved as a PDF before the diaries were returned to the museum. In between the diary pages, loose pages were found. When each diary was scanned as a unit, the loosely inserted pages were kept in their original place and this order was kept for the publication, even though some of these loose pages were inserted later, proven by the notes on them that must have been written by Ingholt later than the origin of the respective diary.[78] This way, it is possible to keep the publication as close as possible to the find situation of the archive, which most likely resembles the state of the diaries as they entered the collection of the Ny Carlsberg Glyptotek. Unlike the paper archive recording the Palmyrene sculpture, the diaries do not seem to have

---

[73] Bobou, Miranda, and Raja 2021.

[74] Bobou, Miranda, and Raja 2021.

[75] Raja 2021b, 43; 2021c, 7.

[76] Diary 1: 1924 (Raja, Steding, and Yon 2021, 85–368); diary 2: 1925 (Raja, Steding, and Yon 2021, 492–676); diary 3: 1925 (Raja, Steding, and Yon 2021, 695–828); diary 4: 1928 (Raja, Steding, and Yon 2021, 877–950); diary 5: Tombs (Raja, Steding, and Yon 2021, 965–1750).

[77] Raja and Sørensen 2015a, 22; 2015b, 22.

[78] Raja and Steding 2021, 6.

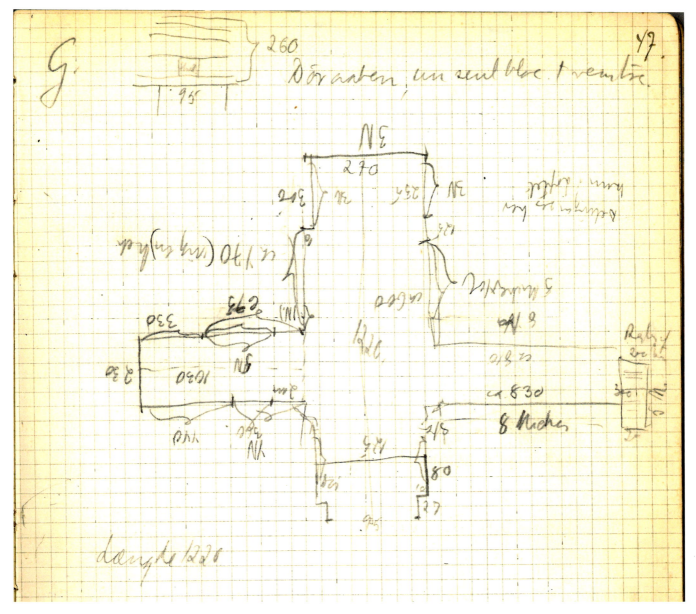

Figure 5.14. Excerpt from diary 3 (p. 47) with the ground plan of hypogeum G.
© Palmyra Portrait Project, courtesy of Ny Carlsberg Glyptotek.

been revisited by anyone since Ingholt donated them to the museum. Even though it is unknown when Ingholt last worked with the diaries and what happened to some of the missing pages, it is likely that the diaries, as they have been published now, closely resemble their state in 1983. However, additional materials — that most likely belong to Ingholt's fieldwork documentation — were only found in 2016 in a box holding diverse materials belonging to the Ingholt Archive.

The diaries became part of the Archive Archaeology Project in 2020, under which their publication was finalized. The decision was taken to publish the diaries in chronological order. Each diary page is printed on the left of a double page, while the right side holds a transcription and translation of the page.[79] The positioning of the transcription and translation mirrors the setup of the original diary page, and it is thus effortless to find the respective part on either the diary page or in the transcription and translation.

---

[79] The scans of the draft diary are included and follow upon diary 1, but have not been transcribed or translated, as it did not have any information that could not be gained from diary 1 (Raja 2021d, 7).

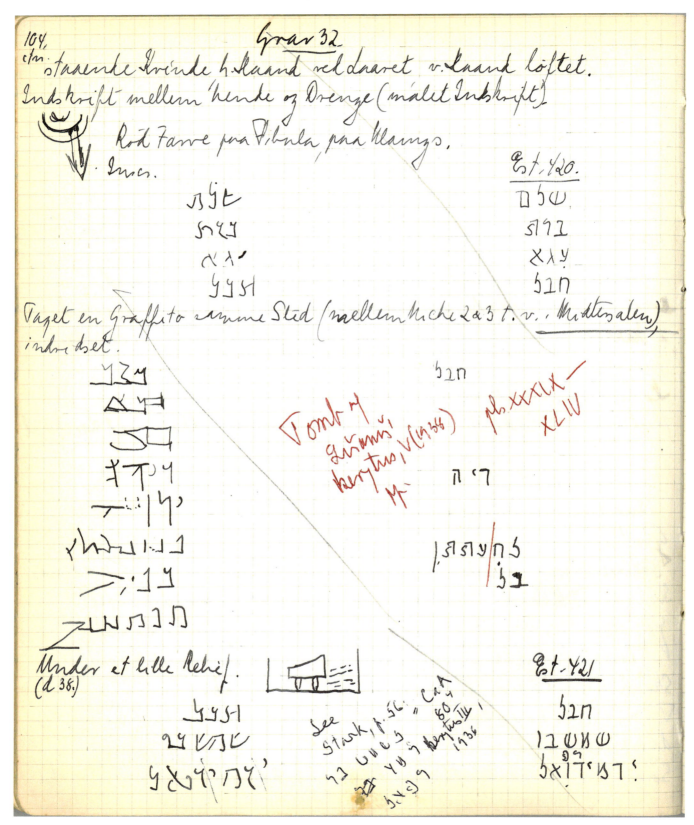

Figure 5.15. Excerpt from diary 1 (p. 104) with transcriptions and a reference to the journal *Berytus*. © Palmyra Portrait Project, courtesy of Ny Carlsberg Glyptotek.

Figure 5.16. Ingholt and a worker with reliefs from the Tomb of Malkû. © Rubina Raja and Palmyra Portrait Project, courtesy of Mary Ebba Underdown.

In the transcription, the different languages used by Ingholt are colour coded.[80] Most of the text is in Danish, but he also wrote in French, English, and German. Some phrases and words are in Arabic, as well as Latin. It was decided to translate the Danish text, but as most scholars read the other modern languages, these were kept in the original language in the translation. The inscriptions in Palmyrene Aramaic and Ancient Greek were transcribed and then translated either in the footnotes or in the translation, depending on the availability of space on each given page and whether an inscription has previously been published or not.

Ingholt revisited his diaries regularly, during and after the field campaigns in the 1920s and in later years. He cross-referenced between the diaries and included relevant literature references to comparative materials and inscriptions.[81] In the 1930s, when he published some of the graves in the journal *Berytus*, he used a red pen to add the publication year and page numbers to the respective diary page he had used in preparation for his publication (Fig. 5.15).[82] In 1971, Jürgen Kurt Stark published a book on the Palmyrene names, and multiple references to this book can be found in red pen in the diaries, proving that Ingholt still revisited the diaries more than thirty years after his last field campaign in Palmyra.[83] Whenever the editors were able to identify a reference, the information was added as a footnote. The diary publication thus holds a bibliography to Ingholt's personal references as well as an updated bibliography to the published information from the diaries.

In the introduction as well as in between the diaries, the publication contains many additional materials, such as photos, newspaper articles, postcards, and documents depicting Ingholt and his family's life over the years (Fig. 5.16). A range of photographs displays various monuments and graves in Palmyra and in the Near East, as well as the work conducted in Palmyra. To facilitate anyone's work with the diaries, a range of concordances was added at the end of the publication, covering the published and unpublished inscriptions as well as the mentioned tombs.[84]

---

[80] Yon 2021, 11.

[81] For an example, see diary 1, p. 48 (Raja, Steding, and Yon 2021, 191), where Ingholt referenced a publication by Moritz (1917) regarding the Sinai cult.

[82] For an example, see diary 1, p. 97 (Raja, Steding, and Yon 2021, 291), where Ingholt referenced his publication of the tombs of Yarḥai, 'Atenuri, and Zabdibol in *Berytus*, 2, published in 1938.

[83] For an example, see diary 1, p. 99 (Raja, Steding, and Yon 2021, 295), where Ingholt referenced the publication of an inscription by Stark in 1971.

[84] Concordance of all tombs: Raja, Steding, and Yon 2021,

Besides the commented publication, the scans of the diaries were also made available online via the platform figshare under a CC-BY 4.0 licence and the *Journal of Open Archaeology Data*.[85] All 645 pages from the diaries and twenty-six loose pieces of paper, as well as a hand-drawn map of the south-west necropolis, are available for download, and anyone interested in the archive can access the files free of charge.

One outcome we would like to highlight is a collaborative project with Klaus Schnädelbach. Due to the combined expertise on the archaeological contexts and the geographical knowledge of the south-west necropolis, it was possible to update the map of the necropolis. The first topographic map of Palmyra with, at the time, all known archaeological remains indicated was published in 2010 by Schnädelbach.[86] On the map section showing the south-west necropolis, only twelve hypogea were known by name, and only seven had a known ground plan. Through the collaboration, thirty-four names and twenty-eight ground plans could be added to the map, and six locations of known tombs were corrected.[87] This shows how much information can be gained by studying the diaries and how a collaborative approach leads to new results and closes research gaps. The updated map of the south-west necropolis and the ground plans are also made available online under a CC BY 4.0 license via the platform figshare.[88]

The diaries have a high archaeological and historical research potential, and with their publication, scholars can engage with the documentation made by Ingholt in the 1920s. As Ingholt himself only published on thirteen graves of the approximately eighty excavated graves,[89] much information is still to be gained from the diaries on the hypogea, including their layout, chronology, inscriptions, funerary sculpture, and preservation at their point of excavation. Furthermore, they are a resource to study excavation techniques as well as the daily life and excavation life in Palmyra.

Conclusion

This contribution has given an overview of what the three Palmyra projects based at Aarhus University have added to the research on Palmyra over the last decade. We have thematized challenges and potentials, and our approach to the material and publication strategy. In doing so, we hope to contribute to further discussions about the value of archival material related to archaeological excavations and post-excavation processes and research foci. Furthermore, we wish to develop systematic ways of publishing such material in a form which, on the one hand makes the raw data freely available to all interested, and on the other hand presents new research results based on the new discoveries made during the course of the work with the material. As described above, the diaries and the archival material turned out to hold much more information than first thought. However, it is crucial to underline that this information only became clear as research on the sculpture was quite progressed, since it was the research on the collection histories and object biographies and the other publications by Ingholt on his excavations, which made it possible to decipher the subtle relationships between the diaries, the archives, and the sculptural corpus over time. While at the outset the idea had been to treat all material, sculptures, diaries, and archival material within the Palmyra Portrait Project, it soon became clear that they could not be treated together all at once but had to be revisited as research on the corpus progressed. At this point, the research has been ongoing for more than ten years, and on some fronts, there is still some way to go. Nevertheless, much has been done and published already, and the raw data made available for future research.

1780–83; unpublished inscriptions: Raja, Steding, and Yon 2021, 1799–1806; published inscriptions: Raja, Steding, and Yon 2021, 1793–97.

85 <https://doi.org/10.6084/m9.figshare.c.5442765>; Raja and Steding 2021.

86 Schnädelbach 2010.

87 Raja, Schnädelbach, and Steding 2022.

88 <https://doi.org.10.6084/m9.figshare.c.5696872>.

89 For the published graves, see Ingholt 1932 (Hypogeum of Ḥairan; Hypogeum of ʿAtenatan); 1935 (Hypogeum of ʿAtenatan; Hypogeum of J. A. Male; Hypogeum of Malkû; Hypogeum of Naṣrallat; Hypogeum of Barʾa); 1938 (Hypogeum of Yarḥai; Hypogeum of Seleukos; Hypogeum of Lišamš; Hypogeum of ʿAbdʾastor); 1966 (Hypogeum of Malkû); 1970–1971 (Hypogeum of Malkû); 1974 (Hypogeum of Bat-Mitrait/Tomb I; Hypogeum of Yarḥibola).

Acknowledgements

This work was supported by the Danish National Research Foundation under the grant DNRF119 — Centre of Excellence for Urban Network Evolutions (UrbNet). The authors thank the directors, former and current, and colleagues at the Ny Carlsberg Glyptotek for allowing access to the material since 2012 and for the rights to publish it. We also thank the ALIPH Foundation and Carlsberg Foundation for generously respectively funding Archive Archaeology: Preserving and Sharing Palmyra's Cultural Heritage through Harald Ingholt's Digital Archives (grant held by Rubina Raja, agreement 2019-1267) and the Palmyra Portrait Project (grant held by Rubina Raja, agreement CF15-0493), as well as the Carlsberg Foundation (grant held by Rubina Raja, agreement CF19-0061) and Augustinus Foundation for the support of the project Circular Economy and Urban Sustainability in Antiquity. Since 2012, when the Palmyra Portrait Project was founded, several individuals have contributed to the digitization and study of the material. The authors wish to thank everyone who has participated in and contributed to the projects over the years.

Works Cited

Ali, C. 2015. 'Palmyra: Heritage Adrift. Detailed Report on All Damage Done to the Archaeological Site between February 2012 and June 2015', *The Association for the Protection of Syrian Archaeology / The American Schools of Oriental Research Cultural Heritage Initiatives*: 1–59 <http://www.asor-syrianheritage.org/wp-content/uploads/2015/06/Palmyra_Heritage_Adrift.pdf> [accessed 12 February 2023].

Bessac, J.-C. 2021. 'Le calcaires de Palmyre face aux autres roches de décoration architecturale et de sculpture', in R. Raja and J. Steding (eds), *Production Economy in Greater Roman Syria: Trade Networks and Production Processes*, Studies in Palmyrene Archaeology and History, 2 (Turnhout: Brepols), pp. 49–70.

Bobou, O., N. Breintoft Kristensen, S. McAvoy, and R. Raja. 2020. 'Archive Archaeology in Palmyra, Syria: A New 3D Reconstruction of the Tomb of Ḥairan', *Digital Applications in Archaeology and Cultural Heritage*, 19: e00164 <https://doi.org/10.1016/j.daach.2020.e00164>.

Bobou, O. and R. Randeris Thomsen. 2021. 'Collecting Then and Now', in O. Bobou, J. V. Jensen, N. Breintoft Kristensen, R. Raja, and R. Randeris Thomsen (eds), *Studies on Palmyrene Sculpture: A Translation of Harald Ingholt's 'Studier over Palmyrensk Skulptur', Edited and with Commentary*, Studies in Palmyrene Archaeology and History, 1 (Turnhout: Brepols), pp. 533–36.

Bobou, O., A. C. Miranda, and R. Raja. 2021. 'The Ingholt Archive. Data from the Project "Archive Archaeology: Preserving and Sharing Palmyra's Cultural Heritage through Harald Ingholt's Digital Archives"', *Journal of Open Archaeology Data*, 9.6: 1–10 <http://doi.org/10.5334/joad.78>.

Bobou, O., R. Raja, and I. Romanowska. 2021. 'Historical Trajectories of Palmyra's Elites through the Lens of Archaeological Data', *Journal of Urban Archaeology*, 4: 153–66 <https://doi.org/10.1484/J.JUA.5.126598>.

Bobou, O., J. V. Jensen, N. Breintoft Kristensen, R. Raja, and R. Randeris Thomsen (eds). 2021. *Studies on Palmyrene Sculpture: A Translation of Harald Ingholt's 'Studier over Palmyrensk Skulptur', Edited and with Commentary*, Studies in Palmyrene Archaeology and History, 1 (Turnhout: Brepols).

Bobou, O., A. C. Miranda, R. Raja, J. Steding, and J-B. Yon (forthcoming). 'Harald Ingholt and Palmyra: Documenting the Oasis City through the Legacy of Berytus' Founder', *Berytus*.

Bobou, O., A. C. Miranda, R. Raja, and J.-B. Yon. 2022. *The Ingholt Archive: The Palmyrene Material; Transcribed with Commentary and Bibliography*, Archive Archaeology, 2 (Turnhout: Brepols).

Butcher, K. 2003. *Roman Syria and the Near East* (Los Angeles: J. Paul Getty Museum).

Cassas, L.-F. 1799. *Voyage pittoresque de la Syrie, de la Phoénicie, de la Palestine, et de la Basse Égypte* (Paris: Imprimerie de la République).

Colledge, M. A. R. 1976. *The Art of Palmyra* (London: Thames and Hudson).

Cuneo, A., S. Penacho, and L. Barnes Gordon. 2015. 'Update on the Situation in Palmyra', *ASOR* <http://www.asor.org/wp-content/uploads/2019/09/Palmyra_UpdateReport_FINAL4reduced.pdf> [accessed 12 February 2023].

Cuneo, A., S. Penacho, M. Danti, M. Gabriel, and J. O'Connell. 2015. 'The Recapture of Palmyra', *ASOR* <https://www.asor.org/wp-content/uploads/2019/09/NEW2_PalmyraSpecialReport3-FINAL.pdf> [accessed 12 February 2023].

Delplace, C. and J. Dentzer-Feydy. 2005. *L'agora de Palmyre* (Bordeaux: Institut Ausonius).

Dentzer-Feydy, J. and J. Teixidor. 1993. *Les antiquités de Palmyra au Musée du Louvre* (Paris: Éditions de la Réunion des musées nationaux).

Dillon, S. 2010. *The Female Portrait Statue in the Greek World* (Cambridge: Cambridge University Press).

Gawlikowski, M. 2021. *Tadmor – Palmyra: A Caravan City between East and West* (Cracow: IRSA).

Hillers, D. R. and E. Cussini. 1996. *Palmyrene Aramaic Texts* (Baltimore: Johns Hopkins University Press).

Ingholt, H. 1928. *Studier over Palmyrensk Skulptur* (Copenhagen: Reitzel).

—— 1932. 'Quelques fresques récemment découvertes à Palmyre', *Acta archaeologica*, 3: 1–20.

—— 1935. 'Five Dated Tombs from Palmyra', *Berytus*, 2: 57–120.

—— 1938. 'Inscriptions and Sculptures from Palmyra II', *Berytus*, 5: 93–140.

—— 1957. *Gandharan Art in Pakistan* (New York: Pantheon).

—— 1966. 'Some Sculptures from the Tomb of Malkû at Palmyra', in M. L. Bernhard (ed.), *Mélanges offerts à Kazimierz Michalowski* (Warsaw: Państwowe Wydawnictwo Naukowe), pp. 457–76.

—— 1970–1971. 'The Sarcophagus of Beʿelai and Other Sculptures from the Tomb of Malkû, Palmyra', *Mélanges de l'Université Saint Joseph*, 46: 171–200 <https://doi.org/10.3406/mefao.1970.1281>.

—— 1974. 'Two Unpublished Tombs from the Southwest Necropolis of Palmyra, Syria', in D. K. Kouymjian (ed.), *Near Eastern Numismatics, Iconography, Epigraphy and History: Studies in Honor of George C. Miles* (Beirut: American University of Beirut), pp. 37–54.

—— 1976. 'Varia Tadmorea', in E. Frézouls (ed.), *Palmyre: Bilan et perspectives; colloque de Strasbourg (18–20 octobre 1973) organisé par le C.R.P.O.G.A. à la mémoire de Daniel Schlumberger et de Henri Seyrig* (Strasbourg: Association pour l'étude de la civilisation romaine), pp. 101–37.

Intagliata, E. E. 2018. *Palmyra after Zenobia 273–750: An Archaeological and Historical Reappraisal* (Oxford: Oxbow).
Krag, S. 2018. *Funerary Representations of Palmyrene Women: From the First Century BC to the Third Century AD*, Studies in Classical Archaeology, 3 (Turnhout: Brepols).
Kropp, A. and R. Raja. 2014. 'The Palmyra Portrait Project', *Syria: archéologie, art et histoire*, 91: 393–408.
—— 2015. 'The Palmyra Portrait Project', in J. M. A. Martínez, T. N. Bassarrate, and R. de Lianza (eds), *Centro y periferia en el Mundo Clásico: actas XVIII Congreso internacional de arqueología clásica* (Mérida: Museo nacional de arte romano), pp. 1223–26.
Millar, F. 1993. *The Roman Near East, 31 BC–AD 337* (Cambridge, MA: Harvard University Press).
Miranda, A. C. and R. Raja. 2021. 'Archive Archaeology: Preserving and Sharing Palmyra's Cultural Heritage through Harald Ingholt's Digital Archives. A Case Study in the Accessibility and Potential of Archives', *Antiquity*, 96.385: 229–37 <https://doi.org/10.15184/aqy.2021.165>.
Moritz, B. 1917. *Der Sinaikult in heidnischer Zeit* (Berlin: Weidmann).
Mortensen, E. and R. Raja. 2021. 'Facing the Palmyrenes: Exploring Life and Death in a Desert City', *Current World Archaeology*, 111: 16–24.
Mortensen, E. 2021. 'A Brief Note on Harald Ingholt — as I Remember Him', in O. Bobou, J. V. Jensen, N. Breintoft Kristensen, R. Raja, and R. Randeris Thomsen (eds), *Studies on Palmyrene Sculpture: A Translation of Harald Ingholt's 'Studier over Palmyrensk Skulptur', Edited and with Commentary*, Studies in Palmyrene Archaeology and History, 1 (Turnhout: Brepols), pp. 29–32.
Musée Impérial Ottoman. 1895. *Antiquités Himyarites et Palmyréniennes: catalogue sommaire* (Constantinople: Musée impérial ottoman).
Nielsen, A. M. 2019. 'Palmyra in the Glyptotek', in A. M. Nielsen and R. Raja (eds), *The Road to Palmyra* (Copenhagen: Ny Carlsberg Glyptotek), pp. 23–40.
Østrup, J. E. 1894. *Skiftende Horizonter* (Copenhagen: Gyldendalske Boghandel Forlag).
—— 1895. *Historisk-topografiske Bidrag til Kendskabet til den syriske Ørken*, The Royal Danish Academy of Sciences and Letters, 16.2 (Berlin: Weidmann).
Poulsen, F. 1921. 'De Palmyrenske Skulpturer', *Tidskrift för Konstvetenskap*, 6: 79–105.
Raja, R. 2013. 'Gravportrætterne i Palmyra: Mellem krig og kunstmarked', *SFINX*, 36.4: 168–69.
—— 2018. 'Palmyrene Funerary Portraits: Collection Histories and Current Research', in J. Aruz (ed.), *Palmyra: Mirage in the Desert* (New York: Metropolitan Museum), pp. 100–09.
—— 2019a 'Harald Ingholt and Palmyra: A Danish Archaeologist and his Work at Palmyra', in A. M. Nielsen and R. Raja (eds), *The Road to Palmyra* (Copenhagen: Ny Carlsberg Glyptotek), pp. 42–64.
—— 2019b. *The Palmyra Collection: Ny Carlsberg Glyptotek* (Copenhagen: Ny Carlsberg Glyptotek).
—— 2019c. 'Reconsidering the *dorsalium* or "Curtain of Death" in Palmyrene Funerary Sculpture: Significance and Interpretations in Light of the Palmyra Portrait Project Corpus', in R. Raja (ed.), *Revisiting the Religious Life of Palmyra*, Contextualizing the Sacred, 9 (Turnhout: Brepols), pp. 67–151.
—— 2021a. 'Adornment and Jewellery as a Status Symbol in Priestly Representations in Roman Palmyra: The Palmyrene Priests and their Brooches', in M. K. Heyn and R. Raja (eds), *Individualizing the Dead: Attributes in Palmyrene Funerary Sculpture*, Studies in Palmyrene Archaeology and History, 3 (Turnhout: Brepols), pp. 75–117.
—— 2021b. '"Den smukkeste Kvindebuste, jeg endnu har set": The Palmyra Excavation Diaries of Harald Ingholt, 1924–1928', in R. Raja, J. Steding, and J.-B. Yon (eds), *Excavating Palmyra: Harald Ingholt's Excavation Diaries; A Transcript, Translation, and Commentary*, Studies in Palmyrene Archaeology and History, 4, 2 vols (Turnhout: Brepols), I, pp. 23–70.
—— 2021c. 'Harald Ingholt and Palmyrene Sculpture: Continuing a Lifelong Relationship a Century Later', in O. Bobou, J. V. Jensen, N. Breintoft Kristensen, R. Raja, and R. Randeris Thomsen (eds), *Studies on Palmyrene Sculpture: A Translation of Harald Ingholt's 'Studier over Palmyrensk Skulptur', Edited and with Commentary*, Studies in Palmyrene Archaeology and History, 1 (Turnhout: Brepols), pp. 1–28.
—— 2021d. 'Reading the Ingholt Excavation Diaries, and Acknowledgements', in R. Raja, J. Steding, and J.-B. Yon (eds), *Excavating Palmyra: Harald Ingholt's Excavation Diaries; A Transcript, Translation, and Commentary*, I: *Introduction and Ingholt's Diaries 1–3*, Studies in Palmyrene Archaeology and History, 4.1 (Turnhout: Brepols), pp. 7–9.
—— 2022. *Pearl of the Desert: A History of Palmyra* (Oxford: Oxford University Press).
Raja, R. and J. Steding. 2021. 'Harald Ingholt's Excavation Diaries from his Fieldwork in Palmyra – an Open Data Online Resource', *Journal of Open Archaeology Data*, 9: 1–9 <https://doi.org/10.5334/joad.84>.
Raja, R. and A. Sørensen. 2015a. *Harald Ingholt og Palmyra* (Aarhus: Fællestrykkeriet).
—— 2015b. *Harald Ingholt and Palmyra* (Aarhus: Fællestrykkeriet).
Raja, R., O. Bobou, and I. Romanowska. 2021. 'Three Hundred Years of Palmyrene History: Unlocking Archaeological Data for Studying Past Societal Transformations', *PLoS ONE*, 16.11 <https://doi.org/10.1371/journal.pone.0256081>.
Raja, R., O. Bobou, and J.-B. Yon (forthcoming). *The Palmyrene Funerary Portraits*, Studies in Palmyrene Archaeology and History (Turnhout: Brepols).

Raja, R., K. Schnädelbach, and J. Steding. 2022. 'A New Map of Palmyra's Southwest Necropolis Based on the Excavation Diaries of Harald Ingholt', *Zeitschrift für Orientarchäologie*, 14: 230–73.

Raja, R., J. Steding, and J.-B. Yon. 2021. *Excavating Palmyra: Harald Ingholt's Excavation Diaries; A Transcript, Translation, and Commentary*, Studies in Palmyrene Archaeology and History, 4, 2 vols (Turnhout: Brepols).

Romanowska, I., O. Bobou, and R. Raja. 2021. 'Reconstructing the Social, Economic and Demographic Trends of Palmyra's Elite from Funerary Data', *Journal of Archaeological Science*, 133: 105432 <https://doi.org/10.1016/j.jas.2021.105432>.

Romanowska, I., J. C. Jiménez, O. Bobou, and R. Raja. 2021. 'Evaluating the Environmental Kuznets Curves through Archaeological Data: A Conceptual and Theoretical Framework', *Journal of Urban Archaeology*, 4: 61–97 <http://doi.org/10.1484/J.JUA.5.126594>.

Sartre-Fauriat, A. 2019. 'The Discovery and Reception of Palmyra', in A. M. Nielsen and R. Raja (eds), *The Road to Palmyra* (Copenhagen: Ny Carlsberg Glyptotek), pp. 65–76.

Sartre, M. 2001. *D'Alexandre à Zénobie: histoire du Levant antique, IVᵉ siècle avant J.-C.–IIIᵉ siècle après J.-C.* (Paris: Fayard).

—— 2005. *The Middle East under Rome*, trans. by C. Porter and E. Rawlings (Cambridge, MA: Belknap).

Sartre, M. and A. Sartre-Fauriat. 2016. *Palmyre: Vérités et légendes* (Paris: Perrin).

Schmidt-Colinet, A. 1995. 'The Quarries of Palmyra', *Aram Society for Syro-Mesopotamian Studies*, 7: 53–58.

—— 2017. 'Die antiken Steinbrüche von Palmyra: Ein Vorbericht', *Mitteilungen der Deutschen Orient-Gesellschaft zu Berlin*, 149: 159–96.

Schnädelbach, K. 2010. *Topographia Palmyrena*, I: *Topography*, Documents d'archéologie syrienne, 18 (Damascus: Deutsches Archäologisches Institut).

Seland, E. H. 2015. 'Palmyrene Long-Distance Trade: Land, River, and Maritime Routes in the First Three Centuries CE', in M. N. Walter and J. P. Ito-Adler (eds), *Long-Distance Trade, Culture, and Society* (Cambridge: Cambridge Institutes Press), pp. 101–31.

—— 2016. *Ships of the Desert and Ships of the Sea: Palmyra in the World Trade of the First–Third Centuries CE* (Wiesbaden: Harrassowitz).

—— 2019. 'The Trade of Palmyra', in A. M. Nielsen and R. Raja (eds), *The Road to Palmyra* (Copenhagen: Ny Carlsberg Glyptotek), pp. 127–36.

Shifman, I. S. 2014. *The Palmyrene Tax Tariff* (Oxford: Oxford University Press).

Simonsen, D. 1889a. *Skulpturer og indskrifter fra Palmyra i Ny Carlsberg Glyptotek* (Copenhagen: Lind).

—— 1889b. *Sculptures et inscriptions de Palmyre à la Glyptothèque de Ny Carlsberg* (Copenhagen: Lind).

Sommer, M. 2018. *Palmyra: A History* (Abingdon: Routledge).

Spencer, C. 2022. *Shifting Horizons: Observations from a Ride through the Syrian Desert and Asia Minor; A Translation of Johannes Elith Østrupt's 'Skiftende Horizonter'*, Archive Archaeology, 1 (Turnhout: Brepols).

Stark, J. K. 1971. *Personal Names in the Palmyrene Inscriptions* (Oxford: Clarendon).

Stucky, R. A. 2008. 'Henri Seyrig: Engagierter Archäologe und Verwalter des Antikendienstes während der Mandatszeit', in Charlotte Trümpler (ed.), *Das Große Spiel: Archäologie und Politik zur Zeit des Kolonialismus (1860–1940)* (Cologne: DuMont), pp. 504–11.

Underdown, H. 2021. 'Preface: An Introduction from the Ingholt-Underdown Family', in O. Bobou, J. V. Jensen, N. Breintoft Kristensen, R. Raja, and R. Randeris Thomsen (eds), *Studies on Palmyrene Sculpture: A Translation of Harald Ingholt's 'Studier over Palmyrensk Skulptur', Edited and with Commentary*, Studies in Palmyrene Archaeology and History, 1 (Turnhout: Brepols), p. xxiii.

Wood, R. 1753. *The Ruins of Palmyra: Otherwise Tedmor in the Desert* (London: Robert Wood).

Yon, J.-B. 2013. 'L'épigraphie palmyrénienne depuis PAT, 1996–2011', *Studia Palmyreńskie*, 12: 333–67.

—— 2021. 'Preliminary Notes', in R. Raja, J. Steding, and J.-B. Yon (eds), *Excavating Palmyra: Harald Ingholt's Excavation Diaries; A Transcript, Translation, and Commentary, Introduction and Ingholt's Diaries 1–3*, Studies in Palmyrene Archaeology and History, 4.1 (Turnhout: Brepols), p. 11.

6. Considerations in Archive Archaeology: Past and Present Colonialism in the Study of Palmyra's Archaeology and History

Amy C. Miranda and Rubina Raja

Centre for Urban Network Evolutions (UrbNet), Aarhus University (acm351@gmail.com, Rubina.raja@cas.au.dk)

Introduction

A black-and-white photograph, almost square, shows a relief sculpture fragment against a black background (Fig. 6.1). The sculpture is of a reclining figure of a priest wearing a modius, his right arm at rest on his elevated knee. His modius overlaps the relief's frame, an inscribed moulding supported below by a band of egg-and-dart. The photograph is taped to a medium brown file folder, oriented vertically, and surrounded by annotations in red and blue ink, as well as pencil. The handwritten notes are scattered across the folder and include such information as a date for the relief, a transcription of its inscription, and several bibliographic references. These annotations are made in English and French, and the relief's inscription is Palmyrene Aramaic — a local dialect of the Semitic language Aramaic developed at Palmyra. The various writing implements, languages, and haphazard arrangement of the notes, along with the torn grey photographic mounts that once held the now taped image all suggest that this piece of file folder was returned to over and over during the course of some time.

The photograph and its accompanying annotations belong to the Danish archaeologist Harald Ingholt (1896–1985, Fig. 6.2), whose research archive contains 2099 sheets of Palmyrene architecture, epigraphy, and funerary sculpture that were collected in the 1920s.[1] This banqueting relief fragment is likely one of the earliest photographs gathered for the archive and is representative of the type of work Ingholt would conduct on Palmyrene funerary archaeology over his lifetime. His archive, published as the Ingholt Archive, is just one of countless examples of archaeological archives.[2] These archives are often vast in size, having been developed over years of archaeological fieldwork, museum collection and object provenance research, or other scholarly activities. These resources can go untouched for years, if not generations, despite holding critical information. Regardless of their intellectual value, archaeological archives still tend to be under-utilized within the discipline of classical archaeology, as researchers prioritize the accumulation of 'their own' data over archival research and data synthetization. However, attitudes are changing, particularly as the so-called archival turn in the humanities continues to gain momentum and increasingly draws the attention of archaeologists. Recent conflicts and crises — the Syrian civil war, COVID-19, or the escalating conflict in Afghanistan after the takeover of the Taliban — have made archives invaluable as documenters of at risk heritage, or as supplement to or replacement of fieldwork. Yet, archives are more than mere sources of information and, as the turn suggests, deserve to be objects of study in their own right. In studying archives, it is essential to consider who has access to archival material, whether making archives available online means they are truly available and not digital colonialism, and whether scholars are fulfilling their larger social corporate responsibility. Archives also require researchers to reflect upon the material itself, the means and times in which the data was collected, and the work it takes to make archives as holistically available to others as is possible. As such, working with archival material requires researchers to be critical not only of their own *modus operandi* but also to critically engage with the historical framework of the time in which an archive came into existence. This, in turn, requires rigorous historiographic research.

---

[1] Regarding the archive sheets, Bobou, Miranda, and Raja 2021 published 2347 sheets. The extra 248 sheets appear not to be original to Ingholt and were likely created by Gunhild Ploug to reflect Palmyrene portraits in the collection of the Ny Carlsberg Glyptotek, Copenhagen. More about the Ingholt Archive and the Ny Carlsberg Glyptotek below.

[2] The Ingholt Archive has been published online as open data (Bobou, Miranda, and Raja 2021) and in print (Bobou and others 2022).

There are, however, recent examples of work on archaeological archives that has performed the extensive historiographic research and placed the archaeological material within the historical framework of its development.³ Such projects demonstrate what deep knowledge of archives can do for the protection of cultural heritage, and have a track record of making primary source data open access.⁴ The aims of these projects, overall, contribute to the preservation of Syrian cultural heritage, disseminate knowledge of this heritage, raise awareness of the plight of Syria (particularly Palmyra), and grapple with the colonialist past of Europeans and their institutions in the Middle East that have created the archive. Simultaneously, decisions made within both projects have had to be self-critical regarding present-day digital colonialism and their larger social responsibility.

To unpack the problems these projects confronted, this article looks at Ingholt's legacy data on Palmyra, Syria that he developed over the course of much of the twentieth century: the Ingholt Archive and his excavation diaries. This case study allows for an exploration into the role and historiography of archives in archaeological practices, which includes a consideration of colonialism in several forms as it has evolved over the years. The article first contextualizes the origins of the Ingholt Archive by introducing the site of Palmyra, and then focuses on Harald Ingholt's biography and publications so as to illustrate the entanglement between the man and the archaeology. These introductions set up an investigation into the Ingholt Archive and his excavation diaries. Charting the archive's development in a parallel investigation to the history of research in Palmyra demonstrates the dynamics between archive and archaeology. This one specific story of an archive — its development, uses, outcomes, and afterlives — not only contributes knowledge of Palmyra's history and archaeology, or a portrait of archaeology in Syria during the twentieth century, it also offers ways forward. The case study of the Ingholt Archive serves as a jumping-off point for a wider discussion on archive accessibility and digital colonialism in classical archaeology. Despite potential pitfalls, the article concludes by advocating for archival study as a means for advancing archaeology.

Palmyra's History and Archaeology⁵

The banqueting relief with the reclining priest seen in Figure 6.1 has a second, non-adjoining piece, also in the Ingholt Archive. This fragment shows a seated female figure in a three-quarters view (Fig. 6.3). She wears a tunic and himation and clutches her veil with her right hand. Like the priest's modius, her head overlaps the egg-and-dart motif that is below an inscribed moulding. Together the two fragments suggest a larger, rectangular relief of a priest and his wife as indicated by the inscriptions: '[- - - daughter of] Šimʿôn son of Ḥairân Firdušî, his wife' and 'Malkû son of Lišamš son of Ḥennibel ʾAʿabeî, year 58'.⁶ The relief was likely part of a substantial decorative programme in one of Palmyra's many lavish tombs (tower tombs, house tombs, and hypogea) and is an example of the culture's portrait habit.⁷ As these portraits were the focus of Ingholt's attention throughout his career and so captured in his archive, a close look at the culture that produced them is necessary to understand the portraits' significance to the field of classical archaeology as well as Ingholt's enchantment with them.

Palmyra, ancient Tadmor, was a rich site full of monumental architecture — some of which has been destroyed by ISIS since 2015 — but was also noteworthy for the sheer quantity of funerary portrait sculptures that it produced.⁸ An oasis city located in the Syrian Steppe Desert (Fig. 6.4), Palmyra reached its zenith during the first three centuries AD having been an integrated part of the Roman world since Pompey the Great's campaigns in the Near East, and since playing a prominent role in the East–West caravan trade. Active in both land and sea trade routes (Palmyrenes owned ships that sailed the Euphrates River, the Persian Gulf, and potentially the Indian Ocean), Palmyra was of significant economic importance to the Roman Empire as a connection with luxury goods and source of taxation.⁹ Palmyra's geo-

---

³ <https://projects.au.dk/archivearcheology/> [accessed 8 December 2021].

⁴ See, for example, Bobou, Miranda, and Raja 2021; Raja and Steding 2021.

---

⁵ General introductions to Palmyrene archaeology and history are Smith 2013 and Veyne 2017. For the archaeology and history of the Roman Near East, see Millar 1993; Sartre 2001; Butcher 2003.

⁶ Translations of the inscriptions from Bobou and others 2022. Cf. *CIS* no. 4458 and 4458bis; *PAT* no. 0818 and 0819.

⁷ Raja 2019c.

⁸ Between 2012 and 2020, the Palmyra Portrait Project has collected 3976 funerary portrait sculptures. This is the largest corpus of portrait sculpture from the ancient Roman world outside of the city of Rome itself. Cf. Kropp and Raja 2014; Raja 2018a; 2019c; 2019d. Earlier studies on the corpus of Palmyrene funerary sculpture include Ingholt 1928 and Colledge 1976.

⁹ Seland 2015; Schörle 2017.

graphic and economic positioning directly shaped its unique culture — rather than provincial, Palmyra should be thought of as a worldly ancient city that was an epicentre of trends and fashions, religious developments and architectural innovations, languages and cultural traditions with a strong local grounding necessitated by its somewhat isolated location in the desert.[10] It is during these three centuries of economic prosperity that Palmyra underwent monumentalization including colonnaded streets, the monumental arch, theatre, and several sanctuaries (Figs 6.5–6.6).[11] In addition to the proliferation of public buildings, Palmyrenes also paid close attention to their private architecture that is seen in the extravagant tombs that populate the city's necropoleis. Although many tombs are underground (hypogea, Fig. 6.7), the landscape just outside the city centre is punctuated with massive tower tombs and smaller temple or house tombs (Fig. 6.8).[12] These tombs, regardless of what form they took, were lavishly decorated with the aforementioned funerary sculptures and wall paintings (Figs 6.9–6.10). The architecture and decorative programmes seen in Palmyra, like many cities in the Roman provinces, have resonances of the city of Rome while still reflecting local traditions.[13]

Palmyra's heyday came to an end in AD 272/273, when the Roman Emperor Aurelian sacked the city twice with his troops.[14] This destruction was a direct result of the Palmyrenes' bid for independence under the famed ruler Zenobia.[15] While she ruled in the stead of her underage son, Wallahbat, following the death of her husband Odeinathus, Zenobia expanded the Palmyrene territory to include Egypt and parts of Asia Minor. The sack of Palmyra likely did not destroy the city entirely as a Roman legion was installed there afterwards, but it certainly lost its centrality to the caravan trade and therefore its fame. The period between the end of the third century and the Early Islamic period as well as the medieval period has only recently begun to attract attention through scholarly investigation.[16]

As Palmyra was impacted by Roman colonialism in the ancient past, so should the city be understood as encumbered by strong colonial interests in the modern period. Palmyra was 'rediscovered' by European travellers on several occasions, and perhaps the most well known were James Dawkins (1722–1757) and Robert Wood (1717–1771) who came to Palmyra in 1751. A 1758 painting by Gavin Hamilton, now in the Scottish National Gallery (NG 2666), shows an idealized version of the Dawkins and Wood expedition and presents an image of Palmyra through the western gaze. This painting was also made as a print, allowing the image to be widely circulated. The publication by Wood and Dawkins documents the ancient city's architecture through description, drawing, and etching, popularizing the site amongst Europeans and making it the focus of many travellers' attention. Shortly after, in 1758, a famous set of drawings was produced by Louis-Francois Cassas (1756–1827) furthering western — not to mention colonial — interests. Despite this early but significant attention from Europe, Palmyra did not fully capture the imagination of the western world until the nineteenth century.[17] The late nineteenth century saw the arrival of both scholars and tourists, the latter of whom were on tours through the Holy Land. The Danish theologian and first Professor of the Study of Islam in Denmark, Johannes Elith Østrup (1867–1938), was one such visitor to Palmyra in the 1890s and his published writings about the journey describe vandalism to the site.[18] According to Østrup, the conditions at Palmyra in the 1890s were not unlike today's looting practices.

---

[10] Nielsen and Raja 2019.

[11] For the development of Palmyra, see Hammad 2010. An earlier study is Schlumberger 1935. See also, Barański 1995; Delplace and Dentzer-Feydy 2005. On the development of Palmyra's sculptural habit in the late first century AD, see Raja 2019d.

[12] For the tower tombs, see Henning 2013. An earlier publication that also includes the underground tombs (hypogea) is Gawlikowski 1970. For the house or temple tombs, see al-Asʿad and Schmidt-Colinet 1985; Schmidt-Colinet 1987; 1992; 1997.

[13] Nielsen and Raja 2019; Raja 2021a.

[14] For a history of Palmyra in the third century AD, see Hartmann 2001; Smith 2013, 175–81.

[15] For recent literature on Zenobia, see Hvidberg-Hansen 2002; Yon 2002–2003; Sartre-Fauriat and Sartre 2014; Andrade 2018.

[16] Intagliata 2018. For further references to late antique and early Islamic Palmyra, see Gawlikowski 2009 and Intagliata 2019.

[17] There are known European visitors to Palmyra in the twelfth (Benjamin of Tudela) and seventeenth (Pietro della Valle) centuries. For the various visitors to Palmyra over the centuries, see Wood 1753; Cassas 1799; Adler 1907; Shifman 2014, 1–14; and Astengo 2016; Starkey 2019. See also the online exhibition at the Getty Research Institute 'The Legacy of Ancient Palmyra': <https://www.getty.edu/research/exhibitions_events/exhibitions/palmyra/exhibition.html> [accessed 28 October 2021].

[18] Østrup 1894; 1895; Raja 2016a; 2017; 2018b; 2019a; 2019b. The destruction of Syrian cultural heritage, while a timely topic, is not restricted to the present day; numerous incidents since the Roman sack of the ancient city have inflicted irreversible damage upon Palmyra's tangible and intangible heritage.

There was money in beheading the figures on the monumental sarcophagi showing banquet scenes, and then trading them as antiquities. In what might be considered a colonialist impulse, Østrup himself purchased several Palmyrene artefacts for the Ny Carlsberg Glyptotek collection, as such transactions were legal at that time. Across Europe, the upper-class collectors and the art market fuelled the systematic looting of Palmyra, which was undertaken both by locals and foreigners given the financial incentive. This looting formed a vicious cycle: Europeans began feverishly collecting antiquities from the Middle East in the late nineteenth century, seen in both private collections and the rapid growth of museum holdings, thereby encouraging looters to continue to vandalize archaeological sites.[19]

The twentieth century saw continued western interventions in Palmyra, but in a more systematic manner with the beginning of formalized excavations.[20] Excavations by archaeological missions would continue throughout the twentieth century and into the twenty-first until all fieldwork was suddenly and indefinitely halted by the outbreak of the Syrian civil war in 2011.[21] Palmyra would gain worldwide attention beyond the scholarly community when, in May 2015, ISIS systematically demolished several of the city's monuments, recording and disseminating news of the destruction.[22]

This most recent devastation of Palmyra's material culture and the diaspora of Syrian nationals due to the ongoing conflict has brought the discussion of cultural heritage preservation to the forefront.[23] The scholarly discussions around the preservation of Syrian, specifically Palmyrene, cultural heritage have developed in parallel with the increased use of archives in archaeological practice. The Ingholt Archive has much potential to generate much scholarship as well as inform the public of what is at stake.[24]

Harald Ingholt: Fieldwork and Scholarship[25]

The creator of the Ingholt Archive, Kai Harald Ingholt (called Harald Ingholt), was born on 11 March 1896. His career as an archaeologist began in 1918 at the University of Copenhagen where, as a student, he would be awarded the gold medal in Semitic and Oriental philology for his master thesis. He would continue his studies at the university, pursuing theology and earning the academic degree of cand. Theol. (Master of Theology) in 1922 (Fig. 6.11).[26] That same year, Ingholt would arrive at Princeton University in New Jersey, United States, on a scholarship that he was awarded by the New York-based American-Scandinavian Foundation (Fig. 6.12). His academic success continued with a position as a research fellow at the Sorbonne in Paris in 1923.

Ingholt conducted his first excavation in Palmyra in 1924. This excavation was funded by the Rask-Ørsted Foundation and was as mentioned a collaboration with the French archaeologist Maurice Dunand (1898–1987; Fig. 6.13).[27] With a permit granted by the High Commissioner of Syria under the French

---

[19] For a recent overview on European collecting practices in the nineteenth and early twentieth centuries, particularly of ancient Near Eastern artefacts, see McGeough 2015.

[20] For a brief overview and additional references on Palmyra's research history, see Sartre-Fauriat and Sartre 2016. Also, Shifman 2014, 1–14; Sartre-Fauriat 2019.

[21] Although most early fieldwork was conducted by French teams due to the mandate, later excavations would be performed by American, Austrian, British, German, Italian, Japanese, Norwegian, and Polish missions in cooperation with the Syrians. For an overview of late nineteenth- and early twentieth-century excavations, see Sartre-Fauriat 2019, also for further references. The bibliography on Palmyra continues to grow, yet no complete overview of the literature is available. Recent examples of general scholarship include Andrade 2012 and Sommer 2017. See also, Raja 2022. For an example of recent excavations in Palmyra, the Syro-German/Austrian Archaeological Mission begun in 1981, see Schmidt-Colinet 2017. For the final publication of the excavation, see Schmidt-Colinet and al-Asʿad 2013. This particular mission was co-directed by Khaled al-Asʿad until 2002. He was for many years the director of antiquities at the site and was brutally executed by ISIS on 18 August 2015, when trying to prevent illegal looting of the site's objects.

[22] The literature on the effects of the Syrian civil war and destruction by ISIS is prolific. For a sweeping approach to the relationship between conflict and cultural heritage, see Weiss and Connelly 2017; Luck 2018. For a focus on how the dismantling of Palmyra has affected the art market, see Raja 2016b.

[23] Several projects have been initiated in the twenty-first century, many using digital technologies to research and preserve ancient Palmyra. For example, 'Experience Ancient Palmyra in 360° and in 3D' <https://www.smb.museum/en/whats-new/detail/experience-ancient-palmyra-in-360-and-in-3d//> [accessed 1 November 2022]; 'The Rediscovery of Palmyra. Le fonds Collart' <https://archeologie.culture.gouv.fr/palmyre/en/fonds-collart> [accessed 1 November 2022]. Attention has also been given to the future of Palmyrene studies, for example Kaizer 2016; Baird and Kamash 2019.

[24] Some potentials of the Ingholt Archive are presented in Bobou, Miranda, and Raja 2022; Miranda and Raja 2021.

[25] For a full biography of Ingholt and his legacy, see Bobou and others (forthcoming).

[26] Raja and Sørensen 2015b, 22; 2015c, 22.

[27] Raja and Sørensen 2015b, 22; 2015c, 22.

Mandate, Ingholt and Dunand began excavations of the city's south-west necropolis where they excavated around thirty tombs.[28] A second campaign in the south-west necropolis took place in 1925 with permission from the French High Commissioner. This time Ingholt worked with the French architect Albert Gabriel (1883–1972), revisiting tombs excavated during the previous campaign and exploring new areas of the necropolis.[29] Concurrently, between 1924 and 1925, Ingholt was a research fellow at the American School of Oriental Research in Jerusalem. He would return to Denmark later in 1925 to begin his five-year tenure as the deputy director of the Ny Carlsberg Glyptotek in Copenhagen.[30] Then, from 1927 to 1930, he served as secretary at the Ny Carlsberg Foundation. During this time, Ingholt was at work on the doctoral dissertation, *Studier over Palmyrensk Skulptur*, which he successfully defenced in 1928 (Figs 6.14–6.15). This same year, Ingholt would conduct a third excavation campaign in Palmyra.

From 1930 to 1938, Ingholt directed the Danish excavations of Hama, Syria, with funding from the Carlsberg Foundation.[31] Living in Beirut, he began his employment as Professor of Archaeology at the American University of Beirut where he was also the curator of the AUB Archaeological Museum.[32] A regional museum founded in 1868, its holdings include a large collection of Palmyrene portraits some of which Ingholt may have assisted the museum in acquiring. Ingholt's activities in Beirut also included founding the journal *Berytus* in 1934, with a focus on the publication of archaeology and history of Lebanon, Syria, Jordan, and Palestine.[33] In addition to publishing the work of many leading archaeologists of the Near East, the journal also published Ingholt's articles on his work in the Levant, including the results of his excavations in Palmyra. For example, *Berytus* volume 2 contains an article by Ingholt that discusses his 1924 and 1925 campaigns.[34] Following the founding of *Berytus*, Ingholt would return his attention to fieldwork in Palmyra. He would excavate in two separate campaigns, first in 1935 and again in 1937, Ingholt's final excavations at the site.[35] Ingholt would move to the United States to continue his career. Even after his retirement in 1964, as Professor Emeritus at Yale University, he remained active by publishing on Palmyra and other areas of interest (Fig. 6.16).[36] Ingholt passed away on 28 October 1985 in his home in Hamden, Connecticut, at the age of eighty-nine.

The Ingholt Archive and the Excavation Diaries from Palmyra

As a fellow at Princeton University in 1922, Harald Ingholt began forming ideas for his higher doctoral dissertation, which he would successfully defend at the University of Copenhagen six years later in 1928. In the introduction to his dissertation, Ingholt reflects upon his year at Princeton and remarks that he 'conceived the plan to make a comprehensive presentation of the Palmyrene portrait busts'.[37] As was a requirement for higher doctoral dissertations, the text would be published that same year as the now canonical work, *Studier over Palmyrensk Skulptur*.[38] The work outlines a chronology of Palmyrene funerary sculpture based on stylistic criteria and divides the sculptures into three main time periods: (1) between AD 1–150, (2) AD 150–200, (3) AD 200–250. The work is so foundational to the study of Palmyrene archaeology that it has recently been translated as part of Aarhus University's Palmyra Portrait Project.[39] The translation allows for a non-Danish reading audience to access the critical text and has already served as the basis for several recent publications and much forthcoming research.[40]

---

28 Raja and Sørensen 2015b, 26; 2015c, 26.

29 Ingholt 1935; 1938.

30 Raja and Sørensen 2015b, 18; 2015c, 18; Nielsen and Raja 2019, 57–58.

31 Ingholt 1940. For Ingholt's work on Hama after 1940, see Mortensen 2021.

32 Raja and Sørensen 2015b, 23; 2015c, 23.

33 <https://www.aub.edu.lb/Berytus/Pages/default.aspx> [accessed 8 December 2021].

34 Ingholt 1935.

35 Raja and Sørensen 2015b, 19; 2015c, 19.

36 Ingholt 1966; 1970–1972; 1974; 1976.

37 Ingholt 1928, 5. For an English translation, see Bobou and others 2021, 39. For Ingholt's time at Princeton, see Raja and Sørensen 2015a, 18; 2015b, 18.

38 Ingholt 1928. It is a testament to the importance of Ingholt's study that a text written in Danish, a language that archaeologists do not often learn (instead focusing on English, German, French, and Italian, for example), should become — and remain — a gold standard in Palmyrene scholarship. This work has recently been translated into English and published with essays contextualizing Ingholt's life and career. See Bobou and others 2021. Such a publication will ensure an even wider readership of this critical text.

39 Bobou and others 2021. For the Palmyra Portrait Project, see <https://projects.au.dk/palmyraportrait/> [accessed 8 December 2021].

40 Bobou, Romanowska, and Raja 2021; Raja, Bobou, and Romanowska 2021; Romanowska, Bobou, and Raja 2021.

Studier over Palmyrensk Skulptur presents the first 545 sculptures in the Ingholt Archive, but given the dissertation's emphasis on chronology and style is not a publication of the archive as such.[41] Ingholt would never publish the archive, since it was his private scholarly archive and never intended for publication, but he would continue adding to it throughout his career. As he added to his archive, the typological and chronological structure falls by the wayside and instead documents when images came into his possession. Ingholt acquired images from a variety of sources such as others' excavations, new publications, or pieces appearing on the art market. Being an avid photographer, many of the photographs were likely taken by Ingholt himself. Over the years, duplicate images were added to the archive, but often Ingholt did not recognize that the sculpture had already been assigned a PS number and would assign a new number.[42] Upon discovery of the duplication, Ingholt would amend the PS number as seen in the case of a male head labelled PS 1405, which is the same sculpture as PS 1314A and PS 615 (Figs 6.17–6.18).[43]

The archive appears to have received Ingholt's sporadic attention until sometime in the late 1970s. Two sheets for PS 1430 contain newspaper clippings from the Beirut *Daily Star* and *Arab News and Views* both dated to 1964, October and December respectively (Figs 6.19–6.20). The articles detail the recent excavation of a relief described as depicting Queen Zenobia, now understood to be a relief with two goddesses.[44] As the relief was newly excavated, Ingholt could have only added it to his archive in 1964 or later, thereby demonstrating his continued attention to the archive's development. On a third sheet for PS 1430, an annotation reads 'On back: Letter from Peder Mortensen. Aarhus, 4. Juli 1971', indicating that this particular photograph came into Ingholt's possession in 1971 (Fig. 6.21).[45] Additionally, Ingholt returned to his sheets to update the bibliographic information. Such references include texts by Józef T. Milik and Malcolm A. R. Colledge.[46] Ingholt continued publishing on Palmyra even after his retirement and into the 1970s raising the possibility that the archive remained a critical resource for him throughout his life.[47]

Ingholt donated his archive to the Ny Carlsberg Glyptotek in 1981 and the material arrived in Copenhagen in 1983 (Fig. 6.22).[48] In Copenhagen, the classical archaeologist Gunhild Ploug began to work on the archival material. Although it is unknown in which state the material arrived at the museum, Ploug is known to have reorganized the archive sheets. The restructuring saw the archive sheets distributed across nineteen folders.[49] Additionally, all sheets above PS 527 — meaning those discussed in the text of *Studier over Palmyrensk Skulptur* — were assigned a new number that appears centred at the top of the sheet (Fig. 6.23). According to Ploug, this new structure formed the foundation for her forthcoming book, *The Relative Chronology of the Palmyrene Funerary Busts*.[50] This manuscript was neither published nor recovered after her death in 2005.[51] Yet, Ploug would leave behind a catalogue of Palmyrene sculpture at the Ny Carlsberg Glyptotek, demonstrating some of her work on the museum's collection.[52] The archive was then digitized in 2012. In 2021, the archive was published online as open data with print and e-book editions in 2022.[53] This marks a new phase in the life of the archive and sets the foundation for much future research just as the use of archives in archaeological scholarship is receiving renewed interest.

The study of archives requires consideration of their formation and how such knowledge was accumulated as well as disseminated. The Ingholt Archive was formed over decades, but its early years and exponential

---

[41] Only sculptures through PS (Palmyrensk Skulptur, or Palmyrene Sculpture) 527 are covered in the body of the text; in footnotes, however, Ingholt refers to sculptures up to PS 545.

[42] 'PS' is an abbreviation used by Ingholt in his thesis, meaning 'Palmyrensk Skulptur'. It is translated to 'Palmyrene Sculpture' in Bobou and others 2021 and Bobou and others 2022.

[43] Bobou and others 2022, PS 615, PS 1314A, PS 1405.

[44] The relief's last known location was in the National Museum of Damascus, Damascus, Syria.

[45] cf. Mortensen 2021.

[46] Milik 1972; Colledge 1976. See Figs 6.1 and 6.2, for example.

[47] For example, Ingholt 1970–1972; 1974; 1976.

[48] Bobou and others 2022.

[49] For Ploug's work on the Ingholt Archive, see Hvidberg-Hansen and Ploug 1993; Ploug 1995.

[50] Ploug 1995, 7.

[51] Raja 2019b, 61; 2021b, 24. Recently, when visiting the private archive of Klaus Parlasca after his death, Raja saw a letter from Klaus Parlasca to Gunhild Ploug, where he comments that he had read her manuscript on the sculptures. This indicates that the manuscript indeed did exist, but somehow has gotten lost.

[52] Hvidberg-Hansen and Ploug 1993. For a more recent publication of the Palmyra collection at the Ny Carlsberg Glyptotek, see Raja 2019a.

[53] Bobou, Miranda, and Raja 2021; Bobou and others 2022.

growth occurred in Syria during the period of the French Mandate (1920–1946, ratified 1923). The mandate was, in the aftermath of World War I and the dissolution of the Ottoman Empire, interference of the colonialist west in the local affairs of the Middle East. Ingholt was working in Syria and Lebanon in the 1930s as a professor at the American University of Beirut and as a curator in the university museum, and during this time facilitated acquisition of pieces of Palmyrene sculpture for the Ny Carlsberg Glyptotek's collection following in the footsteps of the founder's already monumental Palmyrene collection.[54] Since these acquisitions took place long before the 1970 UNESCO convention they are not considered as illegal acquisitions, and Ingholt also held the appropriate export licences for the pieces acquired through him.[55] The formation of the Ingholt Archive raises questions about decolonizing archaeological practices. Ingholt was collecting photographs of hundreds of Palmyrene sculptures as his personal research resource. Yet, with its physical form at the Ny Carlsberg Glyptotek and the archive as the only record of some of the sculptures after the systematic destruction in Syria by ISIS starting in 2015, the archive should be made accessible to better share Syrian heritage to a string of stakeholders, including the local population and institutions. The digitization of the Ingholt Archive and its recent online publication as open data on figshare is a first step in making the archive more widely accessible. However, this too raises questions of colonialist practices in archaeology and heritage preservation, as 'digital colonialism' is increasingly discussed.[56]

Interested parties exist outside academia such as UNESCO and others who work on illicit trafficking of cultural goods: archival research also affects museums, state and private collections, and provenance researchers. Such institutions often strive to keep heritage within the country of origin or at the very least have a detailed provenance history dating back prior to 1970. By contrast, auction houses tend to inspire illegal looting from sites like Palmyra 'white washing' provenances and driving up prices on irreplaceable heritage. Given the broad range of intentions with antiquities, sharing primary source data as open access under a CC-BY 4.0 license is a first step in providing data to assist in the tracking of Palmyrene funerary sculpture from Syria to foreign collections. However, the data, both the Ingholt Archive and the excavation diaries, may be considered risky to share: Might not this information, such as tomb locations, be put to misuse? Although this possibility remains, scholars should remain optimistic that data will be used for good. The alternative, secrecy, means that connections will be missed and collaborations will not occur, leading to a sort of dark age in scholarship in which parties cannot trust each other. There is much good that can stem from open data and the Ingholt Archive and diaries are examples that have already begun to bear fruit.

Case Study

Of the hundreds of images that Ingholt collected many are his own photographs and some are objects that Ingholt himself excavated. Only a handful of the archive sheets contain references to the diaries, but PS 410 is one such sheet (Fig. 6.24). A brown archive sheet with an image mounted at its centre shows a loculus relief with a female bust and a fragment of architectural sculpture, both of which have been photographed against a black backdrop. Ingholt's date for the loculus relief AD 150–200, is written in the sheet's upper left-hand corner. The abbreviation, 'Mus Bey 14' in the sheet's upper right-hand corner indicates the relief's location in the collection of the Musée du Beyrouth, Beirut, during Ingholt's time of writing; however, the relief's last known location was the Palmyra Museum.[57] At the bottom right corner of the image are three annotations: 'Dépôt de Palmyre'; '1925 p. 1'; and '*Inv.* viii, no. 130'. These annotations suggest first that the sculpture was photographed at Palmyra's sculpture depot during fieldwork. The second annotation '1925 p. 1' is a reference to the excavation diary of 1925, page 1, while the third note is a bibliographic citation for the relief's inscription: Jean Cantineau's *Inventaire des inscriptions de Palmyre*, fasc. VIII: *Le dépôt des antiquités* of 1932.[58]

In his 1925 excavation diary, also known as diary 2, Ingholt writes on page 1 (Fig. 6.25):

> 15 March.
> In a tomb near 'tombeau de Malkou', a buste funeraire feminin. Shoulder locks, face mutilated.

---

[54] For a historiographic overview of Palmyrene sculpture in the Ny Carlsberg Glyptotek, see Raja 2019c.

[55] Objects acquired by Ingholt for the Ny Carlsberg Glyptotek are included in the museum's catalogue. See Raja 2019c.

[56] Bobou, Miranda and Raja 2021. For example, Elias 2019; Meskell 2020; Stobiecka 2020.

[57] Starcky 1955, 44.

[58] Cantineau 1932, 84, no. 130. For more on the relief's inscription, see *PAT* no. 1281 and Bobou and others 2022, PS 410.

Hair also done up. Earrings: ⚭. Right hand. L
Left holding on to the veil.
Inscription on right
ṣlmt
ʾḥtʾ
brt ʿqybʾ
ḥbl.
ph. ?
The tomb has 4 niches in the central chamber, all 3 walls, whereas the chamber at right has 5 in the 2 side walls and 4 in the end wall. Under the ceiling of same, an arch: ⌒[59]

In sum, Ingholt is recording that in a tomb close by the Tomb of Malkû, a loculus relief with a female bust was found. Though her face has been damaged, locks of her hair are still discernible cascading over her shoulder. Also visible are her ornate drop earrings — which Ingholt roughly sketches — and the gesture of her hands: her right arm is bent at the elbow with the hand held against her chest (Ingholt draws this as a capital L-shape in the diary) and the left hand pulls back her veil. The inscription, which is on the viewer's right, is not transcribed in the original Palmyrene Aramaic and can be translated as 'Image of Aḥitâ daughter of ʿAqîbâ, alas!'[60] The inscription is followed by the note 'ph?' which must be an abbreviation or shorthand that is presently unclear in meaning. Ingholt concludes his diary entry with a description of the tomb, drawing the archway at the end of the description.

Ingholt devotes the first four pages of diary 2 to March 15 in which he goes on to mention two sarcophagi, PAT 0031 and 0035, which are not in the archive, and detail a visit to the house of a Mr Christineh where Ingholt viewed an inscribed stone.[61] Although it is likely that Ingholt excavated many loculus reliefs, PS 410 is one of few that he cross-references between the archive and the diaries, and it is regrettable that the two sarcophagi mentioned on the same day are seemingly not in the archive. Nevertheless, this first entry of the 1925 campaign together with the image provided in the archive, can help to enrich the current picture of the Tomb of Malkû. The decorative programme was likely not limited to the single loculus relief with a female bust and the two sarcophagi mentioned, yet, at the very least, PS 410 can be recontextualized as part of a tomb assemblage.

The archive and diaries are critical to read together as information is otherwise lost. The archive provides photographic documentation and bibliography to complement the field notes made in the diaries. With both resources available freely online as open data, researchers and interested parties can access this information through the internet. This effort to democratize data can catalyse work on Palmyrene archaeology and history particularly as solutions take shape for preserving Syrian cultural heritage under the shadow of the country's civil war. However, as awareness and efforts in the area increase, the question of colonialism arises as many initiatives stem from western institutions and funding. As such, a discussion of colonialism in the past and present is warranted.

Colonialism's Past and its Digital Present

In the aftermath of World War I came the dissolution of the Ottoman Empire and the dividing up of the Middle East by England, the United States, and France. This action was overseen by the newly formed League of Nations that would strive to maintain international relations through diplomacy and avoid the outbreak of another catastrophic war. The French Mandate of Syria and Lebanon was a League of Nations mandate that was formed in 1920 and later ratified in 1923. Although the mandate states that it was designed to avoid such colonial mistakes that Europe made in Africa during the nineteenth century, so doing by promising to transition to local rule once a degree of stability had been reached, it clearly was an intervention rife with western saviourism.[62] Such attitudes are not a twentieth-century phenomenon; on the contrary, religions have continually laid claim to the Middle East and caused conflict in this area for centuries. This is particularly potent after the dawn of Christianity, at which point Europeans consistently visited the Holy Land — sometimes as pilgrims and at other times crusaders. The western conviction that the Middle East somehow belonged to them continued into the modern period with the birth of biblical archaeology and, shortly thereafter, the founding of western research institutions.[63]

---

[59] Raja, Steding, and Yon 2021, 503.

[60] Bobou and others 2022, PS 410.

[61] Raja, Steding, and Yon 2021, 505–09.

[62] Tauber 1994; Stucky 2008; Grainger 2013.

[63] For example, the German Protestant Institute of Archaeology and the American School of Oriental Study and Research in Palestine were founded in 1900, while the British School of Archaeology in Jerusalem was established in 1919.

Awareness of and attitudes towards colonialism were not the same in the late 1910s to early 1920s as they are a century later, yet a short article written by the Assistant Director of League of Nations News Bureau seems particularly naïve regarding the dangers of colonial interventions. The article begins by asserting that the 'mandatory system began under the League of Nations as one of the best-attested ideas that has ever been realized on paper'.[64] At the moment of its creation, the western world was optimistic that this was the best way forward and would correct colonial mistakes of the past. However, this hubristic language now reflects an embarrassing degree of insensitivity towards what the mandate system would do to the Middle East by subjecting the local populations to the foreign rule of the French and British. The western need to regulate the Middle East following the dissolution of the Ottoman Empire is a clear colonialist impulse, and it is in this environment that Harald Ingholt began his excavations in Palmyra, Syria.

Beginning in 1924, Ingholt would direct five separate field seasons in Palmyra in cooperation with the French authorities and archaeologists.[65] Ingholt would employ local workmen for his excavations, and he recorded many of his daily interactions with them in his excavation diaries.[66] The six diaries record more than excavation details; they also provide some kind of record — although not comprehensive — of Ingholt's social life in Palmyra. Interspersed between drawings of ground plans and accompanying notes on the tombs of Palmyra's southwest necropolis are anecdotes of everyday life. In diary 4, which is dated to 1928, Ingholt wrote on Tuesday, 13 November that while on his way to the necropolis that morning he purchased an 'interesting tessera with a sea nymph on the one side and a Kalathos deity with curled locks' (Fig. 6.26).[67] Later that day, 'on the way out to the hotel to fetch bath towels', Ingholt would purchase another tessera, this one with the busts of two deities on the obverse and a camel on the reverse.[68] Ingholt concludes the entry with a more personal anecdote of bathing in the spring and walking home with Avvar, 'who served dates'.[69] This figure of Avvar is a local one who, in diary 2 (1925–1928), asked Ingholt to '"dalla hôn"; he wanted to be my "halti" (uht–ummik), me to marry his daughter, have children in Palmyra; then I would not leave'.[70] This entry, dated to 21 April, concludes that Ingholt could purchase a wife for 1800 francs and that Avaar was keen on such an arrangement as Ingholt would stay in Syria and Avaar could use the money to buy himself a new wife.[71] The last sentence of the entry states that if Ingholt were to leave, Avvar 'would shoot me down in the "avion"'.[72] These two diary entries not only highlight how casual the collecting of antiquities was in 1920s Syria, but also paint Ingholt as someone with close ties to the local community. Although Ingholt was seemingly respectful of the Syrians he engaged with, his tesserae purchases and exporting of sculptures to institutions worldwide was part of the colonial system at this point in history.

It is also in the cultural climate of the mandate that Ingholt began acquiring the images in his archive. The photographing of hundreds of Palmyrene funerary sculptures is not a colonialist act per se, and this collection was not, during Ingholt's lifetime, a formal archive, but rather a personal research resource that provided the foundation for much of his scholarship.

Upon arrival in Copenhagen in the early 1980s, the Ingholt Archive would be stored with some of the museum's other archival materials in a series of nineteen blue boxes, and it was only accessible with the Ny Carlsberg Glyptotek's permission (Fig. 6.27). This access limitation is, arguably, a form of institutional colonialism. Although potentially an unfair criticism, had the museum declined the offer of the archive, it is unclear what would have happened to this photographic resource: perhaps it would have remained private, thus eliminating any chance of sharing cultural heritage. The restricted access to the paper archive remains a challenge in the preservation and dissemination of knowledge of Palmyrene funerary sculpture. However, since the digitization of the archive in 2012, steps have been taken to make the archive more accessible: mainly its publication online as open freely accessible raw data and as print and

---

64 Myers 1921, 74.

65 Ingholt excavated in Palmyra in 1924, 1925, 1928, 1935, and 1937.

66 Ingholt's excavation diaries have recently been published in an English translation. See Raja, Steding, and Yon 2021.

67 Raja, Steding, and Yon 2021, 905. For the tessera, see illustration 4.1a–b. *RTP* 343. See also Raja 2019a, 431, cat. no. 203.

68 Raja, Steding, and Yon 2021, 905. For the tessera see illustration 4.2a–b. *RTP* 254. See also Raja 2019a, 434, cat. no. 206.

69 Raja, Steding, and Yon 2021, 905.

70 Raja, Steding, and Yon 2021, 613. 'Dalla hôn' = stay here. 'Halti (uht–ummik)' = my aunt (my mother's sister).

71 Raja, Steding, and Yon 2021, 613.

72 Raja, Steding, and Yon 2021, 613.

e-book editions with commentary.[73] Given the restructuring of the Ingholt Archive by Ploug, proper research needed to be conducted on it to understand the nature of the changes. Although the state of the archive upon its arrival at the Ny Carlsberg Glyptotek is not known, the likely original PS system was restored in the publications.

With the diaspora of Syrian nationals due to the now decade-long civil war and systematic destruction of Syrian heritage by ISIS, the Ingholt Archive is a critical source of information, arguably more important than ever. The online publication of the archive in PDF form on figshare as open data is a first step in making the material widely available, but it too has its limitations. In this form, the archive is only available to anyone with internet access, but perhaps more problematic are the language limitations. The online publication of the Ingholt Archive is only the raw data, meaning it is not accompanied by the commentary provided in the print or e-book editions, both of which, due to the sheer size of the archive, will be costly publications. Ingholt annotated the images of Palmyrene sculpture in English, Danish, French, and German. The sculptures' inscriptions are in Palmyrene Aramaic (sometimes transliterated into Hebrew), Ancient Greek, and Latin. Thus, despite the increased accessibility via the internet, it will be challenging for many to interpret the data. The print and e-book editions are not much more inclusive as one must be able to understand English to read the transcriptions and commentary. These publications raise several questions: With whom is this data being shared? Is it really an effort to return cultural heritage to Syria? Are these publications empowering Syrian nationals? Or, despite good intentions, is the archive's online publication just colonialism in a digital form?

The question of digital colonialism is a recent issue in archaeological practice and runs parallel to the disciplinary conversation on decolonizing the field. Postcolonial theory has played a role in archaeological scholarship for decades. Across the humanities, Edward W. Said's seminal work *Orientalism* was published in 1978 and remains a cornerstone for scholars.[74] The influence of authors such as Gayatri Spivak, Homi K. Bhabha, and Dipesh Chakrabarty has brought postcolonial studies through the end of the twentieth century and into the twenty-first.[75] More specifically for the field of classical archaeology, interest in acculturation and the relationship between capitals and colonies has shifted scholarship away from Atheno- and Romano-centric views. Discussions of Hellenization and Romanization have developed into more nuanced studies of the relationship between Greece and Sicily or the Near East, or the city of Rome and its provinces, to name a few examples, that challenge the centre–periphery binary inherent in traditional approaches.[76] In the past decade, globalization has become popular amongst archaeologists, particularly studies of the Roman Empire.[77] Like the term Romanization, globalization is a slippery concept that has been assigned a myriad of definitions, thus one scholar's understanding of the term may not be the meaning used by another. In its origins as a paradigm for understanding the present day, globalization may be taken as something strictly and inherently modern as it can only be applied in a worldwide context. Yet most scholars of the ancient world have found the concept useful for decentring the city of Rome, for example, and approaching pan-imperial connectivity. The usefulness of globalization might be tested against the issue under discussion here, digital colonialism, as a framework for destabilizing western privilege in its political, economic, and other forms.

Globalization is entangled with the development of the internet, which shares networking and relationing as a foundation. In the global internet age, relations and networks have shifted human connections from the physical to the digital, thus leading to the development of digital colonialist practices. Although technology has been shaping everyday life for decades, it is only within the past three years or so that awareness of the colonialist repercussions of western digital domination has come about. Often discussed in terms of its economic impact, digital colonialism is not restricted to Silicon Valley or

---

[73] Bobou, Miranda, and Raja 2021; Bobou and others 2022.

[74] Said 1978.

[75] Spivak 1988; Bhabah 1994; Chakrabarty 2000.

[76] Some key studies on Romanization are Freeman 1993; Barrett 1997; Woolf 1998. For a range of views on the term, see Keay and Terrenato 2001; Mattingly 2002; Millett 1990; Woolf 1992. A scathing review of the concept of Romanization came early with Syme, who described the framework as 'vulgar and ugly' (Syme 1988, 64). A somewhat different approach to Romanization was utilized by Michael Dietler (2010, 123), who suggests that the term 'be reserved for the process of self-definition that was occurring within Rome itself — a process that was obviously linked to the broader colonial world in which it had become entangled and to developments in the provinces'. For more recent work that nuances the relationships between capitals and provinces, see Mattingly 2011; Martin 2017.

[77] For example, see Hingley 2005; De Angelis 2013; Pitts and Versluys 2015; Hodos 2017. The topic has become so prevalent that Cambridge University Press initiated the series 'Antiquity in Global Context' in 2021.

GAFAM (Google/Alphabet, Amazon, Facebook, Apple, Microsoft) and plays a significant role in heritage preservation as well as being pervasive in academia.[78] Digital applications in archaeology are often touted as less destructive or invasive than traditional archaeological excavation and generate immense quantities of data on a specific site. With massive amounts of data now in digital form, this has increased the likelihood of online databases and other forms of digital heritage.[79] Although many consider the internet a democratic medium, it remains debatable whether the digitization of datasets is truly democratic.

Naturally, some forms of sharing data are more transparent and holistic than others. The online publication of the Ingholt Archive as open data is one example of how archaeologists are grappling with how to best disseminate knowledge.[80] The Ingholt Archive, in its digital shape, is available on the free, international repository figshare, which is known for supporting data from many scholarly areas including archaeological datasets, usually under a CC-BY 4.0 license. The high-resolution scans of the so-called archive sheets are available as PDF files to both view and download. Organized into four categories and saved as twenty-one separate files, the publication makes raw data accessible online, thereby eliminating the institutional and geographic restrictions in place with the paper archive. This is an optimistic view of the power of the internet to disseminate knowledge and is a western perspective. The online publication as open data is theoretically available to anyone with internet, yet there are several hurdles that remain in the attempt to return Syrian heritage to its people. Not only do Syrians need to be made aware of the Ingholt Archive as a resource for researching their heritage, across the entire archive of 2347 sheets, Arabic was only used on a few occasions. As such, the good intentions behind making the Ingholt Archive freely available as open data highlights an ongoing problem in the preserving and sharing of cultural heritage: reaching desired audiences. Yet, open data can only go so far. Access to the diaries and archive not only require awareness, but also internet access. Many countries in conflict see powers that turn off or at least regulate internet connections and restrict website access. In the case of wars and revolutions, open data does nothing. Although this fact might incite feelings of helplessness among interested parties, it does support the notion that cultural heritage needs to be supported by many around the globe — the efforts of the many exceed those of the few, meaning that global collaborations are critical to support one another.

A slightly earlier example of an international attempt at sharing Syrian cultural heritage was the reduced-scale replica of Palmyra's triumphal arch following its destruction by ISIS in 2015 (Fig. 6.28). The replica was set up in Trafalgar Square, London in 2016 and toured the western world until 2019. During the time that the replica arch was in London, archaeologist Zena Kamash conducted a related project called Postcard to Palmyra.[81] The project showed that just under half of the public participants had mixed (22 per cent) or negative (18 per cent) feelings about the arch's replication, and these responses frequently cited concerns regarding authenticity, authority, and colonialism.[82] A grave concern was intentionality: For whom was the arch replica created? The publication of the Ingholt Archive and the Postcard to Palmyra project are just two examples of attempts by archaeologists to reach wider audiences in the work to preserve and share cultural heritage. Although each effort will have its critics, they represent a growing awareness of colonialism in archaeological practice even in the twenty-first century.

The Archival Turn and Archaeology

The allure of archives comes from the multiple temporalities captured within them: in the case of the Ingholt Archive there is the moment of the Palmyrene sculpture being made and put in the graves as the monuments testifying to their time of creation, moments of its excavation and photographic documentation, the moment the archive sheet is created, and all the returns to the sheet again and again. The archive sheet seen in Figure 6.3, known as PS 38, bears the signs of many returns: faded pencil annotations are barely legible and even crossed out to the right of the image, multiple changes to the catalogue number on the white label in the sheet's lower right corner, and the different red and blue pens used below the image to make annotations. With its low PS number, the sheet was likely an early addition to the archive and was

---

78 For example, Coleman 2018; Kwet 2019a; 2019b; Mann and Daly 2019; Young 2019; Mouton and Burns 2021.

79 For examples of digital applications and use of 'big data' in recent archaeological fieldwork, see Berggren and others 2015; Cooper and Green 2016.

80 Bobou, Miranda, and Raja 2021.

81 Kamash 2017.

82 Kamash 2017.

published as PS 38 in Ingholt's thesis.[83] Yet, the inclusion of the names 'Colledge' and 'Milik' on the sheet are references to texts that were published in the 1970s, confirming that Ingholt returned to his sheets and updated their information.[84] The sheet, then, is not from a single moment in time, but part of a continual process of history and knowledge formation. As seen in this example, archives have the potential to tell a variety of stories from many points in history. However, in recent years the archive has come to be studied as an object of inquiry in its own right. The so-called archival turn in the humanities has evolved rapidly over the past few decades. A potential point of arrival for the 'turn' comes in 1995 with the publication of Jacques Derrida's article 'Archive Fever: A Freudian Impression'.[85] This is not to say that archives were not utilized and studied prior to Derrida's study, however, this publication was the harbinger of a widespread shift in the study of archive-as-source to archive-as-subject.[86] Archive-as-subject, or a historiography of archives, illustrates how the current shape of archival research in the humanities and archaeology has come to be.

In an investigation of the use of archives in her field, the anthropologist Ann Laura Stoler notes that the need for the study of archive-as-subject was called for as early as the 1950s, with E. E. Evans-Pritchard who wrote in his discussion of the engagement between anthropology and history that anthropologists were often 'uncritical in their use of documentary sources'.[87] Yet, almost two generations of scholars would pass before more rigorous and consistent critical engagement with archives would occur. The moment was noted by Michel De Certeau in his publication of *The Writing of History* in which he argues: 'the transformation of archival activity is the point of departure and the condition of a new history'.[88] Then, as mentioned above, the so-called turn would be heralded with Derrida's 1994 lecture and subsequent publication. In the past twenty-five years, archive use would gradually increase in humanities scholarship including classical archaeology.

Classical archaeology is, arguably, perfectly poised for the utilization of archives as its fieldwork produces so much data that needs to be documented and recorded.[89] Early excavation records, often referred to as legacy data, are necessary to consult prior to fieldwork and research. Yet, archive archaeology, as a term, does not simply refer to the use of archives of archaeological material, such as excavation diaries or reports. Nor is it merely an archaeology of archives, a digging through of legacy data and peeling back the layers of information. Although both these forms of research are part of archive archaeology, a more nuanced understanding would consider the term as a reciprocal engagement between researcher and archive, thus restoring agency to the archive itself. Object agency is certainly not new among archaeological scholarship, particularly since its deployment by Alfred Gell, and it is now readily accepted.[90] It has even been expanded upon as seen in the adoption and exploration of ideas such as Actor-Network Theory (ANT) or Object-Oriented Ontology (OOO).[91] The familiarity of object agency is being pushed to new extremes by proponents of a post-humanist theory and the concept of that takes notions of agency and materiality into a realm in which objects do not need humans. Theories of agency, materiality, and a post-humanist world invite archives to place demands upon their researchers, much as the art historian W. J. T. Mitchell famously asked twenty-five years ago: 'What do pictures want?'[92] As these twenty-first-century theoretical frameworks gain traction within classical archaeology and related humanities fields, the agency of archives in archaeological practice, as well as the entanglement of archives with creators and researchers, should be reviewed and re-evaluated.[93] These frameworks also raise the issue of who archives are for. Understanding what archives want goes hand in hand with for whom they are meant.

[83] Ingholt 1928, PS 38.

[84] Milik 1972; Colledge 1976. See above for the archive's chronology.

[85] Derrida 1995. Derrida notes that the article builds upon his lecture 'The Concept of the Archive' from the conference *Memory: The Question of Archives* held in London in 1994. The holding of such a large international conference suggests that interest in archival studies was already gaining traction in the early 1990s.

[86] Stoler 2009, 44; Baird and McFadyen 2014, 14.

[87] Evans-Pritchard 1962. Cf. Stoler 2009, 44.

[88] De Certeau 1988, 75.

[89] The use of archives in archaeology has seen such a rapid development in recent years that in 2021 Brepols Publishers launched the book series 'Archive Archaeology'.

[90] Gell 1998.

[91] For ANT, see Latour 2005. For OOO, see Harman 2018. However, Harman used the phrase 'object-oriented philosophy' in his 1999 dissertation, published in 2002 (Harman 1999; 2002). See also, Bryant 2010.

[92] Mitchell 1996. Although this first instance occurs in 1996, a longer investigation of this question appeared in 1997 and in book form in 2010 (Mitchell 1997; 2010). Archaeologist Chris Gosden (2005) later asked the same of objects.

[93] Recent usage of OOO in archaeological scholarship, for example, Pitts and Versluys 2021. For archaeology and hyperobjects, see Campbell 2021.

Conclusion

Making material openly accessible in a researched and commented way supports a democratization of accessibility — well-knowing that accessibility is not the answer to everything. Local situations, such as conflict, can hamper the use of accessible material optimally; however, practising responsible open data sharing is intended to push boundaries for international standards for archaeological archives. Although each day and age will have their own pitfalls, a historiographic situating of the material as soundly as possible allows 'owners' of heritage to open up the data to as broad an audience as possible and thereby creating impact. This impact is not only on a scholarly basis but also in a much wider societal sense — working towards what today is termed social corporate responsibility, a term which has come to stay also in the academic world.

As archaeologists continue to develop the best practices for handling legacy data, the archive itself increasingly becomes the object of interest. This can only benefit the academic audience as well as the interested public. It has become clear that in projects evolving around archival material and object histories there is no one fits all approach or easy politically correct way of dealing with the often sensitive data. Issues of digital colonialism, collection histories, and legacy data must be addressed and confronted with respect for both sides of the story, acknowledging that archaeologists of the present day work in entirely different ways than a hundred years ago. Yet, it is worth asking that despite this temporal distance that allows for reflection on past practice, have archaeologists learned all the lessons that they could or should when it comes to colonialism?

Figure 6.1. PS 8. Fragment of a banqueting relief with reclining male figure (© Palmyra Portrait Project, Ingholt Archive at Ny Carlsberg Glyptotek, and Rubina Raja).

Figure 6.2. Harald Ingholt (© Rubina Raja and Palmyra Portrait Project, courtesy of Philip Underdown).

Figure 6.3. PS 38. Fragment of a banqueting relief with seated female figure (© Palmyra Portrait Project, Ingholt Archive at Ny Carlsberg Glyptotek, and Rubina Raja).

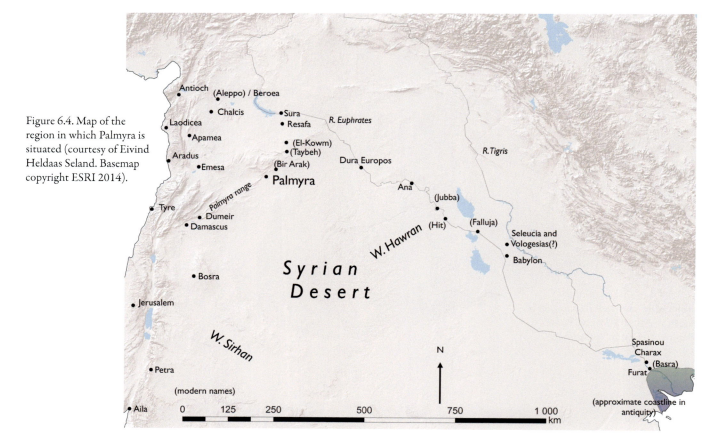

Figure 6.4. Map of the region in which Palmyra is situated (courtesy of Eivind Heldaas Seland. Basemap copyright ESRI 2014).

6. CONSIDERATIONS IN ARCHIVE ARCHAEOLOGY

Figure 6.5. View of Palmyra from the periphery of the city (© Rubina Raja).

Figure 6.6. View of a stretch of the colonnaded main street in Palmyra with consoles for statues (© Rubina Raja).

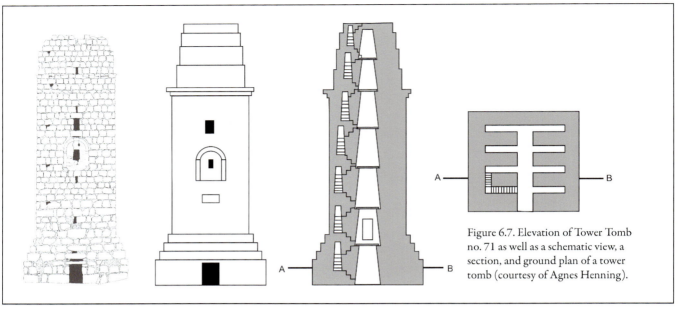

Figure 6.7. Elevation of Tower Tomb no. 71 as well as a schematic view, a section, and ground plan of a tower tomb (courtesy of Agnes Henning).

Figure 6.8. Restored entrance to the underground Tomb of the Three Brothers in Palmyra (© Rubina Raja).

Figure 6.9. Photograph from the Ingholt Archive showing *in situ* sarcophagi in an underground tomb, the so-called Duvaux Tomb. © Rubina Raja and Palmyra Portrait Project.

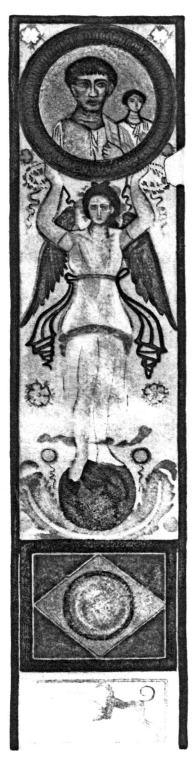

Figure 6.10. PS 1417 showing a wall painting from a tomb (© Palmyra Portrait Project, Ingholt Archive at Ny Carlsberg Glyptotek, and Rubina Raja).

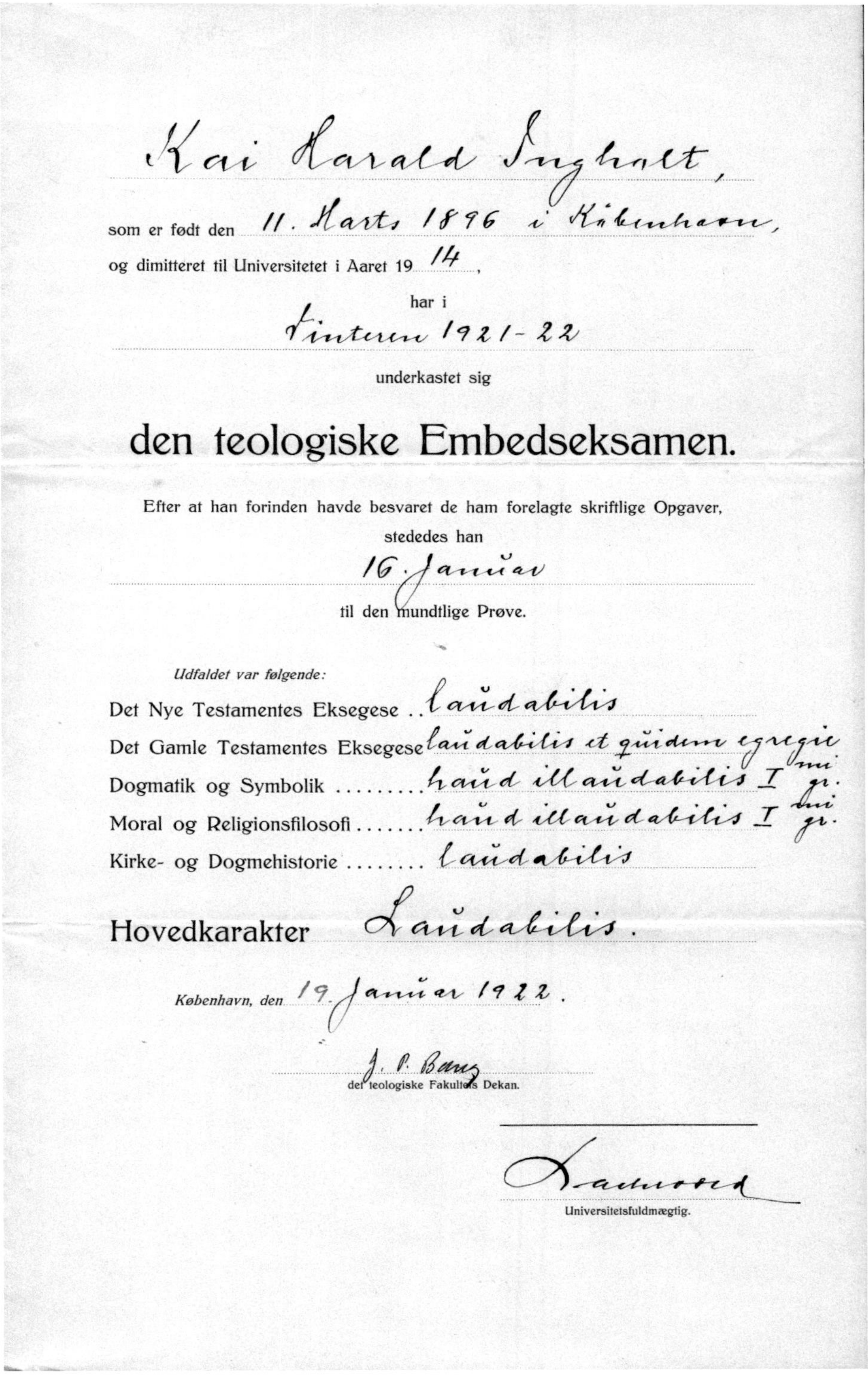

Kai Harald Ingholt,

som er født den 11. Marts 1896 i København,

og dimitteret til Universitetet i Aaret 1914,

har i

Vinteren 1921-22

underkastet sig

den teologiske Embedseksamen.

Efter at han forinden havde besvaret de ham forelagte skriftlige Opgaver,

stededes han

16. Januar

til den mundtlige Prøve.

Udfaldet var følgende:

Det Nye Testamentes Eksegese .. laudabilis

Det Gamle Testamentes Eksegese laudabilis et quidem egregie

Dogmatik og Symbolik .... haud illaudabilis I mi gr.

Moral og Religionsfilosofi ...... haud illaudabilis I mi gr.

Kirke- og Dogmehistorie .... laudabilis

Hovedkarakter Laudabilis.

København, den 19. Januar 1922.

J. P. Bang
det teologiske Fakultets Dekan.

Universitetsfuldmægtig.

Figure 6.11. Ingholt's diploma of Master of Theology, 1922 (© Rubina Raja and Palmyra Portrait Project, courtesy of Mary Ebba Underdown).

THE AMERICAN-SCANDINAVIAN FOUNDATION
25 WEST FORTY-FIFTH STREET
NEW YORK

CABLE ADDRESS: "SCANFOUN NEWYORK"

Hotel d'Angleterre,
Copenhagen, June 7, 1920.

Mr. Harald Inholt,
    Store Kannike Stræde 12,
        Copenhagen.

Dear Mr. Inholt:

    It would be very satisfactory to me if you are lucky enough to become the successful candidate for the Fellowship with stipend of ø 1500.- provided for a Danish or a Norwegian student at Princeton University for the academic year 1921 - 22. I understand that you won the Gold Medal for Oriental Philology in 1918, that you hope to become Cand. theol. in 1921 and to study oriental archaeology with Professor Butler at Princeton University. Both Professor Butler and Professor West, Dean of the Princeton Graduate School, have informed me that you would be a desirable student and very welcome.

    You must make application, accompanied by records of your scholarship, to the American-Scandinavian Foundation's Danske Komité at that time to be designated by the Chairman, Departementchef Weiss.

Very truly yours,
Henry Goddard Leach
Secretary of the Foundation.

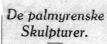

Figure 6.12. Letter from the American-Scandinavian Foundation about a fellowship at Princeton University in 1921–1922 (© Rubina Raja and Palmyra Portrait Project, courtesy of Mary Ebba Underdown).

Figure 6.13. French archaeologist Maurice Dunand performing fieldwork in Palmyra during the 1924 excavation season (© Palmyra Portrait Project, Ingholt Archive at Ny Carlsberg Glyptotek, and Rubina Raja).

Figure 6.14. Newspaper article on Ingholt's defence of his doctoral dissertation, 1928 (© Rubina Raja and Palmyra Portrait Project, courtesy of Mary Ebba Underdown).

STUDIER

OVER

PALMYRENSK SKULPTUR

AF

HARALD INGHOLT

C. A. REITZELS FORLAG — KØBENHAVN
BIANCO LUNOS BOGTRYKKERI
1928

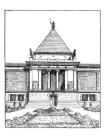

Figure 6.15. Ingholt's monograph from 1928 on Palmyrene sculpture (After Ingholt 1928).

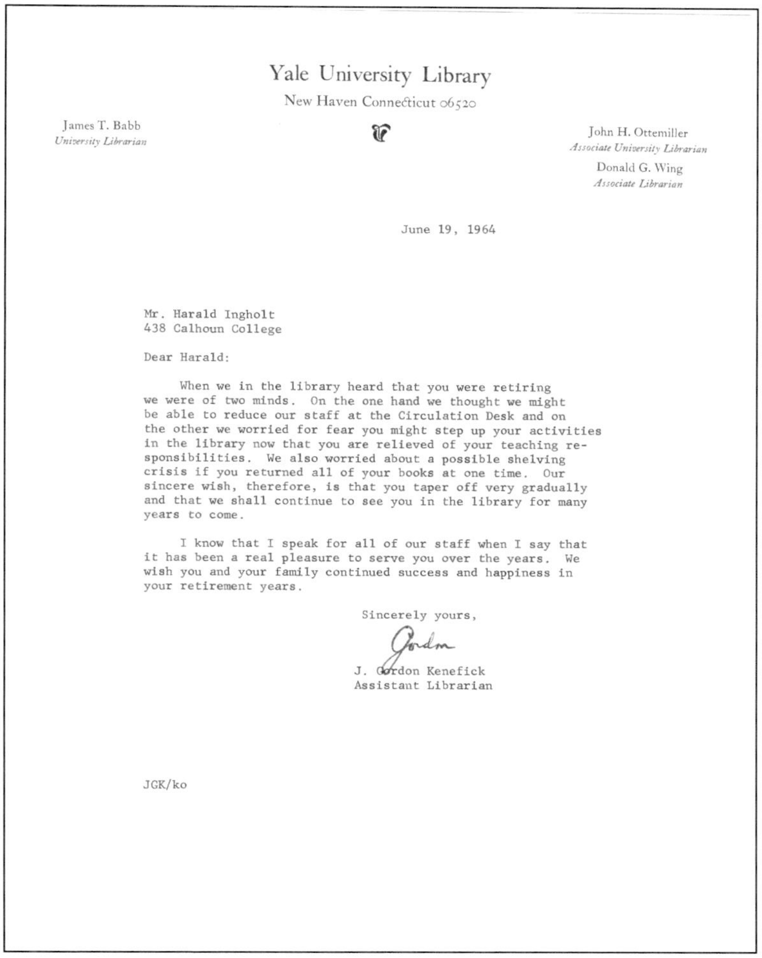

Yale University Library
New Haven Connecticut 06520

James T. Babb
University Librarian

John H. Ottemiller
Associate University Librarian
Donald G. Wing
Associate Librarian

June 19, 1964

Mr. Harald Ingholt
438 Calhoun College

Dear Harald:

When we in the library heard that you were retiring we were of two minds. On the one hand we thought we might be able to reduce our staff at the Circulation Desk and on the other we worried for fear you might step up your activities in the library now that you are relieved of your teaching responsibilities. We also worried about a possible shelving crisis if you returned all of your books at one time. Our sincere wish, therefore, is that you taper off very gradually and that we shall continue to see you in the library for many years to come.

I know that I speak for all of our staff when I say that it has been a real pleasure to serve you over the years. We wish you and your family continued success and happiness in your retirement years.

Sincerely yours,

Gordon

J. Gordon Kenefick
Assistant Librarian

JGK/ko

Figure 6.16. A letter from Yale University Library in relation to Ingholt's retirement, 1964 (© Rubina Raja and Palmyra Portrait Project, courtesy of Mary Ebba Underdown).

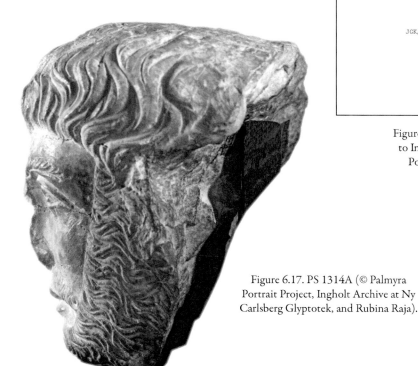

Figure 6.17. PS 1314A (© Palmyra Portrait Project, Ingholt Archive at Ny Carlsberg Glyptotek, and Rubina Raja).

Figure 6.18. PS 615 (© Palmyra Portrait Project, Ingholt Archive at Ny Carlsberg Glyptotek, and Rubina Raja).

Figure 6.19. PS 1430 (© Palmyra Portrait Project, Ingholt Archive at Ny Carlsberg Glyptotek, and Rubina Raja).

Figure 6.20. PS 1430 (© Palmyra Portrait Project, Ingholt Archive at Ny Carlsberg Glyptotek, and Rubina Raja).

Figure 6.21. PS 1430 (© Palmyra Portrait Project, Ingholt Archive at Ny Carlsberg Glyptotek, and Rubina Raja).

Figure 6.22. Letter from the director of the Ny Carlsberg Glyptotek, Copenhagen, Flemming Johansen, thanking Mr and Mrs Ingholt for bequeathing parts of Ingholt's archival material to the museum in 1983 (© Rubina Raja and Palmyra Portrait Project).

Figure 6.23. PS 845. A yellow archive sheet with an image of a loculus relief of a priest. The sheet shows the two different numbering systems used by Ingholt and Ploug (© Palmyra Portrait Project, Ingholt Archive at Ny Carlsberg Glyptotek, and Rubina Raja).

Figure 6.24. PS 410 (© Palmyra Portrait Project, Ingholt Archive at Ny Carlsberg Glyptotek, and Rubina Raja).

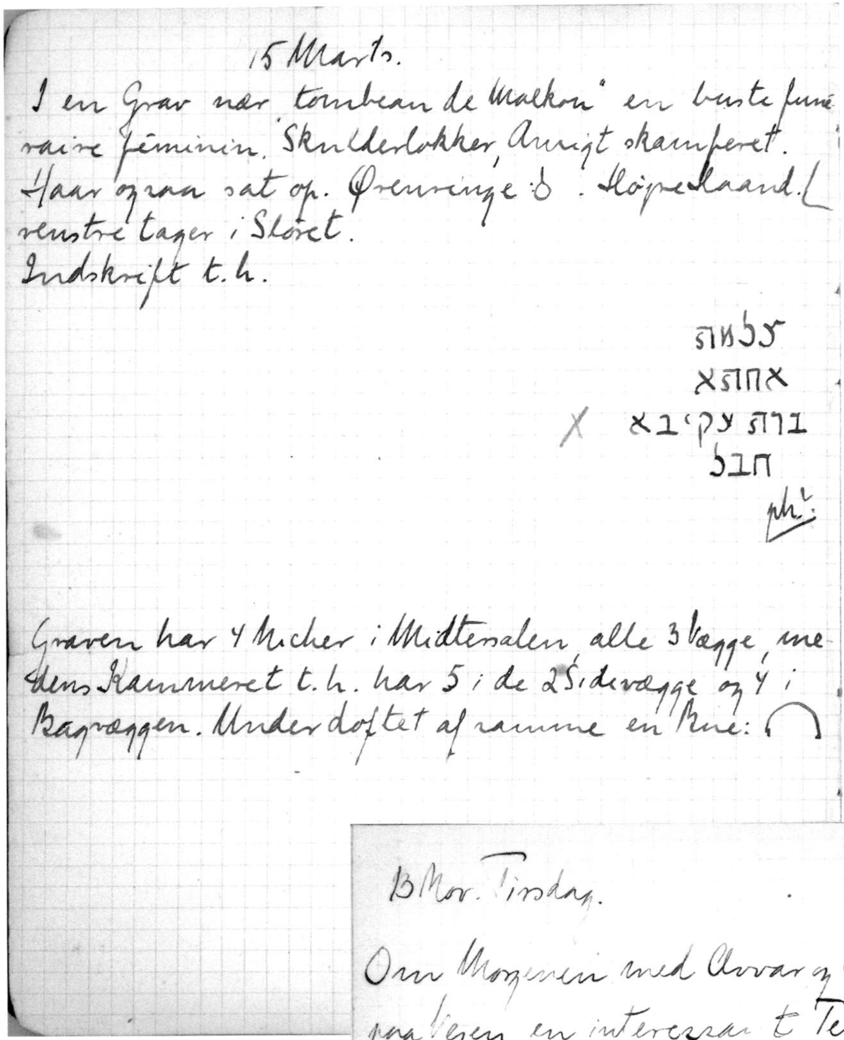

15 Marts.
I en Grav nær tombeau de Malkou en buste funé-
raire féminin. Skulderlokker, Ansigt skamferet.
Haar ogsaa sat op. Ørenringe ð . Højre Haand, L
venstre tager i Stolet.
Indskrift t.h.

לעבד
אתתא
ברעקיבא X
חבל
ph:

Graven har 4 Nicher i Midtersalen alle 3 Vægge, me-
dens Kammeret t.h. har 5 i de 2 Sidevægge og 4 i
Bagvæggen. Under doftet af ramme en Bue: ⌒

Figure 6.25. Excerpt from Ingholt's diary 2, p. 1 (© Rubina Raja and the Palmyra Portrait Project, courtesy of the Ny Carlsberg Glyptotek).

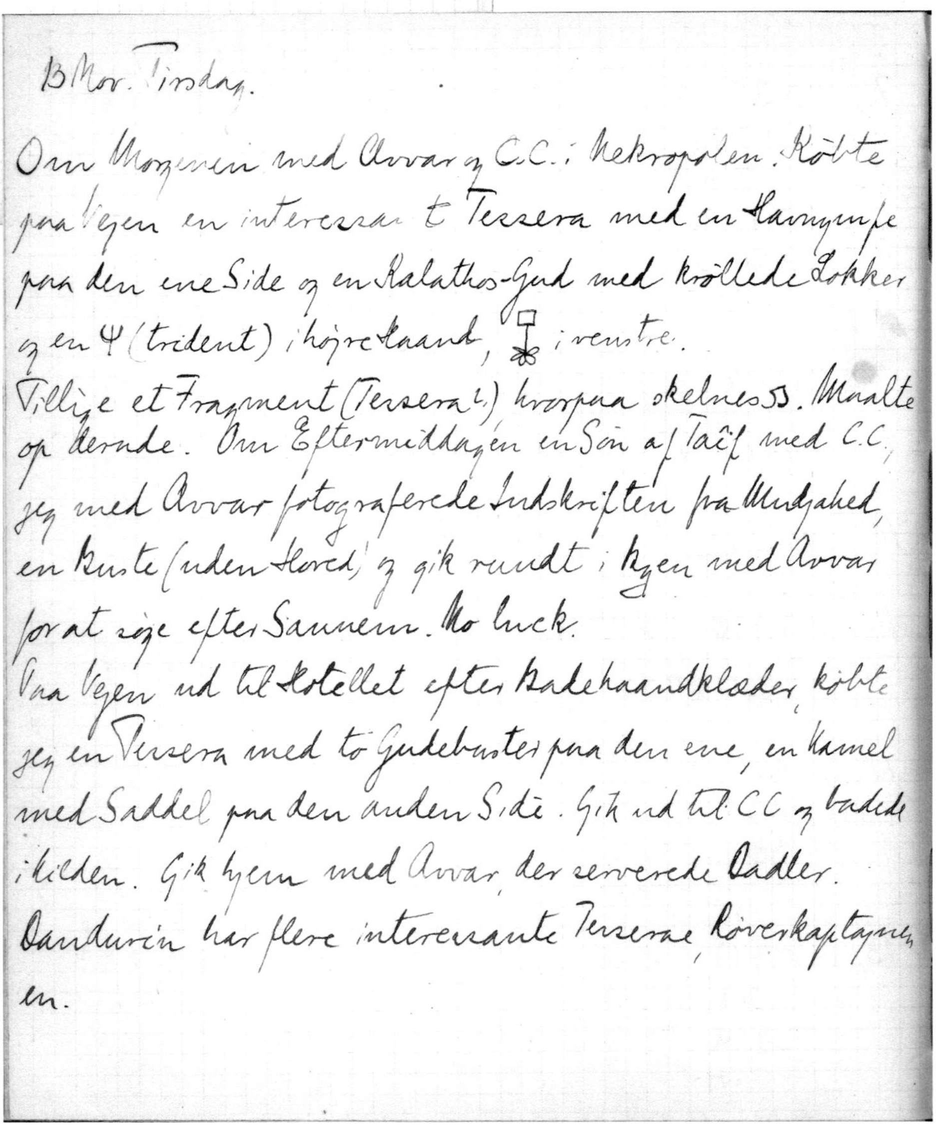

8 Nov. Tirsdag.

Om Morgenen med Anvar og C.C. i Nekropolen. Købte
paa Vejen en interessant Tessera med en Havnymfe
paa den ene Side og en Kalathos-Gud med krøllede Lokker
og en Ψ (trident) i højre Haand, 🜚 i venstre.
Tillige et Fragment (Tessera?) hvorpaa skelnes SS. Maalte
op derude. Om Eftermiddagen en Søn af Taïf med C.C.
jeg med Anvar fotograferede Indskriften paa Mudjahed,
en Buste (uden Hoved) og gik rundt i Byen med Anvar
for at søge efter Sannem. No luck.
Paa Vejen ud til Hotellet efter Badehaandklæder, købte
jeg en Tessera med to Gudebuster paa den ene, en Kamel
med Saddel paa den anden Side. Gik ud til CC og badede
i Kilden. Gik hjem med Anvar, der serverede Dadler.
Dandurin har flere interessante Tesserae, Røverkaptajnen
o.m.

Figure 6.26. Excerpt from Ingholt's diary 4, p. 28, with sketches and descriptions of tesserae from the Dandurin Collection (© Rubina Raja and the Palmyra Portrait Project, courtesy of the Ny Carlsberg Glyptotek).

6. CONSIDERATIONS IN ARCHIVE ARCHAEOLOGY

Figure 6.27. The archive boxes at the Ny Carlsberg Glyptotek (© Rubina Raja).

Figure 6.28. View of the Triumphal Arch on the main street in Palmyra with the Sanctuary of Bel visible in the background (© Rubina Raja).

Works Cited

Adler, M. N. 1907. *The Itinerary of Benjamin of Tudela* (London: Frowde).
al-Asʿad, K. and A. Schmidt-Colinet. 1985. 'Das Tempelgrab Nr. 36 in der Westnekropole von Palmyra: Ein Vorbericht', *Damaszener Mitteilungen*, 2: 17–35.
Andrade, N. J. 2012. 'Inscribing the Citizen: Soados and the Civic Context of Palmyra', *MAARAV*, 19: 65–90.
—— 2018. *Zenobia: Shooting Star of Palmyra* (Oxford: Oxford University Press).
Astengo, G. 2016. 'The Rediscovery of Palmyra and its Dissemination in "Philosophical Transactions"', *Notes and Records: The Royal Society Journal of the History of Science*, 70: 209–30 <http://doi.org/10.1098/rsnr.2015.0059>.
Baird, J. A. and Z. Kamash. 2019. 'Remembering Roman Syria: Valuing Tadmor-Palmyra, from "Discovery" to Destruction', *Bulletin of the Institute of Classical Studies*, 62: 1–29 <https://doi.org/10.1111/2041-5370.12090>.
Baird, J. A. and L. McFadyen. 2014. 'Towards an Archaeology of Archaeological Archives', *Archaeological Review from Cambridge*, 29.2: 14–32.
Barański, M. 1995. 'The Great Colonnade of Palmyra Reconsidered', *ARAM*, 7: 37–46.
Barrett, J. C. 1997. 'Romanization: A Critical Comment', in D. Mattingly (ed.), *Dialogues in Roman Imperialism: Power, Discourse, and Discrepant Experience in the Roman Empire* (Ann Arbor: Journal of Roman Archaeology), pp. 51–64.
Berggren, Å., N. Dell'Unto, M. Forte, S. D. Haddow, I. Hodder, J. Issavi, N. Lercari, C. Mazzucato, A. Mickel, and J. Taylor. 2015. 'Revisiting Reflexive Archaeology at Çatalhöyük: Integrating Digital and 3D Technologies at the Trowel's Edge', *Antiquity*, 89: 433–48.
Bhabah, H. K. 1994. *The Location of Culture* (London: Routledge).
Bobou, O., I. Romanowska, and R. Raja. 2021. 'Historical Trajectories of Palmyra's Elites through the Lens of Archaeological Data', *Journal of Urban Archaeology*, 4: 153–66 <https://doi.org/10.1484/J.JUA.5.126598>.
Bobou, O., J. V. Jensen, N. Breintoft Kristensen, R. Raja, and R. Randeris Thomsen (eds). 2021. *Studies on Palmyrene Sculpture: A Translation of Harald Ingholt's 'Studier over Palmyrensk Skulptur', Edited and with Commentary*, Studies in Palmyrene Archaeology and History, 1 (Turnhout: Brepols).
Bobou, O., A. C. Miranda, and R. Raja. 2021. 'The Ingholt Archive: Data from the Project "Archive Archaeology: Preserving and Sharing Syria's Cultural Heritage through Harald Ingholt's Digital Archives"', *Journal of Open Archaeology Data*, 9: 6 <http://doi.org/10.5334/joad.78>.
—— 2022. 'Harald Ingholt's Twentieth-Century Archive of Palmyrene Sculptures: "Unleashing" Archived Archaeological Material of Modern Conflict Zones', *Journal of Eastern Mediterranean Archaeology and Heritage Studies*, 10.1: 74–101.
Bobou, O., A. Miranda, R. Raja, J. Steding, and J.-B. Yon (forthcoming). 'Harald Ingholt and Palmyra: Documenting the Oasis City through the Legacy of Berytus' Founder', *Berytus*.
Bobou, O., A. Miranda, R. Raja, and J.-B. Yon. 2022. *The Ingholt Archive: The Palmyrene Material, Transcribed with Commentary and Bibliography*, Archive Archaeology, 2, 4 vols (Turnhout: Brepols).
Bryant, L. 2010. 'Onticology: A Manifesto for Object–Oriented Ontology, Part 1', *Larval Subjects* (10 January 2010) <https://larvalsubjects.wordpress.com/2010/01/12/object-oriented-ontology-a-manifesto-part-i/> [accessed 6 October 2022].
Butcher, K. 2003. *Roman Syria and the Near East* (London: British Museum Press).
Campbell, P. 2021. 'The Anthropocene, Hyperobjects and the Archaeology of the Future Past', *Antiquity*, 95.383: 1315–30 <https://doi.org/10.15184/aqy.2021.116>.
Cantineau, J. 1932. *Inventaire des inscriptions de Palmyre*, fasc. VIII: *Le dépôt des antiquités* (Beirut: Imprimerie Catholique).
Cassas, L.-F. 1799. *Voyage pittoresque de la Syrie, de la Phoénicie, de la Palestine, et de la Basse Égypte* (Paris: Imprimerie de la République).
Chakrabarty, D. 2000. *Provincializing Europe: Postcolonial Thought and Historical Difference* (Princeton: Princeton University Press).
Coleman, D. 2018. 'Digital Colonialism: The 21st Century Scramble for Africa through the Extraction and Control of User Data and the Limitations of Data Protection Laws', *Michigan Journal of Race and Law*, 24: 417–40.
Colledge, M. A. R. 1976. *The Art of Palmyra* (London: Thames and Hudson).
Cooper, A. and C. E. W. Green. 2016. 'Embracing the Complexities of "Big Data" in Archaeology: The Case of the English Landscape and Identities Project', *Journal of Archaeological Method and Theory*, 23: 271–304.
De Angelis, F. 2013. *Regionalism and Globalism in Antiquity: Exploring their Limits* (Leuven: Peeters).
De Certeau, M. 1988. *The Writing of History* (New York: Columbia University Press).
Delplace, C. and J. Dentzer-Feydy. 2005. *L'Agora de Palmyre* (Beirut: Institut français du Proche-Orient).
Derrida, J. 1995. 'Archive Fever: A Freudian Impression', *Diacritics*, 25.2: 9–63.
Dietler, M. 2010. *Archaeologies of Colonialism: Consumption, Entanglement, and Violence in Ancient Mediterranean France* (Berkeley: University of California Press).
Elias, C. 2019. 'Whose Digital Heritage?', *Third Text*, 33.6: 687–707.

Evans-Pritchard, E. E. 1962. 'Anthropology and History', in E. E. Evans-Pritchard (ed.), *Social Anthropology and Other Essays* (Glencoe: Free Press), pp. 172–91.

Freeman, P. W. M. 1993. 'Romanization and Roman Material Culture', *Journal of Roman Archaeology*, 6: 438–45.

Gawlikowski, M. 1970. *Monuments funéraires de Palmyra*, Travaux du Centre d'archéologie méditerranéenne de l'Académie polonaise des sciences, 9 (Warsaw: Państwowe Wydawnictwo Naukowe).

—— 2009. 'Palmyra in the Early Islamic Times', in K. Bart and A. al-R. Moaz (eds), *Residences, Castles, Settlements: Transformation Processes from Late Antiquity to Early Islam in Bilad al–Sham; Proceedings of the International Conference Held at Damascus, 5–9 November 2006* (Rahden: Leidorf), pp. 89–96.

Gell, A. 1998. *Art and Agency: An Anthropological Theory* (Oxford: Clarendon).

Gosden, C. 2005. 'What Do Objects Want?', *Journal of Archaeological Method and Theory*, 12.3: 193–211.

Grainger, J. D. 2013. *The Battle for Syria, 1918–1920* (Woodbridge: Boydell & Brewer).

Hammad, M. 2010. *Palmyre: Transformations urbaines; développement d'une ville antique de la marge aride syrienne* (Paris: Geuthner).

Harman, G. 1999. 'Tool-Being: Elements in a Theory of Objects' (unpublished doctoral thesis, DePaul University).

—— 2002. *Tool-Being: Heidegger and the Metaphysics of Objects* (Chicago: Open Court).

—— 2018. *Object-Oriented Ontology: A New Theory of Everything* (London: Pelican).

Hartmann, U. 2001. *Das palmyrenische Teilreich* (Stuttgart: Steiner).

Henning, A. 2013. *Die Turmgräber von Palmyra: Eine lokale Bauform im kaiserzeitlichen Syrien als Ausdruck kultureller Identität* (Rahden: Leidorf).

Hingley, R. 2005. *Globalizing Roman Culture: Unity, Diversity and Empire* (London: Routledge).

Hodos, T. 2017. *The Routledge Handbook of Archaeology and Globalization* (London: Routledge).

Hvidberg-Hansen, F. O. 2002. *Zenobia: Byen Palmyra og dens dronning* (Aarhus: Sfinx).

Hvidberg-Hansen, F. O. and G. Ploug. 1993. *Palmyrasamlingen: Ny Carlsberg Glyptotek; Katalog* (Copenhagen: Ny Carlsberg Glyptotek).

Ingholt, H. 1928. *Studier over Palmyrensk Skulptur* (Copenhagen: Reitzel).

—— 1932. 'Quelques fresques récemment découvertes à Palmyre', *Acta archaeologica*, 3: 1–20.

—— 1935. 'Five Dated Tombs from Palmyra', *Berytus*, 2: 57–120.

—— 1938. 'Inscriptions and Sculptures from Palmyra II', *Berytus*, 5: 93–140.

—— 1940. *Rapport préliminaire sur sept campagnes de fouilles à Hama en Syrie (1932–1938)*, Det Kgl Danske Videnskabernes Selskab: Archaeologisk–Kunsthistoriske Meddelelser, 3.1 (Copenhagen: Munksgaard).

—— 1966. 'Some Sculptures from the Tomb of Malkû at Palmyra', in M. L. Bernhard (ed.), *Mélanges offerts à Kazimierz Michalowski* (Warsaw: Państwowe Wydawnictwo Naukowe), pp. 457–76.

—— 1970–1972. 'The Sarcophagus of Beʿelai and Other Sculptures from the Tomb of Malkû, Palmyra', *Mélanges de l'Université Saint-Joseph*, 46: 171–200.

—— 1974. 'Two Unpublished Tombs from the Southwest Necropolis of Palmyra, Syria', in D. K. Kouymjian (ed.), *Near Eastern Numismatics, Iconography, Epigraphy and History: Studies in Honor of George C. Miles* (Beirut: American University of Beirut), pp. 37–54.

—— 1976. 'Varia Tadmorea', in D. Schlumberger and H. Seyrig (eds), *Palmyre: Bilan et perspectives; colloque de Strasbourg, 18–20 octobre 1973* (Strasbourg: Association pour l'étude de la civilisation romaine), pp. 101–37.

Intagliata, E. E. 2018. *Palmyra after Zenobia AD 273–750: An Archaeological and Historical Reappraisal* (Oxford: Oxbow).

—— 2019. 'The City that Would Not Fall: Palmyra in Late Antique and Early Islamic Times', in A. M. Nielsen and R. Raja (eds), *The Road to Palmyra* (Copenhagen: Ny Carlsberg Glyptotek), pp. 233–50.

Kaizer, T. 2016. 'The Future of Palmyrene Studies – Paul Veyne (aus dem Französischen von Anna und Wolf Heinrich Leube), Palmyra. Requium für eine Stadt (C. H. Beck, München 2016). S. 127 mit 8–seitigem Tafelteil und 13 Farbabbildungen', *Journal of Roman Archaeology*, 29: 924–31 <https://doi.org/10.1017/S1047759400073025>.

Kamash, Z. 2017. '"Postcard to Palmyra": Bringing the Public into Debates over Post-Conflict Reconstruction in the Middle East', *World Archaeology*, 49.5: 608–22 <https://doi.org/10.1080/00438243.2017.1406399>.

Keay, S. J. and N. Terrenato. 2001. *Italy and the West: Comparative Issues in Romanization* (Oxford: Oxbow).

Kropp, A. J. M. and R. Raja. 2014. 'The Palmyra Portrait Project', *Syria: archéologie, art et histoire*, 91: 393–405.

Kwet, M. 2019a. 'Digital Colonialism: South Africa's Education Transformation in the Shadow of Silicon Valley' (unpublished doctoral thesis, Yale University).

—— 2019b. 'Digital Colonialism: US Empire and the New Imperialism in the Global South', *Race & Class*, 60.4: 3–26.

Latour, B. 2005. *Reassembling the Social: An Introduction to Actor-Network-Theory* (Oxford: Oxford University Press).

Luck, E. C. 2018. *Cultural Genocide and the Protection of Cultural Heritage*, J. Paul Getty Trust Occasional Papers in Cultural Heritage Policy, 2 (Los Angeles: J. Paul Getty Trust) <https://www.getty.edu/publications/pdfs/CulturalGenocide_Luck.pdf> [accessed 6 October 2022].

Mann, M. and A. Daly. 2019. '(Big) Data and the North-in-South: Australia's Informational Imperialism and Digital Colonialism', *Television & New Media*, 20.4: 379–95.

Martin, S. R. 2017. *The Art of Contact: Comparative Approaches to Greek and Phoenician Art* (Philadelphia: University of Pennsylvania Press).

Mattingly, D. J. 2002. 'Vulgar and Weak "Romanization" or Time for a Paradigm Shift', *Journal of Roman Archaeology*, 15: 536–40.

—— 2011. *Imperialism, Power, and Identity: Experiencing the Roman Empire* (Princeton: Princeton University Press).

McGeough, K. 2015. *The Ancient Near East in the Nineteenth Century: Appreciations and Appropriations*, II: *Collecting, Constructing, Curating* (Sheffield: Sheffield Phoenix Press).

Meskell, L. M. 2020. 'Imperialism, Internationalism, and Archaeology in the Un/Making of the Middle East', *American Anthropologist*, 122.3: 554–67.

Milik, J. T. 1972. *Dédicaces faites par des Dieux (Palmyre, Hatra, Tyr) et des thiases sémitiques à l'époque romaine* (Paris: Geuthner).

Millar, F. 1993. *The Roman Near East, 31 BC–AD 337* (Cambridge, MA: Harvard University Press).

Millett, A. 1990. *The Romanization of Britain: An Essay in Archaeological Interpretation* (Cambridge: Cambridge University Press).

Miranda, A. C. and R. Raja. 2021. 'Archive Archaeology: Preserving and Sharing Palmyra's Cultural Heritage through Harald Ingholt's Digital Archives. A Case Study in the Accessibility and Potential of Archives', *Antiquity*, 96.385: 229–37 <http://doi.org/10.15184/aqy.2021.165>.

Mitchell, W. J. T. 1996. 'What Do Pictures "Really" Want?', *October*, 77: 71–82 <https://doi.org/10.2307/778960>.

—— 1997. 'What Do Pictures Want? An Idea of Visual Culture', in T. Smith (ed.), *In Visible Touch* (Chicago: University of Chicago Press), pp. 215–32.

—— 2010. *What Do Pictures Want? The Lives and Loves of Images* (Chicago: University of Chicago Press).

Mortensen, P. 2021. 'A Brief Note on Harald Ingholt — as I Remember Him', in O. Bobou, J. Vestergaard Jensen, N. Breintoft Kristensen, R. Raja, and R. Randeris Thomsen (eds), *Studies on Palmyrene Sculpture: A Translation of Harald Ingholt's 'Studier over Palmyrensk Skulptur', Edited and with Commentary*, Studies in Palmyrene Archaeology and History, 1 (Turnhout: Brepols), pp. 29–31.

Mouton, M. and R. Burns. 2021. '(Digital) Neo-Colonialism in the Smart City', *Regional Studies*: 1–12.

Myers, D. P. 1921. 'The Mandate System of the League of Nations', *The Annals of the American Academy of Political and Social Science*, July 1921, vol. 96, no. 185. The Place of the United States in a World Organization for the Maintenance of Peace: 74–77.

Nielsen, A. M. and R. Raja. 2019. 'The Road to Palmyra', in A. M. Nielsen and R. Raja (eds), *The Road to Palmyra* (Copenhagen: Ny Carlsberg Glyptotek), pp. 9–22.

Østrup, J. E. 1894. *Skiftende Horizonter* (Copenhagen: Gyldendalske Boghandel Forlag).

—— 1895. *Historisk-Topografiske Bidrag til Kendskabet til den syriske Ørken* (Copenhagen: Det Kongelige Danske Videnskabernes Selskab).

Pitts, M. and M. J. Versluys. 2015. *Globalisation and the Roman world: World History, Connectivity and Material Culture* (Cambridge: Cambridge University Press).

—— 2021. 'Objectscapes: A Manifesto for Investigating the Impacts of Object Flows on Past Societies', *Antiquity* 95: 367–81 <https://doi.org/10.15184/aqy.2020.148>.

Ploug, G. 1995. *Catalogue of the Palmyrene Sculptures Ny Carlsberg Glyptotek* (Copenhagen: Ny Carlsberg Glyptotek).

Raja, R. 2016a. 'Danske Pionerer i Palmyra: Den Danske Palmyra-Forskning i et Historiografisk Perspektiv', in J. Benarroch, A. M. Nielsen, and P. Thostrup (eds), *Carlsbergfondets Årsskrift* (Copenhagen: Narayana Press), pp. 56–63.

—— 2016b. 'The History and Current Situation of World Heritage Sites in Syria: The Case of Palmyra', in K. Almqvist and L. Belfrage (eds), *Cultural Heritage at Risk: The Role of Museums in War and Conflict* (Stockholm: Axel and Margaret Ax:son Johnson Foundation), pp. 27–47.

—— 2017. 'Danish Pioneers at Palmyra: Historiographic Aspects of Danish Scholarship on Palmyra', in R. Raja (ed.), *Palmyra: Pearl of the Desert* (Aarhus: Sun-Tryk), pp. 21–29.

—— 2018a. 'Compilation and Digitalisation of the Palmyrene Corpus of Funerary Portraits', *Antiquity*, 92: 1–7 <https://doi.org/10.15184/aqy.2018.218>.

—— 2018b. 'Palmyrene Funerary Portraits, Collection Histories and Current Research', in J. Aruz (ed.), *Palmyra: Mirage in the Desert* (New York: Metropolitan Museum), pp. 100–09.

—— 2019a. *Catalogue: The Palmyra Collection, Ny Carlsberg Glyptotek* (Copenhagen: Ny Carlsberg Glyptotek).

—— 2019b. 'Harald Ingholt and Palmyra: A Danish Archaeologist and his Work at Palmyra', in A. M. Nielsen and R. Raja (eds), *The Road to Palmyra* (Copenhagen: Ny Carlsberg Glyptotek), pp. 41–64.

—— 2019c. 'Portrait Habit in Palmyra', in A M. Nielsen and R. Raja (eds), *The Road to Palmyra* (Copenhagen: Ny Carlsberg Glyptotek), pp. 137–54.

—— 2019d. 'Stacking Aesthetics in the Syrian Desert: Displaying Palmyrene Sculpture in the Public and Funerary Sphere', in C. Draycott, R. Raja, K. Welch, and W. T. Wootton (eds), *Visual Histories of the Classical World: Essays in Honor of R. R. R. Smith*, Studies in Classical Archaeology, 4 (Turnhout: Brepols), pp. 281–98.

—— 2021a. '"Den smukkeste Kvindebuste, jeg endnu har set": The Palmyra Excavation Diaries of Harald Ingholt, 1924–1928', in R. Raja, J. Steding, and J.-B. Yon (eds), *Excavating Palmyra. Harald Ingholt's Excavation Diaries: A Transcript, Translation, and Commentary*, vol. 1, Studies in Palmyrene Archaeology and History, 4 (Turnhout: Brepols), pp. 23–70.

—— 2021b. 'Harald Ingholt and Palmyrene Sculpture: Continuing a Lifelong Relationship a Century Later', in O. Bobou, J. Vestergaard Jensen, N. Breintoft Kristensen, R. Raja, and R. Randeris Thomsen (eds), *Studies on Palmyrene Sculpture: A Translation of Harald Ingholt's 'Studier over Palmyrensk Skulptur', Edited and with Commentary*, Studies in Palmyrene Archaeology and History, 1 (Turnhout: Brepols), pp. 1–28.

—— 2022. *Pearl of the Desert: A History of Palmyra* (Oxford: Oxford University Press).

Raja, R., O. Bobou, and I. Romanowska. 2021. 'Three Hundred Years of Palmyrene History: Unlocking Archaeological Data for Studying Past Societal Transformations', *PLoS ONE*, 16:11: e0256081 <https://doi.org/10.1371/journal.pone.0256081>.

Raja, R. and J. Steding. 2021. 'Harald Ingholt's Excavation Diaries from his Fieldwork in Palmyra: An Open Data Online Resource', *Journal of Open Archaeology Data*, 9: 8 <https://doi.org/10.5334/joad.84>.

Raja, R., J. Steding, and J.-B. Yon. 2021. *Excavating Palmyra: Harald Ingholt's Excavation Diaries; A Transcript, Translation, and Commentary*, Studies in Palmyrene Archaeology and History, 4, 2 vols (Turnhout: Brepols).

Raja, R. and A. H. Sørensen. 2015a. *Harald Ingholt og Palmyra* (Aarhus: Fællestrykkeriet Aarhus Universitet).

—— 2015b. *Harald Ingholt and Palmyra*, English version (Aarhus: Fællestrykkeriet Aarhus Universitet).

Romanowska, I., O. Bobou, and R. Raja. 2021. 'Reconstructing the Social, Economic and Demographic Trends of Palmyra's Elite from Funerary Data', *Journal of Archaeological Science*, 133: 105432 <https://doi.org/10.1016/j.jas.2021.105432>.

Said, E. W. 1978. *Orientalism* (London: Routledge & Kegan Paul).

Sartre, M. 2001. *D'Alexandre à Zénobie: histoire du Levant antique, IVᵉ siècle avant J.-C.–IIIᵉ siècle après J.-C.* (Paris: Fayard).

Sartre-Fauriat, A. 2019. 'The Discovery and Reception of Palmyra', in A. M. Nielsen and R. Raja (eds), *The Road to Palmyra* (Copenhagen: Ny Carlsberg Glyptotek), pp. 65–76.

Sartre-Fauriat, A. and M. Sartre. 2014. *Zénobie: De Palmyre à Rome* (Paris: Perrin).

—— 2016. *Palmyre: Vérités et légendes* (Paris: Perrin).

Schlumberger, D. 1935. 'Études sur Palmyre I. Le développement urbain de Palmyre', *Berytus*, 2: 149–62.

Schmidt-Colinet, A. 1987. 'Palmyrenische Grabarchitektur', in E. M. Ruprechtsberger (ed.), *Palmyra: Geschichte, Kunst und Kultur der Syrischen Oasenstadt* (Linz: Druck- und Verlagsanstalt Gutenberg), pp. 214–27.

—— 1992. *Das Tempelgrab Nr. 36 in Palmyra: Studien zur palmyrenischen Grabarchitektur und ihrer Ausstattung*, Damaszener Forschungen, 4 (Mainz: Von Zabern).

—— 1997. 'Aspects of "Romanization": The Tomb Architecture at Palmyra and its Decoration', in S. E. Alcock (ed.), *The Early Roman Empire in the East* (Oxford: Oxbow), pp. 157–77.

—— 2017. 'Thirty Years of Syro–German / Austrian Archaeological Research at Palmyra in Memory of Khaled al-Asʿad', in J. Aruz (ed.), *Palmyra: Mirage in the Desert* (New York: Metropolitan Museum of Art), pp. 66–75.

Schmidt-Colinet, A. and W. al-Asʿad. 2013. *Palmyras Reichtum durch weltweiten Handel: Archäologische Untersuchungen im Bereich der hellenistischen Stadt*, 2 vols (Vienna: Holzhausen).

Schörle, K. 2017. 'Palmyrene Merchant Networks and Economic Integration in Competitive Markets', in H. F. Teigen and E. H. Seland (eds), *Palmyrene Merchant Networks and Economic Integration in Competitive Markets* (Oxford: Oxford University Press), pp. 147–54.

Seland, E. H. 2015. 'Palmyrene Long-Distance Trade: Land, River, and Maritime Routes in the First Three Centuries CE', in M. N. Walter and J. Ito-Adler (eds), *The Silk Road: Interwoven History*, I: *Long-Distance Trade, Culture, and Society* (Cambridge: Cambridge Institutes Press), pp. 101–31.

Shifman, I. S. 2014. *The Palmyrene Tax Tariff*, Journal of Semitic Studies Supplement, 33 (Oxford: Oxford University Press).

Smith, A. M. I. 2013. *Roman Palmyra: Identity, Community, and State Formation* (Oxford: Oxford University Press).

Sommer, M. 2017. *Palmyra: A History* (New York: Routledge).

Spivak, G. C. 1988. 'Can the Subaltern Speak?', in C. Nelson and L. Grossberg (eds), *Marxism and the Interpretation of Culture* (London: Macmillan Education UK), pp. 271–313.

Starcky, J. 1955. 'Inscriptions palmyréniennes conservés au Musée de Beyrouth', *Bulletin du Musée de Beyrouth*, 12: 29–44.

Starkey, P. 2019. 'Rabbi Benjamin of Tudela: A 12th Century Traveler to the Middle East', in N. Cooke (ed.), *Journeys Erased by Time: The Rediscovered Footprints of Travelers in Egypt and the Near East* (Oxford: Archaeopress), pp. 1–15.

Stobiecka, M. 2020. 'Archaeological Heritage in the Age of Digital Colonialism', *Archaeological Dialogues*, 27.2: 113–25.

Stoler, A. L. 2009. *Along the Archival Grain: Epistemic Anxieties and Colonial Common Sense* (Princeton: Princeton University Press).

Stucky, R. A. 2008. 'Henri Seyrig: Engagierter Archäologe und Verwalter des Antikendienstes während der Mandatszeit', in C. Trümpler (ed.), *Das Große Spiel: Archäologie und Politik zur Zeit des Kolonialismus (1860–1940)* (Cologne: DuMont), pp. 504–11.

Syme, R. 1988. *Roman Papers*, IV, ed. by Anthony R. Birley (Oxford: Oxford University Press).

Tauber, E. 1994. *The Formation of Modern Iraq and Syria* (London: Routledge).

Veyne, P. 2017. *Palmyra: An Irreplaceable Treasure* (Chicago: University of Chicago Press).

Weiss, T. G. and N. Connelly. 2017. *Cultural Cleansing and Mass Atrocities: Protecting Cultural Heritage in Armed Conflict Zones*, J. Paul Getty Trust Occasional Papers in Cultural Heritage Policy, 1 (Los Angeles: J. Paul Getty Trust) <http://www.getty.edu/publications/pdfs/CulturalCleansing_Weiss_Connelly.pdf> [accessed 7 October 2022].

Wood, R. 1753. *The Ruins of Palmyra: Otherwise Tedmor in the Desert* (London: Robert Wood).

Woolf, G. 1992. 'The Unity and Diversity of Romanization', *Journal of Roman Archaeology*, 5: 349–52.

—— 1998. *Becoming Roman: The Origins of Provincial Civilization in Gaul* (Cambridge: Cambridge University Press).

Yon, J.-B. 2002–2003. 'Zenobie et les femmes de Palmyra', *Annales archéologiques arabes syriennes*, 45–46: 215–20.

Young, J. C. 2019. 'The New Knowledge Politics of Digital Colonialism', *Environment and Planning A: Economy and Space*, 51.7: 1424–41.

7. Revisiting Harald Ingholt's Excavation Diaries: Zooming in on Two Graves in the South-West Necropolis of Palmyra and their Inscriptions

Rubina Raja and Julia Steding
Centre for Urban Network Evolutions (UrbNet), Aarhus University
(Rubina.raja@cas.au.dk, j.steding@cas.au.dk)

Introduction

Palmyra's archaeology has been the focus of numerous publications for more than a hundred years. Since the late nineteenth century, excavations and field surveys have taken place in the city and its hinterland.[1] Harald Ingholt, a Danish archaeologist, was one of the many scholars undertaking archaeological fieldwork at the site during the French Mandate in Syria, a period of many large-scale archaeological missions.[2] During the 1920s he headed the excavation of about eighty tombs in the south-west necropolis, which he documented in handwritten fieldwork diaries. These diaries, relating to his fieldwork campaigns in 1924, 1925, and 1928, have recently been published in a commented form.[3]

Together with an extensive paper archive, the diaries were donated by Ingholt to the Ny Carlsberg Glyptotek in Copenhagen in 1983 — quite some years after his retirement from a professorship at Yale University in 1964. The paper archive served as a basis for Ingholt's higher doctoral dissertation on the Palmyrene sculptures submitted to the University of Copenhagen and published in 1928.[4] The diaries served as the basic documentation for later publications by Ingholt. Numerous graves, however, remained unpublished; some did not reveal groundbreaking archaeological evidence in Ingholt's view, and others he simply did not seem to have had the time to publish. Within the framework of the Palmyra Portrait Project,

Figure 7.1. Photo of Harald Ingholt (© Rubina Raja and Palmyra Portrait Project, courtesy of Philip Underdown).

the diaries were digitized in 2012. In 2015 the information about the find context of the Beauty of Palmyra in the diaries was published together with a file folder with further information about the excavation of Qasr Abjad.[5] Furthermore, one of the inscriptions from the diaries was published by Jean-Baptiste Yon in the context of a confer-

---

[1] For the research history of Palmyra, see e.g. Sartre-Fauriat 2019 with further references. See also Sommer 2018, ch. 1; Raja 2022, ch. 1.

[2] For Harald Ingholt and his work in Palmyra, see Raja and Sørensen 2015a; 2015b; Raja 2019a; 2019b; 2021a; Bobou and others (forthcoming).

[3] Raja, Steding, and Yon 2021.

[4] Ingholt 1928. For a translated and commented version, see Bobou and others 2021.

[5] Raja and Sørensen 2015a. For the Beauty of Palmyra, see Raja 2019c, 198–201, cat. no. 75.

Figure 7.2. Palmyrene relief portraits exhibited at the Ny Carlsberg Glyptotek in Copenhagen during the special exhibition 'The Road to Palmyra', 2019–2020 (courtesy of Ny Carlsberg Glyptotek, photographer Anders Sune Berg).

ence held within the Palmyra Portrait Project.[6] Within the same context, Annette Højen Sørensen published an article related to the tomb paintings from the Hypogeum of Ḥairan and resituated the respective wall paintings within the tomb based on the excavation diaries.[7] In a recent publication that connected the information from the diaries with the map of the south-west necropolis of Palmyra, the map was updated and several ground plans were added.[8] Another article highlighted the research potential of the diaries and how they can add to our understanding of the excavation practices of the 1920s, the Palmyrene graves, their layout, interior, and state of preservation when excavated, the epigraphy, small finds like tesserae, and Palmyra in the 1920s in general.[9] In this contribution, we revisit and reflect upon the publication process and also take a closer look at two hypogea from the south-west necropolis that were excavated by Ingholt and have not been examined in any further detail so far.

---

[6] Yon 2016, 122.

[7] Sørensen 2016.

[8] Raja, Schnädelbach, and Steding 2022.

[9] Raja and Steding 2022.

Harald Ingholt and his Fieldwork in Palmyra

Harald Ingholt's (Fig. 7.1) interest in Palmyra grew out of long-standing Danish research interests in the Near East. The brewer and art collector Carl Jacobsen (1842–1914) bought numerous funerary portraits through Julius Løytved, the Danish consul in Beirut at the time. Jacobsen seems to have been interested in the Palmyrene portraits as comparanda to Greek and Roman portraits and, at the same time, was genuinely interested in understanding the Palmyrene portraits in their local context.[10] The first Dane, as far as we know, to visit Palmyra was the Danish philologist Johannes Elith Østrup (1867–1938).[11] In 1892 he mapped parts of the Syrian Desert, and during his travels he acquired some Palmyrene funerary portraits and wrote about the vandalism taking place in Palmyra, both in terms of icono-

---

[10] On the collection history, see Nielsen 2019; Raja 2019c; 2021a, 24–26.

[11] Østrup acquired the following objects for the Ny Carlsberg Glyptotek, Copenhagen: I.N. 1130, I.N. 1147, I.N. 1149, I.N. 1150, I.N. 1152, I.N. 1153, I.N. 1155, I.N. 1156, I.N. 1157, I.N. 1159, I.N. 1160, I.N. 1161 (see Raja 2019c).

Figure 7.3. Title page of diary 1 from 1924 (© Rubina Raja and Palmyra Portrait Project, courtesy of the Ny Carlsberg Glyptotek).

clasm but also since European collectors showed a growing interest in the sculptures.¹² However, despite the fact that he criticizes the vandalism, he did not reflect upon whether he contributed to it himself by buying further objects. The objects became part of the Ny Carlsberg Glyptotek's collection (Fig. 7.2), which is, as of today, the largest collection of Palmyrene funerary portraits outside of Syria. This collection also sparked Harald Ingholt's interest in Palmyra, and in 1925 he took up a position as curator at the Ny Carlsberg Glyptotek.¹³ At this time, he had already been excavating in Palmyra. In later years, he initiated excavations at another site in Syria: Hama. He also left his position at the Ny Carlsberg Glyptotek to take up a position at the American University in Beirut, Lebanon, and during his employment there, he founded the journal *Berytus*.¹⁴

Ingholt's first fieldwork in Palmyra was conducted in the year immediately after Syria had come under French control, and the campaign was carried out under French concession. During the early years under French administration, the archaeological service had been reorganized, which naturally led to an increase in foreign missions, mostly French, while excavations by local authorities were largely prohibited.¹⁵ During the mandate period, much of the archaeological work was funded by the French government and, as such, was done within the framework of what was a colonial setting. This is also reflected in Ingholt's work, who worked closely with French colleagues and employed local workers as excavators and workmen. Ingholt's three field campaigns in the 1920s, however, were funded by the Danish Rask-Ørsted Foundation.¹⁶ In 1936, Ingholt returned to Palmyra to excavate the Hypogeum of Malkû and for general follow-up research, but no diaries or any kind of documentation from this time have been found in the archival materials.¹⁷

The Excavation Diaries and their Publication

In total, five chronologically labelled diaries and one draft diary were donated to the Ny Carlsberg Glyptotek (Fig. 7.3). The draft diary served as a basis for diary 1. Diaries 1, 2, and 4 relate to the excavations in 1924, 1925, and 1928, respectively; diary 3 is an inventory of all tombs excavated during the first two campaigns; and diary 5 is a concordance of all tombs investigated by Ingholt.¹⁸ As mentioned above, Ingholt excavated around eighty tombs during his fieldwork campaigns in the 1920s. Only thirteen of these were published by him in the years after the excavations.¹⁹

---

¹² Østrup 1894; 1895. Raja and Sørensen 2019. See also Spencer 2022 for a translation of Østrup 1894.

¹³ Raja and Sørensen 2015b, 8; Raja 2019a, 53–55; 2019b, 118–20; 2021a, 24–26.

¹⁴ Raja and Sørensen 2015b, 23; Raja 2019a, 58; 2019b, 123; 2021a, 32. In later years, Ingholt worked at Aarhus University and Yale University. See Raja and Sørensen 2015b, 22; Raja 2019b,

129–30; 2021a, 39–43. For Ingholt's life and career, see also Bobou and others (forthcoming).

¹⁵ For the French Mandate in Syria, see most recently Ouahes 2018. See also Tauber 1994; Gelin 2002; Grainger 2013; Greenhalgh 2016. See also Delplace's elaboration on the archaeological missions launched in the Near East during this period: <https://heritage.bnf.fr/bibliothequesorient/en/archeology-syria-art> [accessed 12 November 2021]; Stucky 2008.

¹⁶ Ingholt 1935, 13; Raja and Sørensen 2015b, 18, 22.

¹⁷ Ingholt 1935; 1966; 1970–1971; Raja and Sørensen 2015b, 19, 22.

¹⁸ Diary 1: 1924 (Raja, Steding, and Yon 2021, 85–368); diary 2: 1925 (Raja, Steding, and Yon 2021, 492–676), the last few pages of this diary already document the campaign from 1928; diary 3: 1925 (Raja, Steding, and Yon 2021, 695–828); diary 4: 1928 (Raja, Steding, and Yon 2021, 877–950); diary 5: tombs (Raja, Steding, and Yon 2021, 965–1750).

¹⁹ Ingholt 1932 (Hypogeum of Ḥairan; Hypogeum of

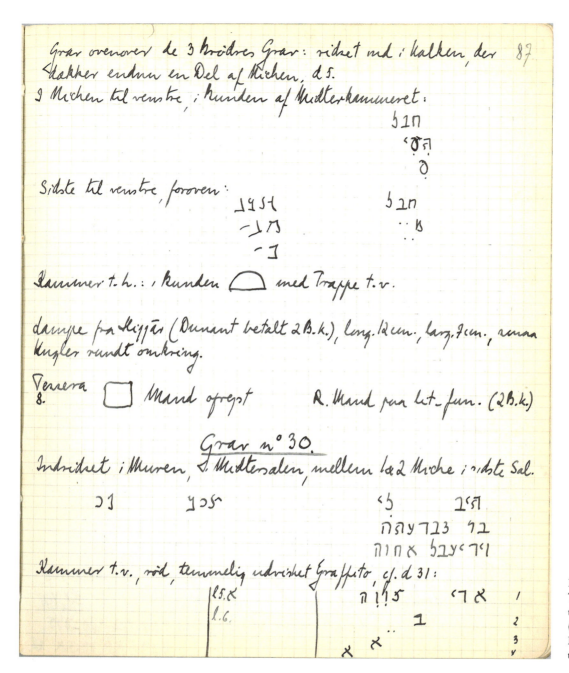

Figure 7.4. Diary 1, p. 87. Transcribed inscriptions and the mention of small finds (© Rubina Raja and Palmyra Portrait Project, courtesy of the Ny Carlsberg Glyptotek).

Through the diaries, we get unique insight into the daily fieldwork and are provided with information on the hypogea located in the south-west necropolis where Ingholt excavated.[20] A strong focus on the inscriptions and the layout of the tombs can be observed, but Ingholt also paid attention to the funerary portraiture, small finds, and inscriptions (founder and cession texts as well as funerary inscriptions and graffiti incised in the plaster).[21] The funerary portraiture and the sarcophagi

---

'Atenatan); 1935 (Hypogeum of 'Atenatan; Hypogeum of J. A. Male; Hypogeum of Malkû; Hypogeum of Naṣrallat; Hypogeum of Bar'a); 1938 (Hypogeum of Yarḥai; Hypogeum of Seleukos; Hypogeum of Lišamś; Hypogeum of 'Abd'astor); 1966 (Hypogeum of Malkû); 1970–1971 (Hypogeum of Malkû); 1974 (Hypogeum of Bat-Mitrait/Tomb I; Hypogeum of Yarḥibola). In total, there are 473 tombs known in Palmyra (based on mapped structures from Schnädelbach 2010).

20 For a complete list of all tombs mentioned in the diaries, see Raja, Steding, and Yon 2021, 1793–97. Through the collaborative work with K. Schnädelbach, it was possible to refine the list: Raja, Schnädelbach, and Steding 2022, appendix 1.

21 For a concordance of all published inscriptions from the

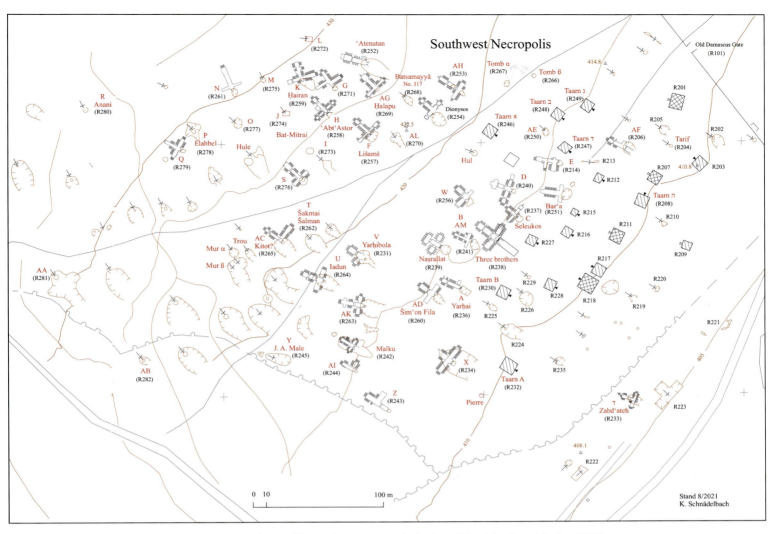

Figure 7.5. Updated map of the south-west necropolis (© Raja, Schnädelbach, and Steding 2022).

are described in detail, and in some cases it was possible to associate the excavated or bought portraits with a later publication or a photograph from the Ingholt Archive of the said object.[22] Small finds were unearthed during the excavations but were also offered for acquisition by locals, who had conducted their own illegal excavations. Ingholt bought sculpture heads, coins, tesserae, and other objects from the locals.[23] Many of the tesserae became part of the collection in the Ny Carlsberg Glyptotek.[24]

Ingholt over the years also added a few funerary sculptures to the collection, among these the famous so-called Beauty of Palmyra, an extraordinary funerary portrait from the elite grave Qasr Abjad.[25]

The tombs are described in detail. When first excavated, Ingholt usually transcribed the inscription over the entrance, described the tomb's ground plan and any reliefs or sarcophagi that he spotted (Fig. 7.4). In diary 3, drawings of the layout are provided with the measurements of the walls and the number of niches on each wall. If any sarcophagi were found, he indicated their location on the drawing. Also in diary 3, Ingholt located many of the tombs. He noted the distance between tombs, how they align with one another and with the grave towers, and the direction of the entrance towards

---

diaries, see Raja, Steding, and Yon 2021, 1793–97, 1807–11. For a concordance of all unpublished inscriptions from the diaries, see Raja, Steding, and Yon 2021, 1799–1806. For the prosopography of the unpublished inscriptions, see Raja, Steding, and Yon 2021, 1813–17. For a short discussion of selected inscriptions from the diaries, see Yon 2016.

22   For the archive, see n. 31. See also the list of diary illustrations in Raja, Steding, and Yon 2021, 21, 875. Whenever possible, the photographs of portraits and further findings were added after each diary.

23   For an example, see Raja, Steding, and Yon 2021, 255 (diary 1, p. 79). Ingholt bought tesserae, a relief, and lamps.

24   For the tesserae at the Ny Carlsberg Glyptotek, see Raja

2019c, cat. nos 140–231. See also Raja, Steding, and Yon 2021, 682–83, figs 5.1–5.2.

25   For the Beauty of Palmyra, see Raja and Sørensen 2015a; Raja 2019c, cat. no. 57; 2021a, 58. For the other reliefs, see Raja 2019c, cat. nos 7–8, 13, 40, 66.

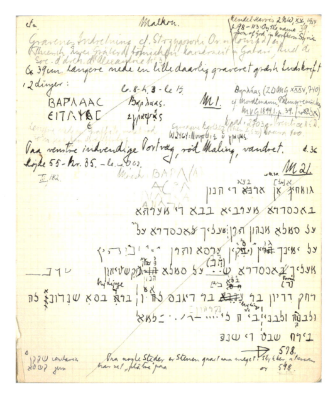

Figure 7.6. A double-page spread from the diary publication, showing the scan, transcription, and translation (© Raja, Steding, and Yon 2021).

geographic north.[26] A few loose pages were found in another box in the Ny Carlsberg Glyptotek, one with a hand-drawn map and one with the angles that indicate the orientation of the entrances.[27] Combining the map with the descriptions in the diaries made it possible to create an updated and more precise map of the southwest necropolis (Fig. 7.5).[28]

The updated map is just one example of the kind of information that can be drawn from the diaries. Their publication was an important addition to our knowledge about Palmyra and will thus be discussed in some more detail here. In 2012, the archive and diaries became part of the Palmyra Portrait Project.[29] Within the framework of the project, the archive sheets were digitized and the portraits were added to a database that now holds almost four thousand portraits from the Palmyrene funerary sphere. The corpus is currently in its last stage of preparation for publication, and numerous publications have

---

[26] Raja, Steding, and Yon 2021, 804–19 (diary 3, pp. 79–87).

[27] Map: Raja, Steding, and Yon 2021, 1780. Additional pages: Raja, Steding, and Yon 2021, 1757.

[28] Raja, Schnädelbach, and Steding 2022.

[29] <https://projects.au.dk/palmyraportrait/> [accessed 7 January 2022].

Figure 7.7. The Ingholt family, 1934 (© Rubina Raja and Palmyra Portrait Project, courtesy of Philip Underdown).

Figure 7.8. Workers in the grave of Malkû, discovering a sarcophagus (© Rubina Raja and Palmyra Portrait Project, courtesy of the Ny Carlsberg Glyptotek).

Figure 7.9. The Great Colonnade in Palmyra (© Rubina Raja and Palmyra Portrait Project, courtesy of the Ny Carlsberg Glyptotek).

already appeared relating to a number of issues concerning the sculptures.[30] The Ingholt archive has been further investigated within the framework of the project Archive Archaeology: Preserving and Sharing Palmyra's Cultural Heritage through Harald Ingholt's Digital Archives,[31] also discussed in this volume.

Another task the project took up was publishing the Ingholt excavation diaries. Project members scanned the pages of all six diaries. All these scans are now available online and openly accessible on the platform figshare under a CC BY 4.0 licence.[32] This allows researchers to engage with the 'raw material', without accessing the physical archive. Everyone can now explore the diaries online and download high-resolution images of each diary page.

The diaries are also published in print (Fig. 7.6).[33] For the publication, the decision was made to transcribe each diary page and include a translation of the Danish into English.[34] The transcription is colour-coded and highlights whenever Ingholt used a language other than Danish. Furthermore, unpublished and published inscriptions in Palmyrene Aramaic, Greek, and Latin were translated. Any published tombs, inscriptions, reliefs, and other objects that are mentioned were provided with references to their publications. Further notes were provided whenever Ingholt made cross-references to other diaries, in order to translate phrases and words from Arabic, and to provide some information on the publications Ingholt used as references. To simplify the work with the diaries, the publication provides concordances of the mentioned tombs as well as all published and unpublished inscriptions.[35] Another appendix offers the prosopography of the unpublished inscriptions.[36] The paper publication also compiles an impressive number of documents, letters, newspaper articles, and photographs depicting Ingholt's life, his family, and the Near East (Figs 7.7–7.9).[37] The paper publication is thus the most efficient tool to work with, but the online availability of the data allows more researchers and the public to access the material from anywhere with an internet connection.

Two Graves from the South-West Necropolis

The research potential of the diaries has been briefly summarized in the above section. In the following, we will discuss the value of the diaries for archaeological research in more detail, based on two case studies. Hypogea AC and AD are both unpublished and add important knowledge on the hypogea from the southwest necropolis. Ingholt diligently described their layout and included notes on the inscriptions and interior, which will all be discussed here.

Tomb No. 39 / Hypogeum AC

Hypogeum AC is first mentioned in diary 1 and finds further mention in diaries 2, 3, and 5. Ingholt introduces it as Tombeau 39 in diary 1 and added, later on and in pencil, the name 'AC' and a cross-reference to page 118 (Fig. 7.10).[38] On page 110 and page 118, he then used the label Tomb no. 39 (Figs 7.11–7.12).[39]

In diary 3 he connects the 'AC' with the name 'Kitôt', which could mean that the descriptions of the Tomb of Kitôt belong to the same grave (Fig. 7.12). The difficulty with this will be discussed below. In diary 5, he names the tomb number alongside AC, but the name Kitôt is not mentioned again.[40]

Location

We learn little about the hypogeum's exact location from the diaries. With the help of small sketches, Ingholt noted the direction of the entrance towards the north for most graves in diary 3, but AC does not appear

---

[30] Raja, Bobou, and Yon (forthcoming).

[31] <https://projects.au.dk/archivearcheology/> [accessed 11 October 2022]. See also Bobou, Miranda, and Raja 2021; (forthcoming); Bobou and others 2022.

[32] <https://doi.org/10.6084/m9.figshare.c.5442765>. See also Raja and Steding 2021.

[33] Raja, Steding, and Yon 2021. See also Raja and Steding 2022.

[34] The draft diary that served as basis for diary 1 was not transcribed or translated, as it did not give more information than that provided in diary 1. The scanned pages are included in the publication, though.

[35] Tombs: Raja, Steding, and Yon 2021, 1780–83; unpublished inscriptions: Raja, Steding, and Yon 2021, 1799–1806; published inscriptions: Raja, Steding, and Yon 2021, 1793–97.

[36] Raja, Steding, and Yon 2021, 1813–17.

[37] Raja 2021a; plenty of photographs are also provided between all diaries, depicting life in Syria and Palmyra, the Palmyrene monuments, work at Palmyra, uncovered objects, the tombs of Palmyra, postcard sent by Ingholt, newspaper articles, and images from other sites in the Near East (e.g. Hama).

[38] Raja, Steding, and Yon 2021, 151 (diary 1, p. 27).

[39] Raja, Steding, and Yon 2021, 297 (diary 1, p. 100), 333 (diary 1, p. 118).

[40] Raja, Steding, and Yon 2021, 1629 (diary 5, p. 121).

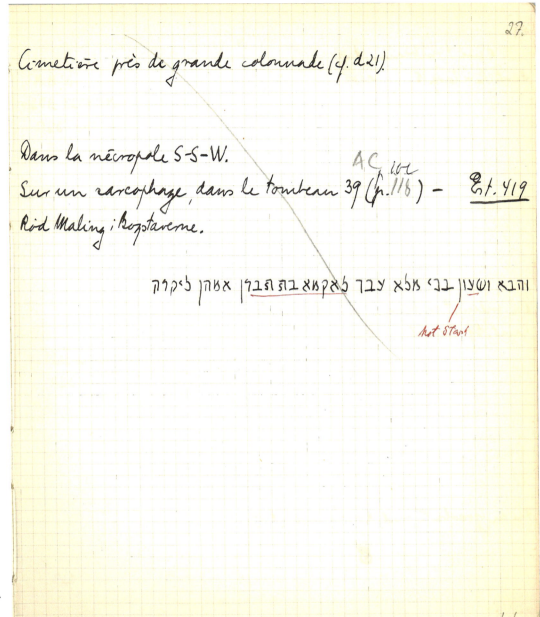

Figure 7.10. Diary 1, p. 27 (© Rubina Raja and Palmyra Portrait Project, courtesy of the Ny Carlsberg Glyptotek).

here.[41] Likewise in diary 3, he made a list of the locations of the tombs in relation to one another and the towers to the south of the necropolis, as well as measurements between the graves.[42] We learn that Tomb AC aligns with the centre of the last tower, and that the distance to the entrance of Tomb T is 21 m and the distance to the entrance of Tomb U is 43 m (Fig. 7.13).[43] Together with the hand-drawn map that was found alongside the diaries on a loose page, the information led to the localization of Hypogeum AC to the west of the Tomb of Šakmai Šalman (R 262).[44] In the Topographia Palmyrena, it thus matches the structure R265 (see also Fig. 7.5).[45] The direction towards the north on the map is hypothetical

---

[41] Raja, Steding, and Yon 2021, 780, 782, 784, 786, 792, 794 (diary 3, pp. 67–69, 72–73).

[42] Raja, Steding, and Yon 2021, 805, 807, 809, 811, 813, 815, 817, 819 (diary 3, pp. 79–87).

[43] Raja, Steding, and Yon 2021, 811 (diary 3, p. 82). The information is repeated in diary 3, p. 87.

[44] For the most recent map of the south-west necropolis that is based on the information from the excavation diaries, see Raja, Schnädelbach, and Steding 2022.

[45] Schnädelbach 2010.

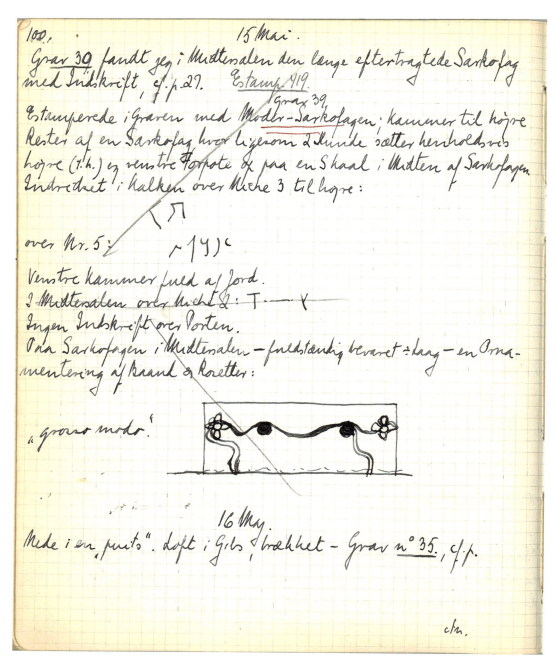

Figure 7.11. Diary 1, p. 100 (© Rubina Raja and Palmyra Portrait Project, courtesy of the Ny Carlsberg Glyptotek).

and based on the orientation of the surrounding tombs where the direction towards the north is known.

Layout

The first description of the layout can be found in diary 1 (1924), where Ingholt gives an overview of the tombs he had been excavating that year. The translated description of Tomb no. 39 reads as follows (Fig. 7.12):

Tomb 39
No inscription. 2 side chambers, just after the entrance. On the left, ceiling caved in.

Side chamber on right: on the left, first 6 niches; next 5 (in all: 11). At the end 4 niches plus the sarcophagus with the dog, cf. p. 100 – On the right, from the portal, 5+6 niches.

Central chamber: on the right, first 6 [niches]; next 4 niches. At the end 3; on the left first 6, and then 3. – Sarcophagus, Wahbâ, etc. cf. p. 27.[46]

---

[46] Raja, Steding, and Yon 2021, 333 (diary 1, p. 118). The mention of p. 100 and p. 27 are cross-references within the same diary.

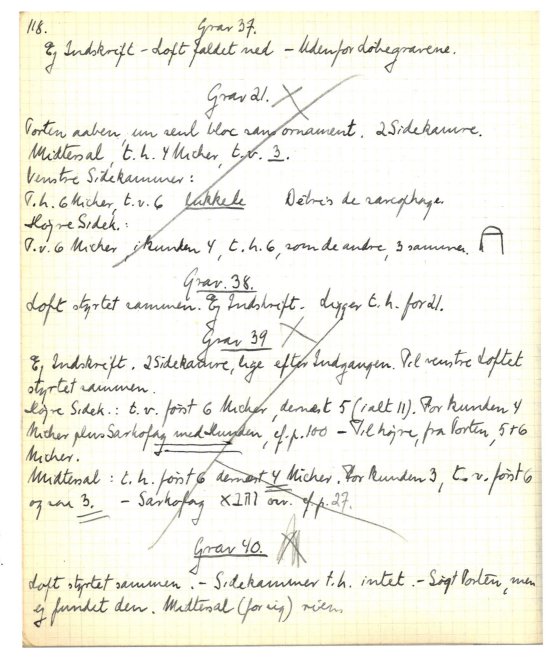

Figure 7.12. Diary 1, p. 118 (© Rubina Raja and Palmyra Portrait Project, courtesy of the Ny Carlsberg Glyptotek).

This description gives us a first impression of the tomb's layout. The hypogeum was of the typical T-shape with a central chamber and two side chambers. In each of the chambers, multiple loculus niches are dug into the three walls. The right chamber had eleven niches in the first part and fifteen niches in the bottom end of the side chamber. The central chamber had twelve niches in the anterior part and nine niches in the posterior part. The left chamber was never excavated as the ceiling had caved in. There are thus at least forty-seven niches in this grave, most likely more when accounting for more niches in the left side chamber. In diary 5, the description is repeated, including a few more details.[47] It is indicated how many niches are on each wall in what interval, and the symbol of a rounded arch most likely indicates that the walls between the niches have arched ceilings, something we can see in other hypogea as well, for example Tomb no. 5 (Hypogeum of Artaban) in the south-east necropolis.[48] It is possible that sarcophagus reliefs were inserted here.

---

47 Raja, Steding, and Yon 2021, 1635 (diary 5, p. 122).

48 The reliefs from the hypogeum are published in Tanabe 1986, 31, pls 229–32. On the pictures the arched ceiling is visible.

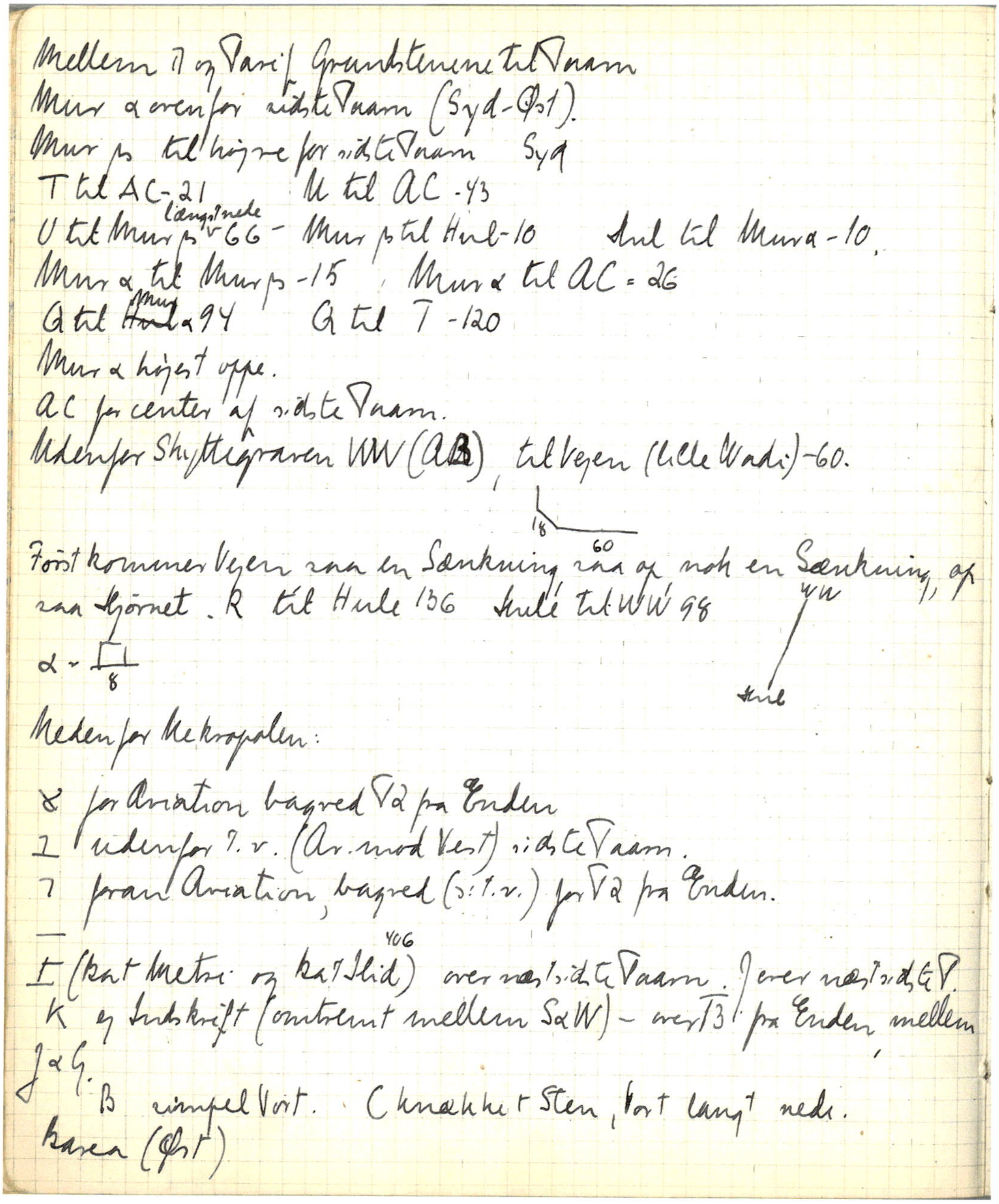

Figure 7.13. Diary 3, p. 82 (© Rubina Raja and Palmyra Portrait Project, courtesy of the Ny Carlsberg Glyptotek).

In diary 5, we are presented with a rough sketch as well as a detailed sketch (Figs 7.14–7.15). The rough sketch depicts a hypogeum with a central chamber and two side chambers.[49] Only the number of niches in the right side chamber is noted; '6 + 5' on the right, '5 + 6' on the left, and four on the main wall. Furthermore, the location of two sarcophagi is roughly indicated, each placed centrally in one of the accessible chambers. Two pages later, Ingholt wrote down the word 'Maal', Danish for 'measurements'. The only information here is, however, that the left chamber had collapsed. On the last page dedicated to Tomb AC, we get a ground plan with much information that led to the reconstruction of the layout by Klaus Schnädelbach (Fig. 7.16).[50] In total, the hypogeum was 17.70 m long. Each wall was measured, and the number of niches was indicated. Again, the sarcophagi are mentioned.

---

[49] Raja, Steding, and Yon 2021, 1631 (diary 5, p. 121a).

[50] Raja, Steding, and Yon 2021, 1639 (diary 5, p. 122b). The ground plan was published in Raja, Schnädelbach, and Steding 2022. It is also freely accessible online on Figshare: <https://doi.org/10.6084/m9.figshare.c.5696872>.

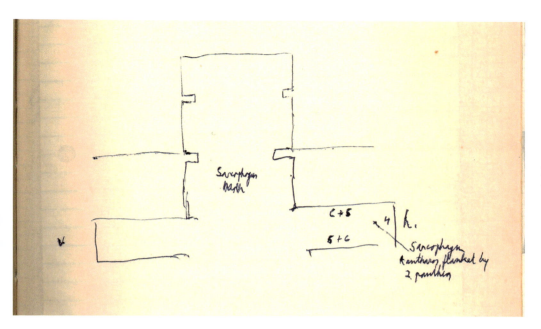

Figure 7.14. Diary 5, p. 121a (© Rubina Raja and Palmyra Portrait Project, courtesy of the Ny Carlsberg Glyptotek).

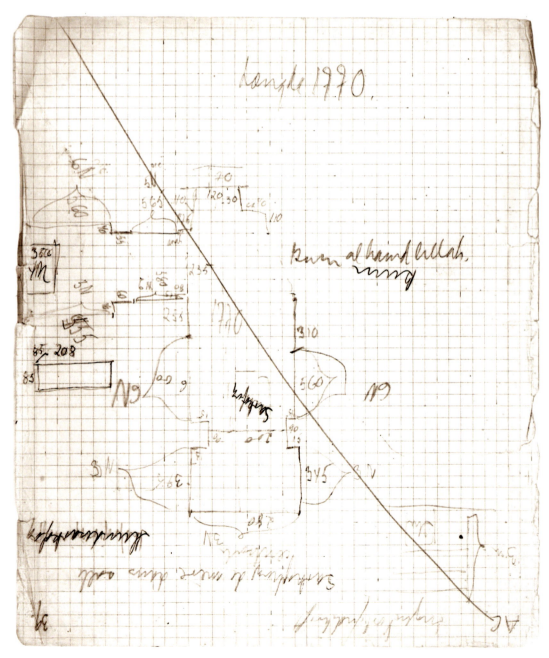

Figure 7.15. Diary 5, p. 122b (© Rubina Raja and Palmyra Portrait Project, courtesy of the Ny Carlsberg Glyptotek).

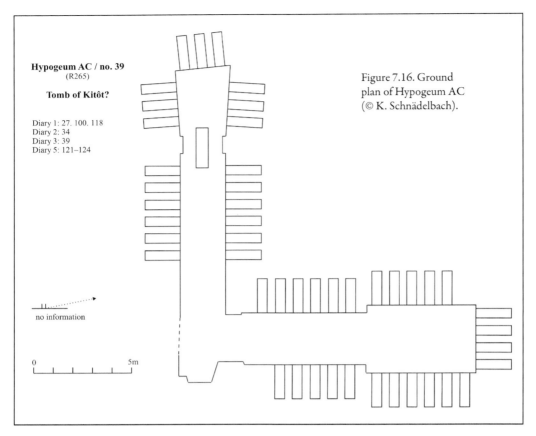

Figure 7.16. Ground plan of Hypogeum AC (© K. Schnädelbach).

This ground plan sketch gives us a good impression of the tomb and its scale (Fig. 7.16). Hypogeum AC has a very common ground plan that is comparable to the hypogea around, for example the Hypogeum of Malkû that Ingholt published in 1935.[51] The hypogeum has, as does Hypogeum AC, a central chamber and two side chambers right at the entrance. Other examples are the Hypogeum of 'Abd'astor and Lišamš, published by Ingholt in 1938.[52] These two are even more comparable to Hypogeum AC, as the central chamber as well as the side chambers have an anterior and posterior part.

Inscriptions

Not many inscriptions were noted down. No inscription seems to have been found above the portal at the time of excavation.[53] An inscription of unknown location was transcribed and translated in 1924: 'Wahba and Šimʿun, sons of Male, have made (this) for Aqma Bat-Tabiran, their mother in her honour.' The inscription was incised in the stone and highlighted with red paint.[54] Possibly, it was on one of the sarcophagi that will be discussed below, as the transcription is mentioned alongside the finding of a sarcophagus and, later on in diary 1, Ingholt calls one of the sarcophagi 'Sarkofag whb', which translates to 'sarcophagus of Wahba.'[55]

Above and next to some of the niches in the chambers, inscriptions were incised into the plaster. One is 'm qn', another one 'zkw'. Furthermore, Ingholt copied (mainly incomplete) inscriptions relating to different niches in the grave.[56]

Not a lot of information is thus gathered about this grave regarding the funder or individuals and families buried in it. The female name on the sarcophagus, Aqma, is not known from the Palmyrene funerary sphere, where only the somewhat similar name Aqmat appears.[57] The name appears in combination with the name At'am, on an altar from an unknown context.[58] The names of the sons that made the sarcophagus for their mother are, however, not unheard of. Šimʿun is a name appearing in relation to an inscription from Tomb no. 112 that Ingholt also excavated. Here we find Šimʿun mentioned in two cession texts; however, no family connections can be made to other tombs.[59] The other son's name, Wahba, only appears twice in the funerary sphere; both times on

---

51 Ingholt 1935, 90–108. The ground plan was published in Ingholt 1962, pl. 1.

52 'Abd'astor: Ingholt 1938, 119–40. The ground plan is published on pl. XLV. Lišamš: Ingholt 1938, 106–19. The ground plan is published on pl. XXXIX.

53 Raja, Steding, and Yon 2021, 297, 1629, 1639 (diary 1, p. 100 and diary 5, pp. 121, 122b).

54 Raja, Steding, and Yon 2021, 151 (diary 1, p. 27).

55 Raja, Steding, and Yon 2021, 297 (diary 1, p. 100).

56 Raja, Steding, and Yon 2021, 333 (diary 1, p. 118).

57 CIS no. 4516, PAT no. 0877, RES no. 347 / PAT no. 1043.

58 See PAT no. 1430.

59 Raja, Steding, and Yon 2021, 531, 533, 535 (diary 2, pp. 16–18); see also Yon 2016, 123–24.

Figure 7.17. Photo of the garland sarcophagus from Hypogeum AC (© Rubina Raja and Palmyra Portrait Project, courtesy of the Ny Carlsberg Glyptotek).

When Ingholt summarized all tombs at the end of diary 1, he repeats the location of the sarcophagus in the central chamber and assigns the name 'Wahbâ' to it (Fig. 7.12).[63] In diary 5 he specifies that the sarcophagus is placed towards the end of the chamber and its orientation was lengthwise.[64] On the sketch that follows the description of the tomb the sarcophagus is placed at the centre, maybe even rather towards the beginning of the central chamber.[65] In total, the sarcophagus was 2 m long, 85 cm deep, and 60 cm high (excluding the lid).[66] In Ingholt's archival material, a photo of a sarcophagus box appears on an unnumbered sheet,[67] showing exactly what Ingholt described in his diary. A reference to the diaries is missing; only the name of the tomb ('Tombeau AC, Palmyra') is mentioned on the sheet (Fig. 7.17).

In the right chamber, the remains of a sarcophagus were found as well. It was located at the end of the side chamber, as we learn from the descriptions as well as the sketch of the layout.[68] At first, Ingholt describes the depiction as dog-like creatures and a bowl, and titles the sarcophagus 'dog sarcophagus' (Fig. 7.11).[69] In diary 5, he refines this to a 'kantharos, flanked by 2 panthers' (Fig. 7.14).[70] The complete description reveals even more information. The left side of the front was fragmented but most likely depicted the leg of a kline, as there was a leg depicted on the right side of the depiction. In the centre was a kantharos with a garland or wreath above it. Two felines flanked it, placing their right paw on the kantharos. A sketch of the right feline's tail indicated that the individual strands of fur are indicated. One or

loculus reliefs dedicated to females.[60] However, there is no detectable connection between the names, and they are thus different individuals.

Interior

With the first mention of Tomb no. 39, Ingholt also noted the presence of the sarcophagus, without further information about where it was found.[61] When Ingholt revisited the tomb during the following days of the excavation, he specified that there was one sarcophagus in the central chamber, which he now calls the 'mother sarcophagus', and one in the right side chamber. From the sarcophagus in the central chamber (holding the inscription discussed above), the box was preserved. It was decorated with ribbons and rosettes. A small sketch accompanies the text, depicting the rosettes at the outer ends of the length side and a ribbon connecting them, as well as ribbons proceeding downwards from them (Fig. 7.11).[62]

---

60 Hatay Arkeoloji Müzesi, Antakya, Turkey, inv. no. 9039 (Krag 2018, 260, cat. no. 350); Rijksmuseum van Oudheden, Leiden, Holland, inv. no. 1977/4.1 (Krag 2018, 356, cat. no. 723). More common is the name Wahbai, which appears in some public inscriptions, e.g. on a statue base (see *PAT* no. 2773) and on a column drum from the Temple of Baalshamin, see *PAT* no. 0163.

61 Raja, Steding, and Yon 2021, 151 (diary 1, p. 27).

62 Raja, Steding, and Yon 2021, 297 (diary 1, p. 100). The same drawing and description can be found in diary 5, p. 122.

63 Raja, Steding, and Yon 2021, 333 (diary 1, p. 118).

64 Raja, Steding, and Yon 2021, 1629 (diary 5, p. 121).

65 Raja, Steding, and Yon 2021, 1631 (diary 5, p. 121a).

66 Raja, Steding, and Yon 2021, 1635 (diary 5, p. 122).

67 Bobou and others 2022, 1714.

68 Raja, Steding, and Yon 2021, 297, 333, 1629, 1631 (diary 1, pp. 100, 118, 121–121a).

69 Raja, Steding, and Yon 2021, 297 (diary 1, p. 100).

70 Raja, Steding, and Yon 2021, 1631 (diary 5, p. 121a).

both animals are strapped into a harness around the neck and covering the torso. Rosettes with six leaves decorate the space over and behind the animals.[71] The location of the sarcophagi today is unknown.

Both decorations are uncommon in Palmyra. The sarcophagus with the inscription from Tomb no. 39 is an unfinished garland sarcophagus, a type well known in the Roman Empire in general,[72] but which is the only attested garland sarcophagus from Palmyra. Garlands appear on other Palmyrene sarcophagi but always in connection with either portrait busts or felines,[73] And they never cover the entire box. As garlands are only depicted on sarcophagi boxes after AD 150,[74] this sarcophagus could give some indication for the dating of the hypogeum.

The second sarcophagus also has an uncommon motif; while feline heads appear regularly in the funerary sphere,[75] no sarcophagus or other form of funerary presentation depicts a whole feline. However, the kline legs are well known and indicate that the box was accompanied by a lid once, depicting one or multiple reclining individuals surrounded by seated or standing family members.[76]

The sarcophagi from this tomb are thus unusual and do not conform with the depiction we usually see.

---

[71] Raja, Steding, and Yon 2021, 1635 (diary 5, p. 122).

[72] For overviews, see e.g. Korkut 2006; Işık, Reynolds, and Roueché 2007; Papagianni 2016.

[73] For an example with portrait busts, see Bobou and Raja 2023, cat. nos 181–82, 187–90 (Temple Tomb no. 186, Tombeau de l'aviation/Tomb Duvaux). For an example of a sarcophagus box with a feline head, see PS 1097 (Bobou and others 2022, 1240). See also <https://doi.org/10.6084/m9.figshare.14980284.v1> [accessed 11 October 2022] for the sheet.

[74] Bobou and Raja 2023.

[75] For examples on sarcophagi, see Musée du Louvre, Paris, inv. no. AO 2630 (Cussini 2019, 74, fig. 4) and Ny Carlsberg Glyptotek, Copenhagen, inv. no. IN 1159 (Raja 2019c, 76–79, cat. no. 6). For examples on loculus reliefs, see Ny Carlsberg Glyptotek, Copenhagen, inv. no. IN 1156 (Raja 2019c, 130–31, cat. no. 25). Lion heads were also used as part of the garland decoration, see sarcophagi from n. 54 (Tomb no. 86). One altar depicts the goddess Allat sitting on a lion-throne (first published in Ploix de Rotrou and Seyrig 1933, 14, pl. IV.1; most recently published in Drijvers 1976, 20, 33, pl. LVIII). Furthermore, they appear as decoration of brooches worn by females, see Colledge 1967, 70, 151, 255; Krag 2018, 103–04 with ns 78, 109.

[76] Turned legs are common in Roman furniture, see Ulrich 2007, 233–34. For the legs depicted in the Palmyrene sarcophagi boxes, see Bobou and Raja 2023, with examples.

Discussion

No inscriptions related to the foundation or cessions have been found in the hypogeum. Looking at another hypogeum with a similar layout, we can get closer to dating the hypogeum. The founder inscription from the Hypogeum of Malkû dates to AD 116.[77] The latest date relating to the tomb is on a cession text from AD 267.[78] The Hypogeum of Lišamš was most likely built in the first half of the second century AD, based on the stylistic analysis of the funerary sculpture.[79] The inscriptions coming from the tomb date to the second half of the second century AD and the first half of the third century AD.[80] The Hypogeum of 'Abd'astor was built in AD 98, according to the founder inscription that Ingholt found in 1937.[81] Some of the funerary sculptures found in the tomb can be stylistically dated to the first half of the second century AD.[82] A cession text can be dated to AD 239, based on the date given in the inscription.[83] The inscriptions and funerary sculpture tell us that the hypogea were all built around AD 100 and were in use for at least 150 years, and they were decorated with sarcophagi.[84] The many similarities in the tombs' layout make it possible to date Hypogeum AC to the second to early third centuries AD. The sarcophagi are contributing little to the dating. Their uniqueness makes it difficult to date them, and the overall style and carving cannot be considered without seeing the sarcophagus boxes.

Another reoccurring phenomenon that can be discussed based on the information concerning Hypogeum AC are cross-references to other diaries. In the case of this hypogeum, there is a cross-reference in diary 5, referring to diary 3. There must thus have been a page dedicated to the tomb as well, missing today, as no page 39 can be found in diary 3.[85] This illustrates very well the lacuna in the evidence we must consider when working with archival materials.

---

[77] Ingholt 1935, 90–91, cat. no. 1.

[78] Ingholt 1935, 102–04, cat. no. 11.

[79] Musée National de Beyrouth, Beirut, inv. no. 698 (Ingholt 1938, 116–17, pl. 42.2).

[80] CIS no. 4194; Ingholt 1938, 106–12, cat. nos 1–3.

[81] Ingholt 1938, 120.

[82] Ingholt 1938, 123.

[83] Ingholt 1938, 125–26.

[84] For the sarcophagi from the Hypogeum of Malkû, see e.g. Ingholt 1976. For the sarcophagi from the Hypogeum of Lišamš, see Ingholt 1938.

[85] Raja, Steding, and Yon 2021, 1633 (diary 5, p. 121b).

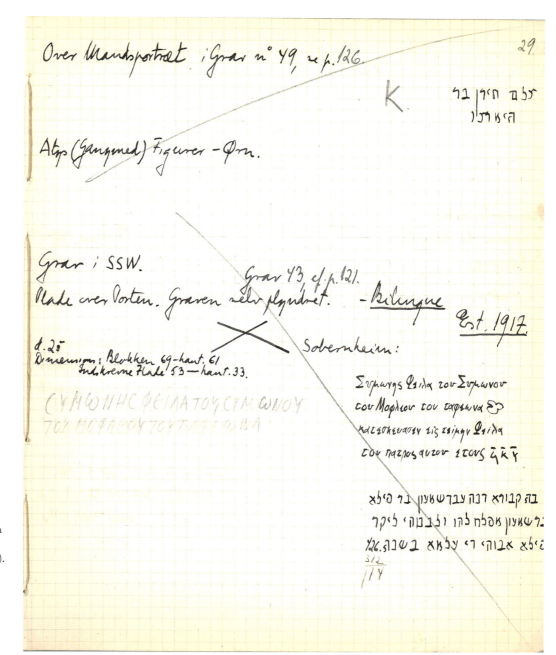

Figure 7.18. Diary 1, p. 29 (© Rubina Raja and Palmyra Portrait Project, courtesy of the Ny Carlsberg Glyptotek).

Lastly we return to the question of whether Tomb no. 39/AC is indeed the same as the so-called Tomb of Kitôt. As mentioned above, the tomb has been associated with the name 'Kitôt' in diary 5. In diary 2, we find a sketch of a tomb that is called 'Kitôt tomb'.[86] It has a large central chamber and two small side chambers, but according to the sketch, there are twenty-three niches; six niches followed by four niches on the side walls and three niches on the central wall. This description does not match with the description Ingholt gave in diaries 1 and 5. It is thus unlikely that the Tomb of Kitôt is the same as Tomb no. 39/Tomb AC. This shows that ongoing research can bring new results — even when studying the same archive.

The information on the hypogeum thus contributes to understanding the layout of the graves in the south-west necropolis and its interior. Even though the sarcophagi's location is unknown today, the detailed descriptions of the iconography will make it possible to identify the sarcophagi (or parts of them) if they ever appear on the art

---

[86] Raja, Steding, and Yon 2021, 569 (diary 2, p. 34).

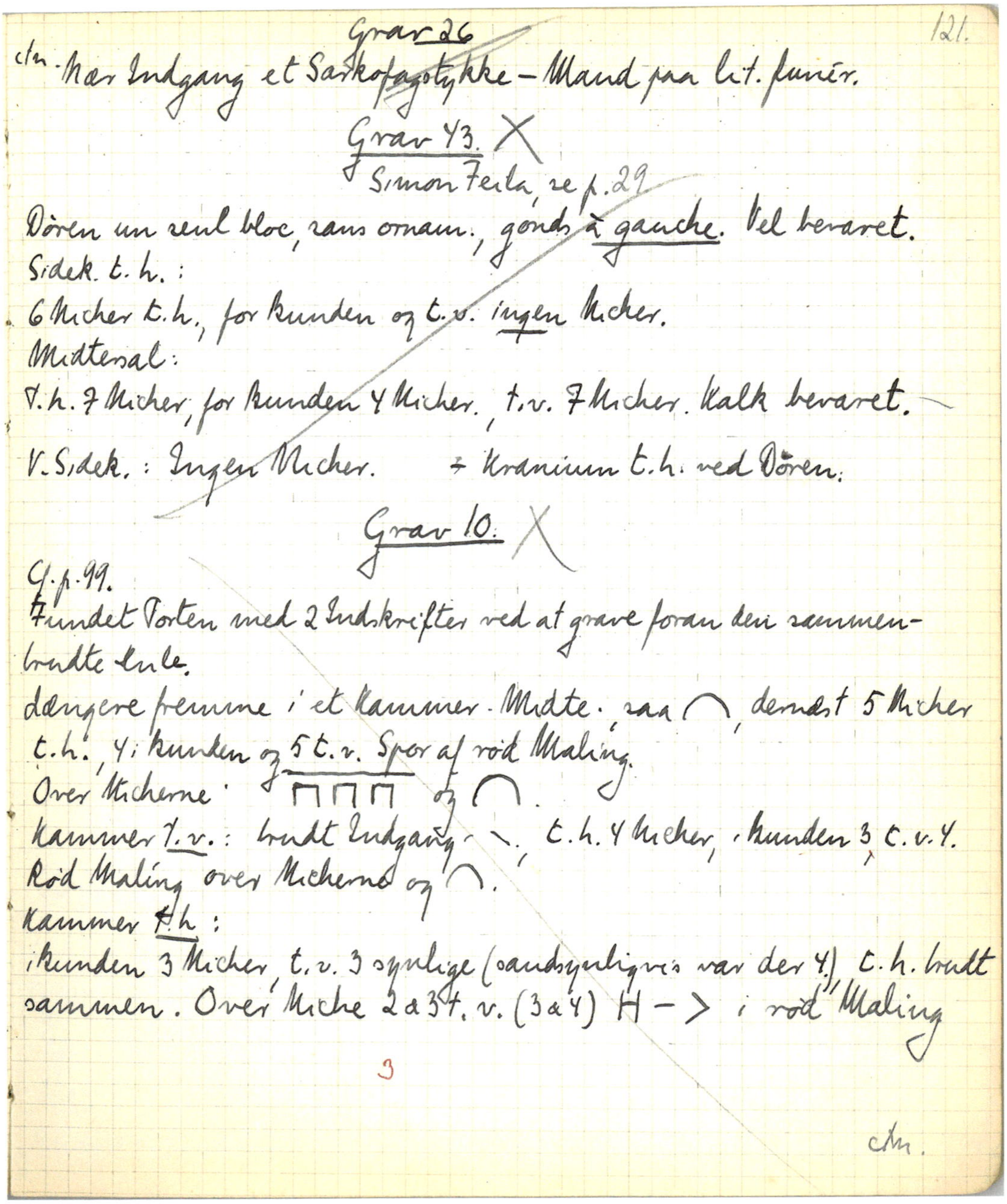
121.
Grav 26
cln. Mar Indgang et Sarkofagstykke – Mand paa l.t. funér.
Grav 43. X
Simon Feila, se p. 29
Dören un seul bloc, sans ornam., gonds à gauche. Vel bevaret.
Sidek. t.h.:
6 Nicher t.h., for Kunden og t.v. ingen Nicher.
Midtesal:
t.h. 7 Nicher, for Kunden 4 Nicher, t.v. 7 Nicher. Kalk bevaret.
V. Sidek.: Ingen Nicher. + Kranium t.h. ved Dören.
Grav 10. X
G. p. 99.
Fundet Porten med 2 Indskrifter ved at grave foran den sammenbrudte Hule.
Længere fremme i et Kammer-Midte, saa ∩, derefter 5 Nicher t.h., 4 i Kunden og 5 t.v. Spor af rød Maling.
Over Nicherne: ⊓⊓⊓ og ∩.
Kammer t.v.: brudt Indgang ⌒, t.h. 4 Nicher, i Kunden 3, t.v. 4.
Rød Maling over Nicherne og ∩.
Kammer t.h.:
i Kunden 3 Nicher, t.v. 3 synlige (sandsynligvis var der 4), t.h. brudt sammen. Over Niche 2 a 3 t.v. (3 a 4) H –> i rød Maling
3
cln.

Figure 7.19. Diary 1, p. 121 (© Rubina Raja and Palmyra Portrait Project, courtesy of the Ny Carlsberg Glyptotek).

market. Furthermore, the diaries help to reconstruct the grave and its interior in quite some detail.[87]

Hypogeum AD

A second unpublished tomb is Hypogeum AD. Ingholt first mentions the hypogeum in 1924 in diary 1, as grave 43. He noted that the grave was robbed[88] but that it was generally well preserved (Figs 7.18–7.19).[89] Later, the tomb number is associated with the name from the founder inscription, Simon Feila (later: Šim'on Fila) (Fig. 7.19),[90] and Sobernheim, who had first published the founder inscription (Fig. 7.20).[91] In 1925, the hypogeum was revisited during May (no day specified, Fig. 7.20).[92]

87 For an example of a reconstructed grave as a 3D model, see e.g. Bobou and others 2020 (also discussed below).

88 Raja, Steding, and Yon 2021, 155 (diary 1, p. 29).

89 Raja, Steding, and Yon 2021, 339 (diary 1, p. 121).

90 Raja, Steding, and Yon 2021, 339 (diary 1, p. 121).

91 Raja, Steding, and Yon 2021, 789, 805 (diary 3, pp. 70, 79).

92 Raja, Steding, and Yon 2021, 789 (diary 3, p. 70).

7. REVISITING HARALD INGHOLT'S EXCAVATION DIARIES

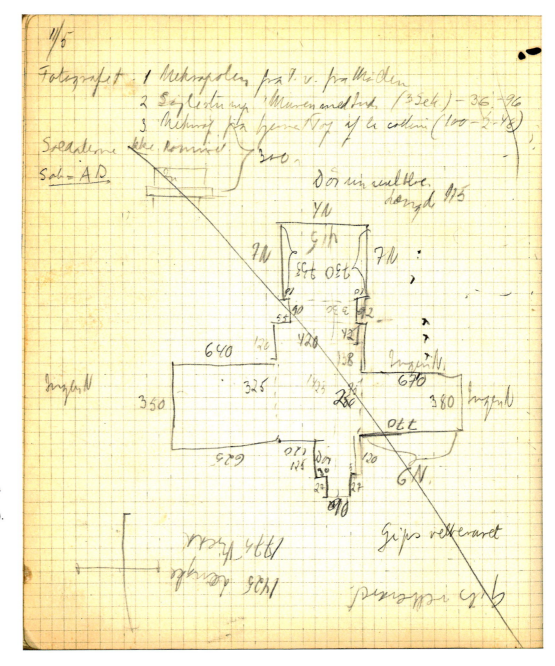

Figure 7.20. Diary 3, p. 70 (© Rubina Raja and Palmyra Portrait Project, courtesy of the Ny Carlsberg Glyptotek).

Location

The tomb is located western of the Tomb of Yarḥai and southern of the Tomb of Naṣrallat. In the Topographia Palmyrena, it is the structure R260 that, until recently, had been assumed to be the Hypogeum of Bar'a.[93] During the work on the diaries and the updated map of the south-west necropolis, some structures were relocated based on the information gained from the diaries. Hypogeum of Bar'a is, in fact, located further north, where structure R251 was mapped in 2010.[94] Structure R260 can now, based on the hand-drawn map found with the diaries, where the relation to Tomb A (Tomb of Yarḥai) and the Tomb of Naṣrallat is indicated, be securely connected to Hypogeum AD (see also Fig. 7.5), even though the hypogeum does not appear on the lists in the diaries giving the distances between tombs. In diary 3, the direction towards the north is indicated with 36° (Fig. 7.19).[95]

---

93 Schnädelbach 2010, 27. Structure R260 is also indicated on the map of the south-west necropolis on p. 65 as Tomb of Bar'a.

94 Raja, Schnädelbach, and Steding 2022.

95 Raja, Steding, and Yon 2021, 793 (diary 3, p. 72).

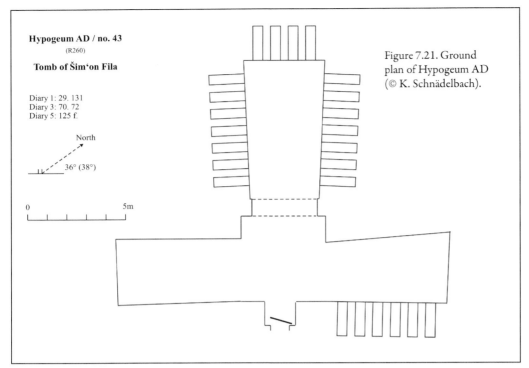

Figure 7.21. Ground plan of Hypogeum AD (© K. Schnädelbach).

Layout

The tomb's layout is comparable to the above-mentioned Hypogeum AC and the comparanda. It has a typical T-shape, with the side chambers located right behind the entrance (Fig. 7.21). A first description is made in diary 1 (Fig. 7.19).[96] The door was made from a single block without any ornaments, and the hinges were on the left side. The right side chamber has six niches dug into the right wall. The other walls were not equipped with niches. The central chamber has seven niches on each side and four niches on the central wall. The left side chamber was carved but without any niches. On a sketch in diary 3, the measurements of the tomb are given, and the number of niches per wall matches the description (Fig. 7.20).[97] There were thus twenty-four niches dug into the walls available for burials. The tomb had plenty more space for further burial niches that were never carved out. It is a common phenomenon in the Palmyrene hypogea; other examples from the south-west necropolis are the Hypogeum of Seleukos (space for more niches on the right side chamber),[98] the Hypogeum of Lišamš (space for more niches in one wall of each side chamber),[99] and the Hypogeum of Zabd'ateh (space for more niches in the left side chamber).[100] Further hypogea only known from Ingholt's diaries have undug niches, but it is not always clear from the descriptions whether there was space for more niches or if these were only partly dug out.[101]

Inscriptions

A squeeze of the bilingual inscription, incised on a slab above the portal, was taken by Ingholt, and he transcribed the Greek and Aramaic texts.[102] He also mentioned the name Sobernheim, which means that this inscription had already been seen and published by the German politician and orientalist when Ingholt first excavated in Palmyra.[103] The inscription was incised on a stone slab, 69 × 61 cm in size. The inscription covered 53 × 33 cm of the slab (Fig. 7.18).[104]

Through the inscription we learn that the tomb was built in the first decade of the second century AD, as the date in Aramaic and Greek states the year 426. Sobernheim calculates the building date to be AD 115–116,[105] Ingholt as AD 114 (Fig. 7.18).[106] This coincides with the foundation date of many of the other tombs in this necropolis, as discussed before.[107]

---

96 Raja, Steding, and Yon 2021, 339 (diary 1, p. 121).

97 Raja, Steding, and Yon 2021, 789 (diary 3, p. 70).

98 Ingholt 1938, 104, pl. XXXVIII.

99 Ingholt 1938, 106, pl. XXXIX.

100 al-As'ad and Taha 1965.

101 For all known ground plans in the south-west necropolis, see Raja, Schnädelbach, and Steding 2022 and <https://doi.org/10.6084/m9.figshare.c.5696872>.

102 The whereabouts of the squeezes, called *estampages* by Ingholt, is unknown. He regularly refers to 'Est.', estampage numbers in the diaries; see also Raja 2021b, 7.

103 Sobernheim 1902, 210–11, no. 6. For the inscription see also *RES* no. 29; *PAT* no. 0512; *IGLS* XVII, 517.

104 Raja, Steding, and Yon 2021, 155, 1651 (diary 1, p. 29; diary 5, p. 125).

105 Sobernheim 1902, 211.

106 Raja, Steding, and Yon 2021, 155 (diary 1, p. 29).

107 See discussion of Tomb no. 39/Hypogeum AC above.

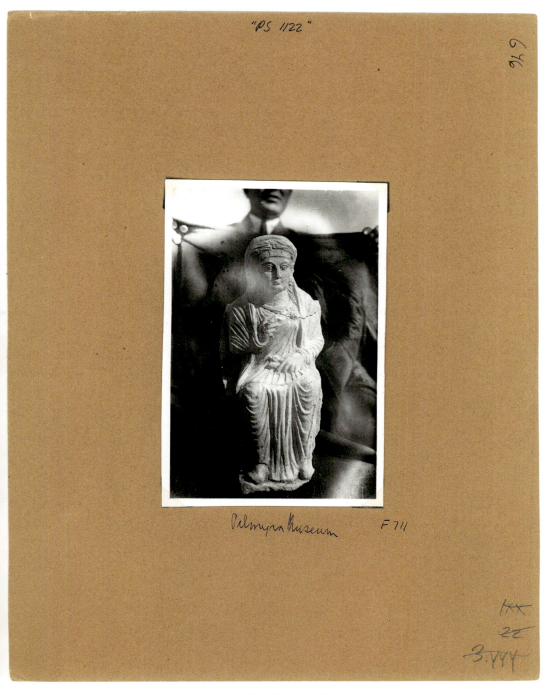

Figure 7.22. Archive Sheet PS 646 (© Rubina Raja and Palmyra Portrait Project, courtesy of the Ny Carlsberg Glyptotek).

context. Due to the lack of cession text or funerary inscriptions from the grave, no more can be said about the individuals and families buried in this hypogeum.

Interior

Very little information is revealed about the interior of the tomb. The funerary sculpture was likely removed from the grave by grave-robbers, as the tomb has been plundered. The only mention of the interior is preserved plaster in the central chamber (Figs 7.19–7.20).[110] In the Hypogeum of Aqraban, the lack of plaster has been related to the collapse of the ceiling,[111] which could mean that the ceiling of Hypogeum AD was still intact.

Discussion

The primary information we gain about Hypogeum AD is the layout and the exact ground plan with all its measurements. The total length of 14.25 m and width of 17.75 m given by Ingholt is challenging to reconstruct based on the measurements given on the sketch, as the sum total of all walls does not add up to the length. This shows quite well the difficulties of fully understanding the notes and connecting them to the archaeological context and material, no matter how detailed the information is.

The date given in the founder inscription reveals that the tomb was built in the twenties of the second century AD, like most of the tombs in the necropolis, as discussed above in relation to Hypogeum AC.

We also learn about the individual who had founded the tomb and his family: Šimʿon, son of Fila, son of Šimʿon Mofliḥ, for himself and his sons.[108] The name Šimʿôn appears in the funerary sphere but never with the same family relations.[109] It is thus not possible to connect this tomb to any of the funerary portraits with unknown

---

108 The Greek equivalents of the names are Sumones, Pheilas, and Sumone Mophleos.

109 See e.g. on a banquet relief, *CIS* no. 4458, *PAT* no. 0810, *RES* no. 727.

110 Raja, Steding, and Yon 2021, 339, 789 (diary 1, p. 121, diary 3, p. 70).

111 al-Hariri 2013, 149.

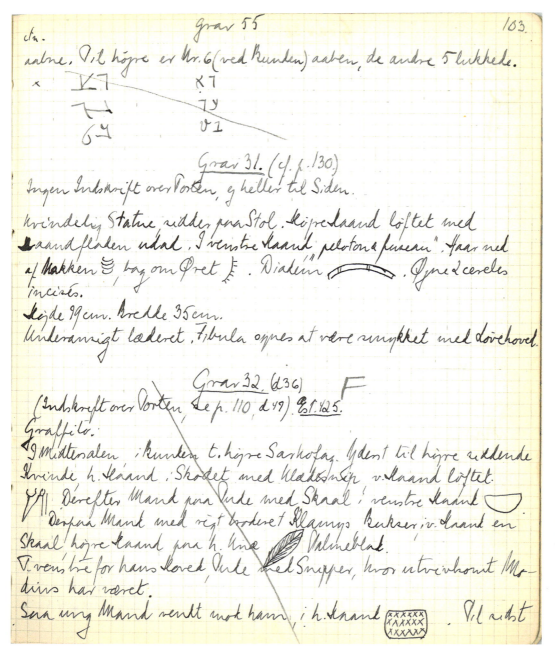

Figure 7.23. Diary 1, p. 103 (© Rubina Raja and Palmyra Portrait Project, courtesy of the Ny Carlsberg Glyptotek).

The Fieldwork Diaries and the Ingholt Archive

In the above-mentioned Ingholt Archive, a paper archive Ingholt kept and added to over several decades to document Palmyrene funerary portraiture and monuments, cross-references to the excavation diaries can be found.[112] Ingholt wrote a Roman numeral (I–V, matching diaries 1–5), the year of excavation, and the pages on which the respective grave was mentioned. He also added references to the paper archive in the diaries by adding the PS number he had assigned to portraits to the description of a funerary portrait.[113]

One example is the sheet PS 646 (Fig. 7.22).[114] The sheet features two photographs, both showing the same

---

[112] For the Ingholt Archive, see Bobou, Miranda, and Raja 2021; 2022; Bobou and others 2022.

[113] See e.g. Raja, Steding, and Yon 2021, 239 (diary 1, p. 72). Here Ingholt added, when revisiting the diaries, the PS number to a bust that he had seen in 1924 and that had, in the meanwhile, been moved to Copenhagen.

[114] The archive sheet will be published as part of the archive publication, Bobou and others 2022. The sheet is also available online, see <https://doi.org/10.6084/m9.figshare.14980284.v1>.

7. REVISITING HARALD INGHOLT'S EXCAVATION DIARIES

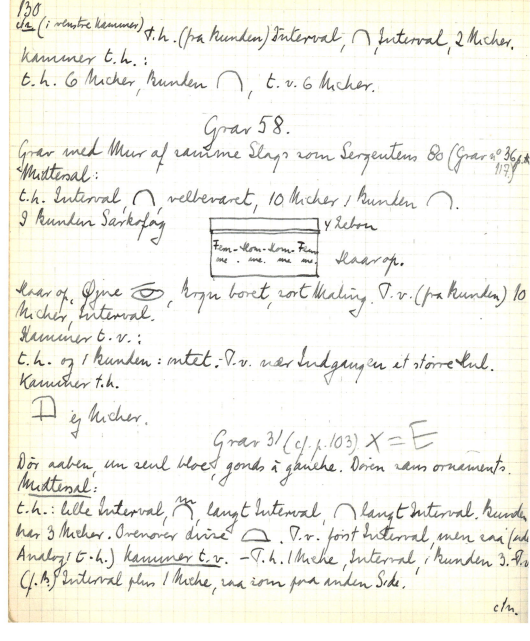

Figure 7.24. Diary 1, p. 130 (© Rubina Raja and Palmyra Portrait Project, courtesy of the Ny Carlsberg Glyptotek).

funerary sculpture of a female.[115] She is seated on a chair, the legs apart, the left arm and left hand are held to the body, and the right hand is slightly raised with the palm pointing forward. The information on the sheet tells us about the dating of the sculpture (AD 100–150), the size of the sculpture (79 × 35), that it was or became part of the collection of the Palmyra Museum (Pal Mus 24), and possibly the inventory number (A 78). A reference to Ingholt's thesis, page 128, footnote 2, PS 334A shows us that the relief was included in his work on the Palmyrene funerary portraiture. The other information can be connected to the diaries. Below the left picture and the reference, it says 'Udgravn 1924', which means that the funerary sculpture was excavated in 1924. Appropriately, under the right picture, Ingholt referred to diary 1 from 1924, pages 103 and 130 ('I, 124, p. 103 og 130'). When looking up the respective pages in the diaries (Figs 7.23–7.24), we find descriptions of Tomb no. 31, also called Tomb E.[116] We find both information,

---

[115] Published in Ingholt 1928, 128; Krag 2018, 238, cat. no. 270.

[116] Raja, Steding, and Yon 2021, 303, 357 (diary 1, pp. 103, 130).

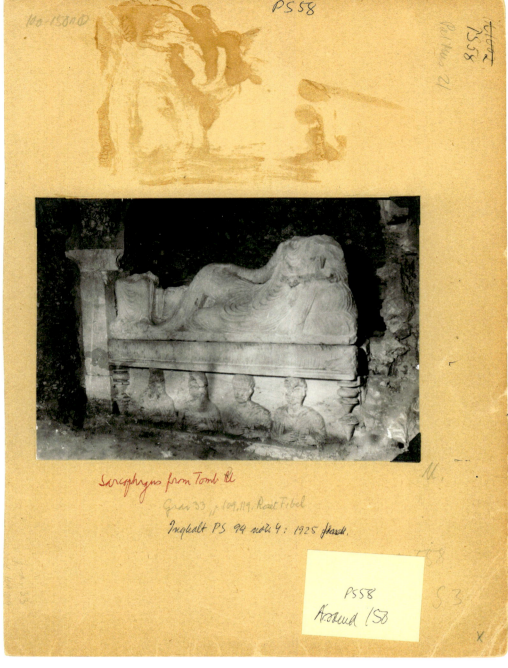

Figure 7.25. Archive Sheet PS 58 (© Rubina Raja and Palmyra Portrait Project, courtesy of the Ny Carlsberg Glyptotek).

the tomb number, as well as the assigned letter, on the sheet.

Another example is the archive sheet PS 58 (Fig. 7.25).[117] Centrally, a photograph of a sarcophagus is placed. In the right corner and centre, the PS number is stated, in the left corner Ingholt dated the sarcophagus to AD 100–150. Three notes connect this sheet with the diaries. In red, right under the picture, 'sarcophagus from Tomb U' is written. At the right lower edge, the letter U is written in pencil. Below, we can read 'Grav 33, p. 109. 119. Roset Fibel', also written in pencil. This information is pointing to diary 1. Tomb no. 33, also called Hypogeum U, was thus first excavated in 1924. The location of the sarcophagus, in the right chamber, on the left side, is mentioned (Fig. 7.26).[118] The sarcophagus is also described, the lid as well as the box. A headless man is reclining on a kline, wearing a chlamys and pants. His right hand is resting on his knee, possibly holding a leaf. A seated female on a chair is on the left side, with her right hand in her lap. The mattress on the kline is decorated with a small bust on the far right. On the box, four busts are depicted. From the right to the left, we see two beardless men, followed by two females. The men wear a himation, with their right arms in a sling created by the clothing. The females are shown with shoulder locks, and both wear a brooch decorated with a rosette.[119] The iconography helps with the dating of the relief, which was, based on stylistic analyses, carved in the first half of the first century AD.[120]

While Ingholt stated, in *Studier over Palmyrensk Skulptur* from 1928, that the sarcophagus was found in 1925, we now know that he already knew of the sarcophagus in 1924.[121] In diary 3, the tomb's ground plan is sketched, including its measurements. On this plan, a sarcophagus is included, so its exact location in the tomb, between

---

[117] See n. 113.

[118] Raja, Steding, and Yon 2021, 315, 335 (diary 1, pp. 109, 119).

[119] Raja, Steding, and Yon 2021, 315 (diary 1, p. 109).

[120] See also Ingholt 1928, 94. For a translation, see Bobou and others 2021, 216–17.

[121] Ingholt 1928, 94 n. 4.

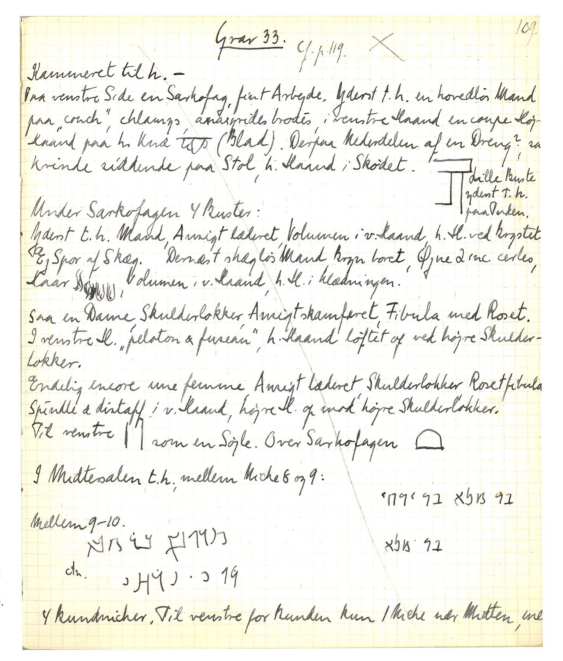

Figure 7.26. Diary 1, p. 109 (© Rubina Raja and Palmyra Portrait Project, courtesy of the Ny Carlsberg Glyptotek).

pilasters, can be reconstructed.[122] In future work, information like this could pave the way for reconstructions of the tombs, as the example of the Hypogeum of Ḥairan highlights. Based on the information from the diaries and the publications by Ingholt on the tomb, it was possible to create a 3D reconstruction of the tomb.[123] It includes the exact measurements of the hypogeum and the chambers, the number of niches on each wall, and interior decorations. Reconstructions like this can possibly be made based on information from the diaries and showcase the great potential of revisiting archives and excavation notes that have not been worked on so far.

Conclusion

This contribution has showcased the type of information on hypogea in the south-west necropolis that can be gained from the diaries, bringing unpublished inscriptions and descriptions of tombs and their interiors to the forefront of current research. We have mainly focused

---

[122] Raja, Steding, and Yon 2021, 747 (diary 3, p. 43).

[123] Bobou and others 2020. For the model, see Raja and McAvoy 2019.

on the information connected to two hypogea that were described in the diaries, and based on the drawings and descriptions, it is possible to reconstruct the graves' layout and interior. This is thus one of the first publications of Palmyrene hypogea from the south-west necropolis since Ingholt last published on them in 1974 — which was late in his long academic career. As only a few other graves from this necropolis have been excavated by archaeologists after Ingholt conducted his fieldwork in the 1920s,[124] every new publication on these tombs sheds new light on the Palmyrenes who used and were buried in the necropolis, the timespan during which the graves were constructed and in use, and the overall knowledge landscape of the Palmyrene hypogea.

The Ingholt diaries are a unique research resource that greatly increases our understanding of the Palmyrene south-west necropolis and the hypogea. Information on excavation techniques, the tombs, and their inscriptions, the south-west necropolis in general, and Palmyra in the 1920s can be drawn from the diaries and the archive. They are thus of interest for archaeologists, epigraphists, historians, and cultural heritage specialists alike, and allow us to study archaeological remains as well as an archaeological excavation and historical setting through the records of Ingholt.

Acknowledgements

The authors thank the Ny Carlsberg Glyptotek for allowing access to the material since 2012 and for the rights to publish it. We also thank the ALIPH Foundation and Carlsberg Foundation for generously respectively funding Archive Archaeology: Preserving and Sharing Palmyra's Cultural Heritage through Harald Ingholt's Digital Archives (grant held by Rubina Raja, agreement 2019-1267) and the Palmyra Portrait Project (grant held by Rubina Raja, agreement CF15-0493). Since 2012, when the Palmyra Portrait Project was founded, several individuals have contributed to the digitization and study of the material. The authors wish to thank everyone who has participated in and contributed to the projects over the years.

---

[124] See al-Asʿad and Taha 1965.

Works Cited

al-Asʿad, K. and O. Taha. 1965. 'Madfan Zabdʿateh al-Tadmuri [The Tomb of Zabdʿateh the Palmyrene]', *Annales archéologiques de Syrie*, 15: 29–46 (in Arabic).

al-Hariri, K. 2013. 'The Tomb of ʿAqraban', *Studia Palmyreńskie*, 12: 149–57.

Bobou, O., J. V. Jensen, N. Breintoft Kristensen, R. Raja, and R. Randeris Thomsen. 2021. *Studies on Palmyrene Sculpture: A Translation of Harald Ingholt's 'Studier over Palmyrensk Skulptur', Edited and with Commentary*, Studies in Palmyrene Archaeology and History, 1 (Turnhout: Brepols).

Bobou, O., N. Breintoft Kristensen, S. McAvoy, and R. Raja. 2020. 'Archive Archaeology in Palmyra, Syria a New 3D Reconstruction of the Tomb of Ḥairan', *Digital Applications in Archaeology and Cultural Heritage*, 19: e00164.

Bobou, O., A. C. Miranda, R. Raja, and J. Steding (forthcoming). 'Harald Ingholt and Palmyra: Documenting the Oasis City through the Legacy of the Journal *Berytus*' Founder', *Berytus*.

Bobou, O., A. C. Miranda, R. Raja, and J.-B. Yon. 2022. *The Ingholt Archive: The Palmyrene Material*, Archive Archaeology, 2, 4 vols (Turnhout: Brepols).

Bobou, O., A. C. Miranda, and R. Raja. 2021. 'The Ingholt Archive: Data from the Project, "Archive Archaeology: Preserving and Sharing Palmyra's Cultural Heritage through Harald Ingholt's Digital Archives"', *Journal of Open Archaeology Data*, 9.6: 1–10.

—— 2022. 'Harald Ingholt's Twentieth-Century Archive of Palmyrene Sculptures: "Unleashing" Archived Archaeological Material of Modern Conflict Zones', *Journal of Eastern Mediterranean Archaeology and Heritage Studies*, 10.1: 74–101.

Bobou, O. and R. Raja. 2023. *Palmyrene Sarcophagi*, Studies in Palmyrene Archaeology and History (Turnhout: Brepols).

Colledge, M. A. R. 1967. *The Parthians* (London: Thames and Hudson).

Cussini, E. 2019. 'Daughters and Wives: Defining Women in Palmyrene Inscriptions', in S. Krag and R. Raja (eds), *Women, Children and the Family in Palmyra*, Palmyrene Studies, 3 (Copenhagen: Royal Danish Academy of Sciences and Letters), pp. 67–81.

Drijvers, H. J. W. 1976. *The Religion of Palmyra* (Leiden: Brill).

Gelin, M. 2002. *L'archéologie en Syrie et au Liban à l'époque du Mandat 1919–1946: histoire et organisation* (Paris: Geuthner).

Grainger, J. D. 2013. *The Battle for Syria, 1918–1920* (Woodbridge: Boydell & Brewer).

Greenhalgh, M. 2016. *Syria's Monuments: Their Survival and Destruction* (Leiden: Brill).

Ingholt, H. 1928. *Studier over Palmyrensk Skulptur* (Copenhagen: Reitzel).

—— 1932. 'Quelques fresques récemment découvertes à Palmyre', *Acta archaeologica*, 3: 1–20.

—— 1935. 'Five Dated Tombs from Palmyra', *Berytus*, 2: 57–120.

—— 1938. 'Inscriptions and Sculptures from Palmyra II', *Berytus*, 5: 93–140.

—— 1962. 'Palmyrene Inscription from the Tomb of Malkû', *Mélanges de l'Université Saint Joseph*, 38: 99–119.

—— 1966. 'Some Sculptures from the Tomb of Malkû at Palmyra', in M. L. Bernhard (ed.), *Mélanges offerts à Kazimierz Michalowski* (Warsaw: Państwowe Wydawnictwo Naukowe), pp. 457–76.

—— 1970–1971. 'The Sarcophagus of Beʿelai and Other Sculptures from the Tomb of Malkû, Palmyra', *Mélanges de l'Université Saint-Joseph*, 46: 173–200.

—— 1974. 'Two Unpublished Tombs from the Southwest Necropolis of Palmyra, Syria', in D. K. Kouymjian (ed.), *Near Eastern Numismatics, Iconography, Epigraphy and History: Studies in Honor of George C. Miles* (Beirut: American University of Beirut), pp. 37–54.

—— 1976. 'Varia Tadmorea', in E. Frézouls (ed.), *Palmyre: Bilan et perspectives; colloque de Strasbourg 18–20 Octobre 1973* (Strasbourg: Association pour l'étude de la civilisation romaine), pp. 101–37.

Işık, F., J. M. Reynolds, and C. Roueché. 2007. *Girlanden-Sarkophage aus Aphrodisias* (Mainz: Von Zabern).

Korkut, T. 2006. *Girlanden-Ostotheken aus Kalkstein in Pamphylien und Kilikien: Untersuchungen zu Typologie, Ikonographie und Chronologie* (Mainz: Von Zabern).

Krag, S. 2018. *Funerary Representations of Palmyrene Women from the First Century BC to the Third Century AD*, Studies in Classical Archaeology, 3 (Turnhout: Brepols).

Nielsen, A. M. 2019. 'Palmyra in the Glyptotek', in A. M. Nielsen and R. Raja (eds), *The Road to Palmyra* (Copenhagen: Ny Carlsberg Glyptotek), pp. 23–40.

Ouahes, I. 2018. *Syria and Lebanon under the French Mandate: Cultural Imperialism and the Workings of Empire* (London: I.B. Tauris).

Østrup, J. E. 1894. *Skiftende Horizonter* (Copenhagen: Gyldendalske Boghandel Forlag).

—— 1895. *Historisk-topografiske Bidrag til Kendskabet til den syriske Ørken* (Copenhagen: Royal Danish Academy of Sciences and Letters).

Papagianni, E. 2016. *Attische Sarkophage mit Eroten und Girlanden* (Wiesbaden: Harrassowitz).

Ploix de Rotrou, G. and H. Seyrig. 1933. 'Khirbet el-Sané', *Syria*, 14.1: 12–19.

Raja, R. 2019a. 'Harald Ingholt and Palmyra', in A. M. Nielsen and R. Raja (eds), *The Road to Palmyra* (Copenhagen: Ny Carlsberg Glyptotek), pp. 41–64.

—— 2019b. 'Harald Ingholt – og Palmyra, Oasen i den Syriske Ørken', in E. Mortensen and R. Raja (eds), *Store danske arkæologer: På jagt efter fortidens byer* (Aarhus: Aarhus University Press), pp. 105–31.

—— 2019c. *The Palmyra Collection: Ny Carlsberg Glyptotek* (Copenhagen: Ny Carlsberg Glyptotek).

—— 2021a. '"Den Smukkeste Kvindebuste, Jeg Endnu Har Set": The Palmyra Excavation Diaries of Harald Ingholt, 1924–1928', in R. Raja, J. Steding, and J.-B. Yon (eds), *Excavating Palmyra: Harald Ingholt's Excavation Diaries; A Transcript, Translation, and Commentary*, I, Studies in Palmyrene Archaeology and History, 4 (Turnhout: Brepols), pp. 23–70.

—— 2021b. 'Reading the Ingholt Excavation Diaries, and Acknowledgements', in R. Raja, J. Steding, and J.-B. Yon (eds), *Excavating Palmyra: Harald Ingholt's Excavation Diaries; A Transcript, Translation, and Commentary*, Studies in Palmyrene Archaeology and History, 4, 2 vols (Turnhout: Brepols), I, pp. 7–9.

—— 2022. *Pearl of the Desert: A History of Palmyra* (Oxford: Oxford University Press).

Raja, R., O. Bobou, and J.-B. Yon (forthcoming). *The Palmyrene Funerary Portraits*, Studies in Palmyrene Archaeology and History (Turnhout: Brepols).

Raja, R. and S. McAvoy. 2019. 'Hypogeum of Ḥairan, Main Reconstruction 3D Model' <https://sketchfab.com/3d-models/hypogeum-of-hairan-reconstruction-822c65461d824f2bb88b442225db5dc3> [accessed 10 February 2022].

Raja, R., K. Schnädelbach, and J. Steding. 2022. 'A New Map of Palmyra's Southwest Necropolis Based on the Excavation Diaries of Harald Ingholt', *Zeitschrift für Orientarchäologie*, 14: 230–73.

Raja, R. and A. H. Sørensen. 2015a. 'The "Beauty" of Palmyra and Qasr Abjad (Palmyra): New Discoveries in the Archive of Harald Ingholt', *Journal of Roman Archaeology*, 28: 439–50.

—— 2015b. *Harald Ingholt and Palmyra* (Aarhus: AU SUN-Tryk).

—— 2019. 'Historiography: Danish Research from Johannes Østrup to the Palmyra Portrait Project', in H. Eristov, C. Vibert-Guigue, W. al-Asʿad, and N. Sarkis (eds), *Les Tombeaux des trois frères à Palmyre: mission archéologique franco-syrienne 2004–2009* (Beirut: Institut français du Proche Orient), pp. 59–64.

Raja, R. and J. Steding. 2021. 'Harald Ingholt's Excavation Diaries from his Fieldwork in Palmyra: An Open Data Online Resource', *Journal of Open Archaeology Data*, 9.8: 1–9.

—— 2022. 'Harald Ingholt's Fieldwork Diaries: Legacy Data of the Early Twentieth Century', in A. C. Miranda and R. Raja (eds), *Archival Historiographies: The Impact of 20th-Century Legacy Data on Archaeological Investigations*, Archive Archaeology, 3 (Turnhout: Brepols), pp. 83–100.

Raja, R., J. Steding, and J.-B. Yon (eds). 2021. *Excavating Palmyra: Harald Ingholt's Excavation Diaries; A Transcript, Translation, and Commentary*, Studies in Palmyrene Archaeology and History, 4, 2 vols (Turnhout: Brepols).

Sartre-Fauriat, A. 2019. 'The Discovery and Reception of Palmyra', in A. M. Nielsen and R. Raja (eds), *The Road to Palmyra* (Copenhagen: Ny Carlsberg Glyptotek), pp. 65–76.

Schnädelbach, K. 2010. *Topographia Palmyrena*, I: *Topography* (Damascus: République arabe syrienne, Direction générale des antiquités et des musées, in collab. with Deutsches Archäologisches Institut, Orient-Abteilung).

Sobernheim, M. 1902. 'Palmyrenische Inschriften', *Beiträge zur Assyriologie und semitischen Sprachwissenschaft*, 4: 207–19.

Sommer, M. 2018. *Palmyra: A History* (Abingdon: Routledge).

Sørensen, A. H. 2016. 'Palmyrene Tomb Paintings in Context', in R. Raja and A. Kropp (eds), *The World of Palmyra*, Palmyrene Studies, 1 (Copenhagen: Danish Academy of Science and Letters), pp. 103–17.

Spencer, C. 2022. *Shifting Horizons: Observations from a Ride through the Syrian Desert and Asia Minor; A Translation of Johannes Elith Østrupt's 'Skiftende horizonter'*, Archive Archaeology, 1 (Turnhout: Brepols).

Stucky, R. A. 2008. 'Henri Seyrig: Engagierter Archäologe und Verwalter des Antikendienstes während der Mandatszeit', in C. Trümpler (ed.), *Das Große Spiel: Archäologie und Politik zur Zeit des Kolonialismus (1860–1940)* (Cologne: DuMont), pp. 504–11.

Tanabe, K. (ed.). 1986. *Sculptures of Palmyra*, I, Memoirs of the Ancient Orient Museum, 1 (Tokyo: Ancient Orient Museum).

Tauber, E. 1994. *The Formation of Modern Iraq and Syria* (London: Routledge).

Ulrich, R. B. 2007. *Roman Woodworking* (New Haven: Yale University Press).

Yon, J.-B. 2016. 'Inscriptions from the Necropolis of Palmyra in the Diaries of H. Ingholt', in A. Kropp and R. Raja (eds), *The World of Palmyra*, Palmyrene Studies, 1 (Copenhagen: Danish Academy of Science and Letters), pp. 118–25.

8. Pompeii as an Archive

Eric Poehler
Classics Department, University of Massachusetts Amherst
(epoehler@classics.umass.edu)

Introduction

In 2011, Kevin Cole, Miko Flohr, and I introduced a collection of essays with a metaphor claiming that 'Pompeii is the great laboratory of the Roman archaeologist'.[1] Our choice of the word 'laboratory' was deliberate.[2] With it, we intended it to convey a sense that the long history of excavation at Pompeii was an evolving scientific endeavour, one that is now approaching the end of its third century of operation. More specifically, we wanted to foreground the notion that Pompeii had been not only the place of inspiration for methodological innovation, but also served as a crucial testing ground for the application of emerging methods, wherever they were invented. Thus, Pompeii famously gave Mau the idea of examining Roman painting within a framework of four illusionistic styles, but as those frescoes decayed from the walls, the city also became a landscape of bare masonry, ripe for analysis with new stratigraphic tools. Yet, this narrow distinction between inspiring and applying methods hides a wider gulf between Pompeii as a place where investigation is conducted, a 'laboratory', and Pompeii as the subject matter of that same investigation. How does the microscope examine itself? The insufficiency of the laboratory metaphor demonstrates that (at least) another is required: Pompeii is also an archive. Yet, as Freud had understood long ago, the excavation of Pompeii and the archive it produces has a similar doubling metaphor, reflecting both the thing being recorded and the record itself. We shape the archive as we record things into it and reshape it again actively as we access the memory it retains or passively as the site labours through time. Indeed, 'the destruction of Pompeii was only beginning now that it had been dug up'.[3]

This paper explores the ancient city of Pompeii through the metaphor of the archive and places the long history of its study and publication within the context of legacy studies, also called archive archaeology. The purpose of this endeavour is threefold. The first goal is to express how much research in contemporary Pompeian studies relies on what might be considered, in another context or at another site, to be legacy information. Therefore, I pose the question 'is Pompeii an archive?' to explore the definitions of legacy studies and archive archaeology before comparing those definitions to the conditions at Pompeii, parsing the distinction between legacy data and legacy materials along the way. The second goal of this paper is to touch upon the long history of Pompeian studies and set out some of the most important conventions and historical factors shaping how one might use those legacy materials. In this, I rely upon Eric Moormann's fulsome history of the reception of Pompeii and Herculaneum, but even more so on the work of Ann Laidlaw's indispensable chapter — 'Mining the Early Published Sources: Problems and Pitfalls'. Here I hope to complement their efforts, at times expanding upon them and setting them within a different frame.[4] Specifically, I divide Pompeii's historiography into four overlapping periods based on the manner in which each era approached the task of organizing, preserving, and/or sharing information. This discussion sets the stage for the paper's final goal: a brief presentation of two contemporary digital humanities projects that serve as large-scale infrastructures for Pompeii's legacy information. Examination of the Pompeii Bibliography and Mapping Project (PBMP) and the Pompeii Artistic Landscape Project (PALP) demonstrates not only that Pompeii is an archive of legacy materials, but also that it can be used effectively as a scaffold for an enormous quantity of legacy data, as well as for previously published and future information.

---

[1] Poehler, Flohr, and Cole 2011, 1.

[2] Subsequently, I have recognized Foss's (2007, 28) similar use of this term and phrasing and suspect his description influenced our own.

[3] Freud 1953–1974, x, 176. See Orrells (2011) for a full discussion of the metaphor.

[4] Laidlaw 2007; Moormann 2015, 7–94.

Defining Legacy Studies at Pompeii

Although this is not the place for an exhaustive examination of legacy studies and archive archaeology, it is useful to set out some basic definitions for the following discussion. In considering these definitions, it is also useful to use Pompeii as a foil, and to test our understanding of legacy studies against the variety of data the ancient city presents. First, then, definitions. Because legacy data exist within most fields of study, their most basic definition is simply 'data from obsolete information systems'.[5] The breadth and vagueness of that definition allow for wide application, but still require some careful thought about the meaning of each term: 'data', 'obsolete', and 'information systems'. Within archaeology, there are definitions that are more specific, but which remain necessarily expansive. For example, archive archaeology has been defined as the management and use of 'the cumulative finds, records, and associated data that result from a piece of archaeological fieldwork, normally but not always excavation'.[6] Similarly, our team at Isthmia understood

> legacy data as any data derived from archaeological research that has not been fully processed and organized, analysed, and interpreted, and — most importantly — published. It is essentially 'old' archaeological data that has been largely or entirely abandoned.[7]

Although broad, these definitions would seem to match the common imagining of legacy data: boxes of unread pottery or bones stacked in storerooms, rows of notebooks or rolls of uninked drawings on bookshelves, and languishing field sites, encroached upon by vegetation.

At first blush, Pompeii might not appear to fit these definitions or our imaging of them. The site is significantly maintained for the millions of annual tourists, thousands of artefacts are arranged for display around the city and in museums, and one can read from a bibliography containing well over twenty thousand titles. A closer look, however, suggests that much of Pompeii is legacy data. To make this claim, one might first appeal to the concepts of age and obsolescence. There is no doubt that the archaeological evidence from Pompeii, *in situ*, in storerooms, and in print, is old. In fact, some parts of Pompeii have been exposed for longer than classical archaeology has been an academic discipline,[8] and some Pompeian buildings have now existed in the modern world longer than they ever did in Antiquity.[9] To give scale to these anecdotes we might consider that in 1859, the year before Giuseppe Fiorelli became superintendent and introduced more stratigraphic methods of excavation, approximately 200,000 m² of the ancient city had already been exposed.[10] These great spans of time also separate us from the people who excavated Pompeii. Indeed, our now six-decade separation from the regular exposure of the landscape of AD 79 is what makes the most recent excavations in Region V (and elsewhere) seem all the more breathtaking.[11]

Such glimpses of the ancient city's long history of excavation might also support the idea that much of Pompeii can be studied as an archive based on the 'finds and associated data' those investigations produced. Such a claim of legacy status could be based on two related issues. One issue is that so much of the data collected for Pompeii is significantly different in format from what is produced today that it must be updated prior to use in contemporary endeavours. This is well illustrated by the series of transformations that earliest excavators' notes have gone through. Beginning as unpublished notes, these early (1748–1860) primary documents were collected by Giuseppe Fiorelli and published in 1860 as the three-volume *Pompeianarum antiquiatum historiae* (PAH).[12] Then, in 2006, these data were republished and collated by Pagano and Prisciandaro who interwove references to other early reports, and organized the notes by date and with reference to modern addresses, appellations, and publications.[13] Although exceedingly helpful, these references still lead back to documents using the legacy systems, some of which remain unpublished.

Age compounds another problem, simple absence, as so much of what is considered valuable today was previously ignored and went unrecorded or unstudied. It is not surprising, perhaps, to imagine that the innovative brickwork within the humble shops found during the first excavations in 1748 were of little interest when the

---

5 Allison 2008.
6 Swain 2012, 351.
7 Ellis, Poehler, and Emmerson (forthcoming).
8 Dyson 2006.

9 For example, the Quadriporticus building was approximately 210 years old when Mt Vesuvius erupted (*c.* 130 BC–AD 79) but was first excavated in 1766, having now been exposed for more than 250 years.
10 Poehler 2022, fig. 1.
11 Osanna 2019.
12 See Laidlaw (2007, 622) for details of the *PAH*'s peculiar organization.
13 Pagano and Prisciandaro 2006.

spectacular remains of the Casa del Torello di Bronzo were only a few doors down. In the twenty-first century, however, a return to their study has produced a detailed depiction of a Pompeian bar, rebuilt in the latest construction techniques.[14] This is one of many such projects to study the standing remains, which, having been exposed for centuries, are no longer covered in painted plaster.[15] We tend not to think of the standing architectural remains of a site as legacy data, but they are not different than a box of pottery, a cache of coins, the baulk of a trench, or a martyra within it. Each of these materials can be studied or restudied as long as they continue to exist.

Although not as visible, Pompeii also has a (depressingly) great quantity of artefactual material that remains unexamined, and only recently has effort been expended to study them or contextualize them. For example, only in the last few years have the ceramics from excavations conducted in the 1970s and 1980s in the forum, suburban baths, and at Tower VIII/Porta di Nola been published.[16] In 2003, Duncan-Jones noted that although Pompeii's 'almost 40,000 coins dwarfs most other groups of Roman-site finds', nonetheless, 'further evidence remains unpublished and a fuller survey [...] remains very desirable'.[17] The most extensive research on finds from older excavations has been done by Penelope Allison in pursuit of a better understanding of room functions, particularly at the Casa del Menandro. But, because so many artefacts were noted (at best) and discarded, the results could not be 'so much a catalogue of the finds from these buildings but rather a spatial analysis of the contents of these buildings'.[18] For the oldest excavations, Pagano and Prisciandaro's compendium is again invaluable, not least for the extensive (more than 3200 records) table of finds, extracted from the daily, narrative entries. These records have now been digitized and mapped (as is possible) by the Pompeii Bibliography and Mapping Project.[19]

The preceding discussion of languishing objects, however, also demonstrates some deficiency in our language on these topics, as alluded to by Freud in the introduction. Thus, while archive archaeology is rightly interested in 'the cumulative finds, records, and associated data', there are significant differences between what might be called *legacy materials* and *legacy data* — the most notable being the methods by which one can study each type. Indeed, the examination of many legacy materials can be done by employing methodologies common in the field today, with an end result — the creation of new data within new systems — often being equivalent to what transpires in a modern, 'non-legacy' investigation. Legacy materials, then, are the physical objects resulting from a previous investigation that might, in the present, be studied or restudied using a variety of archaeological techniques to produce new information. Legacy data, on the other hand, are the resulting records of that previous investigation's actions, the transformation of physical activities and objects into archaeological information, structured (or not) within various documentary systems and media.

This distinction produces its own tension because, if legacy materials can be studied to produce new data in new forms and formats, then these will be hard to reintegrate with the legacy data from the same original project. The use of legacy data, naturally and therefore, requires its own dedicated set of methods and procedures to push the structure of old information into closer proximity to the new data. Such methods are (comparatively) still in their infancy and have tended to focus first on issues of format, especially in digitizing analogue records, which can appear to be relatively straightforward. Embedded within these legacy data, however, are the theoretical and methodological decisions that produced them, which likely gave those legacy data a different shape than those produced today. For example, a spatially defined area excavated fifty years ago, even if that area is given a label and number (e.g. 'Deposit 1'), does not mean it is conceptually or functionally interchangeable with 'Stratigraphic Unit 1' excavated last year in the same location.[20] Archaeological theory, research priorities, and the methodological practices to implement these will have changed, such that the data about 'Deposits' and 'Stratigraphic Units' cannot always occupy the same

---

14   Boman n.d.

15   For a brief history of masonry analysis at Pompeii, see Poehler 2022.

16   Cottica and Curti 2008; De Simone and others 2020; Peña 2020.

17   Duncan-Jones 2003, 162–63. This work is slowly being accomplished by the Rinvenimenti monetali a Pompei project. See Bowes 2022 for the most recent status and application of these publications.

18   Allison 2006, 5; 2004. Allison (2021) has returned to this problem in the search for seasonality at Pompeii.

19   Pompeii Bibliography and Mapping Project 2017.

---

20   See Ellis, Poehler, and Emmerson (forthcoming) for a discussion of the attendant theoretical and methodological issues and their application at the site of Isthmia, Greece.

column in a table, and perhaps not even the same table in a database.

To reconnect these newly generated data from studying legacy material with other legacy information from the original investigation, therefore, still requires reconciliation. In fact, this reconciliation process is one of the essential tasks of studying legacy data and often involves finding and implementing an 'intellectual common denominator' that makes evidence from different eras comparable, if not necessarily perfectly interoperable. Very often that denominator is spatial, with modern records providing a greater resolution than earlier counterparts. A common example from Pompeii is when a fresco, now lost to time, was noted in a given room, but the particular wall it once decorated is unknown. Similarly, it is sometimes possible only to associate the finds recorded in the early notebooks to a building rather than any room within it. In these cases, a researcher must either combine all the data in the more general spatial category — eschewing more fine-grained analyses — or set the legacy data beside the other information as a special case, foregoing its direct integration and using it more sparingly. When the spatial categories are small (e.g. at room level) the former strategy might be tolerable, but when they are large (e.g. at building level) the latter will be preferable. In either case, the integration of legacy data is most fully made through writing and argumentation, explaining how these data were produced, how they are to be used, and asking the reader to endure more ambiguities than might be found in a study of entirely contemporary evidence.

Even these few examples are enough to demonstrate that how information is designed is what makes it useful, extensible, accessible, and sustainable. They also reveal that the word 'system' holds more meaning than 'obsolete' in the definition of legacy data as coming from 'obsolete systems'. Whether one is concerned with legacy materials or legacy data, a fundamental task in their re-examination is coming to terms with the intellectual (i.e. what is recorded and/or recovered) and material (i.e. what objects contain the data) frameworks that gave shape to the data that are available today as an archive. To further consider the metaphor of Pompeii as an archive now requires its examination within the evolving context of the nearly three centuries of excavation (and other methods) and publication (and not) and the identification of some of the systems and frameworks particular to Pompeii.

Pompeii's Long History of Study

As with the definition of legacy studies, this discussion cannot offer a comprehensive intellectual history of Pompeian studies. Instead, the purpose of this section is to make a broad sketch of the historical and academic forces that shaped the outputs of research so that one can be better prepared to use those data appropriately. In large measure, this means grappling with publications, which, like Pompeii itself, is not commonly thought of in the context of legacy studies and archive archaeology. In fact, in one definition, publication was positioned as the antithetical state to legacy status. Nonetheless, the duration of Pompeii's publication history and the volume of its output make this framework appropriate because, just as the evolving archaeological methodologies that exposed Pompeii's physical remains produced differently shaped records, so too did the evolving practices (and audiences) of scholarly communication constrain the form of those records still further. To use an archaeological metaphor, field methods and recording practices serve to sieve information about the past, while the format and organization of publication form a second (narrative) screen through which archaeological data must pass. Therefore, the following section examines Pompeii's long history of scholarship to illuminate the effects of these filters so that one might avoid some of the many 'problems and pitfalls' and better utilize the information one might extract.

Name and Number (1748–c. 1860)

The first decades of excavation at Pompeii were scarcely archaeological and not at all interested in the sharing of knowledge about Antiquity.[21] Excavation was conducted horizontally rather than vertically, controlled by various governments and private interests, and its results were held back by both politics and the limited means of dissemination. In 1891, Furchheim would open his bibliography of the Vesuvian cities by lamenting that 'few are the publications on the excavations of Herculaneum, Pompeii, and Stabia before the middle of the nineteenth century'.[22] Laidlaw's more recent assessment of the documents of the period, for indeed many are not publications, is even more pessimistic: 'especially in the first sixty years or more, the reports consist mostly of long lists of finds and not much

---

21 Parslow 1995, 207–08, 260–62; Foss 2007, 31.
22 Furchheim 1891, xiii.

else'.²³ Conversely, these early excavators helped to establish the concept of the archaeological notebook,²⁴ and by the end of the eighteenth century witnessed a flourishing tradition of grand folios filled with lavish engravings that provide some of the only glimpses of parts of Pompeii and Herculaneum long since disappeared. Works by Saint-Non (1781–1786) and Piranesi (1783) mark the start of this tradition, but it continued well into the nineteenth century, best illustrated by Mazois's four volumes (1824–1838) *Les ruines de Pompéi*.

It is in this period, however, that the bewildering disorganization of Pompeian scholarship begins to require more systematic means of accessing the site and its information. In this process, the tenure of Giuseppe Fiorelli (1860–1875) provides a watershed moment in and for legacy studies at Pompeii. His efforts to organize the city's topography by means of an address system as well as the century-long archival record (mentioned above) were so impactful that one must divide Pompeii's legacy information into periods of before and after Fiorelli. Before Fiorelli's system (i.e. 1868), new buildings were labelled using an idiosyncratic naming convention that highlighted significant finds (e.g. Casa del Chirurgo), characteristics (e.g. Villa delle Colonne a Mosaico), or even modern visitors (e.g. Casa della Regina Carolina). Over time, this system of nomenclature became unwieldy: of the 614 known buildings with given names, nearly half (45 per cent) have at least two names, approximately one tenth shared the same name with another building, and a few buildings acquired as many as fourteen names.²⁵ The natural problems of disambiguation were compounded by contemporary cartographic conventions. Between 1776 and 1830, the only way to locate a building was to number it on a map and add a corresponding label of its name in the margin. This practice both excluded hundreds of places from reference and made the system so cumbersome that by 1851 Overbeck's map used more than one hundred numbers and letters, which were themselves overlain by a grid to help locate such small notations.²⁶

The difficulties of such inexact and inconsistent reference systems undoubtedly elevated the value of numbering every doorway, an idea that had already been advanced by the 1830s. The doorway numbering system had several inherent advantages, not least among them breaking the reliance on (too often not) unique names for places. Unsurprisingly, however, it also had its challenges. First among them was deciding how to apply the numbers and what would be their unit of reference. For example, Carlo Bonucci's (1827–1837) original conception was a 'down-and-back' process in which he labelled all the doorways on one side of a street before returning to the beginning on the opposite side (e.g. Fig. 8.1, strada d'Olconio). This produced numbers in ascending order on one side of the street and descending order on the other. Bonucci's system worked well for streets that were completely excavated, but Domenico Spinelli (1850–1863) recognized that it might be decades before the full length of Via Stabiana was cleared, and it made little sense for his discoveries to be left so long without reference (e.g. Fig. 8.1, strada Stabiana). Spinelli adapted the doorway model into his 'shoelace' system in which each new doorway on a street was numbered as it was discovered, criss-crossing the street as excavation proceeded.²⁷

What united Bonucci's and Spinelli's doorways numbering systems was the notion of the street as the unit of reference, a natural by-product of contemporary excavation procedures that followed streets horizontally and only revealed hints of what was behind the façades. Their street chasing generated a concomitant expectation for how topographical information should be organized, which subsequently influenced how Pompeii's epigraphic record would be catalogued as well. Thus, when Zangemeister and Shoene (1871) published the first volume of inscriptions from Pompeii, individual entries were ordered first by street, then by reference to doorway numbers, and finally by reference to each other. For example, the second entry is under the heading of Via della Fortuna, noted between doorways twelve and thirteen, and recorded as found above the first entry.²⁸ The map published to accompany this volume is remarkable, not only because it shows all these contemporary topographical reference systems deployed at once (i.e. names and numbers, an overlying grid, and both doorway number systems), but also for being the first and only map ever to do so.

Within a few years, Fiorelli's address system superseded all others, though not without controversy, alter-

---

23 Laidlaw 2007, 623.

24 Dyson 2006, 17.

25 Calculations are based on the names reported in van der Poel 1983.

26 Overbeck (1856, 435–38) published three pages of map locations, each with a corresponding grid location.

27 See Borriello 2008, Poehler (forthcoming).

28 Zangemeister and Schöne 1871, 2.

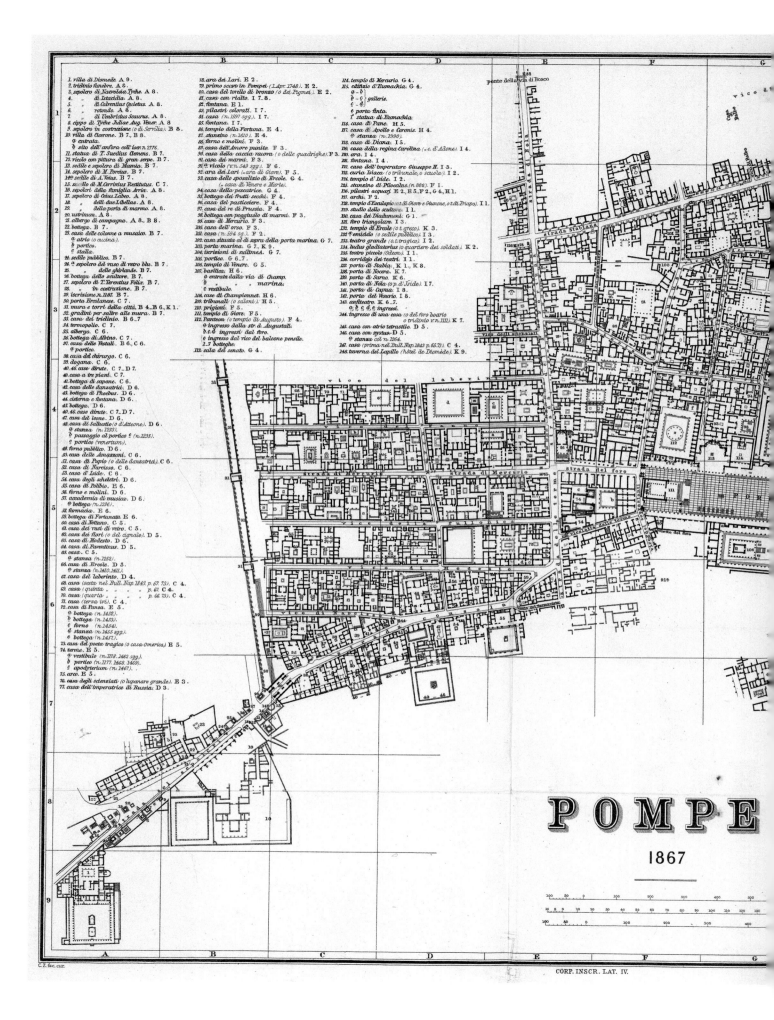

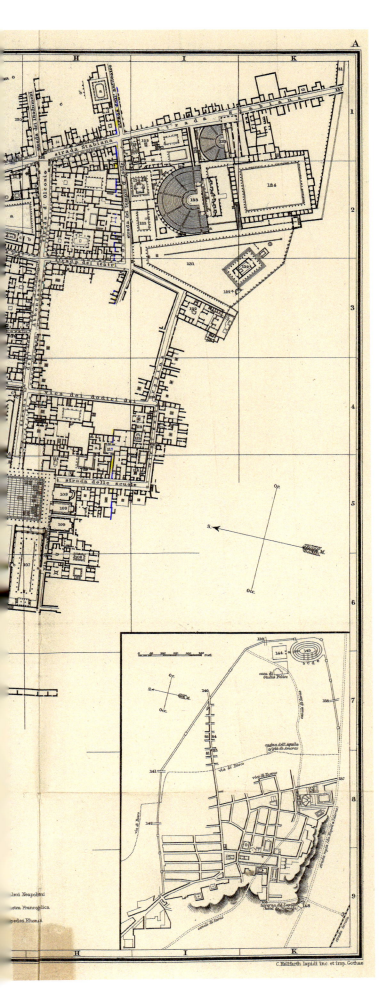

Figure 8.1. Pompei, 1867 (Zangemeister and Schöne 1871).

natives, and revision.[29] Rather than the street as a unit of reference, Fiorelli chose those areas that the streets defined — city blocks, insulae — as his primary units. By grouping these city blocks within nine larger regions and surrounding each block with numbers representing the doorways leading into individual buildings, Fiorelli produced a simple, extensible, and unified system for topographical information. Nearly 150 years later, it remains in use, proving to be an exceptionally durable model.

For our purposes, this history of topographical references highlights the chain of influences shaping Pompeii's legacy information; from field methods, to recording practices, to modes of communication. Thus, an excavation method that privileged the exposure of streets unsurprisingly led to using the street as a crucial element in documenting, locating, and disambiguating what was uncovered. This choice had profound impacts on the form of related scholarship, including underwriting nearly a century of cartography as well as shaping the information design of even the related fields (e.g. epigraphy). Fiorelli's time saw radical changes to Pompeii's excavation method and focus of research, which coincided with the introduction of his new address system and publication models (see below). Yet, because of Fiorelli's successes, a great gulf emerged between the information produced in his time and the preceding century, an unavoidable consequence that has required the creation of expansive concordances to the prior systems and an array of nineteenth-century maps, both of which must be constant companions when using early sources.[30]

Publish and Typologize (*c.* 1820–*c.* 1940)

The divide in the structure of information was exacerbated by the sheer number of works already published in the older systems. By the beginning of Fiorelli's tenure, the rate of publication about Pompeii had already been advancing steadily for several decades, spurred by the return of the Bourbon monarchy to Italy and the

---

29 Poehler (forthcoming).

30 See van der Poel 1981, 505–12 for long lists of concordances between numbering systems. Schefold (1957, 300–56) has useful corrigenda of museum inventory numbers of frescos, reference numbers used by other authors (especially Helbig 1868), and the corresponding address in the city.

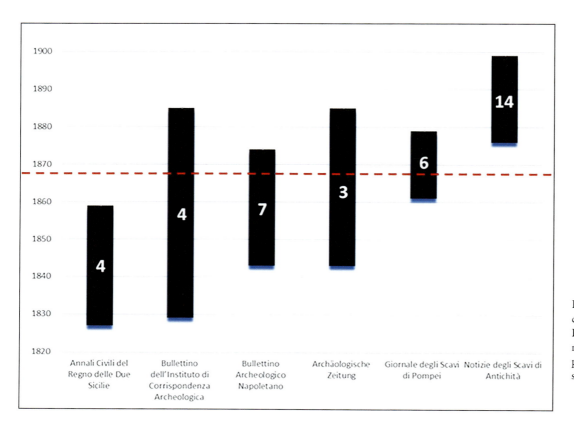

Figure 8.2. Chart of nineteenth-century journals dedicated to Pompeian subjects. The dotted red line indicates the first publication of Fiorelli's address system in 1868 (chart by author).

development of state-sponsored cultural and scientific institutions. These institutions disseminated their results in new, dedicated journals (joined later by others) to produce a steady drum beat of notices regarding the new discoveries. In fact, more than a hundred journals published over 2500 articles about Pompeian material, the great majority in the second half of the century, which both permitted scholars around Europe to keep up with the ongoing archaeological research and exacerbated the gap with pre-Fiorellian systems of nomenclature.[31]

The publication of books also exploded in this period, underwritten not only by improvements in publishing technologies that transformed the book into an industrial product, but also by a public curiosity spurred from increased tourism.[32] In fact, between 1820 and 1860 a great plurality (perhaps one-third) of books published concerning Pompeii were guides, memoires, and travelogues.[33] Perhaps the earliest and most successful of these public-oriented issues was William Gell's *Pompeiana*. First published in 1817–1819, prior to Fiorelli's birth, it was reissued five times, the last in 1875, at the end of Fiorelli's tenure as Pompeii's superintendent. In total, the publication rate for Pompeii quintupled between 1815 and 1900, from twenty-one to 103 publications in those years, respectively.

Within Pompeii's more specialized scientific literature of the nineteenth century were intellectual trends common across many scientific disciplines of the age, most notably the organization of artefacts into classes by material, style, and type.[34] By mid-century, the guidebook to the Musée Royal Bourbon (1854) shows the order of exhibitions to have been first by frescoes, then by mosaics, sculptures, inscriptions, bronze statues, ancient glass, terracotta, and finally precious objects.[35] Likewise, contemporary handbooks to the excavations, such as Overbeck's 1856 *Pompeji in seinen Gebäuden*, also took a typological (and telescopic) approach, describing first the fortifications and streets and plazas, before turning

---

[31] The six early journals illustrated in Figure 8.2 published 70 per cent (481 of 690) of their articles prior to 1869, the first year after Fiorelli's nomenclature system was first published.

[32] Sweet 2015, 248–52.

[33] Of the 2025 books published between 1800 and 1899, 655 contained permutations of the words guide, Italy, itinerary, journey, letter, memoire, Naples, souvenir, tour, travel, visit, or voyage or in the title.

[34] Trigger 2006, 75–79.

[35] d'Aloe 1854.

to public buildings, private houses, tombs, and finally *instrumentum domesticum*.³⁶ In the last quarter of the century, this typologizing spirit would be applied at a city-wide scale, first in Fiorelli's (1873) chronological arrangement of building materials by stone type and later in August Mau's (1882) stylistic approach to fresco painting, based in part on Fiorelli's masonry schema.³⁷

A primary purpose of this typological method, however, was to arrange the subject matter chronologically by appealing to an evolutionary framework that had become the dominant explanatory construct across the century. At Pompeii, the sequence of historically known peoples was deployed to explain building techniques, thus associating the Etruscans with a yellow travertine (i.e. Sarno stone), the Samnites with a grey tuff (i.e. Nocera tuff), and the colonizing Romans with brick and cement. Evolving from a rustic, Italic origin, Fiorelli's late Samnite Pompeii would embrace the progress of 'Hellenic art [that] dominated with majesty and grace in all the plastic manifestations of the spirit',³⁸ producing a golden age in the late second century BC. Nearly seventy years later, Amedeo Maiuri would propose a devolution, arguing that the period following the earthquake of AD 63 witnessed the flight of the noble elite from the city and a collapse in vulgar commercialism.³⁹ For some, this evolutionary model produced a 'creation myth' that endures into current scholarship.⁴⁰

In sum, the impacts of this period of Pompeii's intellectual history on the shape of its legacy data are so common and so broad that they now seem indivisible from the basic scholarly endeavour. That is, by publishing so much and so widely (as was common across all disciplines), this period required future scholars to invest deeply in the practice and the attendant procedures of reading. There became so many resources, in so many far-flung libraries, written in so many languages, that scholars became archivists, bibliophiles, and linguists by necessity. Those who did were rewarded with new common standards and conventions in both form and format that made sharing and synthesizing vast amounts of data possible. At the same time, however, those many voices made consensus appear louder, and new ideas were conceived within an evolutionary model whose iron grip constrained the interpretive world in which those new syntheses could be made.

Catalogue and Describe (*c.* 1920–*c.* 2010)

Even before the era of great clearance excavations closed in the middle of the twentieth century, scholars had come to recognize that the amount of information published in the preceding two centuries was paradoxically both overwhelming and inaccessible. These scholars understood that, although published, the evidence for some subjects required further organization to make those data useful. One of the first such endeavours, of course, was Zangemeister and Schöne's *Corpus Inscriptionum Latinarum* (1871) discussed above, but earlier still was Helbig's 1868 catalogue of fresco paintings, organized by subject matter.⁴¹ Also mentioned already is Friedrich Furchheim, who published the first expansive, multilingual bibliography in 1891. But these efforts were swamped by the continuing rise in publication stemming from the rapid excavation of the eastern half of Pompeii, first under Spinazzola (1911 to 1923) and then under Maiuri (1924 to 1961). To put this in context, this half century saw one publication for every 21 m² of area uncovered, or over eight-eight per year.⁴² Only World War II and the accidental bombing of Pompeii in 1943 could slow the pace of excavation, with clearance excavation coming largely to a halt with the end of Maiuri's tenure as superintendent. It is not surprising, then, that it is in the middle of the twentieth century that the great initiatives to list, to catalogue, and to describe the vast store of information from Pompeii came into being.

Lighting the fuse for these early legacy studies was Tatiana Warscher who, between 1935 and 1961, produced the *Codex topographicus pompejanus*, the first attempt at a comprehensive photographic catalogue.⁴³ Warchser's research has been credited as the basis of the next great cataloguing effort, the *Corpus topographicum pompeiana*,⁴⁴ but

---

³⁶ Overbeck 1856.

³⁷ Fiorelli 1873, 78–86, tav. II–IIII; Mau 1882. See also Poehler (2022, 20–23) for a brief discussion of Mau's use of Fiorelli's model.

³⁸ Fiorelli 1873, 83.

³⁹ Maiuri 1942, 161–64, 216–17.

⁴⁰ See Ball and Dobbins (2013, 462–67) for a (polemical) summary.

⁴¹ Helbig 1868.

⁴² There were 4513 publications between 1911 and 1961 (inclusive), and approximately 98,400 m² of the city was excavated. Compare this to the first 112 years of excavation in which *c.* 200,000 m² were excavated, and only 2817 publications were issued, equalling about one for every 70 m² cleared.

⁴³ Laidlaw (1985, 10–11) documents the extent of Warscher's efforts and provides a concordance of the volumes and their locations in libraries around the world.

⁴⁴ Laidlaw 2007, 622.

the latter's source material and its purview were far greater in scope.⁴⁵ In five volumes, the *Corpus topographicum pompeiana* sought to cover no less than the entirety of Pompeii's toponymy (vol. II), bibliography (vol. III), and cartographic history (vol. V), along with updated maps of the city (vol. III) and its individual buildings (vol. IIIA).⁴⁶ Such grand visions face humbling realities against the ancient city, and 'the sheer size of the site continues to defeat'.⁴⁷ Although the director of the project, Halstead van der Poel, invested his fortune and more than a quarter century to the endeavour, volume I and rest of the maps of vol. III never appeared.⁴⁸ The failures of the *Corpus topographicum pompeiana*, however, are hardly unique, and the enormity of Pompeii as an archive continues to frustrate the ambitious.⁴⁹

Van der Poel's greater success was assembling a team of researchers who could demonstrate the value of legacy information to Pompeian scholars. First among these was Laurentino García y García who continued the work to build a bibliography for Pompeii, culminating in the two volumes of the *Nova bibliotheca pompeiana* in 1998 and a supplement in 2012. The work of mapping the city continued in the cartographic database of the Consorzio Neapolis, which generated new digital plans, one of which likely became the CAD plan that served as the basis for Dobbins and Foss's map sets, published with their 2007 *The World of Pompeii*.⁵⁰ Bringing the map and the source material together for Pompeian topography was the project of Lisolette Eschbach and Jürgen Müller-Trollius, whose catalogue *Gebäudeverzeichnis und Stadtplan der antiken Stadt Pompeji* (based on a lifetime of work by Hans Eschebach) offered basic information on the chronology (phase, date of excavation), finds, decoration, and bibliography for each building in the city.⁵¹ More impactfully, Hans Eschebach's plan of building functions visualized the socio-economic texture of the city for the first time.⁵² The artworks seen in each building were inventoried at this time as well, first in the text catalogues of the *Pitture e pavimenti di Pompei* and then illustrated in eleven massive volumes as *Pompei: pitture e mosaici*. A more targeted set of publications, the *Häuser in Pompeji* series, were devoted to the documentation of Pompeii's best-appointed residences.⁵³

Although not part of the *Hauser* series, the four contemporary volumes documenting the insula of Menander are especially interesting, not only for their completeness, but also for the fact that they examine a house excavated barely fifty years before their study began. Two volumes are dedicated to the architecture's construction history (vol. I) and its decorations (vol. II), and two others describe the materials recovered, including a spectacular silver treasure (IV). It is Allison's volume on the finds (vol. III), however, that is the most illustrative of recent legacy research at Pompeii. Reconciling the published records with the excavators' notes and the objects on the storeroom shelves, Allison described hundreds of artefacts within their contexts of discovery and, in many cases, their places of use. But her examination of this record also reveals a host of problems in using these data, including selective publication of finds, inexact recording practices, and failures in the organization of artefact storage. Above all, Allison's research demonstrates the incredible labour required to bring Pompeii's artefactual record to publication and how, once completed, the expectations for precision of Pompeii's archaeological record could not always be met by the practices that brought it to light. The 'Pompeii premise' (i.e. the idea that Pompeii was a perfect time capsule) was never true, but Allison unapologetically exploded this myth,⁵⁴ and in the process provided a suggestion for why there is comparatively little discussion of finds from Pompeii.

---

⁴⁵ The *Codex* covers only twenty-one city blocks, or 21.3 per cent of the insulas' total area. Additionally, the Getty Research Institute's van der Poel collection shows that Delle Corte's papers were also a core of source material, as were van der Poel's own documents. On the other hand, Warscher (1955) was a driving force for the philosophy behind the *Corpus*, understanding her work as 'a rough draft of a book that someone else must write' and the 'foundations upon which others may build'. Hers was a legacy study destined to be incorporated into another legacy project.

⁴⁶ Van der Poel 1977; 1981; 1983; 1984a, 1984b.

⁴⁷ Wallace-Hadrill 1990, 150.

⁴⁸ In the acknowledgements of vol. II, van der Poel (1983, xii) suggests the work was a life-long endeavour, having developed 'over the past seventy-three years'.

⁴⁹ Allison (2006, 11) notes that a fifth volume of the House of Menander on inscriptions was planned but has not appeared.

⁵⁰ On the Consortio Neapolis, see Ruggiero n.d., 37; Dobbins and Foss 2007. Discussion of more recent mapping efforts can be found in Morichi and others 2011; 2014; Sodo 2011.

⁵¹ Eschebach and Müller-Trollius 1993.

⁵² See Kockel 1985, 514–15. Raper (1977) made important arguments based on Hans Eschebach's (1970) earlier research.

⁵³ The *Häuser* series produced twelve volumes between 1984 and 2002, fulfilling Warscher's (1955) call to the future: 'I have repeatedly urged young students to concentrate their efforts on a single house in the hope that by doing so we shall preserve the fast-vanishing evidence of the excavations'.

⁵⁴ Allison 1992.

Atomize and Share (*c.* 1990–Present)

Allison's research came to publication at the beginning of the twenty-first century, but came to fruition at a time of profound changes in the way scholars imagined they could share information. Once again, this is not the place to define the impact of the digital age on Pompeian studies, but we can identify two important features of it: 1) the understanding that information could be reduced to its 'atomic' form, which supported 2) the impulse to share those organized bits of data as widely as possible. Thus, Allison chose to describe each individual artefact from the insula of Menander within its smallest possible spatial unit, the room. Then, as she had done already for thirty other houses in the city,[55] Allison placed these data in an online catalogue, searchable by room, material, artefact name, or functional type.[56] This change of format, from print page to webpage, did not substantially alter the content, of course, but it has fundamentally changed the manner in which one (and who) could access that information. Such hopes for transparency and democratization of the early web are best represented in BloggingPompeii, a site where hundreds of news items and discussions were shared starting in 2008.[57] A decade earlier, the Pompeii Forum Project had already begun to share not only the details of its project's methods and supplementary publications, but also details of evidence not included elsewhere, including a gallery of high-resolution archival images.[58]

Even more important has been the photographic documentation provided online by the website, Pompeii in Pictures. In many ways the fulfilment of Warchser's *Codex topographicus pompejanus*, Pompeii in Pictures has collected (from multiple sources), organized (by building or part thereof), and captioned over one hundred thousand images of Pompeii and its surrounding sites. Remarkably, the site is funded and maintained by two unaffiliated researchers (for they are by no means amateurs), Jackie and Bob Dunn, whose explicit intent in creating Pompeii in Pictures was to provide access to 'the smaller homes and houses, which seemed ignored but just as interesting.'[59] At the time of this writing, I am working with Pompeii in Pictures to help preserve their work, breaking each image free of its html framework, linking to their high-resolution copies, increasing the spatial resolution down to the individual wall, and providing a means to share each image widely for and into the research of others.[60] These efforts are part of an ongoing set of initiatives to organize and disseminate Pompeii's vast stores of legacy information, which are also the most recent examples of the 'atomize and share' model.

The Pompeii Bibliography and Mapping Project (PBMP) and the Pompeii Artistic Landscape Project (PALP)

Today, many of Pompeii's digital projects take up the mantle — and the data — of the twentieth century's drive to catalogue archival information and then amplify those results in the online world, seeking wider dissemination and more flexible means of interacting with those data. For example, in 2011 García y García moved the *Nova bibliotheca pompeiana* to a new publisher, which immediately produced a series of PDF versions of those volumes. This has improved the ability to search for new terms, but across twenty-six different files. This compromise between a book and a searchable resource may be imperfect, but the PDFs remain online today. Conversely, the ambitious project 'La fortuna visiva di Pompei: Archivio di immagini e testi dal XVIII al XIX secolo' sought to bring archival documents online for use by scholars and the public. Begun in 2002, the project made some materials available, especially the early maps of Pompeii, but by 2020 it was gone from the web.[61]

The Pompeii Bibliography and Mapping Project (PBMP) was undertaken to address both the difficulty of discovering published materials related to Pompeii and the scarcity of digital maps available to the scholar and the lay person alike. To this end, the PBMP has con-

---

[55] This resource is now defunct, but archived at the Internet Archive: <https://web.archive.org/web/20190619221951/http://www.stoa.org/projects/ph/home> [accessed 13 October 2022].

[56] This resource was recently stabilized online as Allison 2021.

[57] Blogging Pompeii is available at: <http://bloggingpompeii.blogspot.com/> [accessed 13 October 2022].

[58] The Pompeii Forum Project is available at: <http://pompeii.virginia.edu/> [accessed 1 November 2022].

[59] See: <https://pompeiiinpictures.com/pompeiiinpictures/R0/help_using_this_site.htm#Welcome> [accessed 13 October 2022].

[60] Over sixty thousand images from Pompeii in Pictures and nineteen thousand from the *Pompei: pitture e mosaici* volumes are now online at the UMass Amherst image collection: <http://umassamherst.lunaimaging.com/> [accessed 13 October 2022].

[61] The project was linked at <http://pompei.sns.it/> [accessed 13 October 2022]. Currently, this address redirects to a security notification.

verted the more than eighteen thousand entries of the *Nova bibliotheca pompeiana* into an online, searchable bibliography and produced maps and published their underlying data on publicly accessible sites.[62] More specifically, the *Nova bibliotheca pompeiana* was reconstituted at its atomic level: the single citation. The effect of this was to break apart the format of the book, which had locked the citations in alphabetical order, thereby making the bibliography far more searchable (by title, date, publisher, and language, etc.) and recombinable. Similarly, the maps of Pompeii were geolocated and redrawn down to the level of the individual property (i.e. each architecturally separate unit), and in some cases deeper still. Giving a digital form to each property allowed these features not only to carry information about themselves from multiple sources (e.g. names and addresses from the *Corpus topographicum pompeiana*, building function from Eschebach and Müller-Trollius, and image links to Pompeii in Pictures), but also made those places searchable by these attributes (and more) or even by their proximity to other features (e.g. location of shops within 20 m of a public fountain).

The PBMP has an additional goal to bring these two types of data not only into close dialogue with one another, but also to make them interoperable to such a degree that one could filter search results by spatial and bibliographic information interchangeably. For example, one might first search for buildings identified by houses, then select only those with publications in the last fifty years, then filter by those houses with an area larger than 400 m². Like the *Corpus topographicum pompeiana*, however, this goal has not been realized as the integration between map and bibliography remains incomplete. At the same time, the bibliographic catalogue continues to grow enormously.[63] Once again 'the sheer size of the site continues to defeat'.[64]

The sister project of the PBMP is the Pompeii Artistic Landscape Project (PALP), which aims to provide detailed descriptions of the artworks at Pompeii.

Since its initial rediscovery, the single greatest source of information for how Romans adorned their world has come from Pompeii's rich and vivid corpus of wall paintings, mosaics, and sculptures. More than mere décor, these artworks reveal innumerable aspects of the ancient world: Roman appetites for food, sex, and mythologies, their identities as revellers, intellectuals, and professionals, and their practices of religion, politics, idyll, and idle. To begin to make use of such remarkable detail, PALP has built upon the mapping data of the PBMP, increasing the spatial resolution from the building level, down to the individual room and even down to the specific wall in that room onto which a fresco was created.[65]

Although this detailed spatial infrastructure is a valuable project in its own right (and indeed, it can serve as the backbone of many other digital projects), it is the thousands of frescoes affixed to those individual walls that PALP seeks to explore. To do this, PALP combines the data from published catalogues (*Pitture e pavimenti di Pompei* and *Pompei: pitture e mosaici*) and images from Pompeii in Pictures, along with our own observations to make specific, individual statements of what is depicted on each wall. In PALP the 'atomic' level is not the room or the wall or even the fresco on that wall, but instead the specific, individual depiction, such as a figure, an object, or a motif. The purpose of freeing each depiction from its description in previous formats is to allow for radical new ways of searching the vast corpus of art at Pompeii. For example, PALP's structure facilitates finding a specific figure, such as Mercury, and the objects associated with him, such as his caduceus. More importantly, the linkages among these depictions will allow for a researcher to immediately explore a new topic, such as the representations of religious objects (e.g. ankhs, cornucopiae, or thrysi) across all of Pompeii, with only a few clicks.

Of course, it is not impossible to make a few of the same analyses with the physical volumes of the PPM, but it can be prohibitively impractical. Each volume contains approximately a thousand pages, weighs over four kilograms, and when open is *c.* 70 cm wide, requiring a table of nearly eight metres in length to lay out all eleven volumes at once. More onerous is the time it takes to find depictions in these books, even if the subject matter was included in volume X's general index. What takes seconds for a database to query and display, will take many minutes for a person to find each of the eight entries

---

62 At the time of writing, the PBMP's current map is the 'Pompeii: Navigation Map 2': <https://arcg.is/1WqOPS> [accessed 13 October 2022]. The map has been accessed approximately seventy-four thousand times since September, 2018.

63 If the average rate of publication in the 1990s (*c.* 270/year) has continued, there are now over 6200 newer publications on Pompeii. Several thousand of these are catalogued in García y García 2012, the first supplement to the *Nova bibliotheca pompeiana* extending from 1999 to 2011 and including references missed in the original publication.

64 See above, n. 47.

65 PALP has currently identified 10,599 rooms, 12,941 doorways, and 86,973 faces of walls.

for Mercury spread across four different volumes.⁶⁶ More importantly, neither the ankh, caduceus, cornucopia, nor thyrsus appears in the PPM's index. The latter three objects are listed in the PPP catalogue's index, but this fact requires reference to yet another four-volume resource that will require more than four hours simply to locate the 253 mentions of these objects.⁶⁷ What no published catalogue can yet do is to utilize the spatial context of a depiction as an important variable for both discovery and analysis. Because of its deep investment in the mapping data, PALP will support searches that compare depictions within room types (e.g. alae vs tablina),⁶⁸ that find depictions facing across a space toward one another, or even multivariate searches that might begin to consider commonalities of style and design in pursuit of the identification of artists' templates, if not entire workshops.⁶⁹ PALP's website, still in active development at the time of writing, is <http://palp.art>.

Conclusion

In many ways, the PBMP and PALP initiatives are the inheritors of Fiorelli's organizational legacy, deepening his spatial identifiers down to the individual artistic motif on a specific wall at Pompeii, and showing once again that the city's own physical structure is one of the best metaphors for organizing information about it. The picture is its own frame. At the same time, these projects are deeply indebted to the efforts of many generations of scholars who brought order to an enormous corpus of legacy information about Pompeii. Naturally, these many generations have generated long chains of legacy data. The bibliographic catalogues, for example, stretch from Furchheim (1891), to van der Poel (1977), to García y García (1998; 2012), and now to the Pompeii Bibliography and Mapping Project (2013–2017). Similarly, artistic compendia begin with Helbig (1868), followed by Schefold (1957), and then evolve into the fifteen volumes of *Pitture e pavimenti di Pompei* (1981–1986) and *Pompei: pitture e mosaici* (1990–2003), before their reconstitution within the Pompeii Artistic Landscape Project (2019–present). Additionally, PALP is further illustrated first by the work of Warscher (1935–1954), whose goals were taken up by Pompeii in Pictures (2004–present).

At the same time, it is necessary to understand that while the data these scholars presented are invaluable, the structure of those data are equally important to their discovery, preservation, and sharing. For example, even if *Pompei: pitture e mosaici* has published more than nineteen thousand images, they are locked into a spatial organization within a cumbersome set of physical objects, preventing their reconsideration within chronological, typological, or other frameworks. Similarly, the *Nova bibliotheca pompeiana*'s alphabetical arrangement of citations based on author name, even now as a set of PDFs, restricts access, searching, and reuse. Even the Pompeii in Pictures website presents its reduced-resolution images in a serial fashion, proceeding from one room to the next, often requiring multiple HTML pages to do so.⁷⁰ These legacy data projects, as products of their age, have spurred their own legacy data initiatives. Indeed, it is the fixed, linear arrangements of data that PALP and the PBMP are now working to disassemble, republishing the data at their most atomic level, as individual catalogue entries, citations, images, and artistic motifs. We hope that such reorganization within digital environments will produce the levels of access and efficiency necessary for scholars to invest in more speculative kinds of research because the barriers and the cost of testing a radical new idea will be sufficiently low.

Finally, it is worth reflecting on the fact that much of the data used by PALP and the PBMP are only twenty to forty years old and are fully published as large physical compendia. According to the narrower archaeological definitions that began this chapter, these works should not be considered legacy data: they are neither 'old', 'abandoned' (unpublished), nor (directly) derived from 'archaeological fieldwork'. Conversely, these objects can be called legacy data under the broader definition, as their data structures and analogue formats require considerable effort to free those data from their 'obsolete systems'. Thus, just as legacy materials that can be re-examined by new methodologies, so too can (must?) even published data be recast as new technologies and platforms are developed. The implications of this observation are potentially enormous, for both the past and

---

66 The calculation assumes a minimum of one minute to find each entry in the index of volume x and then locate the correct page and figure in the appropriate volume.

67 Caduceus, eight references; Cornucopia, fifty references; Thyrsus, 195 references.

68 On decoration by room types, see most recently Cova 2015.

69 On workshops, see most recently Esposito 2009; 2014; Richardson 2000.

---

70 The low resolution of the images is a legacy of the Parco Archeologico di Pompei's desire to control media that represent the site.

the future of archaeological practice and publishing. For the past, we can envision a new, large-scale enterprise of cracking open published narratives in order to extract, curate, and share the atomic level data (e.g. the mention of an artefact) and metadata (e.g. that find's provenance, material, description, etc.) that they contain.[71] Equally, we can imagine books and articles of the future being considered not obsolete, but incomplete, without the data supporting their arguments being described and encoded for interoperability along with the narrative that enlivens them.

When we ponder Pompeii's long legacy of fieldwork and publication with these considerations in mind, we can recognize that a great deal of work is still to be accomplished. Many crates of artefacts languish in storerooms and under-examined architectures remain standing on-site to be studied as legacy materials. Equally, many primary documents reside unacknowledged in scholarly institutions, while centuries of published sources await deconstruction and analysis as legacy data. With so much work still to be done on an archaeological site now nearly three centuries old, perhaps we should understand Pompeii to be, among other things, both laboratory and archive.

---

[71] The Chronika project is already beginning this kind of work for the *Bulletin de correspondance hellénique*: <https://chronique.efa.gr/> [accessed 13 October 2022].

Works Cited

Allison, P. 1992. 'Artefact Assemblages: Not "the Pompeii Premise"', in E. Herring, R. Whitehouse, and J. Wilkins (eds), *Papers of the Fourth Conference of Italian Archaeology*, III.1: *New Developments in Italian Archaeology* (London: Accordia Research Centre), pp. 49–56.

—— 2004. *Pompeian Households: An Analysis of Material Culture*, Monographs, 42 (Los Angeles: Cotsen Institute of Archaeology Press).

—— 2006. *The Insula of the Menander at Pompeii*, III: *The Finds, a Contextual Study* (Oxford: Clarendon).

—— 2008. 'Dealing with Legacy Data: An Introduction', *Internet Archaeology*, 24 <https://doi.org/10.11141/ia.24.8>.

—— 2021. 'Insula of the Menander at Pompeii' (University of Leicester) <https://leicester.figshare.com/articles/dataset/Insula_of_the_Menander_at_Pompeii/14494557/> [accessed 25 November 2021].

Ball, L. and J. Dobbins. 2013. 'Pompeii Forum Project: Current Thinking on the Pompeii Forum', *American Journal of Archaeology*, 117.3: 461–92.

Boman, H. n.d. 'The Swedish Pompeii Project' <https://www.pompejiprojektet.se/house.php?hid=26&hidnummer=3612335&hrubrik=V%201,1.32%20Taberna> [accessed 21 November 2021].

Borriello, M. R. 2008. 'Note per una storia dell'indirizzario di Pompei', *Rivista di studi Pompeiani*, 19: 63–68.

Bowes, K. 2022. 'Tracking Liquid Savings at Pompeii: The Coin Hoard Data', *Journal of Roman Archaeology*, 35.1: 1–27.

Cottica, D. and E. Curti. 2008. 'Il progetto di recupero ed edizione degli scavi I.E. (Impianto Elettrico) 1980–1981 nel Foro di Pompei', in P. G. Guzzo and M. P. Guidobaldi (eds), *Il progetto di recupero ed edizione degli scavi I.E. (Impianto Elettrico) 1980–1981 nel Foro di Pompei* (Rome: L'Erma di Bretschneider), pp. 25–36.

Cova, E. 2015. 'Stasis and Change in Roman Domestic Space: The Alae of Pompeii's Regio VI', *American Journal of Archaeology*, 119.1: 69–102.

d'Aloe, S. 1854. *Nouveau guide du Musée Royal Bourbon* (Naples: Imprimerie Piscopo).

De Simone, G., C. Martucci, A. Simone, and N. Albano. 2020. 'Balnea: l'evidenza ceramica dalla piscina calida delle terme Suburbane di Pompei', in L. Toniolo (ed.), *Fecisti Cretaria: Produzione e circolazione ceramica a Pompei; stato degli studi e prospettive di ricerca* (Rome: L'Erma di Bretschneider), pp. 329–37.

Dobbins, J. and P. Foss (eds). 2007. *The World of Pompeii*, 1st edn (London: Routledge).

Duncan-Jones, R. 2003. 'Roman Coin Circulation in the Cities of Vesuvius', in E. Lo Cascio (ed.), *Credito e moneta nel mondo romano: atti degli incontri capresi di storia dell'economica antica (Capri 12–14 Ottobre 2000)*, Pragmateiai, 8 (Bari: Edipuglia), pp. 161–80.

Dyson, S. 2006. *In Pursuit of Ancient Pasts: A History of Classical Archaeology in the Nineteenth and Twentieth Centuries* (New Haven: Yale University Press).

Ellis, S., E. Poehler, and A. Emmerson (forthcoming). *Isthmia*, XII: *The East Field: Architecture and Stratigraphy*.

Eschebach, H. 1970. *Die städtebauliche Entwicklung des antiken Pompeji, mit einem Plan 1:1000 und einem Exkurs: Die Baugeschichte der Stabianer Thermen nach H. Sulze*, Roemische Abteilung: Ergänzungsheft, 17 (Heidelberg: Kerle).

Eschebach, L. and J. Müller-Trollius. 1993. *Gebäude verzeichnis und Stadtplan der antiken Stadt Pompeji (unter Verwendung des Nachlasses von HANS ESCHEBACH)* (Cologne: Böhlau).

Esposito, D. 2009. *Le officine pittoriche di IV stile a Pompei: dinamiche produttive ed economico-sociali*, 1st edn (Rome: L'Erma di Bretschneider).

—— 2014. *La pittura di Ercolano* (Rome: L'Erma di Bretschneider).

Fiorelli, G. 1873. *Gli scavi di Pompei dal 1861 al 1872: relazione al Ministro della istruzione pubblica* (Naples: Tipografia italiana nel liceo V. Emanuele).

Foss, P. 2007. 'Rediscovery and Resurrection', in J. Dobbins and P. Foss (eds), *The World of Pompeii* (New York: Routledge), pp. 28–42.

Freud, Sigmund. 1953–1974. *The Standard Edition of the Complete Psychological Works of Sigmund Freud*, ed. by Carrie Lee Rothgeb, Anna Freud, and James Strachey (London: Hogarth).

Furchheim, F. 1891. *Bibliografia di Pompei: Ercolano e Stabia* (Naples: F. Furchheim).

García y García, L. 1998. *Nova bibliotheca pompeiana: 250 anni di bibliografia archeologica* (Rome: Arbor Sapientiae).

—— 2012. *Nova bibliotheca pompeiana: 1. supplemento (1999–2011); repertorium bibliographicum pompeianum* (Rome: Arbor Sapientiae).

Helbig, K. 1868. *Wandgemälde der vom Vesuv verschütteten Städte Campaniens* (Leipzig: Breitkopf und Hartel).

Kockel, V. 1985. 'Archäologische Funde und Forschungen in den Vesuvstädten, I', *Archäologischer Anzeiger*, 1985: 495–571.

Laidlaw, A. 1985. 'The First Style in Pompeii: Painting and Architecture', *Archaeologica*, 57: xlvi–358.

—— 2007. 'Mining the Early Published Sources: Problems and Pitfalls', in J. Dobbins and P. Foss (eds), *The World of Pompeii* (New York: Routledge), pp. 620–32.

Maiuri, A. 1942. *L'ultima fase edilizia di Pompei* (Spoleto: Istituto di studi romani).

Mau, A. 1882. *Geschichte der decorativen Wandmalerei in Pompeji* (Berlin: Reimer).

Moormann, E. 2015. *Pompeii's Ashes: The Reception of the Cities Buried by Vesuvius in Literature, Music, and Drama* (Boston: De Gruyter).

Morichi, R., R. Paone, P. Rispoli, and F. Sampaolo. 2014. 'Sulla nuova cartografia digitale di Pompei (II parte)', *Rivista di studi Pompeiani*, 25: 146–49.

Morichi, R., R. Paone, P. Rispoli, F. Sampaolo, and A. Sodo. 2011. 'Sulla nuova cartografia digitale di Pompei', *Rivista di studi Pompeiani*, 22: 133–43.

Orrells, D. 2011. 'Rocks, Ghosts, and Footprints: Freudian Archaeology', in S. Hales and J. Paul (eds), *Pompeii in the Public Imagination from its Rediscovery to Today* (Oxford: Oxford University Press), pp. 185–98.

Osanna, M. 2019. *Pompei: il tempo ritrovato; le nuove scoperte* (Milan: Rizzoli).

Overbeck, J. 1856. *Pompeji in seinen Gebäuden, Alterthümern und Kunstwerken für Kunst- und Alterthumsfreunde: Mit einer Ansicht und einem Plane von Pompeji, zwei chromolithographirten Blättern und gegen dreihundert Holzschnitten* (Leipzig: Engelmann).

Pagano, M. and R. Prisciandaro. 2006. *Studio sulle provenienze degli oggetti rinvenuti negli scavi borbonici del Regno di Napoli: una lettura integrata, coordinata e commentata della documentazione* (Castellammare di Stabia (Na) [Naples]: Longobardi).

Parslow, C. 1995. *Rediscovering Antiquity: Karl Weber and the Excavation of Herculaneum Pompeii and Stabiae* (Cambridge: Cambridge University Press).

Peña, J. T. 2020. 'Evidence for Pottery Production from the Torre VIII/Porta Di Nola Refuse Middens at Pompeii', in M. Osanna and L. Toniolo (eds), *Fecisti cretaria: dal frammento al contesto; studi sul vasellame ceramico del territorio vesuviano*, Studi e ricerche del Parco archeologico di Pompei, 39 (Rome: L'Erma di Bretschneider), pp. 23–32.

Piranesi, F. 1783. *Il teatro d'Ercolano: alla Maestà di Gustavo III re di Svezia &C. &C. &C. promotore munificentissimo delle Belle Arti* (Rome: Stamperia Salomoni).

Poehler, E. 2022. 'Masonry Analysis at Pompeii: The Maturation of a Stratigraphic Method', in D. Rogers and C. Weiss (eds), *A Quaint & Curious Volume: Essays in Honor of John J. Dobbins* (Oxford: Archaeopress), pp. 18–41.

—— (forthcoming). 'The Pompeii Bibliography and Mapping Project and a Brief Discussion of Nearly Three Centuries of Scholarship', in J. Berry and R. Benefiel (eds), *Oxford Handbook to Pompeii and Environs* (Oxford: Oxford University Press).

Poehler, E., M. Flohr, and K. Cole. 2011. 'Introduction', in E. Poehler, M. Flohr, and K. Cole (eds), *Pompeii: Art, Industry and Infrastructure* (Oxford: Oxbow), pp. 1–9.

Pompeii Bibliography and Mapping Project. 2017. 'Artifacts of the Bourbon Excavations', *Pompeii: Navigation Map 2* <https://www.arcgis.com/home/item.html?id=a932a86e11ba4ba28eabfa5976cec33b> [accessed 21 November 2021].

Raper, R. A. 1977. 'The Analysis of the Urban Structure of Pompeii: A Sociological Examination of Land Use (Semi-Micro)', in D. L. Clarke (ed.), *Spatial Archaeology* (London: Academic Press), pp. 187–221.

Richardson, L. 2000. *A Catalog of Identifiable Figure Painters of Ancient Pompeii, Herculaneum, and Stabiae*, 1st edn (Baltimore: Johns Hopkins University Press).

Ruggiero, A. n.d. 'Conservazione delle memorie digitali rischi ed emergenze sei Casi di Studio' <https://www.iccu.sbn.it/export/sites/iccu/documenti/emergenze.pdf> [accessed 27 February 2020].

Saint-Non, J.-B., abbé de. 1781–1786. *Voyage pittoresque ou déscription des Royaumes de Naples et de Sicilie* (Paris: Imprimerie de Clousier).

Schefold, K. 1957. *Die Wände Pompejis: Topographisches Verzeichnis der Bildmotive* (Berlin: Deutsches archäologisches Institut).

Sodo, A. M. 2011. 'Attività SIANV', *Rivista di studi Pompeiani*, 22: 159–60.

Swain, H. 2012. 'Archive Archaeology', in R. Skeates, C. McDavid, and J. Carman (eds), *The Oxford Handbook of Public Archaeology* (Oxford: Oxford University Press), pp. 351–67.

Sweet, R. 2015. 'William Gell and "Pompeiana" (1817–19 and 1832)', *Papers of the British School at Rome*, 83: 245–81.

Trigger, B. 2006. *A History of Archaeological Thought* (Cambridge: Cambridge University Press).

Van der Poel, H. 1977. *Corpus topographicum pompeianum*, IV: *Bibliography* (Austin: University of Texas Press).

—— 1981. *Corpus topographicum pompeianum*, V: *Cartography* (Austin: University of Texas Press).

—— 1983. *Corpus topographicum pompeianum*, II: *Toponymy* (Austin: University of Texas Press).

—— 1984a. *Corpus topographicum pompeianum*, III: *The RICA Maps of Pompeii* (Austin: University of Texas Press).

—— 1984b. *Corpus topographicum pompeianum*, IIIA: *The Insulae of Regions I–V* (Austin: University of Texas Press).

Wallace-Hadrill, A. 1990. 'The Social Spread of Roman Luxury: Sampling Pompeii and Herculaneum', *Papers of the British School at Rome*, 58: 145–92.

Warscher T. 1955. *Codex topographicus pompejanus*, XXXVI: *Regio IX, Insula 3* (Rome).

Zangemeister, C. and R. Schöne. 1871. *Inscriptiones parietariae Pompeianae Herculanenses Stabianae consilio et auctoritate Academiae Litterarum Regiae Borussicae edidit: accedunt vasorum fictilium ex eisdem oppidis erutorum inscriptiones editae a Richardo Schoene; adjectae sunt tabulae lith. LVII* (Berlin: Reimer).

9. Digitizing Knossos Using the Sir Arthur Evans Archive

John Pouncett
School of Archaeology, University of Oxford (john.pouncett@arch.ox.ac.uk)

Andrew Shapland
Ashmolean Museum, University of Oxford (andrew.shapland@ashmus.ox.ac.uk)

Introduction

When Sir Arthur Evans died in 1941, his archaeological papers were donated to the Ashmolean Museum. The task of gathering together the records of a lifetime's work at Knossos and as Keeper of the Ashmolean Museum (1884–1908) fell to Sir Arthur's half-sister, Dame Joan Evans.[1] Despite the constraints of World War II, she ensured that the bequest was removed from his mansion at Youlbury, near Oxford, and deposited in the Ashmolean Museum. This material became the nucleus of the Sir Arthur Evans Archive (Oxford, Ash, AJE; hereafter the Archive). It consists of over ten thousand archival objects, among which are drafts of Sir Arthur Evans's lectures and publications, his correspondence with other scholars, and records of sites and objects including notebooks, photographs, and drawings. Although some of the original order of this material when at Youlbury can be deduced from surviving boxes and folders, no catalogue of the Archive was made upon its arrival. Over the years the Archive has been reordered, catalogued in part, and extensively studied. A number of archival items have been published, often as part of ongoing discussions about the excavations at Knossos. It is only now, with the arrival of a new digital collections management system, that a full catalogue is being produced. As a result, the process of cataloguing is happening alongside the process of digitization. The opportunities that this offers are the subject of this paper.

Sir Arthur Evans began excavating at Knossos in 1900 and worked there until 1931. There he uncovered a grand building known as the 'Palace of Minos' and various surrounding structures including houses and tombs. The Bronze Age Palace at Knossos was clearly a significant structure, but Sir Arthur Evans established it through his writings as the centre of the 'Minoan civilization', a concept that he largely created and popularized. His four-volume work *The Palace of Minos at Knossos*, published between 1921 and 1935, set out this vision of Minoan Knossos and Crete, and remains influential for the archaeology of Bronze Age Crete.[2] By modern standards, however, this is not a final publication of the site, setting out all the data from excavations. The Sir Arthur Evans Archive contains many of the primary records for the excavation, particularly the notebooks kept by Evans and his assistant, Duncan Mackenzie. Archaeologists have continued to draw upon these records in their publications of the site, but Evans's excavations remain essentially unpublished. As a result, the process of digitization is also a form of publication, the implications of which will also be considered here.

Another legacy of Sir Arthur Evans was his work to restore the Palace and surrounding buildings, creating an archaeological site that has become one of the most popular visitor attractions in Greece. With over 950,000 visitors in 2019, it was the second most-visited archaeological site in Greece after the Acropolis in Athens.[3] This also has implications for the digitization of the Sir Arthur Evans Archive: there is a large potential audience for the Archive consisting of people who have a general interest in the site, particularly visitors. This paper will consider how the Archive can be made available to a non-specialist audience. This audience has diverse needs, but a key aim of digitizing the Archive is to provide a tour of the Palace, whether for people at the site itself with their smartphones in their hand or sitting in front of their computers at home. The three-dimensional digital model of the Palace presented here provides one way to engage this audience.

---

[1] Evans 1943, vii.

[2] Evans 1921; 1928; 1930; 1935.

[3] Hellenic Statistical Authority 2022.

Contents

The Sir Arthur Evans Archive contains a variety of different types of material retained by Sir Arthur Evans over the course of his career at the Ashmolean and excavations at Knossos but is far from complete. Since the bequest specified that his archaeological papers should be donated to the Ashmolean, the Archive did not originally contain any personal papers. Some of these were retained by Joan Evans, for writing her biography of Sir Arthur Evans and his ancestors, before coming into the possession of Arthur L. Evans, a relation of theirs. His gift of these papers in 1985 provided the Archive with records of Sir Arthur's childhood, up to the time he went to university, and also some other family papers. After university, Sir Arthur Evans travelled in the Balkans, but the papers from this period of his life were instead bequeathed to the School of Slavonic and East European Studies at UCL (London, UCL, EVA); relevant material later discovered among the Ashmolean bequest was later sent there on loan, although a small number of Balkan-related items remain at the Ashmolean. The papers of Margaret Evans, Sir Arthur's wife until her early death in 1893, went to a relation of hers and were later sold at auction.[4] Other papers related to Sir Arthur's administrative work as Keeper rather than his research, are in the Oxford University Archive. A small amount of material relating to the excavations at Knossos, including some notebooks of Duncan Mackenzie, is held by the British School at Athens (Athens, BSA, Mackenzie Pottery Notebooks). One of the benefits of digitization is that a scattered archive of this kind can be reconnected online, particularly if all institutions adhere to the same basic standards. This point will be developed below.

The focus of this contribution, however, is the material from Knossos. Sir Arthur Evans first visited Crete in March 1894 and met Minos Kalokairinos, a local scholar and businessman, who had started to excavate the Palace of Minos in 1878. Since Crete was at that time part of the Ottoman Empire, his peers had forced him to stop in case his finds were removed to Constantinople Museum. Evans's diary from this period records his visit to Knossos in the company of Kalokairinos, who generously showed him round. Another member of the party was Iosif Hatzidakis, another local scholar, who helped Evans to buy a quarter share of the land on which Kalokairinos's excavations had taken place. This subsequently enabled Evans to buy the remainder of the land, once Crete had gained its independence in 1898, and begin excavating in 1900.[5] Given the historical interest of this diary, it was published in full by Ann Brown, with an image of each page and facing transcription, along with extensive supporting material.[6] One particular point of interest was that the diary recorded the purchases of antiquities made by Evans in this period, many of which are now in the Ashmolean collection (Fig. 9.1). This provides another dimension to the diaries and notebooks, since connections can be drawn with archaeological objects in the Ashmolean collection. Whereas Ann Brown's transcription listed objects in a separate appendix, a digital publication can establish dynamic links between an object in

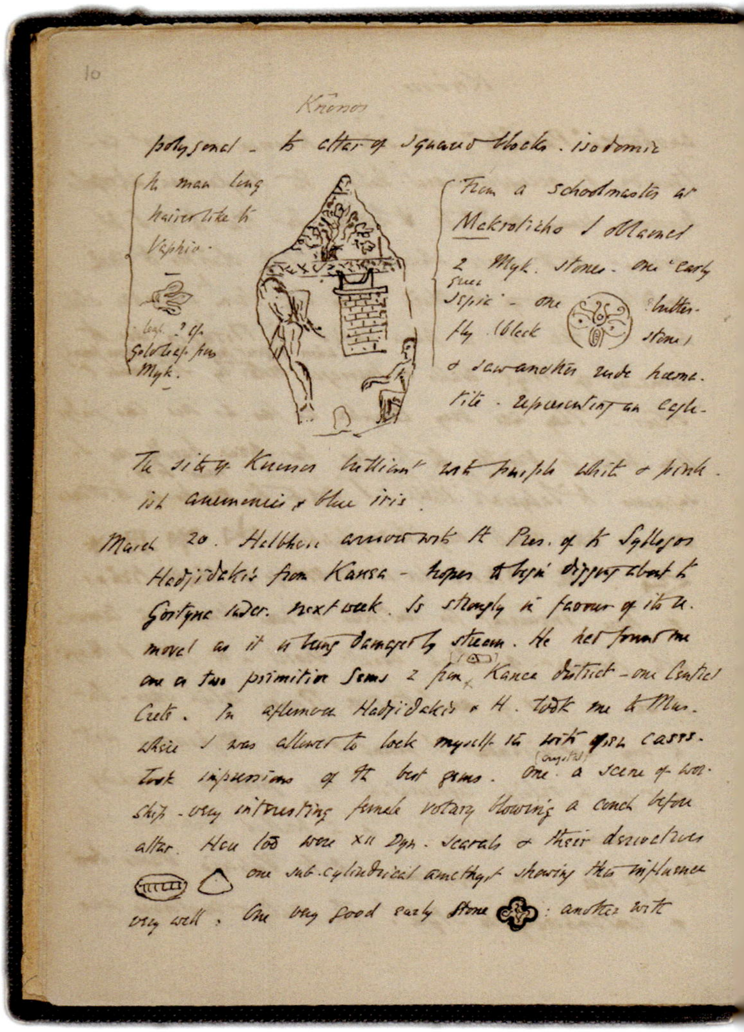

Figure 9.1. Entry for 20–21 March from Arthur Evans's 1894–1899 notebook on Crete (Notebook C), ink on paper, 21.5 × 15 cm, Ashmolean Museum AJE/1/2/1/2 (© Ashmolean Museum, University of Oxford).

---

[4] Pettigrew 2010.
[5] Brown 2000.
[6] Brown 2001.

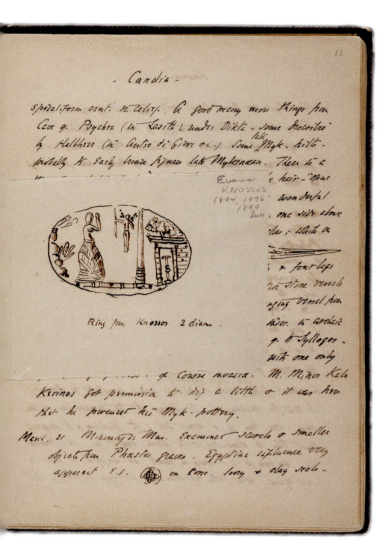

an online collections database and the relevant page in a digitized diary. Although this will be the subject of a future project, it illustrates the different potentials of an annotated online version of a diary versus the published transcription. On the other hand, the printed publication has a permanence that online publications can lack. Similarly, the electronic files for this publication were deposited in the Archive on multiple zip disks. These now need specialist equipment (and software) to read, illustrating the greater permanence and accessibility of the printed version.

The 1894 diary, and forty-nine notebooks related to the excavations of Knossos from 1900 onwards are now in the process of being digitized.[7] These notebooks (sometimes also called daybooks) were kept by Sir Arthur Evans and his employees at Knossos: his assistant, Duncan Mackenzie and the architects Theodore Fyfe and Christian Doll. Together they provide a uniquely important account of the excavations and reconstructions of Knossos, and are often the only record of the find-spots of particular objects. As a result they have been heavily used by archaeologists studying Knossos, and sometimes the subject of fierce debate.[8] They are now too fragile to consult and so facsimiles made in the 1980s are provided to researchers instead (and also exist on microfilm). The current digitization project involves photographing each page or double-page spread, and these will be put on the Ashmolean collections website in due course. The form this will take is currently under discussion: an online reader would ease navigation by enabling users to virtually flip through the pages. Even then, three thousand pages of archaeological observations are of limited interest to most readers. Further work is needed to make them truly accessible: annotation, mentioned above, is one means to do this, as is text encoding to enable them to be searched. A distinction is often made between digitization (i.e. digital photography) and digitalization, which in this case would be the use of digital technologies to increase the accessibility and usefulness of the notebooks. This is a process which the Ashmolean is only just beginning.

Evans employed a number of architects and artists at Knossos and the Archive contains around two thousand original drawings. Of these over a half are object drawings, around four hundred are technical drawings of the excavations, and another four hundred relate to the colourful frescoes that decorated the walls and floors of the Palace and surrounding buildings. Among these are a number of imaginative reconstructions, including Theodore Fyfe's drawing of the Throne Room (Fig. 9.2). The plans, sections, and fresco drawings were digitized in 2004–2005 by the University of Oxford's library (the Bodleian) rather than the Ashmolean Museum. As a result they are available online via the library's digital repository, Digital Bodleian.[9] These drawings are not part of the Bodleian Library's collection, although the Ashmolean and Bodleian are part of the same division of the University (Gardens, Libraries, and Museums). Because these items were digitized by the Bodleian Library, however, they have been given an online presence which the rest of the Archive lacks. On Digital

---

[7] We gratefully acknowledge the support of a grant from the Gladys Krieble Delmas Foundation and an anonymous donor to enable the photography of these notebooks.

[8] Boardman and Palmer 1963.

[9] See <https://digital.bodleian.ox.ac.uk/collections/arthur-evans-archive/> [accessed 20 August 2022].

Figure 9.2. Theodore Fyfe (1875–1945), watercolour reconstruction drawing of the Throne Room, 1901, 38 × 56 cm, Evans Fresco Drawing B/4a (© Ashmolean Museum, University of Oxford).

Bodleian they are presented as individual archival items with limited metadata rather than being contextualized in terms of the excavations at Knossos. The provision of a richer context and metadata for these drawings is one of the aims of the digital model, discussed below.

Another significant aspect of the Archive are around three thousand photographs of the excavations at Knossos including architecture, finds, and workers. There are also a significant number of photographs of related sites and objects. These include some original glass-plate negatives and prints. Many of the prints were numbered and annotated by Evans or Mackenzie and stored in box folders, but after they arrived at the Ashmolean Museum, many were removed and pasted into albums. Although this has enabled them to be viewed more easily, the ordering of the albums is not the same as the box folders. Some of the photographs of pottery were subsequently removed from the albums and ordered by archaeological sequence instead, in new folders. Only a small number of photographs have been digitized, mainly to fulfil commercial image orders. This indicates a general interest in images of the Knossos excavations, but the remainder of the photographs awaits digitization. One of the advantages of putting the photographs in a collections database is that they can be reordered digitally, according to the original numbering system, without the need to remove them from the physical albums.

The Archive also contains material relating to the publications of Sir Arthur Evans, about Knossos and elsewhere. All of the stages of the publication process are represented, from manuscript notes and drafts of text, to page proofs and even some of the original printing blocks for *The Palace of Minos*. Since Evans's ideas have remained influential in Aegean Bronze Age archaeology, the unpublished drafts of some papers are of historical interest for scholars. On the other hand, the thousands of pages of illustration proofs for *The Palace of Minos* are of less interest, although some are annotated by Evans, and are not a candidate for digitization. As a whole this part of the Archive is likely to appeal to a more specialist audience. Related to the publications are the cuttings of press reports kept by Sir Arthur Evans. In some cases (e.g. *The Times*) the relevant article is now available online but some of the reports from undigitized newspapers, such as those printed on Crete, are of interest to researchers.[10]

One of the priorities for digitization is Sir Arthur Evans's correspondence with other scholars. Some of the letters have been published in scholarly articles or biographies of Evans. With the growing interest in the history of archaeology, digitization will allow researchers to trace these networks of interactions between scholars more effectively. Letters are usually straightforward to digitize through scanning, and this will reduce the need for researchers to handle the original, a consideration that applies to other parts of the Archive. Given the age of the letters, most — but not all — are out of copyright, and it is hoped that other institutions will digitize their correspondence relating to the same individuals, allowing links to be made between them. For instance, the Faculty of Classics at Cambridge holds the papers of Alan Wace, a frequent correspondent of Evans (Cambridge, CU, GBR/3437/AJBW).

Work on the Archive

The Sir Arthur Evans Archive has always been available for consultation at the Ashmolean Museum, but it was long seen primarily as a resource for archaeologists to use to understand the excavations at Knossos. This appears to have affected early decisions to sort the material, notably the photographs being removed from box files and placed in albums but also the creation of categories of 'Architectural Plans', 'Fresco Drawings', and so on, since there are indications that Evans kept folders or envelopes of mixed materials on particular subjects. Some of these folders and envelopes survive in the Archive, but often their contents have been removed. The original order of the Archive will never be known, and indeed it is likely to have arrived in a state of disorder. Considerable work in cataloguing and boxing the Archive was undertaken by Ann Brown, administrator in the Department of Antiquities, who also published a number of works based on the material. Further cataloguing work on the correspondence, press-cuttings, and drawings among others was undertaken by Nicoletta Momigliano and Susan Sherratt as part of fellowships at the Ashmolean. As well as the digitization of the drawings, mentioned above, this also resulted in two small exhibitions at the Ashmolean and provided material for a number of publications.[11]

The first overview catalogue of the Archive to ISAD(G) standards was produced by Yannis Galanakis in 2012. This brought together some of the existing item-level catalogues into a coherent structure for the first time and organized the remainder of the Archive at the level of series or file in some cases. This catalogue was placed online, allowing potential users to understand the scope and content of the Archive, but it remained necessary to visit the Ashmolean to see material.[12] The Sir Arthur Evans Archive website itself is now regarded by the University as a 'legacy website' which will no longer be maintained. Sustainability is a perennial problem with digitization, and in future we have decided not to try to maintain a stand-alone website about the Archive. Instead a guide to the Archive will be provided as part of the new collections website. Digital Bodleian has proved a useful lesson because material digitized nearly twenty years ago has remained online as a result of being included in a digital collections resource which the University has a long-term commitment to sustaining in some form.

An ongoing project to update the Ashmolean's Collections Online website has provided an opportunity to put the Archive online in a more sustainable form. Whereas the previous website and collections database supporting it were not able to include archive items, this is now possible. One of the differences between museum objects and archives is that the latter require a hierarchical ordering, which has been enabled by the new collections database. At the same time, a collections database is primarily designed to record information about individual objects or items, and so this has prompted a shift in priorities. Although we are still working on a comprehensive hierarchical catalogue, there is now the possibility of including different identifiers to archive items which could be used to generate different orderings. For instance, a photograph in an album can be recorded

---

[10] Sherratt 2009.

[11] Brown 1983; 1986; 1993; Momigliano 1996; 1999; 2002; Sherratt 2000; 2009.

[12] The work of Yannis Galanakis on the catalogue and website was funded by the Gladys Krieble Delmas Foundation. See <https://sirarthurevans.ashmus.ox.ac.uk/archive/index.html> [accessed 20 August 2022].

with both its original Evans identification number and its album reference page. Although in archival terms the album page is the file within which the photograph is included, it will be possible to reconstruct a different hierarchy based on the box file within which the photograph was previously kept. In addition the database will record other information about photographs, such as subject or date created, that can be used to create different groupings. Items can also be cross-referenced with the publications they appear in or the museum objects they depict. Hence the use of Collections Online for the Archive offers opportunities for presenting it in a non-hierarchical way based on links between items.

A hierarchical catalogue is still in preparation, which will be used as a finding aid and placed online.[13] It is anticipated that it will remain easier to search a discrete catalogue for particular terms rather than a collections website. Another option which is under consideration is the use of Archives Hub, an online service which brings together different UK repositories.[14] This would allow users to search the Sir Arthur Evans Archive alongside other archives in the UK, which is particularly useful for areas such as correspondence. Whereas users might expect the Sir Arthur Evans Archive to include records about Knossos, it might not be the first place to look for a letter from the Nobel Prize-winning author Anatole France for instance.

Why Digitize?

The digitization of an archive requires resources and a long-term commitment to maintaining the digitized files online. The Sir Arthur Evans Archive has always been accessible to scholars by appointment, so it is worth asking what the purpose of digitization is. As a publicly funded institution the Ashmolean Museum has a general commitment to making its collection accessible online, but there are also specific reasons for digitizing this Archive. These relate to the decolonization movement, the publication status of Evans's excavations and the existence of online resources relating to Knossos. There is also a digitalization aspect (see above): using the Archive to complement visitors' experience of the archaeological site of Knossos.

The Ashmolean holds the primary records for Sir Arthur Evans's excavations at Knossos. When Evans began excavating at Knossos in 1900, Crete had recently become independent and passed legislation to allow foreign institutions to conduct excavations.[15] Although there were strict rules about exporting finds, there was no requirement to deposit the excavation archive in Crete.[16] At that time Crete was keen to encourage foreign excavators as a means to establish itself as an independent nation, with a view to union with Greece (which occurred in 1913). Since 1952, the Palace of Knossos has belonged to Greece, having previously been the possession of Sir Arthur Evans and then the British School at Athens. This means that the Ephorate of Antiquities of Heraklion has responsibility for maintaining the site and has conducted extensive conservation work on both the Bronze Age fabric of the Palace and the later concrete restorations undertaken by Evans. The Archive holds, among other things, plans and elevations relating to these restorations as well as a considerable amount of information, particularly photographs, about the way the site looked before it was restored. In this context digitization becomes a form of repatriation, a means of reuniting excavation archive and archaeological site now that they are no longer owned by the same person. In addition, the sharing of information could potentially support the ongoing bid by the Greek Ministry of Culture for Knossos and the other palaces of Crete to be listed as a UNESCO World Heritage Site.[17]

The archaeological site of Knossos is now a major visitor attraction. The visitor experience is largely shaped by the restorations of Sir Arthur Evans and the way in which he interpreted the building. For instance, the Throne Room now sits within a 1930s concrete structure with an unmistakeably modernist air. The room itself was restored with replica paintings of griffins which, although based on the original frescoes found on the walls, are now regarded as being inaccurate.[18] The Sir Arthur Evans Archive holds photographs which show the excavation of the Throne Room, as well as the reconstruction drawings which were then realized in the space itself (Figs 9.3–9.4). There is potential for visitors to be able to access these archival items via their smartphones if they are interested in the history of excavation and

---

[13] Work has continued on Yannis Galanakis's overview catalogue. Further cataloguing was undertaken by Senta German and Alison Roberts in 2016, prior to the work described in this paper which began in 2019.

[14] <https://archiveshub.jisc.ac.uk/> [accessed 8 August 2022].

[15] Carabott 2006.

[16] Panagiotaki 2004.

[17] See <https://whc.unesco.org/en/tentativelists/5860/> [accessed 20 August 2022].

[18] Galanakis, Tsitsa, and Günkel-Maschek 2017.

Figure 9.3. Photograph of the Throne Room of the Palace of Knossos, 1900, Ashmolean Museum AJE/3/1/12/34/2 (© Ashmolean Museum, University of Oxford).

Figure 9.4. Photograph of the Throne Room of the Palace of Knossos, c. 1930, Ashmolean Museum AJE/3/1/12/25/1 (© Ashmolean Museum, University of Oxford).

reconstruction at the site. Indeed, some of this archival material is already shown on display boards at the Palace. There are also commercially available digital tours of the Palace which purport to show the Palace as it was in the Bronze Age. Rather than stripping away Evans's restorations, these simply add another layer of often dubious interpretation. As the material in the Archive shows, Evans's excavations and restorations are an important part of the history of the building. The digital model, to be described below, is one means to present this material.

Although there are numerous publications about Knossos, the Palace and surrounding buildings have never been fully published by modern standards. In his lifetime Sir Arthur Evans published reports on his excavations, particularly during the period 1900–1905 when the Palace was excavated.[19] His four-volume *The Palace of Minos at Knossos* is not a site publication so much as an encyclopaedia of Minoan civilization: there are descriptions of areas of the Palace and surrounding buildings, but these do not list all the finds or give a detailed account of the excavation.

There have been attempts to provide a more complete publication of Knossos. In particular, Sinclair Hood and William Taylor's *The Bronze Age Palace at Knossos: Plans and Sections* included new drawings of the Palace as well as an index, organized by room, to the published sources.[20] Vasso Fotou has compiled an index of references to some of these rooms in the unpublished notebooks in the Archive.[21] Other authors have restudied the excavated material and brought this together with Evans's publications and unpublished material in the Archive in order to produce full publications of particular areas.[22] Given the scale of the task, a digital publication is the most obvious way forward, since this can link together the enormous amounts of data relating to the Palace and its surrounds. It can also draw upon the invaluable work that has been done by these scholars to establish a systematic means of publishing the Palace, by individual room or space.

The Ashmolean can decide whether and how to digitize the Sir Arthur Evans Archive, but there is already a considerable amount of content relating to Knossos and Evans's excavations online. From this point of view, digitization is about contributing to an existing resource rather than initiating a new process. In particular, *The Palace of Minos at Knossos* has already been digitized and made freely available online by the University of Heidelberg.[23] The annual reports published by Evans in the *Annual of the British School at Athens* are available, too, although only to subscribers of JSTOR. Copyright in the published works of Sir Arthur Evans has expired in the UK and EU meaning that there are fewer restrictions on placing his work online. The Ashmolean holds the copyright in nearly all of the unpublished material in the Archive and is committed to making it freely available online, at least for non-commercial use.

In addition to published material, there is a wealth of other data online relating to Knossos. The Pleiades website has resources which provide spatial data about Knossos, including individual rooms of the Palace, and also information about publications.[24] The existence of these place resources means that it is unnecessary for the Ashmolean to create its own spatial data when digitizing the Archive since this is already available online. It is an example, too, of crowdsourcing since anyone can contribute data to this resource. There are other spatial resources, too, including OpenStreetMap or Google Maps. Similarly Wikidata and Wikipedia contain both spatial data and contextual information about Knossos, in a variety of languages. Wikimedia Commons is one example of a website which contains recent images of Knossos, provided by users.[25] Although free to use these images are often not without copyright problems, particularly under Greek law. Nevertheless, these sites show that user-generated content is available which can be incorporated into the digitization process.

Making Links

Our future plans for the digitization of the Archive involve putting it on the Sematic Web, using Linked Open Data (LOD).[26] LOD is a set of standards and tools which allow different datasets on the web to be brought together. These datasets are also machine readable because the data is semantic, that is, structured in a

---

[19] Evans 1900; 1901; 1902; 1903; 1904; 1905.
[20] Hood and Taylor 1981.
[21] Karetsou and Fotou 2004, 586–608.
[22] Examples include: Panagiotaki 1999; Mountjoy 2003; Hatzaki 2005; Oddo 2022.

[23] See <https://digi.ub.uni-heidelberg.de/diglit/evans1921ga> [accessed 20 August 2022].
[24] See <https://pleiades.stoa.org/places/589872> [accessed 20 August 2022].
[25] See <https://commons.wikimedia.org/wiki/Category:Knossos> [accessed 20 August 2022].
[26] Berners Lee 2006.

logical and meaningful way. Museum collections websites typically allow (human) users to search for objects or archive items using a bespoke search interface that cannot be extended to objects in other museum collections without including them in the same underlying database. Even so, online collections databases can be integrated into LOD by ensuring that each item in the database has a unique, unchanging web address, known as a URI (Uniform Resource Identifier). This allows the item to be described in a machine-readable way using a particular standard known as Resource Description Framework (RDF). LOD works by making statements about the item, which are composed using other URIs. For these statements to be machine readable, they need to be in a standard form, known as a triple (subject-predicate-object), and use an agreed set of terms, known as an ontology.

To give an example, the reconstruction of the Throne Room by Theodore Fyfe introduced above can be described using a set of interrelated statements. One might be: 'Evans Fresco Drawing B/4a depicts the Throne Room at Knossos'. As LOD this statement links three URIs: the first is the Ashmolean (or Digital Bodleian) online collections record;[27] the second comes from an ontology used to describe cultural heritage known as CIDOC-CRM, where 'depicts' is property P62;[28] the third comes from Pleiades resource for the 'Throne Room in Palace of Minos'.[29] Similar statements can be made about the date of the drawing, its creator, the collection it belongs to, and so on. If these statements are put into a database known as a triplestore and put online, they can then be queried like any other online database. The difference between a triplestore and the current Ashmolean collections database is that data from different triplestores can be brought together online and queried at the same time. Web users could effectively create their own collections databases which include this drawing because the Semantic Web is structured like a database.

There are a range of tools available which allow users to bring together data in this way. ResearchSpace is one example which provides a platform for visualizing and creating knowledge graphs (sets of linked triples).[30] On ResearchSpace these knowledge graphs can be built to link together different entities, such as archival items, using the CIDOC CRM ontology. There are also tools for annotating texts and images with semantic data such as Recogito.[31] This was an experimental project but showed how texts and images could be linked with the Pleiades spatial resources by annotating them. This tool can be used in conjunction with the Fyfe drawing on Digital Bodleian because of the way it is made available online. This is because Digital Bodleian uses IIIF, a set of standards for images, which are compatible with the principles of LOD.[32] Tools such as ResearchSpace and Recogito allow the creation of content but are primarily means to link together content that is already published elsewhere on the web (for instance in collections databases). As a result they are most useful as means to visualize data rather than long-term sustainable ways of storing data. They provide the next step after an institution has committed to publishing its collections as LOD.

The Archive is not yet available as LOD, but some preparatory work has been done at Oxford, and there are an increasing number of similar examples to use as benchmarks. The Ashmolean has been involved in a pilot project, OXLOD, which examined the feasibility of making collections data available as LOD. This involved mapping it to the CIDOC CRM ontology rather than publishing it. The British Museum did publish its collections as semantic data in 2012, but unfortunately this pioneering resource was not sustained by the museum. A successful example in a related field, Nomisma, allows users to query multiple coin datasets using one interface.[33] These datasets, which include the Ashmolean's coins, are linked by a shared set of LOD standards, partly based on Nomisma's own ontology for numismatics. A current research project is exploring ways of creating LOD from the Ashmolean's exhibition data using the Linked Art Data Model.[34] This will include some items from the Archive.

---

[27] <https://digital.bodleian.ox.ac.uk/objects/59f4aa40-47c3-4707-a28b-29fe30c5a462/> [accessed 20 August 2022].

[28] <https://www.cidoc-crm.org/Property/p62-depicts/version-6.2.1> [accessed 20 August 2022].

[29] <https://pleiades.stoa.org/places/739470591> [accessed 20 August 2022].

[30] Oldman 2021; Oldman and Tanase 2018; <https://researchspace.org/> [accessed 20 August 2022].

[31] Rainer and others 2015; 2017; <https://recogito.pelagios.org/> [accessed 20 August 2022].

[32] See <https://iiif.io/> [accessed 20 August 2022].

[33] <http://nomisma.org/> [accessed 20 August 2022].

[34] *Enriching Exhibition Scholarship: Reconciling Knowledge Graphs and Social Media from Newspaper Articles to Twitter*: <https://gtr.ukri.org/projects?ref=AH%2FW00559X%2F1> [accessed 20 August 2022]; see also <https://linked.art/> [accessed

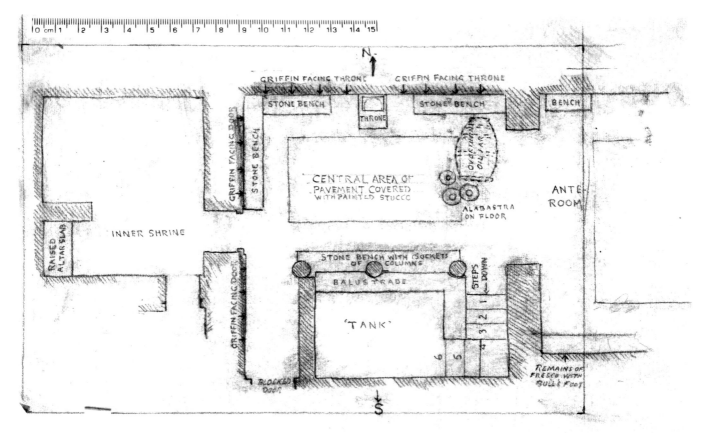

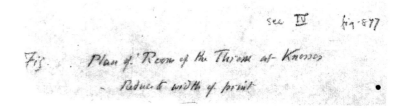

Figure 9.5. Plan of Throne Room, including Inner Shrine and Lustral Basin (draft of Evans 1935, fig. 877), undated, pencil, 25 × 30 cm, Evans Architectural Plans WW/28 (© Ashmolean Museum, University of Oxford).

At the same time as exploring ways to publish the Archive as LOD, we are working on visualizations of it. Traditionally archives are presented in a hierarchical form, and the Archive will appear in this way on the new collections website. This is most useful for users who are already looking for something in particular, whether drawings or correspondence. Our aim is to engage the users who are simply interested in the Palace of Knossos. Rather than browsing an archive, we want to allow them to explore the site. This is the reason for working on a 3D model of the site at the same time as exploring LOD applications. A similar approach is being developed for Pompeii: The Pompeii Bibliography and Mapping Project provides a map of the site, with increasingly rich associated data, and the Pompeii Artistic Landscape Project aims to allow users to discover and explore the associated artworks by publishing them as LOD.[35]

Palace of Minos 3.0

Nearly all of the material from the excavations at the Palace of Minos is split between Oxford and Crete, with the majority of the excavation archive at the Ashmolean Museum, and the objects found during the excavations held in the Heraklion Archaeological Museum and the Knossos Stratigraphical Museum. Perhaps paradoxically, whilst separated by geography, the disparate com-

---

20 August 2022].

[35] <https://digitalhumanities.umass.edu/pbmp/>; <https://palp.p-lod.umasscreate.net/> [accessed 26 August 2022].

Table 9.1. Summary of rooms related to the Throne Room Complex after Hood and Taylor 1981 (Index B. North-West Quarter).

Index no.	Name	Alternative Names(s)	Number on Plan
123	Throne Room Complex	Throne Room System	41–48
124	Antechamber of the Throne Room	Anteroom of the Throne Room	41
125	Throne Room	Room of the Throne, Consistory Hall/Chamber	42
126	Lustral Basin	Bath, Tank	43
127	Loggia	-	Above 42
128	Inner Shrine	Inner Sanctuary, Room of the Stone Lamp	44
129	Room	-	S of 44
130	Room of the Stone Drum	-	45
131	Kitchen	Room of the Plaster Table	46
132	Gallery	-	W of 45/N of 46
133	Room of the Stone Bench	-	47
134	Room of the Lady's Seat	Room of the Woman's Seat, Room of the Cupboard	48
135	Staircase	-	N of 41
136	Corridor of the Stone Basin	-	49

ponents of the excavation can be reunited using a Geographic Information System to create a digital twin of the Palace of Minos — a virtual representation of the Palace to which records and objects from the Archive can be linked. A digital twin of the Palace of Minos is currently being created alongside the ongoing digitization of the Sir Arthur Evans Archive as part of a collaborative project between the Ashmolean Museum and the School of Archaeology at the University of Oxford. Initial work on the digital twin has focused on the Throne Room Complex[36] — a complex of buildings which has been extensively documented and typifies many of the challenges inherent in creating a virtual representation of the Palace that can be used to explore the contents of the Archive. At a fundamental level, any virtual representation created in a Geographic Information System must address two deceptively simple questions — what and where? These questions are particularly challenging when trying to create a virtual representation of an archaeological site excavated over a century ago from legacy data.

What?

The Throne Room Complex was first investigated by Minos Kalokairinos in 1878 when the rounded corner of the façade of an earlier phase of the Palace and the steps at the eastern end of the Antechamber to the Throne Room were discovered during his excavations of Kephala hill.[37] It was later investigated further by Sir Arthur Evans in 1900 during the first season of excavations at Knossos which focused on the West Wing of the Palace when the Antechamber to the Throne Room and the staircase to the north, the Throne Room and Lustral Basin, the Room of the Stone Lamp and adjoining room, the Room of the Cupboard, and the Corridor of the Stone Basin were excavated to floor level.[38] Investigation of the Room of the Cupboard (by then referred to as the Room of the Lady's Seat) and the Corridor of the Stone Basin continued in 1901 during the second season of excavations at Knossos when the Room of the Stone Bench, Room of Stone Drum, the Room of the Plaster Table, and adjoining gallery of three rooms were again excavated to floor level[39] — the block of rooms connected to the Throne Room were referred to collectively in the preliminary excavation report as the Women's Quarter.

The progress of the excavation of the Throne Room Complex can be tracked in the notebooks, photographs, and drawings held in the Archive (Fig. 9.5). Individual entries in the notebooks, photographs, and drawings can typically be related to specific parts of the Throne Room Complex using the names of the rooms used in the preliminary excavation reports published in the *Annual of*

---

[36] Evans 1921, 4–5; 1935, 901–44.

[37] Stillman 1881, 43–49.
[38] Evans 1900, 35–43.
[39] Evans 1901, 31–35.

the British School of Athens and the interpretative synthesis published in *The Palace of Minos at Knossos*. The names of the rooms are interpretative and, as with the Room of the Cupboard/Lady's Seat, changed over time as Evans's theories developed. Whilst interpretations of the Palace have changed since Evans's day, the names of the rooms are a convenient way of linking records in the Archive to the corresponding elements of the Palace. The index created by Hood and Taylor in 1981 to accompany the plans and sections of the Bronze Age Palace at Knossos[40] seeks to decouple the documentation and interpretation of the site, assigning numeric identifiers to rooms (Table 9.1) which have been used to index some, but by no means all, of the unpublished records of the excavations held in the Sir Arthur Evans Archive.[41]

Where?

The locations of the rooms which form part of the Throne Room Complex are shown on the plans by Theodore Fyfe and Christian Doll published in the interim reports of the excavations and *The Palace of Minos at Knossos*.[42] These plans are schematic and typically show the layout and configuration of the rooms, with limited detail showing architectural features and finds central to Evans's interpretation of the site. Additional detail can be found in the sketches and earlier drafts of the plans held in the Archive. Detailed stone-by-stone plans of the Palace, including the Throne Room Complex, have subsequently been produced by Sinclair Hood and William Taylor and the Ephorate of Antiquities of Heraklion at scales of 1:100 and 1:20, respectively.[43] Both plans are accompanied by sections that show the profile of the Kephala hill and elevations of key buildings. The plan of the Palace produced by the Ephorate of Antiquities of Heraklion is accompanied by a series of levels which define the heights of individual architectural elements within the Palace and was produced on a 2 m grid with coordinates that can be used to locate the Throne Room Complex in its correct geographic position. While the Ephorate plan provides a robust basis for the geometry of the digital twin of the Palace of Minos, it shows the Palace as reconstructed by Evans and subsequent generations of archaeologists.

[40] Hood and Taylor 1981.
[41] Karetsou and Fotou 2004.
[42] Evans 1900, pl. XIII; 1901, pl. I; 1928, plans A and C; 1935, fig. 877.
[43] Hood and Taylor 1981.

Later additions related to the reconstruction of the Palace can be identified by cross-referencing the architectural elements shown on the plan with the notebooks, drawings, and photographs held in the Sir Arthur Evans Archive. Although later entries in the notebooks refer to named rooms and can easily be cross-referenced with the plan, earlier entries in the notebooks typically do not specify room names and are harder to cross-reference with the plan. A 10 m grid was established early in the excavations and is shown on the plans of the Palace published in the interim reports. The notebooks kept by Duncan Mackenzie reference this grid, with grid squares denoted by numbers and letters — early entries in the notebooks related to the excavation of the Throne Room Complex are referenced by grid squares K5 and K6. Prior to the establishment of the site grid, the entries in the notebooks refer to regions under active investigation — the area of the Throne Room Complex fell within Region 4 and corresponding entries are typically (but not always) numbered accordingly. Drawings and photographs are either labelled by room or contain distinctive architectural features and consequently can be easily cross-referenced with the Ephorate plan.

Digitization

The Throne Room Complex is shown on four separate sheets of the unpublished plan of the Palace of Minos produced by the Ephorate of Antiquities of Heraklion (Tablets 86/47, 86/48, 87/47, and 87/48), with separate drawings showing rooms on three levels of the Palace (Plans A, B, and Γ). Only Plan A shows the elements of the Throne Room Complex excavated by Evans — Plans B and Γ show the Loggia conjectured above the Throne Room and relate solely to the reconstruction of the Palace. The four separate sheets for Plan A were georeferenced in ArcGIS Pro 3.0 using control points corresponding to the intersections of the gridlines and were added to a mosaic dataset to create a seamless image showing the plan of the Throne Room Complex at ground level. Architectural elements, including walls, floors, benches, and pillar bases, were digitized as 2D polygons with attributes defining the base height and extrusion of each feature based on the levels shown on the plan. The resultant polygons were then extruded to create 3D volumes (multipatch features) representing the built architecture with precise geometry equivalent to Level of Detail 4 or 300 in Building Information Modelling (Fig. 9.6). A virtual representation with a

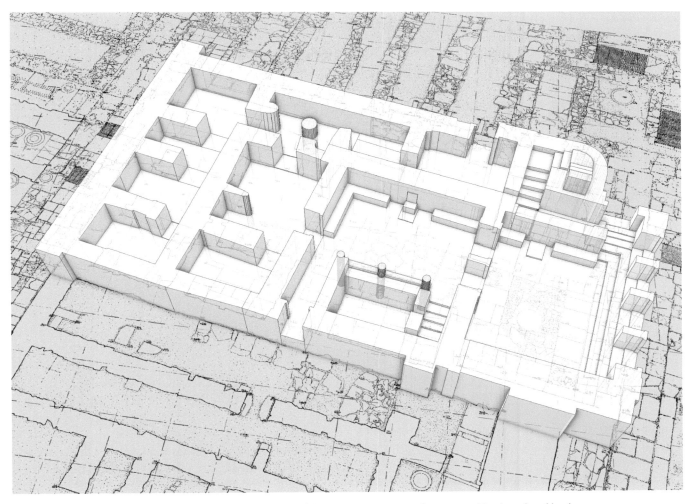

Figure 9.6. Digitized version of the plan of the Throne Room Complex at ground level produced by the Ephorate of Antiquities of Heraklion (courtesy of Heraklion Ephorate of Antiquities and John Pouncett).

higher Level of Detail could in theory be created from the Ephorate plan; however, uncertainty over the scale and extent of modifications related to the reconstruction of the Palace preclude this here.

Photographs published by Evans show the degree of preservation of the Throne Room Complex at the time of the excavation.[44] The western part of the Throne Room Complex was well preserved, with the walls of the Throne Room surviving to a height of c. 1.75 m above the floor level, and the bottom of the Lustral Basin c. 0.75 m below the floor level. In contrast, the eastern part of the Throne Room was less well preserved, with the gypsum block at the north-east corner of the Antechamber to the Throne Room discernible on the surface and only the bases of the bannisters/reveals of the door jambs from the steps at the eastern end of the antechamber sur-

viving. The 3D volumes for individual architectural elements of the Throne Room Complex can be modified to reflect their extent at the time of excavation by georeferencing drawings or by perspective matching photographs from the Sir Arthur Evans Archive. Once the geometry of the multi-patch features has been adjusted, surfaces of the modified 3D volumes can be textured using images extracted from the digitized drawings and photographs.

Additional 3D volumes were created for the rooms/spaces used to denote different components of the Throne Room Complex and index the notebooks, drawings, and photographs held in the Archive, inheriting the geometry of the multi-patch features for the architectural elements where possible and using measurements given in the published and unpublished accounts of the excavation. Individual entries in the notebooks, drawings, and photographs can then be linked to the corresponding multi-patch features using attributes to

---

[44] Evans 1900, fig. 9; 1935, fig. 879.

store text and images directly or to store links pointing to Uniform Resource Identifiers (URIs) or Digital Object Identifiers (DOIs). The enriched multi-patch features were published to ArcGIS online as a scene layer package and hosted feature layer, creating a digital twin of the Throne Room Complex that can be embedded in web-mapping applications that can be tailored to different audiences with Scene Viewers allowing users to explore the contents of the Sir Arthur Evans Archive on their own and Story Maps allowing the construction of narratives that guide users through specific aspects of the Archive. Ultimately, the digital twin will allow visitors to the Ashmolean Museum to view the records and object held in the museum collections in their original context and will allow visitors to the Palace of Minos to access records and objects in the museum collections directly from the site itself.

Conclusion

The Sir Arthur Evans Archive is of particular significance as the primary excavation archive for the Palace of Minos at Knossos, but it has always been accessible to researchers prepared to travel to Oxford. The digitization of over ten thousand items requires significant resources and a continued commitment to sustain those items online. This paper has addressed why the digitization of the Archive is important and what form its digitization and subsequent digitalization should take. A compelling reason for digitization is as a form of digital repatriation of excavation records that relate to a site in Greece. This enables them to be shared with a much wider audience, from those responsible to maintaining and promoting the site now to its hundreds of thousands of visitors. Whereas specialists will be able to find what they are looking for once the Archive is put on the new Ashmolean Collections Online website, this paper has considered how to make these digitized items more accessible, both to machines and humans.

The digitization of Archive items as machine-readable LOD means that they can be linked with other related items on the Semantic Web. Since the Palace of Minos remains unpublished by modern standards, LOD provides a means of digital publication. This will be a form of publication distributed across the web, since there is so much data already available about Knossos already, from published reports to spatial data and images. Publication in this context is a process of giving Archive items URIs and then linking them to other items, within the Archive and on the web. This provides an interesting contrast to traditional hierarchical archival catalogues and also traditional linear print publications. This form of online publication will not supersede either but is complementary since it allows information about the excavations to be ordered and queried in different ways. It is also potentially open-ended, as new Archive items are placed online, and new links are formed.

Alongside the long-term project of online publication of the site, there is also a need for visualizations to enable users and visitors to Knossos to explore the Archive in a more accessible form. The 3D model aims to do this by presenting items from the Archive spatially. This was piloted in an exhibition at the Ashmolean: *Labyrinth: Knossos, Myth and Reality* in the first half of 2023. The longer-term plan is to provide a resource to enable visitors to explore the Palace at Knossos. This will complement the visitor experience of a world-famous archaeological site.

Acknowledgements

We would like to thank Amy Miranda and Rubina Raja for their invitation to participate in a stimulating conference. We would also like to thank Vassiliki Sythiakaki, Elisavet Kavoulaki, and the Ephorate of Antiquities of Heraklion for their collaboration on the 3D model and providing permission to use the 1:20 plan. The work described in this paper has been funded by the Al Thani Collection Foundation (creation of the model), the Gladys Krieble Delmas Foundation (cataloguing of the Archive and digitization of the notebooks), and an anonymous donor. A number of individuals have helped with the ongoing work of cataloguing and digitization of the Archive, among them Ellie Atkins, Aruna Bhaugeerutty, Henny Clare, Vasso Fotou, Yannis Galanakis, Senta German, Nicoletta Momigliano, Chris Monaghan, Jasmin Payne, Alison Roberts, Susan Sherratt, Karl Smith, and Todd Whitelaw.

Archives

Athens, British School at Athens, Mackenzie Pottery Notebooks (1900–1904).
Cambridge, University of Cambridge Faculty of Classics, Wace: The Papers of Alan John Bayard Wace (1879–1957), archaeologist (AJBW).
London, University College London, School of Slavonic and East European Studies, Evans (Arthur) Collection (EVA).
Oxford, Ashmolean Museum, Sir Arthur Evans Archive (AJE).

Works Cited

Berners Lee, T. 2006. 'Linked Data: Design Issues' <https://www.w3.org/DesignIssues/LinkedData.html> [accessed 20 August 2022].
Boardman, J. and L. Palmer. 1963. *On the Knossos Tablets* (Oxford: Oxford University Press).
Brown, A. 1983. *Arthur Evans and the Palace of Minos* (Oxford: Ashmolean Museum).
—— 1986. '"I Propose to Begin at Gnossos": John Myres's Visit to Crete in 1893', *Annual of the British School at Athens*, 81: 37–44.
—— 1993. *Before Knossos: Arthur Evans's Travels in the Balkans and Crete* (Oxford: Ashmolean Museum).
—— 2000. 'Evans in Crete before 1900', in D. Huxley (ed.), *Cretan Quests: British Explorers, Excavators and Historians* (London: British School at Athens), pp. 9–14.
—— 2001. *Arthur Evans's Travels in Crete, 1894–1899* (Oxford: Archaeopress).
Carabott, P. 2006. 'A Country in a "State of Destitution" Labouring under an "Unfortunate Regime": Crete at the Turn of the 20th Century (1898 1906)', in Y. Hamilakis and N. Momigliano (eds), *Archaeology and European Modernity: Producing and Consuming the 'Minoans'*, Creta antica, 7 (Padua: Bottega d'Erasmo), pp. 39–53.
Evans, A. 1900. 'Knossos. Summary Report of the Excavations in 1900: I. The Palace', *Annual of the British School at Athens*, 6: 3–70.
—— 1901. 'The Palace of Knossos: Provisional Report of the Excavations of the Year 1902', *Annual of the British School at Athens*, 7: 1–120.
—— 1902. 'The Palace of Knossos: Provisional Report of the Excavations of the Year 1902', *Annual of the British School at Athens*, 8: 1–124.
—— 1903. 'The Palace of Knossos: Provisional Report for the Year 1903', *Annual of the British School at Athens*, 9: 1–153.
—— 1904. 'The Palace of Knossos', *Annual of the British School at Athens*, 10: 1–62.
—— 1905. 'The Palace of Knossos and its Dependencies: Provisional Report for the Year 1905', *Annual of the British School at Athens*, 11: 1–26.
—— 1921. *The Palace of Minos at Knossos*, I (London: Macmillan).
—— 1928. *The Palace of Minos at Knossos*, II (London: Macmillan).
—— 1930. *The Palace of Minos at Knossos*, III (London: Macmillan).
—— 1935. *The Palace of Minos at Knossos*, IV (London: Macmillan).
Evans, J. 1943. *Time and Chance: The Story of Arthur Evans and his Forebears* (London: Longmans).
Galanakis, Y., E. Tsitsa, and U. Günkel-Maschek. 2017. 'The Power of Images: Re-examining the Wall Paintings from the Throne Room at Knossos', *Annual of the British School at Athens*, 112: 47–98.
Hatzaki, E. 2005. *Knossos: The Little Palace*, British School at Athens Supplementary Volume, 38 (London: British School at Athens).
Hellenic Statistical Authority. 2022. 'Survey on Museums and Archaeological Sites Attendance', press release 14 July 2022 <https://www.statistics.gr/en/statistics/-/publication/SCI21/2022-M03> [accessed 21 August 2022].
Hood, S. and W. Taylor. 1981. *The Bronze Age Palace at Knossos: Plan and Sections*, British School at Athens Supplementary Volume, 13 (London: British School at Athens).
Karetsou, A. and V. Fotou. 2004. 'Research in the Archive of Arthur Evans's Excavations at Knossos', in G. Cadogan, E. Hatzaki, and A. Vasilakis (eds), *Knossos: Palace, City, State*, British School at Athens Studies, 12 (London: British School at Athens), pp. 581–609.
Momigliano, N. 1996. 'Evans, Mackenzie, and the History of the Palace at Knossos', *Journal of Hellenic Studies*, 116: 166–69.
—— 1999. *Duncan Mackenzie: A Cautious Canny Highlander and the Palace of Minos at Knossos*, Bulletin of the Institute of Classical Studies Supplement, 72 (London: Institute of Classical Studies).
—— 2002. 'Federico Halbherr and Arthur Evans: An Archaeological Correspondence (1894–1917)', *Studi Micenei ed Egeo-Anatolici*, 44.2: 263–318.
Mountjoy, P. 2003. *Knossos: The South House*, British School at Athens Supplementary Volume, 34 (London: British School at Athens).
Oddo, E. 2022. *Knossos: The House of the Frescoes*, British School at Athens Supplementary Volume, 51 (London: British School at Athens).

Oldman, D. 2021. 'Digital Research, the Legacy of Form and Structure and the ResearchSpace System', in K. Golub and Y.-H. Liu (eds), *Information and Knowledge Organisation in Digital Humanities* (London: Routledge), pp. 131–53.

Oldman, D. and D. Tanase. 2018. 'Reshaping the Knowledge Graph by Connecting Researchers, Data and Practices in ResearchSpace', in D. Vrandečić, K. Bontcheva, M. C. Suárez-Figueroa, V. Presutti, I. Celino, M. Sabou, L.-A. Kaffee, and E. Simperl (eds), *The Semantic Web: ISWC 2018* (Springer: Cham), pp. 325–40.

Panagiotaki, M. 1999. *The Central Palace Sanctuary at Knossos*, British School at Athens Supplementary Volume, 31 (London: British School at Athens).

—— 2004. 'Knossos Objects: 1904, the First Departure', in G. Cadogan, E. Hatzaki, and A. Vasilakis (eds), *Knossos: Palace, City, State*, British School at Athens Studies, 12 (London: British School at Athens), pp. 565–80.

Pettigrew, A. 2010. 'Lot 211, Christie's Sale 7854' <https://www.christies.com/en/lot/lot-5320073> [accessed 20 August 2022].

Rainer, S., E. Barker, L. Isaksen, and P. de Soto Cañamares. 2015. 'Linking Early Geospatial Documents, One Place at a Time: Annotation of Geographic Documents with Recogito', *e-Perimetron*, 10.2: 49–59.

—— 2017. 'Linked Data Annotation without the Pointy Brackets: Introducing Recogito 2', *Journal of Map & Geography Libraries: Advances in Geospatial Information, Collections & Archives*, 13.1: 111–32.

Sherratt, S. 2000. *Arthur Evans, Knossos and the Priest-King* (Oxford: Ashmolean Museum).

—— 2009. 'Representations of Knossos and Minoan Crete in the British, American and Continental Press, 1900–c. 1930', *Creta antica*, 10: 619–49.

Stillman, W. J. 1881. 'Extracts from Letters of W. J. Stillman, Respecting Ancient Sites in Crete', *Archaeological Institute of America: Appendix to the Second Annual Report of the Executive Committee*, 1880–1881: 41–49.

10. Using Legacy Data to Reconstruct the University of Michigan's Early Twentieth-Century Excavation Methodology at Karanis

Andrew T. Wilburn
Oberlin College, USA (Drew.Wilburn@oberlin.edu)

Introduction[1]

The discipline of archaeology possesses an enormous wealth of unpublished and under-published data. These datasets derive from excavations over the past two centuries at sites throughout the world, including cultural heritage sites currently under threat because of climate change, warfare, or intentional destruction by groups such as the Islamic State.[2] Much of this material is legacy data, a term that refers to records preserved within an obsolete system. Largely moribund in analogue format, hand-drawn maps, lists of finds, printed photographs or negatives, and handwritten or typed excavation diaries, are not easily accessible to scholars and the public.[3] These datasets, however, provide critical contexts for the artefacts housed in museums and storerooms in the United States and abroad and have the potential to open vast reserves of untapped material for contemporary investigations of the past in multiple humanistic disciplines.[4]

Many large legacy datasets were produced through a type of archaeological enquiry that is no longer practised: the 'big dig'. Excavations from the early- and mid-twentieth century employed hundreds of workers who cleared archaeological sites on a scale unimaginable by today's standards. Now, new methods of enquiry, including 'big data' analyses, offer tantalizing opportunities to reassess this material and its geographic distribution, if only it were in an easily searchable format.[5]

The University of Michigan excavations at the site of Karanis, a Graeco-Roman-Egyptian village in the Fayum region of Egypt, recovered more than sixty-five thousand artefacts and documented hundreds of buildings. To translate the legacy data into a usable, contemporary format, the Karanis Housing Project, a research group at Oberlin College, has created digitized versions of the maps in ESRI's ArcGIS and digital records of the finds in PostgreSQL. The process of translating the legacy data into digital formats is providing vital insight into the Michigan team's excavation methodology and recording strategies as well as the inherent biases that structured their interpretations.

---

[1] This work was presented initially as part of the panel 'Secrets Incalculable: Reuse of Documents and Data in Archaeological Research', organized by Jon Frey (Michigan State University) and Fotini Kondyli. My research benefited greatly from the comments of the organizers and the other panellists, including William Caraher, Eric Poehler Andrea De Giorgi, and Sarah W. Kansa. Legacy data from the Michigan excavations at Karanis are now held in the Kelsey Museum of Archaeology in Ann Arbor. I am indebted to the current and recent directors of the museum, Nicola Terrenato, T. G. Wilfong, Elaine Gazda, and Sharon Herbert, as well as Sebastián Encina and Michele Fontenot and the curatorial staff of the museum for their assistance in working with this material. The late Traianos Gagos provided inspiration for this project. Brendan Haug, archivist of the Papyrology Collection, Arthur Verhoogt, and Adam Hyatt assisted in my work with the Michigan Papyrus Collection. I have also benefited from the comments and thoughts of C. Michael Sampson, principal investigator of the Books of Karanis Project, of which I am a collaborator. The Karanis Housing Project team members have included: Ryan Reynolds (Oberlin College, 2014), Miranda Rutherford (Oberlin College, 2015), Olivia Fountain (Oberlin College, 2017), Susanna Faas-Bush (Oberlin College, 2018), Christian Bolles (Oberlin College, 2018), Aaron Henry (Oberlin College, 2018), Emily Hudson (Oberlin College, 2022), Henri Feola (Oberlin College, 2022), Elliot Diaz (Oberlin College, expected graduation 2023), Sadie Pasco-Pranger (Oberlin College, expected graduation 2023), and Grace Burns (Oberlin College, expected graduation 2023). The project has been funded by Oberlin College, an Oberlin-Kalamazoo-University of Michigan Faculty Research Grant, the Thomas F. Cooper '78 Endowed Classics Faculty Support Fund, and the Jody L. Maxmin '71 Classics Department Faculty Support Fund at Oberlin College.

[2] Cunliffe and Curini 2018; Ravankhah and others 2020.

[3] Allison 2008.

[4] Kintigh and others 2014; Bevan 2015.

[5] Kintigh 2006.

The Challenges of Legacy Datasets

Many legacy datasets derive from excavations that were not fully published. The problem of unpublished excavations has long been recognized, and few proposed solutions have been successful. It is likely that in Europe, there are more unpublished excavations than those with a final publication, and for many excavations, the recovered finds are held closely by the original excavator and unavailable to others for study.[6] There are numerous reasons why archaeological data have not been fully published, from lack of funding for publication to the time to conduct research to prepare the publication. Excavators must also overcome their own anxiety about making final pronouncements about the site they excavated and, for some, repress the desire to seek new projects.[7] In the contemporary world, host countries have required projects to publish archaeological finds as a prerequisite for permits, but little can be done to ensure that excavations from the early twentieth century are published.[8]

Working with unpublished legacy archaeological data is complicated by issues endemic to the discipline. The process of collecting archaeological data is inherently destructive; once a site has been excavated, archaeological contexts cannot be put back. Archaeological recovery is fundamentally biased, determined to a large degree by what Bell has termed 'pre-understandings'.[9] These pre-understandings encompass the scaffolding upon which an excavation is conducted — the beliefs and base conceptualization of the excavator regarding the culture and site that is being excavated — as well as any typologies or models that the excavators relied upon in developing and planning the project and its execution. Pre-understandings shape every aspect of archaeological practice, from field collection to artefact analysis.[10] As they structured the collection and interpretation of archaeological data, pre-understandings permitted excavators to obscure the messiness of primary data. For many legacy datasets and unpublished excavations, the pre-understandings of the excavators are lost or obscured by the death of the principal investigators and the absence of published methodologies.

While an archaeological context cannot be fully reconstituted, it is possible to present the excavated material through digital means that will permit new assessments of the data. Numerous projects have built Geographic Information Systems (GIS) and databases from archival material, with productive and informative results.[11] GIS offers a scalable interface that can permit researchers to engage with the totality of an archaeological project while also seeing linkages between datasets. The processes involved in digitizing the archival data can be complex, often requiring researchers to make adjustments to the original recording terminology or system to fit a new methodological and recording schema.[12] Typologies have long been critical to archaeological scaffolding, and the task of reconstructing an archaeological project forces contemporary investigators to reassess and critique the ways in which data were structured and organized.[13] Throughout the process of reconstructing legacy data, modern researchers must maintain a record of their findings, written into the metadata associated with newly produced digital data sources.[14]

Karanis, modern Kom Aushim, was a medium-sized agricultural settlement located in the Egyptian Fayum. The value of the site derives largely from its excavation history. In the late nineteenth century, Grenfell, Hunt, and Hogarth, using contemporary papyri, affirmed the importance of Karanis in the network of towns and villages of the Fayum, an opinion presented initially by Flinders Petrie.[15] The difficulty of excavating houses and the scarcity of papyri led these early excavators to abandon work at the site.[16] It was not until 1924 that the University of Michigan would undertake systematic excavations at the instigation of Francis W. Kelsey, professor of Latin.[17] The Michigan excavations, conducted each year until 1935, were undertaken on a scale that is unimaginable today. In the first season, the excavation employed sixty or seventy men, many from Qift and originally trained by Petrie, and 120 boys and girls.[18]

---

[6] Tilley 1989, 276.

[7] Karageorghis 2000, 4.

[8] Hadjisaavas and Karageorghis 2000, 109; Muhly 2000.

[9] Bell 2014, 45.

[10] Wylie 2017, 204.

[11] Witcher 2008; Lawrence, Bradbury, and Dunford 2012; Bell 2014; González-Tennant 2016; Woywitka and Beaudoin 2017; Loy, Stocker, and Davis 2021.

[12] Esteva and others 2010; Clarke 2015; Loy, Stocker, and Davis 2021.

[13] Wylie 2017, 213; Boozer 2014.

[14] Clarke 2015, 322.

[15] Hogarth and Grenfell 1895, 15; Petrie and others 1891, 32; on early excavation at the site, see Davoli 1998, 74–76.

[16] Hogarth and Grenfell 1895, 16; for a reconstruction of Grenfell and Hunt's brief foray, see Montserrat 1996.

[17] Pedley 2012, 330–32.

[18] Boak and Peterson 1931, 2.

Over the next ten years, more than sixty-five thousand artefacts were recovered, including household objects, written documents on papyri and ostraca, ceramics, lamps, and statuary, as well as the organic remains of seeds, bulbs, and grain. As artefacts were unearthed, each was recorded according to its find-spot: either a room within a building or an open area. These architectural features were associated with an occupation layer, a relative chronology employed on the site on the premise that different periods of habitation could be recognized through building processes. Through the recovered artefacts, architecture, papyri, and ostraca, the site provides an unparalleled glimpse of life in antiquity. The fact that nearly all its documentation is in legacy formats makes it extremely difficult for non-specialists to access this rich archive.

Early twentieth-century excavations present unique challenges due to the varied quality and quantity of record-keeping; the legacy data from a site such as Karanis cannot be simply dumped into a digital format. To make the site accessible to a wider audience, project team members have digitized the architecture as recorded in the scale maps in a Geographic Information System. The Michigan team utilized a complex, site-specific system of recording finds, so it has been necessary to generate and refine a digital record for each artefact discovered at the site, ensuring that the records are machine-readable. As records are completed, they are integrated into a PostgreSQL database that is linked to the GIS map. While the process of digitizing the archival material is not yet complete, the project has identified several critical issues:

1. Numerous objects and artefacts have been listed as part of an excavation unit, but were not retained and lack photographs, drawings, and descriptions.

2. The interpretation of the occupation of the site relied on a restricted chronological framework that did not consider all dating evidence.

3. The Michigan team employed an inconsistent system of identifying and assigning buildings, excavation units, and artefacts to occupation strata.

The inconsistencies and chronological problems can be closely tied to the excavation methodology, which prioritized delineating a strict phasing of the site. This contribution first will review the types of legacy data generated in the excavation and evaluate some of the key problems with these datasets. Then, I will turn to the methods the Karanis Housing Project has employed to mitigate some of these complications.

A Brief History of the Michigan Excavations at Karanis

A team from the University of Michigan excavated Karanis between 1924 and 1935, first under the direction of J. L. Starkey (1924–1926), and subsequently with Enoch E. Peterson at the helm (1926–1935). Before the arrival of the Michigan team, the mining company Daira Agnelli Gianotti had exercised a permit to extract the nutrient-rich fertilizer, or *sebbakh*, that was found at the site.[19] The company removed as much as 200 m³ from the centre of the mound each day. Boak and Peterson described the condition of the site at the arrival:

> A large area in the heart of the mound, apparently about the centre of town, had been cleared down to bed rock by the *sebbakhin*, so that it had the appearance of the crater of some extinct volcano for which the high sides of the mound supplied the rim.[20]

The first excavation season, 1924–1925, focused on parts of the site that had been cleared partially by the mining company, designated Area A and Area B, with A located to the west of the central crater and B to the east (Fig. 10.1). Over a week in March 1925, the team also cleared the area immediately south of the North Temple, marked as Area F on an early sketch plan.[21]

Throughout the first few years of the excavation, the mining company held a permit to extract *sebbakh*, but in subsequent seasons, the Michigan team was able to determine where excavation would occur and could approach the site scientifically. Each season, the team had to remove sufficient sand and debris to supply the mining company until the following season commenced; should the company run out of material for fertilizer, they could return to the mound and restart their extraction.[22] As buildings were revealed and excavated, the team catalogued the finds and drew the architectural structure. The upper strata of buildings were often demolished to permit the investigation of lower, earlier strata. The resulting destruction means that few mud-brick structures remain from the areas in which the Michigan team worked.

---

[19] Boak and Peterson 1931, 1.
[20] Boak and Peterson 1931, 3.
[21] Boak 1933, 3.
[22] Boak and Peterson 1931, 3.

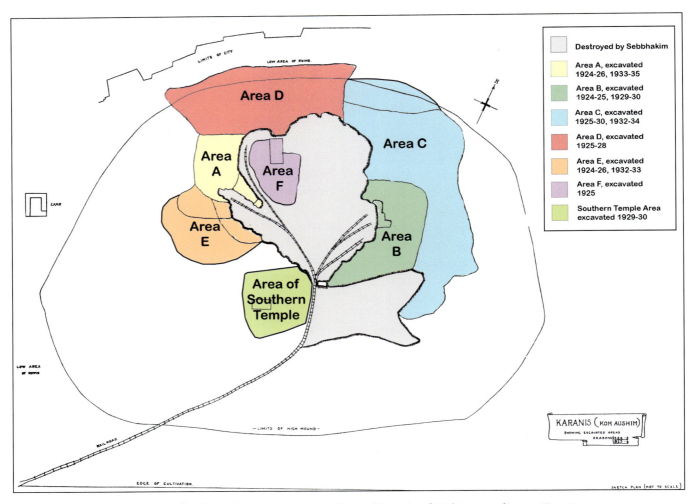

Figure 10.1. Sketch map showing areas excavated by the University of Michigan expedition to Karanis (adapted from Boak and Peterson 1931, plan I. Original image from a glass slide surrogate, GL00426 from the Karanis Excavation Papers, courtesy of the Kelsey Museum of Archaeology, University of Michigan).

During the 1925–1926 season, the focus of excavation shifted. On the west side of the site, excavation moved both north and south to new areas, D to the north, and E to the south. On the east side, excavation opened a new area, C, to the north-east of Area B.[23] During the 1927–1928 season and the 1928–1929 season, work continued in the B and C sections on the eastern side.[24] The Southern Temple, dedicated to Pnepheros and Petesouchos, and its surroundings were excavated in the 1929–1930 season. During the 1931–1932 season, the excavation team began work at another site, Soknopaiou Nesos, to provide comparative data. Work resumed at Karanis in 1932, focusing on the east side. In 1933, the team mostly worked on the west side, in the area to the north of the Southern Temple. In the final season of excavation, 1934–1935, the Michigan team investigated the nearby site of Kom Abou Billou, ancient Terenouthis. Work at Karanis produced few artefacts, as the excavators returned to structures first investigated in 1924. The excavation closed in 1935.

After the completion of field excavation each year, a smaller team continued to work in the dig house, cataloguing the finds and finalizing the maps of the areas that had been excavated.[25] Once the team had left to return to Ann Arbor, guards maintained the site over the summer and were sometimes responsible for recovering artefacts. These objects are identified through the notation SG (Summer Guard), typically without an accompanying locus or provenance. The site was not backfilled, and

---

23 Boak and Peterson 1931, 4.
24 Boak and Peterson 1931, 39.

25 Boak and Peterson 1931, 2.

remained exposed to the elements, leading to the decay of the mud-brick structures, sometimes resulting in the loss of architectural features in as little as a single season. For example, photographic evidence demonstrates the deterioration of a vaulted ceiling in granary C123 between the 1929/1930 season and the 1930/1931 season.[26] The damage to the site since the close of excavations in 1935 has been immense.[27]

After the final season, Peterson returned to Ann Arbor and began to assess the massive amount of accumulated data. Peterson spent the next four decades working on this material, producing an 867-page manuscript on the architecture and topography of the site that was typeset and edited in 1973. This document was never published due to funding constraints. Elinor Husselman soon undertook the task of editing the manuscript and produced a condensed report on the topography and architecture, a year after Peterson's death in 1978.[28] In the eighty-five years since the end of the excavation, publications from the site have followed an approach that is typical of traditional archaeology — the presentation of specialist reports on individual classes of artefacts.[29] The corpus of excavated papyri and artefacts recovered at Karanis remains unparalleled in the Graeco-Roman Mediterranean, and numerous studies have engaged with intersection of texts and the lived environment at the site.[30] Many of these works drew on the artefacts that were housed at Michigan or Cairo and relied on the chronology established by the original excavators and recorded in the early publications and the field notebooks; only recently have some works begun to reassess the papyri and artefacts with an eye to the problems inherent in the archaeological data.[31] To this day, the site lacks a final comprehensive publication of the topography and architecture, and much of the work of reassessing and presenting the data remains to be done.

The Legacy Data from Karanis

Nearly all the legacy records from the Karanis excavations are currently housed at the University of Michigan, with most of the material kept in the Kelsey Museum of Archaeology. Other archival material is kept in the Papyrology Collection, the Bentley Historical Library, and the Ruthven Museum of Anthropology. The records are diverse, comprised of maps of the site and plans of individual buildings, expansive lists of all the finds recovered, documents related to the elevations of buildings and architecture, and a rich photographic archive, which also includes a series of films taken at the site. The Karanis Housing Project has focused on the maps of buildings and the lists of finds, as these data can be used to contextualize the artefacts and papyri that are currently housed in Cairo, Karanis, Ann Arbor, Athens, and at other locations around the world.

Maps and Plans

H. Falconer served as site surveyor in the 1924–1926 seasons, assisted by S. Yeivin. In 1926, J. Terentieff assumed the role of surveyor. Falconer's first triangulation map, intended to geospatially locate the excavated features, was flawed. Terentieff created a new triangulation map, drawn at 1:2000, that marked the locations of datum points, labelled A–Z, which were used to facilitate mapping the structures and recording the elevation of structures and features.[32] The triangulation map overlays a grid onto the site, with the x-axis numbered 0–16, and the y-axis assigned the values A–P (I and J were left out for clarity). Each of the 224 grid squares measured 70 m on each side.[33] A topographic map, also drawn at 1:2000, documented the contours and elevation of the site and included the temples and the datum points. For each of the five excavator-assigned layers, a 'Key Plan' was drawn at 1:400 scale; these maps include only the outlines of each building.

Detailed plans at 1:100 scale were drawn for many of the 70 m excavation squares, with separate maps created for each of the excavator-assigned occupation layers (on the layers, see below). The plans indicate that individual buildings, features, or architectural elements

---

26 Claytor and Verhoogt 2018, 12.

27 Barnard and others 2016.

28 Husselman 1979.

29 Gagos, Gates, and Wilburn 2005. The period between the 1930s and 1990s witnessed the output of separate volumes on glass: Harden 1936; coins: Haatvedt, Peterson, and Husselman 1964; ceramics: Johnson 1981; lamps: Shier 1978; and terracotta figurines: Allen 1985; papyri: Youtie, Schuman, and Pearl 1936; Youtie and Pearl 1944; Youtie and Winter 1951; Husselman 1971.

30 van Minnen 1994; Terpstra 2014.

31 Claytor and Verhoogt 2018; Sampson (forthcoming).

32 Yeivin 1928, 1. In the first few years of the excavation, the team had not demolished the mud-brick structures (though some 'insignificant parts had been destroyed'), so it was possible to redraw the exposed architecture. Terentieff 1929, 1.

33 Peterson 1973, 10.

Figure 10.2. Plan showing excavation square F10. Features attributed to the top (A) layer are shown without fill; the second (B) layer is indicated by diagonal fill, while the third layer is shown with dark crosshatched lines (Kelsey Museum of Archaeology, negative 4-2976. Image courtesy of the Kelsey Museum of Archaeology, University of Michigan).

were believed to be continuously occupied through different periods. At times, features or portions of buildings were incorporated into new structures or alterations were made within buildings. These patterns of continued occupation or reuse are differentiated through shading and cross-hatching, with features assigned to the C-Layer, for example, indicated through crosshatching, B-Layer features are filled using diagonal lines, and A-Layer features were indicated without fill (Fig. 10.2). It should be noted that the excavator's rationale for assigning walls or features to a given layer is seldom explained. One method may have been construction materials, as

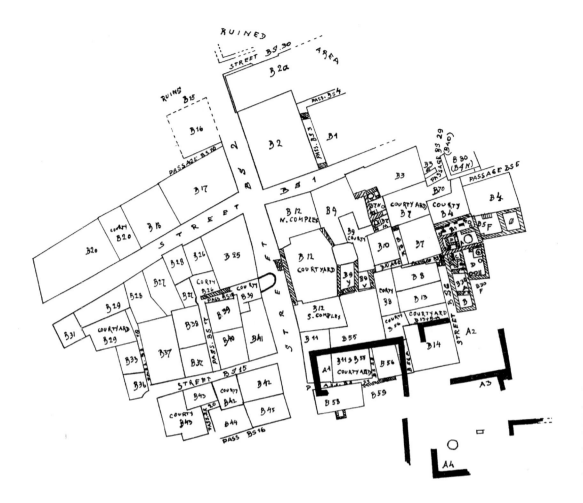

Figure 10.3. Sketch plan of Area G (reprinted with permission the University of Michigan Press, from Boak and Peterson 1931, plan II, from the Karanis Excavation Papers, Kelsey Museum of Archaeology, University of Michigan).

mud bricks were used as a diagnostic tool; the Michigan team assessed the size, shape, and inclusions of bricks and hypothesized dates from this.[34] The Kelsey Museum archives include the sketch maps that were used to record the elevation points taken for these structures.

Cross-sections of the site, keyed to the excavation squares, were created to document the superposition and arrangement of the buildings and to provide a visual record of the excavator-assigned layers that was correlated to metres above sea level. Typically, the excavators created both an east–west and a north–south cross-section of each triangulation square. These plans provide elevation drawings of the buildings positioned along the centre transects of the square and are particularly useful in assessing the elevation of the structures and the assignment of layers. Some individual buildings that were believed to be significant, such as the large granaries, were documented with elevation drawings.

Even with this extensive documentation, some areas of the site are only known from sketch plans, rather than scale drawings. For the 1926–1927 season, buildings excavated in Area G, located to the west and south of Area E, are recorded only on a sketch map (Fig. 10.3). Detailed plans of houses B1, B2, and B3 are preserved, showing both the floor-plan and elevation of the structures. House B1 was a significant structure, as excavators discovered two important papyrus documents in room C: letters from Apollinarius, serving in the fleet at Misenum, to his mother, Taësis.[35] The majority of the structures in this area, however, lack precise plans and cannot be accurately located at the site.

Other structures are very difficult to identify. 'Record of Objects: Karanis 1924–1925: 10–82, XIV–XXI, 010–053, 100–344, 4001–4048, 5000–50096' (these volumes are discussed below), associates objects with

---

[34] Peterson 1973, 5, 34, 43; Husselman 1979, 9.

[35] Boak and Peterson 1931, 7–9; *P.Mich.* VIII.490 (TM 27100) and *P.Mich.* VIII.491 (TM 27101). On Area G and the recovery of papyri, see Sampson (forthcoming).

buildings numbered 10–82 as well as units numbered 010–053, but I have not been able to locate these numbers on the unpublished maps. It seems clear that units that begin with a '0' are different from those that do not, so unit 27 should be distinguished from unit 027. Annotations in the 'Record of Objects' volumes give tantalizing clues about where the team was excavating, but this information does not necessarily aid in identifying where the units were located. Excavation unit 027 was a 'Crocodile grave s.w. section of excavation 4 ft. from rail line', while unit 030 was a large open area to 'the west of the temple'. It is probable that all these '0'-prefixed units were excavated near the Northern Temple, close to the areas in which the *sebbhakim* were extracting fertilizer. Perhaps because these areas were extensively damaged in the process of extraction, or because they were demolished before 1926, they were not effectively mapped.[36]

The double-digit units without the '0' prefix appear to have been renumbered over the course of the excavation season, probably as part of an attempt to bring the buildings in line with the newly designated occupation layers (see below, next section) while also reflecting a more nuanced understanding of the architecture as it came to light. Unit 27, which is described as 'level on top of wall', includes an annotation that this unit was given a new number, 5007. The 'Record of Objects' volume for 1924 lists seven objects for unit 27, and an additional 912 for unit 5007. Like some other renumbered buildings, 5007 is shown on a sketch map drawn by Yeivin (Yeivin Map 3). Certain units were given multiple new numbers, so that unit 29 should be associated with unit 4001B as well as unit 4039. There are additional artefacts attributed to both 4001B and 4039, suggesting that the new numbers were assigned as the architecture was revealed further and indicated the presence of two distinct buildings.

There are additional problems inherent in the legacy maps which make it difficult to translate the maps into modern topography. The triangulation map and the topographic map are not aligned with a modern projection, but rather used twenty-five Egyptian Deodetic Survey Bench marks.[37] Recent excavations at the site by the URU Fayum Project were unable to locate these original survey points.[38] Accurate geospatial measurements can be taken from the four corners of the two temples, but only the Southern Temple appears on the 1:100 scale maps.[39] Fieldwork by Bethany Simpson has revealed further inaccuracies between the detailed maps when compared to the standing mud-brick structures.[40] The maps show the relative locations of excavated spaces, but geospatially locating the excavated features proves to be a greater challenge.

Recording Buildings and Structures

The earliest years of excavation provided the Michigan team with an interpretive framework that would guide subsequent seasons and dominate the canonical dating of the site. In the first season, along the eastern face of the central pit created by the mining company, three strata of houses were visible, each separated by a layer of sand. The excavators believed that these strata, identified as the upper, middle, and lower, corresponded to periods of occupation. The sand that separated the strata was assumed to represent breaks in occupation, when this part of the site lay dormant. The layers were less clear on the north-west scarp of the pit, where buildings appeared to be superimposed on one another.[41] From this view of the site, the excavators developed a chronology based on occupation layers, believing that they could identify discrete phases through changes in architecture. The numbering systems that were employed on the site soon were modified to reflect their beliefs about the occupation phases.

During the 1924–1925 and 1925–1926 seasons, buildings were numbered sequentially. On the east side, Area B, the buildings were numbered 1–1000, while the buildings uncovered on the west, Area A, were given designations between 4000–5000. Buildings associated with the middle, or second layer were numbered 5000–6000. From the 1926–1927 season under Enoch Peterson onwards, a more radical numbering system was employed, and buildings were identified according to one of five different occupation layers, A–E, with A representing the layer below the surface; E, at the bottom, was believed to correspond to the second and first centuries BC.[42] Buildings without a layer prefix ('undesignated') lay just below the surface (although this is not always the case). The new notation system codified the interpretation of the phasing of the site, effectively inscribing the perceived

---

36 Curiously, Yeivin's 1924–1925 report lists the houses that were excavated, assigning them to levels, but his list begins with building 100. Yeivin 1926; Yeivin n.d.

37 Peterson 1973, 10.

38 Barnard, pers. comm.

39 Barnard and others 2015, 57.

40 Simpson, pers. comm.

41 Boak and Peterson 1931, 4.

42 Boak and Peterson 1931, 6–7.

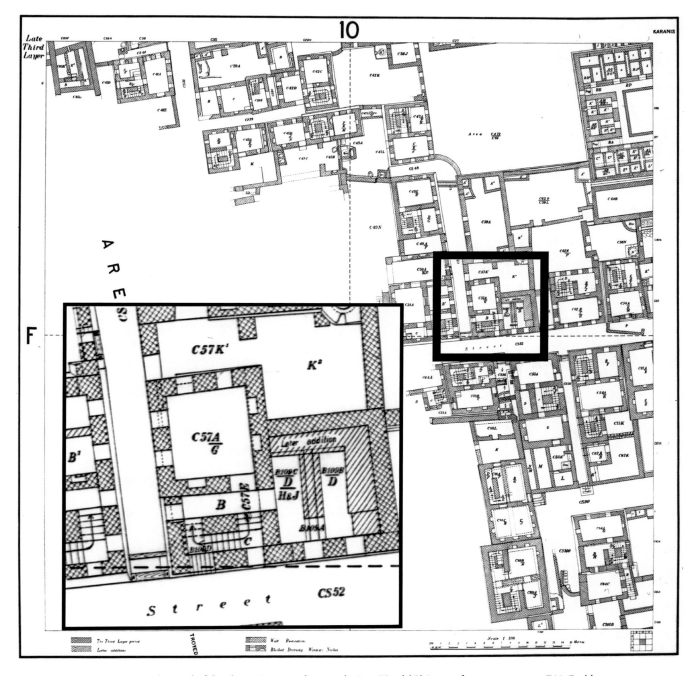

Figure 10.4. Detail of the plan in Fig. 10.2 showing the Late Third (C) Layer of excavation square F10. Buildings of the C- and B-Layers are shown, with room designations separated by a horizontal line (Kelsey Museum of Archaeology, negative 5-7785. Image courtesy of the Kelsey Museum of Archaeology, University of Michigan).

dating into the maps. Structures excavated during the first two seasons were not comprehensively renumbered. Only when a building was reassessed or excavation continued in a particular area, might a building be assigned a new number. In such cases, the new nomenclature was added to the map; the original number was written above a horizontal line, while the new number was placed below. This method of indicating the two separate designations is identical to that used to mark the presence of multiple units within the same area.

As buildings were unearthed, each room within the structure was assigned a letter. Features, such as bins or ovens, were also distinguished by letters. In some rooms, the maps show multiple letter designations for a single space, with the different designations separated by a horizontal line. There is also some variation in how designations might be arranged, with multiple letters placed either above or below the line. So, for example, in the Late C Layer, excavation square F10, building C57, shows four rooms and a stairwell (Fig. 10.4).

The multiple designations may suggest different strata, in which the upper letter indicated a higher elevation for the finds. This may be the case for room C57A/G, where the same four walls enclose two different letters. Finds are recorded for both rooms C57A and C57G, which suggests that the excavators differentiated these spaces in some way. The excavators may have decided to assign a new unit based on changes in the structure of the building, such as new construction or blocked doorways. In other cases, the letters may refer to different parts of the excavation unit. C57D and C57C likely are different parts of a stairway.

An asterisk was used in conjunction with the letter to indicate a special context, most often when objects were discovered beneath a floor, such as B224B*. Streets also were numbered, but an 'S' was used as prefix to the designation. When no walls were readily apparent, the space was designated an 'Area'. The occupation periods of the site were slotted into a chronology based on papyrological and numismatic evidence. The earliest attestations for Karanis in the papyri date from the third century BC. The site appears in three of the Zenon papyri, which provide relatively secure dates for the mid-third century.[43] Excavators believed that the site was founded under Ptolemy II, likely as part of the expansion and reclamation of the Fayum region. Little papyrological or numismatic evidence was found that post-dated the reign of Marcian (AD 450–457) leading the excavators to place the end of the settlement in the mid-fifth century AD.[44]

Peterson's unpublished 1973 manuscript proposed a general reading of the layers at the site. The earliest occupation, the E- and D-Layers, were dated to between the second and mid-first centuries BC.[45] The C-, Late-C-, and B-Layers were associated with the greatest expansion and prosperity of the city, dated to the mid-first–third centuries AD. Finally, the top layer was believed to date to the fourth or fifth century AD. Husselman's 1979 publication reiterated and refined this general chronology, aligning it with known historical events. Ptolemaic remains were slim and included the two temples. The E-Layer was associated with the second and first centuries BC. The D-Layer was dated to the late first century BC,[46] while the C-Layer stretches from the mid-first century AD through the mid-second century AD. Husselman suggests that a significant break may have existed between the C- and B-Layers, although the 1931 publication had stated that these layers were difficult to distinguish.[47] The end of the C-Layer of occupation was associated with the Antonine Plague of AD 165, and the B-Layer marked a subsequent resurgence of the town, stretching through the third century. Another occupation break was believed to exist above the B-Layer, with few architectural features surviving from the previous periods. The top, or A-Layer, marked the final period of occupation, between the third and fifth centuries, culminating in the total abandonment of the site.[48]

Excavation around the Southern Temple to Pnepheros and Petesouchos in 1929–1930 identified four Layers, F, Late F, E, and D, that do not align well with the broad chronology recorded by Peterson and Husselman. The excavators suggested that this area was laid out in the first century BC–early part of the first century AD (Layer F), with the construction of the temple (Layer Late F), dated to the second half of the first century and the early second century AD. Layer E was dated to the second and third centuries AD, while the uppermost layer, Layer D, was dated to the third and early fourth centuries AD.[49] This dating schema is quite confusing, as Layer D in the temple area corresponds chronologically to the B- or A-Layer in other areas of the site. In the area around the Southern Temple, the layers appear to have been identified based on their elevation above sea level. Comparable dating problems can be noted in Area G. In this region of the site, excavators suggested that the B-Layer should be associated with the late third or early fourth century AD.[50]

In the field, the assignment of buildings to layers appears to have coupled the analysis of architectural remains with an assessment of the finds as they were unearthed. The presence of sand between architectural features was taken as evidence of an occupation break. In the absence of such clear indicators, different layers probably were distinguished when the excavators noted changes in architectural construction. When a building was assigned to a new occupation layer, the structures

---

[43] *P.Col.Zen.* II.117, TM 2355; *P.Cair.Zen.* III.59491, TM 1129; III.59361, TM 1004.
[44] Boak and Peterson 1931, 5.
[45] Peterson 1973, 11–13.
[46] Husselman 1979, 10.
[47] Boak and Peterson 1931, 30.
[48] Husselman 1979, 9.
[49] Boak and Peterson 1931, 20.
[50] Boak and Peterson 1931, 9.

were often given a new number, sequentially following the other structures in that layer; these new numbers were seldom related to the number assigned for the later (higher) layer. Even with this general framework, the assignment of layers was not always consistent. In building 242, for example, the excavators noted changes that suggested an earlier occupation. Rather than assign a new number to the building, they merely noted in the 'Record of Objects' book that some objects were likely from an earlier occupation period.[51] In another case, the finds from houses C136, C137, and C138, suggested that the structures should be associated with the D-Layer of occupation. The buildings were recorded on the D-Layer maps but retained the C-Layer designation, making it difficult to distinguish to which phase the excavators assigned the artefacts.[52] It is unclear whether these are isolated incidents.

The 'Record of Objects' Volumes

Perhaps the most important archival materials from the Karanis excavations are the 'Record of Objects' volumes, which documented many of the finds that were recovered at Karanis, Soknopaiou Nesos (excavated 1931–1932), and Terenouthis (excavated 1935). These comprise eleven bound volumes, each titled with the archaeological contexts that are included within, such as 'Record of Objects: Karanis 1928: 102*-242*, B108-172, CS23-CS130', which numbers 821 pages. The volumes contain the typed pages created in the field, presumably copied from handwritten notes. Each page consists of an entry for a street, area, or a single room in a building.[53] Contexts with extensive finds stretch over multiple pages. Some rooms, areas, or streets were excavated over multiple seasons, and are documented in multiple volumes. For particularly unusual or important finds, the excavators included a notation that indicated the approximate location, such as 'in the niche' or 'very low in filling'.

The first twenty-six artefacts recovered in a unit were designated by upper case letters, proceeding sequentially from A–Z. In the first season, additional objects were catalogued with the designations AA–AZ, then AAA–AAZ. In the 1925–1926 season, excavators began to assign the annotation AI, BI, CI [...] ZI (letter with an appended Roman numeral 'I'), then AII, BII, CII [...] ZII. Finds of ceramic vessels are numbered sequentially using lower case letters, a–z, with additional ceramics indicated with a lowercase number and Roman numeral, such as aI, bI, cI [...] zI. Objects of the same type found in a given room, whether textiles, papyri, or beads, frequently were recorded using only a single designation. The artefact description records how many of each object were discovered. As an example, building 5048, excavated in 1924 contained '20 coins' (AS), 'papyri, 2 lots' (AV), or '4 pottery disks' (AAH). It is unclear how many papyri were discovered, as the marginalia only reads 'Box in Cairo'. The same context also disclosed textiles (AX); twenty-two fragments were later accessioned into the Kelsey Museum. Coin hoards typically were given a single letter; in the 1933 season, for example, excavation in house C418, room E recovered 2964 coins found in a ceramic vessel; all were given the designation 'D'. In other cases, the excavators marked multiple examples with annotations such as 'x 2' (times 2).

The 'Record of Objects' volumes provide a basic system that can be used to generate a unique field number for each artefact, except when multiple objects are grouped together. Both the Kelsey Museum of Archaeology and the University of Michigan Papyrus Collection employ this annotation, where artefacts and papyri are designated by year of excavation, building, room, and artefact number. As an example, a Harpocrates figurine, discovered in 1933, in building C409, room J would be indicated as 33-C409J-R.

As early as the first season, the Michigan team developed typologies to document and record the ceramic vessels and the lamps. The ceramic typology is a different system from that used to number the artefacts, even though the same basic elements (Latin letters, Roman numerals, and Arabic numerals) are employed. In the 'Record of Objects' volumes, most ceramic vessels were designated by an Arabic number that is used to indicate a specific vessel shape; 584 distinct vessel types are known.[54] These types are grouped into a rough typology that employs a series of Roman numerals and letters, such as 'I a' (Shallow bowls with round bases) or 'IV b ii' (Dishes with a flat base; moulded rim; convex out-

---

[51] Boak and Peterson 1931, 44 n. 1.
[52] Peterson 1973, 30.
[53] Wilfong 2014a, 15–16. Wilfong lists each of the 'Record of Objects' volumes.

[54] It seems likely that the Arabic number was assigned first, in the field, and the typology developed later. The 1924 'Record of Objects' includes typeset Arabic numbers for the ceramic vessels, with the classification (e.g. XI c i) added later by hand. In later years, both the Arabic number and the typology are typeset.

splayed sides). The 'Record of Objects' books, however, typically list only the type, such as 366 without further explanation, so it is necessary to translate and expand the typology to understand the finds.[55] In some cases, only the general type of vessel (such as Ia) is indicated. Most importantly, the typology represents the only record for a substantial number of ceramics discovered at the site, as these objects were often abandoned in the field and not retained. A comparable typology was created for the lamps, using a large Roman numeral, a capital Latin letter, and a small Latin letter (e.g. XIII B a, field number 24-114D-AQ, identified as a fine red slipped pottery lamp). The code has not yet been deciphered, nor has the key been found.[56]

The 'Record of Objects' volumes document many of the identifiable artefacts discovered in a building or unit, but the data are far from total. It is nearly certain that smaller, less-easily identified objects were thrown into the spoil heaps. Other finds were documented and annotated with the letters 'N.T.H.' an abbreviation for 'Not Taken Home'. Any objects lacking an accession number were presumably left in the field. The 'Record of Objects' books include 68,438 entries, some of which include multiple finds. As was customary for the time, the finds were divided between the sponsoring organization and the Egyptian government. The Egyptian Antiquities Service distributed 2462 artefacts to the Cairo Museum, the Coptic Museum, the Agricultural Museum, and several provincial museums. Thirty-eight thousand and eleven field entries, representing at least 46,415 artefacts, made their way into the collections of the Kelsey Museum; 2603 ostraca, papyri, and wax tablets were catalogued in the Papyrology Collection of the University of Michigan. More than 24,989 artefacts were left in the field.[57]

The loose typeset sheets documenting the finds were bound and annotated in Ann Arbor. The current volumes include references to the maps and plans as well as photographs that show the archaeological contexts. Marginal notes for individual artefacts list the museum or collection and accession numbers. For papyri, ostraca, and coins, dates are provided, either approximate (third century) or precise (11 Nov 301 AD), were added as publications revealed additional information.

The 'Record of Objects' volumes provide a vital resource for understanding the scope of the Karanis excavations and piecing together the archaeological contexts as they were uncovered. The museum collections into which Karanis artefacts were accessioned can only tell part of the story, as much of the recovered material is now lost. These documents, however, present unique challenges. The recording system included letters, special characters such as the asterisk, and Roman numerals. Such an array of field designations makes it difficult to transfer the records into a modern database or to conduct effective searches or analyses.

The Photographic Archive

The Kelsey Museum retains a detailed photographic archive from the excavations. Photographs were taken of many of the structures during excavation, and the field team also took images of interesting or unusual finds as they were unearthed. Two 'Division Albums', one from each of the two main divisions of finds between the Michigan team and the Egyptian government, contain photographs that lay out the artefacts by type; these images were taken before the objects were divided between the University of Michigan, the Cairo Museum, and other stakeholders, such as the National Museum of Athens. The artefacts are annotated, with the objects retained by Egypt sometimes marked with an 'x'. These photographic records, like the field photographs, document the condition of the finds soon after they were unearthed. Some of the artefacts shown in the photographs have been lost or damaged in the intervening years.[58] At the initiative of Francis W. Kelsey, George R. Swain, the site photographer, produced about four hours of silent movie footage of the excavation. This material has not been fully catalogued, but it provides a unique window into the excavation as it was occurring.[59]

---

[55] The 'key' that explains the typology was lost for many years and was not employed by Johnson in her publication. In 2014, I located some loose sheets of paper in the archives that explained the typology, and Nicholas Hudson currently is using this document to reassess the Karanis ceramics as part of the Books of Karanis Project.

[56] As most of the lamps were retained and are currently in Cairo and Ann Arbor, it may be possible to reconstruct the typology from the artefacts. Chi Shu (Oberlin College, 2022) and Sydney Fagerstrom (Oberlin College, expected graduation 2023) have begun work on this project. Preliminary findings suggest that the typology was employed to note the design impressed on the lamp, rather than the form or material of the artefact.

[57] Wilfong 2014a, 16–18.

[58] Wilfong 2014a, 18–20.

[59] Wilfong 2014b.

Interpretive Problems

The published and unpublished records from the Michigan excavations present a picture of the excavation as orderly and scientific. The 'Record of Objects' volumes suggest a structured recovery of all finds, which were documented as they were removed from the earth. Karanis seemed to follow the vicissitudes of the Roman Empire as a whole, fitting neatly into a pattern of expansion, contraction, and eventual abandonment. Digging deeper, however, reveals problems with the recording methods and hints at the ways in which the excavators' methodology and pre-interpretation of the site structured the documentation of architecture and artefacts. The excavators believed that they might find a clear sequence of occupation at the site, attested by the finds in a particular building. With this framework in mind, they assigned layers or periods to buildings and rooms, reifying their pre-understandings within the field diaries, maps, and other excavation records.

The dating proposed by the Michigan team reflected the chronology attested by most of the numismatic and papyrological evidence but did not adequately account for other data sources, particularly ceramics, which were less well understood at that time. Two very late coins are attested, both surface finds. One dates from the reign of Justinian I (527–565, KMA 0000.06.6689) and another from the reign of Heraclius (610–641, KMA 0000.06.6890).[60] Even after nearly a century of publication, the latest dated papyrus from Karanis, a complaint about water scarcity, is securely dated to 15 May 439.[61]

When the ceramic evidence is incorporated into the analysis, however, the picture changes dramatically. Using African Red Slip and transport amphora excavated in the 1920s and 1930s, Nigel Pollard has argued that Karanis flourished into the fifth and even early sixth centuries.[62] Thomas Landvatter, relying on the rediscovered ceramic key, demonstrated that building B224, dated by the excavators to the second layer of occupation, late second to third centuries AD, should be dated to the early fifth century. The finds from room A included a vessel of excavator-assigned type 401, which is a dish with a flat base in African Red Slip, catalogued by Hayes as form 62B. Amphora fragments dated to the fifth century or later were also recovered in adjacent rooms and spaces.[63] This new, down-dated chronology has been confirmed by the URU Fayum Project excavations at the site, which has proposed a fourth-century expansion of the site to both the west and east.[64] Ceramic evidence from a storage facility in the eastern portion of the site indicates that this structure was occupied from the second to the sixth centuries. Evidence of late Roman amphora types demonstrates continued occupation and trade connections at the site through the end of the sixth century, up until the period of the Arab conquest.[65]

The excavators relied on a chronology of the site that posited occupation between a Ptolemaic foundation and the fourth or fifth century AD. Artefacts and other materials recovered at the site were situated within this chronology. Most of the finds were dated through association with the layers or with securely dated papyri and coins. In addition, the excavators tied their compressed chronology to known historical events, such as the Antonine Plague or the economic crisis of the third century, which would have affected the entire village. The result was a circular argument that sought archaeological evidence of major crises at the level of individual buildings and fed this back into the schema, reinforcing the chronological interpretation.

At the level of individual structure, the excavators suggested changes in occupation — whether the building or room should be assigned to the C- or B-Layer, for example — from limited evidence. Alterations in architecture, such as the decision to block a doorway or rebuild a wall, might be taken to represent a new phase in the use of the building. While clear occupation breaks such as a layer of sand might have represented a period of abandonment, it does not seem that such evidence was always used to assign a building or room to a new layer. The excavators also based their layer assignments on the artefacts discovered within a given room, particularly those that could be dated with precision. Analysis of the archival records indicates that the Michigan team reassessed the excavation data at a later date, either at the dig house or perhaps even after the season ended, retroactively distinguishing different occupation layers in single architectural units.[66] In some cases, this resulted in the assignment of artefacts found in adjacent rooms and possibly the same soil stratum to different layers.

---

60 Haatvedt, Peterson, and Husselman 1964, 346–48; Wilfong and Ferrara 2014, 104–05.

61 *P.Haun.* III.58; TM 11456; Rea 1993.

62 Pollard 1998.

63 Landvatter 2016, 1501–02.

64 Barnard and others 2015.

65 Gupta-Agarwal 2010.

66 Claytor and Verhoogt 2018, 9; Sampson 2022.

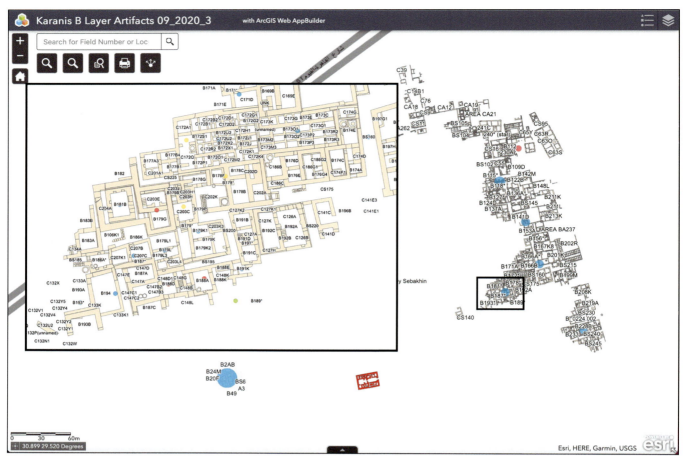

Figure 10.5. Screenshot from <https://karanishousingproject.org> [accessed 29 October 2022], showing the distribution of artefacts in the B-Layer. The inset image shows a detail of the south-eastern part of the excavated area. Artefacts are associated with only a select number of rooms in a building (copyright: Andrew T. Wilburn and the Karanis Housing Project).

Thomas Landvatter's analysis of structure B224 provides a glimpse of the chronological and documentation problems that may have been endemic on the site. B224 is located on the south-east of the site, excavation squares H11–12 and K11–12, in an area that was occupied during the A-, B-, and C-Layers. During the C-period of occupation, a large, paved thoroughfare, CS 190, ran east–west in line with the Southern Temple. An insula block including houses numbered C178–C182 lay to the north of CS190, while another insula block, with houses C184–C189 was positioned south of the street. B224 was built above this street CS190, effectively blocking it. In the B-Layer site plans, the houses to the north were modified slightly, and given new nomenclature as B221, B222, and B223; to the south the insula block included renamed houses B226–B233. Although the construction of B224 was an important modification to the urban landscape, this may not have resulted in major occupational changes to the insulae to the north and south, where modest modifications led to the assignment of new identifiers. Landvatter noted that no excavation unit included artefacts that were associated with both the B-Layer and C-Layer. So, for example, room B227A contained artefacts associated with the B-Layer, but the adjacent room B232A had none; rather, artefacts in this space were assigned to C191K.[67] No finds are associated with the A-Layer, even though some architectural elements continued to be used.

A comparable discrepancy in the assignment of artefacts was noted by Arthur Verhoogt and Robert Stephan in their analysis of the archive of Tiberianus, a Roman legionary, found in building B167/C167. In their study of the archive of papyri from this building, Verhoogt and Stephan note that finds are only recorded for the B-Layer of occupation; no finds are attributed to the

---

[67] Landvatter 2016, 1498–1500.

C-Layer. For some of the objects, however, the find-spots are listed as rooms found only on the C-Layer maps, such as C167 D^2, identified as one of three niches under the stairway where the archive of Terentianus was discovered.[68] The Karanis Housing Project has demonstrated that this pattern can be noted for the distribution of artefacts across the site in the B-Layer, where artefacts only appear in a select number of rooms in each building (Fig. 10.5). Artefacts surely were more evenly distributed across buildings and rooms, as adjacent rooms within a single building would preserve contemporary occupation debris. The excavation records, however, suggest that two nearby rooms might be filled with material deposited in different centuries.

Re-analysis of the artefacts found within the excavator-assigned layers indicates that the dating of the site has significant flaws. The distribution patterns of the finds highlights problems with the recording methods used both during the excavation and during preliminary analyses of the finds. Some of these problems can be tied to flawed pre-understandings of the chronology as well as ignorance of the formation processes that generated the archaeological record at the site. The finds are deceptive; the detritus of daily life, some of which, like the glass vessels, appear to be in pristine condition, are not, for the most part, from primary archaeological contexts. Unlike Pompeii, no cataclysm led to the departure of the residents.[69] At Karanis, it seems likely that some abandoned buildings would have stood empty for a period of time, collecting material that was cast aside by other residents; other structures may reflect a lengthy period of gradual abandonment.[70] There are some contexts, however, that indicate different formation processes. The 'Record of Objects' volumes and the photographic archive reveal a small number of excavation units that reflect primary deposits, such as the intentional burial of objects. For example, a group of papyri were discovered placed within the threshold between rooms D and E of House 5026, and the site has yielded numerous coin hoards were likely hidden intentionally by their owners.

Karanis proved to be a difficult site to understand, with an immense amount of material to sift through. In his 1973 manuscript, Peterson recognized some of the problems with the phasing that took place in the field, noting that 'certain constructions of late date are found contiguous to buildings that were obviously of earlier origin'.[71] To effectively study the site of Karanis and its finds, scholars must first reassess the archival material to determine the extent of the problems with the archaeological data and identify the pre-understandings of the excavators. This will permit contemporary researchers to reconcile excavator biases with the recording strategies that were employed. An appraisal of the entirety of the site can provide an overarching view of how excavation methodologies may have changed over the course of the excavation. Such a broad assessment can evaluate artefact phasing and retention strategies. Peterson's manuscript and the excavator notations that are documented in the 'Record of Objects' volumes caution against any analysis that does not engage in a parallel enquiry of insulae blocks and individual contexts. A nuanced study of the Karanis material requires both the holistic comprehension of the site as well as detailed analysis of individual contexts. This will permit contemporary researchers to assess adequately the depositional processes that may have led to the distribution of finds within a building or room. Through the generation of a full digital map of the site, the Karanis Housing Project intends to provide the framework upon which holistic reassessments of the site may be undertaken.

The Karanis Housing Project

The goal of the Karanis Housing Project is to generate a systematized, digital record of the excavation, accessible through a public digital interface. Ideally, the project will permit scholars and the public to understand the archaeological contexts of the finds, to assess earlier publications, and to use the site and its artefacts as a resource for contemporary research. The legacy data from the site are unwieldy, distributed among many different volumes, and preserved in maps and plans in different media and at different scales. The initial impetus of the project is to use the legacy data to generate an inclusive view of the site by bringing these disparate materials together within a single framework.

To maintain coherence with the original field records, the Karanis Housing Project has structured the digital work around the artefacts that were recovered and the find-spots in which they were found. The 'Record of Objects' volumes can aid in identifying the finds and assessing which material is still preserved, and what artefacts have been lost. The maps and plans, digitized

---

68 Stephan and Verhoogt 2005, 196–97.
69 Keenan 2003.
70 Landvatter 2016, 1502–04.

71 Peterson 1973, 2; Husselman 1979, 7.

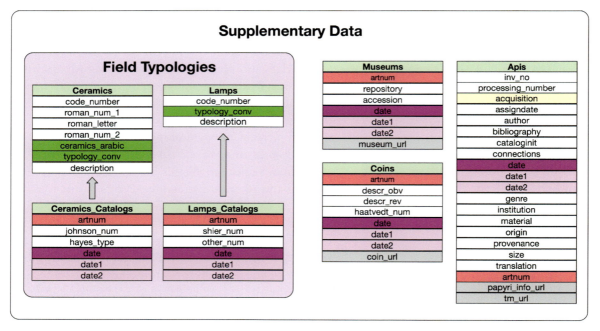

within a Geographic Information System (GIS), can be used to chart the progress of excavation. When paired with the artefact records, this material can help scholars to understand the recording strategies for the artefacts and architecture.

One central goal of the project is to catalogue all artefacts documented in the 'Record of Objects' volumes into a relational database. The database structure (Fig. 10.6) is flexible and employs metadata standards outlined in Archaeocore, established by the Institute for Fine Arts at NYU, and the Archaeological Resource Cataloging System, developed by Ethan Watrall and Jon Frey at Michigan State University. Additional fields hold information derived from the archival documents. The primary record for each artefact, derived from the 'Record of Objects' books, is stored in the **Artefacts** table.[72] The

Figure 10.6. Schematic image of the PostgreSQL database for the Karanis Housing Project (copyright Andrew T. Wilburn and the Karanis Housing Project).

[72] Sebastián Encina at the Kelsey Museum of Archaeology provided a digital version of the 'Record of Objects' books in Microsoft Excel format. Several undergraduate students, under Sebastian Encina's direction, transcribed the 'Record of Objects'

Table 10.1. Table showing examples of original field numbers and converted field numbers (copyright Andrew T. Wilburn and the Karanis Housing Project).

Field Number (fldnum_orig)	Artefact Number (artnum)	Artefact Description from the 'Record of Objects' volumes
25-5072-C	5072-005_003	Conical shaped stone pestle, speckled red granite?
27-C54E-E	C_0054-005_005	Terracotta figure of Isis and Harpocrates. Stand about 0.16 m high. Badly worn.
28-265*-CII	0165.^_081	Fragments of bone pins
30-B203K*-m	B_0203-011.^_c013	159, VII, b. (ceramic vessel: bowl with flat base; convex side with incurving rim)
30-C123CQ9-A	C_0123-003.017.009_001	Bone die found in pot c.
33-B501G-C	B_0501-003_007.0001	1103 coins — apparently had been stored in a cloth bag

project is committed to preserving the original entries from the 'Record of Objects' volumes, while enabling the data to be integrated into a machine-readable format. This table includes the original field number (generated from the year of excavation, layer, building, room, and artefact number), a description of the object, marginalia from the 'Record of Objects' books, and additional metadata related to the original field record. The Artefacts table collates data from each of the excavator-assigned layers, as well as undesignated artefacts and those found by the Summer Guards (SG). Within the Artefacts table, supplemental fields draw on these artefact descriptions to make the data more usable and integrate the project with other datasets related to the ancient world. Project team members have characterized the artefacts using key terms from the Getty Art and Architecture Thesaurus (Artefacts > getty_descr) to facilitate comprehensive searches over the entirety of the site.

Karanis Housing Project team members have worked with OpenRefine, an open-source tool for cleaning data, to assign new, machine-readable field numbers based on the original field designations, entered as 'artnum'.[73]

Examples of the original field number and the new field number are shown in Table 10.1. The new field number uses the underscore to separate the elements of the original field number (the excavator-assigned layer, the building and room, and the artefact number), the hyphen to separate the building and room numbers, and the period to rectify certain problematic data elements. Although the excavator-assigned layers (A-Layer, B-Layer, and so on) are problematic, they have been retained, as the same house numbers might be used for buildings in different areas of the site. For example, structure 199 is located on the eastern side of the site, while structure B199 is located further to the south in a different excavation square. In order to standardize the numbering system, the structure designation was expanded to four numerical places, with initial zeroes added to fill out structures such as 199 or 25. Rooms, originally assigned by using letters, have been converted to a three-digit numerical sequence, where A is 001, B is 002, and so. In cases where room numbers included multiple letters and numbers, such as 123CQ9, a bin in granary C123, the period divides the three component parts, resolving to 003.017.009. Excavation loci that include an asterisk have replaced this symbol with the caret (^). The new nomenclature, Layer — Building — Room is paralleled in the GIS map. As the excavation assigned units according to the presence of architecture, such as walls, the GIS map employs polygons, inscribed within the shapefiles representing the walls, to serve as containers for the artefacts. Polygons are employed to represent other architectural features, such as bins, streets, or open areas.

An underscore separates the locus designation from the artefact number. The letters used to characterize artefacts have been converted to a three-digit number. Artefact designations beyond Z (026), such as AI, BI, and so on, continue the sequential numbering, so that AI is converted to 27, B1 to 28. In the example above, 28-165*-CII, has been resolved to 0165.^_108. Ceramic objects, originally denoted by using lowercase letters, have been given a 'c' prefix, and follow the same conversion as other artefacts, where 'm' would be renumbered as c013. When multiple artefacts are represented by a single field number, the project team has appended a period followed by a four-digit sequence, starting with 0001; four digits are used because several of the coin hoards include more than a thousand coins. Each artefact represents a unique value, allowing the project team eventually to associate a permalink with the individual record.

---

books, assessing the artefact descriptions and classifying the objects by type and name.

[73] The field 'locnum_new' records only the converted locus number (the first part of the field number) to provide a link to the GIS map.

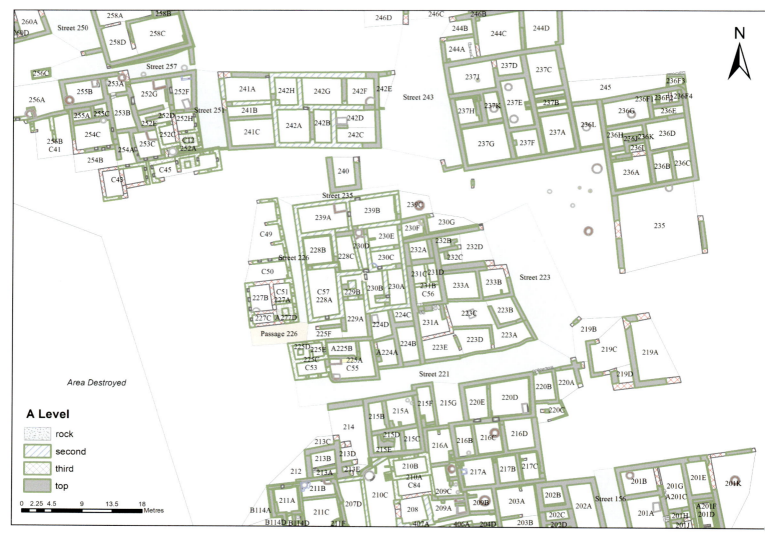

Figure 10.7. Map produced in ArcGIS 10.8, showing south-eastern part of the excavation from the Geographic Information System. The image shows the top or A-Layer, digitized from excavation square F10, shown in Figure 10.2 (copyright Andrew T. Wilburn and the Karanis Housing Project).

The database includes additional tables (grouped as **Supplementary Data**) that expand the original artefact data and can be associated with other sources of linked open data. The table for the ceramics (**Ceramics**), for example, contains information derived from the recently re-discovered pottery 'key', a document that explains the typology used in the field to record the ceramic objects. The typology, used for most of the ceramic entries in the 'Record of Objects' volumes, has been converted to machine-readable text and is complemented by two new fields, one with the Arabic number representing the type (e.g. 205), and the other recording a converted version of the pottery typology, in which the Roman numerals and letters have been replaced by a three-digit sequences, separated by periods (VI b ii = 004.002.002). A description of the vessel type, such as 'Dishes with flat base; moulded rims; concave out-splayed sides', has be added into the artefact record. This table can be used to interpret the vessel number or typology abbreviation given in the 'Record of Objects' entries, so that each artefact record can include the expanded vessel description. The Ceramics table can incorporate information from the 'Ceramics_Catalogs' table, which will be propagated as analysis of the ceramics progresses. Because the ceramic vessels stored at the Kelsey Museum of Archaeology have served as a critical resource for developing pottery typologies for the eastern Mediterranean (e.g. Hayes 1972), the Karanis Housing Project will be able to assign dates to many of the data types. Comparable tables for the lamps have been established, but not yet filled with data.

Where possible, artefacts are linked to other open data sources. The inclusion of Kelsey Museum accession numbers in the 'Record of Objects' volumes has permitted the project to generate URLs to link to the Kelsey Museum Art[e]facts Database. Papyri and ostraca have been linked to data contained in two major papyrological repositories, papyri.info and Trismegistos. The University of Michigan's Papyrus Collection hosts the

Advanced Papyrological Information System (APIS) an online repository for texts and translations of papyri and ostraca, at Michigan, many of which were excavated at Karanis. Each APIS records for a papyrus or ostracon discovered at Karanis include the original field number, allowing the project to scrape the University of Michigan's internally assigned processing number. This processing number provides a unique reference for the recto and verso of each document. The processing number is used by papyri.info and Trismegistos as one field in each of their records. The project can populate the in-house records with chronological and interpretive data that is available for coins, papyri, ostraca, and other artefacts held in the Kelsey Museum and the University of Michigan Papyrology Collection. This will result in a more robust collection of Karanis material than was previously possible.

Locus information and spatial data are collected in three tables, grouped as **GIS/Geographic Data** in Figure 10.6. 'GIS Rooms' is a geospatial table generated by ArcGIS. Ryan Reynolds (Oberlin College '14) digitized the original 1:100 scale maps of each layer using ESRI's ArcGIS.[74] Each group of houses or insula block (defined by shared walls and surrounded by streets) was digitized as a separate ArcGIS layer, retaining the excavator-assigned designations. In each feature, such as the walls that define building A427, the metadata table includes information that was present in the original maps, such as which wall segments were believed to be reused from previous occupation layers. These data can be used to adjust the display properties, allowing the visualization of the excavator-assigned phasing. Working within ArcGIS, project team members have drawn polygon features within the walls and other architectural units to create containers for the artefacts found in each excavation unit. Polygons also have been created to represent ovens, bins, streets and open areas (Fig. 10.7).

'GIS Rooms' includes the geometry for each of the room polygons, the original field number of the excavation unit and the revised (new) field number, a description of the type of space, and the rooms that are listed above and below (separated on the maps by horizontal lines), and a field that indicates whether the location has been deemed accurate. The revised (new) field number provided for each polygon establishes a relate between the artefact records in the database and the GIS map, allowing a user to query which artefacts were found in a discrete unit. The room polygons can also be used to associate spatial data with each artefact, stored in the 'centroid' table. Each artefact can be given longitudinal and latitudinal coordinates and imported into the GIS map as a series of points. The integration of these data into the map allows users to search for individual artefacts, artefact types, and even names derived from the papyri and ostraca. 'Alt-Numbers' provides additional excavation unit numbers that might be associated with each locus, such as the problematic numbers from the early years of the excavation that were discussed above.

There are several cases in which artefacts cannot be spatially located with precision. The buildings that do not appear on the 1:100 scale maps, including those in Area G that are only preserved on a sketch map, have been incorporated into the GIS map with an accompanying annotation stating that the location is not accurate. In some cases, artefacts appear in the 'Record of Objects' volumes as associated with a known building, but with a room designation that is not shown on the map. In such cases, a polygon is drawn over the entirety of the appropriate structure, and the location is annotated as not accurate. The project has not yet determined the best solution for surface finds and those recovered by the Summer Guards.

ArcGIS Online offers a relatively simple method of sharing the map and finds data, accessible through the project webpage (Fig. 10.5).[75] The artefacts are presented as points situated in the centre of the GIS polygon that represents the excavation unit and are colour-coded according to artefact type. Where multiple examples of a particular artefact type, such as lamps or coins, were discovered in the same excavation unit, the map renders a scaled symbol to quantify the number of represented artefacts. A larger dot indicates additional artefacts. Users can search for an archaeological locus, either through the original field number, such as E103, or

---

[74] The triangulation map was spatially located using longitude and latitude lines; each of the 1:100 grid squares were aligned along the triangulation map. The resulting map was internally consistent according to the 1920s and 1930s site plans, but displaced by approximately 10–20 m, in part due to the absence of a modern map projection. Using ArcGIS Pro 2.8 and the spatial data published by the Fayum Project, the project team has been able to increase the accuracy of the GIS maps, although precise geo-spatial rectification may not be possible. Bethany Simpson (pers. comm.) has noted that the preserved mud-brick structures may align with some portions of the 1920s and 1930s plans, but the legacy maps are less accurate when structures are divided by open spaces.

[75] <https://karanishousingproject.org/map.html> [accessed 29 October 2022].

through our revised, new field number, E_103. The map will return the polygon with this designation. Selecting the symbol in the centre of the excavation unit point produces a pop-up window with the records for each of the artefacts found within the unit. Users can also search for artefacts or artefact types over the entirety of the site; such a search will return all the locations where the requested artefact or search term might be found.

Conclusion

The Karanis Housing Project endeavours to provide a holistic view of the site through the legacy data generated in the 1920s and 1930s. The project has attempted to reconstruct the process of excavation and uncover the interpretive framework of the original excavators. By integrating the legacy archaeological data into a contemporary schema and linking it with other datasets, the project has worked to establish a robust foundation for future analyses of the Karanis material. The scale of the original excavation produced a massive amount of data, and the work of reassessing these data is far from complete. To date, the project has generated entries for around sixty thousand artefacts.

One of the most promising avenues for future work lies in refining the dating of the site and assessing the excavator-assigned layers within the context of individual houses or insula blocks. The database structure can link artefacts with other data sources to provide dates for the ceramics or other datable material with an excavation unit; these data can then be sifted up for each excavation locus, allowing the user to create a map that shows a *terminus post quem* for the locus. Continued data entry and refinement will permit the GIS and artefact datasets to open new possibilities for 'big data' analyses. In some ways, this approach to the data, which can extract large-scale pictures of artefact use, may prove the most suitable avenue to investigate sites with flawed or problematic recording systems.

As caretakers of the past, our calling is to preserve and share our cultural heritage. Legacy datasets, including the excavation records from Karanis, offer enormous potential for enquiry, due in part to the sheer quantity of material recovered in these big digs. Digitization provides one means by which this remarkable material can be preserved, updated, and brought into the twenty-first century. At the same time, we must expand access to these enormous quantities of material that are largely understudied and under-published for our mutual benefit.

Works Cited

Allen, M. L. 1985. 'The Terracotta Figurines from Karanis: A Study of Technique, Style, and Chronology in Fayoumic Coroplastics' (unpublished doctoral thesis, University of Michigan).

Allison, P. M. 2008. 'Dealing with Legacy Data: An Introduction', *Internet Archaeology*, 24 <https://doi.org/10.11141/ia.24.8>.

Barnard, H., W. Z. Wendrich, B. T. Nigra, B. Simpson, and R. T. J. Cappers. 2015. 'The Fourth Century AD Expansion of the Graeco-Roman Settlement of Karanis (Kom Aushim) in the Northern Fayum', *Journal of Egyptian Archaeology*, 101: 51–67.

Barnard, H., W. Z. Wendrich, A. Winkels, J. E. M. F. Bos, B. L. Simpson, and R. T. J. Cappers. 2016. 'The Preservation of Exposed Mudbrick Architecture in Karanis (Kom Aushim), Egypt', *Journal of Field Archaeology*, 41.1: 84–100.

Bell, M. 2014. 'Experimental Archaeology at the Crossroads: A Contribution to Interpretation or Evidence of "Xeroxing"?', in R. Chapman and A. Wylie (eds), *Material Evidence: Learning from Archaeological Practice* (New York: Routledge), pp. 62–78.

Bevan, A. 2015. 'The Data Deluge', *Antiquity*, 89.348: 1473–84.

Boak, A. E. R. 1933. *Karanis: The Temples, Coin Hoards, Botanical and Zoological Reports, Seasons 1924–31*, University of Michigan Studies, Humanistic Series, 30 (Ann Arbor: University of Michigan Press).

Boak, A. E. R. and E. E. Peterson. 1931. *Karanis: Topographical and Architectural Report of Excavations during the Seasons 1924–28*, University of Michigan Studies, Humanistic Series, 25 (Ann Arbor: University of Michigan Press).

Boozer, A. L. 2014. 'The Tyranny of Typologies: Evidential Reasoning in Romano-Egyptian Domestic Archaeology', in R. Chapman and A. Wylie (eds), *Material Evidence: Learning from Archaeological Practice* (New York: Routledge), pp. 92–109.

Clarke, M. 2015. 'The Digital Dilemma: Preservation and the Digital Archaeological Record', *Advances in Archaeological Practice*, 3.4: 313–30.

Claytor, W. G. and A. Verhoogt. 2018. *Papyri from Karanis: The Granary C123 (P. Mich. XXI)*, Michigan Papyri, 21 (Ann Arbor: University of Michigan Press).

Cunliffe, E. and L. Curini. 2018. 'ISIS and Heritage Destruction: A Sentiment Analysis', *Antiquity*, 92.364: 1094–1111.

Davoli, P. 1998. *L'archeologia urbana nel Fayyum di età ellenistica e romana* (Naples: Procaccini).

Esteva, M., J. Trelogan, A. Rabinowitz, D. Walling, and S. Pipkin. 2010. 'From the Site to Long-Term Preservation: A Reflexive System to Manage and Archive Digital Archaeological Data', in *Archiving 2010: Proceedings of the IS&T (Digital) Archiving Conference 2010, Den Haag, Netherlands, 1–4 June 2010* (Springfield: Society for Imaging Science and Technology), pp. 1–6.

Gagos, T., J. Gates, and A. Wilburn. 2005. 'Material Culture and Texts of Graeco-Roman Egypt: Creating Context, Debating Meaning', *Bulletin of the American Society of Papyrologists*, 42: 171–88.

González-Tennant, E. 2016. 'Recent Directions and Future Developments in Geographic Information Systems for Historical Archaeology', *Historical Archaeology*, 50: 24–49.

Gupta-Agarwal, S. 2010. 'The Final Curtain Call: The Abandonment of Karanis in Light of Late Roman Amphorae', *Coptica*, 10.10: 61–76.

Haatvedt, R. A., E. E. Peterson, and E. Husselman. 1964. *Coins from Karanis: The University of Michigan Excavations, 1924–1935* (Ann Arbor: University of Michigan Press).

Hadjisaavas, S. and V. Karageorghis (eds). 2000. *The Problem of Unpublished Excavations* (Nicosia: Department of Antiquities, Cyprus, and the Anastasios G. Leventis Foundation).

Harden, D. 1936. *Roman Glass from Karanis* (Ann Arbor: University of Michigan Press).

Hayes, J. W. 1972. *Late Roman Pottery* (London: British School at Rome).

Hogarth, D. G. and B. P. Grenfell. 1895. 'Cities of the Faiyúm I: Karanis and Bacchias', *Egypt Exploration Fund Archaeological Report*, 1895: 14–19.

Husselman, E. M. 1971. *Papyri from Karanis, Third Series*, Michigan Papyri, 9 (Cleveland: Case Western Reserve University Press).

—— 1979. *Karanis Excavations of the University of Michigan in Egypt 1928–1935: Topography and Architecture; A Summary of the Reports of the Director, Enoch E. Peterson*, Kelsey Museum of Archaeology Studies, 5 (Ann Arbor: University of Michigan Press).

Johnson, B. 1981. *Pottery from Karanis: Excavations of the University of Michigan*, Kelsey Museum of Archaeology Studies, 7 (Ann Arbor: University of Michigan).

Karageorghis, V. 2000. 'It's Publish or Perish, and We Do Not Want to Perish', in S. Hadjisaavas and V. Karageorghis (eds), *The Problem of Unpublished Excavations* (Nicosia: Department of Antiquities, Cyprus, and the Anastasios G. Leventis Foundation), pp. 1–4.

Keenan, J. G. 2003. 'Deserted Villages: From the Ancient to the Medieval Fayyūm', *Bulletin of the American Society of Papyrologists*, 40: 119–39.

Kintigh, K. W. 2006. 'The Promise and Challenge of Archaeological Data Integration', *American Antiquity*, 71.3: 567–78.

Kintigh, K. W., J. H. Altschul, M. C. Beaudry, R. D. Drennan, A. P. Kinzig, T. A. Kohler, W. F. Limp, H. D. G. Maschner, W. K. Michener, T. R. Pauketat, P. Peregrine, J. A. Sabloff, T. J. Wilkinson, H. T. Wright, and M. A. Zeder. 2014. 'Grand Challenges for Archaeology', *Proceedings of the National Academy of Sciences*, 111.3: 879–80.

Landvatter, T. 2016. 'Archaeological and Papyrological Inquiry at Karanis: Problems and Potentialities', in T. Derda, A. Łajtar, and J. Urbanik (eds), *Proceedings of the 27th International Congress of Papyrology Warsaw, 29 July–3 August 2013* (Warsaw: Faculty of Law and Administration, University of Warsaw), pp. 1493–1518.

Lawrence, D., J. Bradbury, and R. Dunford. 2012. 'Chronology, Uncertainty and GIS: A Methodology for Characterising and Understanding Landscapes of the Ancient Near East', *eTopoi*, 3: 353–59.

Loy, M. P. A., S. R. Stocker, and J. L. Davis. 2021. 'From Archive to GIS: Recovering Spatial Information for Tholos IV at the Palace of Nestor from the Notebooks of Lord William Taylour', *Internet Archaeology*, 56 <https://doi.org/10.11141/ia.56.5>.

Minnen, P. van. 1994. 'House-to-House Enquiries: An Interdisciplinary Approach to Roman Karanis', *Zeitschrift für Papyrologie und Epigraphik*, 100: 227–51.

Montserrat, D. 1996. '"No Papyrus and No Portraits": Hogarth, Grenfell, and the First Season in the Fayum, 1895–6', *Bulletin of the American Society of Papyrologists*, 33: 133–76.

Muhly, J. D. 2000. 'The Problem of Unpublished Excavations', *International Journal of Cultural Property*, 9.1: 158–61.

Pedley, J. G. 2012. *The Life and Work of Francis Willey Kelsey: Archaeology, Antiquity, and the Arts* (Ann Arbor: University of Michigan Press).

Peterson, E. 1973. 'The Architecture and Topography of Karanis' (unpublished manuscript, Kelsey Museum of Archaeology, University of Michigan).

Petrie, W. M. F., A. H. Sayce, E. L. Hicks, J. P. Mahaffy, F. L. Griffith, and F. C. J. Spurrell. 1891. *Illahun, Kahun and Gurob: 1888–90* (London: D. Nutt).

Pollard, N. 1998. 'The Chronology and Economic Condition of Late Roman Karanis: An Archaeological Reassessment', *Journal of the American Research Center in Egypt*, 35: 147–62.

Ravankhah, M., A. Chliaoutakis, M. J. Revez, R. de Wit, A. V. Argyriou, A. Anwar, J. Heeley, J. Birkmann, A. Sarris, and M. Žuvela-Aloise. 2020. 'A Multi-Hazard Platform for Cultural Heritage at Risk: The STORM Risk Assessment and Management Tool', *IOP Conference Series: Materials Science and Engineering*, 949: 012111.

Rea, J. R. 1993. 'P.Haun. iii 58: Caranis in the Fifth Century', *Zeitschrift für Papyrologie und Epigraphik*, 99: 89–95.

Sampson, C. M. 2022. 'New Light on P. Mich. 15 686', *Pylon*, 2 <https://doi.org/10.48631/pylon.2022.2.92968>.

—— (forthcoming). 'Area G and the Digging of Kom Aushim', in S. Perrone and F. Maltomini (eds.), *Greek Literary Papyri in Context*, Trends in Classics, 15.2 (Berlin: De Gruyter).

Shier, L. A. 1978. *Terracotta Lamps from Karanis, Egypt: Excavations of the University of Michigan*, Kelsey Museum of Archaeology Studies, 3 (Ann Arbor: University of Michigan Press).

Stephan, R. P. and A. Verhoogt. 2005. 'Text and Context in the Archive of Tiberianus (Karanis, Egypt; 2nd Century AD)', *Bulletin of the American Society of Papyrologists*, 42: 189–201.

Terentieff, J. 1929. 'Report on the Surveying Work of the University of Michigan Near East Research, Kom Aushim, Fayoum, Egypt' (unpublished manuscript, Kelsey Museum of Archaeology, University of Michigan).

Terpstra, T. T. 2014. 'The Materiality of Writing in Karanis: Excavating Everyday Writing in a Town in Roman Egypt', *Aegyptus*, 94: 89–119.

Tilley, C. 1989. 'Excavation as Theater', *Antiquity*, 63: 275–80.

Wilfong, T. G. 2014a. 'Notes on Three Archival Sources for the Michigan Karanis Excavations: The Record of Objects Books, the Division Albums, and the "Peterson Manuscript"', in T. G. Wilfong and A. W. Ferrara (eds), *Karanis Revealed: Discovering the Past and Present of a Michigan Excavation in Egypt*, Kelsey Museum Publication, 7 (Ann Arbor: Kelsey Museum of Archaeology), pp. 15–24.

—— 2014b. 'Silent Movies from the Michigan Expedition to Egypt', in T. G. Wilfong and A. W. Ferrara (eds), *Karanis Revealed: Discovering the Past and Present of a Michigan Excavation in Egypt*, Kelsey Museum Publication, 7 (Ann Arbor: Kelsey Museum of Archaeology), pp. 25–34.

Wilfong, T. G. and A. W. Ferrara (eds). 2014. *Karanis Revealed: Discovering the Past and Present of a Michigan Excavation in Egypt* (Ann Arbor: Kelsey Museum of Archaeology).

Witcher, R. 2008. '(Re)Surveying Mediterranean Rural Landscapes: GIS and Legacy Survey Data', *Internet Archaeology*, 24 <https://doi.org/10.11141/ia.24.2>.

Woywitka, R. and A. B. Beaudoin. 2017. 'Legacy Databases and GIS: A Discussion of the Issues Illustrated by a Case Study of Archaeological Site Data from Southeast Alberta, Canada', *The Canadian Geographer*, 53.4: 462–72.

Wylie, A. 2017. 'How Archaeological Evidence Bites Back: Strategies for Putting Old Data to Work in New Ways', *Science, Technology, & Human Values*, 42.2: 203–25.

Yeivin, S. 1926. 'Report on the Architecture at Kaum Aušim Seasons 1924–1925, 1925–1926' (unpublished manuscript, Kelsey Museum of Archaeology, University of Michigan).

—— 1928. 'Report for the Season 1927–1928' (unpublished manuscript, Kelsey Museum of Archaeology, University of Michigan).

—— n.d. 'Appendix II: List of Karanidian Houses Classed in their Respective Period Layers' (unpublished manuscript, Kelsey Museum of Archaeology, University of Michigan).

Youtie, H. C. and O. M. Pearl. 1944. *Papyri and Ostraca from Karanis*, Michigan Papyri, 6; University of Michigan Studies, Humanistic Series, 47 (Ann Arbor: University of Michigan Press).

Youtie, H. C., V. B. Schuman, and O. M. Pearl. 1936. *Tax Rolls from Karanis*, Michigan Papyri, 4; University of Michigan Studies, Humanistic Series, 42–43 (Ann Arbor: University of Michigan Press).

Youtie, H. C. and J. G. Winter. 1951. *Papyri and Ostraca from Karanis*, Michigan Papyri, 8; University of Michigan Studies. Humanistic Series, 50 (Ann Arbor: University of Michigan Press).

11. Placing the Container before the Content
The Cases of the 'Iron Field' and 'Mosaic Field' at Eski Kâhta at the Dörner Archive — Forschungsstelle Asia Minor, Münster

Emanuele E. Intagliata
Università degli Studi di Milano (emanuele.intagliata@unimi.it)

Introduction

When studying an archive, the attention of archaeologists is often directed towards its content rather than its container. In other words, how a collection has come into existence is usually of lesser interest to scholars than the subject of the collection itself — whether an individual artefact, a monument, an entire site, or a group of sites. The cause behind this tendency is likely to be sought in the nature of our discipline and the quantity and quality of documents in an archive. The archaeologist's research agendas tend to focus on the study of artefacts and structures. Information on possible data transfers, meetings, requests for funding, and budgets are generally overlooked or ignored to the advantage of careful examinations of photographs, drawings, and plans. In addition, not all archives necessarily contain information on how their documents and photographs were acquired.

Whenever possible, however, studying the history of a collection is advisable. Not only does such a study provide a solid framework upon which to build up archaeological knowledge, but it can also clarify the quantity and quality of a dataset, help reflect on its limitations, and contribute to understanding the rationale behind the research agenda of the people who created or collated the archived material. Photographs are certainly helpful towards achieving this goal. Yet, another type of document that is particularly apt to cast light on these queries is the private letter. Private correspondence can be veins of information regarding how data were collected, managed, and stored by an archaeological team, how events such as conferences or workshops contributed to speed up or slow down research activities, how funding concerns helped shape the research agenda, and how local communities were perceived. In addition, because of the nature of this document, letters rarely include detailed information on monuments and sites. However, they can provide insights that are otherwise missing in technical reports when they do.

The issue of approaching archives as subjects of study per se is not new.[1] In line with modern literature, this chapter aims to raise further awareness about the importance of the study of the history of archival collections in archive archaeology by reflecting on the formation of the Dörner Archive at the Forschungsstelle Asia Minor, University of Münster (henceforth, Forschungsstelle). The Dörner Archive is home to the original documentation of the excavation of F. K. Dörner and his team at Eski Kâhta (Adıyaman, north-east Turkey) in the 1950s and 1960s. These excavations proved that the site, which had originally attracted the attention of Dörner because of its Hellenistic phase, underwent a significant occupation also in Late Antiquity and the medieval period. Given the extent of the collection in the Dörner Archive, this contribution will only focus on two batches of documents pertaining to the so-called 'Iron Field' and, to a lesser extent, the 'Mosaic Field', two sectors of the site whose excavations yielded the remains of iron productive facilities and a bathhouse. Although the Iron and Mosaic Fields were the objects of major excavations in the 1960s, they were never fully published. The collection of documents from these sectors of the site in the archive is patchy: the material of the Mosaic Field consists only of photographs, while those of the Iron Field lack crucial data on certain types of artefacts such as coins and pottery. The lacunose state of the documentation is exemplificative of what can usually be found in an archive. Although these documents remain to be systematically examined, this contribution aims to start examining how documents associated with these excavations found their way into the archive and how data were collected during fieldwork by Dörner and his team. In so doing, it will also provide the necessary background for future studies on this site based on archive material.

---

[1] See, e.g., Baird 2011; Baird and McFadyen 2014.

Figure 11.1. The area of the Iron Field ('Feld I') excavated in 1963 (© Forschungsstelle Asia Minor, 1963.34.32).

Figure 11.2. Still from a 1963 film showing excavators sorting and cleaning iron slag in the 'Ironfeld' (© Forschungsstelle Asia Minor).

Figure 11.3. Iron slag collected in 1963 (© Forschungsstelle Asia Minor, 1963.34.36).

F. K. Dörner and the Excavation at Eski Kâhta

Dörner first visited Commagene in the late 1930s.[2] Back in the early twentieth century, Commagene was still mostly unknown to many, and iconic sites such as Nemrud Dağ still had to be fully investigated. His involvement in the region continued after World War II. In 1951, an original plan to start conducting research at Nemrud Dağ was diverted to address the until-then unknown site of Eski Kâhta in the Adıyaman province. The site of Eski Kâhta is characterized by two prominent hills: Yeni Kale, where there are imposing remains of a Mamluk fortress, and Eski Kale. The discovery of the Great Cult Inscription by Dörner in 1951 on the latter hill proved that the site was Arsameia-on-the-Nymphaios — the burial place (hierothesion) of King Mithradates I, father of Antiochos I. Excavation on the slope of Eski Kale started in 1953 and concluded in 1955, the results being published in 1963 in a volume co-authored with T. Goell.[3]

Excavations resumed at Arsameia only in 1963. This new round of fieldwork had the aim of understanding the occupation on the plateau of Eski Kale but also investigating the remains of the alleged city of Arsameia mentioned in the Great Cult Inscription.[4] To reach the latter objective, numerous trenches were excavated in the surroundings of Eski Kale and particularly at Yeni Kale, Flur Köyönü, the Mosaic Field, and the Iron Field. Although these trenches were not successful in identifying any traces of the Hellenistic city, they nonetheless proved the existence of important phases of occupation dated to Late Antiquity and the medieval period. Subsequent excavations had the opportunity to expand former trenches but also excavate new ones, such as in the case of the 1965 dig of the Iron Field — see below. Despite the effort to excavate the surrounding of Eski

---

[2] Dörner and Naumann 1939. For the history and archaeology of Commagene, see, e.g. Blömer and Winter 2012; Brijder 2014; Blömer and others 2021.

[3] Dörner and Goell 1963.

[4] Dörner and Goell 1963, 41.

Kale, which continued well into the end of the decade, growing disagreement among the members of Dörner's circle and lack of funding caused the research to stall. The volume 'Arsameia II', which would have included the results of the excavations of all sectors of Eski Kâhta, was never published as planned by Dörner. Eventually, W. Hoepfner managed to publish a volume with the same title, but the content was radically different from the one originally intended by the head of the expedition, for it only included the results of the excavations of the plateau at Eski Kale.[5]

The Iron Field

Excavation of the Iron Field

The Iron Field is situated to the west of Yeni Kale (Figs 11.1–11.3). Excavations in the area started in June 1963 under the direction of W. Winkelmann after a survey had identified significant quantities of iron slag. In that year, two 3 × 10 m and one 2 × 17 m test trenches were opened in what would later be called 'Feld I'. These revealed a set of walls and the remains of a furnace for metal production. The latter was the object of much controversy in Dörner's circle. It was initially published as a furnace by Winkelmann. However, it was reinterpreted by W. Nowothnig as being a bread oven. Later, K. Roesch reassessed the remains and republished it as a multi-purpose iron production facility that could also have served as a bloomery. The results of this first excavation were the object of two interim reports and an article authored by Dörner on iron production in Commagene.[6]

After a short hiatus, excavation in the Iron Field resumed in 1965 under the direction of W. Nowothnig, of whom more will be said below. The work in 1965 aimed first at clarifying the situation in 'Feld I', which had been investigated two years before, and then expanding the research into unexcavated sectors of the site. The latter were 'Feld II', which was situated approximately 20 m to the north of 'Feld I', and 'Feld III', which was situated to the south, by the main road leading to Eski Kâhta.

By the end of the 1965 excavation season, the total area uncovered in the Iron Field by Dörner had extended to 440 m². The results of the 1965 investigations were published in two interim reports.[7] Dörner was fully aware of the potential of the Iron Field to attract investment (particularly from the German iron industry) to continue his excavations at Eski Kâhta. The flurry of publications dedicated to the Iron Field that followed the 1965 excavation is proof of this.[8] This contrasts with other sectors of the site, such as the Mosaic Field, which did not seem to attract the same level of attention from Dörner and his associates.[9] However, further excavations of the Iron Field were never conducted again, despite Dörner's continued work at Eski Kale in the subsequent years.

The Corpus of Letters Pertaining to the Excavation of the Iron Field

The batch of documents associated with the excavations of the Iron Field at Eski Kâhta consists of fifty-nine plans and profiles, 135 drawings of metal artefacts including side notes about their exact find-spot, one list of drawings including short descriptions of each artefact, several hundred photographs, one list of photographs detailing the location and subject of each shot, several abridged versions of already-published preliminary reports with side notes by Dörner, and even a short film taken in 1935 for a general audience (Fig. 11.2).

More importantly for the scope of this contribution, the archive contains 180 private letters exchanged between Dörner and people associated in various capacities with the research conducted by the team in the Iron Field. The documents were written between January 1964 and May 1979 and often have as writers or addressees Nowothnig and Roesch; other people, such as public servants, scholars, pupils, and others (e.g. Nowothnig's wife) rarely appear. The topic treated in these letters var-

---

[5] Hoepfner 1983.

[6] Dörner 1965a, 29–31; 1965b; Dörner and others 1965a, 222–31.

[7] Dörner and others 1965b, 139–45; Dörner and others 1968, 41–44.

[8] Particularly telling in this sense are two publications on *Stahl und Eisen*, which was the flagship journal of the VDEh (Dörner 1966; Nowothnig 1969). See also, e.g. Roesch 1975. The Iron Field also appears in a video preserved in the archive. Winkelmann and other workers are shown sorting and washing iron slag from the site. The video was presumably produced to target the general audience.

[9] Dörner 1965a, 31–33; Dörner and others 1965a, 231; Dörner and others 1965b, 134–39; Dörner and others 1968, 37–41. The Mosaic Field also appears briefly mentioned in Brödner 1983, 131. As opposed to the Iron Field, the Mosaic Field is not present in the issue of *Antike Welt* dedicated to Commagene (Dörner 1975) or in Dörner's popular book on the history and archaeology of this region (Dörner 1981).

ies widely, ranging from requests to send documentation (e.g. plans and photographs) to personal matters that slowed the research down and from invitations to personal gatherings and meetings to amendments of drafts to preliminary reports. Besides the importance of these letters as historical documents to reconstruct the history of the excavation at Eski Kâhta, their content sheds light on the activities of Dörner's research team after the excavations, how data was gathered and processed, and the circumstances under which the documents entered the archive.

Research Activities Conducted after the Excavations of the Iron Field

The letters do not detail the planning stage of the 1963 and 1965 excavations. Yet, they provide important insights into how research developed after this fieldwork. After the 1963 excavations conducted by Winkelmann, Dörner deemed it necessary to invite a specialist in archaeometallurgy to the excavation of this sector of the site. It is not clear when Nowothnig entered the scene, but by January 1964, the archaeologist had already started an intense letter correspondence with Dörner about the results of the fieldwork in 1963. At that time, Nowothnig was already an employee of the Niedersächsisches Landesverwaltungsamt — Dezernat Bodendenkmalpflege (Lower Saxony State Administration Office — Department for the Preservation and Care of Registered Landmarks) in Hanover. He was considered by Dörner particularly apt for this task, having conducted a series of investigations on iron production sites in the north German lowlands and the Harz Mountains.[10] Nowothnig participated in the 1965 expedition to Arsameia as a lead archaeologist and authored a series of interim reports on the Iron Field. He was tasked to produce a final report detailing the results of the excavations for the second volume dedicated to the excavations of Arsameia ('Arsameia II'), which, however, never materialized, as discussed below.

In 1969, a feud arose between Nowothnig and Roesch about the accessibility of the data from the Iron Field. Probably already at that time, Roesch was an honorary member of the history committee of the Verein Deutscher Eisenhüttenleute (VDEh) (Association of German Steel Manufacturers) and was working on a study on the early history of iron. After attending a lecture delivered by Nowothnig at Münster, he contacted Dörner asking for details on the excavations and informing him that he intended to include the Iron Field in a lecture soon to be delivered at the VDEh. Dörner informed Nowothnig and asked him to send out the relevant documentation. In a letter dated 25 March 1969, Nowothnig appears irritated by Roesch's line of questioning and attempts to gain unpublished data for his research.[11] However, considering that the VDEh had sponsored the excavation, Dörner invited Nowothnig to be collaborative.[12] In a letter addressed to Roesch, Nowothnig agreed to cooperate. In the same document, the archaeologist stressed more than once that he was certain that the iron facilities were dated to the medieval period.[13] He also shows some scepticism towards Roesch's dating of the furnaces, which he believed to have been contemporary with the votive inscriptions of Jupiter Dolichenus based on his reading of the 1960s interim reports.[14]

Dörner never put in doubt Nowothnig's involvement as the sole author of the chapter about the Iron Field for the second volume on the excavations of Arsameia. However, personal health issues slowed down the writing. In August 1971, W. Nowothnig passed away without having completed the chapter. Consequently, Dörner

---

[10] L. 17.05.1965.

[11] 'In 35 jähriger wissenschaftlicher Arbeit ist mir noch nie vorgekommen, daß jemand in laufende noch nicht abgeschlossene und ihrer Gesamtheit noch nicht publizierte Forschungsarbeiten eingegriffen hat und ohne Kenntnis der Objekte darüber zu arbeiten begann.' L. 25.03.1969.

[12] 'Hat doch der VDEh unsere Kampagne von 1965 tatkräftig gefördert und wird sicherlich auch weitere Unternehmungen von uns auf diesem Gebiet seine Hilfe, wenn wir sie brauchen, zuteil werden lassen.' L. 04.04.1969; Roesch was well aware of his leverage position, as he made indirectly clear in another letter addressed to Nowothnig: 'Für die Erforschung der Frühgeschichte des Eisens in dem Land Ubi ferrum nascitur wurden von dem VDEh erhebliche Beträge zur Verfügung gestellt, die Ihnen direkt oder indirekt diese Forschungsreise ermöglichten.' L. 12.04.1969.

[13] '[...] war und bin ich über die von Ihnen dem VDEh in Ihrem Schreiben vom 7.3.69 vorgetragenen Folgerungen und Datierungen im Anschluss an meine Grabungen in Eski Kahta überrascht. Sie sind für mich als dem Ausgräber der rein mittelalterlichen Schmieden, an deren mittelalterlicher Datierung auch nicht im geringsten zu zweifeln ist, unfassbar' and further below: 'Für ältere, [sic] als die ergrabenen mittelalterlichen befunde gibt es weder Beweise noch Anhaltspunkte.' L. 07.04.1969.

[14] 'Die Weihetafeln des Jupiter Dolichenus sind so weitfassend, dass sie hier nur mit allen Vorbehalten erwähnt werden konnten, sich aber keineswegs, davon bin ich überzeugt, auf die Schmiedewerkstatten von Eski Kahta beziehen und bezogen werden können.' L. 07.04.1969.

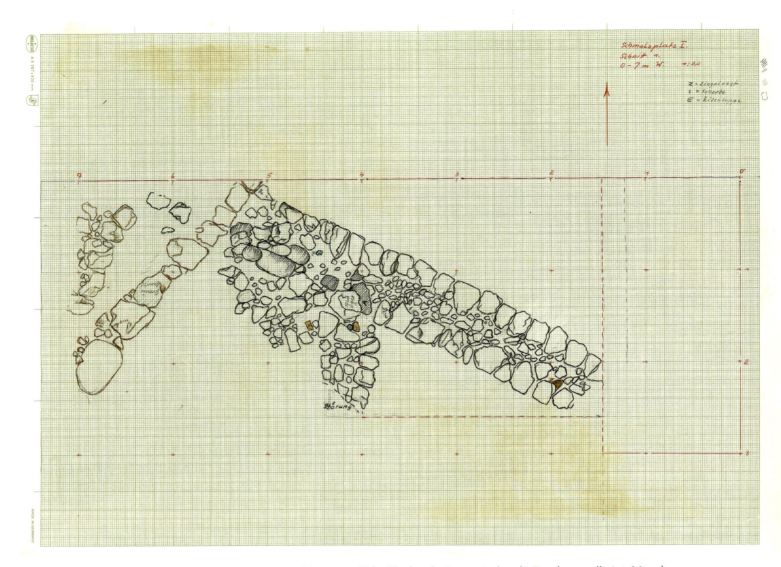

Figure 11.4. One of the drawn plans of the Iron Field ('Feld II') at the Dörner Archive (© Forschungsstelle Asia Minor).

wrote to Nowothnig's wife and asked for the original documentation of the excavations to be posted to him.[15] It is under these circumstances that the batch of documents on the Iron Field entered the Dörner Archive at the Forschungsstelle.[16] It is possible that Dörner at that time was considering appointing E. Lucius as responsible for the publication of the excavation of the Iron Field, therefore replacing Nowothnig in this task. Until then, Lucius had been tasked to prepare the report of the ceramic material found on the site.[17] However, as mentioned above, no chapters were produced.

Roesch did not replace Nowothnig's role in publishing the totality of data from the Iron Field but used the results of the excavations as a way to reflect upon the long history of iron production in the region.[18] He stayed in touch with Dörner and E. Schwertheim in the following years to develop his study on the early history of iron. After 1969, he never questioned Nowothnig's medieval dating of the furnaces in his letters again.[19] However, he

---

[15] L. 18.10.1971.

[16] For a brief history of the Forschungsstelle, see Schwertheim 2017.

[17] L. 29.01.1973: 'Herr Dr Lucius hat mir bereits vor einiger Zeit ein Manuskript geschickt, in das er die gesamte Keramik eingearbeitet hat, die im Bezirk der von Ihrem Mann ausgegrabenen Öfen gefunden worden ist. Sie können sich denken, wie sehr Dr Lucius auf eine Publikation drängt.'

[18] See, e.g. L. 13.10.1970: 'Aufgrund der Funde von R. Pleiner in Böhmen und der Abmessungen eines Rennfeuers mit Schacht auf einer attischen Vase kann man eindeutig sagen, dass die Form der bei Arsameia entdeckten Rennfeuer die gleiche Bauart zeigten wie diese bereits um 600 v. Chr. allgemein Anwendung gefunden hat. Zur Erzeugung eines guten Rennfeuereisens sind die alten Hüttenleute aufgrund jahrhundertalter Erfahrungen und vielen Misserfolgen an eine ganz bestimmte Ofenbauart gekommen, deren Querschnitt durch die Muskelkraft zur Bedienung der Blasebalge bedingt war.'

[19] '[...] die Funde von Arsameia stammen aus dem Mittelalter.' L. 2.11.1970.

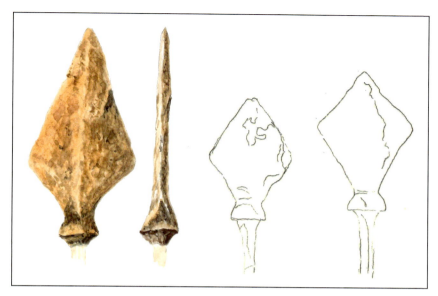

Figure 11.5. Selected drawings of metal artefacts from the Iron Field. Two arrowheads in watercolour and two in pencil (© Forschungsstelle Asia Minor).

was rather critical of Nowothnig's interpretation of the installation in 'Feld I' as an oven.[20] Based on comparanda with iron production sites in other regions, including Germany, Spain, and Corsica, Roesch believed that this facility could have functioned as a bloomery.[21] Besides Roesch's publications, which are limited to several furnaces at the site, the totality of the dataset concerning the Iron Field, including all plans, drawings of metal artefacts, and photographs, remain to be fully published.

Data Collection

There is little information on how the excavation team collected data on-site and managed them in the letters. However, insight into this can be obtained based on an examination of other documents, particularly plans and profiles, drawings of artefacts, and photographs.[22] A total of fifty-nine plan sheets pertaining to the Iron Field are housed in the archive (see, e.g. Fig. 11.4).[23] These cover different areas of the site. Five of these sheets show only the preparatory grid, while others are incomplete. A cursory examination of these documents demonstrates that not all sectors of the excavations were fully drawn. This is the case, for example, with 'Feld II' in which, based on photographs, archaeologists unearthed a series of walls orientated east to west. Given that all documents about the 1965 excavation were sent to Dörner at the death of Nowothnig, this lacuna is probably not the result of documents going missing. Most likely, certain sectors of the sites were simply not documented at the time of the excavations.

In contrast to this lacunose state of documentation, one might notice that several structures were drawn more than once in certain sectors of the site. This is, for example, the case for rooms 4 and 5 in the battery of furnaces in 'Feld I'. These rooms were drawn twice — first, when the furnaces still had to be fully brought to light and secondly, when they were completely unearthed. The same applies to the furnace excavated in 1963, which was uncovered again in 1965 and redrawn by Nowothnig.

Such a degree of selectiveness is shown in other documents in the archive associable with the Iron Field. These include photographs, which were mostly taken in 'Feld I', rarely in 'Feld II' and 'Feld III',[24] and drawings. Out of 351 metal artefacts registered in the surviving catalogue, slightly over 130 have been drawn; these include weapons, tools (pickaxes, chisels), and everyday objects such as metal vessels, keys, and locks (Fig. 11.5). In the case of drawings of finds, however, the incompleteness of the documentation may have been the result of time constraints.

With hindsight, it is easy to criticize Dörner and his team for their selective data collection strategy, which must have been prompted by the large extent of the sector brought to light, time constraints, and limited workforce. However, what has been collected remains impres-

---

[20] 'Die von Herrn Winkelmann ausgegrabenen Ofenmulden, die Herr Nowothnig als Wärme- und Backofen bezeichnete, sind nicht anderes als die häufig benutzten Unteröfen von Rennfeuern.' L. 28.1.1970 and further in L. 5.2.1970. It is possible, but still to be proven through a careful examination of the material, that his accusation related to the fact that Nowothnig did not report the presence of iron slag in proximity to the alleged bread oven of 'Feld I' in his interim reports.

[21] L. 2.11.1970; L. 10.11.1971.

[22] In the future, further information could be obtained by the examination of two handwritten excavation diaries about the fieldwork of the Iron Field and returned to Dörner after the death of Nowothnig by Nowothnig's wife.

[23] No attempt has yet been made to gather all the plans from the authors into a single a document; however, this is a feasible aim, considering that all the drawings are provided with an internal coordinate grid.

[24] Photographs from the Iron Field still have to be fully quantified and catalogued.

Figure 11.6. The Mosaic Field, 'Mosaik I' being documented (© Forschungsstelle Asia Minor, 1965.25.5).

Figure 11.7. Rooms with suspensurae in the Mosaic Field (© Forschungsstelle Asia Minor, 1965.20.13).

sive in its quantity and quality. For example, plans show an exceptional level of detail that include the exact location of iron slag and patches of clay deposits. Similarly, profiles demonstrate careful attention to the guiding principles of archaeological stratigraphy. It is thanks to this methodical approach and the extensive documentation stored in the archive that it would still be possible to reconstruct the spatial and chronological arrangement of this sector of the site in the future.

Notes on the Documents of the Mosaic Field

The Mosaic Field is situated to the south-east of Eski Kale (Figs 11.6–11.7). The area started attracting the attention of Dörner in 1963 when a local shepherd boy reported the find of a mid-third-millennium BC seal. A test trench in the same year, directed by Winkelmann, uncovered the remains of two mosaics (one bearing a geometrical pattern — 'Mosaik I' — and the other white monochrome — 'Mosaik II'). Excavation resumed in the Mosaic Field on 16 August 1965, under the direction of E. Brödner and B. Freiin von Freytag-Löringhoff and continued until 30 September of the same year. In this season, the remains of a large complex with at least three heated rooms and associated units were uncovered. Further test trenches in this site brought to light storerooms and, allegedly, a brick kiln. Four interim reports on the results of the 1963 and 1965 fieldwork were published in *Archäologischer Anzeiger*, *Türk Arkeoloji Dergisi*, and *Istanbuler Mitteilungen*.[25] These summarized the results of the excavations and proposed the dating of the building to the Hellenistic–Early Roman period. The building is further briefly mentioned in E. Brödner's *Die Römischen Thermen und das Antike Badewesen* from 1983. Brödner shortly describes it as a complex dated presumably to the first half of the first century BC; the heated rooms to the north of it are said to have been constructed some decades later than the room with 'Mosaik I'. However, despite these publications, the results of these excavations were never systematically made available to the scholarly community.

The fate of the documentation of the excavation in the Mosaic Field after 1965 is difficult to follow. Of this fieldwork, only a collection of 120 photographs somehow found their way into the Forschungsstelle and is now part of the Dörner Archive. These photographs are currently being studied; their examination has so far provided important insights into the spatial development of the compound and its chronology, which is likely much later than the one proposed by its excavators.[26] Given its incompleteness, the archive material related to the Mosaic Field is not particularly useful in clarifying the history of the collections of the Dörner Archive. However, comparing this information with that retrieved from the documentation of the Iron Field can be used as a starting point to discuss how data were collected and managed by Dörner and his team.

The photographs from the Mosaic Field can be divided into two broad categories, namely photographs showing work in progress, which include people working as subjects, and photographs with scales, some of which are likely meant for publication. Although a full quantification of photographs by subject has yet to be made for this particular batch of documents, it is clear by just cursorily examining them that, quite like the photographs of the Iron Field, the documentation was erratic and the rationale behind the choice of subject subjective. Therefore, 'Mosaik I', 'Mosaik II', and the rooms with suspensurae, for example, are generally better documented than any other rooms in the compound. This leaves an important gap in the documentation that is difficult to disentangle. Further difficulties in assessing this evidence are generated by the fact that no plan of the compound is present in the archive.

Implications for the Study of the Material of the Dörner Archive

Although what has been presented in this contribution is based on a preliminary examination of the archive material, it is nonetheless useful as it provides insights into how data were managed by the excavation team and the limitations of the dataset for archaeological research. Based on the letters associated with the excavation of the Iron Field, one can conclude that Dörner put considerable trust in the people responsible for the excavation and final publication of the results and did not interfere much with the research activities of his collaborators. His role in the project appears to have been that of a manager; he coordinated the activities of the team to produce (or push the

---

[25] See above, note 8.

[26] The geometric pattern and, more importantly, quality of the craftmanship point to a late antique dating for the creation of this mosaic. The fact that the bathhouse is situated close to a storage unit suggests that the compound might have belonged to a rural estate or, less likely, a village. On this, see the preliminary observations in Blömer and Intagliata 2022.

experts towards the completion of) research outputs and facilitate data transfer whenever needed.

Despite his central role, however, Dörner never felt the need to keep all data in one place. After each excavation season, all drawings of artefacts, profiles, plans, and photographs were kept by individual experts or trench supervisors. Only at the time of publication would selected data converge again in Dörner's hands in the form of preliminary reports to be commented on or corrected. This data management system had its downsides, for every time Dörner needed a particular photograph or a plan for a presentation, he had to ask his collaborators. This decentralization of data, which was relatively common practice at that time, was caused by the fact that not all his experts were based at Münster (Nowothnig, for example, was in Hanover) and the difficulty of duplicating and sharing large quantities of documents in the 1950s and 1960s — some of them, such as plans, larger than others.

This way of managing the dataset also has important repercussions for the study of this collection. The first and most obvious is that not all data from these excavations are present in the archive. The presence of plans and drawings of artefacts from the Iron Field in the Dörner Archive is an exception to the norm; these were obtained after the death of Nowothnig only because Dörner himself asked Nowothnig's widow specifically for them. Other important datasets are missing because they were left in the hands of experts but never retrieved. For example, after the 1965 excavation, all coins were left in Ankara, where they were given to a local expert to study. A letter dated 26 February 1971 written by Dörner to Nowothnig informs the addressee that the scholar had finally received a list of forty-five coins from Ankara that included details on their legends, dating, and mints; this list was attached to the letter. Two versions of this list exist, one in German and the other in Turkish. The letter specifies that the document was produced by I. Ebcioğlu in Istanbul and translated into German by S. Şahin, one of Dörner's pupils. It also details that the list was not complete as it did not include medieval coins ('Memlükler, Eyyübiler, Akkoyunlular, Ilhanogullari, Selçuklular, Osmanlilar').[27] The reason for this (Dörner's research agenda? Time pressure?) is not clear. However, a list of the latter never reached Dörner, and the coins' fate remains unknown. Similarly, data on the pottery from this site, which was studied by E. Lucius, is not present in the archive. A letter written by Dörner to Nowothnig suggests that Lucius was responsible for writing a ceramic report for the Iron Field, of which there is no trace in the archive.[28] The same patchy situation is visible, as discussed above, in the documents of the Mosaic Field.

A second consequence of this decentralization of data pertains to the fact that there is no standard methodology in the way data were collected. Although it is plausible that Dörner had a role in deciding what to document, at this stage of the archive research it seems reasonable to conclude that the creation of plans, the drawing of artefacts, or the decision to ignore documenting a profile were the results of subjective choices made by scholars with different professional backgrounds and sometimes in disagreement, as detailed above. Therefore, plans could either have a legend or not, and photographs were taken not systematically but based on the importance assigned by the excavators to their subject.

The Potential of the Dörner Archive for Future Research

The discussion above provides an example of what can be achieved at the Dörner Archive if one looks at this collection not simply as a passive depository of archaeological data but as a source to critically examine how the archive was formed. Letters have been used to cast light on the history of the study of the Iron Field, which would have otherwise gone unpublished. Their examination has also clarified the reasons behind the lacunose state of the batch of documents and photographs of this sector of Eski Kâhta and the Mosaic Field. In addition, private correspondence, photographs, and plans have been employed to start addressing questions related to data collection and management strategies. Future studies on these documents will certainly contribute to better refining our understanding of these issues.

However, much more can be achieved. Focusing on the photographic material of Dura-Europos now held at the Yale University Art Gallery, J. Baird and L. McFadyen have pointed out how this type of document in archaeological archives can be used to write 'alternate archaeological histories and knowledge'.[29] Detailing what is present and what is missing in a photograph can allow researchers to clarify what the photographer deemed important and thence shed light on, for example, how

---

[27] L. 26.02.1971.

[28] L. 28.3.1966; another letter (L. 29.1.1973) mentions a pottery report sent by Lucius to Dörner. This document could not be found.

[29] Baird and McFadyen 2014, 16.

local communities were perceived by the excavators. In the case of the Dörner Archive, we are in the fortunate position of being able to cast light on the latter issue by integrating information gathered from an analysis of the photographs with that of the extensive collection of private letters written by Dörner and his associates.

In a recent contribution dedicated to the potential of the Dörner Archive for future research, by focusing on a batch of photographs about Dörner's fieldwork in Bithynia, the writers have calculated that 11 per cent of the photographs taken during this survey portray people, 18 per cent landscapes, and 13 per cent modern buildings.[30] Although the conditions in which the photographs were taken in Bithynia were considerably different from those taken in Commagene, the high number of photos about subjects other than archaeology is indicative of Dörner's appreciation for contemporary Turkey and its people. Through the photographs of this archive, Dörner emerges not only as a historian and epigrapher but also as a passionate and curious ethnographer. Systematic examination of these photographs and the study of the archive's private correspondence letters will help assess how Dörner and his team perceived these local communities and thence fit this scholar and his research into a much wider perspective.

Concluding Remarks

When studying archive material, archaeologists are naturally prone to examine documents directly associated with their subject of study — whether a monument, a site or a collection of sites — and that can help shed light on their chronology or spatial development. This does not do justice to the 'container', the archive. This contribution aimed to go beyond a traditional approach towards legacy data and explore archives as subjects of study themselves. It has focused on selected documents from the Dörner Archive at the Forschungsstelle to begin to cast light on how the documentation of the excavation of the Iron Field and the Mosaic Field at Eski Kâhta found their way into the Dörner Archive and how data was collated on-site and managed after the excavation.

The analysis of selected material from these sectors of Eski Kâhta has contributed to shedding light on these matters. Even if it was not possible to clarify how the photographs of the Mosaic Field entered the archive, we now have a good understanding of how the batch of documents of the Iron Field entered the collection thanks to the study of private correspondence. The letters also provide clues on the reasons that led the research on this sector of the site to eventually halt. Much could also be said about data collection and management strategies. Dörner appears to have been the central figure behind the project, but he was never responsible for keeping all data in one place. This decentralized way of managing data caused the dispersal of documents and lack of standardization in data collection, with the evident consequence of the loss of crucial parts of the dataset — including pottery and coins.

In an archive showing evident uniformity in the subject treated, such as the one discussed in this contribution, this research has demonstrated much heterogeneity in the quantity and quality of the material. Each batch of documents taken as a case study in this contribution appears to have its own history, which is impossible to disentangle in the case of the Mosaic Field fully. Studying these micro-histories, which are often ignored in publications, has proven to be pivotal not only to clarify the modes and ways in which individual batches of documents found their way into the Forschungsstelle but also to identify the existence and formation of critical gaps in the documentation and the reasons behind these gaps.

However, much more can be achieved with a systematic study of this collection and an approach that seeks to address the archive and those responsible for its existence as subjects of study. Particularly useful in this sense would be to examine in detail the vast collection of photographs and letters to explore how Dörner perceived the local communities and, therefore, shed light on the character of a scholar who significantly contributed to shaping the course of classical archaeology in the twentieth century.

Acknowledgements

This contribution was the result of a research trip conducted in November 2021 and funded by the Danish Institute in Damascus. Parts of this research were also funded by the Danish National Research Foundation under the grant DNRF119 — Centre of Excellence for Urban Network Evolutions (UrbNet). I am grateful to all members of the Forschungsstelle for having allowed me to peruse the archive, and particularly to Prof. Dr M. Blömer for having read and commented on the first draft of this paper. I also thank the editor of this volume for their helpful suggestions. Any mistakes, however, remain wholly my own.

---

30 Blömer and Intagliata 2022.

Works Cited

Baird, J. A. 2011. 'Photographing Dura-Europos, 1929–1937: An Archaeology of the Archive', *American Journal of Archaeology*, 115: 427–46.

Baird, J. A. and L. McFadyen. 2014. 'Towards an Archaeology of Archaeological Archives', *Archaeological Review from Cambridge*, 29.2: 14–32.

Blömer, M. and E. E. Intagliata. 2022. 'Archive Archaeology at the Forschungsstelle Asia Minor, University of Münster: The Untapped Potential of the Dörner Archive', in O. Bobou, A. C. Miranda, and R. Raja (eds), *Archival Historiographies: The Impact of Twentieth-Century Legacy Data on Archaeological Investigations*, Archive Archaeology, 3 (Turnhout: Brepols), pp. 145–59.

Blömer, M. and E. Winter. 2012. *Commagene: The Land of Gods between Taurus and Euphrates* (Istanbul: Ege Yayınları).

Blömer, M., S. Riedel, M. J. Versluys, and E. Winter (eds). 2021. *Common Dwelling Place of All the Gods: Commagene in its Local, Regional, and Global Context*, Oriens et Occidens, 34 (Stuttgart: Steiner).

Brijder, H. A. G. 2014. *Nemrud Dağı: Recent Archaeological Research and Conservation Activities in the Tomb Sanctuary on Mount Nemrud* (Berlin: De Gruyter).

Brödner, E. 1983. *Die römischen Thermen und das Antike Badewesen: Eine Kulturhistorische Betrachtung* (Darmstadt: Wissenschaftliche Buchgesellschaft).

Dörner, F. K. 1965a. 'Zusammengassender Bericht über die Aisgrabungen in Arsameia 1963', *Türk Arkeoloji Dergisi*, 12.2 (1963): 24–33.

—— 1965b. 'Kommagene: Das Land – ubi ferrum nascitur', *Anzeiger der phil.-hist. Klasse der Österreichischen Akademie der Wissenschaften*, 1965: 1–7.

—— 1966. 'Kleinasien – Ursprungsland des Eisens? Bericht über Ausgrabungen in Kommagene', *Stahl und Eisen*, 86.1: 1–7.

—— (ed.). 1975. *Kommagene: Geschichte und Kultur einer antiken Landschaft*, Antike Welt Sondernummer, 6 (Küsnacht: Raggi-Verlag).

—— 1981. *Kommagene: Götterthrone und Königsgräber am Euphrat* (Bergisch Gladbach: Lübbe).

Dörner, F. K. and T. Goell. 1963. *Arsameia am Nymphaios: Die Ausgrabungen im Hierothesion des Mithradates Kallinikos von 1953–1956* (Berlin: Mann).

Dörner, F. K. and R. Naumann. 1939. *Forschungen in Kommagene*, Istanbuler Forschungen, 10 (Berlin: Deutsches Archäologisches Institut).

Dörner, F. K., K. Böhne, E. Brödner, E. Lucius, and W. Nowothnig. 1965b. 'Arsameia am Nymphaios Bericht über die Grabungskampagne 1965', *Istanbuler Mitteilungen*, 16: 130–56.

—— 1968. 'Über die Ausgrabungen in Arsameia 1965', *Türk Arkeoloji Dergisi*, 15.1 (1966): 35–57.

Dörner, F. K., W. Hoepfner, H. Müller-Beck, and W. Winkelmann. 1965a. 'Arsameia am Nymphaios. Bericht über die 1963 und 1964 ausgeführten Ausgrabungen', *Archäologische Anzeiger*, 2: 189–235.

Hoepfner, W. 1983. *Arsameia am Nymphaios, II: Das Hierothesion des Königs Mithradates I. Kallinikos von Kommagene nach den Ausgrabungen von 1963 bis 1967* (Tübingen: Wasmuth).

Nowothnig, W. 1969. 'Mittelalterliche Schmiedeplätze von Eski Kâhta, Anatolien (Südsstürkei)', *Stahl und Eisen*, 89.18: 1022–23.

Roesch, K. 1975. 'Kommagene – das Land ubi ferrum nascitur', in F. K. Dörner (ed.), *Kommagene: Geschichte und Kultur einer antiken Landschaft*, Antike Welt Sondernummer, 6 (Küsnacht: Raggi-Verlag), pp. 15–17.

Schwertheim, E. 2017. 'Professor Dr Friedrich Karl Dörner (1911–1992), die Forschungsstelle Asia Minor und die deutsch-türkischen Altertumswissenschaften an der WWU', in P. Leidinger and U. Hillebrandt (eds), *Deutsch-Türkische Beziehungen im Jahrhundert zwischen Erstem Weltkrieg und Gegenwart: Grundlagen zu Geschichte und Verständnis beider Länder; 100 Jahre Deutsch-Türkische Gesellschaft Münster* (Münster: LIT), pp. 339–45.

12. Excavating Time and Space: The Archive of the Hama Expedition in the National Museum of Denmark

Anne Haslund Hansen and John Lund
Collection of Classical and Near Eastern Antiquities, Modern History and World Cultures,
The National Museum of Denmark (Anne.Haslund.Hansen@natmus.dk, John.Lund@natmus.dk)

Introduction

The Collection of Classical and Near Eastern Antiquities in the Danish National Museum is home to archives of several Danish archaeological expeditions to the Mediterranean,[1] which we strive to make accessible to researchers. It is to be hoped that these archives may be made freely accessible online in a not-too-distant future, not only in order to preserve the information for posterity but also — and perhaps principally — to enable scholars to re-examine the data and test the results using contemporary methods. That is easier said than done, however, in part because archives are created by individuals using different methodologies and in part because archaeological fieldwork is dependent on the practices of its time that may not be up to the standards of today.

This is a case study of the problems and prospects raised by the large and complex archive of the Danish excavations at Hama in Syria, from 1931 to 1938. In keeping with the practice of the time, a part of the finds was allotted to Denmark. These finds entered the Danish National Museum as gifts from the Carlsberg Foundation,[2] and thereafter, archaeologists and other specialists have for more than seventy years studied and interpreted them in order to unravel the history of the site. They have all depended on the same field data, which are encapsulated in the Hama archive.

In our view, it is necessary to reassess the evidence in order to determine the extent to which an archive — be it digitized or not — is capable of generating new information. In the case of Hama, we wish to explore two central aspects:

– How was each trench documented in 'time and space', and would it be possible to reactivate some of the collected data, if assembled anew, and with a different approach from that chosen in the published volumes?

– Could the data, if assembled and examined anew, enable us to address some of the lost or overlooked aspects and intangibilities, such as work processes, methodological differences and finally the social dynamics of the participants, in terms of cultural status and assigned roles?

Until the final volume of the Hama series appeared in print in 2007 the data from the project was somehow in a *continuum*, but the time has now come to approach both the raw data and its published interpretations as a historical collective. In order to do so, it is necessary to examine how the data was produced: Who did what, saw what, and how was this information fixed into writing or images? It is essential, also, to pay attention to different modes of documentation, and to how the accumulated datasets interact or even counteract. In addition, we need to recognize the important yet insufficiently understood role played by the Egyptian and local excavators, who worked for the Danish team.

---

* The authors wish to thank Stephen Lumsden for his valuable comments on and improvements to the text. Lasse Sommer Schütt and Maximilian Holmström kindly helped with digitizing images.

[1] In addition to the Hama Archive, the Collection of Classical and Near Eastern Antiquities keeps archives from the following projects: the Carlsberg expedition to Rhodes, Greece (1902–1914); the excavations at Tell Sailun/Shiloh, Israel, the West Bank (1926, 1929, 1932, and 1963); the excavations at Bithia, Sardinia (1953–1955); the Carlsberg expedition to Phoenicia, Syria (1958–1961, 1963); the Danish expedition to the Zagros Mountains, Iran (1962–1964, 1974–1975, 1977); the excavations of the Maussolleion of Halikarnassos/Bodrum, Turkey (1966–1967, 1970, 1972–1974, 1976); excavations at Carthage, Tunisia (1975, 1977–1978, 1981, 1984); the Tunisian-Danish survey and excavations in the Segermes region, Tunisia (1984, 1987–1989), cf. Rathje and Lund 1991, nos 1, 7, 13, 14, 17, 23–24, Thrane 2015 and Petersen 2019.

[2] Some archive theorists might argue that the objects form part of the archive, but the present authors prefer to think of the two as separate but inseparable entities, cf. Manoff 2004.

Figure 12.1. Harald Ingholt and a local workman on the Citadel of Hama, 1938. Photo courtesy of Nationalmuseet, Copenhagen.

The Creation of the Archive

The Hama archive was primarily generated by the expedition's director, Harald Ingholt (1896–1985), a Semitic philologist, theologian, and archaeologist (Fig. 12.1).[3] Following a promising trial excavation of the Hama Citadel in 1930 (Fig. 12.2), Ingholt obtained a grant from the Carlsberg Foundation to conduct a large-scale expedition to the site.[4] A first field season was carried out in 1931, with consecutive campaigns lasting until 1938, when the project was discontinued due to the uncertain political situation. The main components of the archive are:

- Ingholt's diaries with summaries of the key events during a given day, such as decisions and orders regarding the running of the excavation, meetings, and letters written. Once the excavation began, the diary also included summaries of the finds in each of the active squares and occasional sketches of the uncovered architecture.[5]
- 'Daily' sketch plans by associated architects (unpublished)
- Numerous inked drawings of the architectural remains based on the sketch plans, by the architects of the expedition
- An index file with the registration of the numbered finds
- Inked drawings of numerous objects
- More than 7500 photographic negatives, and a corresponding number of prints
- Maps and other documentary material concerning northern Syria
- A huge amount of drafts and preparatory material for the various publications, including *c.* one hundred boxes of sheets with attached positives and brief data
- Letters to and from the expedition members
- Administrative documents

Poul Jørgen Riis (1910–2008),[6] one of the participants in the excavations, eventually became 'custodian' of the archive and its legacy in the National Museum. His own personal archive, which is kept in the Royal Library,[7] also contains relevant documents, e.g.:

- Two albums with his personal observations and images from the daily life of the expedition
- Life-long correspondence with collaborators from Denmark, Syria, and other places

---

[3] See Eidem 2008, 152–53; Raja and Sørensen 2015; Raja 2019; Bobou, Raja, and Steding 2022.

[4] Haslund Hansen 2021, 260.

[5] The diary entries are brief and comprise little more than the identification of the square (or squares) dug on the day in question, together with a list of finds deemed to be particularly important. The diaries also record the daily life and tribulations of the members and workforce.

[6] Mortensen 2019. Riis later became Professor of Classical and Near Eastern Archaeology at the University of Copenhagen and President of the Royal Danish Academy of Sciences and Letters.

[7] Riis: Efterladte papirer. Acc. 2008/80. The Royal Library.

Figure 12.2. Aerial photo view of the Citadel of Hama, 1936. Photo courtesy of Nationalmuseet, Copenhagen.

Figure 12.3. Ejnar Fugmann A view of the Citadel behind the waterwheel el-Muhammadiya, 1934. Reproduced with the permission of Nationalmuseet, Copenhagen.

A Place in Time

The historical town of Hama, which is now home to some 850,000 inhabitants, is situated on the Orontes River between Damascus to the south and Aleppo to the north, and some 75 km from the Mediterranean coast. Its centrepiece is an ancient town mound or *tell*, and later Citadel, where human habitation can be traced back to the Neolithic period (Fig. 12.3). Prior to the Danish project, Hama was mainly known from the Old Testament and other written sources as one of the capitals of the kingdoms of Upper Syria,[8] and from accounts by travellers such as the orientalist Johann Ludwig Burckhardt, who had discovered Hieroglyphic Luwian inscriptions at the site.[9]

---

8 Riis and Buhl 1990, 9–10.

9 Porter 2010, 54; Payne 2012, 1–2.

Figure 12.4. Members of the Danish expedition, 1936: Fugmann, Hornemann, Ingholt, Riis, Jensen (Visti), and Terentieff, 1936. Photo courtesy of Nationalmuseet, Copenhagen.

The Hama project came about in what has been termed 'the Golden Age of archaeology in the Near East', i.e. the 1920s and 1930s,[10] when priority was given to sites with a biblical connotation, and the 'unique phenomenon of the tell site dominated the archaeological agenda in the Levant [...]. Large-scale excavations were the order of the day in Syria and Palestine'.[11] Ingholt had previous field experience from his excavations at Palmyra in Syria in 1924–1925 and 1928,[12] where he focused on tombs, because 'excavation of buildings in the central part of the site would have demanded far more workers than were at our disposal'.[13] The Citadel of Hama, which measures c. 400 × 300 m and rises c. 45 m above the surrounding plain, posed a far more complex challenge.

Ingholt met this by copying the organization of the Oriental Institute of Chicago's excavations at Megiddo in Israel, where he spent two days in 1930 as a guest of the British field director P. L. O. Guy,[14] examining 'all details of the working methods' of the excavation, which Ingholt described as 'from a technical point of view surely the best equipped of all those [...] that are currently working in the Near East' in a report to the Carlsberg Foundation.[15] He stated that 'the excavations at Megiddo are the best sorted in the Middle East and the Englishman proceeds extremely systematically. The mound on which the finds are made, is peeled off layer by layer'.[16]

An International Team

Alongside Ingholt, the other permanent participant was the architect Ejnar Fugmann (1896–1965),[17] and — from 1932 — Riis, who started out as a student (he graduated in 1936). The sculptor and Egyptologist Bodil Hornemann (1894–1994) also became a staple from 1932 onwards. She worked as a photographer and was the only permanent female team member (Fig. 12.4).[18]

Another fixture was the conservator and craftsman Frode Jensen, later Frode Visti (1901–1963), who had travelled in the Middle East since his youth and spoke Arabic. He had field experience from the Danish excavations at Tell Sailun/Shiloh, and was later to take part in excava-

---

[10] Davis 2003, 55–56; Porter 2010, 54; Chevalier 2012, 48–49, 62–65; Stevenson 2019, 147.

[11] Davis 2014, 35–39.

[12] Raja 2019; Raja and Steding 2021.

[13] Ingholt 1930, 342; a small house to the west of the Temple of Bel was excavated in 1924. For Ingholt, see further Raja 2019.

[14] Riis 1987, 12–13; Haslund Hansen 2021, 268–70. The career of Guy has recently been discussed by Green 2009, and the excavations at Megiddo by Cline 2020.

[15] "Dr Ingholts Redegørelse til Carlsbergfondets Direktion vedrørende Prøvegravningen i Hama i Aaret 1930", quoted from a typed copy in the Hama archive ('Udgravningerne i Hama Journal 1931–1935', 8).

[16] Berlingske Politiske og Avertissementstidende 27 marts 1930.

[17] Nilsson 2002.

[18] Haslund Hansen 2021, 274–80.

12. EXCAVATING TIME AND SPACE

Figure 12.5. Scene from a bakery at Hama, photographed by Elo, 1931. Photo courtesy of Nationalmuseet, Copenhagen.

Figure 12.6. Egyptian diggers from Quft at Hama: Reis Khalil, Reis Ali, Reis Muhammed Hussain, and Reis Ahmad Ibn Khalil, son of Khalil. Photo courtesy of Nationalmuseet, Copenhagen.

tions at Tell Sukas, Bahrain and in Nubia. The sculptor Mathilius Schack Elo (1887–1948) only participated as a conservator in the 1931 campaign (Fig. 12.5), but he later became responsible for the reconstruction of a monumental lion statue of basalt (see below, 'Jour de Grand Lion'). Other architects associated with the excavation were: Charles Christensen (1931), who had earlier participated in the excavations at Tell Sailun/Shiloh and Palmyra,[19] Jørgen Rohweder (1932 and 1933), the Russian-born Georges Tchalenko (1905–1987) (1934, 1935, 1938), I. Terentieff (1936), who had worked in Megiddo in 1928, and Marc Le Berre (1937).[20] They all left traces of themselves in the documentation, in terms

---

[19] Andersen 2019; Bobou, Raja, and Steding 2022, 68–76.
[20] Fugmann 1958, 10.

Figure 12.7. Fieldwork: men carrying baskets; to the right the Egyptian Reis may be seen.
Photo courtesy of Nationalmuseet, Copenhagen.

of style and technique, but of course also in the way they read and translated what they saw in the field.

Ingholt, Jensen, and Christensen were the most experienced excavators of the Danish team, but as at Megiddo, the crew also included skilled Egyptian diggers, hired for each season, who made up a crucial part of the workforce (Fig. 12.6).[21] They are commonly referred to as Quftis since they originated from the small Egyptian village Quft. Their continuous presence in excavations, stretching back to the late nineteenth century, had long been known, but their crucial role was only recently acknowledged properly.[22] Letters from some of the Quftis who worked at Hama are preserved: these are formal and brief, and usually reflect the financial importance of the excavations to the Quftis. Unfortunately, there are no known field notes from them, and it must therefore be assumed that knowledge was transferred orally, possibly via translation from Arabic. The Egyptians lived with the Western excavators but in separate quarters. The workforce also included local Syrians who, apart from digging, helped handle the finds, register and preserve them, and were responsible for the daily running of the expedition house.

Retracing the Methodology

Ingholt never published an account of the excavation method he employed at Hama. The archive, however, makes it clear that he followed the approach taken at Megiddo in opening up large areas simultaneously, and in removing architectural remains successively to

---

21 Haslund Hansen 2021, 271–73.
22 Quirke 2010; Doyon 2018; Cline 2022.

Figure 12.8. Egyptians recognizable by their long robes, standing at some distance from the actual digging, observing and giving directions to the team. Photo courtesy of Nationalmuseet, Copenhagen.

Figure 12.9. Mohammed Hussein keeps an eye on the diggers while Fugmann takes measurements. Photo courtesy of Nationalmuseet, Copenhagen.

clear the way to the lower layers (Figs 12.7–12.9).[23] The Citadel was divided into squares measuring 20 × 20 m,[24] each referenced by a letter (from A to U) and a number (1 to 20) like the fields of a chess board (Fig. 12.10).[25] In some periods up to four hundred workmen were engaged in the excavation simultaneously, and it was not unusual to have more than a hundred working in a square at the same time, all of whom were apparently supervised by a single archaeologist and/or architect.[26] The architects regularly drew sketch plans of the progress in each square, occasionally indicating the location of the important finds.

---

[23] The Megiddo system was set up by Clarence S. Fisher, who established the methodology of American archaeology in Palestine in the 1920s, see Davis 2003, 56 and Cline 2020, 48–49. The procedure is now known to be problematic, cf. Cline 2020, 51–52: 'There are almost always pits, trenches, remodelling, renovations, and other aspects of human behaviour and construction that can render both the initial excavation and the subsequent reconstruction of habitation of each level difficult.'

[24] At Megiddo, the squares measured 25 × 25 m, cf. Cline 2020, 49.

[25] Haslund Hansen 2021, 269.

[26] Riis 1987, 20–21.

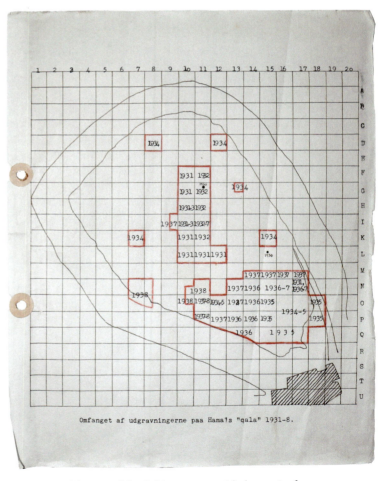

Figure 12.10. The mound divided into squares with the year/s of their excavation indicated. From the transcript of Ingholt's diary. Photo courtesy of Nationalmuseet, Copenhagen.

The excavation journal contains few references to layers and/or stratigraphy with the partial exception of a deep sounding dug in 1933 below a cistern from the Islamic period.[27] This could hardly have been otherwise, since 'the first archaeologists to consider stratification of urban centres for the purposes of dating' were Sir Mortimer Wheeler and Kathleen Kenyon.[28] The method derived from the former's excavations at Verulamium (1930–1935), and was refined by Kenyon at Jericho (1952–1958).[29] The first preliminary report of the Hama project from 1934 accordingly only included a few references to a *couche arabe* or *islamique*, which is not otherwise described.[30] It needs to be said, though, that some of Fugmann's cross-sections certainly included stratigraphical features,[31] and in the second preliminary report from 1940, Ingholt distinguished twelve levels (*niveaux*),[32] but these were apparently only to a limited extent derived from stratigraphical observations made during the digging.[33] This was probably why he used the word 'level' rather than 'stratum' or 'layer',[34] two terms that have occasionally been applied to some of them later.[35]

The twelve levels became the conceptual framework of the final series of Hama publications, beginning with the earliest settlement, Level M (the Late Neolithic period, dated *c.* 5500–5000 BC), and followed by Level L (the Chalcolithic period, *c.* 4300–3400 BC), Level K (the Early Bronze Age I–III, *c.* 3400–2600 BC),[36] J (the Early Bronze Age IV, *c.* 2600–1900 BC),[37] H (the Middle Bronze Age, *c.* 1900–1600 BC),[38] G (the Late Bronze Age, *c.* 1600–1200 BC),[39] F and E (the Iron Age, *c.* 1200–720 BC),[40] D, C, and B (the Graeco-Roman and Byzantine periods, *c.* 200 BC to AD 636),[41] and A (the medieval period, *c.* AD 636–1401),[42] when the Citadel was conquered and destroyed by the Mongols. It was uninhabited since then and remained so when the Danish excavators arrived.[43]

Recording the Finds

The objects unearthed during the excavation were taken to the dig house for cleaning, restoration, and photography.[44] This documentation was important, as these finds would later be divided between Syria and Denmark. An inventory number was allotted to those deemed to be of special importance,[45] which was either written directly on the object or attached to it on a paper label. The inventory number began with an Arabic numeral, which indicated the year of the field campaign, from 2 (1932) to 8 (1939).[46] Then came a letter, from A to Y, followed by a number (from 1 to 999). Hence, the number A 999 was followed by B 1, etc.[47] The square from whence it

---

[27] Thuesen 1988. Note, however, that the excavation journal states: 'The excavation proceeded in stages ["etaper"], marked by letters or figures. Each of the first (a-j) brought the sounding *c.* 20 cm further down; the remaining (1–35) *c.* 25–30 cm.' In Rohweder's section, Thuesen 1988, 18, fig. 8, the stages are labelled 'paniers' (i.e. baskets).

[28] Scholars had, of course, been aware of the existence of stratigraphic sequences since at least 1669, when the Dane Niels Steensen 'suggested that the shell-bearing strata beneath ancient Rome must be older than the ancient city itself', Stein 2005, 244–45.

[29] The development of a stratigraphic approach to excavations in Syro-Palestinian archaeology is described by Holladay, Jr. 2003, 35–38.

[30] Ingholt 1934, 12, 27, 37, and 43; reference is made to a 'couche de crépi' on p. 9.

[31] See, for instance, Pentz 1997, pl. 1.

[32] Ingholt 1940, 20: 'Aux douze différents niveaux de civilisation que nous avons rencontrés pendant les fouilles, nous avons donné comme signes caractéristiques les douze premières lettres de l'alphabet. La première strate déblayée, le niveau arabe, a été désignée par la lettre A, et ainsi de suite jusqu'à la lettre M, qui représente la dernière et plus ancienne strate trouvée. Afin de donner une idée plus claire du développement de la civilisation d'un niveau à l'autre, nous commençons notre description des trouvailles principales par celles du niveau M, pour remonter jusqu'au niveau A.'

[33] Nigro 2007, 369 n. 21.

[34] Fisher also used the term "level" at Megiddo, cf. Cline 2020, 51.

[35] For instance Riis and Poulsen 1957, 17–29. Pentz (1997, 34–36), who published the remains from the medieval period at Hama, characterized the stratigraphy as 'a refined construction on the basis of the layers found; these layers were naturally much more numerous than illustrated by the four strata'.

[36] Fugmann 1958, 12–48; Thuesen 1988.

[37] Fugmann 1958, 49–85.

[38] Fugmann 1958, 86–116; Thuesen 2000; Riis and Buhl 2007.

[39] Fugmann 1958, 117–34.

[40] Fugmann 1958, 135–269; Riis and Buhl 1990.

[41] Papanicolaou Christensen and Friis Johansen 1971; Ploug 1985; Papanicolaou Christensen, Thomsen, and Ploug 1986. The evidence from the Hellenistic period is discussed in Lund 2003, and the dates of Periods C and B in Lund 1995, 144–45.

[42] Riis and Poulsen 1957; Ploug and others 1969; Pentz 1997.

[43] Pentz 1997, 24.

[44] Haslund Hansen 2021, 269–70.

[45] A great many finds were not numbered individually, and we have no indication of where or when they were found. A certain amount of pottery was discarded — mostly undecorated, supposedly undiagnostic, plain and coarse wares, but apparently no sigillata sherds, cf. Lund 2003, 254.

[46] The number was omitted in the first field season.

[47] This cumbersome system was probably devised in order to

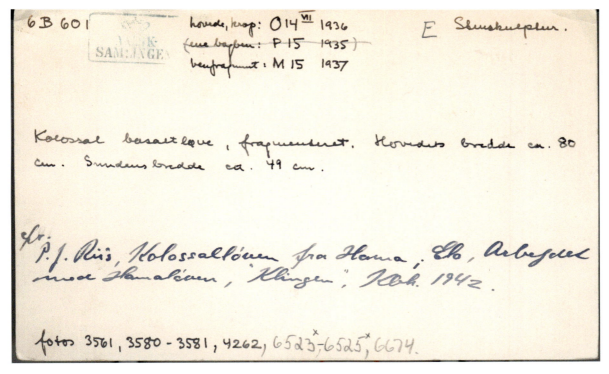

Figure 12.11. The registration card for the Hama lion, 6B601. Photo courtesy of Nationalmuseet, Copenhagen.

came was added occasionally (for instance F 11), as was the date of the find (e.g. 7/3 1931). Beginning in the second campaign, the actual date was often replaced by 'a Roman numeral followed by an Arabic numeral, e.g. III5', which implies that it was found on the fifth day of the third week of the excavation season.[48] When all of this information is present within the inventory number, we can discern the year and date of the find and the square in which it was brought to light, even if the place of finding can only be fixed within a square measuring 20 × 20 m.[49] More exact find-spots were occasionally recorded by the architects, who recorded the place on their sketch plans, or they can be worked out from Ingholt's excavation diaries.

The numbered finds were documented in the expedition house, where they were described on index cards (Fig. 12.11), in the so-called excavation file (*udgravningskartotek*), which comprised approximately 29,553 index cards.[50] For reasons that are difficult to fathom, the high-

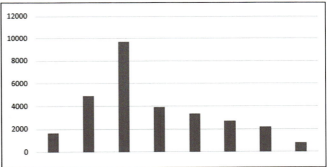

Figure 12.12. The number of specially recorded finds from each excavation campaign; data compiled by the authors.

est number of finds was recorded in 1933 (Fig. 12.12), which was by no means the longest field season. The high number may in part be due to the previously mentioned deep sounding, which was dug in the same year. The information on the index cards is extremely brief, but measurements and references to negatives are given, and some objects are illustrated by sketches. Most of the numbered finds were photographed, many were also drawn, and exact pottery profiles were drawn using a template — a procedure that allegedly set a new standard for the registration of ceramics in the Near Eastern excavations.[51]

---

separate the consecutive numbers from the first digit, which marked the year of the campaign.

48 Thuesen 1988, 11 which goes on to say: 'To complicate the situation the week was sometimes counted not from the beginning of the season, but from the beginning of work in that particular square.'

49 This issue was raised by John W. Hayes (1975) in his review of Papanicolaou Christensen and Friis Johansen 1971.

50 The number of recorded finds is somewhat higher, because two or more objects were occasionally recorded on one index card.

51 Riis 1987, 15.

Journ. Nr. 39/38 *Plade Nr.* 3561,3580/1 4262,6523ˣ- 6525+,6674 01 380 or881,6944 *Inv. Nr.* 6B 6o1.

Findested: Hama,O14 VII,1936. P 15,1935. M 15,1937. *Opstillet under:* Restaurationsgaarden. (Hama E).

Erhvervet 1938 *gennem* Gave fra Carlsbergfondet.

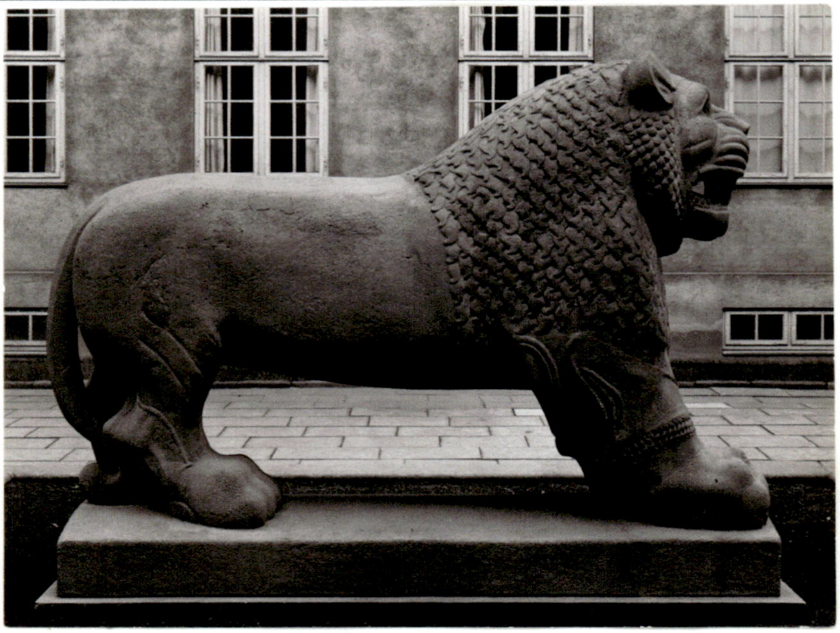

H,245 cm. L.295 cm. Br.9o cm.

Kolossalløve af Basalt. Fragmenteret men restaureret. Bevaret er Torsoen m.Hoved, Forben og Dele af Forpoterne,h.Bagben med lidt af Bugen og v.Laar. "Flammet" Mankeparti, opretstaaende Ører, Snuden kraftigt modelleret som i Palmetter med svungne Blade, aabent Gab og kraftige Hjørnetænder.

Ingholt, Rapport II,p.111ff.,pl.XXXVII,3.
"Klingen", Kbh.1942: P.J.Riis, Kolossalløven fra Hama.
Elo, Arbejdet med Hamaløven.
P.J.Riis, Hama Samlingen, 1943,p.2o,Fig.14.
Fra Nationalmuseets Arbejdsmark 1943, p.50,Fig.14.
Antiksamlingen: Vejledning 1948 side 77 afb. tavle 9
W. ORTHMANN, UNTERSUCHUNGEN ZUR SPÄTHETHITISCHEN KUNST, 1971, p. 102,103, 145, 160, 168 anm 84, 485 (Hama C1), Taf. 7, e.
VEND!

Figure 12.13. Registration card, *springbind*, for the Hama lion, 6B601. Photo courtesy of Nationalmuseet, Copenhagen.

up in the mid-nineteenth century. They consist of very brief descriptions, e.g. 2A958 'Astarte tc [i.e. terracotta] fragmented'. The electronic database also gives the object's present location.[52] Another descriptive format was also established in the museum, namely a set of larger cards (*springbindssedler*) with images and descriptions (Fig. 12.13), but these only comprise relatively few artefacts. The descriptions are occasionally in-depth and accompanied by a glued-on photo and/or a drawing copied from the publications. An additional feature to these cards are references to publications dealing with the objects in later literature. While this data is not necessarily complete, it remains very valuable. These cards have all been digitized and linked with the database entries.

Mining the Archive

Ingholt's diary lists, albeit unsystematically, the square/s dug on any given day, together with the name of the foreman in charge, testifying to a link between field observations and particular individuals. The work methods of the foremen and workers are also attested in many of the photographs taken by Hornemann and others. Our preliminary study of these

The objects that later entered the Danish National Museum have been entered electronically in a museum registry, which currently contains at least 12,412 records, but the actual number of artefacts is larger, as some entries cover more than one object, and some objects and samples are not inventoried. The information in the database is based on registration cards, which were drawn

52 A small selection of objects is currently deposited in the Museum of Ancient Art at Aarhus University. During the mid-twentieth century, some pieces were donated to other institutions.

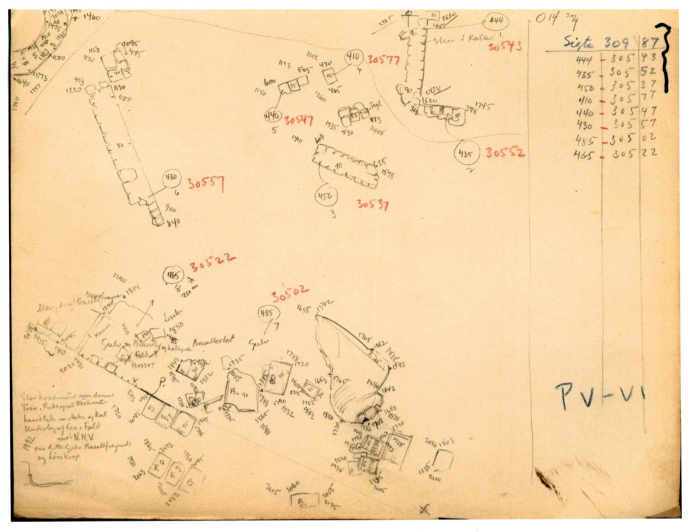

Figure 12.14. Ejnar Fugmann, sketch of the location of the largest fragment of the Hama lion. Photo courtesy of Nationalmuseet, Copenhagen.

sources indicates that it will be possible to draw up a much more detailed understanding of how the crews operated on a daily basis and how the knowledge was transferred from these agents to their Danish supervisors.

The 1937 season began with 208 workers and four foremen working a total of six squares: Muh[ammed] Hussein in M17 and M16, Ahmed in N15, Raif (a local Syrian) in N14, and Arabo (a local Syrian) in O13 and N13.[53] This distribution of workmen continued for the next five days (Tuesday 23 until Saturday 27 February), but the entries primarily focus on two squares, namely N15 and N14. In these two squares, the work had already begun in the previous season, while the remaining four are only mentioned once or not at all. The following week the setting was adjusted, with Raif and Muh[ammed] Hussein working in the same squares, while the two other foremen were assigned elsewhere. If this data were to be systematically combined with the dated images and finds, our understanding of how knowledge was gained and transmitted during the excavation would surely be enhanced.[54]

That it is possible to obtain an idea of how often a given square was worked in, and by who, is shown by the discovery of the monumental sculpture of the so-called Hama lion (i.e. 'Hamaløven') in square O14, which was opened during the 1936 campaign. Ingholt first men-

---

53 Diary, Ingholt, 1937.

54 The Hama archive also holds an undated payroll ledger with the names of the workmen under each foreman and of the staff of the expedition house. However, it does not appear to be a complete log of all seasons.

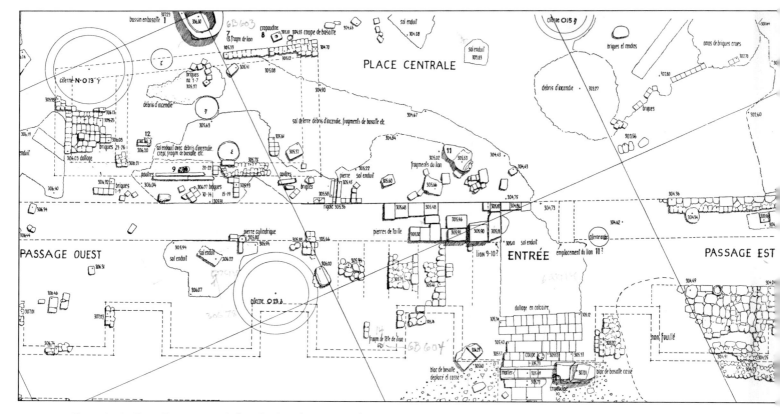

Figure 12.15. From Fugmann 1958, fig. 265. Detail. Location of the largest fragment of the Hama lion (the lion is marked 11).

Figure 12.16. Photo of the Hama lion *in situ*. Photo courtesy of Nationalmuseet, Copenhagen.

tions this square on 27 February, when he assigns Ahmed to it. On 6 March, Raif substituted for Ahmed, and he seems to have remained there until the end of the season. Ingholt reports activity in the square, but also, importantly, days of no activity ('Ej arbejdet'). This of course raises the question of what took place in the squares that were active, but not reported on.

Ingholt recorded activity in O14 for about thirty days of the season, and for twelve of these days, Fugmann or Terentieff produced the drawn 'daily' sketch plans (Fig. 12.14), with annotations alternating between Danish and English. It would surely be worthwhile to carry out a closer study of how these sets of documentation correlated, not only with regard to the finds but also to ascertain how the preparatory sketches ended up as inked drawings in the final publications (Fig. 12.15). The diary contains summaries of the finds in square O14, including fragments of basalt, some of which belonged to the monumental lion, as a constant. Interestingly, there are also frequent mentions of what Ingholt terms 'Arab', i.e. at least in most cases, ceramics from the medieval period, which seems to indicate that the soil may have been disturbed by pits or — as is perhaps less likely — that the square was occasionally excavated in smaller sections.

'Jour de Grand Lion'

One of the most significant days of the excavation was 17 April 1936. On this day, also known as the 'Jour de grand lion', the monumental basalt sculpture of the 'Hama Lion' resurfaced. The lion was photographed *in situ*, lying on its side (Fig. 12.16). Numerous pieces of the same sculpture were found in a larger area and over an extended period of time,[55] and the fragmented lion

---

[55] The torso was found in O14. Fragments in squares P15 and M15.

12. EXCAVATING TIME AND SPACE

Figure 12.17. One of the Syrian conservators posing with the Hama lion. Photo courtesy of Nationalmuseet, Copenhagen.

Figure 12.18. A 3D jigsaw: Elo at work reassembling the lion in the Ny Carlsberg Glyptotek. Photo courtesy of Nationalmuseet, Copenhagen.

was immediately recognized as an object of particular importance, as witnessed by a photo of a Syrian conservator posing next to it (Fig. 12.17).

In Copenhagen, the lion was later restored by Elo, the conservator who worked at the Ny Carlsberg Glyptotek (Fig. 12.18). The elaborate and years-long process of restoration (1939–1942) was documented in images and presented to the public in a high-end art magazine, containing an article by P. J. Riis who argued that the lion was an impressive representative of biblical Hama.[56] The heavily restored sculpture was transported on an open lorry from the Glyptotek to the National Museum as Copenhageners looked on (Fig. 12.19). It was placed in one of the inner courtyards of the museum, which was henceforth referred to as 'The Lion Courtyard', perhaps echoing the lure of the famous 'Court of Lions' at Alhambra (Fig. 12.20).[57] Sadly, it had to be removed in

Figure 12.19. The lion being transported from the Glyptotek to the National Museum. Photo courtesy of Nationalmuseet, Copenhagen.

---

56 Elo 1942, 87–92.
57 Haslund Hansen 2021, 260.

Anne Haslund Hansen and John Lund

Figure 12.20. Menu card from the restaurant of the National Museum in the 'Court of the Lion'. Photo courtesy of Nationalmuseet, Copenhagen.

Figure 12.22. Ejnar Fugmann, Khan Rustam Pasha, watercolour — from 1936 to 1938 the expedition was housed in the Khan Rustam Pasha. 1932. Photo courtesy of Nationalmuseet, Copenhagen.

Figure 12.21. Cartoon by Fugmann from 1933 in which the members of the expedition appear downcast because the finds allegedly had not lived up to their expectations. In reality, the 1933 season yielded more finds than other campaigns. Photo courtesy of Nationalmuseet, Copenhagen.

the late 1980s, when the National Museum was undergoing a grand-scale refurbishment. Since the reconstruction coincided with the construction of a new local museum in Hama, which opened in 1999, the sculpture was returned to Syria on long-term loan.

The Hama lion remains not only one of the most impressive Iron Age sculptures from north-western Syria but also represents a clear example of an object with an agency far beyond its historical framework.[58] As with other archaeological objects, it was, and is, an asset, which can be used to address cultural heritage.

Developing New Object Narratives

All artefacts found during an excavation contribute to the collective narrative that constitutes our attempt at reconstructing the past in the most accurate way. The Hama project was an early example of what might be called a 'democratic' approach, wherein the archaeologists did consider and paid attention to all of the chronological phases. Nevertheless, the team also had a story to pitch, in this case that of the biblical Hamath, i.e. the Iron Age (Periods F and E) (Fig. 12.21).[59] This is evident from Ingholt's funding application to the Carlsberg

---

[58] Incidentally, the Arabic word for lion is *assad*, and rumour had it that the then president, Hafęz al-Assad (1928–2000) laid claim to being the only lion of Syria.

[59] This period continues to attract the attention of researchers and the public alike, as shown by a recent exhibition at the Louvre in Paris on the 'Royaumes oubliés, de l'Empire hittite aux Araméens', which included a selection of finds from the Danish excavations at Hama, cf. Lund 2019.

Figure 12.23. Photo of the Khan Rustam Pasha from 1935. It includes features left out by Fugmann, such as telephone poles and a bus stop. Photo courtesy of Nationalmuseet, Copenhagen.

Foundation, which focused on furthering our knowledge of this period, previously based mainly on written sources.[60] The same chronological focus prevailed, when the excavation was first transformed into an exhibition in the National Museum in the 1940s, as is perhaps most evident from a three-dimensional model which was created for the display, in which the architecture of the Iron Age was frozen in time.

The excavators no doubt prioritized the periods they considered crucial (J, F–E, and A), leaving one to wonder how the 'less crucial' periods were registered and documented. Likewise, certain types of finds received a heightened level of attention in the field, which is reflected in their publication history and the later dissemination of the results. Such selective excavation and documentation biases must be made as transparent as possible. A good example of this selective practice is the written evidence found in the excavation, consisting of a small number of cuneiform tablets. Discoveries of this kind hold a prominent place in the documentation — first and foremost in Ingholt's diary, where the most pivotal event was labelled 'Jour des tablettes cunéiformes'. At the site, such discoveries meant that soil was re-sieved, and the engaged workers received higher *bakshish*.[61] Riis worked tirelessly to aid and encourage the study and publication of the tablets, but it proved difficult to achieve in full — let alone to disseminate their contents to a wider public. While a selection of the cuneiform tablets was published in 1956 and 1990, it was only in 2023 that Assyriologist Troels Pank Arbøll published a complete corpus and contextualization of this important text group.[62] His research (supported by Edubba Fonden) was part of a larger project financed by the Carlsberg Foundation aimed at digitizing and publishing the Assyrian cuneiform tablets in the National Museum.[63]

---

60 See also Haslund Hansen 2021, 267.

61 See 1936, 27/4 and 30/4.

62 Arbøll 2023. A preliminary discussion can also be found in Arbøll 2020.

63 <https://www.carlsbergfondet.dk/da/Nyheder/Nyt%20fra%20fondet/Nyheder/Stor%20kileskrift%20samling%20digitaliseres%20og%20tilgaengeliggoeres> [accessed 20 June 2022].

Figure 12.24. Ejnar Fugmann, pencil drawing of Sunday activities in the courtyard of the headquarters of the expedition. Photo courtesy of Nationalmuseet, Copenhagen.

Figure 12.25. Ejnar Fugmann, pencil sketch of Ingholt overseeing the excavations at Hama in the manner of Napoleon at Wagram. Photo courtesy of Nationalmuseet, Copenhagen.

A grant given by the Independent Research Council of Denmark in 2021 to the project 'Ordinary Lives in Extraordinary Times: A New View of the Earliest Urban Societies in Bronze Age Syria' is another example of the continued interest in engaging with the results of the Hama expedition. The research programme, which was initiated by two colleagues from the National Museum,[64] will investigate the early development of cities in Bronze Age Syria, based on a new assessment of the Hama archive and the archaeological finds in the museum. The three-year project, which was launched in September 2021, focuses on the Bronze Age and comprises among other things the digitization of the field archives in order to develop a GIS-based three-dimensional representation of the site's stratigraphy and architecture, and to re-evaluate the spatial associations and contexts of the finds.[65] Additionally, this new initiative offers a unique opportunity to test the potential of extracting new information from the Hama archive in order to answer the research questions of today.

Documenting the Other Now

Unsurprisingly, the documentation of the Hama project also includes information on the historical, political, and social fabric of Hama from the time of the expedition. Ingholt's diaries contain a wealth of data as to how he interacted with the local and regional power structures. In his writings, Riis also comments on Hama in the thirties and the archive itself holds a fair number of photographs of life in the city at the time.

The expedition, however, also produced another type of documentation, namely watercolours by Fugmann. On Sundays, during the Christian holy day, he would seek out motifs in the historical part of Hama, which he then painted on-site. As the seasons came to an end, he had produced around a hundred pieces, many of which are held in the National Museum.[66] Being an architect, Fugmann's main interest was architecture(Fig. 12.22, compare photo Fig. 12.23), but the motifs also comprise scenes of daily life .[67] He also documented the daily life of the expedition in pencil sketches with a humorous overtone (Figs 12.21 and 12.24–12.25).[68]

Fugmann's watercolours are to some degree both nostalgic and somewhat orientalizing, but together with the other documentation in the archive, they constitute a valuable source of information on the daily life and social conditions of Hama in the 1930s. This remains a largely untapped source,[69] and a graphic reminder of the changes the city has undergone since the 1930s. Modernization and urban development of the twentieth century have played their parts, but more significant was the extensive damage to the city, which occurred during the tragic events of 1982.

A Concluding Perspective

The interest in making archaeological archives accessible online has grown steadily over the last decades, as reflected in the digitization of Harald Ingholt's archives and other similar initiatives.[70] All archaeological projects — and the archives generated by them — reflect the state of art at the time of their creation, which is why no two archives are exactly similar. That should, however, neither deter us from attempting to define the common denominators and the 'best practice', nor from utilizing their full potential not only as repositories of data but also as springboards for gaining new insights. To reinterpret the results of any excavation is, however, a huge and time-consuming endeavour, which should not be underestimated. If we wish to assess which problems are capable of being solved, and which are not, it is necessary to begin by analysing the formation processes and composition of the archive in question. To digitize the Hama archive will not by itself answer the questions one may pose to the material today. But if made available online, the depth and breadth of such digitized content will be at the disposal of contemporary and future scholarship.

---

[64] The principal investigator is Mette Marie Hald, senior researcher at Environmental Archaeology and Environment Science, with Assistant Curator Stephen Lumsden from the Collection of Classical and Near Eastern Antiquities as key person of the in-house team. <https://dff.dk/forskningsprojekter?SearchableText=Syrien&period%3Alist=all&instrument%3Alist=all&filed_method%3Alist=all> [accessed 19 June 2022].

[65] Stephen Lumsden, pers. comm. [June 2022].

[66] Nilsson 2002.

[67] See Riis 1990 and Nilsson 2002.

[68] Riis 1987, 32–41.

[69] See Reilly 2002 and Ahmad 2014. However, see now Lumsden and others 2023.

[70] Bobou, Miranda, and Raja 2021; Bobou, Raja, and Steding 2022; Bobou and others 2023. See also, for instance <https://agora.ascsa.net/research?v=default/> [accessed 26 June 2022], and Nordquist and Lindblom 2020.

Works Cited

Ahmad, A. 2014. 'Survey of the Old Town of Hama: Documentation and Monuments', in K. Bartl and M. al-Maqdissi (eds), *New Prospecting in the Orontes Region: First Results of Archaeological Fieldwork*, Orient-Archäologie, 30 (Rahden: Leidorf), pp. 137–45.

Andersen, B. 2019. 'Arkæologen og museumsinspektøren Hans Kjær', *Lokalhistorie fra Sydøstjylland*, 2019: 21–80.

Arbøll, T. P. 2020. 'Magical and Medical Knowledge on the Fringe of the Neo-Assyrian Empire: The Cuneiform Tablets from the Danish Excavations of Hamā in Syria (1931–1938)', *State Archives of Assyria Bulletin*, 26: 1–22.

—— 2023. *The Cuneiform Texts from the Danish Excavations of Hama in Syria (1931–1938)*. Scientia Danica. Series H. Humanistica 4, Vol. 11. Copenhagen: The Royal Danish Academy of Sciences and Letters.

Bobou, O., A. C. Miranda, and R. Raja. 2021. 'The Ingholt Archive. Data from the Project "Archive Archaeology: Preserving and Sharing Palmyra's Cultural Heritage through Harald Ingholt's Digital Archives"', *Journal of Open Archaeology Data*, 9.6: 1–10 <https://doi.org/10.5334/joad.78>.

Bobou, O., A. C. Miranda, R. Raja, and J.-B. Yon. 2023. *The Ingholt Archive: The Palmyrene Material*, Archive Archaeology, 2 (Turnhout: Brepols).

Bobou, O., R. Raja, and J. Steding. 2022. *Excavating Archives: Narratives from 20th-Century Palmyra* (Aarhus: Centre for Urban Network Evolutions (UrbNet)).

Cline, E. H. 2020. *Digging up Armageddon: The Search for the Lost City of Solomon* (Princeton: Princeton University Press).

—— 2022. 'Invisible Excavators: The Quftis of Megiddo, 1925–1939', *Palestine Exploration Quarterly* <https://doi.org/10.1080/00310328.2022.2050085>.

Chevalier, N. 2012. 'Early Excavations (pre-1914)', in D. T. Potts (ed.), *A Companion to the Archaeology of the Ancient Near East*, I (Oxford: Wiley-Blackwell), pp. 48–69.

Davis, T. W. 2003. 'Levantine Archaeology', in S. Richard (ed.), *Near Eastern Archaeology: A Reader* (Winona Lake: Eisenbrauns), pp. 54–59.

—— 2014. 'History of Research', in M. L. Steiner and A. E. Killebrew (eds), *The Archaeology of the Levant, c. 8000–332 BCE* (Oxford: Oxford University Press), pp. 35–43.

Doyon, W. 2018. 'The History of Archaeology through the Eyes of Egyptians', in B. Effros and G. Lai (eds), *Unmasking Ideology in Imperial and Colonial Archaeology* (Los Angeles: UCLA Cotsen Institute of Archaeology Press), pp. 173–200.

Eidem, J. 2008. '"Harald Ingholt et l'archéologie syrienne" and "Les fouilles archéologiques danoises à Hama"', in M. Al-Maqdissi (ed.), *Pionniers et protagonists de l'archéologie syrienne 1860–1960: D'Ernest Renana à Sélim Abdulhak*, Documents d'archéologie syrienne, 14 (Damascus: Direction générale des antiquités et des musées), pp. 153–55.

Elo, M. S. 1942. 'Arbejdet med Hama-løven', *Klingen*, 1942: 87–92.

Fugmann, E. 1958. *Hama: Fouilles et recherches 1931–1938*, II.1: *L'architecture des périodes pré-hellénistiques* (Copenhagen: Nationalmuseet).

Green, J. D. M. 2009. 'Archaeology and Politics in the Holy Land: The Life and Career of P. L. O. Guy', *Palestine Exploration Quarterly*, 141.3: 167–87.

Haslund Hansen, A. 2021. 'Den skjulte by En arkæologisk ekspedition til Hama 1931–1938', in J. Kurt-Nielsen and C. Sune Pedersen (eds), *Dansk Ekspeditionshistorie: For fremskridtet og nationen i imperialismens tidsalder 1850–1945* (Copenhagen: Gads), pp. 256–87.

Hayes, J. W. 1975. Review of A. Papanicolaou Christensen and C. Friis Johansen. 1971. *Hama*, III.2: *Les poteries hellénistiques et les terres sigillées orientales* (Copenhagen: Nationalmuseet), *Journal of Hellenic Studies*, 95: 297–98.

Holladay, J. S. 2003. 'Method and Theory in Syro-Palestinian Archaeology', in S. Richard (ed.), *Near Eastern Archaeology: A Reader* (Winona Lake: Eisenbrauns), pp. 33–47.

Ingholt, H. 1930. 'Paa udgravning i Palmyra', *Tilskueren: Månedsskrift for litteratur, samfundsspørgsmål og almenfattelige videnskabelige skildringer*, November 1930: 336–47.

—— 1934. *Rapport préliminaire sur la première campagne des fouilles de Hama*, Det Kongelige Danske Videnskabernes Selskab. Archæologisk-kunsthistoriske Meddelelser, 1.3 (Copenhagen: Levin & Munksgaard).

—— 1940. *Rapport préliminaire sur les sept campagnes de fouilles à Hama en Syrie (1932–1938)*, Det Kongelige Danske Videnskabernes Selskab. Archæologisk-kunsthistoriske Meddelelser, 3.1 (Copenhagen: Ejnar Munksgaard).

Lumsden, S., G. Mouamar, A. Haslund Hansen, and M. M. Hald. 2023. *Hama on the Rebel River: A Syrian Town in the 1930s through the Eyes of Danish Archaeologists*, Proceedings of the Danish Institute in Damascus, 18 (Aarhus: Aarhus University Press).

Lund, J. 1995. 'A Fresh Look at the Roman and Late Roman Fine Wares from the Danish Excavations at Hama, Syria', in H. Meyza and J. Młynarczyk (eds), *Hellenistic and Roman Pottery in the Eastern Mediterranean: Advances in Scientific Studies* (Warsaw: PAN), pp. 135–61.

—— 2003. 'Hama in the Early Hellenistic Period', in M. Sartre (ed.), *Actes du colloque sur 'La Syrie hellénistique'*, Topoi: Orient-Occident, Supplement, 4 (Paris: De Boccard), pp. 253–68.

—— 2019. 'L'histoire et le découvertes du site de Hama', in V. Blanchard (ed.), *Royaumes oubliées: de l'empire hittite aux Araméens* (Paris: Le Louvre), pp. 272–82, 286–92.

Manoff, M. 2004. *Theories of the Archive from across the Disciplines*, MIT Libraries Research Collection <https://dspace.mit.edu/handle/1721.1/35687> [accessed 20 June 2022].

Mortensen, E. 2019. 'P. J. Riis: – og Hama og Tell Sukas, der forbandt Middelhavet med Mellemøsten', in R. Raja and E. Mortensen (eds), *Store danske arkæologer: På jagt efter fortidens byer* (Aarhus: Aarhus Universitetsforlag), pp. 187–213.

Nigro, L. 2007. 'Towards a Unified Chronology of Syria and Palestine: The Beginning of the Middle Bronze Age', in P. Matthiae, L. Nigro, L. Peyronel, and F. Pinnock (eds), *Proceedings of the International Colloquium 'From Relative Chronology to Absolute Chronology: The Second Millennium BC in Syria-Palestine' (Rome 29th November – 1st December 2001)* (Rome: Bardi), pp. 365–90.

Nilsson, A. 2002. *Hama and Jabla: Watercolours 1931–1961 by the Danish Architect Ejnar Fugmann*, Proceedings of the Danish Institute in Damascus, 2 (Aarhus: Aarhus University Press).

Nordquist, G. and M. Lindblom. 2020. 'Curating the Past: Asine and PRAGMAT', in I. B. Mæhle, P. B. Ravnå, and E. H. Seland (eds), *Methods and Models in Ancient History: Essays in Honor of Jørgen Christian Meyer*, Papers and Monographs from the Norwegian Institute at Athens, 9 (Athens: Norwegian Institute at Athens), pp. 285–94.

Papanicolaou Christensen, A. and C. Friis Johansen. 1971. *Hama*, III.2: *Les poteries hellénistiques et les terres sigillées orientales* (Copenhagen: Nationalmuseet).

Papanicolaou Christensen, A., R. Thomsen, and G. Ploug. 1986. *Hama*, III.3: *The Graeco-Roman Objects of Clay, the Coins and the Necropolis* (Copenhagen: Nationalmuseet).

Payne, A. 2012. *Iron Age Hieroglyphic Luwian Inscriptions*, Writings from the Ancient World, 29 (Atlanta: Society of Biblical Literature).

Pentz, P. 1997. *Hama*, IV.1: *The Medieval Citadel and its Architecture* (Copenhagen: Nationalmuseet).

Petersen, N. M. 2019. 'Den glemte tempeludgravning på Sardinien', *Sfinx*, 42.2: 18–23.

Ploug, G. 1985. *Hama*, III.1. *The Graeco-Roman Town* (Copenhagen: Nationalmuseet).

Ploug, G., E. Oldenburg, E. Hammershaimb, R. Thomsen, and F. Løkkegaard. 1969. *Hama*, IV.3: *Les petits objets médiévaux sauf les verreries et poteries* (Copenhagen: Nationalmuseet).

Porter, B. W. 2010. 'Near Eastern Archaeology: Imperial Pasts, Postcolonial Presents, and the Possibilities of a Decolonized Future', in J. Lydon and U. Z. Rizvi (eds), *Near Eastern Archaeology: Imperial Pasts, Postcolonial Presents, and the Possibilities of a Decolonized Future* (London: Routledge), pp. 51–60.

Quirke, S. 2010. *Hidden Hands, Egyptian Workforces in Petrie Excavation Archives, 1880–1924* (London: Duckworth).

Raja, R. 2019. 'Harald Ingholt and Palmyra. A Danish Archaeologist and his Work at Palmyra', in A. M. Nielsen and R. Raja (eds), *The Road to Palmyra* (Copenhagen: Ny Carlsberg Glyptotek), pp. 42–64.

Raja, R. and A. Høyen Sørensen. 2015. *Harald Ingholt and Palmyra* (Aarhus: Fællestrykkeriet, Aarhus Universitet).

Raja, R. and J. Steding. 2021. 'Harald Ingholt's Excavation Diaries from his Fieldwork in Palmyra' <https://openarchaeologydata.metajnl.com/articles/10.5334/joad.84/> [accessed 26 June 2022].

Rathje, A. and J. Lund. 1991. 'Danes Overseas – A Short History of Danish Classical Archaeological Fieldwork', *Acta Hyperborea*, 3: 11–56.

Reilly, J. A. 2002. *A Small Town in Syria: Ottoman Hama in the Eighteenth and Nineteenth Centuries* (Oxford: Lang).

Riis, P. J. 1987. *Hama: Danske arkæologers udgravninger i Syrien* (Copenhagen: Rhodos).

—— 1990. 'Ejnar Fugmann, the Architect, as a Portrayer of the Syrian Town Hama in the Islamic Period', in E. Keck, S. Søndergaard, and E. Wulff (eds), *Living Waters: Scandinavian Orientalistic Studies Presented to Professor Dr Frede Løkkegaard on his Seventy-Fifth Birthday, January 27th 1990* (Copenhagen: Museum Tusculanum Press), pp. 305–20.

Riis, P. J. and M.-L. Buhl. 1990. *Hama*, II.2: *Les objets de la période dite syro-hittite (Âge du Fer)* (Copenhagen: Nationalmuseet).

——. 2007. *Hama*, I.2: *Bronze Age Graves in Hama and its Neighbourhood* (Copenhagen: Nationalmuseet).

Riis, P. J. and V. Poulsen. 1957. *Hama*, IV.2: *Les verreries et poteries médiévales* (Copenhagen: Nationalmuseet).

Stein, J. K. 2005. 'Principles of Stratigraphic Succession', in C. Renfrew and P. Bahn (eds), *Archaeology: The Key Concepts* (London: Routledge), pp. 243–48.

Stevenson, A. 2019. *Scattered Finds: Archaeology, Egyptology and Museums* (London: UCL Press).

Thuesen, I. 1988. *Hama: Fouilles et recherches 1931–1938*, I: *The Pre- and Protohistoric Periods* (Copenhagen: Nationalmuseet).

Thrane, H. 2015. 'A Valley in the Zagros Mountains – the Danish Expedition to Luristan', in B. Bundgaard Rasmussen (ed.), *The Past in the Present* (Copenhagen: National Museum of Denmark), pp. 95–112.

13. The Mosaics from the 1928–1929 Campaigns of the Joint British-American Expedition to Gerasa: Drawings by Grace and Dorothy Crowfoot

Lisa Brody
Department of Ancient Art, Yale University Art Gallery (lisa.brody@yale.edu)

Rubina Raja
Centre for Urban Network Evolutions (UrbNet) and Classical Studies, Aarhus University (Rubina.raja@cas.au.dk)

Gerasa and Early Twentieth-Century Archaeological Explorations

The monumental ruins of the ancient city of Gerasa have been known and visited since the nineteenth century, when travellers began to make their way to the site in larger numbers (Fig. 13.1). One of the first of these was Jasper Ulrich Seetzen, who identified the remains as those of the Decapolis city, Gerasa.[1] Sporadic surface exploration took place for some years, culminating in small-scale investigations during the first few years of the twentieth century and marked by the excavation in 1907 of a Roman mosaic, fragments of which today are in several museums and private collections, including the Yale University Art Gallery (Fig. 13.2).[2] After World War I, with the establishment of the British protectorate of Transjordan, the newly founded Palestine Department of Antiquities expressed interest in launching a systematic excavation of the site. The British School of Archaeology in Jerusalem initiated work at Gerasa in 1925, led by architect George Horsfield. The work undertaken in 1925 and 1926 consisted mostly of clearing the site, repairing the visible archaeological remains, collecting inscriptions and other fragments from the surrounding area and village, and making the site more accessible in general.

In the meantime, Yale Divinity School professor Benjamin Wisner Bacon had become interested in Gerasa. He had visited the site in 1906 while serving as director of the American School of Oriental Research in Jerusalem. Professor Bacon petitioned Yale's Archaeological Committee to embark upon a collaborative expedition at Gerasa with the British School of Archaeology in Jerusalem. Bacon's goal for the project was to understand the site's many Christian churches, and the permit specifically granted permission to excavate these monuments. The joint campaign was co-directed by Bacon and John Winter Crowfoot, who was then director of the British School and served as field director; the results from the initial Yale-British excavations in 1928 were published in the *Bulletin of the American Schools of Oriental Research*.[3]

Bacon remarks upon 'the highly appreciated and able services of Director Crowfoot,'[4] and this opinion of Crowfoot's archaeological abilities was shared by many contemporary colleagues. His daughter Elizabeth recalls

> all his excavations, including Samaria and representatives from the Palestine Exploration Fund, the British Academy, the British School of Archaeology in Jerusalem, Harvard and Yale Universities, and he was admired by all who worked with him for his tact and skill in handling a team of archaeologists with very diverse trainings and qualifications.[5]

In the Gerasa Excavation Archive at the Yale University Art Gallery is a set of twenty-five drawings of floor mosaics, most of which are unpublished. They can be ascribed to various churches and to the hands of known and unknown people, among them Grace Mary Crowfoot and Dorothy Crowfoot (later Hodgkin). These drawings are the focus of this paper.

---

[1] Stinespring 1938, 1. Also see Lichtenberger and Raja (forthcoming) for a comprehensive collection and commentary of travel accounts written between Seetzen's visit and the publication of Gottlieb Schumacher.

[2] Lichtenberger and Raja 2020. For the research history, see Mortensen 2018. Fragments at Yale University Art Gallery: YUAG 2004.2.1–5.

[3] Fisher 1930.

[4] Bacon 1931, 2.

[5] Crowfoot 2004, 13.

Figure 13.1. View from the North-West Quarter towards the south. In the foreground the remains of the so-called Synagogue Church (now the Church of the Electi Justiniani) are visible. © Rubina Raja.

Figure 13.2. Mary and James Ottaway Gallery of Ancient Dura-Europos, Yale University Art Gallery, showing installation of fragments from the Gerasa mosaic. Jessica Smolinski, Yale University Art Gallery.

13. THE MOSAICS FROM THE 1928–1929 EXPEDITION TO GERASA

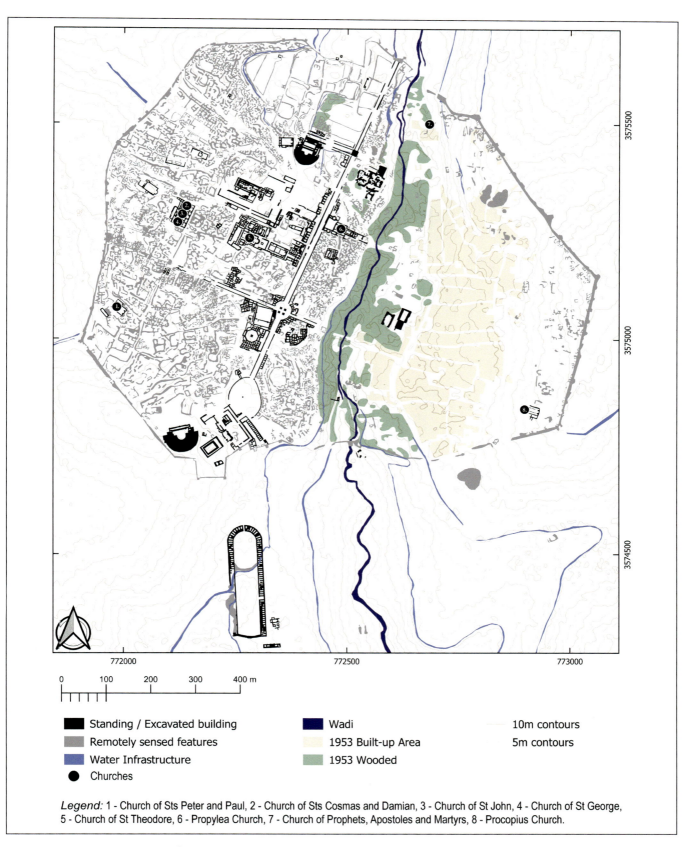

Figure 13.3. Map of Gerasa marking the churches from which the mosaic drawings stem. After the plan from the Danish-German Jerash Northwest Quarter Project, amended by Katarína Mokránová and Rubina Raja.

Figure 13.4. Flag-hoisting in Gerasa in 1929. The woman in the photo (standing third from left) is Grace Crowfoot.

The drawings pertain to mosaic pavements in the following nine churches: the Church of Sts Cosmas and Damian, the Church of the Prophets, Apostles, and Martyrs, the Procopius Church (Church of Bishop Paul), the Church of St George, the Propylaea Church, the Church of St Theodore, the Church of Sts Peter and Paul, and the church described to be part of the stables and house of Bakir Ibrahim (Fig. 13.3).

The Women behind the Scenes: Grace and Dorothy Crowfoot's Mosaic Drawings

John Winter Crowfoot and Grace Mary Crowfoot were married in 1909 and subsequently had four daughters: Dorothy Mary (born in 1910), Joan (born in 1912), Elisabeth Grace (born in 1914), and Diana (born in 1918).[6] John's career took him to Egypt for many years, beginning in the Ministry of Education in 1901, and the couple's first three children were born in Cairo.[7] Grace shared her husband's interest in ancient history and archaeology; her grandfather had been a collector of Egyptian antiquities.[8] Grace herself had an interest in and prior experience with scientific illustration, having published a book of detailed botanical drawings of plants that she observed during the couple's years living in Sudan.[9]

Due to World War I, Dorothy and her sisters spent much of their childhood apart from their parents.[10] While living in Cairo, Grace had met and hired a nanny, Kate Stevens, who ultimately looked after the children for nine years.[11] In 1914, Grace settled the children and Kate in a home near John's parents in Sussex and then rejoined her husband in Egypt.[12] John and Grace moved to the Sudan in 1916 when he was named director of the Gordon College in Khartoum, and their youngest daughter Diana was born there.

John Crowfoot worked as director of the Department of Antiquities in the Sudan for nearly a decade, resigning in 1926. His retirement was short-lived as he shortly afterwards accepted a new job as director of the British School of Archaeology in Jerusalem.[13] John Crowfoot directed the first two campaigns of work at Gerasa, the first from March to June, 1928, and the second in the spring and fall of 1929 (after which he became director of the excavations at Samaria, and work at Gerasa continued under the auspices of Yale and the American School of Oriental Research in Jerusalem).[14] His wife Grace was also a member of the excavation team (Fig. 13.4).

Grace Crowfoot performed multiple roles on the Gerasa excavation (just as, for example, Susan Hopkins

---

6   Crowfoot 2004, 6.
7   Ferry 1998, 9.
8   The collection was sold at Sotheby's in 1923. Crowfoot 2004, 2.
9   Crowfoot 1928.
10 Crowfoot 2004, 9.
11 Ferry 1998, 13.
12 Ferry 1998, 14.
13 Rosenberg 2008.
14 Bacon 1931, 2.

did while her husband Clark was field director of the other Yale excavation in the 1920s: Dura-Europos).[15] She was responsible for organizing the camp and the household staff and for managing many of the day-to-day logistics, while also working with and recording finds. Archaeologist Kathleen Kenyon, who worked with the Crowfoots at Samaria, wrote about Grace in her obituary:

> When I arrived, the camp was set up and all the organization in being. It was typical of Mrs Crowfoot that it was not till long afterwards I realized what this all implied; domestic arrangements all running so smoothly that one took them for granted, everything in order for the recording and examination of finds, a warm welcome for all newcomers, and all with a minimum of fuss. She was the ideal coadjutor for a Director of Excavations. Not only did she undertake most of the routine organization at the dig headquarters, both archaeological and domestic, but she was a first-class archaeologist herself.[16]

Grace focused particularly on the glass discovered at Gerasa, and her diligence and patience with this material was noteworthy.[17] During the 1928 season, she worked 'over a period of two weeks' with hundreds of excavated fragments and was able to restore at least one mostly complete stemmed goblet.[18]

In 1928, when the initial Yale-British excavation season at Gerasa was being planned, then eighteen-year-old Dorothy Crowfoot had been accepted to Oxford's Somerville College for the study of chemistry. As she was preparing to enter college in September of that year, her parents invited her to join them as a member of the excavation team for a few months in the meantime (April–June). Other members of the team included Arnold Hugh Martin Jones and Robert William Hamilton from Jerusalem, C. C. Roach from Yale, architects Ignaz Reich and Clarence Fisher, and photographer Joseph Schweig.[19] The focus of the first season of excavation was understanding the site's Christian churches (see Appendix 1 for the excavation permit), particularly the Church of St Theodore and the adjacent Fountain Court, the Procopius Church (Bishop Paul's Church), and the Propylaea Church according to the field report from the season (see Appendix 2 for the field report).[20] Other churches were excavated in 1929, including the Synagogue Church, the Church of St John the Baptist, the Church of St George, and the Church of Sts Cosmas and Damian.[21] The Crowfoots' second-oldest daughter, Joan, accompanied her parents to Gerasa in the 1929 season.[22] She ultimately made archaeology her career as well and became a renowned scholar specializing in lithics and Predynastic Egypt.[23] It is unclear what tasks were assigned to Joan on the excavation, perhaps cleaning and recording finds. At least there is no evidence that she made any of the drawings of mosaics.[24]

Dorothy Crowfoot's time on the excavation of Gerasa was clearly a momentous experience for her; she focused on it in an entire chapter of her unpublished autobiography, calling it 'a blessed interlude'.[25] She recalled approaching the site: 'And then we came to a great triumphal arch on the open hill side and looked down to Jerash. It seemed to me one of the most beautiful places on earth.'[26] Dorothy was first assigned the task of cleaning finds, particularly coins. But as the archaeologists uncovered the mosaic floors of the site's numerous churches, she instead began to work on making accurate colour copies of these elaborate floors. She was fascinated by the intricate designs and describes one as follows: 'The pattern in the nave was of linked octagons, and there were small panels, square or diamond-shaped, generally with decorative motifs between them [...] I began to think of the restraints imposed by two-dimensional order in a plane.'[27] She made elegant line drawings of an assortment of floral scroll borders in the mosaics, which were published in 1931.[28]

---

15 Goldman and Goldman 2011. Also see Raja (forthcoming).

16 Kenyon 1957, 154.

17 Working on the glass finds is mentioned among Grace's tasks in the excavation report for 1928, held in the Gerasa Excavation Archives, Yale University Art Gallery. See Baur 1938, 513. Grace also co-wrote an article on the glass lamps: Crowfoot and Harden 1931.

18 Robertson 1928, 211.

19 British School of Archaeology 1930, 26.

20 Stinespring 1938, 6. In the field report it is stated that a copy of the field diary from the 1928 campaign was sent to Yale University, however, this diary is not in the Yale University Art Gallery's Gerasa Excavation Archives.

21 Crowfoot 1938, 234 and 241.

22 Crowfoot 1931, 1.

23 Moorey 2003, iv–v.

24 Biebel (1938, 305) mentions using the drawings of the mosaics in his discussion of their colour: 'All indications of colour throughout the text, unless otherwise noted, are based on the careful colour notes and facsimiles made by Mrs G. M. Crowfoot, Miss Dorothy Crowfoot, and Mr I Reich, all members of the excavation staff.'

25 Ferry 1998, 38.

26 Ferry 1998, 38.

27 Ferry 1998, 39.

28 Crowfoot 1931, 45, diagram 2.

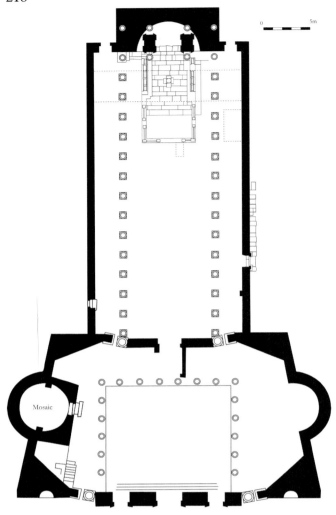

Figure 13.5. Plan of the Propylaea Church. Adapted from Kraeling 1938, plan XXXV by Katarína Mokránová and Rubina Raja.

For the watercolour drawings, Dorothy would have recorded careful measurements and notes in the field, making sketches and diagrams on-site, and she then took her work back to Jerusalem at the end of the season. She was originally going to draw the outline of the tesserae, at a scale of 1:10, and add just enough colour to show the range of shades and pattern in the pavement. But in Jerusalem she met Père Louis-Hugues Vincent, a French archaeologist with experience excavating mosaics, and he encouraged her to complete the drawings entirely in colour. As a result, she says that 'I did not finish the job in Jerusalem, but took it to Oxford with me, and slowly in the course in my first two years at college completed the two most important drawings.'[29] One of Dorothy's close friends at Oxford saw one of these drawings in early 1930 and wrote home about it with enthusiasm:

> It came out that what [she] has been so busy on (which we thought was work — since she has been busy every Sunday and weekdays too) is a marvellous painting of the tessellated pavement her father excavated at Jerash. She made a rough sketch of it two years ago when she was there and has been on work on it ever since [...] The painting is to be photographed and is then being sent to Yale [...] It was simply beautiful — both the painting and the actual mosaic — lovely soft colouring — and she had done it most exquisitely. I wonder she didn't go blind doing all the tiny squares.[30]

It was clear to all who observed Dorothy's drawings of the Gerasa mosaics that she had rare qualities of observation as well as a high level of artistic skill. Even subsequent references for her applications to research and teaching positions draw attention to this part of her background:

> She spent a part of one vacation in analysing the colouring matter of early Palestinian mosaics, thus relating two of her main interests, chemistry and archaeology. To the latter subject she has already done valuable service by making exquisite drawings to be reproduced and published of early Christian mosaic floors. She is a most skilful draftsman, working with sensitive accuracy.[31]

Mosaic Drawings in the Gerasa Excavation Archives at the Yale University Art Gallery

In the archives from the Yale-British Excavations at Gerasa held at the Yale University Art Gallery are several watercolour drawings of floor mosaics. Some of these are signed by Grace M. Crowfoot, some by Dorothy M. Crowfoot, and some are unsigned.[32] The two largest and most elaborate drawings were made by Dorothy and are those that she continued to work on in Jerusalem and Oxford, after the excavation season was completed. One of these, illustrated in Crowfoot's publications of the churches, is of the Diaconia in the Propylaea Church, a small circular room on the north side of the atrium probably intended to receive and/or store offerings (Figs 13.5–13.6).[33] This mosaic had been discovered

---

[29] Ferry 1998, 39; Crowfoot 1931, pl. IV.b.

[30] Ferry 1998, 55 (letter from K. M. Elisabeth Murray to her family, 1930).

[31] Ferry 1998, 71 (letter of reference from Margery Fry, held in Dorothy Crowfoot Hodgkin file, Somerville College Archives at Oxford).

[32] In addition, the paintings of the mosaics from the Church of St John the Baptist and the Church of Sts Peter and Paul were made by Ignaz Reich: Crowfoot 1931, pls VII and XII.

[33] Crowfoot 1931, pl. IVb; Crowfoot 1938, 228–29, pl. XLIIb.

Figure 13.6. Drawing of mosaic in the Propylaea Church by Dorothy Crowfoot. Published in Kraeling 1938, pl. LXII.b. Dimensions: 76.5 × 63 cm (30 × 24 ¾ in.). Unless otherwise indicated, all images in this chapter are reproduced courtesy of the Gerasa Collection, Yale University Art Gallery.

prior to the Yale-British excavations, under field director George Horsfield.[34]

The Propylaea Church was built into the propylaea of the monumental Sanctuary of Artemis, in an area that extended beyond the main part of the sanctuary and in fact was located on the east side of the main street bordering the steep wadi where a bridge in Antiquity would have crossed the River Chrysorrhoas.[35] Incorporated into the mosaic design of the Diaconia are two Greek inscriptions: one in the centre of the floor and one running around the perimeter. The latter identifies the room and dates it to AD 565.[36] This is the only unequivocal date associated with the church and probably refers to the major period of construction for the entire building. Like the majority of the Byzantine mosaics at Gerasa, the floor of the Diaconia was created of limestone tesserae in a range of natural colours including pink, yellow, red,

---

[34] Crowfoot 1938, 227.

[35] Raja 2009; 2012, ch. 5; Brizzi 2018.

[36] Crowfoot 1938, inscription no. 331.

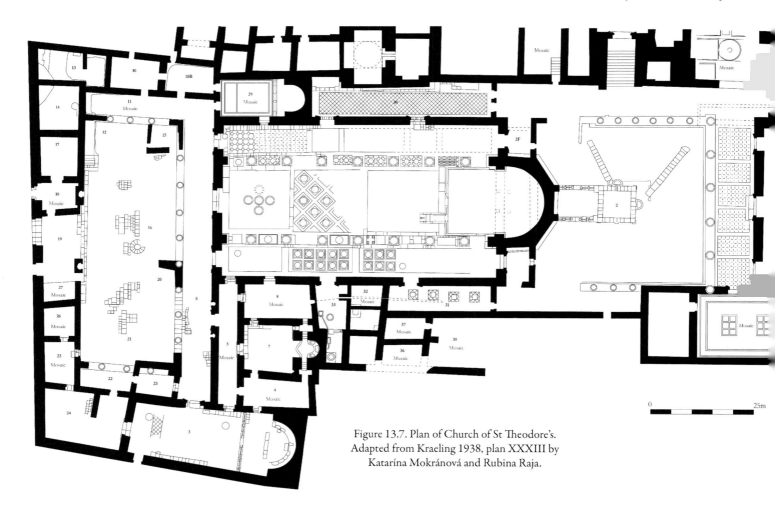

Figure 13.7. Plan of Church of St Theodore's. Adapted from Kraeling 1938, plan XXXIII by Katarína Mokránová and Rubina Raja.

blue, brown, and black. The field just inside the perimeter inscription is a continuous guilloche band. The primary pattern includes another guilloche that intersects and overlaps with a curvilinear rainbow-coloured band as well as two rectilinear designs of interlocking lines, filled with variable checkerboard designs, creating an inner octagon. The central inscription is set within a circular wave pattern. The most external band, apparently interrupted with architectural elements, is divided and includes both diamond and Maltese cross designs.

The mosaic in the Diaconia is one of the best-preserved and significant discoveries from the site, as Biebel notes:

> Perhaps because it was entirely non-representational in character, this mosaic escaped destruction. Because of its excellent preservation, the high quality of its workmanship, and its important geometric design, it is one of the most valuable of the mosaic pavements uncovered at Gerasa.[37]

Crowfoot adds: 'In color and design the mosaics on this floor are some of the most pleasing in Gerasa.'[38]

The other large mosaic drawing in Yale's Gerasa Excavation Archive is of the floor in the north-west chapel of the Church of St Theodore. Although not signed, this work of art is identified as being by Dorothy in Crowfoot's 1938 publication in the volume edited by Kraeling (Figs 13.7–13.9).[39] The Church of St Theodore is one of a complex of buildings around the so-called Fountain Court that were constructed over several centuries; while part of the complex appears to date to the second century AD, most of the buildings date to the fourth and fifth centuries.[40] An inscription found near the central doorway of the Church of St Theodore shows that the foundation of the church was laid in AD 494 and the lintel erected in AD 496.[41] Most of the rooms and

---

[37] Biebel 1938, 317.

[38] Crowfoot 1938, 228.

[39] Crowfoot 1938, pl. LXIa.

[40] Raja 2015; Brenk, Jäggi, and Meier 1995; 1996.

[41] Welles 1938, 477, no. 300.

Figure 13.8. Photo of Church of St Theodore.

chapels associated with the church were paved with marble floors or mosaics, some of which Crowfoot dismissed as being 'of no great merit'.[42]

In the north-west chapel of the Church of St Theodore, however, the excavators discovered another of the site's well-preserved and intricate geometric mosaics.[43] Biebel dates it slightly after the construction of the main church to the early sixth century AD.[44] The limestone tesserae use the same colour palette as contemporary mosaic floors at Gerasa: pink, dark red, yellow, blue, and white, though here yellow is the dominating colour. The border of the rectangular floor space is composed of small, connected circles, essentially the same pattern on a smaller and simpler scale as one of the motifs in the Diaconia mosaic. Then about one-third of the floor, at the western end of the room, is covered with a field of diamonds and small triangles. The remainder of the floor contains a large circle; at the four corners of the square that contains the circle are images of two-handled amphorae. The circle itself contains three overlapping and interlocking shapes — similar to a kidney shape but symmetrical, pinched in evenly on both sides — each of which bears its own pattern: a rainbow, a ribbon pattern, and a two-strand braid. In the six curved triangles created by the intersections of these shapes are two each of the following motifs: a bunch of grapes, a leaf, and a trefoil. The centre, a hexagon with concave sides, is filled with overlapping triangles.

The excavation archives at Yale also include several small drawings of other floor mosaics from Gerasa. Among these is one particularly detailed, completely coloured rendering of the floor mosaic in the north aisle of the Procopius Church (earlier also called the Church of Bishop Paul) (Figs 13.10–13.11). It bears a carefully handwritten label identifying it and giving its scale (1:10). The initials 'D. M. C.' on the back of the paper identify Dorothy as the artist. Also on the back is a note: 'I am not certain that the outside pattern is fitted in correctly to the circle as I have drawn it in from memory.' The other drawing that is without doubt by Dorothy's hand is rendering on graph paper; it is labelled (Fig. 13.12):

Mosaic in Room #4
Southwest Corner
Church of St Theodore – Jerash

---

[42] Crowfoot 1938, 225.
[43] Crowfoot 1938, 224.
[44] Biebel 1938, 315.

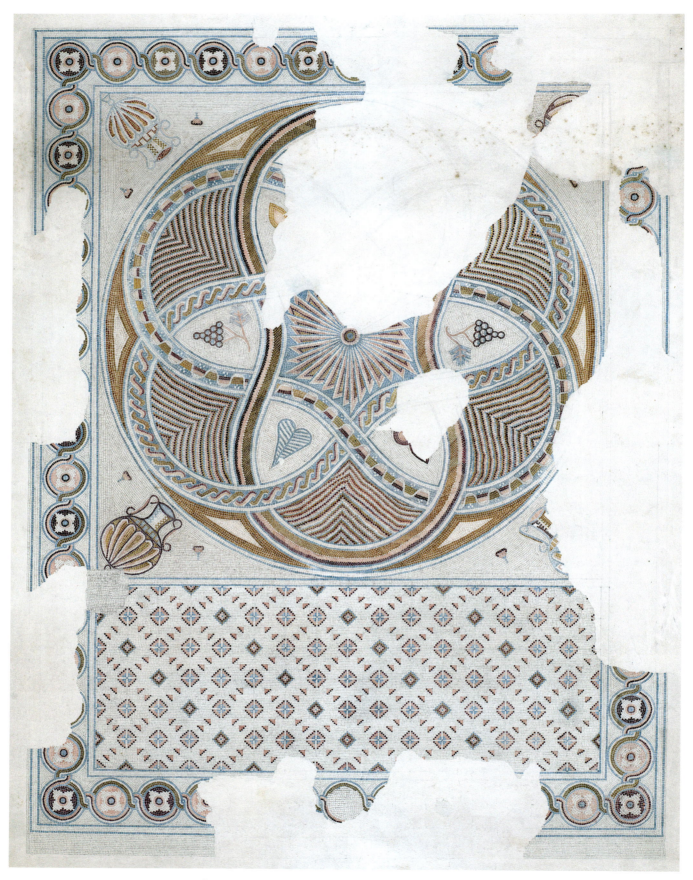

Figure 13.9. Drawing of mosaic in Church of St Theodore by Dorothy Crowfoot. Published in Kraeling 1938, pl. LXI.a. Dimensions: 56 × 76 cm (22 × 30 in.).

13. THE MOSAICS FROM THE 1928–1929 EXPEDITION TO GERASA

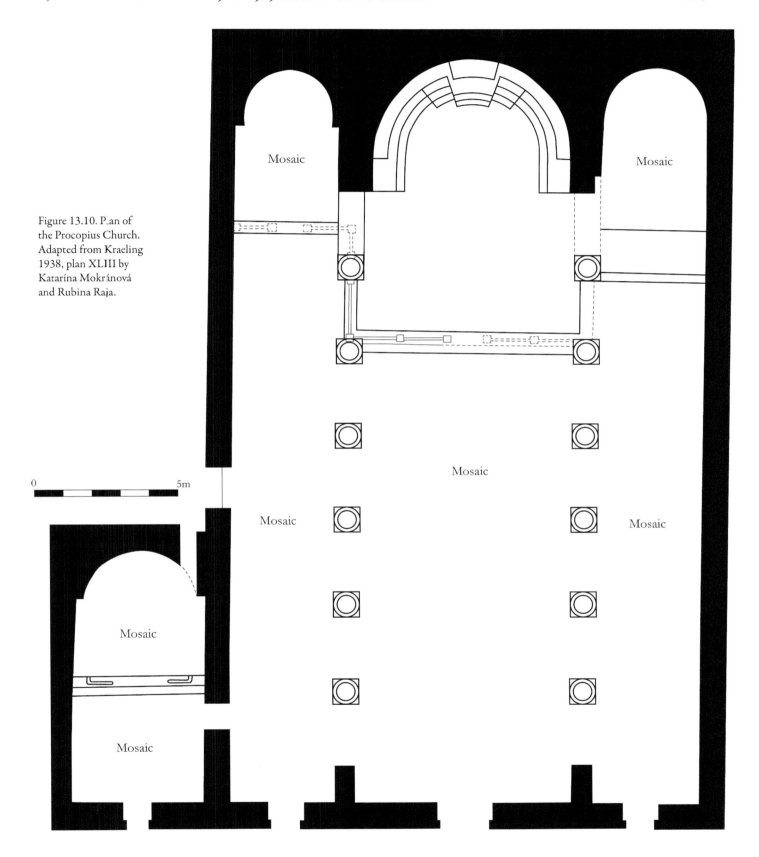

Figure 13.10. Plan of the Procopius Church. Adapted from Kraeling 1938, plan XLIII by Katarína Mokránová and Rubina Raja.

Figure 13.11. Drawing of mosaic in north aisle of Procopius Church by Dorothy Crowfoot, 1928.
Dimensions: 17 × 24 cm (6 7/8 × 9 ½ in.).

13. THE MOSAICS FROM THE 1928–1929 EXPEDITION TO GERASA

Figure 13.12. Drawing of mosaic in room 4, south-west corner of Church of St Theodore by Dorothy Crowfoot, 1928. Dimensions: 44 × 23 cm (17 ½ × 9 in.).

In the lower right corner are the words 'Watercolor by D. Crowfoot'. Along the top edge she has provided the original dimensions: '2 m 5 cm'.

Also preserved among the small drawings of mosaics in the Gerasa excavation archives are four works signed by Grace Crowfoot ('G. M. Crowfoot'). All show mosaics from the Procopius Church. Two of the four show geometric patterns and are done on graph paper (Figs 13.13–13.14):

> North east intercolumniar Pattern
> between columns 5 & 6
> in Bishop Paul's Church
> Side of tessera = 1 cm approx.
>
> Pattern from front of South Apse
> of Bishop Paul's Church
> Side of Tessera = 1 cm approx.

In pencil on both, the identification of the church is clarified ('Procopius'), and information about the colours used is given: 'Colours used: Blue Black, Dark Red, Light Red, Vermillion Red, Pink (mauve when dry), Yellow Brown' (the drawing from the south apse adds 'and Grey' to this list). The other two drawings by Grace show a floral frieze identified as being from the 'Northwest Chapel, Bishop Paul's Church, Jerash' and a tree ('The Cypress Tree') from the 'North Side of South Apse, Bp. Paul's Church, Jerash' (Figs 13.15–13.17). The Yale University Art Gallery's Gerasa Excavation Archive contains photographs of the mosaics from the Procopius Church, taken during and after excavation. These show several elaborate mosaics and give a vivid impression of their quality (Figs 13.18–13.36). Some of the mosaics themselves are also in the collection of the Yale University Art Gallery (Figs 13.37–13.38).

Additional Mosaic Drawings from the Archive

In addition to the drawings by Dorothy and Grace Crowfoot described above, there are several other unpublished drawings in the Yale University Art Gallery's Gerasa Excavation Archive. One of the drawings, which does not carry a name or initials of the artist, is simply a colour scheme with samples of colours accompanied by a description of each (Fig. 13.39). This drawing shows that Grace and Dorothy worked systematically and would have had a consistent reference chart for rendering the colour palette of the mosaic stones.

From the Procopius Church, on the east side of the river in the area where the village was located, stem a total of nine drawings. Of those, four can be assigned as

Figure 13.13. Drawing of mosaic in north-east intercolumniar pattern between columns 5 and 6 in Procopius Church by Grace M. Crowfoot, 1928. 19.25 × 28.5 cm (7 ½ × 11 ¼ in.).

13. THE MOSAICS FROM THE 1928–1929 EXPEDITION TO GERASA

Figure 13.14. Drawing of mosaic in front of south apse in Procopius Church by Grace M. Crowfoot, 1928. Dimensions: 17.5 × 28.75 cm (6 7/8 × 11 ¼ in.).

Figure 13.16. Drawing of mosaic of cypress tree in south apse in Procopius Church by Grace M. Crowfoot, 1928. Dimensions: 13.75 × 22.75 cm (5 ½ × 9 in.).

Figure 13.15. Drawing of mosaic in north-west chapel in Procopius Church by Grace M. Crowfoot, 1928. Dimensions: 29.25 × 21.5 cm (11 ½ × 8 ½ in.).

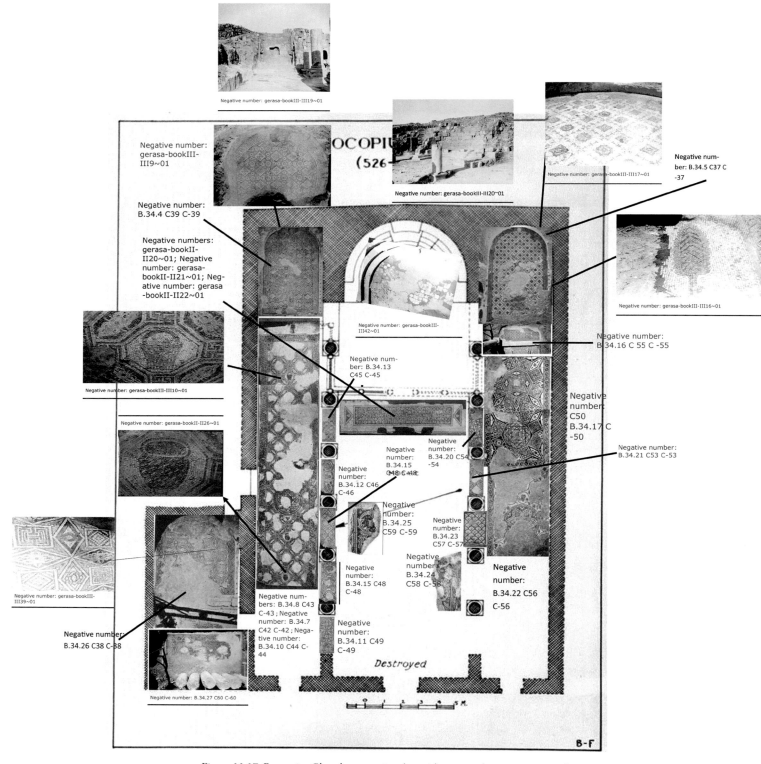

Figure 13.17. Procopius Church composite plan with mosaic photos incorporated.

13. THE MOSAICS FROM THE 1928–1929 EXPEDITION TO GERASA

Figure 13.18. Photo of Procopius Church, mosaic in north chancel.

Figure 13.19. Photo of Procopius Church, mosaic in south chancel.

Figure 13.20. Photo of Procopius Church, mosaic in north aisle, east end.

Figure 13.21. Photo of Procopius Church, mosaic in north aisle, centre.

Figure 13.22. Photo of Procopius Church, mosaic in north aisle.

Figure 13.23. Photo of Procopius Church, mosaic in north aisle.

Figure 13.24. Photo of Procopius Church, mosaic in north aisle.

Figure 13.25. Photo of Procopius Church, mosaic in north aisle.

Figure 13.26. Photo of Procopius Church, mosaic in south aisle, west end.

Figure 13.27. Photo of Procopius Church, mosaic in south aisle.

Figure 13.28. Photo of Procopius Church, mosaic in south aisle.

Figure 13.29. Photo of Procopius Church, mosaic in south aisle.

Figure 13.30. Photo of Procopius Church, mosaic in south aisle.

Figure 13.31. Photo of Procopius Church, mosaic in nave.

Figure 13.32. Photo of Procopius Church, mosaic in nave.

Figure 13.33. Photo of Procopius Church, mosaic in north chancel.

13. THE MOSAICS FROM THE 1928–1929 EXPEDITION TO GERASA

Figure 13.34. Photo of Procopius Church, mosaic in chapel.

Figure 13.35. Photo of Procopius Church, mosaic in south aisle.

Figure 13.36. Photo of Procopius Church, mosaic in north aisle.

Figure 13.37. Mosaic with inscription, from nave of Procopius Church, *c.* AD 526. The Yale-British School Excavations at Gerasa. Yale University Art Gallery, 1929.419.

Figure 13.38. Mosaic with geometric design, from south aisle of Procopius Church, *c.* AD 526. The Yale-British School Excavations at Gerasa. Yale University Art Gallery, 1929.418.

13. THE MOSAICS FROM THE 1928–1929 EXPEDITION TO GERASA

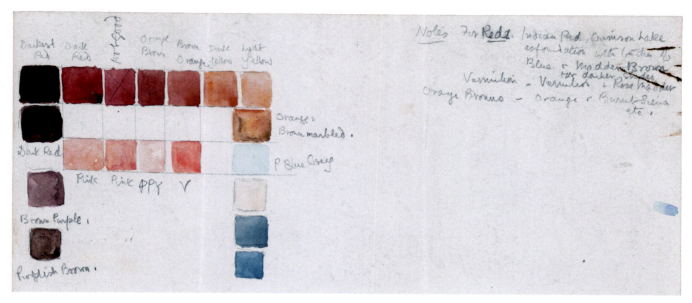

Figure 13.39. Colour scheme for drawings of mosaics. Dimensions: 22.5 × 14 cm (8 7/8 × 5 ½ in.). Unpublished. Artist not known.

Figure 13.40. Pencil drawing on reverse of colour scheme showing pattern in the north aisle of Procopius Church. No initials or name written on the drawing. Published in Kraeling 1938, pl. LXXXIII.a–b. Dimensions: 22.5 × 14 cm (8 7/8 × 5 ½ in.).

described above to Grace Crowfoot and one to Dorothy Crowfoot. Four have no names or initials on them. One of them also has no church name on it but can be ascribed to the Procopius Church since a photograph of exactly that pattern is published in Kraeling 1938, pl. LXXXIII (Fig. 13.40).[45] The other three can be identified as drawings of sections of mosaics from the same church. One drawing shows two baskets (Fig. 13.41), one is a detail of the intercolumnar pattern (Fig. 13.42), and the last one shows details in pencil and colour of the mosaic in the north aisle of the church (Fig. 13.43). Since these are all drawings from the Procopius Church, which was explored in the 1928 excavation season, we can assume that they were drawn by either Grace or Dorothy.

From the Church of the Prophets, Apostles, and Martyrs, also located on the east side of the river in the northern end of the city, stems one drawing with a floral scroll. It does not carry the name of the artist (Figs 13.44–13.45).

The last two drawings are fascinating since they give their locations as 'the house of Bakir Ibrahim' and 'the sta-

---

45 Kraeling 1938, pl. LXXXIII.a–b.

Figure 13.41. Drawing of mosaic in chancel of north aisle in Procopius church.
Dimensions: 20 × 25 cm (7 7/8 × 9 7/8 in.). No initials or name written on the drawing.

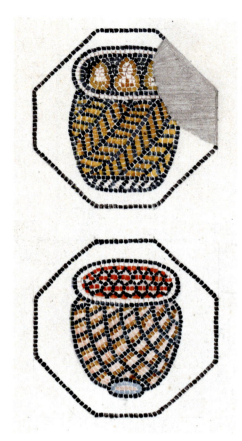

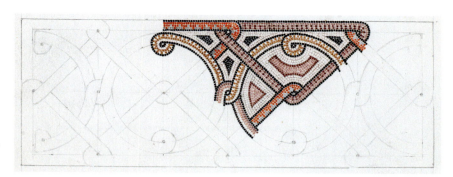

Figure 13.43. Drawing of mosaic with of intercolumnar pattern in Procopius Church. No initials or name written on the drawing. Dimensions: 30 × 16.5 cm (11 ¾ × 6 ½ in.).

Figure 13.42. Drawing of mosaic of two baskets from centre octagons in north aisle in Procopius Church. No initials or name written on the drawing. Dimensions: 12.25 × 20 cm (4 7/8 × 7 7/8 in.).

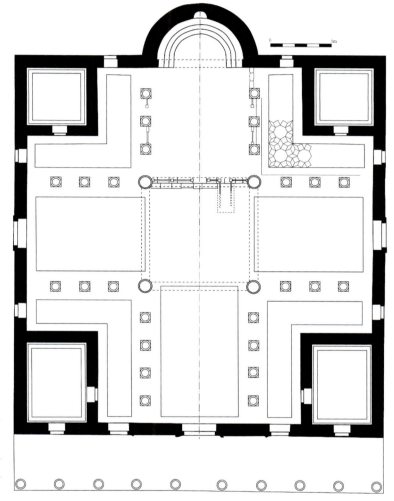

Figure 13.44. Plan of Church of the Prophets, Apostles, and Martyrs. Adapted from Kraeling 1938, plan XLI by Katarína Mokránová and Rubina Raja.

Figure 13.45. Drawing of mosaic with floral scroll from Church of the Prophets, Apostles, and Martyrs. No initials or name written on the drawing. Dimensions: 25.25 × 17.75 cm (10 × 7 in.).

Figure 13.46. Drawing of mosaic in the stable of Bakir Ibrahim. No initials or name written on the drawing. Dimensions: 24.75 × 20 cm (9 ¾ × 7 7/8 in.).

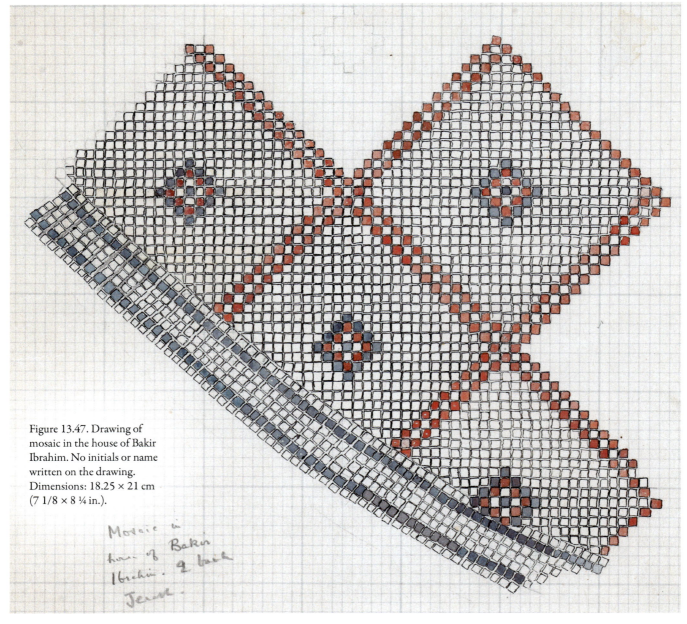

Figure 13.47. Drawing of mosaic in the house of Bakir Ibrahim. No initials or name written on the drawing. Dimensions: 18.25 × 21 cm (7 1/8 × 8 ¼ in.).

bles of Bakir Ibrahim'. One of them is also dated 21 April 1928 (Figs 13.46–13.47). They do not carry the name of the artist. We assume that these mosaics were located on private grounds on the east side of the river where the village was located. Potentially, these mosaics were located in what by Schumacher was termed Roman house or church in his 1902 publication and were given the number 13 on the legend of the map published by the Danish-German Jerash Northwest Quarter Project (Fig. 13.48).[46]

From the Church of St Theodore, located on the west side of the river close to the main street and the Sanctuary of Artemis, comes a total of six drawings (Figs 13.49–13.54). Two of them are labelled as such and bear the name of Dorothy Crowfoot on them (Figs 13.9 and 13.12), and one of them was published in Kraeling 1938 as mentioned above.[47] The other one is a reddish patterned one from room 4 (Fig. 13.12). Four drawings have no initials or names, nor is the church name given. However, based on comparisons with room numbers on the plan marking the mosaics found of the Church of St Theodore in Kraeling's 1938 publication, these numbers match up with the ones on the drawings. We may therefore assume that these four drawings copied fragmented mosaics found in those rooms.[48] One of them shows small square decorations found in room 26 (Fig. 13.49). The others all show details of geometric mosaic patterns with variations on decorative schemes with rosettes and squares centrally placed in the different units and decorated borders, respectively from rooms 13, 25, 36, and 37 (Figs 13.50–13.53). We have here made an attempt to incorporate these mosaics into the plan of the Church of St Theodore according to the room numbers on the plan published in Kraeling 1938 (Fig. 13.54). These might well have been done by either Grace or Dorothy, since at least Dorothy worked on mosaics in the church during the campaign.

From a church complex that consisted of three linked churches — those of St George, St Paul, and Sts Cosmas and Damian — stems three drawings. One is from the Church of St George and depicts a peacock in an elaborate decorative setting (Figs 13.55–13.56). The drawing is not labelled, but the peacock and the surrounding motif appears in a photo in Kraeling 1938; thus, the location of the mosaic can be identified.[49] From the Church of Sts Cosmas and Damian stem another two drawings,

whereof neither carries the name of the artist, and only one carries the name of the church and location of the mosaic (Figs 13.57–13.58). The second one is, however, recognizable as coming from the Church of Sts Cosmas and Damian by its patterning.

From the Church of Sts Peter and Paul stem two mosaic drawings (Figs 13.59–13.60). These have no names or initials of the artist on them, but one of them holds the name of the church; the mosaic pattern can be recognized from excavation photos as well (Fig. 13.61). The second drawing holds no name of the church, but the pattern is recognizable from drawn plans in Kraeling and Michel (Fig. 13.62).[50]

It is tempting to try to attribute the remaining unsigned drawings to either Grace or Dorothy through study of the paper, pigments, brush strokes, or technique. This is exceedingly difficult, however, as they were certainly using the same materials. Even studying the drawings from a connoisseurship standpoint is problematic as they may well have shared artistic style and technique. Furthermore, some of the drawings were perhaps made in the field, while others were certainly done back in a studio (Jerusalem, Oxford, or elsewhere). In some cases, the handwritten labels are carefully printed, while in others they are clearly quickly written notes. However, since Dorothy only participated in the excavations in 1928, we can in fact get further with the attribution of the drawings to her mother Grace. In the chapter on the Christian churches written by John W. Crowfoot and published in 1938, it is clearly stated that the Churches of Sts Cosmas and Damian and St George, as well as that of Sts Peter and Paul and that of the Prophets, Apostles, and Martyrs were only examined and excavated in the 1929 campaigns.[51] The first two between 20 March and 30 May and the third between 20 March and 11 April, while the last church was only partly surveyed and sounding made in the autumn campaign of 1929. This means that the 1929 drawings can almost certainly be ascribed to the hand of Grace Mary Crowfoot.

Dorothy, however, did not only take back to Oxford her field sketches to create the final mosaic drawings for publication. She also took with her some glass tesserae from other excavated mosaics. We do not know which ones exactly. But we do know that she undertook chemical analysis of the glass tesserae at Oxford in order to study their composition. Some of her correspondence with her parents attests to this:

---

[46] Schumacher 1902.
[47] Kraeling 1938, pl. LXI.a.
[48] Kraeling 1938, plan XXXIII.
[49] Kraeling 1938, plan XXXVII.

[50] Kraeling 1938, pl. LXXII.c.
[51] Crowfoot 1938, respectively 241, 251, 256 for excavation dates.

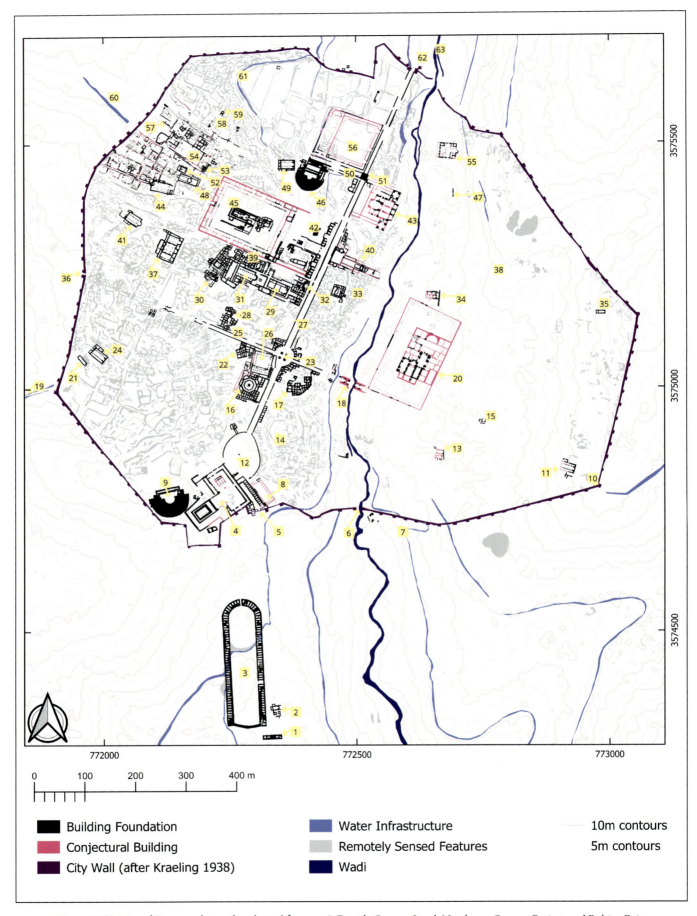

Figure 13.48. Map of Gerasa and its archaeological features. © Danish-German Jerash Northwest Quarter Project, and Rubina Raja.

MAP OF GERASA LEGEND

1. Extramural arch ('Hadrian's Arch')
2. Church of Bishop Marianos
3. Hippodrome
4. Sanctuary of Zeus Olympios
5. South Gate
6. Water Gate
7. City walls
8. Shops and structures along the South Gate street
9. South Theatre
10. South-East Gate (blocked)
11. Procopius Church
12. 'Oval Piazza'
13. Roman house or church
14. 'Camp Hill' (location of modern museum)
15. Byzantine villa
16. Agora ('Macellum')
17. Area of the House of the Blues
18. South Bridge
19. Possible South-West Aqueduct
20. East Baths
21. Mortuary Church
22. Late Antique and Early Islamic structures
23. South Tetrapylon
24. Church of Sts Peter and Paul
25. Side street ('South Decumanus')
26. Mosque
27. Main Street ('cardo')
28. Early Islamic domestic quarter
29. Cathedral complex
30. 'Temple C'
31. Church of St Theodore and Fountain Court
32. Nymphaion
33. Buildings west of the Wadi
34. Small Eastern Baths
35. Chapel of Elia, Mary, and Soreg
36. South-West Gate
37. Churches of Sts George, John, Cosmas, and Damian
38. Approximate location of 'House of the Poets and Muses'
39. Ecclesiastic complexes and Baths of Placcus
40. Propylaea Church
41. Church of Bishop Genesius
42. Ottoman House
43. West Baths
44. Large rock-cut cistern
45. Sanctuary of Artemis
46. North Theatre
47. Spring (Ain Karawan)
48. Synagogue/Church of the *Electi Iustiniani*
49. Church of Bishop Isaiah
50. Side street ('North Decumanus')
51. North Tetrapylon
52. Hall of the *Electi Iustiniani*
53. Umayyad houses
54. Middle Islamic hamlet (and large courtyard)
55. Church of the Prophets, Apostles, and Martyrs
56. Large open area ('forum') and basilica
57. Roman edifice and cistern
58. Middle Islamic structures
59. Circassian house
60. North-West Aqueduct
61. Early modern water channel
62. North Gate
63. Chrysorrhoas/Wadi Jerash

This letter is being written in the OCD [Old Chemistry Department] on Monday evening, with all my pots and pans boiling merrily all round me. I have been feeling so miserable this weekend but have quite cheered up now. This afternoon I found the slightest trace of my old friend Titanium in the blue glass — isn't that good news! Perhaps Mummy will remember the other time in my life I met titanium — in Khartum with Dr Joseph from the ilmenite Joan and I extracted from our gadwell [she was not quite 14 at the time]. I carefully wrote down and kept the test he taught me and now after all these years I have used it again!

I had a tragedy on Saturday and lost all the cobalt from the dark blue glass so I had to go to the Ashmolean on Monday and extract Mr Harden's last-but-one piece of it. So if you are prowling round Jerash and likely to find some more bits of it — you might bring them back.

Next week I hope to send you a full analysis of the blue glass and possibly too of some green![52]

Not only did Dorothy Crowfoot display talent for making archaeological drawings, but she also undertook some of the earliest archaeological science which we know about today. On that background it might not be so surprising that she, with this creativity and talent combined with intelligence, went on to be awarded the Nobel Prize in Chemistry in 1964.

The study of archival documents and drawings from historical excavations, such as the Yale University and British School of Archaeology at Jerusalem project at Gerasa, is essential to subsequent study of ancient sites. The importance of artistic copies and renderings, in addition to photographic documentation, is particularly heightened when considering a period when on-site photography was only available in black-and-white. For study of wall paintings or mosaics, the work of excavation artists is immensely powerful and significant. The colour paintings by Herbert Gute, for example, are consistently cited in publications on the wall paintings of the Synagogue at Dura-Europos. Due to the fact that the Gerasa Excavation Archive at Yale is smaller and less well studied than that of Dura-Europos at the same institution, the drawings done by Dorothy Crowfoot and her mother, Grace Mary Crowfoot, are less well known. By conserving, digitizing, and publishing this material, it is hoped that their work will come to be fully appreciated both for its artistic merit and for its archival and historical significance.

---

[52] Letter from Dorothy Crowfoot to her parents, 1929, reproduced in Ferry 1998, 53.

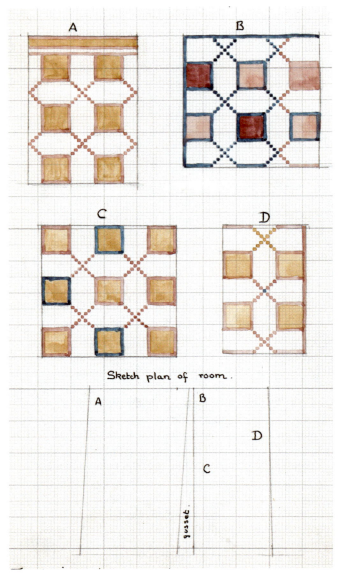

Figure 13.49. Drawing of mosaic from room 26, most likely Church of St Theodore. Dimensions: 12.5 × 20 cm (4 7/8 × 7 7/8 in.). No initials or name written on the drawing.

Figure 13.51. Drawing of mosaic from room 25, most likely Church of St Theodore. Dimensions: 12.5 × 20.25 cm (4 7/8 × 8 in.). No initials or name written on the drawing.

Figure 13.50. Drawing of mosaic from room 18, most likely Church of St Theodore. Dimensions: 20.25 × 12.5 cm (8 × 4 7/8 in.). No initials or name written on the drawing.

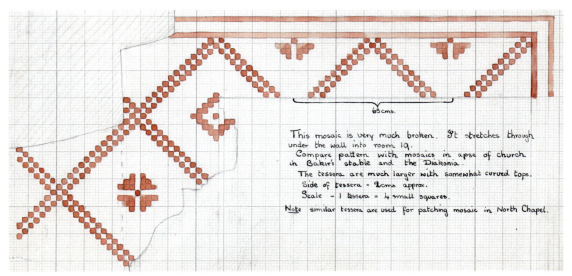

13. THE MOSAICS FROM THE 1928–1929 EXPEDITION TO GERASA 243

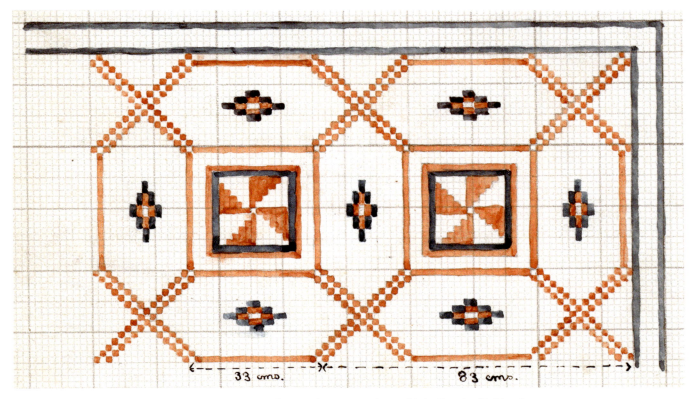

Figure 13.52. Drawing of mosaic from room 36, most likely Church of St Theodore.
Dimensions: 12.5 × 16.5 cm (4 7/8 × 6 ½ in.). No initials or name written on the drawing.

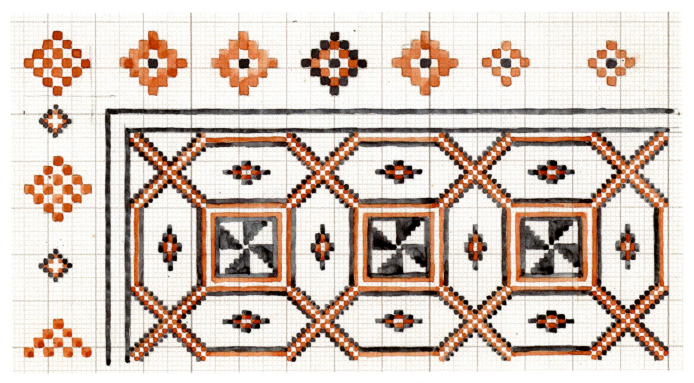

Figure 13.53. Drawing of mosaic from room 37, most likely Church of St Theodore.
Dimensions: 20.25 × 12.5 cm (8 × 5 in.). No initials or name written on the drawing.

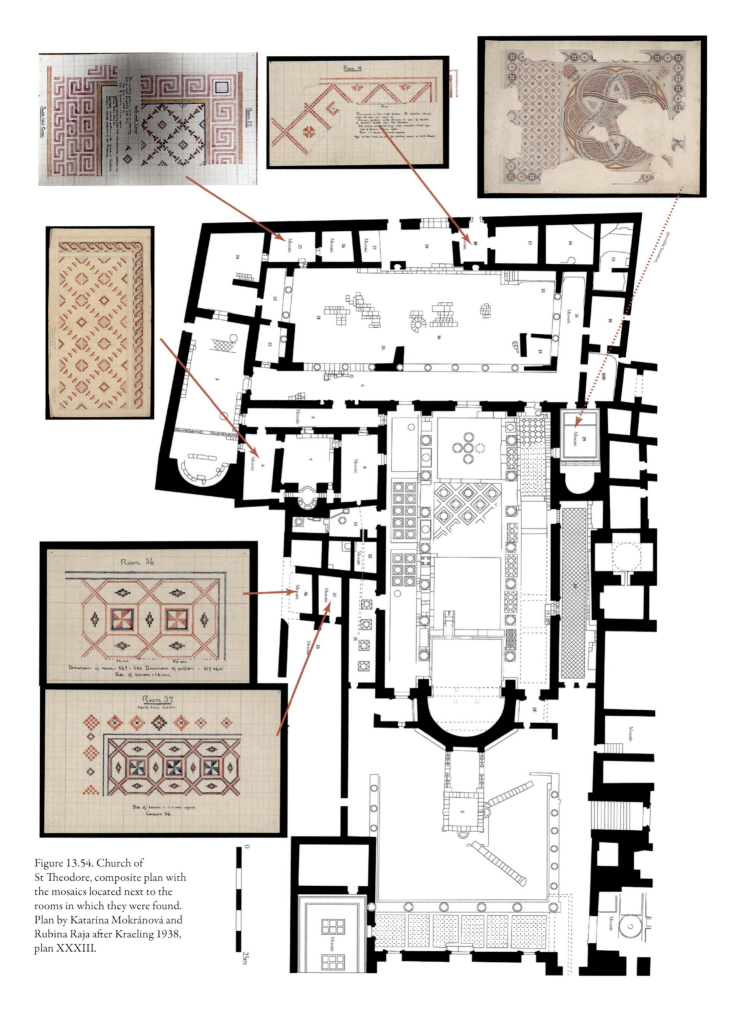

Figure 13.54. Church of St Theodore, composite plan with the mosaics located next to the rooms in which they were found. Plan by Katarína Mokránová and Rubina Raja after Kraeling 1938, plan XXXIII.

13. THE MOSAICS FROM THE 1928–1929 EXPEDITION TO GERASA

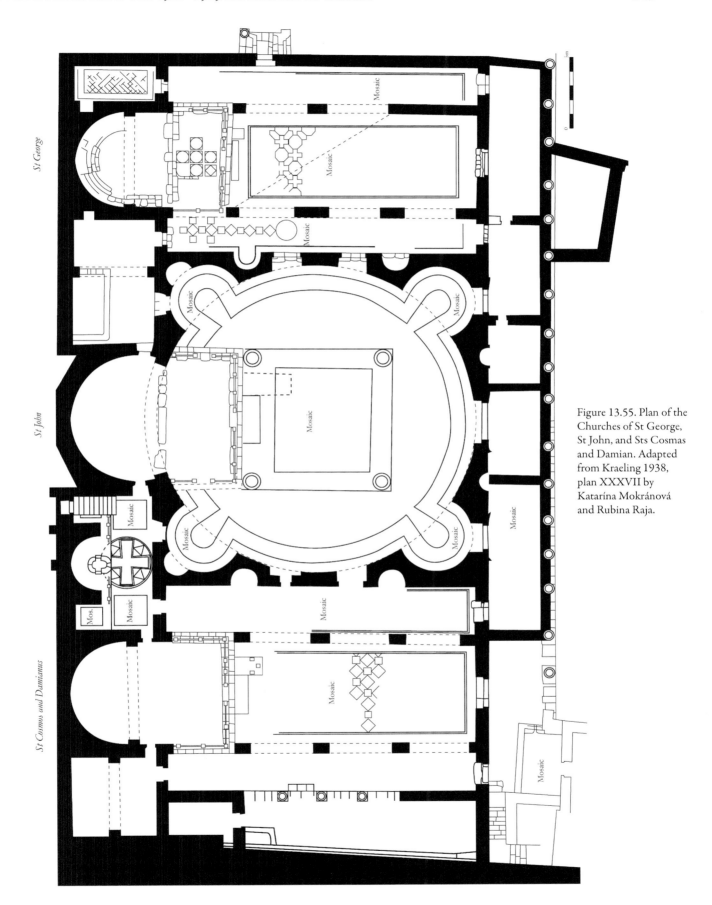

Figure 13.55. Plan of the Churches of St George, St John, and Sts Cosmas and Damian. Adapted from Kraeling 1938, plan XXXVII by Katarína Mokránová and Rubina Raja.

Figure 13.56. Drawing of mosaic with peacock from Church of St George. Dimensions: 30 × 21.75 cm (11 ¾ × 8 ½ in.). No initials or name written on the drawing. A photo is published in Kraeling 1938, pl. LXXII.c.

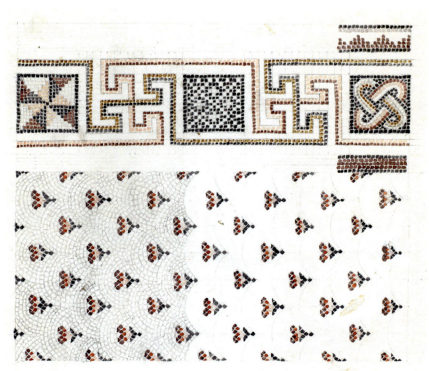

Figure 13.57. Drawing of mosaic from north aisle in Church of Sts Cosmas and Damian. Dimensions: 21.5 × 26 cm (8 3/8 × 10 ¼ in.). No initials or name written on the drawing.

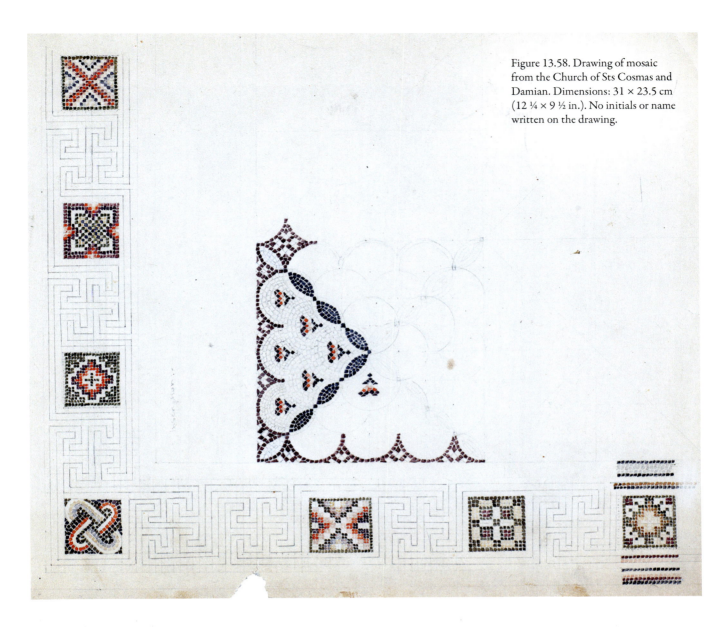

Figure 13.58. Drawing of mosaic from the Church of Sts Cosmas and Damian. Dimensions: 31 × 23.5 cm (12 ¼ × 9 ½ in.). No initials or name written on the drawing.

Figure 13.59. Photo of the Church of Sts Peter and Paul.

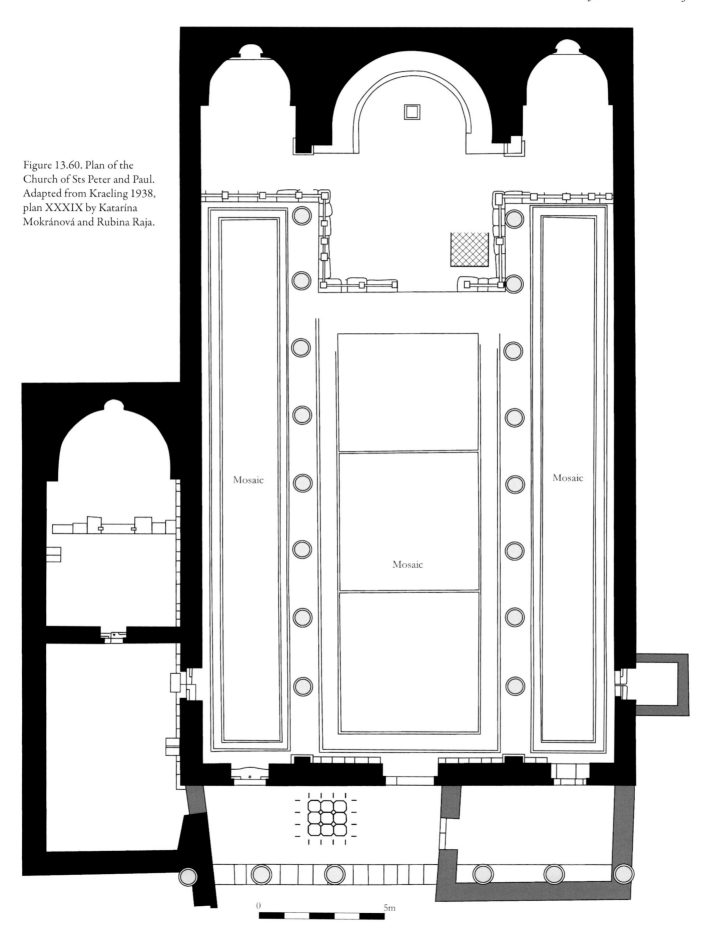

Figure 13.60. Plan of the Church of Sts Peter and Paul. Adapted from Kraeling 1938, plan XXXIX by Katarína Mokránová and Rubina Raja.

13. THE MOSAICS FROM THE 1928–1929 EXPEDITION TO GERASA

Figure 13.61. Drawing of mosaic from south aisle in Church of Sts Peter and Paul. Dimensions: 30.25 × 16 cm (11 7/8 × 6 3/8 in.). No initials or name written on the drawing.

Figure 13.62. Drawing of mosaic from the Church of Sts Peter and Paul. Dimensions: 21.5 × 31.5 cm (8 3/8 × 12 3/8 in.). No initials or name written on the drawing.

APPENDIX 1: EXCAVATION PERMIT — THE CHURCHES.
GERASA COLLECTION, YALE UNIVERSITY ART GALLERY

YALE - BRITISH SCHOOL EDPEDITION TO JERASH, 1928.
==

1. The joint expedition to Jerash in 1928 was first proposed in September 1927 at a meeting in the American School which was attended by the Director and by representatives of the Trans-Jordanian Government, Yale University and the British School of Archaeology in Jerusalem. The expedition was designed to give effect to two projects which had been in the air for some months previously. The first of these was a proposal to excavate the Church of St. Theodore at Jerash and to make soundings in other churches there, a proposal which emanated from Yale. A verbal application for permission to undertake these excavations had been made to the Palestine Department of Antiquities in December 1925, and the request approved in principle by the Trans-Jordanian Government a few months later, Dr. Albright, who had put forward the original application, being invited to submit detailed proposals in May 1926. Before any detailed proposals had been submitted, a second project had taken shape: this originated in November 1926 in a request addressed to the Director of the British School by Professor Garstang, then Director of Antiquities in Jerusalem, for assistance in preparing for publication the inscriptions recently found at Jerash: squeezes of a large number of these inscriptions were handed over to the British School, and some work on them begun by Mr. FitzGerald, then Assistant Director, and the Director, who visited Jerash together in April 1927.

- 2 -

At the meeting last September the position was reviewed, and an outline of a scheme of cooperation between the two interested parties which should cover both projects was sketched out. This scheme was approved by the respective authorities in America and England, and sufficient financial support was provided to enable work to be started in the following spring as soon as the weather permitted.

2. In February 1928, as Director of the proposed expedition, I went to Amman to visit the authorities of the Trans-Jordanian Government and discuss the terms of the concession. It was arranged that the terms of the concession should be the same as those given to Professor Guidi for the excavation of the citadel at Amman, and that no fee should be charged for the concession. A copy of the concession is attached to this report (Enclosure A). I had hoped to go on to Jerash to arrange further details on the spot, but a heavy fall of snow made the road between Amman and Jerash impassable, and I was obliged to return to Jerusalem, where the next few weeks were spent in purchasing equipment for the expedition, including a motor car, in arranging for the engagement of two Egyptian foremen through the good offices of Mr. Alan Rowe, Field Director of the University Museum of the Pennsylvanian expedition to Beisan, and in final details with regard to the personnel.

3. Mr. Robertson and I proceeded to Jerash with one servant on the 24th March in the Expedition car, and the two Egyptian foremen arrived in a lorry with the tents, tools and other equipment, a few hours later. Arrangements

- 3 -

for building huts were made the next day and the building started on the 26th. A local foreman was engaged at the same time and the excavation of St. Theodore's site was begun on the 27th. The excavations were carried on from the 27th March until the 7th June continuously except for two breaks, one at Easter (6th to 9th April) and the second at Bairam (28th May to 1st June), the total number of full working days being 56.

4. The members of the expedition, the dates of their arrival and departure, and the principal services rendered by each, were as follows:-

1. Mr. J. B. Robertson, Two Brothers Fellow, Yale University. Business manager and photographer of work in progress, assisted generally in the supervision of the field work, and particularly in the minor works (see 5(b)(c)(d)): drove the car. 24th March to 9th June.

2. Mr. A.H.M. Jones, Fellow of All Souls, Oxford. Kept the archaeological record of objects found, and collected and studied the inscriptions of Jerash and the neighbourhood. Assisted in supervision. 17th April to 8th June.

3. Mr. A. G. Buchanan, Lt. Commander R.N. Ret. and student of the British School. Made all the plans of the work with theodolite and level. 17th April to 9th June.

4. Mrs. Crowfoot. Managed the household economy and accounts. Red Cross work. Studied the glass and assisted with the Object Register. 9th April to 8th June.

- 4 -

5. **Mrs. Jones.** Late student of Somerville College and of the British School at Rome. Drew to scale the objects for the Object Record Cards and the architectural details, and transferred the former to the Register. 17th April to 8th June.

6. **Miss Dorothy Crowfoot.** Cleaned the coins and other metal objects. Prepared and coloured drawings to scale of the Mosaics, and assisted with the Object Register. 8th April to 8th June.

The organization and supervision of the field work naturally was the main work of the Director, who also kept in duplicate the Diary of the Expedition, one copy of which has been sent to Yale. The objects were entered on cards and transferred in duplicate to an object Register prepared by Dr. Clarence G. Fisher, Archaeological Adviser to the American School; one copy of the Object Register has been sent to the Department of Antiquities in Amman and one to Yale. The second copy of the Diary and the Record Cards are kept in the British School.

5. It is impossible in the limits of the Report to give more than a bare summary of the work of the past season. All the churches of Jerash were included in our concession, but special reference was made to the Church of S. Theodore, and it was agreed that the clearance of this site was to be the main objective of the 1928 expedition, though a little work was carried out in three other places.

- 5 -

(a.). The Church of S. Theodore.

All that we knew about this Church before our work began may be resumed in a few sentences. Its position in the centre of the old town, close to the temple of Artemis, suggested that it was the most important, if not the largest, of the Christian churches in Jerash. A few courses of masonry at the west end, fewer still in the apse at the east end, and the drums of some broken columns between these points, were all the remains that were visible last March; and it was impossible to see even how many aisles the church once possessed. Beyond the west front of the church remains of the west wall of what we presumed to be an atrium rose above the ground, and two important inscriptions had been discovered, one near the entrance to the atrium, the other near the central doorway at the west end of the church; from the latter, some words in which were missing, it was known that the foundations of the church were laid in the autumn of 494 A.D. and the lintel two years later, and that the church was dedicated to the martyr S. Theodore. The knowledge with which we started, therefore, was very meagre.

Our excavations have proved that the Church and Atrium, which we set out to clear, were part only of a much larger complex of ecclesiastical buildings, reaching from the boundary wall of the Atrium in the west down to the colonnaded street which ran north and south through the heart of ancient Jerash. From east to west this complex measures nearly 150 metres in length, and the level of the western threshold of the Atrium is about 19 metres above the level of the street. The whole

- 6 -

complex falls into five main divisions: the western atrium, the Church of S. Theodore with the buildings adjoining it north and south, a pillared court with a tank in the middle of it and two flights of stairs which we shall refer to as the Fountain Court, a second large church, and a third court which must once have contained further flights of stairs. In our description we will go from West to East, following the order in which we have enumerated the above divisions.

(1) The west atrium.

This division was rhomboid in shape and measured over 21 metres from west to east and about 50 from north to south. Three doorways led originally from a street on the west into an entrance hall paved with mosaics. and three steps descended from this into an open court, surrounded formerly by covered colonnades on the north, east and south. The columns in these colonnades had Ionic capitals, and the floor was once paved with mosaics: the floor of the open court was partly cut in the rock, partly paved with larger slabs of stone. West of the court there were three rooms on each side of the entrance hall, and three more north of the north colonnade: two of the rooms south of the entrance contained patterned mosaics (Nos. 25 and 26).

On each side of the steps leading to the court there were two large niches, which the authorities in Jerusalem with whom I have discussed them, consider to be seats occupied by Bishops or priests in a service for the absolution of penitents.

There were two subterranean tombs cut in the rock under the atrium: one of these, which was opposite to the south wall of the church, was cleared, and two chambers which had been made in Byzantine times were found in it but they contained nothing of interest. The second is very much larger and was discovered too late in the season to be cleared.

According to the inscription at the doorway this atrium was laid out by the 'all wise and pious hierophant' (= Bishop?) Aeneas in a place formerly fouled by the carcases of dead animals: this inscription is identical in style with that recording the dedication of S. Theodore's church, and the two buildings must therefore be contemporaneous: it is the more curious that the doorways into the atrium are not concentric with those of the church. According to a new undated inscription found by us on one of the columns the colonnade or Stoa was erected by the Proedros Symmachus: the ppor lettering would suggest that the Stoa was later than other parts of the Atrium, but the use of the phrase ΑΓΑΘΗ ΤΥΧΗ may indicate that the columns of the Stoa were taken from an earlier pagan building: in this case the bad lettering would be the result of careless workmanship.

The most northerly of the three doorways of the atrium was reduced in size at some later period and there were several other signs of late occupation, cross-walls, pots in earthenware and bronze, and a few coins, all indicating that this part of the complex was inhabited down to the 8th century at least. The curious way in which the large stones forming the central doorway have fallen suggests that the place was finally ruined by a violent earthquake.

(ii) S. Theodore's Church and the adjoining buildings.

The Church of S. Theodore was entered by three doorways from the east portico of the Atrium. It had a nave and two aisles and ended in an apse which was externally polygonal: the accumulation inside nowhere exceeded two metres in depth and was composed of building debris.

-8-

The walls were built with two faces, the outer one of hard limestone, the inner of the soft stone called *nari* here, as in Jerusalem. The inner face was cased with panels of limestone, fastened with bronze nails and divided from each other by marble spacers, exactly like the marble casing round the innermost piers in the Dome of the Rock. The outer face was composed almost entirely of fragments from earlier buildings, good material but indifferently arranged, architectural mouldings with the mouldings turned inwards, sections of engaged columns used as stretchers with the round side inwards, inscriptions and so forth. The floor was originally of slabs of different coloured stone and marble, laid in varied patterns, but it had been largely destroyed and only a few of the patterns could be reconstructed. The apse had been vaulted with stone originally decorated with glass mosaics, but the roof over the body of the church must have been of timber covered with tiles, and from the complete absence of stone architraves we concluded that the architraves above the columns were also of wood. The columns, fourteen in number, with their Corinthian capitals, were all lying where they had fallen, not a single drum had been removed but not a single one was upon its base: in the west half of the church the columns had fallen inwards, across each other, but in the east half most of them had fallen to the north **after** the collapse of the side walls, both of which in this part had fallen to the south. Masons' marks on the sections of the column drums showed that these columns had been used previously for the same building as the engaged columns and certain other carved blocks which we found built into the side walls: the style of the Corinthian capitals suggests that this earlier building may have belonged to the beginning of the 3rd century.

The church originally had twelve doors: all of these except three, which led into adjoining rooms or chapels, had moulded jambs, all of which, except one perhaps, had been taken from earlier buildings, as was the string-course which ran round the apse. Indeed the only architectural moulding which seems to have been carved for the church originally is the moulding above the two inscriptions: this, though Byzantine in the flatness of the profile, is otherwise entirely classical in character. One of the doors, the most easterly on the north side, had been reduced in size, like the north door in the atrium, and subsequently blocked up, showing two phases in the decay of the building, but there was no sign that any part of the church proper had been re-used for a secular purpose. A rare feature in the ground plan is the position of the two doors at the east end of the aisles, in the place usually occupied by the Pastophoria, the Prothecis and the Diaconicou: this is to be explained by the importance of the ceremonies in the Fountain Court below. The opening of the chancel screen leading to the Ambo, from which the Gospel was read, is another rare, if not unique, feature. The chancel screen, as is usual at this period, was a low one, and one of the small pillars, which divided the panels of which it was composed, is still lying broken under the column nearest the ambo: the fittings of the church were therefore probably intact when the columns fell.

On the north side of the church there are two buildings, the first a chapel at the west end, with a brilliant mosaic on the floor, which may have been built in commemoration of some benefactor; the second a long passage paved with mosaics laid in red and yellow diagonal squares, and leading east to the stairs going down into the Fountain Court: two doors opened from this passage into the Church, and on the other side of the passage were various constructions belonging to some Baths which had been built some forty years before our church according to an unpublished inscription: these constructions included a furnace which served as a hypocaust.

On the south side of the church there was a long passage parallel to the east portico of the Atrium: the west wall of this passage was simply a continuation of the west wall of the church, carried on without a break or even a straight joint, therefore built at the same time. This passage led from the main church to a smaller one at the south west corner of the complex: this smaller church had been paved with slabs of stone and marble, nearly all of which have disappeared, and the church walls, the southern one of which coincides with the south wall of the precinct, are set out in curious lines which can only be explained by the presence of some earlier building of which we found no traces. There were three rooms between the two churches, all communicating with each other and with the passage first mentioned: the central of these was a baptistery with a built font for immersion at the east end, and steps leading into it on each side from the two side chambers, which may have been reserved for men and women, respectively: above the font there were some curious constructions like bins with seats in them of a diminutive size, which may have been used in the ceremonies of anointment which accompanied baptism. The side chambers were paved with patterned mosaics, the central room with slabs which have almost all disappeared. In the most southerly of

-11-

these (No.4) the north and east walls had been taken down, and the stones of which they were composed stacked in regular lines over the floor, with a packing between them and the mosaics, evidently to protect the latter: It looks as if some work of reconstruction was in progress just before the place was finally deserted. In the most northerly room (No.8) there were about 6 inches of fine ashes above the mosaics and above this layer about 250 roof tiles were found, another probable indication of reconstruction works: some marble slabs which fit the chancel screen in the small north chapel were also found in this room. Immediately east of this series of rooms there was a splendidly built cistern, filled perhaps originally from the church roof, from which no doubt the baptistery had been supplied; and further still east a passage (No.31) from which admission was gained both to the church and to the south flight of steps into the Fountain Court, and some more rooms with patterned mosaic floors.

(iii) The Fountain Court.

The Fountain Court is the heart of the whole complex, in position certainly, possibly in more than position. Epiphanius refers to a spring in Gerasa 'in the Martyrium' at which water was turned into wine on the anniversary of the miracle at Cana in Galilee, which was also the anniversary of the Epiphany. It appears likely that a Christian festival of this kind took the place of some Pagan ceremony previously celebrated at the neighbouring Nymphaeum, and that its growing popularlity led to the erection of the larger church of St. Theodore in addition to the earlier church which lies still unexcavated to the east.

-12-

This is put forward only as a probable hypothesis on which more light may be thrown by later investigations which may conceivably reveal the existence of another church with better claims to be the site of the miracle.

As it is now, the Fountain Court is an open paved court some 20 metres across with a square tank in the middle. The pavement of the court is more than 5 metres lower than the floor of S. Theodore's, and the remains of the apse towering between two flights of steps still dominate the west side; on the opposite side a portico of six Corinthian columns opened into a church as long as S. Theodore's, and the whole court may be regarded as the atrium of the second church. On the north and south sides of the court there were lower colonnades with Ionic columns, that on the south being broken by a wall belonging to some building which still awaits investigation.

The fountain, after which we have named the court, is a square tank, more than $4^{1/2}$ metres across and about 90cms. high, with a basin on the east side: the mouldings and little pilasters on its walls suggest that it is a work of the 4th century or even earlier, but in later days it had a heavy superstructure which we cannot with any certainty restore. The fountain was connected with the apse of S. Theodore's by two later arches probably in the 6th century, and under these were low rails like those across the chancel of the church: a stone seat stood against the wall of the apse facing the fountain, and the whole space enclosed by the rails was about 15 cms. higher than the pavement of the court: the west side of the fountain was decorated with carved blocks from some coffered ceiling of the classical period. In the 7th and 8th century the rails between the fountain and the

-13-

apse were replaced by walls of the poorest masonry with steps on one side and a row of crude conical coping stones.

Three water channels radiated from, or to, the fountain under the paving stones of the court. The most important contained fine leaden pipes about 30 cm. in diameter, which conducted water towards the centre of the tank from under the steps on the north side of the court, just below the first landing, beyond which there was a clumsy stone bowl of large dimensions through which the water must have poured. On the opposite side, at the south west corner of the tank, there was an earthenware pipe which apparently carried the water off to the south. There was a third channel just below the paving, cut in the rock and unpiped: this started from the basin on the east side and ran towards the north east corner, being joined on the way by a branch channel from the north side of the tank: this drain evidently carried off the overflow from the basin or basins. In addition to these, there was an open gutter running all round the court, which was graded to carry off the water in the north half of the court towards the north east, and the water in the south half towards the south west corner, from which it may have flowed into some cistern that has not been yet located.

We have mentioned the Fountain and the water system first, but in its present state the most striking features in the Court are the two flights of steps which lead up to the level of S. Theodore's. In the north east corner there are 24 steps leading in two stages to a landing from which two short flights originally branched one, now broken, going south to a platform in front of the door at the east end of the north

-14-

aisle, the other still running straight on to the passage along the north wall of the church. In the south west corner the plan was rather different, the steps were more regular and steeper, and here 15 steps only led up to a second landing, from which two short flights once branched, as on the north side. The two flights vary in arrangement and in execution, the southern one being much the better in style, they are probably the work of different hands, but they balance admirably one against the other, and the discovery was as welcome as it was unexpected, for not one step was visible when our work began nor was the existence of these flights suspected.

It seems to us, however, probable that, spectacular as they are, these flights were an afterthought on the part of the architect. The church proper, the apse, that is, and the two side aisles lie between the two main flights of stairs which lead straight to the passages along side the church, and it is the walls which carry the church plus the side passages which form the west boundary of the court. Now the two lower walls of the church thus extended north and south of the apse are pierced each by two doors on the level of the court, one on each side under the vaults formed by the stairs and one on each side between the stairs and the apse, and these four doors now lead nowhere. At first we thought they might lead to a very early crypt under the east end of the church, but shafts which we sank from the floor above prove that no such crypt ever existed and that one of these doors at least never led anywhere. We can only explain their presence on the assumption that the architect intended to build steps under the aisles and passages, and subsequently changed his mind and built external flights of steps instead. This would explain also some other difficulties in the existing arrangements: the flight of steps on the north side cuts right into the base of one of the pillars in the colonnade, and on both sides the steps at the top cut into the middle of a course of the church wall which was evidently laid before they were planned. Furthermore, the existing arrangement involved spanning the space between the stairs and the apse in order to provide an approach to the doors at the east end of the aisles: it was necessary therefore to provide supports for beams to span this space and these supports were in fact provided by cutting 'put-log' holes in the existing wall, a procedure which would never have been adopted if the wall had not been constructed before this necessity arose. These difficulties disappear if we assume that the plan was changed just after the east wall of the church had been carried up to the level of the floor.

The plan ultimately adopted provided a long room in each corner at the west end of the Court, and the contents of these lower rooms, especially of the parts nearest the apse, proved of considerable interest. On the top we found a stratum of heavy stones from the wall of the church and the door-jambs, below these were blocks from the steps, under these a number of timber beams, joists both rough and squared, in a surprisingly good state of preservation: those so far identified were of pine (pinus pinea) and cypress (cupressus sempervireus). Below this last stratum there was on the north side an enormous quantity of broken glass and ashes, much of the former apparently stored in stone pigeon-holes which had been erected against the apse wall: among this broken glass the bottoms of some 300 glass

- 16 -

lamps were identified, belonging mainly to two types which have survived in mosques and churches to the present day.

The Fountain Court has had a long history but it is only the later stages just before the final destruction and desertion that we can thus hope still to recover. It existed in its present form before S. Theodore's apse was built, for in some places the paving stones underlie the bottom course of the apse and in other places they had been broken to make way for it. How much earlier was the Court? In two of the pits which we sank in the floor at the east end of the church we found fragments of pottery which go back to the Hellenistic period, but these may have been carried from a distance when the platform on which the church stands was filled in. In the pit under the apse we found a small patch of Roman mosaic still in position on the level of the court about $5^{1/2}$ metres below the church floor: this mosaic probably goes back to the 2nd or 3rd century A.D. and the rock on which the paving stones of the court stand must therefore have been levelled by the 3rd century at least. The paving stones may have been laid in the 3rd or 4th century: we found two re-used stones among them, one an inscription, the other a piece of moulding like that used in the string-course round the apse. The Corinthian portico at the east end might perhaps be assigned to the 4th century, but on this it would be well to reserve judgment until the church to which it leads has been excavated. The Ionic columns on the north and south sides have masons' marks which are quite different in character from those on the drums of the Corinthian columns in the church: the form of the letters used indicates a much later date, it resembles that of the letters on the Ionic columns in the 'forum' and, less closely, that of the letters on the Theodore inscription: these colonnades therefore may be tentatively assigned to the latter decades of the 5th century A.D. The debris which we cleared away contained masses of worked stones, including several fine fluted columns to which we could assign no place in the later disposition of the court: what it was like therefore in pre-Christian days we can hardly hope to recover.

(iv) The church at the east end of the Fountain Court was only discovered later in the season, and we had not time to do more than clear the west front and make soundings inside at the south-west corner and at the east end. From west to east this church measured over 40M. in length and ended in an internal apse. The masonry was much better than in S. Theodore's, but here too, it was composed of re-used materials, and a course of huge stones nearly a metre square had originally been built above three smaller courses at the west end, just as is the case in the west front of S. Theodore's between the central and the southern door-ways. One architrave and three of the Corinthian columns on the south side of the nave are still standing. The floor was paved with slabs of stone. The door jambs at the west end were moulded: in those of the central doorway one stone had been fully carved and the others only blocked out: in the southern doorway all the stones had old mouldings carved on them and some of them, as a double set of masons' marks showed, had been already re-used once at least before they were placed in their present position.

At the east end where the masonry is very finely jointed, the outer face is bulging dangerously outwards, and it may be

-18-

necessary to re-set the stones before this wall is cleared.

There can be no doubt that this church is earlier than S. Theodore's, but we should not be justified at present in dating it more closely.

(v) The last section in our complex is the area between the east end of the last named church and the main street. This area is about 30 m. from west to east and there is a fall of more than 10 metres between the floor of the last church and the street. It is evident that there must have been flights of steps leading up from the street to the church, but there is nothing a present to show how they ran. The whole area is covered with heavy building material.

(b) The Fore Court of the Propylaea.

An interesting mosaic was discovered a few years ago by the Trans-Jordan Department of Antiquities in a circular chamber, north of the courtyard which lies across the road east of the great Gateway to the Temple of Artemis. This mosaic was again uncovered by us and fully recorded. The building in which the mosaic lies is described as a Diaconia, which appears to have been a place where alms were distributed: the mosaic is dated A.D.564.

A few men were employed to examine a corresponding circular building on the south side of the same Court, but no trace of a mosaic was found there.

(c) The Nymphaeum Road.

The Department of Antiquities discovered a fine glass chalice last year in a road just north of the Nymphaeum, and a

-19-

few men were employed for a few days making a further clearance in this neighbourhood in the hope of finding the missing fragments of this chalice. The road was completely cleared at the point indicated and the soil sifted, but nothing more was found.

(d) The Church of Bishop Paul.

At the request of the Department of Antiquities, work was undertaken on a church at the south end of the modern town close to the town walls, as mosaics were known to exist here and, as the site lies outside the controlled Antiquities area, there was reason to fear that they might suffer damage. The church proved to be a building of the basilica plan, partly cut in the rock, with a nave and two aisles, ending in three internal apses, and a side chapel on the north side like that in S. Theodore's. The features of most interest were the seats in the central apse at the east end, the differences in the ground plan between the Prothesis and the Diaconicou, and the wonderful series of mosaics with which the floor was covered. An inscription in mosaic gave the date of the church, A.D.526, and the names of the founders, a certain Bishop Paul and two others. Originally, the whole floor with the exception of the central apse had been covered with mosaics, but the scene in the nave and the representations in some of the medallions elsewhere had evidently given offence to some one at some time: they had consequently been destroyed and the vacant place filled with pinkish cement. The fragments of panels from the screen dividing the central apse from the Pistophoria had also been defaced: these originally represented two sheep or lambs with an elaborate circular device between them and crosses and pomegranates above, and on them almost every trace of the sheep or lambs had been carefully chiselled out. The mutilation of the mosaics had obviously been carried out before the church was deserted, otherwise the gaps would not have been repaired. It is probable that the offending portions represented pagan scenes and symbolic figures of the seasons or the months or some such subject, and that the destruction was due to ignorant fanatics, Persian or Arab perhaps, who may have thought that any representation of the human form might be connected with the Christian religion, and did not know how strongly the Christians themselves were opposed to the representation of any religious subject on a pavement. (A devout Syrian, to whom I showed the mosaic in the Diaconia mentioned above, was genuinely shocked at the idea of treading on a verse from Psalm 86 which surrounded the principal pattern). More probably perhaps the destroyers, whoever they were, simply wished to annoy a defeated enemy.

There were also remains of an ugly painting on the steps on the north side of the apse: it represented a number of white circles with squiggly red objects inside them on a dark red field, and looked like an enormous magnification of a diagram of parasites in white corpuscles floating in a red medicine!

(e) Epigraphic work.

Throughout the period of his stay at Jerash Mr. Jones devoted all the time that could be spared from the archaeological record of our finds, to the study of the inscriptions, new and old, in Jerash and the neighbourhood. Some of these copied by previous visitors have since disappeared, but many remain and in several cases improved readings were obtained: the number of new ones found during the excavation works undertaken by the present Government is considerable, and these throw fresh light on the history of the buildings in Gerasa. The most interesting epigraphic discovery made in the course of our own work was that of the missing fragments of the inscription recording the dedication of the church to S. Theodore: only about ten letters were missing from each of the four long lines which this inscription contained, and it is amusing to note that not a single one of the conjectural emendations put forward by the five or six scholars who have described this inscription was confirmed by the actual discovery!

6. Further programme.

In the foregoing section it has been shown that another season's work will be necessary to complete the clearance of the complex to which St. Theodore's Church belongs.

In the first place, the church east of the Fountain Court must be completed: there are some very heavy stones at the west end of this church, but there is no great accumulation anywhere, and this work should present no particular difficulties. There is reason to believe that this church is the oldest church in the complex and, though it seems to have been grievously pillaged, the results should be most interesting.

Secondly, the area between the east end of the last named church and the main street must be cleared. It is probable that this rapid drop may be due in part to the slope of the rock, and if the rock rises, say, 5 or 6 metres higher here at the west end than it is at the east end, the work of

-22-

clearance will be proportionately lightened, but it promises to be heavy in any case, and new and difficult dumping problems will have to be solved.

Thirdly, it may prove desirable to extend our excavations a few metres to the south all along the eastern half of the complex, especially in the Fountain Court section. The large cave under the atrium should also be explored and it would be interesting also to work further on the north side of the complex, but there are old dumps to be removed here and the results might not be commensurate with the expenditure.

Besides the work immediately connected with the main work of the last season, there is a little further work to be done at Bishop Paul's church, apart altogether from the removal of the mosaics, if this is decided on, and there is a mosaic in the North East of the town to be uncovered and recorded.

There are three more churches also on the high ground west of the main street which should be cleared; one of these, the church west of the temple of Artemis, could be excavated without great expenditure, but the other two would involve a heavier outlay. The church in front of the Propylaea might be cleared in conjunction with a classical expedition.

There is no reason why several of these works should not be undertaken simultaneously if staff and funds are available, and there would be some reduction in the overhead charges if this were possible. It would also permit earlier publication, as these various churches may be expected to throw great light on each other and it will be impossible to

-23-

speak positively on many points connected with the history of Gerasa in the Christian period until all the evidence is before us. The work carried out during the last season cost less than £1,200: the programme above sketched could probably be completed in a single season for about twice this sum if a suitable staff were available. A 'suitable staff' should include one architect with experience of Byzantine work and one trained architectural draughtsman: the latter at least might be recruited in Palestine.

7. Acknowledgements.

There remains only the pleasant duty of expressing our thanks to those who have assisted us during the past season.

The first mention should be made of those whose generous benefactions made the work possible.

The British School has to thank the University of Oxford for a grant from the Craven Fund, the Byzantine Research Fund and Mr. Henry G. Patten, for special donations.

The American contributors I am unable to mention by name.

For permission to undertake the work, and for never failing support and assistance throughout the season we are under a deep debt to the Government of His Highness the Amir of Trans-Jordania and especially to the local representative of His Highness' Government, Mr. G. Horsfield and to Mr. Horsfield's assistants, Signor Ricci and Rashid Bey.

Mr. Alan Rowe, Field Director of the University of Pennsylvanian Expedition to Beisan, provided us with two of his foremen: he visited us himself in the course of our work and helped considerably both with personal advice on the

-24-

planning of the site and with the loan of instruments.

Mr. A.St.B.Harrison, Chief Architect to the Palestine Government, not only helped us with his advice on the spot but has kindly allowed us to have our plans traced by members of his staff.

We learned much also from a visit paid us by an expert in Eastern Church ritual, the Rev. C. Bridgman of St, George's in Jerusalem, and he added to this debt by sending us references from books in Jerusalem libraries during the course of the work.

Lastly, as leader of the expedition, I should like to be permitted to close this note with an acknowledgement of the admirable support received from the whole staff on each and every occasion.

=====

(Signed) J. W. Crowfoot

5th July 1928

EXCAVATION PERMIT No. 2

ISSUED UNDER

TRANS JORDAN ANTIQUITIES ORDINANCE

TO

EXCAVATE THE CHURCHES OF JERASH.

=========

PERMIT No. 2.

PERMIT TO EXCAVATE THE CHURCHES OF JERASH.

Subject to the conditions set forth hereunder, a Permit for one year from the date hereof, is hereby granted to the Yale University - British School of Archaeology Expedition to excavate the Churches of Jerash in an area defined by plan including the Church of St. Theodore.

(1) The excavation will be under the direct supervision of Professor John Crowfoot, and will be carried out in accordance with the terms of the Trans-Jordan Antiquities Ordinance.

(2) The Official appointed to supervise the work on behalf of the Trans-Jordan Government shall be the Inspector of Antiquities and no part of the salary or expenses of this Official shall be at the charge of the Yale University - British School of Archaeology Expedition.

(3) In case of dispute as to the division of objects found or as to the indemnity payable in lieu of the excavators' share of the antiquities found, the Director may, and if requested by the Yale University - School of Archaeology Expedition, shall call in two members of the Archaeological Advisory Board of the Palestine Government to assist him.

(4) That the operations on the site for which the Permit is granted shall continue during a period of two months at least unless the excavations be completed within a shorter time.

(5) The excavators shall furnish to the Department of Antiquities as soon as possible after discovery a detailed list of all antiquities found.

(6)/

-2-

(6) That all objects discovered in the course of the excavations shall be open to the Department of Antiquities.

(7) That the excavations shall at all times be open to the inspection of the officers of the Department of Antiquities.

(8) That any person or persons specially authorised by the Director of Antiquities may at such times as may be arranged enter upon and view the excavations.

(9) That the person to whom this Permit is granted shall be responsible for the care of all objects found during the excavations and shall, if requested, maintain a guard over the excavations.

(10) That the excavators shall, within four months of the conclusion of the season's digging, supply in a form suitable for publication, a summary report of the main results of their works.

(11) That the Expedition to whom this Permit is granted shall produce within a period of two years after the completion of the excavations of Antiquities (unless this period be extended by the Director of Antiquities) an adequate scientific publication of the results of the excavations.

(12) If the proceeds of the excavations have been disposed of a record of allocation of the various objects shall be included therein.

(13) That copies of all printed publications relating to the excavations issued by the excavator or by the body which he represents, shall be deposited in the Archives of the Amman Museum.

(14) The acceptance of this Permit shall be deemed to constitute a contract between the Government and the person to whom the Permit is given in accordance with

the

-3-

the conditions laid down therein.

(15) In case of a breach of any condition of the Permit the Director of Antiquities may forthwith require the suspension of the work of excavation, or withdraw the Permit.

25/3/28.　　　　(Sgd) G. Horsfield.
　　　　　　　　　Inspector of Antiquities.
　　　　　　for Director of Antiquities.

CONFIRMED.

25/3/28.　　　　(Sgd)

　　　　　　CHIEF MINISTER

ACCEPTED

25/3/28.　　　　(Sgd) John W. Crowfoot.
　　　　　　for YALE UNIVERSITY - BRITISH SCHOOL
　　　　　　　　OF ARCHAEOLOGY EXPEDITION.

Works Cited

Bacon, B. W. 1931. 'Early Christian Archaeology in Palestine', unpublished report, Gerasa Excavation Archives, Yale University Art Gallery.

Baur, P. V. C. 1938. 'Glassware', in C. Kraeling (ed.), *Gerasa: City of the Decapolis* (New Haven: American Schools of Oriental Research), pp. 505–46.

Biebel, F. M. 1938. 'Mosaics', in C. Kraeling (ed.), *Gerasa: City of the Decapolis* (New Haven: American Schools of Oriental Research), pp. 297–354.

Brenk, B., C. Jäggi, and H.-R. Meier. 1995. 'The Buildings under the "Cathedral" at Gerasa: The Second Interim Report on the Jerash Cathedral Project', *Annual of the Department of Antiquities of Jordan*, 39: 211–20.

—— 1996. 'Neue Forschung zur Kathedrale von Gerasa: Probleme der Chronologie und der Vorgängerbauten', *Zeitschrift des Deutschen Palästina-Vereins*, 112.2: 139–55.

British School of Archaeology. 1930. 'British School of Archaeology in Jerusalem. Report for the Season 1928–29', *Palestine Exploration Quarterly*, 62.1: 26–31.

Brizzi, M. 2018. 'The Artemis Temple Reconsidered', in A. Lichtenberger and R. Raja (eds), *The Archaeology and History of Jerash: 110 Years of Excavations*, Jerash Papers, 1 (Turnhout: Brepols), pp. 87–110.

Crowfoot, E. 2004. 'Grace Mary Crowfoot (1877–1957)', in G. M. Cohen and M. S. Joukowsky (eds), *Breaking Ground: Women in Old World Archaeology* (Ann Arbor: University of Michigan Press) <https://www.brown.edu/Research/Breaking_Ground/bios/Crowfoot_Grace.pdf> [accessed 12 February 2023].

Crowfoot, G. M. 1928. *Flowering Plants of the Northern and Central Sudan* (Leominster: Orphans' Printing Press).

Crowfoot, G. M. and D. B. Harden. 1931. 'Early Byzantine and Later Glass Lamps', *The Journal of Egyptian Archaeology*, 17: 196–208.

Crowfoot, J. W. 1931. *Churches at Jerash: A Preliminary Report of the Joint Yale-British School Expeditions to Jerash, 1928–1930*, British School of Archaeology in Jerusalem, Supplementary Papers, 3 (London: Council of the British School of Archaeology in Jerusalem).

—— 1938. 'The Christian Churches', in C. Kraeling (ed.), *Gerasa: City of the Decapolis* (New Haven: American Schools of Oriental Research), pp. 171–264.

Ferry, G. 1998. *Dorothy Hodgkin: A Life* (London: Granta).

Fisher, C. S. 1930. 'Yale University – Jerusalem School Expedition at Jerash: First Campaign', *Bulletin of the American Schools of Oriental Research*, 40: 2–11.

Goldman, B. M. and N. W. Goldman. 2011. *My Dura-Europos: The Letters of Susan M. Hopkins, 1927–1935* (Detroit: Wayne State University Press).

Kenyon, K. M. 1957. 'Obituary. Grace Mary Crowfoot', *Palestine Exploration Quarterly*, 89.2: 153–55.

Kraeling, C. (ed.). 1938. *Gerasa: City of the Decapolis* (New Haven: American Schools of Oriental Research).

Lichtenberger, A. and R. Raja. 2020. 'Late Hellenistic and Roman Antiochia on the Chrysorrhoas, also Called Gerasa: A Reappreciation of the Urban Development in the Light of the Findings of the Danish-German Jerash Northwest Quarter Project (2011–2017)', in A. Lichtenberger and R. Raja (eds), *Hellenistic and Roman Gerasa: The Archaeology and History of a Decapolis City*, Jerash Papers, 5 (Turnhout: Brepols), pp. 7–54.

—— (eds) (forthcoming). *By the Gold River: Gerasa through the Eyes of 19th and Early 20th Century Visitors*, Jerash Papers, 2 (Turnhout: Brepols).

Moorey, R. 2003. 'In memoriam: Joan Crowfoot Payne (1912–2002)', *Levant*, 35.1: iv–v.

Mortensen, E. 2018. 'The Early Research History of Jerash: A Short Outline', in A. Lichtenberger and R. Raja (eds), *The Archaeology and History of Jerash: 110 Years of Excavations*, Jerash Papers, 1 (Turnhout: Brepols), pp. 167–86.

Raja, R. 2009. 'The Sanctuary of Artemis in Gerasa', in T. Fischer-Hansen and B. Poulsen (eds), *From Artemis to Diana: The Goddess of Man and Beast*, Acta Hyperborea, 12 (Copenhagen: Museum Tusculanum Press), pp. 383–401.

—— 2012. *Urban Development and Regional Identity in the Eastern Roman Provinces, 50 BC–AD 250: Aphrodisias, Ephesos, Athens, Gerasa* (Copenhagen: Museum Tusculanum Press).

—— 2015. 'Bishop Aeneas and the Church of St Theodore in Gerasa', in É. Rebillard and J. Rüpke (eds), *Group Identity and Religious Individuality in Late Antiquity* (Washington, DC: Catholic University Press), pp. 270–92.

—— (forthcoming). 'This Is a Man's World: Accompanying Wives and Daughters of Male Travellers and Archaeologists in Gerasa in the Nineteenth and Early Twentieth Century', in N. Koefoed and R. Raja (eds), *Women of the Past*, Women of the Past, 1 (Turnhout: Brepols).

Robertson, J. B. 1928. 'Gerasa the Golden', *Art and Archaeology*, 26.6: 203–14.

Rosenberg, S. G. 2008. 'British Groundbreakers in the Archaeology of the Holy Land', *Minerva*, 19.1: 26–28.

Schumacher, G. 1902. 'Dscherasch', *Zeitschrift des Deutschen Palaestina-Vereins*, 25: 111–77.

Stinespring, W. F. 1938. 'The History of Excavation at Jerash', in C. Kraeling (ed.), *Gerasa: City of the Decapolis* (New Haven: American Schools of Oriental Research), pp. 1–10.

Welles, C. B. 1938. 'The Inscriptions', in C. Kraeling (ed.), *Gerasa: City of the Decapolis* (New Haven: American Schools of Oriental Research), pp. 355–493.

14. Digitizing the Archaeological Finds and the Photographic Archive of the German Excavation Campaigns in Samarra (1911–1913) at the Museum für Islamische Kunst in Berlin

Miriam Kühn

Museum für Islamische Kunst, Staatliche Museen zu Berlin — Preußischer Kulturbesitz (m.kuehn@smb.spk-berlin.de)

Introduction

Founded in 1904 as the Islamic Department of the Royal Museums, the Museum für Islamische Kunst in Berlin houses the most extensive collection of Islamic art and archaeology in the German-speaking world. The largest part of its holdings derives from archaeological excavations conducted by museum staff. In addition to the finds themselves, the museum maintains the corresponding excavation documentation consisting of photographs and archival material such as find journals, notes, and correspondence.

The excavation at Samarra, an archaeological site located in present-day Iraq, was one of the most significant excavations for the museum's collection and the discipline of Islamic art history and archaeology. It was here, that the first systematic excavations of an Islamic site took place between 1911 and 1913, shaping the foundation of the field.

From October 2021 to February 2022, the NEUSTART KULTUR programme, funded by the Federal Government Commissioner for Culture and Media (BKM), provided funds for the indexing and digitization of the photographic documentation of the Museum's two excavation campaigns in Samarra. This should serve as a starting point for some reflections on the potential of digitizing archaeological archives, rendering their content significant and useful to both researchers and the general public. The example of the Samarra excavation is clearly demonstrating the complexity of an archaeological archive, heavily characterized by the dispersion of finds, but also of their documentation.

If the digitized archive is considered an offering, it presents infinite possibilities for approaching the material and subsequently utilizing it. This article will present two approaches that will illustrate the potential of digitizing excavation archives: their use for researchers and their use for a broader audience. In both cases, digitization serves as the fundamental basis for disseminating knowledge and rendering the archive more relevant and significant.

The article first discusses the significance of Samarra for Islamic history and the field of Islamic archaeology and art history. It then briefly describes the dispersal of finds and their archival documents after the completion of the excavations, resulting in a network of museums worldwide holding both finds and archival material. The positive impact of digitizing scattered archival components for the indexing and documenting of the photographic holdings at the Museum für Islamische Kunst is demonstrated through a few examples.

The article then examines the opening of the photographic archive from another perspective: the recently digitized photographs were used for an exhibition featuring new ways of approaching the material, which is typically perceived as mere illustrations for research on Samarra's artistic and cultural achievements. Finally, the article looks towards the future, envisioning the digitized archive, as an offering for all respective users according to their specific interests, be they archeologists or the interested public.

Samarra: An Eminent Site of Islamic (Art) History

Located approximately 125 km north of Baghdad, the city of Samarra in present-day Iraq is one of the most significant sites in Islamic art history and archaeology. It was the temporary seat of government for the Abbasid caliphs between 836 and 892, and during this time, it replaced Baghdad as the actual capital. Samarra was the centre of one of the largest empires in Islamic history, geographically spanning from North Africa to western Central Asia. The Abbasid Empire served as the cultural, political, and economic hub of the entire Middle East in the ninth century, maintaining close trade relations with Byzantium, Europe, and East Asia.

The city of Samarra was founded by the Abbasid caliph al-Muʿtasim (r. 833–842) in 836. The reasons behind his decision remain debated.[1] He built a large caliphal palace complex, the Dar al-Khilafa, and government buildings for the administration of the Abbasid Empire, buildings for the army, as well as mosques and numerous residential buildings. Only shortly afterwards, the caliph Mutawakkil (r. 847–861) changed the cityscape fundamentally.[2] He built, amongst other things, a new palace, the so-called Balkuwara Palace[3] and the Great Mosque (849–852), of which the enclosure walls and iconic spiral minaret, known as al-Malwiyya, still stand today.[4] However, Mutawakkil's most significant impact on the city was the foundation of a new imperial city named after him, al-Mutawakkiliyya, located north of Muʿtasim's city. Here he built another congregational mosque,[5] an imperial palace, markets, and military buildings. Altogether, the city itself spanned almost 40 km along the Tigris River with a width of 8 km.[6]

Both palaces and private houses in Samarra were adorned with lavish decorations such as stucco and wooden wall panels, tiles, and wall paintings. Finds of ceramics with lustre decoration, imported Chinese porcelain, and exquisitely cut glass vessels provide insight into the opulence of the caliphal court.

After 892, the caliph and his court moved to Baghdad, and large parts of the city were abandoned. However, it remained an important provincial centre after the tenth century, housing the tombs of the tenth and eleventh Shi'a imams, Ali al-Hadi and Hasan al-Askari. Their shrine is still an important Shiite pilgrimage site.[7] Samarra with its archaeological sites has been a UNESCO World Heritage Site since 2007, while also being on UNESCO's list of World Heritage in Danger.[8]

---

[1] Bosworth 2012; Terzi 2014, 10.

[2] Northedge 2012.

[3] Leisten 2003, 81–104.

[4] See for the building activities of caliph al-Mutawakkil, e.g. Leisten 2003, 35; for an assessment of the congregational mosque, see Leisten 2003, 35–57.

[5] Leisten 2003, 58–68.

[6] See for a compact appraisal of Samarra: <https://archive.archnet.org/authorities/3929> [accessed 4 November 2022].

[7] See for the shrine: <https://www.archnet.org/sites/5525> [accessed 4 November 2022].

[8] <https://whc.unesco.org/en/list/276> [accessed 26 April 2022].

Samarra: Excavation, Finds, and Documentation

Excavating Samarra

Samarra is of outstanding importance for understanding the urban planning of early Islamic imperial cities and the architecture and material culture of the Abbasid Empire. Baghdad, established as the capital of the Abbasid Empire by caliph al-Mansur in 762, has since been densely populated and subject to reconstruction. Similarly, al-Raqqah in Syria, founded as a garrison city by al-Mansur only shortly after in 771, was already an extensively looted excavation site by the end of the nineteenth century.[9] In contrast, Samarra has largely preserved the original layout of the city, which was abandoned in large parts relatively soon after its founding. This lack of constant rebuilding and development made it an ideal site for archaeological investigations.[10] It was here that the first systematic excavations of an Islamic archaeological site were conducted.

In 1908, Friedrich Sarre (1865–1945), the director of the Islamic Department of the Royal Museums in Berlin, today's Museum für Islamische Kunst, and the archaeologist Ernst Herzfeld (1879–1948) visited Samarra together.[11] In July/August 1910, Sarre obtained a two-year excavation permit from the Ottoman sultan, who ruled the territory of present-day Iraq at that time.[12]

Ernst Herzfeld led the excavation work on the site in two campaigns: from 9 January to 9 October 1911[13] and from 1 December 1912 to 18 June 1913.[14] Over the course of sixteen months, three caliphal palaces, the congregational mosque, and various residences were partly excavated: the congregational mosque, several residences, and the Balkuwara Palace in 1911[15] and parts of the Dar al-Khilafa (also known as Jawsaq al-Khaqani) in 1912/1913.[16]

---

[9] Jenkins 2006, 21–22; Tütüncü Çağlar 2017, 112–14.

[10] Today, however, it is endangered by extensive and uncontrolled agriculture.

[11] Kröger 2014, 238–40.

[12] Kröger 2014, 248, 262. See also Terzi 2014, 11–12; Leisten 2003, 9.

[13] Kröger 2014, 266–67; see for different dates Terzi 2014, 13 (13 October); Leisten 2003, 11 (3 December).

[14] Kröger 2014, 279.

[15] Kröger 2014, 266.

[16] Kröger 2014, 278.

Some of Herzfeld's methods,[17] such as inventorying small finds by groups rather than individual items,[18] and missing trenches[19] pose challenges today when trying to assign finds to their find-spots. However, it should be acknowledged that Herzfeld was almost solely responsible for the extensive scientific documentation, which included photography, drawing, excavation diaries, and a find journal, as well as organization of the work, including management of around three hundred workers temporarily[20] on a vast site within a limited time frame.[21]

Aside from the challenge of assigning finds to their find-spots in Samarra, researchers also face obstacles due to the division of finds after World War I, the destruction of finds during World War II in Berlin, and the dispersal of finds and excavation records around the world.

The Dispersal of Material Originating from the Excavation in Samarra 1911–1913

When Sarre and Herzfeld began their investigation of Samarra, the Ottoman authorities were responsible for the archaeological site. In 1906, a new Ottoman decree declared that all recently discovered antiquities belonged to the state and were to be conserved and stored in Ottoman imperial museums, and were not to be taken out of the country.[22] However, Halil Edhem Bey, the general director of the Ottoman imperial museums, who was also in charge of archaeology and excavations in the empire, allowed Sarre and Herzfeld to take individual material samples from Samarra for technical investigations.[23] After the second excavation campaign ended in May 1913, thirty-four boxes of wall paintings and stucco panels, including originals and casts, were sent to Berlin.[24]

After completing the excavation, Herzfeld stored a total of 104 boxes of small finds, 116 bundles of ornaments, and three hundred pieces of detached wall panels in the Serail of Samarra in vaulted halls. Originally, they were scheduled to be transported to Istanbul, but political instability in the Ottoman Empire in 1913 and the outbreak of World War I in August 1914 prevented this from happening.[25] Only five boxes with 134 finds were sent to Istanbul for technical investigations in 1913.[26]

During World War I, when the British Army took over Iraq in 1917, the boxes stored in Samarra came under their control. The British War Trophies Committee awarded them to the British Museum in London in May 1918. However, only seventy-nine boxes arrived at the British Museum in London between March and June 1921.[27] Herzfeld was invited to examine the finds in London from mid-July to September 1921 and wrote a final report of his investigations, in which he also recommended distributing the finds. For Berlin, he proposed finds that were indispensable for the final excavation publications.[28] He also recommended sending a large part of the finds to a museum in Samarra or Baghdad.[29] In early 1922, the Secretary of State divided the finds between Herzfeld, the British Museum, the Victoria and Albert Museum, and the Mesopotamian government.[30] The objects that according to the Trustees Standing Committee were supposed to be awarded to Herzfeld, were sent to the Kaiser-Friedrich-Museum in Berlin.[31] The Louvre received the boxes left by Henri Viollet in Samarra, which had also been brought to London.[32] The remaining fragments were sent as 'type-sets' to seventeen museums, including museums in Ann Arbor, Boston, Cleveland, New York, Toronto, and Cairo.[33]

In addition to the remarkable excavation finds, it is also worth noting the extensive amount and high quality of the documentary material that Herzfeld produced and/or gathered. In an article reporting on the results of the second campaign, which was published in 1914, Herzfeld listed the various materials that resulted from the two campaigns:[34]

---

17 See for an assessment Kröger 2014, 324–26.

18 Herzfeld 1914, 204.

19 Cf. Leisten 2003, 120; Northedge 2005, 391–92; Kröger 2014, 267–68, esp. 268 n. 211, 324–26.

20 Kröger 2014, 264.

21 See for an assessment of the excavation also Kröger 2014, 324–27.

22 Ottoman Empire: Règlement sur les antiquités, 1324/1907 (22 April 1906).

23 Kröger 2014, 290–92; Terzi 2014, 14.

24 Kröger 2014, 291–92.

25 Kröger 2014, 288–90.

26 Kröger 2014, 289, Terzi 2014, 14.

27 Kröger 2014, 298–99.

28 Kröger 2014, 300.

29 Kröger 2014, 301.

30 Kadoi 2014, 29.

31 Kadoi 2014, 30, esp. n. 13; Kröger 2014, 305, 308–09.

32 Kröger 2014, 306.

33 Kröger 2014, 303–04, 306; Kadoi 2014.

34 Herzfeld 1914.

The scientific material amounts to about 300 photographic plates of architectures, 150 of decorations, 115 of paintings, 24 coloured plates, 310 plates with small finds, about 250 Kodak photographs of architectures. In addition three 1:23,000 Ordnance Survey sheets, a 1:100,000 map, a reconstruction of the historic city plan, a Routiers sheet of the wider surroundings. Drawings of about 130 plans, sections, perspective views, and architectural details, 300 sheets of ornaments, 100 watercolours of paintings. Finally, an inventory of 1004 'numbers' of small finds,[35] most of which are not inventoried according to individual pieces, but according to groups, and of which each piece is recorded in drawings, the more important also in photographs, watercolours, squeeze papers, and moulds.[36]

Furthermore, Herzfeld kept excavation diaries and a find journal,[37] 'in der Art, wie es bei den Expeditionen der Deutschen-Orient-Gesellschaft üblich ist'.[38] In his find journal, he catalogued 1161 items, again with many individual items being inventoried by group.

After completing the excavation in 1913, Herzfeld sent this extensive documentation to Berlin.[39] Kröger assumes that this material was kept as property of the Samarra expedition in the Islamic Department in Berlin.[40] Thus Sarre[41] and Lamm[42] were able to use the find journal, sketchbooks, and watercolours in their publications, as they worked in Berlin in 1922/1924 and 1926/1927. They also made extensive use of the Islamic Department's negative collection.[43]

From an unknown date — Kröger assumes between 1927 and 1935 — Herzfeld came into possession of the find journal, sketchbooks, and watercolour drawings.[44] After World War II, Herzfeld sold parts of his records to American Institutions, including the Metropolitan Museum of Art in New York, which currently holds watercolour drawings of Samarra finds and photographic albums with pictures from Samarra.[45] However, the majority of Herzfeld's scholarly legacy was given to the Freer Gallery of Art in Washington in 1946.[46]

Samarra Finds in Berlin

According to archival records, there were thirty-four boxes in Berlin at the end of the excavation in July 1913 and at the beginning of World War I on 1 August 1914. Among them were seventeen boxes containing one hundred stucco panels, of which eighteen were original and seventy-eight were mouldings.[47] Another seventeen boxes contained fragments of wall paintings and small finds.[48] In June 1922, eight more boxes of finds were sent from London to Berlin after the division of finds.[49] In November/December 1921, the Museum für Islamische Kunst inventoried stucco casts and originals.[50] The small finds and wall paintings retained or were given numbers based on Herzfeld's find journal.[51]

However, the grouping of the finds rather than recording them individually, the dispersion of the objects and their documentation, and the destruction and looting of the Berlin museums during World War II have led to a loss of information about them. Therefore, identifying and documenting the objects is an ongoing project.

The Samarra Archive in Berlin

The Archival Records

As previously noted, there is an abundance of documentation available regarding the Samarra excavation. Archival records are divided between two locations within the Staatliche Museen zu Berlin: the excavation

---

35 Cf. also Terzi 2014, 13.

36 Herzfeld 1914, 204, my translation; cf. Kröger 2014, 285–86.

37 Digitized: <https://edan.si.edu/slideshow/viewer/?damspath=/Public_Sets/FS/FSA/FSA_A.06_07.01> [accessed 14 July 2022].

38 Kröger 2014, 249, private employment contract Sarre and Herzfeld 1910.

39 Kröger 2014, 309.

40 Kröger 2014, 309–11.

41 Sarre 1925, V–VI.

42 Lamm 1928, 3.

43 Kröger 2014, 309–10.

44 Kröger 2014, 310.

45 Referred to as 'Ernst Herzfeld Papers in the Department of Islamic Art, Metropolitan Museum of Art'. Root 1976; Kröger 2014, 310; Nagel and Woody 2014, 22–23.

46 Referred to as 'Herzfeld Papers, Freer Gallery of Art and Arthur M. Sackler Gallery Archives'. Upton 1978; Kröger 2014, 310.

47 Kröger 2014, 292, 294. The mouldings were produced by the gypsum technicians Theodor Bartus and Karl Beger, whom the Berlin museums had sent to Samarra especially for this purpose (Kröger 2014, 286–88).

48 Kröger 2014, 292.

49 Kröger 2014, 305.

50 See inventory of the Museum für Islamische Kunst, III: <https://storage.smb.museum/erwerbungsbuecher/IV_ISL-B_SLG_NC_3401-4900_LZ_1921-1927.pdf> [accessed 14 July 2022] for: I. 3467–3547, I. 4524–I. 4528. Cf. Kröger 2014, 294.

51 Kröger 2014, 292.

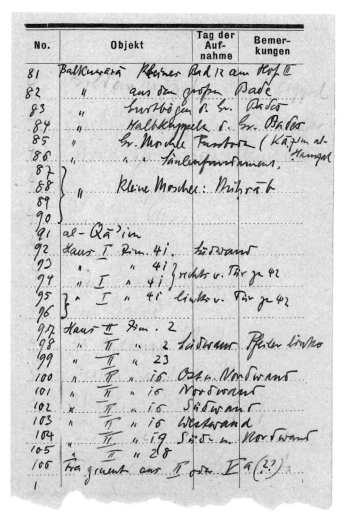

Figure 14.1. Ernst Herzfeld: photographic list of the first campaign, 1911 (Staatliche Museen zu Berlin, Museum für Islamische Kunst, Samarra Archiv, Kiste 3).

archive in the museum itself and in the Central Archive (Zentralarchiv der Staatlichen Museen zu Berlin). Unfortunately, as there is no list of the Samarra files prior to 1945, it is unclear to what extent the documents stored at the Pergamonmuseum may have been lost during the turmoil of 1945.[52]

The Samarra Archive in the Museum für Islamische Kunst is organized thematically, with documents relating to the excavation organization, including official documents, excavation reports, photo/negative directories, account books from the two campaigns, and accounts from 1911 to 1914. The collection also includes find books, sketchbooks, drawings, watercolour drawings, photographic prints, scientific papers, materials for publications, newspaper clippings from 1911 to 1926, and miscellany. The correspondence includes letters between Sarre and Herzfeld, Halil Edhem to Sarre, and more.[53]

Official letters from Sarre and Herzfeld as well as from Wilhelm Bode to higher authorities and their replies, but also invoices that were not to be paid and registered by the Samarra expedition but by the General Administration of the museums, are stored in Zentralarchiv der Staatlichen Museen zu Berlin.[54]

The Photographic Records

The Samarra excavation is well documented through photographic records, which currently include 778 glass plate negatives, 472 plastic negatives, and thirty large-format coloured slides or autochromes. Herzfeld served as the photographer during both campaigns and captured images of the architecture, decoration, wall paintings, and small finds in both group and single shots.

Throughout the excavation, Herzfeld created photo lists that recorded the number of the negative and the corresponding subject (Fig. 14.1).

Several of these lists are preserved in the archive of the Museum in Berlin. The recorded numbers correspond with numbers inscribed on some of the negatives kept at the museum in Berlin and signed by Herzfeld with 'E.H. [number]' at the lower left edge (Fig. 14.2). It is likely that Herzfeld marked these negatives after their development, suggesting that he may have had them developed in Iraq during the excavation campaign and sent them later to Berlin.[55]

However, the majority of the glass and film negatives were sent to Berlin for development.[56] All negatives were assigned new consecutive numbers, covering the range from 1 to 1307,[57] which do not match those given by Herzfeld. The large-format autochromes received Latin numerals to identify them as a separate stock. At an unknown date after he began working at the museum in 1927, Kurt Erdmann prepared a handwritten list of the negatives (Fig. 14.3).

---

52 Kröger 2014, 310.

53 Cf. Kröger 2014, 235.

54 Kröger 2014, 310–11.

55 Cf. Kröger 2014, 260; cf. Leisten 2003, 190 citing Herzfeld's letter to Sarre from 15 February 1911, mentioning in § 4 that thirty-six photographs are going to be developed by Donatossian in Baghdad.

56 Kröger 2014, 260.

57 *c.* 1250 negatives are preserved today and have been digitized.

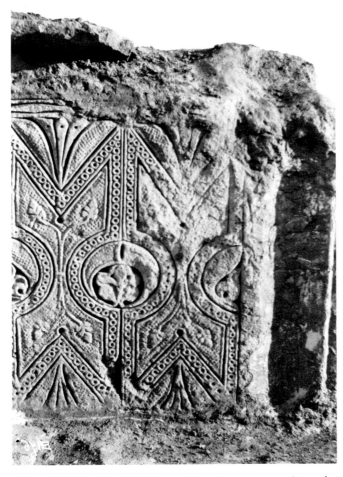

Figure 14.2. Ernst Herzfeld: Samarra, Haus II, stucco, room 41, south wall, east of door, 1911, glass negative, 13 × 18 cm (Staatliche Museen zu Berlin, Museum für Islamische Kunst, Fotoarchiv, inv. no. Pl. Sam 1170, Public Domain Mark 1.0).

No	Gegenstand	No.	Bem.
1159	Moderne Gräber : Khān Mushāludah		Tafel 7×11
1160	Grab des Harbah		"
1161	Pendjāh 'Ali		"
1162	" Samarra		"
1163	" "		"
1164	"		"
1165	"		"
1166	"		"
1167	Privathäuser Stuck: Haus II. Zimmer 41	0.222	"
1168	" " II " 41	0.222	"
1169	" " II " 41	0.219	"
1170	" " II " 41	0.205	"
1171	" " II " 41	0.205	"
1172	" " III " 2	0.117	"
1173	" " III " 2	0.277	"
1174	" " III " 16	0.221	"
1175	" " III " 16	0.228	"
1176	" " III " 16	0.224	"
1177	" " III " 16	0.235	"
1178	" " III " 18	0.241	"
1179	" " III " 23	0.266	"
1180	" " III " 28	0.184/	"
1181	" " IV " 6	0.91	"
1182	" " IV " 6	0.91	"
1183	" " IV " 7	0.126	"
1184	" " V " 1	0.129	"
1185	" " V ? " 2 ?	0.62	"
1186	" " VII " 3	0.	"
1187	" " XI/6	0.270	"

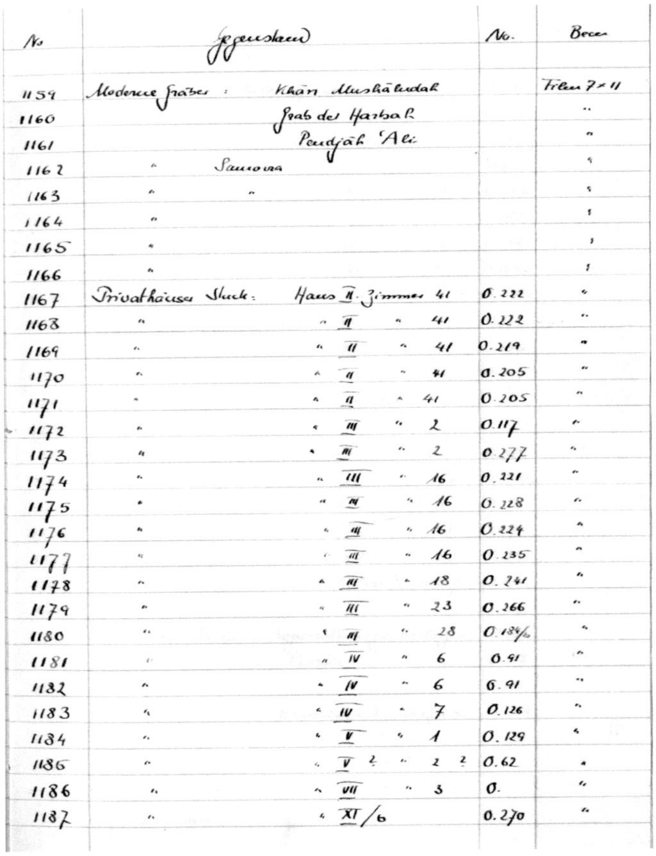

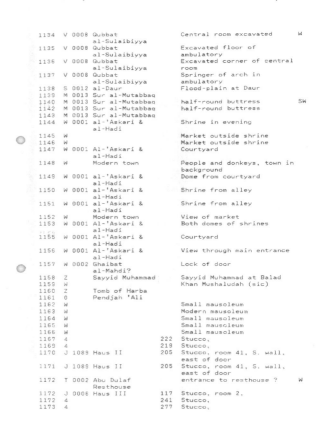

Figure 14.3. Kurt Erdmann: list of glass negatives from Samarra with an appendix of colour photographs, after 1927 (Staatliche Museen zu Berlin, Museum für Islamische Kunst, Fotoarchiv).

1134	V	0008	Qubbat al-Sulaibiyya		Central room excavated	W
1135	V	0008	Qubbat al-Sulaibiyya		Excavated floor of ambulatory	
1136	V	0008	Qubbat al-Sulaibiyya		Excavated corner of central room	
1137	V	0008	Qubbat al-Sulaibiyya		Springer of arch in ambulatory	
1138	S	0012	al-Daur		Flood-plain at Daur	
1139	M	0013	Sur al-Mutabbaq			
1140	M	0013	Sur al-Mutabbaq		half-round buttress	SW
1142	M	0013	Sur al-Mutabbaq		half-round buttress	
1143	M	0013	Sur al-Mutabbaq			
1144	W	0001	al-'Askari & al-Hadi		Shrine in evening	
1145	W				Market outside shrine	
1146	W				Market outside shrine	
1147	W	0001	Al-'Askari & al-Hadi		Courtyard	
1148	W		Modern town		People and donkeys, town in background	
1149	W	0001	al-'Askari & al-Hadi		Dome from courtyard	
1150	W	0001	al-'Askari & al-Hadi		Shrine from alley	
1151	W	0001	al-'Askari & al-Hadi		Shrine from alley	
1152	W		Modern town		View of market	
1153	W	0001	Al-'Askari & al-Hadi		Both domes of shrines	
1155	W	0001	Al-'Askari & al-Hadi		Courtyard	
1156	W	0001	Al-'Askari & al-Hadi		View through main entrance	
1157	W	0002	Ghaibat al-Mahdi?		Lock of door	
1158	Z		Sayyid Muhammad		Sayyid Muhammad at Balad	
1159	W				Khan Mushaludah (sic)	
1160	Z		Tomb of Harba			
1161	O		Pendjah 'Ali			
1162	W				Small mausoleum	
1163	W				Modern mausoleum	
1164	W				Small mausoleum	
1165	W				Small mausoleum	
1166	W				Small mausoleum	
1167	4			222	Stucco,	
1169	4			219	Stucco,	
1170	J	1089	Haus II	205	Stucco, room 41, S. wall, east of door	
1171	J	1089	Haus II	205	Stucco, room 41, S. wall, east of door	
1172	T	0002	Abu Dulaf Resthouse		entrance to resthouse ?	W
1172	J	0006	Haus III	117	Stucco, room 2.	
1172	4			241	Stucco,	
1173	4			277	Stucco,	

Figure 14.4. Alastair Northedge: computer-generated list of the Samarra photographic archive, 1990 (Staatliche Museen zu Berlin, Museum für Islamische Kunst, Fotoarchiv).

Erdmann compiled the directory by indicating the number and the motif of the negatives, along with Herzfeld's ornament numbers referring to his classification of wall decoration[58] and the medium used. Additionally, he included remarks in keywords. It is possible that he had Herzfeld's photo lists available while preparing the directory.

In 1990, Alastair Northedge conducted research in the photo archive at the Museum für Islamische Kunst and created a typewritten list in English (Fig. 14.4). He included site numbers that corresponded to his own publication[59] and added the compass direction of each photograph. While the descriptions are mostly the same as those on Erdmann's list, Northedge's descriptions of the depicted architecture are more detailed in some cases. For example, he provided a more specific descrip-

58 Cf. Herzfeld 1923, 4–9.

59 Northedge and Kennet 2015, II, 1.

Figure 14.5. Ernst Herzfeld: Samarra, excavation in congregational mosque, 1911, plastic negative, 7 × 11.7 cm (Staatliche Museen zu Berlin, Museum für Islamische Kunst, inv. no. Pl. Sam 967, Public Domain Mark 1.0).

tion of the glass plate negative Pl. Sam 967 in Berlin, which shows workers in front of a wall (Fig. 14.5).

While the list of negatives only provides a generic description of the motif as 'excavation shot',[60] Northedge was able to identify the depicted architecture as the congregational mosque.[61] Small finds were described less precisely,[62] as they were not the focus of Northedge's research.

To avoid the need to constantly handle the original negatives, yet still to know what they show and be able to work with them, the museum in Berlin created so-called blueprints sorted thematically into nine folders.[63] It appears that Erdmann also played a role in their preparation.[64]

Additionally, a group of 162 slides, copied from selected negatives and not taken during the excavation, is also part of the collection (Fig. 14.6).

The majority of these slides are labelled as Herzfeld's property, suggesting that he likely commissioned them. It is possible that Ernst Kühnel later used them. Kühnel was appointed as an honorary professor for 'Islamic art history with special consideration of its relations to occidental culture' on 4 September 1935. From the winter semester of 1935 until the winter semester 1944/1945, he gave lectures and held exercises on Islamic art at the Friedrich Wilhelm University's Institute of Art History in Berlin. It is highly likely that he discussed Samarra during his lectures on *Art under the Abbasids* (winter semester 1939), *Exercise on Islamic Ornament* (1940, 1941) and *Style* (winter semester 1938, 1940, 1941).[65] Erdmann also compiled a list of these slides. Even though they are only copies of the original negatives, they are significant sources because some of the negatives that were used as originals are no longer preserved today (Fig. 14.6).

The Museum für Islamische Kunst also preserves the original prints in addition to the negatives. These prints are further important sources, as they were made before the negatives showed any signs of decomposition, and in some cases, the negative is completely missing. However, not all the negatives have prints available.

Researching, Publishing, and Exhibiting Samarra in Berlin

The Samarra finds have been on display in the museum's permanent exhibition since 1922. Although the original stucco panels and mouldings sent to Berlin in 1913 were prepared for display upon their arrival, they could not be exhibited due to the outbreak of World War I in 1914. Starting in 1922, thirty-six stucco panels were displayed

---

[60] Herzfeld identified the subject in one of his handwritten lists of photographs in the Museum für Islamische Kunst as 'Excavation in the Haram of the Great Mosque' (EH 16).

[61] He refers to his publication by citing the congregational mosque as building H3 (Northedge and Kennet 2015, II, 1, 84–85).

[62] Cf. the description of Pl. Sam 170 by Erdmann as 'al-Dschausaq al-Chaqani, Harem, Kleinfunde, Perlmutt, a. Glas, Rekonstruktion' and by Northedge as 'Glass'.

[63] Parent topics are amongst others architecture, excavation shots, ceramics, small finds, landscapes, painting, stucco and 'types'.

[64] I thank Jens Kröger for his appraisal of the handwriting.

[65] I thank Jens Kröger for sharing this information.

Figure 14.6. Ernst Herzfeld: Samarra, al-Mutawakkiliyya, Abu Dulaf Mosque, south hall, 1911, slide reproduced from a now-missing glass negative, 8.5 × 10 cm (Staatliche Museen zu Berlin, Museum für Islamische Kunst, inv. no. Dia Sam 77, Public Domain Mark 1.0).

in the Samarra Room in the Kaiser-Friedrich-Museum,[66] and they have remained a cornerstone in educating audiences on the visual language and material culture of the Abbasid caliphate. The most recent update to the Samarra gallery occurred in 2013 to commemorate 101 years of research on Samarra.[67] In 2027, when the new permanent galleries will open, Samarra will continue to hold a prominent position.

The excavations' findings were published in several volumes between 1923 and 1948.[68] However, researchers continue to study the artefacts kept at the Museum für Islamische Kunst in Berlin[69] and publish their findings in articles[70] and monographs.[71]

Over the last two decades, the excavation and its key figures have become the subject of significant interest and research. A conference was held in Berlin in 2014, and its proceedings serve as a milestone for this undertaking.[72] Jens Kröger's chronicle of the Samarra excavation, included in the publication, is a fundamental contribution that summarizes the current state of research to date in a profound and concise manner.[73] This work offers a good starting point for new research directions.

Digitizing Samarra

Several museums housing Samarra finds have been actively displaying their collections online, including the Victoria and Albert Museum[74] and the British Museum.[75] In particular, the Victoria and Albert Museum has created a blog to accompany a project that is dedicated to researching, cataloguing, photographing, and conserving the collections of material excavated by Herzfeld at Samarra.[76]

In addition, the various institutions have been actively digitizing their Samarra archival material for some time. The Archives of the Freer Gallery of Art and the Arthur M. Sackler Gallery in Washington, DC, have played a pioneering role in this effort. They systematically catalogued their archival material as early as in the 1970s, and digitized and published it online in the early 2010s.[77] Similarly, in the 1970s, the Metropolitan Museum in New York catalogued their collection of Herzfeld papers[78] and published photographic albums, original watercolours, and drawings related to Herzfeld's excavations in Samarra online.[79]

Since 2004, Gert Audring has made the correspondence between Eduard Meyer (1908–1930) and Herzfeld available online on the website of the Humboldt University of Berlin, mainly from the archives of the Berlin-Brandenburg Academy of Sciences and Humanities.[80]

---

66 Kröger 2014, 294. The Islamic department moved to the Pergamonmuseum only in 1932.

67 <https://www.smb.museum/en/exhibitions/detail/samarra-centre-of-the-world/> [accessed 14 July 2022].

68 For a discussion of the publication, see Kröger 2014, 311–24.

69 <https://www.smb.museum/en/museums-institutions/museum-fuer-islamische-kunst/collection-research/research-cooperation/samarra-and-the-art-of-the-abbasids/> [accessed 14 July 2022].

70 See e.g. Schibille and others 2018.

71 Saba 2022. Works in progress: Simone Struth's dissertation on the stucco work of Samarra.

72 Gonnella and Abdellatif 2014.

73 Kröger 2014.

74 *c.* three hundred objects online.

75 *c.* 2650 objects online.

76 <https://samarrafindsproject.blogspot.com/> [accessed 14 July 2022].

77 See for details Nagel and Woody 2014.

78 See Root 1976; Szostak 2020.

79 See Szostak 2020: <https://networks.h-net.org/node/7636/discussions/36479/resource-ernst-herzfeld-papers-metropolitan-museum%E2%80%99s-department> [accessed 14 July 2022].

80 <https://www.geschichte.hu-berlin.de/de/bereiche-und-lehrstuehle/alte-geschichte/forschung/briefe-meyer/herzfeld> [accessed 14 July 2022].

Figure 14.7. Screenshot, museum documentation system (Staatliche Museen zu Berlin, Museum für Islamische Kunst).

Digitizing Samarra Finds in Berlin

From 2012 to 2017, an interdisciplinary team consisting of art historians, archaeologists, photographers, museologists, and conservators conducted a comprehensive survey, documenting and photographing a representative selection of the Museum für Islamische Kunst's collection in Berlin. The project aimed to publish eleven thousand objects online and was generously funded by Yousef Jameel.[81] The team collected crucial metadata of the artefacts such as date, origin, materials, and production techniques of each artefact. Furthermore, they took various photographs of the objects from different angles. The information was entered into the museum's database and has been made available to the public through the online catalogue of the Staatliche Museen zu Berlin since 2017. As part of this initiative, the team also documented and published online a large portion of the Samarra excavation finds, which amount to around nine hundred data sets.[82] Nonetheless, surveying, documenting, and photographing the remaining parts of the Samarra finds is still an ongoing process.

Another digitization project conducted by the Hochschule für Technik und Wirtschaft in Berlin, which ran from 2013 to 2015, created highly accurate three-dimensional captures of Samarra's stucco panels and three-dimensional digital simulations of substantial areas of the archaeological site. These developments will eventually enable scholars and educators to contextualize museum objects using virtual images.[83]

Digitizing the Photographic Archive of the Samarra Excavation in Berlin

In October 2021, the Museum für Islamische Kunst received funding from the Deutsche Digitale Bibliothek to survey and digitize the photographic documentation of Herzfeld's two excavation campaigns. In preparation for the digitization, the museum recorded the depot locations of the 1250 glass plate or film negatives and 192 slides in various formats, assessed and documented the condition of the originals, and prepared the objects for transport. Due to their fragile state of preservation, the objects required the highest demands on the process of digitization, with regard to material conservation and

---

81 <https://www.smb.museum/en/museums-institutions/museum-fuer-islamische-kunst/collection-research/research-cooperation/yousef-jameel-digitalization-project/> [accessed 14 July 2022].

82 <https://recherche.smb.museum/?language=de&question=%22Fundort%3A+Samarra+%28Irak%29+%28Ort%29%22&limit=15&controls=none> [accessed 14 July 2022].

83 <https://gamedesign.htw-berlin.de/en/dehive/research/mosys3d/> [accessed 14 October 2022]; <https://www.smb.museum/en/museums-institutions/museum-fuer-islamische-kunst/collection-research/research-cooperation/samarra-and-the-art-of-the-abbasids/> [accessed 14 July 2022].

Figure 14.8. Wall painting, mud, baked; plastered, black painting, Samarra, 836–892, Museum für Islamische Kunst, inv. no. Sam 514.1 (© Staatliche Museen zu Berlin, Museum für Islamische Kunst/Christian Krug).

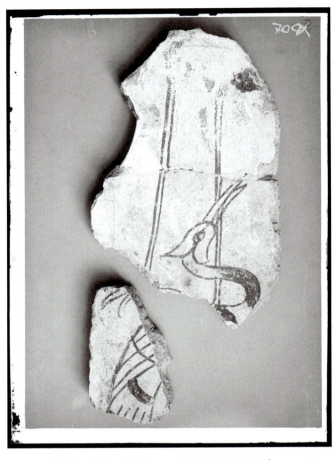

Figure 14.9. Ernst Herzfeld: Samarra, Haus XVI, 1911, glass negative, 13 × 18 cm (Staatliche Museen zu Berlin, Museum für Islamische Kunst, inv. no. Pl. Sam 709, Public Domain Mark 1.0).

minimized exposure to light and heat. Therefore, the museum decided to use repro-photography on a transmitted light unit (transmitted light photography) and contracted an external service provider with relevant experience to carry out the digitization.

The museum's staff also digitized and analysed finding aids, such as the above-mentioned blueprints and photo lists, to compile relevant metadata, which they entered into the museums database along with the digitized photographs (Fig. 14.7). The direct incorporation of all information into the museum database facilitated easy publication of the content online, and ensured sustainable maintenance and updates.

To enhance the value of the project, the digitized data was integrated with the existing documentation of Samarra excavation finds in the museum database. Thus, this project has filled a gap in the documentation of the Samarra excavation by linking the already digitized finds kept at the museum with the photographs that depict the finds in their original archaeological context and state of preservation. This has provided a crucial point in the object biographies that is now transparent. Furthermore, these unique photographs capture the historical condition of this World Heritage Site.

However, the project's goal was not only to digitize but also to promptly publish the digitized material. The datasets are now accessible on the Museum für Islamische Kunst's website, highlighting its collection.[84] This enables not only a small group of interested researchers but also the broader public to benefit from this unique source for reconstructing the rich and eminent material culture of Samarra. As a result, users of the website can now develop their own inquiries, relevant to them, regarding historical excavation practices, knowledge production protagonists, participation, and provenance.

---

84 <https://recherche.smb.museum/?language=de&question=%22Aufnahmeort%3A+Samarra+%28Irak%29+%28Ort%29%22&limit=15&controls=none> [accessed 14 July 2022].

Potentials of Digitization

Making the Collection Accessible for Researchers: Recontextualization of (Lost) Find Contexts

Researchers often face difficulties in bringing together archival material and objects due to incomplete documentation. Missing documents, missing object labels, or newly assigned inventory numbers by the administering museum are common reasons for such difficulties.[85] Several cases shall demonstrate the potential of collating different digital resources available on the internet to gain a broader understanding of excavations, their findings, analysis, and interpretation.

Web sources prove useful in re-establishing the excavation inventory number, which is again crucial for identifying the find context. This will be demonstrated on a fragment of a wall painting on plaster in the Samarra collection in Berlin (inv. no. Sam 514.1) showing herons with long, slender legs (Fig. 14.8).[86]

The assembled fragment depicts two herons, one standing on top of the other and the lower one 'nipping' the upper one in the leg. The upper bird is facing left, while the lower bird is facing right. Unfortunately, the object does not have an inscribed inventory or excavation number. Therefore, it was temporarily listed as the internal number Sam I. 372 at the museum to manage it for lending, exhibiting, and publishing purposes.[87]

Fortunately, among the negatives of the Samarra excavation in Berlin are two glass plate negatives of this object, Pl. Sam 665[88] and Pl. Sam 709 (Fig. 14.9).[89]

These negatives have been instrumental in identifying the object and providing further context for its discovery. Both negatives display the wall-painting fragments in their state before their various fragments were joined together.

The fragments' find context can be deduced from the list of Samarra negatives and the Museum für Islamische Kunst's blueprint collection, which refer to Haus XVI.[90]

Additionally, the Metropolitan Museum's holdings include a watercolour drawing by Herzfeld that features the fragment, with a focus on the legs of the upper and the head of the lower heron.[91] The drawing also displays the excavation inventory number IN 514.[92] Herzfeld's find journal,[93] kept at the Freer Gallery in Washington, records that IN 514 was discovered in the rubble of a room with plaster stucco decorations, possibly with a fountain.[94] Other fragments found under the same number depict women's heads, fish, and a lion. These pieces were registered on 9–11 December [1911]. A note in red ink refers to the Latin number XVI relating to Haus XVI, which is consistent with the documentation in Berlin.[95] However, a pencil note next to it indicates [Haus] XII as the find-spot.[96]

By utilizing the various available (digital) resources, the excavation inventory number of the object was successfully identified, and the interim museum inventory number replaced. Furthermore, additional information regarding the archaeological context of the object was added to the museum records. Nevertheless, this example highlights the challenging and time-consuming

---

[85] Cf. Nagel and Woody 2014, 23.

[86] <https://id.smb.museum/object/1529718/fragment-wandmalerei> [accessed 14 July 2022].

[87] See e.g. Dreßen 2003, 159, no. 610.

[88] <https://id.smb.museum/object/2753539/malereien-al-dschausaq-al-chaqani%2C-harem%2C-t%C3%A4nzerin> [accessed 14 July 2022]. A print of the negative/photographic print of Pl. Sam 665 can be found in the collection of the Freer Gallery (FSA A.06 04.PF.21.071). <https://collections.si.edu/search/detail/ead_component:sova-fsa-a-06-ref26011?q=bartus+house&fq=object_type%3A%22Photographs%22&fq=topic%3A%22Mural+painting+and+decoration%22&record=1&hlterm=bartus%2Bhouse&inline=true> [accessed 14 July 2022].

[89] Pl. Sam 709 served as a model for the publication in Herzfeld's volume on the wall paintings of Samarra (Herzfeld 1927, pl. LVI above).

[90] Northedge and Kennet 2015, II, 92, no. H28.

[91] <https://libmma.contentdm.oclc.org/digital/collection/p16028coll11/id/1112/rec/101/> [accessed 14 July 2022]. A version of this watercolour drawing is published in Herzfeld 1927, fig. 44.

[92] Furthermore, a photo number 232 is mentioned. However, the entries for photo number 232 on the lists held at Berlin do not correspond with this motif.

[93] <https://edan.si.edu/slideshow/viewer/?damspath=/Public_Sets/FS/FSA/FSA_A.06_07.01> [accessed 14 July 2022], uan: FS-FSA_A.06_07.01.44.

[94] Cf. Leisten 2003, 180 § 83, publishing an excerpt of Herzfeld's diary Samarra III from 11.11.

[95] See for this house: Northedge and Kennet 2015, II, 92, no. H28.

[96] Northedge and Kennet 2015, II, 90, no. H14. Northedge's description of the location of H14 rather corresponds to Herzfeld's description in the find journal: 'House between Sur Isa and river.' However, no wall painting is mentioned by Northedge for this building, but for XVI. Herzfeld has changed the numbering system of the houses (Northedge 2005, 387 n. 6). For the different numbering of the houses by Herzfeld see also the table collated by Leisten 2003, 122.

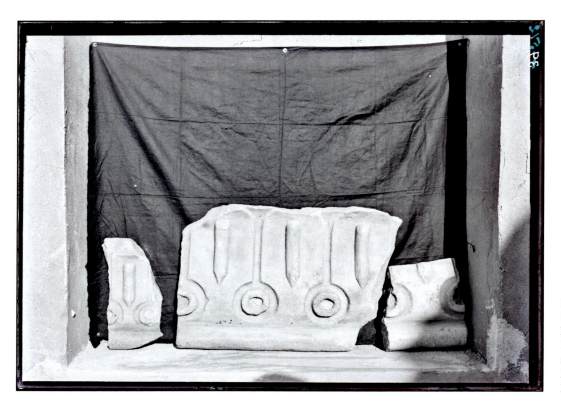

Figure 14.10. Ernst Herzfeld: Samarra, marble (Ornament No. 22), 1911, glass negative, 13 × 18 cm (Staatliche Museen zu Berlin, Museum für Islamische Kunst, inv. no. Pl. Sam 512, Public Domain Mark 1.0).

No	Gegenstand		No.	Bem
497	Privathäuser Stuck:	Haus III Zimmer 18	0. 241	
498	" "	Haus östl. Bab Qātūn	0 253	
499	" " :	Haus III Zimmer 23	0. 264/6	
500	" " :	" III	0 268/9	
501	" " :	Haus XI/b	0 270	
502	" " :	"	0.273	
503	" " :	Haus III Zimmer 23	0.274	
504	" " :	" II grosser Hof	0. 271	
505	" " :	Haus II grosser Hof	0. 272	
506	" " :	" II Zimmer 2	0. 277	
507	" " :	" XI/a Hof	0. 281	
508	" " :	" XI/a Hof	0. 284	
509	" " :	" XI/a Hof	0. 281/3	
510	" " :	" XI/a Hof	0. 281	
511	" " :	" XI d	0. 286	
512	Marmor-, Gips und Holz:	Marmorfragmente	0. 22	
513	" :	"	0 23	
514	" :	"	0. 22	
515	" :	"	0. 27	
516	" :	"	0. 27	
517	" :	"	0. 26	
518	" :	"	0. 26	
519	" :	"	0. 27	
520	" :	"	0. 279	
521	" :	"	0. 135	
522	" :	"	0. 135	
523	" :	"	0. 135	
524				
525	" :	"	J.N. 268 u. 0. 135 (2)	

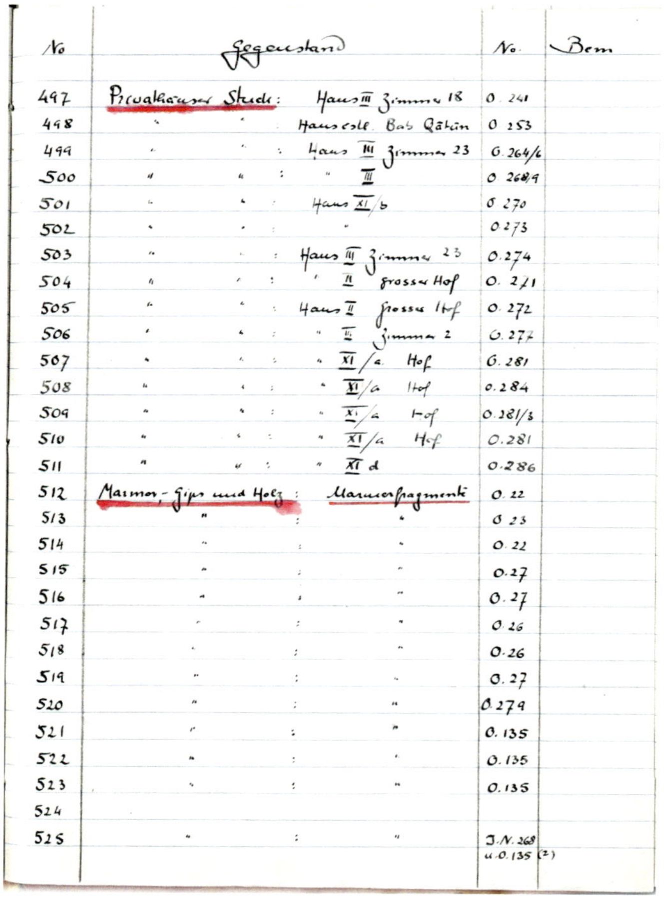

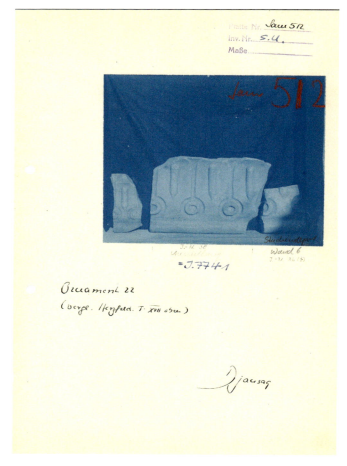

Figure 14.11. Kurt Erdmann: list of glass negatives from Samarra with an appendix of colour photographs, after 1927 (Staatliche Museen zu Berlin, Museum für Islamische Kunst, Fotoarchiv).

Figure 14.12. Kurt Erdmann: blueprint collection, folder: Samarra, small finds, Sam 512, after 1927 (Staatliche Museen zu Berlin, Museum für Islamische Kunst, Fotoarchiv).

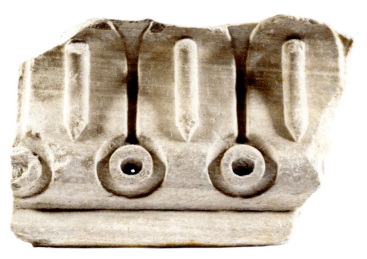

Figure 14.13. Front of a fragment of a large marble panel, marble, cut, drilled, polished, Samarra, 836–892, Museum für Islamische Kunst, inv. no. I. 7741 (© Staatliche Museen zu Berlin, Museum für Islamische Kunst/Christian Krug).

Figure 14.14. Back of a fragment of a large marble panel, cut, drilled, polished, Samarra, 836–892, Museum für Islamische Kunst, inv. no. I. 7741 (© Staatliche Museen zu Berlin, Museum für Islamische Kunst/Christian Krug).

process of reconstructing the find context — even with relatively detailed documentation.

Moreover, web sources can be helpful in determining the find contexts. For instance, glass plate negative Pl. Sam 512 kept in Berlin features three marble frieze fragments (Fig. 14.10).

The list of Samarra negatives indicates that marble fragments of Herzfeld's ornament type no. 22 are depicted on this negative (Fig. 14.11). The information available in the blueprint collection is more extensive (Fig. 14.12). It includes a reference to Herzfeld's publication[97] and identifies the centrepiece as being exhibited in the Museum für Islamische Kunst and bearing the museum inventory number I. 7741 (Fig. 14.13).

This number was given to this and other marble pieces in 1987,[98] which is rather unusual since only stucco plates and mouldings from Samarra were inventoried until then, and this was done only in 1921 (Fig. 14.16).

However, the centrepiece is furthermore identified as excavation number IN 38, a number also appearing in red on the back of the object (Fig. 14.14).

In the find journal in Washington, it is stated that for IN 38 there is a drawing in Sketchbook I on page 9 and a reference to the photo number 39. It is also mentioned that the piece was found in the city without a clearly identified find-spot, presumably from the Bait al-Khalifah.[99] In Herzfeld's sketchbook 'Samarra 1' in Washington, the indication 'presumably from Bait al-Khalifah or al-Quwair' is also mentioned.[100]

The possible provenance Bait al-Khalifah is also confirmed by a letter from Herzfeld to Sarre dated 2 February 1911, in which he mentions that inhabitants of Samarra brought him several marble pieces and vessels.[101] He goes on to describe the marble fragment in detail and assumes that it originates from the 'Bet al-Khalifah'.[102]

The original caption of a photographic print of the negative in the Freer Gallery also mentions that the object was not found on the spot, but was purchased.[103]

---

[97] Herzfeld 1923, pl. XVII above.

[98] Cf. Inventory of the Museum für Islamische Kunst, v: <https://storage.smb.museum/erwerbungsbuecher/IV_ISL-B_SLG_NC_6351-7755_LZ_1935-1988.pdf> [accessed 14 July 2022].

[99] FS-FSA_A.06_07.01.05.

[100] <https://edan.si.edu/slideshow/viewer/?damspath=/Public_Sets/FS/FSA/FSA_A.06_07.12>: FSA_A.06_07.12.06.JPG [accessed 14 July 2022]. In Herzfeld's sketchbook 'Samarra 1' in Washington, the piece is drawn in frontal view and in profile on page 9 with more precise measurements recorded. This drawing is published in Herzfeld 1914, as fig. 29. In the Herzfeld material at the Metropolitan Museum of Art, we find furthermore an ink drawing: <https://libmma.contentdm.oclc.org/digital/collection/p16028coll11/id/1183/rec/231> [accessed 14 July 2022].

[101] Cf. also Herzfeld's entry in his diary on 20 January 1911 (FS-FSA_A.06_07.06.18), <https://edan.si.edu/slideshow/viewer/?damspath=/Public_Sets/FS/FSA/FSA_A.06_07.06> [accessed 14 July 2022]; Leisten 2003, 154 § 21.

[102] Leisten 2003, 187 § 6, app. IV.

[103] <https://collections.si.edu/search/detail/ead_component:sova-fsa-a-06-ref25597?q=ernst+herzfeld+marble&record=17&hlterm=ernst%2Bherzfeld%2Bmarble&inline=true> [accessed 14 July 2022].

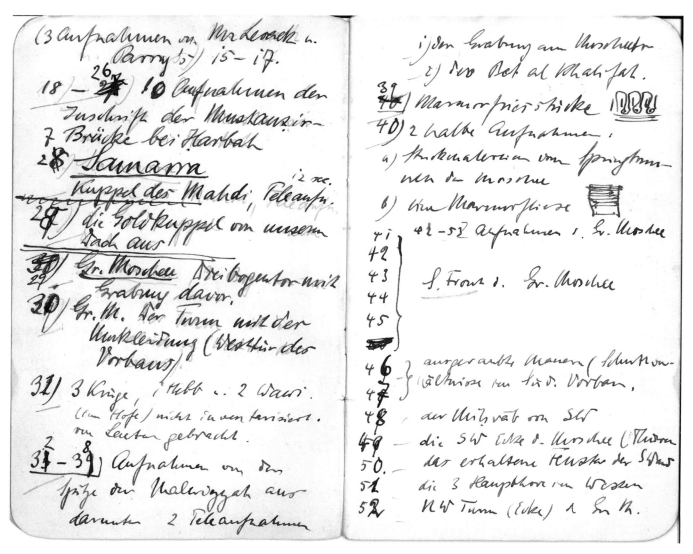

Figure 14.15. Ernst Herzfeld: Photographic list of the first campaign, 1911 (Staatliche Museen zu Berlin, Museum für Islamische Kunst, Samarra Archiv, Kiste 3).

This caption also includes a reference to 'Photo 39', which corresponds to Herzfeld's photo list of the first campaign in the archives of the museum in Berlin. This list records 'marble frieze pieces' under 39, and a small sketch is included (Fig. 14.15).

On closer inspection of the glass plate negative Pl. Sam 512 in Berlin (Fig. 14.10), it becomes apparent that the inscription '39' in white, which likely corresponds to Herzfeld's photo number mentioned in various documents, has been crossed out. Therefore, the current plate number '512' was assigned at a later point in time by the museum.

This example is noteworthy for several reasons. It illustrates how holding institutions utilize their own classification systems, not only for the objects they acquire but also for their documentation. However, without these numbers, the objects' find context can get lost. For example, the entry for I. 7741 in the inventory book of the Museum für Islamische Kunst does not reference the find context or excavation inventory number (Fig. 14.16).

It is understandable that holding institutions need to have a consistent numbering system for keeping and handling their inventoried objects, including changing the numbering system of the negative plates. Herzfeld's photo lists, held at the Museum für Islamische Kunst in Berlin, show that although he used numbers very consistently within his lists, he started each list from number 1, creating twin numbers eventually. However, when new numbers are assigned, there is a risk that information accessible via the excavation numbers may be lost.

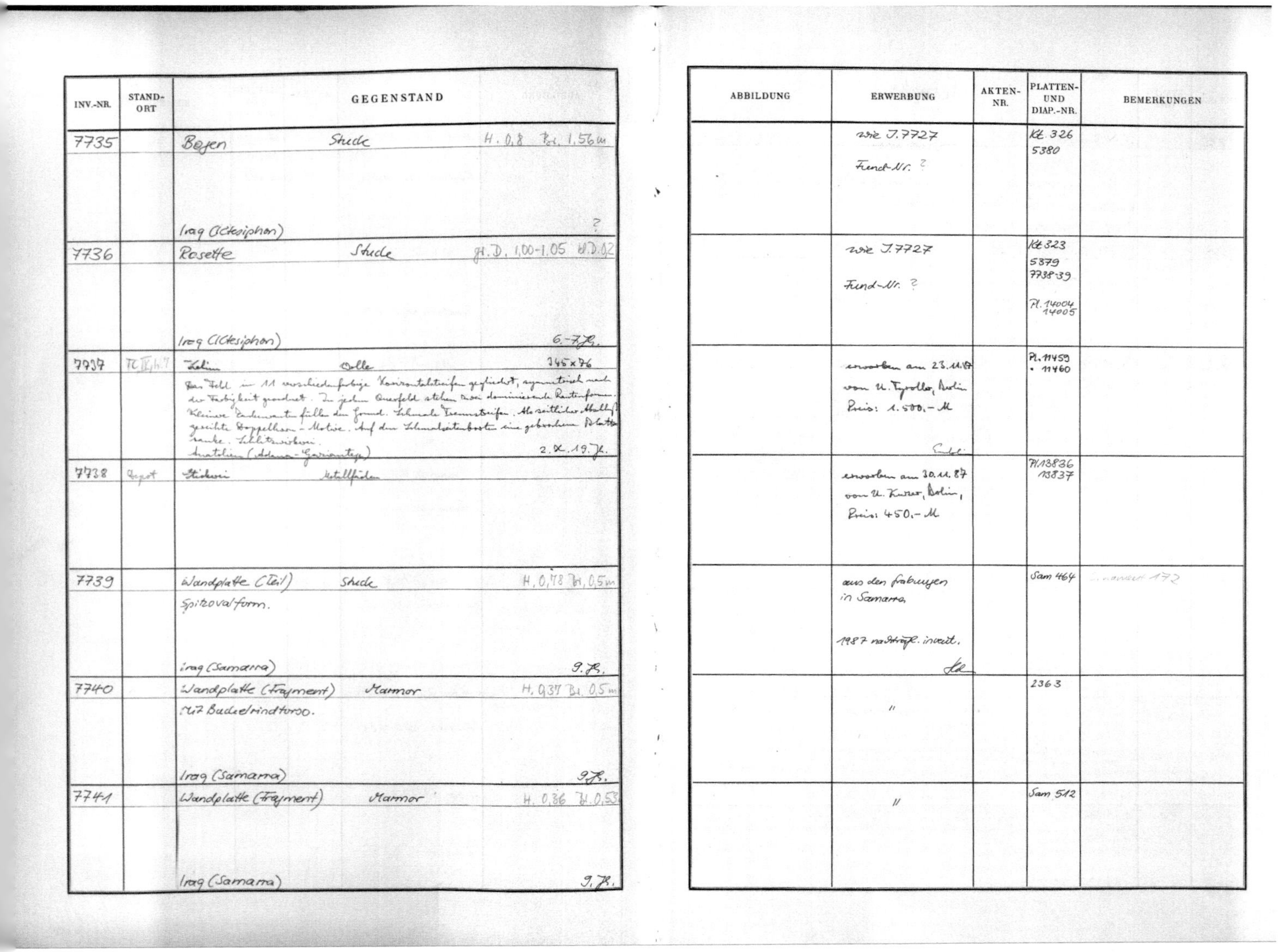

Figure 14.16. Museum für Islamische Kunst, *Inventarbuch*, v (Staatliche Museen zu Berlin, Museum für Islamische Kunst).

Identifying Actors

The glass negative Pl. Sam 978 in Berlin depicts two horsemen in front of the Bab al-Ammah in Samarra (Fig. 14.17).

The building's identification can be deduced from the list of Samarra negatives. The inscription 'EH 21' at the lower left edge of the picture corresponds to an entry in one of Herzfeld's handwritten photo lists in the Museum, which contains the following additional information: 'Guyer and Ali in the river garden of the B.[ait] al-Kh.[alifah]'[104] (Fig. 14.18).

Dr Samuel Guyer, the first excavation commissioner, supported Herzfeld during the first excavation campaign.[105] 'Ali' seems to have been portrayed in yet another of Herzfeld's photographs,[106] depicting a man named 'Ali' in the excavation house in Samarra, and Herzfeld also refers to 'Ali' in his diaries.[107] However, as

---

104 A print of this plate is found in the album in the Metropolitan Museum of Art with the handwritten inscription 'Guyer and Ali in front of Djausaq' (New York, Metropolitan Museum of Art, ANE.2.2.1; Photo Album-1, p. 7 (ANE.2.2.1_007), <https:// libmma.contentdm.oclc.org/digital/collection/p16028coll11/id/7999/rec/3> [accessed: 14.07.2022]).

105 Kröger 2014, 262, 270–71.

106 New York, Metropolitan Museum of Art, ANE.2.2.1; Photo Album-1, p. 3 (ANE.2.2.1_003), left above.

107 Cf. Leisten 2003, 181 § 95; 159 § 74 (Excerpts from Diary Samarra III, Herzfeld Papers Document S-8).

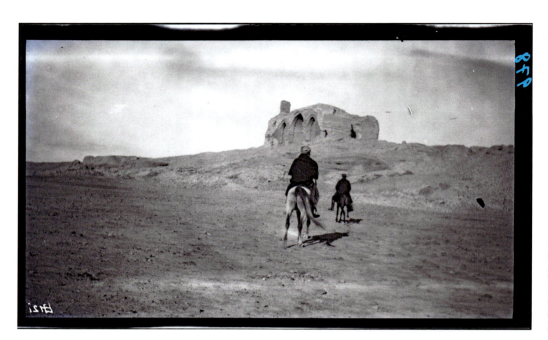

Figure 14.17. Ernst Herzfeld: Samarra, Bab al-ʿAmma, 1911, plastic negative, 7 × 11.5 cm (Staatliche Museen zu Berlin, Museum für Islamische Kunst, inv. no. Pl. Sam 978, Public Domain Mark 1.0).

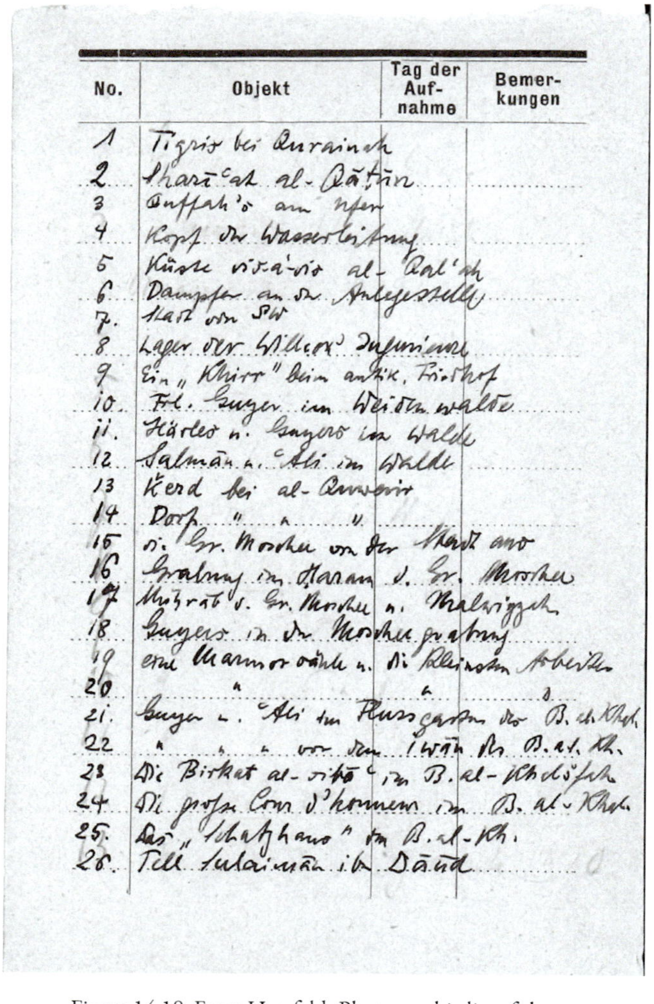

No.	Objekt	Tag der Aufnahme	Bemerkungen
1	Tigris bei Quraineh		
2	Sharīʿat al-Qāṭūn		
3	Buffalo's am Ufer		
4	Kopf der Wasserleitung		
5	Küste vis-à-vis al-Qal'ah		
6	Dampfer an der Anlegestelle		
7.	Stadt von SW		
8	Lager der Willcox' Ingenieure		
9	Ein „Khirr" beim antik. Friedhof		
10.	Frl. Guyer im Weidenwalde		
11.	Härles u. Guyers im Walde		
12.	Salmān u. ʿAli im Walde		
13	Kerd bei al-Quwair		
14	Dorf " " "		
15	d. Gr. Moschee von der Stadt aus		
16	Grabung im Haram d. Gr. Moschee		
17	Miḥrāb d. Gr. Moschee u. Malwiyyah		
18	Guyers in der Moscheegrabung		
19	eine Marmorsäule u. die kleinsten Arbeiter		
20	" " "		
21.	Guyer u. ʿAli im Flussgarten des B. al-Khal.		
22	" " " vor dem Iwān des B. al. Kh.		
23	Die Birkat as-sibāʿ im B. al-Khalīfah		
24	Die große Cour d'honneur im B. al-Khal.		
25.	Das „Schatzhaus" im B. al-Kh.		
26.	Tell Sulaimān ibn Dāūd		

Figure 14.18. Ernst Herzfeld: Photographic list of the first campaign, 1911 (Staatliche Museen zu Berlin, Museum für Islamische Kunst, Samarra Archiv, Kiste 3).

'Ali' is a common name and no further specifications are given, it is difficult to identify this person/these persons.

Identification of some of the 'nameless' excavation workers in the photographs is possible by cross-referencing various sources of information.[108] For instance, while the portraits of workers are listed as 'types' in the blueprint collection and the list of negatives in the Museum für Islamische Kunst, the man on Pl. Sam 917 (Fig. 14.19)[109] is identified by Herzfeld's handwritten caption of a photographic print in the album in the Metropolitan Museum of Art as Muhammad.[110]

108 See for a discussion of the recording of names of European or North American scholars in photographs, but not those of local workers: <https://projects.au.dk/archivearcheology/cultural-heritage-resources/virtual-exhibition-excavating-archives-narratives-from-20th-century-palmyra/excavating-archives-narratives-from-20th-century-palmyra/14-archive-archaeology#c140705> [accessed 14 July 2022].

109 <https://id.smb.museum/object/2763616/mann> [accessed 14 July 2022].

110 New York, Metropolitan Museum of Art, ANE.2.2.1; Photo Album-1, p. 6 (ANE.2.2.1_006), <https://libmma.contentdm.oclc.org/digital/collection/p16028coll11/id/7999/rec/3> [accessed 14 July 2022]. Cf. also the photographic print in Washington and its caption: 'Muhammad. Photos of Arab workmen at Samarra.' Probably the foremen (a): <https://collections.si.edu/search/detail/ead_component:sova-fsa-a-06-ref25626?q=crew&fq=object_type%3A%22Photographs%22&fq=place%3A%22S%5Cu0101marr%5Cu0101%5Cu02BC+%28Iraq%29%22&record=9&hlterm=crew&inline=true> [accessed 14 July 2022].

Figure 14.19. Ernst Herzfeld: Man, 1911–1913, glass negative, 13 × 18 cm (Staatliche Museen zu Berlin, Museum für Islamische Kunst, inv. no. Pl. 917, Public Domain Mark 1.0).

Figure 14.20. View of the exhibition 'Samarra Revisited: Excavation Photographs from the Caliph's Palaces Revisited' at the Museum für Islamische Kunst in Berlin

However, Herzfeld does not give his surname, making identification more challenging. There are also other individuals named Muhammad in Herzfeld's album photographs,[111] and their images are not very clear, making it difficult to ascertain whether any of them are the person identified as Muhammad on Pl. Sam 917.

What seems to be clear is that Herzfeld seemed to value his staff. Leisten noted that he planned to include information on their daily life during excavation in the first volume of a series of publications on Samarra.[112] Further research on the staff, similar to the information available on Shaul ibn Salman,[113] who served as an excavation secretary, is a desideratum.[114]

These examples of collating (digitized) materials illustrate the advantages of having online access to the finds and their documentation. It is also evident that the photos, being physical objects in various surrogates, are not only a source of visual content but are also circulated, (re-)classified, and (re-)arranged.[115] Considering this can add new perspectives to the historiography of the excavation of Samarra.[116]

---

[111] New York, Metropolitan Museum of Art, ANE.2.2.1; Photo Album-1, pp. 6, 16, 23 (ANE.2.2.1_006, ANE.2.2.1_016, ANE.2.2.1_023). <https://libmma.contentdm.oclc.org/digital/collection/p16028coll11/id/7999/rec/3> [accessed 14 July 2022].

[112] Leisten 2003, 31. Cf. the album at the Metropolitan Museum.

[113] New York, Metropolitan Museum of Art, ANE.2.2.1; Photo Album-1, p. 8, middle below (ANE.2.2.1_008). <https://libmma.contentdm.oclc.org/digital/collection/p16028coll11/id/7999/rec/3> [accessed 14 July 2022].

[114] Kröger 2014, 262–63.

[115] Cf. for this perspective also the Florence declaration (Kunsthistorisches Institut in Florenz 2022); Caraffa 2019, 16; Bärnighausen and others 2019, 49–50, 52.

[116] Cf. also Schwartz 2019, 313.

Participation and Outreach

The aforementioned examples highlighted the advantages of digitization for researchers. However, museums as public institutions also strive to make their collections more relevant and accessible to the public. Furthermore, curators and archaeologists find it rewarding to share their enthusiasm and expertise with a larger audience. As a result of the digitization project, the Museum für Islamische Kunst held the exhibition 'Samarra Revisited: Excavation Photographs from the Caliph's Palaces Revisited' from 4 March to 28 August 2022.[117]

Prior to digitization, the negatives of the Samarra photographic archive were only partially accessible due to their fragile state of preservation. Prints and finding aids, such as the blueprints, were not available for all negatives, and even the museum staff did not have a complete overview of the collection. To address this issue, colleagues were invited to examine the now completely digitized and available collection of Samarra negatives. Twenty-four current and former staff members were asked to select five negatives each that were connected to their respective fields of work. The participants chose one photograph that they found particularly meaningful, which was exhibited in the museum's book-art cabinet, along with their commentary on the image (Fig. 14.20). The other selected photographs and explanations for their selection were available in a media station.

Five main themes emerged from this, showing the broad spectrum of possible approaches for the use of excavation photographs. Archaeologists and provenance researchers used the photographs to contextualize finds, to reconstruct buildings in their urban environment and/or landscape, thus also mapping their impact and agency in space.

Photographers and conservators were interested in the technical aspects and conditions of photography. Photography has been used to document objects or find-spot in great detail, capturing the situation before it is lost forever through excavation work. New photographic techniques, such as autochromes, were used to capture not only the shape and size of the objects but also their colour scheme.[118] Even simple tools, like scales, were considered crucial. Other photographers, artists, and interpreters focused on the aesthetic qualities of the photographs and their potential for use in art and education.[119]

The excavation work and the working conditions of the local labour force sparked the greatest interest among participants, as the photographs also capture the hard physical labour involved.[120] The images thus also served as points of reference for current social debates on labour practices and worker rights.

In May 2022, this exhibition was transformed into a series of stories for the newly launched website *Islamic Art* of the Museum für Islamische Kunst, with the aim of promoting key concepts of the museum to wider audiences.[121] As the featured stories cover a wide range of perspectives they encourage visitors to look beyond the conventional approach to these materials as mere illustrations for research publications on Samarra and to develop their own ways of looking at and inquiring into these photographs.[122]

This exhibition was just the first step towards unlocking the photographic archive of the Samarra excavation and gaining fresh, personalized perspectives on it. The digitization of the archive made it accessible and serves as the foundation for any future endeavours involving the photographic collection.

Outlook

The present study aimed to illustrate two key benefits that derive from digitizing the excavation archives of Samarra. On the one hand, the collation and interpretation of digitized material make research more convenient for specialists and researchers, as a wealth of information is already available online and only needs to be linked. On the other hand, the efforts of other collections in making their Samarra material available online have helped the Museum für Islamische Kunst benefit

---

[117] <https://www.smb.museum/ausstellungen/detail/samarra-revisited/> [accessed 14 July 2022].

[118] See for the problem of reproducing colours Männig 2019, 286–88.

[119] Mehrad Sepahnia commenting on Pl. Sam 490 and Pl. Sam 670: 'I have been looking for faces on the excavation finds. Two types I find particularly exciting: abstract geometric patterns that look like hidden faces and self-explanatory examples.'

[120] Antonia Krappe commenting on Pl. Sam 135: 'I like the photos of the unjustly unknown people who worked like "ants" on this huge project. Without them it would have been impossible to uncover Samarra. The dimension of the excavation becomes even clearer through the juxtaposition of the depicted man and ruins.'

[121] <https://islamic-art.smb.museum/stories/samarra> [accessed 16 March 2023].

[122] Cf. Schwartz 2019, 312–13.

extensively for surveying and indexing the museum's photographic archive. As a result, the museum is also committed to making further Samarra material available online, including archival records. The digitization of the finds and negatives is just the start of this process.

I fully concur with the concluding remarks of Alexander Nagel and Rachel Woody's paper in the 2014 conference proceedings on Samarra. They expressed the objective of creating a 'digital research tool for a divided collection'[123] that could facilitate the collation of all the preserved Samarra finds and their identification using the find journal, photographs, sketchbooks, and other archival materials. This could serve as the foundation for a larger international collaborative project on the history and historiography of the excavation of Samarra.[124]

However, it is not just researchers who benefit from digitizing the Samarra archives, but larger audiences as well. Samarra provides an excellent example of turning what may seem like a challenge — the distribution of finds and their documentation across the globe — into a benefit. As many documents are kept in English-speaking countries, they have been indexed and some of them have even been translated into English.[125] This is a gain for non-German speakers, as all of the excavation documentation was originally written in German. It is important to emphasize that German institutions should provide their documentation in English as well.

To further expand access and usage of digitized archives, archives and museums should encourage the wider audience to explore and choose their own approaches. To achieve this, language and access barriers should be lowered.[126] Furthermore, institutions must think innovatively by gathering diverse voices[127] and testing new avenues of usage beyond traditional research, for instance by drawing inspiration from the individual insights of a broad range of museum staff members. Digitization is merely the first step towards this goal.

---

[123] Nagel and Woody 2014, 23–24.

[124] Cf. also Kadoi 2014, 28 n. 2; Kröger 2014, 302.

[125] See for this e.g. the translated captions of Herzfeld's photographs in the Freer Gallery archive, where also the finds journal has been translated: <https://samarrafindsproject.blogspot.com/2013/05/meeting-lubkins.html> [accessed 14 July 2022].

[126] Cf. Agostinho 2019.

[127] See e.g. Geismar 2018; Durgun 2020.

Works Cited

Agostinho, D. 2019. 'Archival Encounters: Rethinking Access and Care in Digital Colonial Archives', *Archival Science*, 19.2: 141–65 <https://doi.org/10.1007/s10502-019-09312-0>.

Archnet.org, 'Marqad al-Imamayn' <https://www.archnet.org/sites/5525> [accessed 4 November 2022]

Bärnighausen, J., S. Klamm, F. Schneider, and P. Wodtke. 2019. 'Photographs on the Move: Formats, Formations, and Transformations in Four Photo Archives', in J. Bärnighausen, C. Caraffa, S. Klamm, F. Schneider, and P. Wodtke (eds), *Photo-Objects: On the Materiality of Photographs and Photo Archives* (Berlin: Max-Planck-Gesellschaft zur Förderung der Wissenschaften), pp. 33–66 <https://doi.org/10.34663/9783945561409-03>.

Bosworth, C. E. 2012. 'al-Muʿtaṣim Bi 'llāh', in P. Bearman, T. Bianquis, C. E. Bosworth, E. van Donzel, and W. P. Heinrichs (eds), *Encyclopaedia of Islam*, 2nd edn <http://dx.doi.org/10.1163/1573-3912_islam_SIM_5656>.

Caraffa, C. 2019. 'Objects of Value: Challenging Conventional Hierarchies in the Photo Archive', in J. Bärnighausen, C. Caraffa, S. Klamm, F. Schneider, and P. Wodtke (eds), *Photo-Objects: On the Materiality of Photographs and Photo Archives* (Berlin: Max-Planck-Gesellschaft zur Förderung der Wissenschaften), pp. 11–32 <https://doi.org/10.34663/9783945561409-02>.

Dreßen, W. (ed.). 2003. *Ex oriente: Isaak und der weiße Elefant; Bagdad, Jerusalem, Aachen; Eine Reise durch drei Kulturen um 800 und heute; Katalogbuch in drei Bänden zur Ausstellung in Rathaus, Dom und Domschatzkammer Aachen vom 30. Juni bis 28. September 2003* (Mainz: Von Zabern).

Durgun, P. 2020. *Digging Digital Museum Collections* <https://alexandriaarchive.org/digging-digital-museum-collections/> [accessed 21 October 2022].

Geismar, H. 2018. *Museum Object Lessons for the Digital Age* (London: UCL Press).

Gonnella, J. and R. Abdellatif (eds). 2014. *Beiträge zur Islamische Kunst und Archäologie*, IV (Wiesbaden: Reichert) <https://doi.org/10.29091/9783954906024>.

Herzfeld, E. 1914. 'Mitteilung über die Arbeiten der zweiten Kampagne von Samarra', *Der Islam*, 5: 196–204.

—— 1923. *Der Wandschmuck der Bauten von Samarra und seine Ornamentik*, Forschungen zur islamischen Kunst, 2 (Berlin: Reimer).

—— 1927. *Die Malereien von Samarra*, Forschungen zur islamischen Kunst, 2 (Berlin: Reimer).

Jenkins, M. 2006. *Raqqa Revisited: Ceramics of Ayyubid Syria* (New York: Metropolitan Museum of Art).

Kadoi, Y. 2014. 'The Samarra Finds in the New World: A Fragment of 'Abbasid Artistic Legacy in American Museums', in J. Gonnella, S. Struth, and R. Abdellatif (eds), *Beiträge zur Islamische Kunst und Archäologie*, IV (Wiesbaden: Reichert), pp. 28–37.

Kröger, J. 2014. 'Chronik der Ausgrabungen von Samarra 1911–1913: Eine kulturhistorische Studie zur Forschungs- und Förderungsgeschichte der Islamischen Archäologie im 20. Jahrhundert', in in J. Gonnella, S. Struth, and R. Abdellatif (eds), *Beiträge zur Islamische Kunst und Archäologie*, IV (Wiesbaden: Reichert), pp. 234–346.

Kunsthistorisches Institut in Florenz 2022 — Max-Planck-Institut, 'Florence Declaration' <https://www.khi.fi.it/en/photothek/florence-declaration.php> [accessed 19 March 2022].

Lamm, C. J. 1928. *Das Glas von Samarra*, Forschungen zur islamischen Kunst, 2 (Berlin: Reimer).

Leisten, T. 2003. *Architecture: Final Report of the First Campaign 1910–1912*, Baghdader Forschungen (Mainz: Von Zabern).

Männig, M. 2019. 'Bruno Meyer and the Invention of Art Historical Slide Projection', in J. Bärnighausen, C. Caraffa, S. Klamm, F. Schneider, and P. Wodtke (eds), *Photo-Objects: On the Materiality of Photographs and Photo Archives* (Berlin: Max-Planck-Gesellschaft zur Förderung der Wissenschaften), pp. 275–90 <https://doi.org/10.34663/9783945561409-17>.

Nagel, A. and R. Woody. 2014. 'Excavations in the Archive. An Update on the Ernst Herzfeld Online Resources at the Freer|Sackler in Washington DC', in J. Gonnella, S. Struth, and R. Abdellatif (eds), *Beiträge zur Islamische Kunst und Archäologie*, IV (Wiesbaden: Reichert), pp. 18–27.

Northedge, A. 2005. 'Ernst Herzfeld, Samarra, and Islamic Archaeology', in A. C. Gunter and S. R. Hauser (eds), *Ernst Herzfeld and the Development of Near Eastern Studies 1900–1950* (Leiden: Brill), pp. 385–403 <https://doi.org/10.1163/9789047406587_017>.

—— 2012. 'Sāmarrā', in P. Bearman, T. Bianquis, C. E. Bosworth, E. van Donzel, and W. P. Heinrichs (eds), *Encyclopaedia of Islam*, 2nd edn <http://dx.doi.org/10.1163/1573-3912_islam_SIM_6573>.

Northedge, A. and D. Kennet. 2015. *Archaeological Atlas of Samarra*, 3 vols (London: British Institute for the Study of Iraq).

Root, M. C. 1976. 'The Herzfeld Archive of The Metropolitan Museum of Art', *Metropolitan Museum Journal*, 11: 119–24 <https://www.metmuseum.org/art/metpublications/Herzfeld_Archive_of_The_Metropolitan_Museum_of_Art_The_Metropolitan_Museum_Journal_v_11_1976> [accessed 14 October 2022].

Saba, M. 2022. *Impermanent Monuments, Lasting Legacies: The Dar al-Khilafa of Samarra and Palace Building in Early Abbasid Iraq*, Studies in Islamic Art and Archaeology, 3 (Wiesbaden: Reichert).

Sarre, F. 1925. *Die Keramik von Samarra*, Forschungen zur islamischen Kunst, 2 (Berlin: Reimer).

Schibille, N., A. Meek, M. T. Wypyski, J. Kröger, M. Rosser-Owen, and R. Wade Haddon. 2018. 'The Glass Walls of Samarra (Iraq), Ninth-Century Abbasid Glass Production and Imports', *PloS One*, 13.8: e0201749 <https://doi.org/10.1371/journal.pone.0201749>.

Schwartz, J. M. 2019. '"In the Archives, a Thousand Photos that Detail our Questions": Final Reflections on Photographs and Archives', in J. Bärnighausen, C. Caraffa, S. Klamm, F. Schneider, and P. Wodtke (eds), *Photo-Objects: On the Materiality of Photographs and Photo Archives* (Berlin: Max-Planck-Gesellschaft zur Förderung der Wissenschaften), pp. 311–20 <https://doi.org/10.34663/9783945561409-00>.

Szostak, D. 2020. *Guide to the Ernst Herzfeld Papers in the Department of Ancient Near Eastern Art, Metropolitan Museum of Art: Finding Aid Prepared by Daira Szostak Based on the Work of Matthew Saba and Rebecca Lindsey in the Department of Islamic Art, Adapted from the 1974 Catalogue Compiled by Margaret Cool Root* (New York: Metropolitan Museum of Art) <https://libmma.contentdm.oclc.org/digital/collection/p16028coll11/id/9846/> [accessed 21 October 2022].

Terzi, A. 2014. 'Samarra Excavations in Ottoman Bureaucracy', in J. Gonnella, S. Struth, and R. Abdellatif (eds), *Beiträge zur Islamische Kunst und Archäologie*, IV (Wiesbaden: Reichert), pp. 10–15.

Tütüncü Çağlar, F. 2017. 'From Raqqa with Love: The Raqqa Excavations by the Ottoman Imperial Museum (1905–06 and 1908)' (unpublished doctoral thesis, University of Victoria) <https://dspace.library.uvic.ca/handle/1828/7803> [accessed 21 October 2022].

Upton, J. M. 1978. *Catalogue of the Herzfeld Archive* (Washington, DC: Freer Gallery of Art).

15. Analogue Problems through a Digital Lens: Reconsidering Underlying Issues with Archaeological Archival Practice Using the Digitization of the Samarra Archives

Rhiannon Garth Jones
Centre for Urban Network Evolutions (UrbNet), Aarhus University
(rhiannon.garthjones@cas.au.dk)

Introduction

Digitization of archaeological archives can appear to be an exciting and even inspirational opportunity to address multiple long-standing concerns of archaeological archives, as so many of the contributions here highlight. Such concerns include opening up new sources of information for researchers, increasing and improving access (including for the public), reconsidering what and who archives are for, as well as responding to a curation crisis of rapidly increasing archives without the physical space or personnel to best manage them.[1]

However, greater use of digitization faces obstacles that are familiar concerns to traditional archaeologists and archivists, frequently because digitization is not, in fact, a solution to those problems. The practicalities of expertise, funding, manpower, and storage in archives remain, as do the difficulties of data management, both practical and theoretical. Archive archaeologists must still address: 'What is worth saving? What is worth saving in its original form?'[2] And the way archives can silence, such as by privileging one perspective,[3] frequently remain because the underlying causes have not been addressed. Ethical issues around the use of indigenous materials are not necessarily solved by digitized archives nor, as I shall discuss, does digitization of collections necessarily resolve debates around repatriation.

Here, I work from the argument that a digital archival practice that is grounded in analogue archival practice will replicate and frequently magnify both the strengths and weaknesses of that practice.[4] However, I argue that viewing the problems of archival methods through the magnifying glass of digitization can help us better understand and address those issues across our whole practice — so the very problems of digitization have the potential to transform archives in a different way than is commonly envisioned. In particular, I believe, the way digitized archives make underlying issues visible on a greater scale might help us reconsider 'what or who are archives for?' The results of that reconsideration could then inform discussions on best practice for the digitization of archaeological archives going forward.

Case Studies and Background

I use this magnifying glass approach on two case studies. Firstly, the recently digitized archives of Samarra at the Museum für Islamische Kunst in Berlin and that institution's work on 3D documenting part of the archives. And, secondly, archaeological data management systems and the possibility of expanding them into systems suitable for big data trend spotting, applying current commercial best practice to this type of project. Both of these are deliberately high-profile opportunities of digitized archives, in order to push the 'magnifying' approach and allow for the clearest view of the underlying issues and thus some learnings for future best practice.

The Samarra archives contain the material and written records of one of the most important sites of Islamic art history and archaeology. The archives are essential to my own research, and I have been working with them both in person and online as part of my PhD project. I will discuss the potential of digitizing these archives, the problems these types of digital archives highlight, and how a better understanding of these problems can inform our everyday practice and point us towards other possible solutions.

3D documentation of cultural heritage is a practice that receives a lot of attention, and many institutions are increasingly making 3D images available as part of open access initiatives. For example, the Smithsonian Institution and twenty-five other museums and cultural

---

[1] Bauer-Clapp and Kirakosian 2017, 221.
[2] Bauer-Clapp and Kirakosian 2017, 221.
[3] Christen 2018, 404.
[4] See, for example, Evans, McKemmish, and Rolan 2017, 10; Christen 2018, 404.

organizations have made more than 1600 3D images available as part of open access initiatives on Sketchfab, the main online repository of 3D images and models.[5] However, the practice remains rare. In fact, only outstanding artefacts are usually recorded for 3D digital simulations because of the complex workflows required for deriving datasets.[6] The process is lengthy, often requires locational expertise, and demands powerful, expensive technology.

The applied methodology of digitizing a cultural heritage site can vary significantly — it is not just dependent on the research questions at hand but the spatial scales involved, the type of objects being recorded, and the technical equipment and expertise available or required. For example, different items require different data acquisition processes. 3D scanners, photogrammetry, and multispectral imaging all have different strengths and weaknesses depending on the items in question and the resolution, accuracy, and range required. What works well for one item, such as a stucco panel, may work poorly on another within the same collection, such as a glass fragment. Often, there is a certain amount of manual input required in the data acquisition process, even where the technology can mostly be automated. Likewise, post-processing of the images usually requires a certain amount of manual input for optimum results.[7]

Case Study 1: 3D Digitization in Samarra through MOSYS-3D

Samarra as a Site

Samarra was the first systematic excavation on Islamic ruins and remains one of the richest archaeological sites in the ancient world, stretching over 57 km². The first excavations were carried out by archaeologist Ernst Herzfeld in 1911 and 1912–1913; at the end of which, Herzfeld had recorded 1161 finds, including ceramics, glass, wall painting, stucco, and other media.[8] Some of his finds were shipped to Berlin and a smaller portion to Istanbul, but the largest portion remained in Samarra during World War I. After the war, the material and its documentation were split up and distributed to museum collections worldwide, including the Museum für Islamische Kunst in Berlin, the Louvre Museum in Paris, the V&A in London, and the Freer Gallery of Art and Arthur M. Sackler Gallery Archives at the Smithsonian Institution, in Washington, DC. This creates a familiar problem for students of the site — a thorough understanding of the excavated remains requires travel to multiple locations, access to multiple institutions, and induction into multiple different archival practices.[9]

There are other issues. Funding and time concerns during the excavation meant that there were problems, for example, with limited recording of the site in the field compared with other explorations by Herzfeld or his peers, and much of what he saw *in situ* is now damaged. This has led to a situation where later research on Samarra has often been done on the basis of Herzfeld's accounts and sketches. For instance, Herzfeld's skill as a draughtsman means his paintings have often been republished and used for analysis of the so-called 'Samarra style', despite some important differences between his paintings and the original materials.[10]

Increased digitization of the main archives of Samarra would allow researchers and the public access to all the original materials, making it possible to see a more exhaustive picture of the remains without having to travel. This would reduce inequalities of economic access as well as environmental impact. Moreover, it would open up the possibility of a combined archaeological database of the different collections that could enable much more detailed and comprehensive analysis. It should be noted, as I will return to, that a lack of data standardization in physical records, which follow from different methodologies of either the original excavations teams or later archivists and curators, will always make it difficult to usefully unify different archives even with institutional interest and funding.

However, many of the archives containing Herzfeld's material have recently been, or are currently being, digitized, which gives me the opportunity to explore some theoretical concerns of archival digitization. In 2013, the British Institute for the Study of Iraq (BISI) funded an effort to digitize the V&A's collection. A similar project was undertaken at the Freer-Sackler Gallery (Washington, DC).

---

[5] <https://sketchfab.com/Smithsonian> and <https://sketchfab.com/smkmuseum> [both accessed 1 November 2022].

[6] Kai-Browne and others 2016, 397.

[7] Kai-Browne and others 2016, 399.

[8] Kadoi 2014, 28.

[9] For a more detailed discussion of this issue, as well as the process of digitizing the archives of the campaigns in Samarra, please see Miriam Kühn's contribution to this volume. See also Gonella 2014, 7.

[10] Hoffman 2008, 114.

MOSYS-3D Project

The Museum für Islamische Kunst in Berlin (SMK), which has a large number of Samarra remains, systematically documented much of their collection for the first time in 2012, with more work in 2021. That work is available online and is further explored within the permanent exhibition of the Museum of Islamic Art at the Pergamon Museum, part of the SMK. The museum has also used this digitization work to explore the creation of 3D digital replicas and simulations of much of the archaeological site to provide a foundation for subsequent scientific investigations and give scholars a range of approaches to help contextualize museum objects virtually, such as placing individual objects in a three-dimensional reference space to demonstrate their original context.

From February 2013 to September 2015, the interdisciplinary research project 'MOSYS-3D' (Mobile, Modular System for Highly Accurate 3D Documentation of Cultural Heritage) between the University of Applied Sciences Berlin and SMK investigated different aspects of the process of 3D documentation and simulation, 'ranging from the efficient acquisition of 3D data, automating pre- and post-processing steps and finding new ways for visualizing these datasets for knowledge transfer and scientific research questions'[11] to simplify the workflow. The aim was to collect and analyse historic photographs, excavation plans, and Herzfeld's field notes to enable the exact localization of digitized stucco panels within individual rooms of different buildings, with the archaeological excavation plans of Herzfeld forming the groundwork for the complete 3D reconstruction of certain buildings.

This project demonstrated how the applied methodology of digitizing a cultural heritage site can vary so significantly and the difficulties involved even with technical and specific archival expertise involved. The stucco decoration in SMK's Samarra collection required different methods than the excavation plans, for example. A robotic arm to automatically position single 3D scans was less efficient than hoped because of a number of factors, including the limited space and lighting of the location of the objects as well as software and technical stumbling blocks. Both the manual input required in the data acquisition process and the post-process of images remained an issue, although MOSYS-3D were able to further automate part of both processes.

MOSYS-3D made important progress in the next stage of processing, which is usually one of the most difficult as enormous file sizes have to be significantly reduced while maintaining the very high degree of detail required. This is hugely time consuming, requires intensive manual labour as well as powerful computers, and demands multiple individual pieces of software that do not interact with one another. The project developed a script to automate many of the processes and create a model in a standardized 3D data format appropriate for multiple end-uses, including simple web-based applications and a more impressive 3D visualization using a game-engine to provide the power and detail needed to tackle the previously identified research questions.

Overall, the project concluded that:

> Significant achievements could be made in the area of processing the 3D-data. The time necessary for the data reduction and preparation for the use within game-engines or web-based viewer was reduced drastically, while still retaining high accuracy and fine details, which can be captured by modern close-range scanners. The manual labor was reduced to a fraction of the time spent before. The developed workflow enables an easy way to automatically reduce hundreds of objects with hardly any manual interference.[12]

MOSYS-3D did not specify if the techniques they developed would be applicable across all the Samarra collections but, even if they were, to accomplish those results in an entirely different set of archives would require training in all these techniques and access to the technologies, as well as — very likely, the adaptation of those techniques to different archives with different particularized needs and opportunities. The expertise required could not reasonably be provided within current training opportunities, nor is the technology within most budgets. But specialized manpower would still be required, meaning projects could not simply be outsourced. This tension between resources and expertise might be resolved on bigger projects, like SMK's Samarra archive, but, of course, few archives have such options. Those same issues would apply to restoration and conservation opportunities, where access to and training in the relevant software and additive manufacturing technologies and techniques would be required.

---

[11] Kai-Browne and others 2016, 398.

[12] Kai-Browne and others 2016, 406. The paper itself contains a much more detailed explanation of the processes I have only summarized here, and I recommend it for anyone interested in the technical procedures.

The problem of resources in the analogue practice are not solved by digitization; they might even be made worse. 3D digitization of archives is an exciting tool for archivists and archaeologists — but it is still only a tool. The scale of its potential is likely to be determined by the resources and expertise of the user and their organization. Users might choose to focus their resources on partial 3D digitization of an archive, for example, to maximize their resources — and, in selecting some items over others, would silence parts of their collection. Those archives with more resources could develop further, inspiring others. But those without would be left further behind, unable to adapt those methods to their own collections. Moreover, archivists would also still be faced with concerns around publishing sensitive material at sites where looting is a concern.[13] Some Indigenous concerns around the appropriation of published materials they consider sacred would not necessarily be addressed.[14] In both these cases, in fact, it is easy to see how such problems could easily be exacerbated.

The contrast between paper files and 3D projections of images can seem stark, a juxtaposition of the past and the future. But traditional archival skills and expertise are still required in fully digitized archives because traditional archival problems remain, even with a non-traditional approach. Digitization and 3D documentation advance what archives can do, but they are not solutions to existing problems.

Discussion

3D and Repatriation

I have already demonstrated how digitization of archives magnifies existing issues, while heightening strengths. Next, I take that magnifying approach further and consider the particular role of an archaeological archive combined with the resources to 3D visualize that archive and physical collection.

One argument that is often made in favour of capturing artefacts in 3D is that it renders the discussion of whether museums, art galleries, or other collections should repatriate their cultural items obsolete, since they can both return them and keep a copy — the rather reductive, 'everyone is a winner!' argument. My position is that repatriation of items should be the default if and when places of origin ask for them. There are also concerns around digital colonialism that have been particularly highlighted with 3D replicas.[15] What I want to explore, however, is the role of archives within a 3D visualization of a collection for institutions and members of the public (rather than necessarily archaeologists, for whom, of course, working with a replica has very different considerations). There is a lot of complexity and variety in this discussion — different objects have differing values that might have changed over time, and that might change again, which inform the wider conversation. And there are a number of really interesting examples connected to this discussion. For instance, the Smithsonian Institution and the Tlingit community of south-east Alaska have collaborated on several initiatives to 3D digitize, preserve, and repatriate important cultural objects.[16]

An increasing number of museums globally are starting to use virtual reality as part of their exhibits, a trend that has risen over the past two years, as institutions looked to find new ways to improve access.[17] However, there are currently no virtual exhibitions that explicitly include access for the user to the digitized archive, which is my focus here. So I have used a hypothetical to continue magnifying the underlying issues. My hypothetical is this: What if the SMB created a large-scale 3D simulation that enabled visitors to visually immerse themself in the Samarra site, exploring building reconstructions based on the digitized archive, accessing original field notes from the digitized archive, and touching replica objects, and then transferred every item in its Samarra collection to the National Museum of Iraq? What would that mean for the museum experience? What would it tell us about repatriation? And what would it tell us about digitization of archives?

Many people would argue that a copy, no matter how perfect, cannot replicate the museum experience of the original, whether that is about the affective quality of the items or rather the premium that many museums have put on the authenticity of their objects and the way that

---

[13] For example, Palmyra, see Raja 2016.

[14] Christen 2018, 407; I should stress that indigenous concerns vary and a 'one size fits all' approach cannot be taken. The example here is specific to and inspired by the Blackfoot people, it would neither necessarily address other concerns of the Blackfoot people or other indigenous groups.

[15] For example, Kamash 2021.

[16] Hollinger and others 2013.

[17] One example is the Getty museum, seen here: <http://www.getty.edu/news/get-closer-to-ancient-mesopotamia-than-ever-before/> [accessed 23 September 2022].

translates to the perception of their audiences.[18] There is a lot of research on this that is outside the scope of this paper. But it is worth highlighting that there are many famous copies, and the V&A Museum in London is an excellent example of a collection initially famous in part for its copies.

I believe that a deeper understanding of an archaeological archive can offer a different, possibly greater experience than objects alone. A virtually immersive exhibition such as my hypothetical would, I suggest, change engagement with the archive as a whole, and it could change future curation of the archive to drive further engagement. For example, using Herzfeld's field notes in such a way and replicating his 'view' of the site could demonstrate how much our understanding of Samarra is permeated by his initial impressions and work, emphasizing the subjectivity of an archive to the audience while allowing them to engage with the process creating it.

Repatriation: Return or Reparation?

But that hypothetical combination of 3D technology, an excavation archive, and a former collection could combine to create an incredibly prestigious exhibition, in an already prestigious museum, whose prestigious reputation and the resources to create that exhibition were partly built on those now, hypothetically, repatriated items. Such an exhibition, I think, would entrench the power and resources imbalance that has existed from the moment of archive creation, even after the excavated items were no longer present.

For some, it might be that the ultimate end-goal of repatriation of cultural objects is simply their return, and so this hypothetical has nothing further to say. Moreover, of course, there are many different, complex factors at play within this issue; this paper only focuses on one aspect as it relates to this specific conversation around digitization of archives. However, I would argue that, for example, the National Museum of Iraq having the SMK's Samarra collection and the SMK having this hypothetical virtually immersive exhibition is not a satisfactory response to calls for repatriation but rather an example of where a so-called digital 'solution' entrenches the flaws of its analogue practice while it enhances its apparent strengths. This approach would, in fact, exemplify 'contemporary colonial technocracy in heritage politics'.[19] Increasingly, 3D technologies are a significant dimension of current archaeological practice, and those technologies are frequently, as currently constituted, 'merely the extension of the *coloniality of power and Being*'.[20] Repatriation that makes use of digital technologies in any way has to engage seriously with that scholarship, including (but not limited to) building greater capacity in local museums to take advantage of these technologies and adding the insights and interpretations of local museums to the digitized archives, to share their expertise more broadly and acknowledge the significance of multiple perspectives.[21]

Case Study 2: Trend Spotting

Data Management Systems

Another high-profile opportunity of archival digitization is archaeological data management systems and the possibility that they might allow 'big data trend spotting'. There are many excellent data management systems available that combine state-of-the art software with expertise from heritage professionals from around the world to not only create digital archives of resources but explore and establish relationships between those resources. Examples of these are the ARCHES open source software platform[22] or Linked Open Data projects like the Pelagios Network,[23] which links geographic data with cultural heritage data. Such databases often also allow data and metadata from multiple different field excavations to be stored, organized, and networked, allowing archaeologists from other projects and different locations to access the data.

However, these are not the same as a cross-project archaeological database or an archaeological data management system (ADMS) that allows 'big data' analysis, where archaeologists or other researchers could try to identify trends across time and space from vast quantities of data. The quantities of data available, the time and manpower saved, and the insights gleaned could generate significant results for both theoretical and field archaeologists. Data management systems with this level of functionality, however, are difficult to create and use even in fields where data collection standards and categories can be imposed.

---

[18] Fyfe 2006, 41.

[19] Stobiecka 2020.

[20] Stingl 2016, xvii, original emphasis.

[21] See, for example, Mickel 2020.

[22] <https://www.archesproject.org/> [accessed 23 September 2022].

[23] <https://pelagios.org/> [accessed 23 September 2022].

Any content management system requires high-quality data to be more than a storage system. To be effectively searchable by non-project users and, in an ideal world, to be able to run useful analysis on the data, it has to be standardized across different projects. It also has to be available from different locations. To be effectively usable for individual projects, it has to be customizable and, ideally, available offline locally. Data management systems in other fields have addressed issues of standardization (having the same categories available for each project) and normalization (the same method of entering data into those categories to ensure consistency — a very simple example would be measurements in metric rather than imperial) by creating a central database that 'reads', uploads, and 'corrects' or 'normalizes' individual project data within the central database to make it searchable. Flexibility can be introduced with multiple tags[24] to allow for different categorization approaches within a search function (particularly relevant to archaeological datasets), and analysis is made possible by algorithms built to identify similarities across tags, allowing data from whole projects or subsets of projects to be identified and pulled into a new dataset for the user. Natural Language Processing can be used to allow for users to work in their preferred language.

Such data management systems can, therefore, be built. Personalized online marketing systems are based on sophisticated versions of these data management systems, with algorithms that enable incredibly nuanced targeted advertising (albeit not always accurately). Such systems, however, rely on vast raw datasets initially being made available to them by users online, whether, for example, that is personal information about individuals on social media platforms or online websites. This is a very different data acquisition and collection process than digitized archives, where information is not volunteered and inputted by the subject. Moreover, categories in such datasets are determined by the requirements of the end-user. Both of these present problems for building an ADMS inspired by the outputs of such data management systems, beyond the other very practical issues of cost, resources, technical expertise, time, etc.

Archaeologists might theoretically agree on 'what might be called methodological meta-standards'[25] but the practicalities of fieldwork make any kind of standardization difficult, across both geography and time. For instance, a Palaeolithic site in France is very different than a nineteenth-century farmstead in Nova Scotia.[26] One site team might record every individual potsherd, while another only records diagnosable sherds; one site team might sieve the earth, while another site does not, with implications for bone counts. Archaeology is a highly nationalized discipline, and practice differs within a small geographical area — for example, from France to Germany to Italy. The resources that excavation teams have access to vary widely, with consequences for excavation approaches and recording methods. What constitutes a meaningful category or description changes over time, and archived notes do not always have clear explanations. Aside from the cost of creation, an ADMS that allowed for such complexity would likely have serious hosting and accessibility issues — even if such complexity could be achieved.[27] Any reduction in complexity would limit the potential of the database accordingly.[28]

Drawing Conclusions from Data

The impact of algorithm bias on data has been much discussed elsewhere.[29] As a simple but illuminating example, I once checked the demographic information that Google had recorded on my behalf, interpreting my age and gender through my search history. Its algorithms had categorized me as a man aged forty-five–sixty. I was twenty-five at the time and I am a woman. The data it had collated from my search history did accurately reflect my interests, but the algorithm that analysed them was incorrect in the conclusions it drew from that data.

This example highlights a few crucial issues: (1) data is not 'neutral', it can replicate biases (for example, science, sports, and guitar music do not indicate age or gender); (2) data analysis struggles to account for silences in the data[30] (for instance, those are not my only interests, I have many more); (3) our end goals determine our categories, with implications for data reuse.

The example demonstrates flaws in categorization that are inherent in most commercial database management systems that partially inspire attempts to create

---

24 One aspect of the potentials of 'tagging' within online archaeological databases is explored in Boast and Biehl 2011.

25 Watrall 2011, 171.

26 Watrall 2011, 171–72.

27 Pajas and Olivam 2009, 191.

28 For further discussion on standardization in digitized datasets, see Hirst, White, and Smith 2018.

29 For example, with reference to racial bias, see Noble 2018; for the impact on Google Scholar see Jacsó 2005.

30 Huggett 2020.

archaeological big data projects. Commercially, they are insignificant to the overall outcomes. When applied to an archaeological database management system, however, such flaws have considerably greater significance for meaning and interpretation. Moreover, those problems will only be amplified the further the original data goes from its original archivist or in any attempt at a multiple user archaeological data management system for big data analysis.

These concerns are also significant because of the ways Google is increasingly important for research scholars. Tools such as Google Dataset Search and Google Scholar are integral for many. Although Google has made commitments to open source data in these projects,[31]

> The search results will be subject to the definitions and expectations of the guidelines, which, although released and open for feedback from the developers, are controlled not by a group of peer scholars but a group of researchers working for profit.[32]

While those structures are built on open source data, they are still susceptible to the biases and algorithmic challenges that have been highlighted in the Google Search engine.[33]

Archaeologists and archivists are better placed than most to appreciate how the creation of categories to organize data can flatten context, nuance, and gaps in information.[34] But data standardization and normalization to make functional, searchable, and analysable datasets replicate this problem on a truly enormous scale, across quantities of data that make it incredibly challenging to revisit the original material to check the assumptions and interpretations involved. Again, the expertise and resources required would be beyond most institutions, exacerbating existing inequalities.

I am not suggesting that large-scale data analysis is impossible, but rather that we have to be extremely cautious in using any conclusions that are drawn from this type of work. The resources required to make a truly functional, analysable archaeological data management system are significant. For any analysis generated to be reliable, it is likely that a team of researchers would then have to go back through those results to reintroduce nuance of meaning and check for any incorrectly imposed categories in the standardization process, adding another layer of resources required. Introducing greater flexibility of meaning through 'tagging' would allow for much more nuance, although introducing too much flexibility might render meaningful analysis impossible, with any single search returning a relatively large proportion of the dataset as a result. To do this well is possible, but it is not necessarily practical or the best use of resources.

What about my earlier suggestion of a smaller combined digital collection of the various Samarra archives? Even with every archive of the site in existence, we would still be talking about a very small data management system compared with the vast systems that would allow big data analysis. But this is an example where tagging would allow for differences of practice without reducing meaning, because there is a shared, specialized context that all contributors are working within. Its specialization would be its strength, rather than its vast scope. Individual researchers or small teams would be able to use such a collection meaningfully. It could also open up access in a different way, bringing in a diverse range of contributors, because 'tagging' like this is a widely understood practice from social media. Indeed, this method is already being experimented with in some digital heritage collections.

Discussion

Standardization or Multiplicity of Meaning?

I argue that we need to consider how far greater standardization of data is a useful goal. Practice differs for a reason and an enforced standardization of data collection is likely to impose the type of bias I demonstrated earlier but on a grander scale.

'Tagging' might not be the difference in making a large dataset analysable, but it could have a significant impact on the way we consider, use, and show categories, especially when digitizing archives. Using tags could allow for fidelity to the original recording approach in the paper archive while also acknowledging the limitations of that approach in the digital archive. It would update understandings — and allow for future updates to those understandings. It would acknowledge that many items can and do have multiple uses over time and space and that there are differing perspectives on meaning.[35] It would make archives more searchable for expert

---

31 Burgess and Noy 2018.
32 Canino 2019, 4.
33 Noble 2018.
34 Christen 2018, 404.

35 Hodder and Hutson 2003, 3.

and non-expert users alike, shifting from available to accessible archives. It could also support efforts to convey the complexity of archaeological research to non-experts, in public reporting and understanding.

Compared with the grand vision of running data analysis on huge sets of cross-project archaeological datasets, 'tagging' might initially seem rather small as a 'solution'. But thinking about how tagging can introduce flexibility into digitization of archives opens up important possibilities for data management, for researchers themselves, and for public communication and use of digitized archives.

Conclusion

In both of these examples, I have tried to show that while digitization of archives presents some exciting opportunities, it also replicates and reinforces problems of the paper archives. But identifying the continuation of those problems allows us to better understand the origins of those problems and possible responses or alternatives.

Creating an immersive 3D archive and collection has huge potential value for preservation and research, as well as conveying the subjectivity of archives, but, in many cases, it might also entrench existing power imbalances. Recognizing that allows us to think more deeply about the purpose of repatriation, as well as museum and archive experiences.

Flattening the nuance, ignoring the silences, and imposing assumptions on large datasets reminds us that data is not neutral and questions the value of standardizing meanings and creating fixed categories, and how we can convey that to a wider audience.

In both cases, examining these problems through the magnifying lens of digitization allows us to reassess our goals and reconsider 'what or who are archives for?' Do we want them to be accessible to multiple audiences? If so, how do we balance those different audiences and their respective priorities? A 3D replica of an object has different possibilities and problems for an archaeologist than an interested member of the public, for example. But an immersive 3D exhibition that combines the paper archives and replica objects of a collection with the expertise built up from curation of those archives seems likely to educate and engage a public audience better than a traditional exhibition, or an exhibition of 3D replicas only. How does that influence the decisions of institutions?

Lastly, if public engagement is a goal for archivists, digitization immediately reduces obvious physical barriers to access, which is important. But, as we have discussed, availability is not accessibility. If an archive cannot be understood in its current form, or could be easily misunderstood, how does that inform the way we digitize it to remove other barriers to access? And who do we listen to and include when considering how to make our archives better understood? Who is an 'expert' in this instance? And how does reconsidering expertise in this instance inform the way we use and study archives as researchers?

That is a lot of questions and I suspect we will have many different answers if we applied them to our own research interests. However, I hope that I have demonstrated that considering digitization of archives as a magnifying glass can be a valuable process in itself to help us recognize and articulate problems in a way that can be constructive in improving our archival practice — as well as some suggestions for doing that, in small and large ways.

Works Cited

Bauer-Clapp, H. and K. Kirakosian. 2017. 'Archaeologists and Archives: Revisiting an Old Challenge', *Advances in Archaeological Practice*, 5.3: 220–26.

Boast, R. and P. Biehl. 2011. 'Archaeological Knowledge Production and Dissemination in the Digital Age', in E. C. Kansa, S. Whitcher Kansa, and E. Watrall (eds), *Archaeology 2.0: New Approaches to Communication and Collaboration* (Los Angeles: Cotsen Institute Press), pp. 119–56.

Burgess, M. and N. Noy. 2018. 'Building Google Dataset Search and Fostering an Open Data Ecosystem', web log message retrieved from Google AI Blog <https://ai.googleblog.com/2018/09/building-google-dataset-search-and.html> [accessed 22 September 2022].

Canino, A. 2019. 'Deconstructing Google Dataset Search', *Public Services Quarterly*, 15.3: 248–55.

Christen, K. 2018. 'Relationships Not Records: Digital Heritage and the Ethics of Sharing Indigenous Knowledge Online', in J. Sayers (ed.), *Routledge Companion to Media Studies and Digital Humanities* (Routledge: Taylor and Francis), pp. 403–12.

Evans, J. E., S. M. McKemmish, and G. Rolan. 2017. 'Critical Approaches to Archiving and Recordkeeping in the Continuum', *Journal of Critical Library and Information Studies*, 1.2: 1–38.

Fyfe, G. 2006. 'Sociology and the Social Aspects of Museums', in S. Macdonald (ed.), *A Companion to Museum Studies* (Malden: Blackwell), pp. 33–49.

Gonella, J. 2014. 'Studying Samarra Today', in J. Gonnella, S. Struth, and R. Abdellatif (eds), *Beiträge zur Islamische Kunst und Archäologie*, IV (Wiesbaden: Reichert), pp. 7–9.

Hirst, C. S., S. White, and S. E. Smith. 2018. 'Standardisation In 3D Geometric Morphometrics: Ethics, Ownership, and Methods', *Archaeologies*, 14.2: 272–98.

Hodder, I. and S. Hutson. 2003. *Reading the Past: Current Approaches to Interpretation in Archaeology*, 3rd edn (Cambridge: Cambridge University Press).

Hoffman, E. R. 2008. 'Between East and West: The Wall Paintings of Samarra and the Construction of Abbasid Princely Culture', *Muqarnas: An Annual on the Visual Culture of the Islamic World*, 25: 107–32.

Hollinger, R. E., H. Jacobs, L. Moran-Collins, C. Thome, J. Zastrow, A. Metallo, G. Waibel, and V. Rossi. 2013. 'Tlingit-Smithsonian Collaborations with 3D Digitization of Cultural Objects', *Museum Anthropology Review*, 7.1–2: 201–53.

Huggett, J. 2020. 'Capturing the Silences in Digital Archaeological Knowledge', *Information*, 11.5: 278.

Jacsó, P. 2005. 'Google Scholar: The Pros and the Cons', *Online Information Review*, 29.2: 208–14.

Kadoi, Y. 2014. 'The Samarra Finds in the New World: Fragments of 'Abbasid Artistic Legacy in North American Museums', in J. Gonnella, S. Struth, and R. Abdellatif (eds), *Beiträge zur Islamische Kunst und Archäologie*, IV (Wiesbaden: Reichert), pp. 28–37.

Kai-Browne A., K. Kohlmeyer, J. Gonnella, T. Bremer, S. Brandhorst, F. Balda, S. Plesch, and D. Lehmann. 2016. '3D Acquisition, Processing and Visualization of Archaeological Artifacts', in M. Ioannides, E. Fink, A. Moropoulou, M. Hagedorn-Saupe, A. Fresa, G. Liestøl, V. Rajcic, and P. Grussenmeyer (eds), *Digital Heritage: Progress in Cultural Heritage; Documentation, Preservation, and Protection; 6th International Conference, EuroMed 2016, Nicosia, Cyprus, October 31 – November 5, 2016; Proceedings*, I, Lecture Notes in Computer Science, 10058 (Cham: Springer), pp. 397–408.

Kamash, Z. 2021. 'Rebalancing Roman Archaeology: From Disciplinary Inertia to Decolonial and Inclusive Action', *Theoretical Roman Archaeology Journal*, 4.1: 1–41.

Mickel, A. 2020. 'The Proximity of Communities to the Expanse of Big Data', *Journal of Field Archaeology*, 45 (suppl): 51–60.

Noble, S. U. 2018. *Algorithms of Oppression: How Search Engines Reinforce Racism* (New York: New York University Press).

Pajas, J. A. and A. S. Olivam. 2009. 'Assessment, Dissemination and Standardization of Geometric Data Recording of Archaeological Heritage Obtained from 3D Laser Scanning', *Virtual Respect*, 4: 187–93.

Raja, R. 2016. 'The History and Current Situation of World Heritage Sites in Syria: The Case of Palmyra', in K. Almqvist and L. Belfrage (eds), *Cultural Heritage at Risk* (Stockholm: Axel and Margaret Ax:son Johnson Foundation), pp. 27–47.

Stingl, A. 2016. *The Digital Coloniality of Power: Epistemic Disobedience in the Social Sciences and the Legitimacy of the Digital Age* (Lanham: Lexington).

Stobiecka, M. 2020. 'Archaeological Heritage in the Age of Digital Colonialism', *Archaeological Dialogues*, 27: 113–25.

Watrall, E. 2011. 'iAKS: A Web 2.0 Archaeological Knowledge Management System', in E. C. Kansa, S. Whitcher Kansa, and E. Watrall (eds), *Archaeology 2.0: New Approaches to Communication and Collaboration* (Los Angeles: Cotsen Institute Press), pp. 171–84.

16. Digital Data and Recontextualization: The Case of South Italian Pottery

Vinnie Nørskov

Museum of Ancient Art, Aarhus University (klavn@cas.au.dk)

Marie Hélène van de Ven

School of Culture and Society — Department of History and Classical Studies, Aarhus University (m.h.vandeven@cas.au.dk)

Introduction

This contribution stems from our work with archaeological material influenced by large-scale looting in the southern part of Italy in the second half of the twentieth century: South Italian red-figure pottery.[1] The project investigates different methodologies to recontextualize objects that have lost their archaeological provenance because they have been illegally excavated and exported from their country of origin into the international art market. Our case study is a group of fragments of Apulian red-figure pottery discovered in the art dealer Robin Symes's warehouse in Geneva in 2014.[2]

Evidence from the warehouse points to the material being looted, partly restored, and deposited in the warehouse in the late 1980s/early 1990s as the objects were wrapped in newspapers from this period.[3] How the objects came to the warehouse, from where, and through which channels are less clear from the material at hand. The question we want to pursue in this paper is how digital archives can facilitate the recontextualization of such orphaned objects and reconnect them to possible find contexts in Apulia, where we suspect the material was looted in the 1980s. In the paper, we investigate digitization in the area of South Italian red-figure pottery to identify possible tools in this process.

The Case of South Italian Pottery: A Research History Framework Informing Digital Archives

Archives reflect the ontology and paradigms of former and current research traditions. The research field of South Italian red-figure pottery has developed immensely in the last ten to fifteen years but is still profoundly influenced by the tradition of connoisseurship.[4] Scholarship in the field has a long trajectory, as figure-decorated pottery from the region has been found and collected in Italy ever since the Renaissance, and it spread to other parts of Europe in the late eighteenth century through the activities of Sir William Hamilton, who sold the first major collection outside of Italy to the British Museum in 1772.[5] The art-historical and antiquarian approach of the early research focused on the vases as carriers of images. First, an interest in the symbolic meanings of the images was in focus, and then — inspired by the research in Attic black- and red-figure pottery — studies moved to the production of the vases looking specifically to identify workshops and painters' hands.[6] This has had a profound influence on the categorization and publications during the twentieth century, culminating with the publication of the volumes by Arthur D. Trendall and Alexander Cambitoglou between 1936–1982, where South Italian figure-decorated pottery was organized stylistically in geographical regions and individual styles using the method of connoisseurship, developed on Attic vase painting by John D. Beazley.[7] The research on

---

[1] The project Illicit Antiquities in the Museum is financed by the Independent Research Fund Denmark 2020–2023. The loan of the materials from Robin Symes's warehouse has been possible through the cooperation with the Ny Carlsberg Glyptotek in Copenhagen, Denmark and the Ministry of Culture in Italy. We are grateful to the Ny Carlsberg Glyptotek and Italian authorities for this possibility and to Jan Kindberg Jacobsen for his engagement in facilitating our project. We are also grateful to the Carlsberg Foundation for supporting 3D scanning of several vases from the material corpus.

[2] Tsirogiannis 2016.

[3] Agnoli and others 2019; Nørskov 2022.

[4] Carpenter, Lynch, and Robinson 2014; Kästner and Schmidt 2018.

[5] For collections in Italy, see Masci 2014. For Hamilton, see Jenkins and Sloan 1996; Masci 2007.

[6] Carpenter 2009.

[7] Trendall 1936 (Paestan); Trendall 1967–1983 (Lucanian, Campanian, and Sicilian); Trendall and Cambitoglou 1978–1982;

the workshops has produced a complex chronological network of workshops covering a period of *c.* 150 years that is still used today as the main classification tool and has become the primary tool in geographical studies on production and use as about 80 per cent of the known corpus of vases lack a proper archaeological provenance. The approach has been criticized as it treats archaeological objects as works of art. Still, it is an effective categorization method involving clay, production, shape, decoration, and iconography analyses.[8]

The development of archaeology in the second half of the twentieth century has moved away from objects to contexts, from production to consumption, requiring a much firmer theoretical and contextual archaeological approach. This has, however, had little impact on the archaeology of southern Italy until the twenty-first century. There has been intensive research into the Iron Age and the question of cultural encounters, 'colonialism', and the questions of identities. Still, only in the last twenty to thirty years has the role of figures painted on pottery in the context of the different villages of the indigenous population received more interest.[9] Studies such as Daniel Gräpler's and Andreas Hoffman's investigations on rituals and burials in Taranto based on material excavated and documented have contributed to a much deeper understanding of the local social interactions around these vases. Still, they simultaneously illustrate the central problem with the lack of archaeological information and research to find the context of the figure-decorated pottery.[10] These studies were working with extensive empirical data material gathered in databases using data analysis tools. These databases are, however, not made publicly accessible. Like in so much archaeology, the huge work on assembling the empirical data for this specific analysis is not accessible to anyone other than the author and those who might be close to him.

The 2012 three-volume publication *La ceramica a figure rosse della Magna Grecia e della Sicilia* edited by Luigi Todisco impressively collects the present research situation treating technical, quantitative, chronological, iconographic, and iconological aspects that have been a part of the research for a long time. Moreover, factors such as provenance, archaeological and historical context, international trade, and collecting have been added.[11] In 2018, Edward Herring published a quantitative study based on Trendall's catalogues, identifying patterns to better understand the use of choices of potters, painters, and their clientele. However, this type of research is still based on the objects as a corpus and less on archaeological context.

Digitization and Databases on South Italian Red-Figure Pottery

Digital tools have made their way into current research on South Italian red-figured pottery in the last twenty to twenty-five years in the form of digital databases, catalogues, excavation registration, online archives for GIS applications to create landscape surveys and 3D analyses, and dissemination. In the following, digital archives or tools relevant for research into South Italian pottery are presented in three different categories:

1. Archaeological data covering excavation registrations used in fieldwork. These often show more widespread and connected information. However, the reports published online are often quite general and do not usually show detailed information such as a catalogue of specific objects.

2. Object data covering databases on single objects, for instance museum databases. These often have quite detailed descriptions of the object itself and corresponding literature, but they are not well connected across different databases. Moreover, entries in this type of database rarely cover the finding place of an object in a detailed manner.

3. Research data covering datasets that have been collected around a specific subject. These show a more detailed and encompassing view of a single object and can be connected to different types of databases.

Archaeological Data

Today much excavation data are born digitally, but this does not mean that the data are accessible. Publication of excavations, both in traditional excavation publications or online reports, is a long and sometimes deprioritized

---

1983; 1990–1991 (Apulian); Arias 1997; Williams 1996.

  [8] For example, Roscino 2018.
  [9] Saxkjær 2018.
  [10] Gräpler 1997; Hoffmann 2002.

  [11] The series consists of three volumes, the first one a catalogue of vases organized according to the attribution of painters' workshops; the second several informative papers on topics such as the cultural exchange between the indigenous inhabitants of Apulia and the Greeks, literary sources, history of scholarship, production of the vases, archaeological context, iconography, and more; and the third volume contains images and indices.

part of archaeology. Public archaeology — in Italy called *archeologia pubblica* — is a key element in the present policy on digitization in the Italian Ministry of Culture and a significant part of the current academic debate.[12] A reform of the Italian heritage sector in 2014 changed the structure of the organization, intending to further a better integration of culture and tourism, including goals for more open and accessible communication of research and other activities carried out by cultural institutions. However, it made the situation for archaeology more complex because museums and the archaeological authorities were separated. The role of the cultural ministry in archaeological research is essential in Italy, as it oversees all archaeological activity. Different actors create excavation data: preventive archaeology is mostly carried out by private companies whereas research excavations are carried out by universities and other institutions such as foreign schools, but data are stored in the archives of regional soprintendenze.[13] Scholars are generally able to access these archives through a written request, but access and a lack of a clear, tangible, and uniform policy somehow remain problematic. Due to laws on transparency passed in the last decade, cultural ministries have been obliged to publish their documents such as contracts, but archaeological information has been excluded from such rules. Therefore, there is a need for open access policies regarding the publishing of archaeological data and documentation.[14]

Since 2016, a central body established under the Ministry of Culture (MIBACT), the Central Institute for Archaeology, has had the task of defining guidelines and standards of archaeological data, including assessing the digital archives and open access.[15] One of their objectives is:

> effettua la ricognizione e la pubblicazione on line degli archive di dati archeologici anche in formato di open data, procedendo al recupero sistematico della documentationzione pregressa, anche in vista di un sistema unico nazionale di messa in rete dei risultati dell'archeologia preventiva, definendo in parallelo i termini dei diretti di pubblicazione.[16]

In this process, it has been recognized that there is a very diversified landscape of practices.[17] In an overview published by Calandra and others (2021), they concluded that repositories and databases for internal use are still the most widespread practice.

One of their larger projects is the 2017 National Geoportal for Archaeology (GNA).[18] The project aims to create an online platform for all kinds of material from archaeological projects under the Ministry of Culture as well as projects under the universities and other bodies — in short, to create one single access point for the archaeological heritage data in Italy and relating it to spatial data.[19]

For the GNA project, three areas were defined as 'pilot regions' in 2018: Piedmont, Tuscany, and Puglia. At this moment, many websites can be accessed through the web portal of the institute. There is a technical geoportal to show the geographical and cartographical information of Puglia, including datasets that can be used in GIS applications. Then, there is a charter of cultural heritage where the archaeological sites and other points of interest (such as museums) are displayed. As for the actual archaeological data, the GNA project has had some troubles in its implementation of uniform data entries for excavations and object databases. Archivers find it difficult to guarantee long-term sustainability and technical updating, which results in the data not always having been uploaded or being difficult to search through in a web browser. In addition, there is a high level of heterogeneity in how information is collected, organized, and published, which makes it difficult to compare different information sources.[20] This is primarily difficult for quantitative analyses, perhaps less so for qualitative analyses, of a specific site, for example. Due to these difficulties, the project has not yet been able to present a working version of the GNA in the pilot regions.

---

[12] Nucciotti, Bonacchi, and Molducci 2019.

[13] Boi, Marras, and Santagati 2015, 138; Calandra and others 2021.

[14] Boi, Marras, and Santagati 2015. Problems and topics of discussion: Which data and documents, held in superintendencies' archives, can be considered 'public data' and published as open access; who owns the intellectual property rights; who has the right — and the duty — to decide on the publication; which kind of licences should be used to allow for the reuse of data; how and who should guarantee for data quality; how and who should guarantee for the long-term preservation; who has to pay for the creation and the management of the platform?

[15] Calandra and Boi 2018; <http://www.ic_archeo.beniculturali.it/it/141/istituto> [assessed 6 July 2022].

[16] <http://www.ic_archeo.beniculturali.it/it/141/istituto> [assessed 6 July 2022].

[17] Calandra and others 2021.

[18] Geoportale Nazionale is an online archive of GIS maps; they also have maps of Italy roughly from 1988 to 1998: <http://www.pcn.minambiente.it/mattm/servizio-wms/> [assessed 6 July 2022].

[19] Ronzino, Acconcia, and Falcone 2018.

[20] Calandra and Boi 2018, 70.

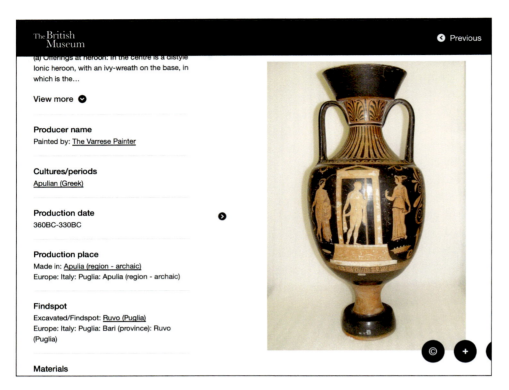

Figure 16.1. British Museum database: screenshot of database entry of an Apulian amphora by the Varrese Painter, British Museum, London, inv. no. 1856,1226.205.
© The Trustees of the British Museum <https://www.britishmuseum.org/collection/object/G_1856-1226-205> [accessed 7 February 2022].

Figure 16.2. Catalogue of the Italian cultural ministry: Catalogo generale dei Beni Culturali: screenshot of the database entry of an Apulian volute krater by the Arpi Painter, Museo Civico di Foggia, Foggia, inv. no. 132731, cat. no. 1600011775 <https://catalogo.beniculturali.it/detail/ArchaeologicalProperty/1600011775> [accessed 7 February 2022].

Figure 16.3. Apulian red-figure volute krater by the Arpi Painter, RVAp 28/92, Museo Civico di Foggia, Foggia, inv. no. 132731 (photo: Vinnie Nørskov).

It seems necessary that a uniform mode of communication of information will be established; otherwise, projects such as these (and the ARIADNE Plus database that we return to below), might solely be useful in big data analyses and will provide fewer opportunities for those interested in landscape archaeology and contextual analyses of a site or a class of objects. Moreover, uniformity here is a difficult goal due to the high level of heterogeneity in archaeological and historical data.

Calandra and her colleagues argue that the use of digital tools would facilitate the democratization of archaeological knowledge and information as an alternative to analogue archives that are usually only accessible to specialists.[21] It is important to note that one of the main aims is the 'creation of a minimum knowledge base about archaeological heritage'.[22] While a significant step forward, it is not yet enough to conduct detailed contextualized analyses that require detailed archaeological reporting, for which excavation catalogues, reports, and the elusive 'grey literature' is necessary.[23]

The aim is to integrate the GNA into the EU-funded ARIADNE Plus project that merges online archaeological databases in Europe. This project is an online data aggregator and network of digitized European archaeology. Here, researchers can search for sites, different periods, types of objects, and more. In the case of southern Italy, users are mainly redirected to the FASTI online website when interested in excavation reports. They include short summaries of excavations, which are not detailed regarding their findings. Relevant to our case, the looting that occurred at a specific site is sometimes included.[24] However, especially in the case of southern Italy, excavation reports and general information are sorely lacking and contain obvious errors.[25] There are, for example, through the ARIADNE Plus database no entries on an important site such as Arpi.

---

21 Calandra and others 2021.

22 Calandra and others 2021.

23 Gardin 1999, 63; Niccolucci 2020, 37. Grey literature refers to unpublished archaeological reports and catalogues of material found.

24 <https://www.fastionline.org/excavation/micro_view.php?fst_cd=AIAC_601&curcol=sea_cd-AIAC_5484> [assessed 6 July 2022].

25 <https://www.fastionline.org/excavation/micro_view.php?fst_cd=AIAC_4421&curcol=sea_cd-AIAC_9040> [assessed 6 July 2022]. Using the filters: Foggia and -600 to -300 reveal only one entry of an excavation conducted in 2015–2016, which only mentions two findings both from the Late Roman period.

Moreover, applications such as the ARIADNE Plus project and Fasti Online are aimed at big data archaeology and otherwise quantitative analyses. The archaeological reports currently available through an aggregator such as ARIADNE Plus are quite general and consist of perhaps half a page of a summary without details. In the case of discovering a specific context of an object, specialized, detailed, and meticulous research is required, as one is trying to ascertain how a certain object might fit within the archaeological landscape. To do that, a detailed understanding of an area is necessary, with a focus on not only location but a relatively short period of time as well (for example, the attribution method can often determine the decade an object was made). The problem, then, with archaeological aggregators such as these, in our case, is a high level of heterogeneity in its records, faulty information, its lack of detailed information, and difficult implementation.

Object Data: Museum and Private Collections

During the last thirty years, we have seen a growing presence of digital museum collections online, accompanied by theories on how digital knowledgescape changes collection practices.[26] Most larger museums are today presenting their entire collection through accessible databases, such as, for instance, the Louvre, the British Museum, and the Metropolitan Museum in New York, just to mention some collections with extensive collections of South Italian red-figure pottery. The data made accessible in these databases differ among the institutions that have published these online. However, looking for information about archaeological find contexts, these are often lacking — either because they are not known or because they are just referred to by a place name, for instance, an Apulian red-figure amphora by the Varrese Painter in the British Museum, bequeathed by Sir William Temple in 1856.[27] The database entry has a field called Findspot: Excavated/Findspot, and here the entry is Ruvo (Fig. 16.1). In general, this is the kind of provenance information found in museum databases.

In Italy, very few museums have made their collections accessible through online databases. A survey made in 2016 by the Italian National Institute of

---

26 See, for instance, Cameron and Robinson 2007.

27 The British Museum, London, inv. no. 1856,1226.205. Trendall and Cambitoglou 1978–1982, 338, no. 6. (RVAp 13/6). The catalogue from Henry Walters from 1896 just mentions 'from Ruvo', Walters 1896, 168 (F333).

Statistics revealed that about half of Italian museums did not even have a dedicated website.²⁸ Thus, digitization and accessibility of Italian collections are still in their infancy. However, at the beginning of the century, the Italian Ministry of Culture established a centralized catalogue for cultural heritage, Catalogo Generale dei Beni Culturale. This system is a centralized registration of all movable and immovable heritage sites and objects, thus an enormous task. On the homepage of the Ministry of Culture, this online catalogue is described as a databank that shows and organizes the information (or knowledge) of cultural heritage in Italy, the 'fruits of the research activities by different institutions on the territory'.²⁹

Some Italian museums have published an online catalogue on these websites. Museo Civico di Foggia is one of the museums that has several objects available here. This main museum for archaeology in the Daunian region does not have an independent homepage but is present here. There are 197 objects from the museum. The entries can be downloaded as PDF files, and you can also find digitization of the old catalogue cards (Fig. 16.2). The example here is an Apulian red-figure volute krater found in 1972 in a tomb in Arpi and attributed to the Arpi Painter (Fig. 16.3).³⁰ The find-spot information appears on the scanned registration card available under *documentazione allegata/scheda storica*, but not in the database.³¹

The general catalogue is and will be an excellent tool when more objects have been registered, especially when searching for specific vases. You need a high level of knowledge to properly work with this catalogue, and it is not easy to search for groups of objects through typologies, motifs, or other characteristics at the moment. It is also difficult to find material using non-professional terms; thus, the accessibility might not fulfil the aims of *archeologica pubblica* but provides scholars with access to data when working with questions of contextualization.

Research Data

This large group of data comprises all kinds of collections defined through specific research questions. Research data covers a wide range of different digital datasets, but they are all research-driven data, collected with specific questions in mind, meaning they are not always interoperable.³² For South Italian pottery, the largest is the Corpus Vasorum Antiquorum, a catalogue begun in the early twentieth century with the aim to publish all known Greek vases, including South Italian vases. The publication is partly digitized and available as a digital publication through the web portal from the University of Oxford. However, few collections of South Italian red-figure vases have been published here as this group of Greek pottery has had low priority among scholars, and it is not a database but 'just' a digital publication, like for instance the vase catalogues from the British Museum published in the second half of the nineteenth century.

The most developed database on painted pottery is the Beazley Archive built on the work of John Davidson Beazley on Attic black- and red-figure pottery but extended to south Italian red-figure by Arthur Dale Trendall. Trendall's archive from his many years of work is today located at La Trobe University in Melbourne. It holds forty thousand personal photographs of Arthur Trendall and is an invaluable source of information for those studying South Italian pottery, but plans related to its online publication have unfortunately been much delayed.³³ The plan was to include it in the Beazley Archive that today features over ninety thousand vases, of which approximately 3400 are Apulian, 1972 Campanian, 1179 Gnathian, and 331 Lucanian. They are included because they have been published in the CVA and not as part of the Trendall archive — the digitization of which is still not realized. Approximately half of those included feature at least one image, and a fair amount have some details that make (tentative) attribution possible.³⁴

Another, quite different, type of pottery database is the Kerameikos database. The creators of this database

---

²⁸ Orlandi and others 2018, 80. <https://www.museonazionaledimatera.it/la-collezione-rizzon-online/comunicazioni/> [accessed 21 May 2022].

²⁹ <http://www.iccd.beniculturali.it/it/150/archivio-news/5165/> [assessed 8 July 2022]; <https://www.catalogo.beniculturali.it> [accessed 6 July 2022].

³⁰ Museo Civico di Foggia, Foggia, inv. no. 132731, cat. no. 1600011775; Trendall and Cambitoglou 1978–1982, 925, no. 92 (RVAp 28/92); <https://www.catalogo.beniculturali.it/detail/ArchaeologicalProperty/1600011775> [accessed 7 February 2022].

³¹ <http://www.sigecweb.beniculturali.it/images/fullsize/ICCD1039335/ICCD13416582_1600011775.PDF> [accessed 8 July 2022].

---

³² FAIR principles.

³³ Video transcript from 2012: <https://studylib.net/doc/15143429/the-legacy-of-arthur-dale-trendall-transcript> [assessed 6 July 2022].

³⁴ Gruber and Smith 2014.

have set up an online aggregator of information on pottery not based on 'textual strings', which are quite diverse due to the different languages used in open databases and even a lack of consistent vocabulary in the same language, but on HTTP URIs.[35] As such, it has allowed for a 'thesaurus of the simplest typologies to model' for pottery, in particular for the categories 'production place, person or organisation responsible for some aspect of production, shape, material, style, period, ware, and technique', as well as its dimensions and the collection it is currently in. This website also allows for visualization and analysis based on these categories, in the form of graphs and geographical locations (to a certain extent).[36] Its categories are still somewhat limited, and for further information one is directed to the database of the museum. The main focus on Greek pottery on this website is visible, as there are not many Apulian painters included in the database, and the area 'Apulia' is a square that just encompasses Foggia until Cerignola and already fails to include important areas such as Canosa di Puglia and Minervino Murge.

At the moment, seven museum collections from the US and UK have been included, providing only 114 objects when searching for Apulia. However, if more collections could be related, this method for automatic data aggregation will be helpful to solve some of the problems regarding the lack of heterogeneity, as it translates the relevant terms in different languages to the same in readable and connected entries. The technique used to aggregate data is useful for quantitative analyses. Aside from that, this program is already a near copy of the earlier project Nomisma.org, which uses a similar method to aggregate information on numismatic concepts. Therefore, it should be possible to apply this to South Italian pottery as well. This method will allow for automatic data aggregation leading to a more encompassing view of the South Italian pottery that can be found online, as it links to museum records directly.[37]

What is clear is that the form and records of these archives, and thus the information they provide, are determined by the dominant methodologies of a given discipline or speciality, and as such, these are focused on the attribution method.[38] Newer online projects have different agendas. The Feminicon project of the École française de Rome is focused on the iconographical aspect of studies into South Italian pottery, which in 2005 was about 28 per cent of the scholarly publications.[39] Feminicon aims to study gender identity in Greek iconography, with a focus on funerary archaeology, representations of women, the difference between the sexes, and the role of women through images.[40] Within this database, it is possible to search based on iconographical representations, from themes to specific objects such as torches. Another project is Agorha (Accès global et organisé aux ressources en histoire de l'art), a database of the Institut national d'historie de l'art in Paris focusing on the history of Greek pottery as registered in old publication and auction catalogues.[41] This specific part of the database has been shaped by the LASIMOS project, named after a vase that had an interesting collection history.[42] Archival research has allowed researchers to reconstruct the history of the object from its first mention in the seventeenth century. In 1688 the vase was in the collection of Giuseppe Valletta in Naples. In 1688 it was acquired by Francesco de' Ficoroni for the collection of Cardinal Filippo Antonio Gualtieri in Rome, and in 1730 by Pope Clemens XII for the Biblioteca Vaticana, where it was on display from 1734. In 1797 it was brought to Paris by Napoleon and has been in the Louvre in Paris since 1799. However, the documents that tell us this are not available in the database right now, but the collection history of the vase is added to the entry in text form. The database allows researchers to immediately access information on find-spots, collection history, conservation history, and their current location. Moreover, it provides links (often in the same Agorha database) to ancient documentation and the history of studies that the vase was included in.

It is clear that digital databases with South Italian red-figure pottery have developed in the last decades, but still there are relatively few collections accessible online. There are two obvious problems: first, there is a

---

35 Gruber and Smith 2014. URI is short for 'uniform resource identifier' and refers to a sequence of characters referring to an abstract or physical resource on the internet.

36 Gruber and Smith 2014.

37 <http://kerameikos.org/id/apulia> [assessed 6 July 2022].

38 Lippolis and Mazzei 2005. From 1956 to 2005, about 40 per cent of published research on Italic ceramics were presentations and stylistic analyses of objects in private and public collections without archaeological context. <https://books.openedition.org/pcjb/2799> [accessed 8 February 2022].

39 <https://www.efrome.it/feminicon> [accessed 8 July 2022]; Lippolis and Mazzei 2005.

40 <https://magnagrecia.huma-num.fr/s/feminicon/page/presentation> [accessed 8 February 2022].

41 Annoepel-Cabrignac 2011.

42 Denoyelle and Masci 2009.

clear lack of a unified vision of how databases on pottery should be formed and how all relevant information can be included; and secondly, there are no clear connections with archaeological data or grey literature. The different types of archives would be most well served if they could, in some way, be combined and anchored in some way, for example geographically. This is an option using geographical and archaeological information systems (GIS and AIS), which have been used in studying looting in Apulia and the management of sites that have been excavated over long periods, resulting in diverse archaeological reporting, partly resolving the problems that come with this type of heterogeneity found in these different datasets.

GIS Methodology and AIS: Involving the Ancient and Current Landscape

A recent development in archaeology has been GIS analyses using satellite imagery and aerial photography used to survey the archaeological landscape. In southern Italy, it has led to the discovery of important sites, such as the Daunian settlement Arpi, situated near modern-day Foggia, as well as the extent of the looting that has occurred in the local landscape.[43] A developing speciality in archaeology is that of remote sensing to monitor looting, which has mostly been used in areas where looting and other destruction are most rampant.[44] Specifically, imagery from Google Earth can help in the identification of looted areas as well, as can be seen in the case of Syria.[45] Here, it is necessary to be able to make a comparative and diachronic analysis of the imagery. Using similar techniques, GIS analyses using satellite imagery and aerial photography have been used to survey the extent of the looting that has occurred in the local landscape. Especially the work of Fabio Fabrizio and the GIS lab in Lecce has led to an extensive survey of illegal activities in the Puglian landscape.[46] However, this technique is not yet applicable to the period of the 1980s, when most of the looting of South Italian ceramics in Puglia occurred. Nonetheless, it might be possible to conduct comparative analyses, comparing photos from two different dates. Then, it becomes possible to gain a tentative overview of the looting that occurred at a certain location, which could be cross-referenced with information from excavations that might have taken note of the looting, if any exist.

An example of a GIS/AIS project based on different datasets, which consists of multiple layers of maps, is the Imago Project.[47] Here, research into the topography of Rome has been combined to construct a map of Rome with different layers, from its ancient roots to more modern cadastral maps, with information added by different scholars and institutions. However, a point of critique here is that the project lacks a unified vision of epistemological methods, and the needs of different users have not been taken into account.[48] Again, this example shows that there is a need for a cultural meta-system, that provides 'concrete [...] archaeological data and knowledge through different suitable digital interfaces' to which access is continuously guaranteed, and that is 'tailored on specific users requirements'.[49] Similar to the example of Kerameikos, this could be achieved by creating tags that can be easily used by people in their language, while still connecting the data. Open access should be granted to the corresponding object, documentation, and archaeological grey literature of a certain area. If different user interfaces can be constructed, for example, specialized in detailed archaeological reports and/or settlement development using (archaeological) maps, perhaps cross-referenced with a modern map of looting that occurred during the 1990s–2000s, a versatile and encompassing tool would become available to conduct complicated research into looting and which areas it has affected.

An aggregator that does something similar can be found on the American School of Classical Studies website, where all information on the site of Corinth can be found in one place.[50] Here, GIS maps have been uploaded, including many different types of archaeological information based on excavations, as well as archival information and even 3D models of structures found on the site. Archives of the excavations are available as well, even though some are not available online. Of course, without the benefit of having a site that has been excavated by one institution, in the case of South Italian pottery, institutional collaboration is necessary.

---

43 Guaitoli 2003.
44 Casana 2015, 151–52.
45 Casana and Panahipour 2014.
46 Fabrizio 2017.

47 Serlorenzi and others 2015.
48 Serlorenzi and others 2015, 8.
49 Serlorenzi and others 2015, 9.
50 <https://www.ascsa.edu.gr/excavations/ancient-corinth/digital-corinth> [accessed 8 February 2022]; <https://www.ascsa.edu.gr/excavations/ancient-corinth/collections-archives> [accessed 8 February 2022].

An existing open-source software tool that enables such collaboration is Arches. This tool integrates layers of information on people, materials, activities, historic events, objects, and iconography while anchored in a digital geographical map. Such maps facilitate discoveries of previously unknown connections, as they allow access to information related to all the aforementioned aspects. The Arches website presents the software platform as follows: 'Institutions that deploy Arches can create digital inventories that describe types, locations, extent, cultural periods, materials, and conditions of heritage resources and establish the numerous and complex relationships between those resources.'[51] This software is open source and could be applied to red-figure vases in Italy and the archaeological sites in which they were found as well as the collections they are a part of currently. One could select a broader area such as a site, connecting the relevant archaeological reports (perhaps spanning decades of different campaigns), including drawings and photographs, to specific areas within that site as well as material that has been found there.

3D Methodologies

There is significant potential in 3D technologies to further the conservation and dissemination of ancient pottery and provide tools to analyse pottery. Perhaps most importantly, it allows broader access to archaeological material worldwide without the need for (time-)expensive travel. For example, 3D reconstructions of archaeological artefacts can be shared and visualized. These reconstructed images are especially popular in museum exhibitions, for instance in the reconstruction of the Regolini Galassi tomb.[52] It allows museums to present archaeological material visually intact and in context as well as provide a closer look at a specific vase.[53] An example thereof is the Ipogeo della Medusa, part of a tomb found in Arpi, which had been ravaged by looters and was recontextualized thanks to the work of Marina Mazzei, a prominent archaeologist of the area, and the carabinieri.[54]

Similar to the example of reconstructed 3D analyses in museums, these can be used in research in the case of pottery allowing for 'non-intrusive, detailed visual examination of both the exterior and the interior of the object', which makes it a relevant alternative for researchers interested in the attribution method.[55] Besides that, it allows for the digital preservation of objects, and functions as a tool for the dissemination of information, similar to the application of 3D models in museums. These efforts are, as of yet, not well coordinated and difficult to locate. However, these could be added to the 3D models of the 3D reconstructed tombs, as shown earlier, to show the context of South Italian vases.

An example of 3D analyses used in research is the application of methods to reconstruct or reassemble broken artefacts, even if only a relatively small section of the fragments is available.[56] A Greek study, using a replica of an Apulian red-figured vase, shows the application of the Thickness profile method. A handmade replica was made of the vase, which was then smashed on purpose. Then after selecting part of the available material (primarily the medium and large sherds), the fragments could be levelled based on the inner horizontal traces that the potter left. Then, when the sherds are aligned, they can be photographed all around, consisting of about thirty images, so they could be converted to 3D images. After that, a vertical line is drawn on the 3D model of the sherd, so a thickness profile can be extracted. The thickness profiles of these sherds can then be compared by an algorithm, and that way, the sherds can be matched.[57] This has led to results in which these vases can be securely and non-intrusively reconstructed.

Conclusions

The challenges in the digitization of archaeology in southern Italy are manifold. One element is that many sites have been explored over a very long period, and the historical documentation and archaeological reports are diverse and sometimes inaccessible. Another is a complex history of illicit excavations, which has led to the loss of valuable archaeological contextual information leading to an object-centred research agenda. Moreover, there is a constant fear of guiding looters to sites of possible objects, meaning that low transparency is sometimes the more

---

51 <https://www.archesproject.org/wp-content/uploads/2019/09/Arches_Factsheet_August2019_eng.pdf> [accessed 8 February 2022].

52 Hupperetz and others 2013.

53 Tucci, Cini, and Nobile 2011.

54 Mazzei 1995; <https://www.youtube.com/watch?v=OsAPNCmL0Js&t=81s> [assessed 6 July 2022].

55 Acke and others 2021, 273.

56 Stamatopoulos and Anagnostopoulos 2018.

57 Stamatopoulos and Anagnostopoulos 2018.

prudent course of action. The main problems concerning (online) archaeological databases are a lack of uniform, systematic handling of data which leads to data deluge, inefficient databases, and the lack of openness and accessibility regarding grey literature necessary for thorough contextual analyses. Throughout the discussion of the available pottery databases, these challenges have led to a lack of uniformity and no unified vision, leading to a data deluge and limited access to material online, which might lead to miscommunications of research and inefficiency. Policies such as the FAIR data principles (Findable, Accessible, Interoperable, and Reusable) have helped push many researchers to publish their data online. Still, without a clear, uniform implementation guideline for archaeological data that considers its complex nature, the level of reusability is relatively low. Miscommunication can quickly occur.[58] A similar problem can be found when studying online databases that are primarily about or include South Italian pottery. As such, there are many points of information on the internet in different types of databases dealing with the same objects. This is not necessarily an issue as these types of information could supplement each other, allowing for a more encompassing understanding of an object. The problem is that these different databases do not always communicate, meaning gathering all available information on a single object or site is difficult. The solution to this problem would then be to create a clear overview of all relevant databases, using a single entry point.

A specialized online archive or aggregator of datasets and archives would be a welcome tool to create an overview of existing databases on South Italian red-figure pottery, which in turn could provide a unified vision for online research and dissemination. Such an aggregator already exists to an extent, in the form of the ARIADNE Plus project. As the ARIADNE project serves as a general aggregator of existing databases on all types of cultural heritage, its use favours researchers interested in questions that can be answered using qualitative methodologies, as the data available in there is quite general and broad.[59] Furthermore, the lack of communication between these different types of online databases leads to a high level of heterogeneity of databases that contain similar or even the exact same information on sites and/or specific objects. This makes data aggregation difficult. To function as an online archive where qualitative research is possible instead of (or as well as) quantitative, it is necessary to decrease the scope in comparison to a broad aggregator such as the ARIADNE Plus project and increase the detail and depth of information to answer different and more complex research questions when studying South Italian red-figure pottery. Moreover, access to reports and bibliography should be more explicit, and it is necessary to be able to create new relationships between archaeological, object, and historical data.

Arches software could be used to create a more extensive specialized database or aggregation of archaeological, object, and collection data. In our case, it is not unthinkable to develop an option to connect specific workshops of vase painters and information about the locations some of these vases were found in and where they are now in collections. For example, suppose the aforementioned vase from Arpi, currently in the Museo Civico in Foggia (Fig. 16.3), attributed to the workshop of the Arpi painter, is selected.[60] In that case, this program could be used to show other vases of the same workshop and where they were found if the provenance is known (including the relevant archaeological report or archaeological publications). This facilitates the possibility of creating relationships with the museum, university, or collection of vases from the same workshop, as well as relationships to extensive documentation datasets related to the vase.[61] Furthermore, 3D reconstructions of tombs and vases can be added, allowing researchers to come quite close to the actual archaeology and objects, increasing the accessibility of red-figure vases and the archaeology of southern Italy as well as allowing for non-invasive studies of pottery. Reconstructions of vases without archaeological context such as ours can then be added to such a tool through the relationships with the relevant workshops that made them. Additionally, relationships between the grey literature and the sites they describe could be made within this tool, making it easier for researchers to ask for specific information and reports to consult from cultural ministries and museums that oversee these.

Within Arches, the history and reality of looting can be included as well. Relationships can be made to layers of maps that show looting that has occurred at a site, using, for example, Fabrizio's work to be able to have an

---

[58] Niccolucci 2020, 40. Information might be overlooked because it is not viewed as relevant, even if it is, due to for example different terminologies.

[59] Niccolucci 2020.

[60] See n. 30.

[61] See 'relationships': <https://www.archesproject.org/features/> [accessed 8 February 2022].

overview of which areas have been looted concerning the material that has been found there in regular excavations. This will result in a more complete and contextualized overview of looting in specific sites, making it possible to analyse what kind of material might have been taken from certain sites and focus on their archaeological reality, too, instead of solely focusing on the spread and patterns in looting in the current landscape.

A program like Arches could provide a clear overview of the available online databases, bibliographies, and references to grey literature. However, it cannot immediately solve the lack of heterogeneity of datasets in existing pottery databases. One way to partly overcome this problem concerning the lack of uniformity and increase how searchable resources are is to use tags that can be translated clearly, or an automatic dictionary that can facilitate direct translation, similar to the technique used in the Kerameikos project. For example, instead of having multiple entries of the same object, a tag can be created that can be searched using 'vasi apuli' (Apulian vases), 'céramique apulienne', etc. If one of these searches is made, all relevant entries are still displayed, even if they were initially registered in a different language. Then, three separate searches can be fulfilled in one, possibly adding searches that one would not have thought of (for example, using the same word in a less obvious language when studying South Italian pottery, such as Dutch). Heterogeneity in reports and data cannot be eliminated, but this way it is possible to search for and access all relevant data entries, nonetheless.

Works Cited

Acke, L., K. de Vis, S. Verwulgen, and J. Verlinden. 2021. 'Survey and Literature Study to Provide Insights on the Application of 3D Technologies in Objects Conservation and Restoration', *Journal of Cultural Heritage*, 49: 272–88.

Agnoli, N., L. Bochicchio, D. F. Maras, and R. Zaccagnini. 2019. *Colori degli Etruschi: tesori di terracotta alle Centrale Montemartini; catalogo della mostra* (Rome: Gangemi).

Annoepel-Cabrignac, S. 2011. 'AGORHA: The New Multimedia Database at the Institut National d'Histoire de l'Art (INHA) in Paris', *Art Libraries Journal*, 36.3: 31–33.

Arias, P. E. 1997. 'La situazione della ricerca sulla ceramica greca e italiota dopo il Beazley e il Trendall', *Athenaeum*, n.s., 85: 199–203.

Boi, V., A. M. Marras, and C. Santagati. 2015. 'Open Access and Archaeology in Italy: An Overview and a Proposal', *Archäologische Informationen*, 38: 137–47.

Calandra, E. and V. Boi. 2018. 'Tra riproduzione e condivisione dei beni culturali: il ruolo dell'istituto centrale per l'archeologia', *Archeologia e calcolatori*, 29: 63–72.

Calandra, E., V. Boi, A. Falcone, V. Acconcia, S. Di Giorgio, F. Massara, and P. Ronzino. 2021. 'Policy and Practice for Digital Archaeological Archiving in Italy', *Internet Archaeology*, 58 <https://doi.org/10.11141/ia.58.27>.

Cameron, F. and H. Robinson. 2007. 'Digital Knowledgescapes: Cultural, Theoretical, Practical, and Usage Issues Facing Museum Collection Databases in a Digital Epoch', in F. Cameron and S. Kenderdine (eds), *Theorizing Digital Cultural Heritage: A Critical Discourse* (Cambridge, MA: MIT Press), pp. 165–91.

Carpenter, T. H. 2009. 'Prolegomenon to the Study of Apulian Red-Figure Pottery', *American Journal of Archaeology*, 113.1: 27–38.

Carpenter, T. H., K. M. Lynch, and E. G. D. Robinson. 2014. *The Italic People of Ancient Apulia: New Evidence from Pottery on Workshops, Potters and Customs* (Cambridge: Cambridge University Press).

Casana, J. 2015. 'Satellite Imagery-Based Analysis of Archaeological Lootings in Syria', *Near Eastern Archaeology*, 78.3: 142–52.

Casana, J. and M. Panahipour. 2014. 'Satellite-Based Monitoring of Looting and Damage to Archaeological Sites in Syria', *Journal of Eastern Mediterranean Archaeology and Heritage Studies*, 2: 128–51.

Denoyelle, M. and M. E. Masci. 2009. 'Lasimos and CVA: History of Collections. Presentation from a Meeting of International Directors in Oxford 2009' <https://www.cvaonline.org/cva/authors/lasimos.pdf> [assessed 6 July 2022].

Fabrizio, F. 2017. 'Application of Satellite Images for Detection of Illegal Excavation in Puglia (Italy)', *SCIRES*, 7.2: 43–50.

Gardin, J.-C. 1999. 'Calcul et narrativité dans les publications archéologiques', *Archeologia e calcolatori*, 10: 63–78.

Gräpler, D. 1997. *Tonfiguren im Grab* (Munich: Biering und Brinkman).

Gruber, E. and T. Smith. 2014. 'Linked Open Greek Pottery', in F. Giligny, F. Djindjian, L. Costa, P. Moscati, and S. Robert (eds), *CAA2014: 21st Century Archaeology; Concepts, Methods and Tools; Proceedings of the 42nd Annual Conference on Computer Applications and Quantitative Methods in Classical Archaeology* (Oxford: Archaeopress), pp. 204–14.

Guaitoli, M. 2003. *Lo Sguardo di Icaro* (Rome: Campisano).

Hoffmann, A. 2002. *Grabritual und Gesellschaft: Gefassformen, Bildthemen und Funktionen unteritalisch-rotfiguriger Keramik aus der Nekropole von Tarent*, Internationale Archäologie, 76 (Rahden: Leidorf).

Hupperetz, W., E. Pietroni, D. Pletinckx, C. Ray, and M. Sannibale. 2013. *Etruscanning: Digital Encounters with the Regolini Galassi Tomb* (Amsterdam: Allard Pierson Museum).

Jenkins, I. and K. Sloan (eds). 1996. *Vases and Volcanoes: Sir William Hamilton and his Collections* (London: British Museum).

Kästner, U. and S. Schmidt. 2018. *Unteritalische Vasenmalerei zwischen Griechen und Indigenen: Proceedings of the International Conference Berlin 26.–28. Oktober 2026*, CVA Supplements, 8 (Munich: Verlag der Bayerischen Akademie der Wissenschaften in Kommission beim Verlag C.H. Beck).

Lippolis, E. and M. Mazzei. 2005. 'La ceramica apula a figure rosse: aspetti e problemi', in M. Denoyelle, E. Lippolis, M. Mazzei, and C. Pouzadoux (eds), *La céramique apulienne* (Naples: Publication du Centre Jean Bérard), pp. 11–18.

Masci, M. E. 2007. 'The Birth of Ancient Vase Collecting in Naples in the Early Eighteenth Century: Antiquarian Studies, Excavations and Collections', *Journal of the History of Collections*, 19.11: 215–24.

—— 2014. 'Apulian and Lucanian Red-Figure Pottery in Eighteenth Century Collections', in T. H. Carpenter, K. M. Lynch, and E. G. D. Robinson (eds), *The Italic People of Ancient Apulia: New Evidence from Pottery on Workshops, Potters and Customs* (Cambridge: Cambridge University Press), pp. 283–302.

Mazzei, M. 1995. *Arpi: L'ipogeo della Medusa e la necropoli* (Foggia: Banca del Monte di Foggia).

Niccolucci, F. 2020. 'From Digital Archaeology to Data-Centric Archaeological Research', *Magazén*, 1.1: 35–54.

Nørskov, V. 2022. 'Collecting and Communicating Greek Painted Pottery in the Twenty-First Century', in M. Salvadori, E. Bernard, L. Zamparo, and M. Baggio (eds), *Beyond Forgery: Collecting, Authentication and Protection of Cultural Heritage* (Padua: Padua University Press), pp. 401–17.

Nucciotti, M., C. Bonacchi, and C. Molducci. 2019. 'Introduzione', in M. Nucciotti, C. Bonacchi, and C. Molducci (eds), *Archeologia pubblica in Italia* (Florence: Firenze University Press), pp. 11–16.

Orlandi, S. D., G. Calandra, V. Ferrara, A. M. Marras, S. Radice, E. Bertacchini, V. Nizzo, and T. Maffei. 2018. 'Web Strategy in Museums: An Italian Survey Stimulates New Visions', *Museum International*, 70.1–2: 78–89.

Ronzino, P., V. Acconcia, and A. Falcone. 2018. 'Towards the Integration of Spatial Data through the Italian Geoportal for Archaeological Resources', in A. C. Addison and H. Thwaites (eds), *Proceedings of the 2018 3rd Digital Heritage International Congress (DigitalHERITAGE) Held Jointly with 2018 24th International Conference on Virtual Systems & Multimedia (VSMM 2018) (San Francisco: IEEE)*, pp. 1–5 <https://doi.org/10.1109/DigitalHeritage.2018.8810132>.

Roscino, C. 2018. *Corpus vasorum antiquorum: Italia*, LXXXIV: *Collezione Jatta Fasc. V. Ruvo di Puglia* (Rome: L'Erma di Bretschneider).

Saxkjær, S. G. 2018. 'The Emergence and Marking of Ethnic Identities: Case Studies from the Sibaritide Region', *Analecta Romana Instituti Danici*, 42: 7–31.

Serlorenzi, M., I. Jovine, G. Leoni, A. De Tommasi, and A. Varavallo. 2015. 'A Retrospective on GIS and AIS Platforms for Public Archaeology in Italy: Searching Backward for Roots and Looking Onwards for New Methodological Road-Maps', in F. Giligny, F. Djindjian, L. Costa, P. Moscati, and S. Roberts (eds), *Proceedings of the 42nd Annual Conference on Computer Applications and Quantitative Methods in Archaeology, CAA 2014, 21st Century Archaeology* (Oxford: Archaeopress), pp. 1–12.

Stamatopoulos, M. I. and C. N. Anagnostopoulos. 2018. 'Simulation of an Archaeological Disaster: Reassembling a Fragmented Amphora Using the Thickness Profile Method', in M. Ioannides, E. Fink, R. Brumana, P. Patias, A. Doulamis, J. Martins, and M. Wallace (eds), *Digital Heritage: Progress in Cultural Heritage; Documentation, Preservation, and Protection; EuroMed 2018* (Cham: Springer), pp. 162–73.

Todisco, L. 2012. *La ceramica a figure rosse della Magna Grecia e della Sicilia*, 3 vols (Rome: L'Erma di Bretschneider).

Trendall, A. D. 1936. *Paestan Pottery: The Study of Red-Figured Vases of Paestum* (London: British School at Rome).

—— 1967–1983. *The Red-Figured Vases of Lucania, Campania and Sicily*, 2 vols + suppl. (London: Clarendon).

Trendall, A. D. and A. Cambitoglou. 1978–1982. *The Red-Figured Vases of Apulia*, 3 vols (Oxford: Clarendon).

—— 1983. *First Supplement to The Red-Figured Vases of Apulia* (London: Institute of Classical Studies).

—— 1991–1992. *Second Supplement to The Red-Figured Vases of Apulia* (London: Institute of Classical Studies).

Tsirogiannis, C. 2016. 'Attitudes in Transit: Symes Material from Market to Source', *Journal of Art Crime*, 2016: 79–86.

Tucci, G., D. Cini, and A. Nobile. 2011. 'Effective 3D Digitization of Archaeological Artifacts for Interactive Virtual Museum', *International Archives of the Photogrammetry, Remote Sensing and Spatial Information Sciences*, 38.5/W16: 413–20.

Walters, H. B. 1896. *Catalogue of the Greek and Etruscan Vases in the British Museum*, IV (London: British Museum).

Williams, D. 1996. 'Dale Trendall: An Eye of an Eagle', *Bulletin of the Institute of Classical Studies*, 41: 6–16.

17. From Paper to Open-Air Archive: Reconstructing Illegal Excavations and Art-Market Circulations of Archaeological Objects in the Case of the Archaic Sanctuary on Timpone della Motta, Southern Italy

Gloria Mittica
The Danish Institute in Rome (mittica@acdan.it)

Carmelo Colelli
Soprintendenza Archeologia Belle Arti e Paesaggio per la provincia di Cosenza (carmelo.colelli@cultura.gov.it)

Jan Kindberg Jacobsen
The Danish Institute in Rome (jaki@glyptoteket.dk)

Introduction [JKJ]

The Timpone della Motta hill close to present-day Francavilla Marittima in Calabria, southern Italy, is undoubtfully one of the archaeological sites in Magna Grecia which has suffered most from illegal excavations. Located on the northern bank of the Raganello River, the hill rises some 280 m above sea level (Fig. 17.1). Immediately to the east, the Macchiabate necropolis in located, which was in use from the late ninth century to the sixth century BC.[1] Archaeological remains on Timpone della Motta cover the time span from the Middle Bronze Age to the fifth century BC. Archaeological excavations have been conducted on the site both before and after the period of illegal digs, and today an archaeological reading of the cultural transformation and associated material culture is available.[2] Notably the summit of Timpone della Motta witnessed extensive illegal diggings between the 1970s and 1980s.

Here a Greek sanctuary flourished during the Archaic period of the seventh and sixth centuries BC on the remains of what was probably already an indigenous cult place during the eighth century BC. The illegal excavators were attracted by tens of thousands of precious votive objects which had been deposited within the sanctuary during the Archaic period. Figure-decorated Greek pottery, terracotta figurines, and objects in bronze, faience, and ivory were sought objects on the international illegal art market, and buyers, museums, and private collectors alike, had little, if any, concern for the provenance of the objects or how they had reached the market in the first place. That Italy and other Mediterranean countries were the site of massive illegal excavation must have been well known beyond the borders of the Mediterranean Sea — if not for other reasons, then for the fact that a steady stream of priced Etruscan, Greek, and Roman objects, and artworks without information of collection history or provenance reached collections throughout Europe and North America. Acquiring objects without this kind of information was not considered particularly problematic. In fact, although difficult to prove, we might wonder if an intuition of an object's illegal pedigree might have been an additional reason for buying it? At least in some cases. As it remains the case today, the curatorial foundation for most larger public and private collections displaying ancient art rested on art-historical connoisseurship in which the capability to distinguish fake from original stands at the very centre. Accidently acquiring a fake with trusted funds would have been a nightmare scenario for museum directors and curators responsible for ancient art collection.[3] A hint that an object was recently excavated might very well just have

---

[1] Guggisberg and Colombi 2021, with reference to earlier publications.

[2] For the research history of older excavations, Colelli 2014; Kleibrink 2010; de Lachenal 2007. For later excavations in the sanctuary, see Boschetti and others (forthcoming); Mittica 2021; Jacobsen and others 2021; 2018; Jacobsen, Saxkjær, and Mittica 2017a; 2017b; Mittica and Jacobsen 2018; Mittica and others 2018; Mittica and Perrone 2018.

[3] A high-profile case of ancient art fraud which surely must have contributed to a certain anxiety throughout the museum world during the 1970s might have been the series of colossal terracotta figures acquired by the Metropolitan Museum in 1933. It took the Metropolitan twenty-eight years to come to terms with their inauthenticity before they finally left the museum display in 1962 after having fooled famous classical archaeologists such as John Marshal and Gisela Richter. The sculptures were eventually found to be forgeries manufactured by the notorious Riccardi brothers, see von Bothmer and Noble 1961.

Figure 17.1. Timpone della Motta seen from the west (photo: the Danish Institute in Rome).

offered the right kind of assurance for its authenticity. The tide turned when a photo archive belonging to art dealer Giacomo Medici was seized in a raid in Geneva Freeport in 1995, to be followed by the confiscation of other archives belonging to art dealers Robin Symes, Gianfranco Becchina, and Robert Hecht. For more than four decades, these four dealers supplied the art market with illegally exported archaeological objects through galleries in Basel, Geneva, London, New York, and Los Angeles.[4] Based on these archives, Italian authorities launched a broad investigation, eventually leading to the repatriation of a vast number of archaeological objects from North American and European public and private collections.[5]

Discovering Timpone della Motta [CC]

On 12 January 1793, Luigi Serra, the duke of Cassano (1747–1825) sent a letter to the king of Napoli in which he asked permission to initiate an archaeological excavation in the dukedom of Cassano in Calabria, south Italy. The permission was granted by the Crown in Napoli four days later, 16 January 1793. The dukedom of Cassano included the area which would later become the commune of Francavilla Marittima, but it is unknown if Luigi Serra intended to excavate in the area of Francavilla Marittima or elsewhere in the territory, which, among others, also covered the Greek colony of Sybaris and the later cities of Copia and Thurii.[6] The earliest confirmed information about excavations in the vicinity of Francavilla Marittima dates to 1843. During February that year, a member of the local nobility, D. Abramo Saladini, wrote a letter to the superintendent of nearby Castrovillari in which he communicated the excavation of numerous archaeological objects which, in the opinion of Saladini, were evidence for the presence of an ancient settlement. Information on these excavations can be traced through archived letters. From the letters it transpires that objects were excavated c. 1.6 km south-west of Francavilla Marittima, which corresponds to the location of Timpone della Motta and the nearby Macchiabate necropolis.[7] Saladini continued in claiming

---

[4] For all for dealers, see Watson and Todeschini 2006. On Becchina and Hecht, see also Paoletti 2014, 7–10; 2017.

[5] For a recent account on investigation and repatriation to Italy, see Gill 2018.

[6] Colelli and Scavello 2020, 485–88.

[7] The excavations are described in three letters sent between

Figure 17.2. Marquis Gaetano Gallo (1822–1908) of Castrovillari (photo: Reproduced from E. Miraglia. 2021. *Carlo Maria L'Occaso: Patriota e letterato calabrese* (Il Pollino: Castrovillari), p. 37.

Figure 17.3. Letter signed by Giuseppe Fiorelli, 21 June 1879, instructing to safeguard archaeological objects (photo: Carmelo Colelli).

that he had discovered the remains of ancient Lagaria. According to ancient sources, Lagaria was founded by Epeios, the mythical craftsman loved by Athene, who according to the Homeric poems built the Trojan horse.[8] It is today unknown where the material from these excavations ended up, but it is likely to assume that a part arrived in Napoli where they entered the collection of the Minister for Internal Affairs, Nicola Santangelo, who during that period was actively assembling a large collection of archaeological objects in the capital of Kingdom of the Two Sicilies. Some of the objects are today probably to be found in the collection of the Museo Archeologico Nazionale di Napoli where notably some mould-made terracotta pinax fragments of the so-called 'dama di Sibari'-type unquestionably arrived from Francavilla Marittima in the light of the fact that fragments from the same mould have come to light during excavations on Timpone della Motta.[9] From less than two decades later, we again have confirmed information about finds of archaeological objects in the area of Timpone della Motta. In spring 1879, during the construction works of the provincial road 263, a notable number of archaeological objects were collected from the areas today known as the Macchiabate necropolis and Area Rovitti at the southern foothill of Timpone della Motta. Some of the objects were collected by the Marquis Gaetano Gallo (1822–1908) in Castrovillari, who was forming his own collection during the years following the unification of Italy (Fig. 17.2).[10]

2–24 February 1843, two from Saladini to the soprintende in Castrovillari Alliata and one from Alliata to the superintendent in Cosenza with c.c. to Saladini, see Colelli 2014, 301–06 and app. 2 and attachments 1–3. The excavations might be the ones mentioned in a local publication about the history of Francavilla Marittima published fifteen years later, see Piccirillo 1857, 94.

8 Colelli 2017.

9 On the collection of Nicola Santangelo and the terracotta pinax, see Paoletti 2014, 17–20.

10 Colelli 2014, 306–10 and app. 2 and attachments 4–9.

Figure 17.4a. Archaeological stratigraphy exposed during roadworks in 1879 (photo: the Danish Institute in Rome).

Figure 17.4b. Oinotrian-Euboean fragments from the eighth century BC on display in the Museo Civico Archeologico di Castrovillari (photo: the Danish Institute in Rome).

The discoveries of 1879 led to the first publications of the archaeology of Francavilla Marittima by Gaetano Gallo in the regional newspaper *Il Calabrese* under the title 'Terre cotte e Bronzi antichi rinvenuti negli scavi della strada del Pollino' as well as a scientific preliminary report by the then Direttore Generale per le antichità in Rome, Giuseppe Fiorelli (1823–1896), in *Notizie degli Scavi dell'Accademia dei Lincei*, respectively.[11] Once again we do not know the whereabouts of the archaeological objects which came to light during the construction works in 1879. What, however, is certain is that Fiorelli gave specific instructions to the prefect of Cosenza in a letter from 21 June 1879 in which he stated that 'the found objects should be safeguarded in order to enter the collection of the provincial museum', today's Museo Civico dei Bretti e degli Enotri di Cosenza (Fig. 17.3).[12]

It is unknown if these instructions were ever accommodated, but the objects can today not be located in the collection of the Museo Civico dei Bretti e degli Enotri di Cosenza. As noted above, Marquis Gaetano Gallo in Castrovillari was assembling his own collection during the same period, and it is plausible that some, if not all, objects reached his collection in Castrovillari rather than the prefect of Cosenza. Following the death of Gaetano Gallo in 1908, most of his collection was dispersed, and today only a minor group of objects are preserved in the Museo Civico Archeologico di Castrovillari. However, among these are a few particular Iron Age pottery fragments belonging to the so-called Oinotrian-Euboean pottery class, which is mainly found on Timpone della Motta and in notable amounts in Area Rovitti at the southern base of the hill located just a few metres to the north of provincial road 263. During the 2016 research campaign conducted by the Danish Institute in Rome, an archaeological stratigraphy intercepted by the 1879 road work was identified along provincial road 263 in a position of *c.* 5 m to the south of the excavation field in Area Rovitti. Pottery extracted from the stratigraphy as well as that from the excavation field closely corresponds to the fragments in the Museo Civico Archeologico di Castrovillari, rendering it likely that they were collected in this location (Fig. 17.4a–b).[13]

During the four decades following the 1879 discoveries, no records are known about additional finds from Francavilla Marittima. Only during the 1930s, new communications emerged about findings of archaeological objects from the Iron Age in various locations including Timpone della Motta, Area Pietra Catania, Timpa del Castello, Area Foresta, and the property of Saverio De Leo (today's Macchiabate necropolis).[14] Additional information related to a find from Area Rovitti was communicated as 'remain of a square terracotta with vertical perforations' found on 'the property of Antonio

---

[11] Gallo 1879; Fiorelli 1879, 155–56 which includes a list of found objects. On the argument, see also Colelli 2014, 309–10.

[12] 'Devo pregarla a custodire gli oggetti rinvenuti, i quali dovranno far parte del Museo Provinciale', Colelli 2014, app. 2, attachment 9.

[13] For the recontextualization of the fragments, see Jacobsen and others 2018, 30–31. On Area Rovitti, see Jacobsen and Handberg 2012; Mittica and Jacobsen 2019.

[14] Galli and d'Ippolito 1936, 77–83.

Rovitti'.[15] The description of the object corresponds to fragments of Iron Age pottery kilns attested during the excavations of the Danish Institute in Rome in Area Rovitti.[16] A substantial part of the objects which came to light during the 1930s can today be identified in the collection of the Museo Civico dei Bretti e degli Enotri di Cosenza.[17] Additional donations of archaeological objects from Francavilla to the museum in Cosenza were made by the local De Santis family. A total of three donations from Agostino De Santis (1897–1961) are recorded. A first lot found in 1934 reached Cosenza in 1936, the content of which was described in an article in *Notizie degli scavi di Antichità*.[18] According to a written receipt signed by the director of the museum in Cosenza, Giacinto d'Ippolito, a second donation of fifty-one archaeological objects was donated by Agostino De Santis on that date, followed by a third donation of one object on 6 April of the same year.[19] In the aftermath of World War II, Agostino De Santis retained his firm interest in the archaeology of Francavilla Marittima and he created his own collection of archaeological objects.[20] Upon his death in 1960, his son, Tanino De Santis (1928–2013), continued the work but now with a scholarly and international outlook, leading to the first regular archaeological excavations under the direction of the Italian archaeologist Paola Zancani Montuoro (1901–1987) assisted by the Dutch archaeologist Maria W. Stoop (1924–2004).

An International Puzzle of Archaic Greek Vase Fragments [JKJ]

Since 2002 Danish and Italian archaeologists, led by Gloria Mittica and Jan Kindberg Jacobsen, have been trying to identify archaeological objects in collections which have been illegally excavated on Timpone della Motta.[21] In many cases, it has been possible to establish joining fragments between regularly excavated material and material in a number of Italian and foreign collections. This has been done by consulting printed museum catalogues as well as through physically examining fragments in museum collections. Additional joining fragments could be established through university photo archives. Here, especially, that vast collection of photos of Corinthian ceramics held in the Department of Archaeology at the Free University of Amsterdam has surfaced several fragments from Timpone della Motta.[22] In the last decade, an increasing number of predominantly American museums have provided full access to photo archives of unpublished and often not displayed archaeological objects.[23] This has proven a useful tool to establish joins with fragments in American museums which have been inaccessible until recently.

Reconstruction of the Illegal Excavations of the 1970s and 1980s [JKJ]

The majority of the archaeological objects illegally excavated on Timpone della Motta during the first half of the 1970s reached the market during the second half of the same decade. Whereas archival and material studies, which will be discussed below, have clarified where many of these objects ended up, the dynamics of the illegal excavations at the site are far less known. A reason for this information void is undoubtedly the absence of any legal proceedings in the aftermath of the illegal excavations. Elsewhere in Italy these dynamics have often been mapped in detail through court files and not least through the sworn testimonies of the illegal excavators themselves which generally provides information about when and by whom the objects were excavated.[24] In our case, the absence of these kinds of official files renders locally obtained hearsay the only — and admittedly patchy — source of evidence. The local hearsay, however, finds a degree of support when confronted with material evidence collected during the recent system-

---

15 'Resto di terracotta quadrato con base forata' found 'nella proprietà di Antonio Rovitti', Galli and d'Ippolito 1936, 83.

16 Jacobsen and others 2018, 30–31.

17 Cerzoso and Vanzetti 2014.

18 Gianniti 2020, 35–96; Galli and d'Ippolito 1936.

19 Gianniti 2020, 97–99.

20 Colelli 2019.

21 For an overview, Jacobsen and Mittica 2019.

22 The archive was collected over decades by the leading specialist on Corinthian vase painting, Prof. Kees W. Neeft who kindly granted access to Jan Kindberg Jacobsen in 2005.

23 The following three photo archives have been of notable relevance in establishing joining fragments or close similarity with fragments from Timpone della Motta: Metropolitan Museum of Art: <https://www.metmuseum.org/art/the-collection> [accessed 4 April 2022]; the Princeton University Art Museum: <https://artmuseum.princeton.edu/collections> [accessed 4 April 2022]; Michael C. Carlos Museum, Atlanta: <https://collections.carlos.emory.edu/objects/images> [accessed 4 April 2022].

24 As in the case of the Morgantina Goddess acquired by the Getty Museum in 1987 and repatriated to Italy following an agreement signed in 2007, Raffiotta 2011.

atic excavations in 2022. In the local narrative, extensive illegal excavations started up around 1970 and continued throughout the 1980s and — still relying on local sources — the excavations were undertaken by inhabitants from the nearby towns of Castrovillari and Doria. The left-behinds of the excavators in the form of soda cans, beer, and wine bottles confirm the period of illegal excavations. These items can be regarded as an open-air archive, which provides information about the periods and the areas of the excavations on the site. During the 2022 excavation campaign, a systematic survey of items-distribution was conducted within the sanctuary on the summit of the hill as well as on the southern and northern slopes of the hill.[25] The results show that illegal excavations seem to have been limited to the southern part of the sanctuary during the 1970s. Here a reoccurring item was Fanta soda cans used by the Italian distributor SONBIL S.p.A during the second half of the 1970s (Fig. 17.5a).[26]

Whereas these cans could be collected in many places at the southern part of the sanctuary as well as on the southern slope directly below the sanctuary, none could be found at the northern part of the sanctuary nor on the northern slope. However, the survey towards the north revealed many beer bottles, of which the most

Figure 17.5a. Fanta cans from the second half of the 1970s (photo: the Danish Institute in Rome).

Figure 17.5b. Perlenbacher beer bottle from the 1980s (photo: the Danish Institute in Rome).

Figure 17.6. 1980s wine bottle from the Magna Grecia factory in Doria (photo: the Danish Institute in Rome).

Figure 17.7. Handwritten note on the donation of Agostino De Santis to the Museo Civico Archeologico in Castrovillari in 1957 (photo: the Danish Institute in Rome).

---

[25] The collected items have been categorized and dated using obtainable information online and on occasion by enquiring locally when certain products were sold in southern Italy. Additional information has been sought by contacting beer and soda companies, but replies were not received before the deadline of the current article.

[26] From 1975 SONBIL S.p.A. produced Fanta soda at Nogera on behalf of the Coca-Cola Company, according to the company website: <https://it.coca-colahellenic.com/it/chi-siamo/inostristabilimenti/our-plants--nogara-> [accessed 4 April 2022].

Figure 17.8a. Joining fragments from Corinthian seventh-century BC pyxis lid (photo: the Danish Institute in Rome).

Figure 17.8b. Fragments from seventh-century Corinthian lekythos, probably belonging to the same vessel (photo: the Danish Institute in Rome).

recognizable type is from the German beer company Perlenbacher, which used these kinds of bottles during the 1980s (Fig. 17.5b). Many beer bottles were collected in several places over a one-hundred-metre east–west range, which clearly shows that they were left behind over a period of time and not on a single occasion. Interestingly, a wine bottle from the 1980s collected on the northern slope still preserved its cap on which the wine manufacturer is clearly readable as 'Magna Grecia – Doria (CS)' (Fig. 17.6).

We have not been able to find any published information about the manufacturer, and an answer to our enquiry to the regional commercial chamber in Cosenza is still pending. Nevertheless, by seeking information from the public in the town of Doria itself, it was revealed that the company produced wine during the 1980s to a mainly local market. The town of Doria, located some 15 km to the south of Francavilla Marittima, was in fact mentioned by local hearsay as one of two towns out of which the illegal excavators allegedly operated, and the described bottle might be understood within this context. While the confirmation of Doria as the base of illegal excavators rests on the shaky ground of a single wine bottle, firm evidence is available when it comes to the second town, Castrovillari. In 2019, the Danish Institute in Rome signed an accord of collaboration with the Municipal Museum in Castrovillari (Museo Civico Archeologico di Castrovillari) and the regional office of the Italian Ministry for Cultural Heritage (Soprintendenza Archeologia, belle arti e paesaggio per la provincia di Cosenza). The objective of the collaboration, which is still in progress, is to produce a joined scientific publication of the museum's collection of archaeological objects. A selection of objects from Francavilla Marittima had already reached the museum as a donation from local Francavilla doctor Agostino De Santis in 1957, which is confirmed by small handwritten notes accompanying each object (Fig. 17.7).

In the same manner, Agostino De Santis had also donated a minor collection to the Municipal Museum of Cosenza.[27] A second group of displayed objects mainly consisting of Greek pottery fragments from the seventh and sixth centuries BC with the generic label 'Santuario – Timpone della Motta' forms part of the collection of the Museo Civico Archeologico in Castrovillari. The group is intriguing since no specific information exists on how it reached the museum. A specific recontextualization on this latter group of objects was done in 2018 when a few joining fragments could be established between the regular excavations and the material held in the museum. On other occasions, fragments from the museum and the regular excavations clearly appeared to pertain to the same vessel (Fig. 17.8a–b).[28]

An additional examination of the material in 2020 established more joining fragments between museum and excavation. Based on these it was possible to reconstruct that most of the material must have been removed from the south-western part of the sanctuary from votive

---

[27] Cerzoso and Caputo 2021; Malacrino, Paoletti, and Costanzo 2018; Cerzoso and Vanzetti 2014.

[28] Jacobsen and Mittica 2019, 37–38.

Figure 17.9. Votive deposit to the south of Building Vd during excavation in 2002. A hole dug by illegal excavators can been seen in the lower part of the photo (photo: Jan Kindberg Jacobsen).

deposits to the immediate south of the so-called Building Vd.[29] Here excavations conducted between 2000 and 2004 had revealed evidence for massive illegal excavations targeting rich archaic votive deposits (Fig. 17.9). Minor parts of the deposits had been untouched by the illegal dig, and from these, fragments were excavated which could be joined directly together with fragments in the collection of the Ny Carlsberg Glyptotek in Copenhagen.[30]

The Copenhagen fragments had been acquired in 1978, indicating that they had been unearthed during the first half of the 1970s. A observation which was corroborated by soda cans left behind by the illegal excavators. Considering the fact that the fragments from the Municipal Museum in Castrovillari can be joined with fragments from the same contexts, these fragments must have been excavated at the same time. The quantity of fragments in the museum is notable, counting some 150 displayed pieces together with an estimated five hundred still uncleaned fragments in the museum's store-rooms. Little is known about the circumstances in which the material entered the collection, apart from it having been donated by locals sometime during the late 1980s, but there are no records of who made the donation. Nevertheless, the presence of the material in the museum established a clear link between the illegal excavations on Timpone della Motta and the town of Castrovillari.[31]

Identifying Material in European and American Collections [GM]

Notwithstanding that illegally excavated material could be identified in the Municipal Museum of Castrovillari, the larger part of the objects appears to have reached foreign collections in Denmark, America, and Switzerland, while a minor group of the most pristine objects including terracotta figurines and intact Corinthian vessels were put on auction in 1976 by Gallery Palladion Antike Kunst in Basel, owned by the infamous Italian art dealer Gianfranco Becchina (Fig. 17.10).[32] A photo archive seized from Becchina in 2001 contains a higher number of objects from Timpone della Motta than what was offered for sale in the 1976 auction. From the archive a total of forty-eight complete minor Protocorinthian and Corinthian vessels can be listed. The shapes predominantly belong to aryballoi and alabastra and to a lesser

---

[29] For these votive deposits, see Jacobsen and Handberg 2010, 36–41.

[30] Jacobsen and Petersen 2002.

[31] After establishing the connection between the material and the illegal excavations of the 1970s, the fragments have been included in a wider collaboration between the Museo civico Archeologico di Castrovillari, the Danish Institute in Rome, and the Museo Nazionale Archeologico della Sibaritide, aimed at recontextualizing the material.

[32] *Palladion Antike Kunst* 1976.

Figure 17.10. Photos of Corinthian vessels from the archive of Gianfranco Becchina (photo: courtesy of *Comando Carabinieri Tutela Patrimonio Culturale*).

degree lekythoi, pyxis, and miniature kotylai. Many of the vessels are shown to be in a clearly uncleaned state of preservation while others have been hastily restored. The whereabouts of these vessels today is unknown.

In 1995, an international collaboration was founded between the Ny Carlsberg Glyptotek, the J. Paul Getty Museum, the art collection of the Archaeological Institute at the University of Bern, and the Italian Ministry for Cultural Heritage.[33] Together, they progressively addressed the problems relating to a vast number of high-value archaeological objects in the collections of the three foreign institutions which had been illegally excavated in the 1970s from Timpone della Motta. The collections acted after the illegal provenance of the objects had been highlighted by Prof. Marianne Kleibrink in 1994.[34] Kleibrink's assertions were not based on join-

ing fragments but on the well-founded suspicion that the chronological, stylistic, and typological similarities between material excavated by the Groningen Institute of Archaeology and that of the material in the three collections were too coherent to be a coincidence. The same conclusion had already been reached by another Dutch archaeologist, Maria W. Stoop, who oversaw excavation in the sanctuary between 1963 and 1969 and who allegedly confronted the then director of the Ny Carlsberg Glyptotek, Frederik Poulsen, with her findings immediately after the museum had acquired sixty-five objects from the sanctuary.[35] Stoop had first-hand knowledge about the material from the sanctuary due to her excavations of three temple structures and a minor part of a large votive deposit, labelled 'Stipe 1' at the south-western part of the sanctuary. The excavation of Stipe 1 was not completed, and subsequent recontextualization has concluded that most of the material from the three collections which can be dated to the seventh century BC came from this votive deposit.[36] In synergy, the institutions brought the largely fragmented objects together to be restored and published. In 2002, the objects from the University of Bern and the Getty were repatriated, followed by those from the Ny Carlsberg Glyptotek in 2016. The Ny Carlsberg Foundation went a step further: when receiving information in 2002 that Danish archaeologists excavating in the sanctuary on Timpone della Motta had identified original and undisturbed parts of the material assemblages from which the mentioned objects had been illegally excavated during the 1970s, the foundation recognized the importance of securing the archaeological objects and scientific information about precise find-spots and contextual observations. In the light of this, the Ny Carlsberg Foundation financed a team of archaeologists from Aarhus University to be sent to Francavilla Marittima with the task of excavating the

---

33 On the collaboration, see Serio and Proietti 2003.

34 Prof. Marianne Kleibrink and Prof. Peter Attema directed the excavations conducted on Timpone della Motta between 1991 and 2004 on behalf of the Groningen Institute of Archaeology, University of Groningen, The Netherlands. For a summary of the excavations in the sanctuary, see Kleibrink 2018.

35 As reported by Marianne Kleibrink 2010, 90. The site of Timpone della Motta was, however, not mentioned in articles and museum catalogues later published by the Ny Carlsberg Glyptotek, cf. Christiansen 1977; Fischer-Hansen 1992; Johansen 1994. Only in 2002 did than curator of ancient art at the Ny Carlsberg Glyptotek, Jette Christiansen, publish the connection between the object and Timpone della Motta: Christiansen 2002, 19–34.

36 For Stipe 1, see Stoop 1988; Kleibrink 2010, 88; 2017, 182–83. For additional excavations, see Stoop 1974–1976; 1979; 1983; 1985; 1987; 1989; 1990.

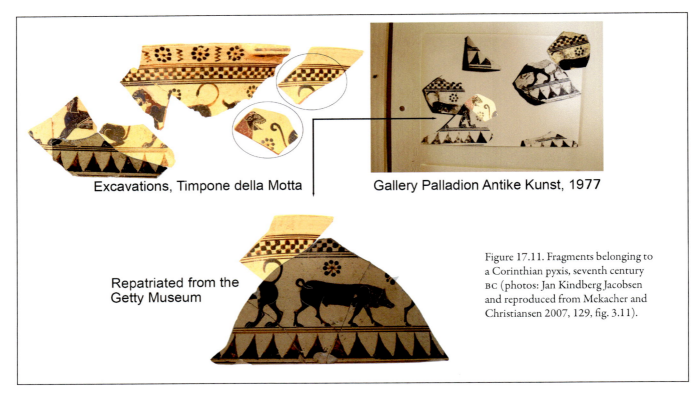

Figure 17.11. Fragments belonging to a Corinthian pyxis, seventh century BC (photos: Jan Kindberg Jacobsen and reproduced from Mekacher and Christiansen 2007, 129, fig. 3.11).

undisturbed object assemblages and thereby redeeming a substantial part of the scientific information lost during the 1970s illegal excavations. The excavations were focused on the aforementioned votive deposits to the immediate south of Building Vd. The object assemblages were found to have been deposited during the seventh century BC. The objects had been deposited in an disorderly manner; many vessels of small dimensions were found intact while larger vessels had been fragmented in Antiquity, and pieces had been deposited along the south side of Building Vd.[37] Many of the unearthed fragments from decorated pottery vessels could be fitted directly together with fragments from the three collections, in many cases leading to an almost full reconstruction of the original vessels.[38] In this manner, the specific place of origin within the sanctuary could be established for the illegally excavated pottery. The findings from the excavations were supplied to colleagues at the three museum institutions with preliminary observations on specific find-spots just in time to be included in the joint publication of the repatriated material, which appeared in the journal of the Italian Ministry of Culture, *Bollettino d'arte*, between 2004 and 2008.[39] Archive studies conducted in the aftermath of these publications had added more fragments to semi-complete vessels, both from the Stoop excavations of Stipe 1 as well as other American museums and art dealers. A case in point is, for example, the international distribution of fragments belonging to a small concave pyxis from the Late Protocorinthian period (Fig. 17.11).

The vessel itself is a small masterpiece of Corinthian vase painting, decorated with lavish drawings of animals in black-figure style. Fragments from this pyxis came to light during the regular excavations conducted by the Groningen Institute of Archaeology in the area to the south-east of Building Vd.[40] An additional seven fragments from the same vessels were repatriated in 2002. Of these, six came from the Getty and one from the Archaeological Institute in Bern.[41] A photo showing another five fragments from the pyxis is held in the photo archive of the Department of Archaeology at the Free University of Amsterdam. The fragments were photographed by Prof. Kees W. Neeft at the Gallery Palladion Antike Kunst in Basel in 1977. Neeft also photographed a fragment of a small Early Corinthian oinochoe in the H.A.C. Kunst der Antike gallery in

---

[37] Jacobsen and Handberg 2010, 36–41.

[38] Jacobsen and Mittica 2019, 38–40.

[39] Papadopoulos 2003, van der Wielen van Ommeren and de Lachenal 2007; 2008.

[40] Jacobsen and Handberg 2010, 150–51 n. A518.

[41] Mekacher and Christiansen 2007, 129 n. 11, fig. 3.11.

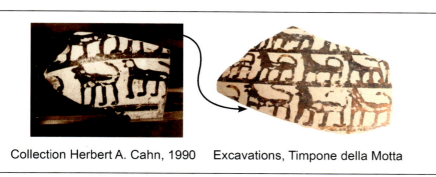

Figure 17.12. Joining fragments from Corinthian oinochoe, later seventh century BC (photos: Jan Kindberg Jacobsen).

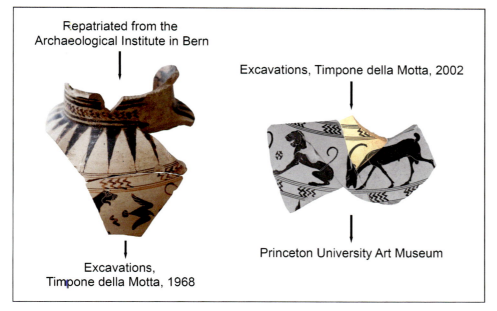

Figure 17.13. Joining fragments from Corinthian oinochoe, middle of the seventh century BC (photos: Gloria Mittica; Nadja Schulz, and Princeton University Art Museum).

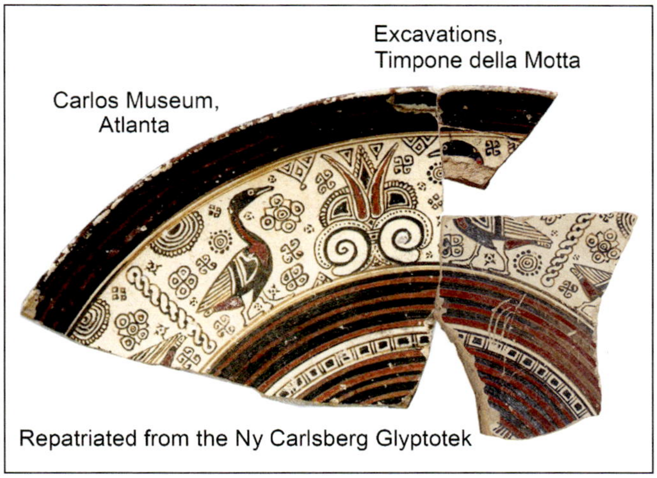

Figure 17.14. Fragments from an East Greek plate from the Ny Carlsberg Glyptotek and the Carlos Museum in Atlanta while a third fragment was excavated on Timpone della Motta (photos: Jan Kindberg Jacobsen, Giovanni Murro, and Michael C. Carlos Museum).

Basel seen on Figure 17.12, which joins together with a fragment excavated in the area of Building Vd.[42]

By consulting online photo archives, it has been possible to identify fragments from the Timpone della Motta in other American museums. Here a concrete example is the fragments from a Middle Protocorinthian oinochoe illustrated in Figure 17.13. Fragments from the vessel were excavated both by Maria Stoop and the Groningen Institute of Archaeology, and further fragments were repatriated from the Archaeological Institute in Bern.[43] Finally, to these can be joined two fragments in the collection of the Princeton University Art Museum, acquired in 1996.[44] In the same manner, fragments from a late seventh-century East Greek plate excavated to the south of Building Vd can be joined with a fragment repatriated from the Ny Carlsberg Glyptotek and a fragment in the collection of the Michael C. Carlos Museum in Atlanta (Fig. 17.14).[45]

---

[42] Jacobsen and Handberg 2010, 208–09 n. A814.

[43] Stoop 1988, 85, fig. 45; Jacobsen and Handberg 2010, 206–07 n. A806; van der Wielen van Ommeren and Christiansen 2007, 197–98 n. 5.61.

[44] <https://artmuseum.princeton.edu/collections/objects/5093> [accessed 4 April 2022].

[45] Jacobsen and Handberg 2010, 294 n. B2; Tsiafakis 2008, 11–12 n. C1. The Carlos Museums traces the collection history of

Figure 17.15. Area view of the MS3 area at the central south side of the sanctuary (photo: Gloria Mittica, the Danish Institute in Rome).

Figure 17.16. Pottery vessels repatriated from the Ny Carlsberg Glyptotek in 2016 (photo: Giovanni Murro).

Recontextualizing Material in the MS3 Area on Timpone della Motta [GM]

Prompted by the successful recontextualization of seventh-century objects that was made possible by the intervention of the Ny Carlsberg Foundation, new excavations at the site were initiated in 2008, this time with the support of the Carlsberg Foundation. A main objective of the new excavations was to attempt a recontextualization of the slightly later repatriated material dating to the sixth century BC, which accounts for roughly 50 per cent of the total lot.

From 2008 to 2010 and again from 2017 to 2022, the so-called MS3 area at the entrance of the sanctuary was investigated (Fig. 17.15). The excavations brought to light limestone alters from the sixth century BC together with evidence for animal sacrifices and ritual dining, areas for receiving pilgrims, as well as a possible enclosure for sacrificial animals. In addition, a sacred road and an access ramp connecting to the main square of the sanctuary were excavated. Numerous deposits of votive gifts were likewise excavated, and they were found to contain pottery vessels, clay figures, and many bronze, silver, ivory, and glass objects. Terracotta figurines from MS3 indicate that the area was probably dedicated to the goddess Artemis.[46] During excavation it was found that several of the illegally excavated objects had been taken from this area. At the same time, it could nevertheless be concluded that large parts of the MS3 area had been left untouched by the illegal excavations, thereby providing an excellent possibility to define a far-reaching and detailed description of the ritual activities that had taken place in the sanctuary during the sixth century BC. Hence, the repatriated archaeological objects could now be understood in light of their intended ritual function. As an example, decorated Greek vases from the hand of some of the most noted Greek vase painters, known for the particular style and beauty of their vase paintings, could now for the first time be associated with an ancient religious context. The 2008–2010 excavations revealed that the MS3 area covered an extensive field of some 1000 m² in the southern part of the sanctuary, but the time schedule and financial means only permitted the excavation of 200 m² of the area.

In 2017, the Danish Institute in Rome founded a Danish-Italian mission in Francavilla Marittima with the purpose of excavating the remaining c. 600 m² of the MS3 area.[47] The scientific studies were supported by the Carlsberg Foundation, while the excavations were supported by the University of Copenhagen and Aarhus University. The new excavations coincided with the repatriation of the objects from the Ny Carlsberg Glyptotek (Fig. 17.16). Accordingly, one of the first initiatives of the Danish Institute was the organization of a temporary exhibition with the title *Francavilla Marittima: Un Partimonio Ricontestualizzato* in the town of Francavilla Marittima. The exhibition included the objects from the Glyptotek, presented in dialogue with the scientific results from the Danish excavations as well as objects from these.

As an integrated part of the exhibition, a recontextualization was conducted on a limited number of repatriated fragments which could be joined together with fragments excavated in the MS3 area. However, the continuing efforts to join fragments have proven to be more difficult than was the case in the area to the south of Building Vd. This is directly related to a shift in the manner of ritual depositing, which must have taken place in the sanctuary at the very end of the seventh century BC. Even though, dispersed over many square metres, the fragments (repatriated and excavated) at Building Vd could for the most part be joined into complete or semi-complete vessels, showing that when they had broken in Antiquity, all fragments had been collected and deposited. In the MS3 area the situation was found to be fundamentally different. The most recurring find in the area was made up of tens of thousands of burned and deliberately fragmented animal bones from the hind legs of sheep. These pertain to the main religious activity to have taken place in the MS3 area, namely animal sacrifices to the gods and communal dining for the pilgrims participating in religious festivals. This kind of sacrifice is known from ancient Greek literary sources as Thysia sacrifices, and it is well attested in several Greek sanctuaries.[48] The Thysia was an animal sacrifice followed by a feast for the participants in the sacrifice. In conducting the ritual, parts of the animals would be burned on a stone altar as a sacrifice to the gods, and the remaining

---

the fragment back to 1976: 'Ex private collection, New York, 1976. Ex coll. Peter Sharrer, New Jersey. Purchased by MCCM from Sotheby's New York, June 7, 2005, lot 23.' <https://collections.carlos.emory.edu/objects/12941/wild-goat-style-plate-fragment-with-water-birds-and-palmette?ctx=ea25e8648b269ec76c5b32200f431c78eb9b2c2b&idx=13> [accessed 4 April 2022].

[46] For MS3, see Mittica 2019b.

[47] Mittica 2019b; Mittica and Perrone 2018, 237–63.

[48] Trantalidou 2013. For the evidence for *Thysia* sacrifices in the MS3 area, Mittica and Perrone 2018, 251–59.

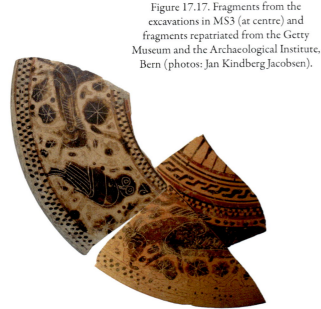

Figure 17.17. Fragments from the excavations in MS3 (at centre) and fragments repatriated from the Getty Museum and the Archaeological Institute, Bern (photos: Jan Kindberg Jacobsen).

Figure 17.18. Laconian fragment excavated in the MS3 area on 25 July 2022 (photo: Louise Møller).

Figure 17.19. Fragments from a Laconian cup in the collection of the Carlos Museum, Atlanta, and joining fragment from the MS3 area (photo: Nadja Schulz, the Danish Institute in Rome, and Michael C. Carlos Museum).

part of the animals would be prepared for serving to the pilgrims. At the end of the ritual, most objects used in the performance of sacrifice and feast show clear signs of having been deliberately destroyed and thereby consigned to the eternal sphere of the gods. In practice, this meant a fragmentation of decorated pottery vessels, terracotta figures, bronze vessels, jewellery, and other objects. Hereafter, the material was deposited around the sacrificial area; or rather, it appears that a part of the material was deposited. Notwithstanding that votive deposits have been excavated in an area covering almost 300 m², joining fragments has proven extremely difficult. At best, two or three fragments from the same vessel can be identified, either through direct joint or typo-stylistic coherency. Only in a handful of cases, of which one will presented below, has it been possible to establish semi-complete vessels. In the period between 2017 and 2022, an estimated fifteen thousand decorated Greek fragments have been excavated in the MS3 area. The limited success in joining these fragments seems to indicate that only a part of the destroyed material was deposited in the MS3 area, acting as a *pars pro toto* for the complete quantity of destroyed material.[49] Nevertheless, the continuing material study of the excavated material and the attempt to connect it to the repatriated material is slowly increasing the number of recontextualized fragments like the ones belonging to a Corinthian pyxis lid seen on Figure 17.17.

What is more, it has been possible to identify additional objects from Timpone della Motta in foreign collections. The latest example came to light during the 2022 excavation campaign. Here a fragment from a sixth-century BC Laconian drinking bowl was excavated in the western part of the MS3 area, in an area which

---

[49] On *pars pro toto* deposits in sanctuaries, see Haynes 2013, 12–14. For ritual destruction in the MS3 area, see Mittica and others (forthcoming).

Repatriated from the Getty Museum

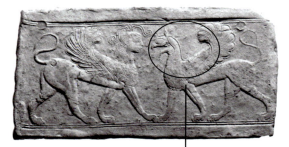

Harvard University Art Museum

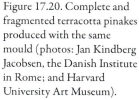

Excavations, Timpone della Motta (2009)

Figure 17.20. Complete and fragmented terracotta pinakes produced with the same mould (photos: Jan Kindberg Jacobsen, the Danish Institute in Rome; and Harvard University Art Museum).

had been severely damaged during the illegal excavations of the 1970s, attested through the occurrence of numerous holes dug in modern times and finds of the abovementioned Fanta soda cans. The fragment is an important addition to the material record of the sanctuary where it is the first piece of figure-decorated Laconian to have been attested so far. The motif is recognizable as a depiction of the Capture of Silenos, and the style can be ascribed to the so-called 'Hunt Painter' (Fig. 17.18). The fragment can be joined with seven other fragments in the collection of the Carlos Museum, Atlanta, with the provenance information: 'Gift from Dietrich von Bothmer. From Ex coll. Ines Jucker (1922–2013), Switzerland. Ex coll. Dietrich von Bothmer (1918–2009), New York, New York, by 1985' (Fig. 17.19).[50]

Dietrich von Bothmer is a well-known name in classical archaeology. Being a leading scholar of ancient Greek pottery, he held the position as head of the Department of Greek and Roman Art at the Metropolitan Museum of Art from 1959 to 1990. From the late 1960s and onwards, he created a personal study collection of Greek vase fragments, which at the time of his death in 2009 had amounted to some sixteen thousand fragments. Most of the collection was donated to the Metropolitan Museum of Art, which accepted them with an understanding with the Italian Ministry for Cultural Heritage, while minor lots were given to the Carlos Museum, the Princeton Museum of Art. Through joining the Laconian fragments, the collection of Dietrich von Bothmer can now — for the first time — be linked to the illegal excavations on Timpone della Motta, which poses the obvious question of whether more fragments donated by Dietrich von Bothmer to the above cited museums may have originated from the site.[51]

The recontextualization of pottery fragments to the MS3 area is conclusive once joining fragments have been identified. The repatriated material, however, also includes many fragments of terracotta figurines and bronze objects which have proven more difficult join with fragments from the archaeological excavations based on a photo documentation alone. Currently, it has not been possible to establish joining fragments among the terracotta and bronze material, but it will be attempted in the near future through direct physical examination of the repatriated material.[52] Meanwhile, some successful

---

[50] <https://collections.carlos.emory.edu/objects/23855/blackfigure-cup-fragment-with-komasts-at-volutekrater-in-t?ctx=438cef12ca4d144077cb6608eda7c34997b28c40&idx=3> [accessed 4 April 2022]. The fragments are published in Gaunt 2013, 42, fig. 4.

[51] A limited number of Corinthian fragments donated by Dietrich von Bothmer to the three collections are of notable interest since they closely resemble the Corinthian pottery from Timpone della Motta in regard to type, date, and state of conservation. The Dietrich von Bothmer fragments can be consulted directly in the museums' online photo archives, Metropolitan Museum of Art: <https://www.metmuseum.org/art/the-collection> [accessed 4 April 2022]; the Princeton University Art Museum: <https://artmuseum.princeton.edu/collections> [accessed 4 April 2022]; Michael C. Carlos Museum, Atlanta: <https://collections.carlos.emory.edu/objects/images> [accessed 4 April 2022].

[52] The repatriation terracotta figurines are currently being prepared for publication by the team of the Danish Institute in Rome in collaboration with Dr Eukene Bilbao Zubiri, École française de Rome.

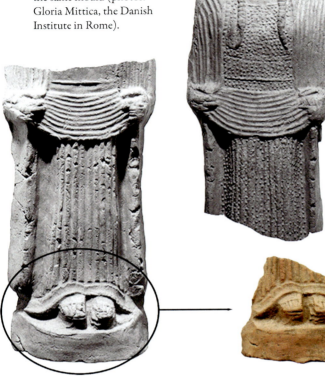

Figure 17.21. Terracotta figurines repatriated from the Getty Museum and from Area MS3, all produced with the same mould (photos: Gloria Mittica, the Danish Institute in Rome).

cases of recontextualization of mould-made terracotta objects can be presented, not based on joining fragments but on the identification of objects produced in the same mould. This permitted the connection of important, but decontextualized, mould-made terracotta pinakes repatriated from the Getty Museum to the MS3 area. Further, it has permitted the identification of a terracotta pinax in the collection of the Harvard University Art Museum acquired in 1980, which in all probability originated from the sanctuary (Fig. 17.20).

The type in question is decorated with a confronting sphinx and griffin. Such a fragment was excavated from a votive assemblage in the MS3 area. A detailed comparison with a complete pinax repatriated from the Getty Museum and an almost-complete pinax from Harvard leaves little doubt that all three were stamped from the same mould, giving a strong indication that they were all excavated at the same site.[53] A couple of terracotta figurines in the repatriated material depict a standing female holding textile in her hands. They should most likely be interpreted as dedicants presenting textiles to a goddess (Fig. 17.21).[54]

However, not having been encountered during regular excavations, the type could until recently not be associated with any structure or area within the sanctuary. This depiction is of notable importance for the understanding of the continuity of cult rites in the sanctuary from the Iron Age to the Archaic period. Excavations of the eighth-century BC so-called Building Vb and Vc conducted by the Groningen Institute of Archaeology to the west of MS3 have produced ample evidence for textile production through the finds of hundreds of loom weights and spindle-whorls.[55] Textile production remained in the cultic sphere during the seventh century BC but now expressed through the dedication of miniature wool baskets (*kalathoi*) in pottery, and symbolic spindle-whorls in faience and glass paste.[56] Until 2017 the regular excavations in the sanctuary had produced scarce evidence for the continuation of textile-related dedications during the sixth century, apart from some occasional finds of loom weights. The excavations in the MS3 area from 2017 onwards seem to underline that textile production remains an important aspect during the sixth century BC, seen both through the dedications of many loom weights as well as the find of fragments belonging to the described terracotta figurines depicting textile dedicants.

Concluding Remarks [JKJ]

Although being recognized as an important archaeological site from the beginning of the twentieth century, large illegal excavations did not commence before the first half of the 1970s. In the absence of written or oral accounts, we have tried to reconstruct the dynamics of the illegal excavations and the international distribution of the excavated objects differently, by treating the excavators left-behinds as an open-air archive and by using documentation from online photo archives and closed archives with analogue photo documentation, respectively. In doing so, it is possible to list several objects from the sanctuary which at times were available on the

---

53 Mitten 2003, 272 and <https://harvardartmuseums.org/collections/object/288249?position=1> [accessed 4 April 2022] (Harvard); Dierichs 1993, 34 (Getty); Jacobsen and Mittica 2019, 44, fig. 14a. (Timpone della Motta).

54 Mittica 2006.

55 Kleibrink 2016; 2017.

56 On the role of textile production in the sanctuary, see Mittica 2021; Saxkjær, Jacobsen, and Mittica 2017.

art market but for which the whereabouts are unknown today. Hopefully, this will provide information for their retrieval sooner or later. Traditionally, repatriation dialogues at large have often been conducted in a tense climate, which prevents collaborations rather than cultivating them. In contrast, the sanctuary on Timpone della Motta has constituted the framework for more than two decades of synergetic collaborations between universities, private foundations, museums, the Italian Ministry of Cultural Heritage, and not least the Comando Carabinieri Tutela Patrimonio Culturale — institutions which do not always share the same points of interest but who, in the case of Timpone della Motta, have teamed up around common values and goals: the repatriation of illegally excavated objects from the sanctuary and their recontextualization to the greatest extent possible.

Works Cited

Boschetti, C., J. K. Jacobsen, G. Mittica, G., E. Mortensen, and R. Raja (forthcoming). 'Glass Beads, Ritual Deposits, and Laser Beams: A Sanctuary on Timpone della Motta Entangled in Networks of Trade and Resettling', *Current World Archaeology*.

Bothmer, D. von and J. V. Noble. 1961. *The History of the Terracotta Warriors: An Inquiry into the Forgery of the Etruscan Terracotta Warriors in the Metropolitan Museum of Art*, Metropolitan Museum of Art Papers, 11 (New York: Metropolitan Museum of Art).

Cerzoso, M. and F. Caputo. 2021. 'Francavilla Marittima e la collezione De Santis: materiali inediti dal Museo dei Brettii e degli Enotri di Cosenza', in T. Grasso and S. Medaglia (eds), *Tra paralia e mesogaia: studi e ricerche per il decennale del Laboratorio di Topografia antica e Antichità calabresi* (Corigliano-Rossano: Ferrari), pp. 151–77.

Cerzoso, M. and A. Vanzetti (eds). 2014. *Museo dei Brettii e degli Enotri: catalogo dell'esposizione* (Soveria Mannelli: Rubbettino).

Christiansen, J. 1977. 'Gudinder, skøger, hustruer eller slaver?', *Meddelelser fra Ny Carlsberg Glyptotek*, 34: 131–56.

—— 2002. 'En Røverhistorie', in A. M. Nielsen (ed.), *Gaveregn: Ny Carlsbergfondets Gaver til Ny Carlsberg Glyptotek gennem hundrede år*, Meddelelser fra Ny Carlsberg Glyptotek (Copenhagen: Ny Carlsberg Glyptotek), pp. 19–34.

Colelli, C. 2014. 'La "questione Lagaria" e le ricerche archeologiche a Francavilla Marittima', in P. Brocato (ed.), *Studi sulla necropoli di Macchiabate a Francavilla Marittima (Cs) e sui territori limitrofi*, Ricerche supplementi, Collana del Dipartimento di studi umanistici, sezione archeologia, Università della Calabria (Rende: Consenso), pp. 335–85.

—— 2017. *Lagaria: mito, storia e archeologia*, Ricerche supplementi, Collana del Dipartimento di studi umanistici, sezione archeologia, Università della Calabria (Rende: Consenso).

—— 2019. 'Francavilla, Sibari e la Sibaritide nella collezione De Santis', in G. Mittica (ed.), *Francavilla Marittima: un patrimonio ricontestualizzato* (Vibo Valentia: Adhoc), pp. 49–57.

Colelli, C. and R. S. Scavello. 2020. 'Scavando tra gli archivi: ritrovamenti archeologici di età preunitaria nella Provincia di Calabria Citeriore', in C. Malacrino, A. Quattrocchi, and R. Di Cesare (eds), *L'antichità nel Regno: archeologia, tutela e restauri nel Mezzogiorno Preunitario, atti del Convegno internazionale di studi Reggio Calabria, 26–29 aprile 2017*, MArRC, Convegni, 3 (Reggio Calabria: Kore), pp. 483–91.

de Lachenal, L. 2007. 'Francavilla Marittima, per una storia degli studi', in F. van der Wielen van Ommeren and L. de Lachenal (eds), *La Dea di Sibari e il Santuario ritrovato: studi sui rinvenimenti dal Timpone della Motta di Francavilla Marittima*, I.1: *Ceramiche di importazione, di produzione coloniale e indigena*, special volume, Bollettino d'arte (Rome: Istituto poligrafico e zecca dello stato) pp. 17–81.

Dierichs, A. 1993. 'Ein Terrakottarelief mit Sphinx und Greif', *Studia Varia from the J. Paul Getty Museum*, 1: 33–54.

Fiorelli, G. 1879. 'XX: Francavilla Marittima', *Notizie degli scavi di Antichità*, 3rd ser., 1879: 125–66.

Fischer-Hansen, T. 1992. *Campania, South Italy and Sicily* (Copenhagen: Ny Carlsberg Glyptotek).

Galli, E. and G. d'Ippolito. 1936. 'Francavilla Marittima: Scoperte fortuite', *Notizie degli scavi di Antichità*, 6th ser., 12: 77–84.

Gallo, G. 1879. 'Terre cotte e bronzi antichi rinvenuti negli scavi della strada del Pollino', *Il Calabrese*, 11: 17.

Gaunt, J. 2013. 'Two Archaic Bronze Κρατῆρες Λακωνικοί? The Dedications of Phanodikos Son of Hermokrates of Prokonnesos and of Phalaris Tyrant of Akragas', *Bulletin Antieke Beschaving*, 88: 39–54.

Gianniti, P. 2020. *Agostino e Tanino De Santis la scoperta della necropoli di Villafranca Marittima e la valorizzazione storico-archeologica della Sibaritide* (Corigliano Calabro: Aurora).

Gill, D. W. J. 2018. 'Returning Archaeological Objects to Italy', *International Journal of Cultural Property*, 25: 283–321.

Guggisberg, M. and C. Colombi. 2021. *Macchiabate: Ausgrabungen in der Nekropole von Francavilla Marittima, Kalabrien, 2009–2016; Die Areale Strada und De Leo* (Wiesbaden: Reichert).

Haynes, I. 2013. 'Advancing the Systematic Study of Ritual Deposition in the Greco-Roman World', in G. Lindström, A. Schäfer, and M. Witteyer (eds), *Rituelle Deponierungen in Heligtümern der hellenistisch-römischen Welt: Internationale Tagung Mainz, 28.–30. April 2008* (Mainz: Generaldirektion Kulturelles Erbe Rheinland-Pfalz), pp. 7–19.

Jacobsen, K. J., P. J. Attema, C. Colelli, J. Ippolito, G. P. Mittica, and S. G. Saxkjær. 2018. 'The Bronze and Iron Age Habitation on Timpone della Motta in the Light of Recent Research', *Analecta Romana Instituti Danici*, 43: 25–90.

Jacobsen, J. K. and S. Handberg. 2010. *Excavations at the Timpone della Motta: Francavilla Marittima 1992–2004*, I: *The Greek Pottery*, Bibliotheca archaeologica, 22 (Bari: Edipuglia).

—— 2012. 'A Greek Enclave at the Iron Age Settlement of Timpone della Motta', in *Atti del L Convegno di studi sulla Magna Grecia (1–4 ottobre 2010)* (Taranto: Istituto per la storia e l'archeologia della Magna Grecia), pp. 683–718.

Jacobsen, J. K., F. Larocca, J. Melander, and G. Mittica. 2021. 'Seasonality of Timpone della Motta (Northern Calabria) during the Iron Age and the Archaic Period', in A. Lichtenberger and R. Raja (eds), *The Seasonality of Archaeology*, Studies in Classical Archaeology, 11 (Turnhout: Brepols), pp. 143–64.

Jacobsen, J. K. and G. Mittica. 2019. 'Alcuni casi di ricontestualizzazione del patrimonio francavillese', in G. Mittica (ed.), *Francavilla Marittima: Un patrimonio ricontestualizzato* (Vibo Valenzia: Adhoc), pp. 35–48.

Jacobsen, J. K. and J. H. Petersen. 2002. 'International Puzzle of Archaic Greek Potsherds', *Tijdschrift voor Mediterrane Archeologie*, 27: 30–36.

Jacobsen, J. K., S. G. Saxkjær, and G. P. Mittica. 2017a. 'Observations on Euboean Koinai in Southern Italy', in S. Handberg and A. Gadolou (eds), *Material Koinai in the Greek Early Iron Age and Archaic Period: Acts of an International Conference at the Danish Institute at Athens (Athens 2015)* (Aarhus: Aarhus University Press), pp. 169–90.

—— 2017b. 'Cultural Dynamics in the Seventh-Century Sibaritide (Southern Italy)', in X. Charalambidou and C. Morgan (eds), *Interpreting the Seventh-Century BC: Tradition and Innovation* (Oxford: Archaeopress), pp. 330–38.

Johansen, F. 1994. *Greece in the Archaic Period* (Copenhagen: Ny Carlsberg Glyptotek).

Kleibrink, M. 2010. *Parco archeologico 'LAGARIA' a Francavilla Marittima presso Sibari: guida* (Rossano: Grafosud).

—— 2016. *Excavations at Francavilla Marittima 1991–2004: Finds Related to Textile Production from the Timpone della Motta*, V: *Spindle Whorls*, British Archaeological Reports, International Series, 2806 (Oxford: British Archaeological Reports).

—— 2017. *Excavations at Francavilla Marittima 1991–2004: Finds Related to Textile Production from the Timpone della Motta*, VI: *Loom Weights*, British Archaeological Reports, International Series, 2848 (Oxford: British Archaeological Reports).

—— 2018. 'Architettura e rituale nell'Athenaion di Lagaria: Timpone della Motta (Francavilla Marittima)', *Atti e memorie della Società Magna Grecia*, 5: 171–253.

Malacrino, C., M. Paoletti, and M. D. Costanzo (eds). 2018. *Tanino de Santis: Una vita per la Magna Grecia*, MArRC, cataloghi, 10 (Reggio Calabria: Kore).

Mekacher, N. and J. Christiansen. 2007. '3. Pissidi', in F. van der Wielen van Ommeren and L. de Lachenal (eds), *La Dea di Sibari e il Santuario ritrovato: studi sui rinvenimenti dal Timpone della Motta di Francavilla Marittima*, I.1: *Ceramiche di importazione, di produzione coloniale e indigena*, special volume, Bollettino d'arte (Rome: Istituto poligrafico e zecca dello stato), pp. 125–52.

Mitten, D. G. 2003. 'Fragmentary Pinax with Relief of Sphinx and Griffin', in J. M. Padgett and W. A. P. Childs (eds), *The Centaur's Smile: The Human Animal in Early Greek Art* (Princeton: Princeton University Art Museum), pp. 272–73.

Mittica, G. 2006. 'Kalathìskoi dall'Athenaion del Timpone Motta: Piccoli doni ricolmi di lana', in P. Altieri (ed.), *Atti della IV Giornata Archeologica Francavillese (Francavilla Marittima 2005)* (Stampa Ventura: Francavilla Marittima), pp. 9–20.

—— 2019a. 'Dal rimpatrio all'allestimento della mostra', in G. Mittica (ed.), *Francavilla Marittima: Un patrimonio ricontestualizzato* (Vibo Valentia: Adhoc), pp. 25–34.

—— 2019b. 'Espressioni votive e rituali nel santuario arcaico di Timpone della Motta', in G. Mittica (ed.), *Francavilla Marittima: Un patrimonio ricontestualizzato* (Vibo Valentia: Adhoc), pp. 65–73.

—— 2021. 'Creazioni artigianali di preziose fusaiole in ambito locale?', in T. Grasso and S. Medaglia (eds), *Tra paralia e mesogaia: studi e ricerche per il decennale del Laboratorio di topografia antica e antichità calabresi* (Corigliano-Rossano: Ferrari), pp. 179–215.

Mittica, G. and J. K. Jacobsen. 2018. 'Recenti ricerche nel Santuario di Timpone della Motta a Francavilla Marittima', in C. Malacrino, D. Costanzo, and M. Paoletti (eds), *Tanino de Santis: Una vita per la Magna Grecia*, MArRC cataloghi, 10 (Reggio Calabria: KORE), pp. 131–38.

—— 2019. 'Il quartiere artigianale dell'età del Ferro. Area Rovitti: ricerche e scavi 2008–2009/2018–2019', in G. Mittica (ed.), *Francavilla Marittima: Un patrimonio ricontestualizzato* (Vibo Valentia: Adhoc), pp. 79–85.

Mittica, G., J. K. Jacobsen, M. D'Andrea, and N. Perrone. 2018. 'Pratiche rituali nel santuario di Timpone della Motta', in C. Colelli and A. Larocca (eds), *Il Pollino: Barriera naturale e crocevia di cultura*, Ricerche supplementi, Collana del Dipartimento di studi umanistici, sezione archeologia, Università della Calabria, 12 (Rende: Consenso), pp. 95–112.

Mittica, G., J. K. Jacobsen, J. Melander, N. Perrone, and N. Schulz (forthcoming). *Mapping Ritual Destruction on Timpone della Motta during the Archaic Period*, Acta Hyperborea.

Mittica, G. and N. Perrone. 2018. 'Espressioni votive e rituali nel santuario arcaico di Timpone della Motta: Le novità dagli scavi DIR 2017', *Analecta Romana Instituti Danici*, 43: 237–63.

Palladion Antike Kunst: Katalog 1976. 1976 (Milan: GEA).

Paoletti, M. 2014. 'La necropoli enotria di Macchiabate, Lagaria e la "dea di Sibari"', in P. Brocato (ed.), *Studi sulla necropoli di Macchiabate a Francavilla Marittima (Cs) e suoi territori limitrofi*, Ricerche supplementi, Collana del Dipartimento di studi umanistici, sezione archeologia, Università della Calabria (Rende: Consenso), pp. 7–21.

—— 2017. 'Un'introduzione a Lagaria. Gli "splendidi trovatelli" di Francavilla Marittima', in C. Colelli (ed.), *Lagaria: Mito, storia e archeologia*, Ricerche, Suppl. 7 (Arcavacata di Rende: Università della Calabria), pp. xi–xxvi.

Papadopoulos, J. 2003. *La Dea di Sibari e il Santuario ritrovato: studi sui rinvenimenti dal Timpone della Motta di Francavilla Marittima*, II.1: *The Archaic Votive Metal Objects*, special volume, Bollettino d'arte (Rome: Istituto poligrafico e zecca dello stato).

Piccirillo, G. 1857. 'Francavilla', in F. Cirelli, *Storia del Regno delle Due Sicilie descritto ed illustrato: opera dedicata alla maestà di Ferdinando II*, XI (Naples: Calabria Citerione), pp. 93–96.

Raffiotta, S. 2011. 'La "Venere" di Morgantina. Torna a casa un capolavoro dell'arte classica', *Archeologia viva*, 146: 30–38.

Saxkjær, S. G., J. K. Jacobsen, and G. Mittica. 2017. 'Building V and Ritual Textile Production at Timpone della Motta', in C. Brøns and M. L. Nosch (eds), *Textile and Cult in the Ancient Mediterranean* (Oxford: Oxbow), pp. 91–103.

Serio, M. and G. Proietti. 2003. 'Premessa', in J. Papadopoulos (ed.), *La Dea di Sibari e il Santuario ritrovato: studi sui rinvenimenti dal Timpone della Motta di Francavilla Marittima*, II.1: *The Archaic Votive Metal Objects*, special volume, Bollettino d'arte (Rome: Istituto poligrafico e zecca dello stato), pp. vii–ix.

Stoop, M. W. 1974–1976. 'Acropoli sulla Motta', *Atti e memorie della Società Magna Grecia*, 15–17: 107–67.

—— 1979. 'Note sugli scavi nel santuario di Atena sul Timpone della Motta (Francavilla Marittima), 1–2', *Bulletin Antieke Beschaving*, 54: 77–90.

—— 1983. 'Note sugli scavi nel santuario di Atena sul Timpone della Motta (Francavilla Marittima – Calabria), 4', *Bulletin Antieke Beschaving*, 58: 17–53.

—— 1985. 'Note sugli scavi nel santuario di Atena sul Timpone della Motta (Francavilla Marittima – Calabria), 5: Un base di ricinto', *Bulletin Antieke Beschaving*, 60: 4–11.

—— 1987. 'Note sugli scavi nel santuario di Atena sul Timpone della Motta (Francavilla Marittima – Calabria), 7: Oggetti di bronzo vari (animali, ornamenti, personali, armi, varia)', *Bulletin Antieke Beschaving*, 62: 21–31.

—— 1988. 'Note sugli scavi nel santuario di Atena sul Timpone della Motta (Francavilla Marittima – Calabria), 8: Il materiale protocorinzio – una scelta', *Bulletin Antieke Beschaving*, 63: 29–37.

—— 1989. 'Note sugli scavi nel santuario di Atena sul Timpone della Motta (Francavilla Marittima – Calabria), 9: La ceramica attica', *Bulletin Antieke Beschaving*, 64: 50–60.

—— 1990. 'Note sugli scavi nel santuario di Atena sul Timpone della Motta (Francavilla Marittima – Calabria), 10: Il materiale corinzio – una prima scelta', *Bulletin Antieke Beschaving*, 65: 29–37.

Trantalidou, K. 2013. 'Dans l'ombre du rite: vestiges d'animaux et pratiques sacrificielles en Grèce antique. Note sur la diversité des contextes et les difficultés de recherche rencontrées', in G. Ekroth and J. Wallesten (eds), *Bones, Behaviour and Belief: The Zooarchaeological Evidence as a Source for Ritual Practice in Ancient Greece and Beyond*, Skrifter utgivna av Svenska Institutet i Athen, 4°, 55 (Stockholm: Swedish Institute in Athens), pp. 61–86.

Tsiafakis, D. 2008. 'The East Greek and East Greek-Style Pottery', in F. van der Wielen van Ommeren and L. de Lachenal (eds), *La Dea di Sibari e il Santuario ritrovato: studi sui rinvenimenti dal Timpone della Motta di Francavilla Marittima*, I.2: *Ceramiche di importazione, di produzione coloniale e indigena*, special volume, Bollettino d'arte (Rome: Istituto poligrafico e zecca dello stato), pp. 7–56.

Watson, P. and C. Todeschini. 2006. *The Medici Conspiracy: The Illicit Journey of Looted Antiquities-From Italy's Tomb Raiders to the World's Greatest Museums* (New York: PublicAffairs).

Wielen van Ommeren, F. van der and J. Christiansen. 2007. '5: Oinochoai', in F. van der Wielen van Ommeren and L. de Lachenal (eds), *La Dea di Sibari e il Santuario ritrovato: studi sui rinvenimenti dal Timpone della Motta di Francavilla Marittima*, I.1: *Ceramiche di importazione, di produzione coloniale e indigena*, special volume, Bollettino d'arte (Rome: Istituto poligrafico e zecca dello stato), pp. 175–209.

Wielen van Ommeren, F. van der and L. de Lachenal. 2007. *La Dea di Sibari e il Santuario ritrovato: studi sui rinvenimenti dal Timpone della Motta di Francavilla Marittima*, I.1: *Ceramiche di importazione, di produzione coloniale e indigena*, special volume, Bollettino d'arte (Rome: Istituto poligrafico e zecca dello stato).

—— 2008. *La Dea di Sibari e il Santuario ritrovato: studi sui rinvenimenti dal Timpone della Motta di Francavilla Marittima*, I.2: *Ceramiche di importazione, di produzione coloniale e indigena*, special volume, Bollettino d'arte (Rome: Istituto poligrafico e zecca dello stato).

18. The History and Implications of the American Center of Research's (ACOR) Archival Digitization

Pearce Paul Creasman and Ryder Kouba
American Center of Research, Amman (pcreasman@acorjordan.org, rkouba@acorjordan.org)

Introduction

Established in 1968, the American Center of Research (ACOR; formerly the American Center of Oriental Research) is an independent non-profit institution whose mission is advancing knowledge of Jordan and the interconnected region, past and present. The American Center promotes the preservation, creation, and dissemination of knowledge and supports research across a broad swath of the social, natural, and physical sciences, the humanities, and the arts, embracing both tangible and intangible cultural heritage. It does so through knowledge sharing, including by means of lectures, digital resources, print publications, workshops and training programmes, archaeological research, and cultural heritage preservation. ACOR's primary efforts are conducted through an extensive library and archive, fellowship and scholarship programmes, public lectures and workshops, language instruction, and publication of open access resources. Our *raison d'être* is to engage with members of the public, students, and scholars at all stages of their careers through the multifaceted cultural sector: project foci include archaeology (from prehistory to the Islamic period), art history, cultural heritage management, and intercultural seminars for educators. The cultural heritage and intellectual legacies of scholars from the United States and other North American countries working in Jordan and the broader region are tended by ACOR. During the past six decades, ACOR has undertaken work directly or supported the efforts of others at hundreds of sites and other types of projects in Jordan, Syria, Saudi Arabia, Yemen, and elsewhere in the region. Above all, the American Center serves as a conduit for cultural and intellectual exchange among Americans, Jordanians, Canadians, and the people and institutions of the wider region. For fifty-four years, we have been preserving the primary historical and cultural record of the region and ensuring the long-term and wide availability of, and access to, these records for scholars, teachers, and the public alike.

Since its founding, the American Center of Research has worked diligently to collect library and archival materials that document both Jordan and the wider region. In its early years, a large amount of collected content was related solely to the archaeology of Jordan, and as ACOR has grown, other subjects and locations have increased in importance. Today, the American Center of Research holds over one hundred thousand photographic images — mostly as 35 mm slides but also including photographic prints, negatives, and born-digital media — that are a valuable tool for researchers and students interested in archaeology, anthropology, the environment, ethnography, architecture, and a host of other subjects relating to the region. In addition to such visual resources, the collections include scholarly works and publications, archaeological excavation notebooks, and assorted other materials. Donors of collections have included ACOR directors and staff, academics, and archaeologists, as well as journalists and photographers. While the earliest photographs in the collection date to World War II, a significant portion of the images are currently from the 1970s to the 1990s, often allowing users to compare sites over decades of immense change in the area.

In addition to personal collections, the archives incorporate the institutional content of ACOR, with collections documenting ACOR-funded archaeological projects such as the American Expedition to Petra's Temple of the Winged Lions excavations and Amman Citadel projects, recordings of lectures hosted by ACOR in a variety of formats since the early 1980s, and 1500 maps of Jordan and surrounding countries.

The value of these collections is manifold: while Petra, Palmyra, and other well-known and well-documented archaeological sites are well represented in the collections, less well-documented sites of the region — and many sites that are now destroyed or drastically altered — are also included. Besides a diverse range of geographical locations represented in the collections, temporally, the images span eight decades. Images of Iraq al-Amir (among many others) from its excavation in the 1960s up to the early 2000s can be compared and changes within the site and surrounding area noted. Having documentation of archaeological excavations and landscapes over time can be valuable for researchers in a host of ways. Images of the workers, their families, and the communities around archaeological sites are valuable documentation that stretch beyond the stones and mortar of the ruins to social histories yet to be constructed.[1] Several collections also feature images from cultural heritage sites under threat from conflicts, most notably in Syria and Yemen. Preserving and providing access to documentary photos of cultural heritage is a valuable component of the ACOR Archive.

The increasing need for digital resources of the region has been apparent since even before the COVID-19 era. In 'Research without Archives? The Making and Remaking of Area Studies Knowledge of the Middle East in a Time of Chronic War', Laila Hussein Moustafa demonstrates that those researching countries in the Middle East face serious barriers to archival materials, which is severely limiting knowledge of the region.[2] The problem is widespread: in Moustafa's 2016–2017 survey of two hundred Middle East area studies researchers, 93 per cent of respondents stated that prior to 2016 they had travelled to the region for their research. Recent restrictions, however, caused 75 per cent of respondents to cite new funding limitations as an impediment to their ability to travel to the Middle East to conduct research.[3] For example, the 2021–2022 Fulbright Middle East and North Africa Regional Research Program was not expecting to fund research or lectures in Yemen, Iraq, Syria, Iran, Lebanon, and Turkey. Unsurprisingly, the survey results demonstrated a significant change in researchers' destination countries for travel within the region, with a marked decrease in those intending to travel to Egypt, Lebanon, and Turkey and a rise in those intending to travel to Jordan and Morocco. Since 2016, the ACOR archive has digitized archival photographs of Yemen, Iraq, Syria, Iran, Lebanon, and Turkey, making research and engagement with the region possible even when regional travel is restricted.

When asked about alternatives if physical archives were inaccessible or destroyed, 37 per cent stated that they would use digitized materials instead.[4] More than two-thirds of respondents stated that they used archival resources *every time* they conducted research in the region, illustrating the utmost importance of these archives to Middle Eastern studies as a field. This is true for the variety of disciplines within this field, including linguistics, humanities, and the social sciences, as well as political science, in which an 'archival turn' is leading to an increase in archive use even for a field traditionally rooted in contemporary affairs. In the current regional political climate, online archives are essential for researchers in Middle Eastern studies to continue to advance knowledge and deepen understanding about the region where access to physical archives may be restricted or unobtainable, especially for U.S. nationals, due to travel/funding prohibitions and safety concerns. Access to recorded conversations and discussions from past decades in ACOR's archives would be a considerable boon to these fields.[5]

History of Archival Digitization Efforts

Early efforts — and understanding the full scope of what ACOR holds and what to do with it — started in 1999.[6] A grant provided by the U.S. Department of Education (2000–2002), helped to organize the materials and funded an early attempt at digitization. While slides and photographs were digitized, a public platform to provide access to them was not created. Slides were also scanned at what was at the time a reasonable resolution, but today it does not meet current standards, such as those set out by the Federal Agencies Digital Guidelines Initiative.[7] There being no way to provide public access to digitized surrogates, the slides largely remained unused, an untapped research resource for scholars and researchers of Jordan and archaeology. Furthermore, little by way of descriptions accompanied the collections created or posted publicly, leaving them difficult for researchers — as well as ACOR staff — to discover and use.

---

[1] Rowland 2014; Beck 2021; Lumb 2020.
[2] Hussein Moustafa 2018.
[3] Hussein Moustafa 2018.
[4] Hussein Moustafa 2018.
[5] The preceding two paragraphs include contributions of John D. M. Green, Jessica Holland, and Noreen Doyle, while on staff at ACOR, with thanks.
[6] Zamora 2000.
[7] See: <https://www.digitizationguidelines.gov/> [accessed 16 October 2022].

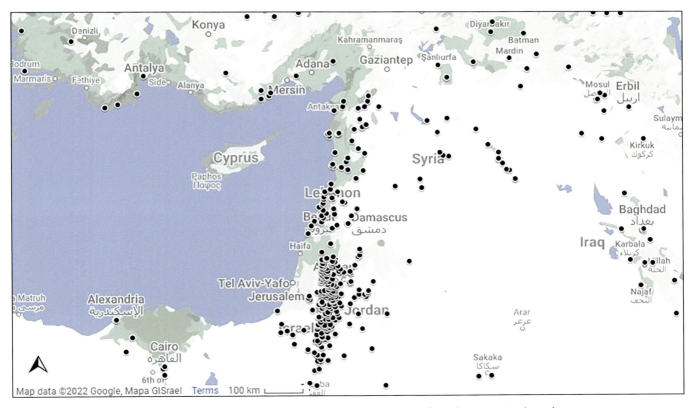

Figure 18.1. Map of sites covered in the ACOR Digital Archive as of October 2022. Map by authors, map data: © 2022 Google, Mapa GISrael <https://bit.ly/3EPFUni> [accessed 16 October 2022].

In 2016, efforts were renewed and ACOR began a U.S. Department of Education Title VI-funded grant to digitize, describe, and provide access to thirty thousand slides and photographic prints.[8] Images are hosted on the ACOR Photo Archive, an online platform created as part of the grant.[9] The collections selected for digitization to date were largely — but not entirely — archaeologically focused. Notable archaeological collections selected include that of Paul and Nancy Lapp, documenting their work in Jordan in the 1960s and 1970s.[10] Highlights include their aforementioned excavation of the Byzantine site of Iraq al-Amir: the process of unearthing the ruins is well documented, as are the various workers on the project. The collection of former ACOR director Bert De Vries highlights his excavation of Umm el-Jimal in Jordan as well as ACOR's institutional history during his term as director.[11] In addition to materials from archaeologists, 35 mm slides and photographic negatives from journalist Rami Khouri documenting daily life in the Middle East (as well as archaeological sites) were digitized,[12] as were images from the ACOR institutional collection, which showcase the history of the organization, both in terms of archaeological projects and in events and facilities. Besides digitization, finding aids were created for collections for the first time; these provide more context about the collections and their creators.

Following the success of the 2016 grant, in 2020 ACOR embarked on another U.S. Department of Education Title VI grant to digitize twenty thousand more slides and begin converting the photo archive to a multimedia archive.[13] The slides to be digitized, described, and made accessible as part of the 2020 grant are from the Barbara Porter collection (which documents archaeological sites, architecture, and scenes of

---

8 Green and Holland 2021.

9 See: <https://photoarchive.acorjordan.org/> [accessed 16 October 2022].

10 See: <https://photoarchive.acorjordan.org/paul-and-nancy-lapp-collection/> [accessed 16 October 2022].

11 See: <https://photoarchive.acorjordan.org/1177-2/> [accessed 16 October 2022].

12 See: <https://photoarchive.acorjordan.org/rami-khouri-collection/> [accessed 16 October 2022].

13 Holland 2021.

Figure 18.2. Results of a search in the ACOR Digital Archive (© American Center of Research) <https://photoarchive.acorjordan.org/> [accessed 16 October 2022].

daily life from around the region during the 1970s to early 2000s), photographic prints and slides from the Brian Byrd collection (related to his archaeological excavations in Jordan, most notably at 'Ain Ghazal), and slides from the Petra Church Project. Excavated between 1992 and 1998 by ACOR with funding from the United States Agency for International Development (USAID) and support from the Jordanian Ministry of Tourism and Department of Antiquities, the Petra Church Project revealed an important Byzantine church. Besides the church and its famous mosaic floor, the excavation revealed the Petra scrolls: 140 papyri documenting a wide range of activities (particularly legal actions) in Byzantine Petra. Furthermore, this grant will feature a significant educator-engagement component for teachers in the United States.

As of June 2022, there are sixteen countries represented in the ACOR Digital Archive (Fig. 18.1), although images from Jordan represent almost three-fourths of the total. Other countries with large numbers of photos include Syria, Turkey, and Lebanon. These ratios are liable to change over time as new collections are acquired and made accessible; awareness of what regions or sites ACOR is lacking can also help drive collecting and outreach efforts.

In addition to photographic materials, also digitized will be audio-visual formats, largely consisting of audio and video recordings of ACOR lectures from the 1980s and 1990s. The lectures include both singular events and multi-lecture courses taught at ACOR. These will complement ACOR's existing lectures from the past half-decade that are currently available on YouTube[14] and will hopefully provide insight into how the teaching of archaeology has changed over the past forty years. Unfortunately, while the clicking and scratching of chalk is clearly audible on the early recordings, no record exists (that we have found yet) of what was being drawn on the chalkboard. In the future, the goal is to provide online access to written archaeological records to complement the photographs and lectures.

Providing easy access to researchers and other users is a necessary step, given the complex digital library environment. While the sharing of archival resources has been practised for a long time (as evidenced by Photostat copies shared between archives a century ago), digital libraries began only around the end of the twentieth century and have continued to grow rapidly over the past twenty years. Researchers are flush with choices as universities and educational/research organizations around the world are continually placing new historical materials online, generally free to access and frequently either in the public domain or with very few restrictions as to how the material can be used. Content is also being provided by individuals who share photographs with metadata through Wikimedia Commons, Flickr, personal websites, and other online venues.

Digitization

Digitization and public access are necessary to maximize the use of our holdings by both researchers and the general public. Besides the limitations that physically visiting Jordan imposes on some potential users (particularly during the COVID-19 era), the physical formats themselves are not as easy to use as many may be accustomed to. Binders of 35 mm slides, which require a light table and jeweller's loupe to view, are neither as convenient nor as expeditious as digital folders of digitized images

---

14 See: <https://www.youtube.com/c/ACORJordan1968/> [accessed 16 October 2022].

Figure 18.3. Photographic slides with labels, potential sources of digital metadata. Jane Taylor Collection, American Center of Research.

viewed on a screen (Fig. 18.2). Indeed, the slide collections were rarely used by researchers who visited ACOR; this is even more so for other formats: for example, wheeling out a television and a thirty-year-old Betamax player, although once standard, is today not an ideal way to access videos. Moreover, the repeated use of fragile archival materials is well known to have a deleterious effect on their long-term preservation. While digitization is not equivalent to preservation of physical items, it can help extend the lifespans of objects through reduced use of and reduced need to rehouse the materials. The ACOR Archive's digitization procedures and policies follow the best practices set out by the Federal Agencies Digital Guidelines Initiative, with the goal of creating digital surrogates that accurately capture the colour and condition of the physical objects. To help provide for long-term access, digital files are stored on multiple servers, external hard drives, and our digital asset management system.

Metadata

Of course, digitization is only half the battle. Allowing users to actually find what they are searching for among tens of thousands of images requires accurate and useful metadata. The intended audience of the project is the general public, but browsing through forty thousand images is not feasible or desirable for users of any class.

For this reason, Simple Dublin Core[15] fields were created, providing searchable descriptions, locations, and keywords to help users find the content they seek. Following standard descriptive practices, the donor's description (e.g. inscription or label on a slide frame; Fig. 18.3) is recorded and often used as the public description that users will see, with other fields added for standardized keywords, locations, and time period. Data provided by donors can vary wildly, even within the same collection. Some have systemic descriptions providing detailed descriptions and specific dates for each slide. Other slides may have no description at all other than being in a box labelled 'Istanbul'. Researching and creating the metadata for individual slides is the most time-consuming part of the process and requires judgement on what is most important or useful for the end users. Does it meet the needs of our users to label a slide 'Ruins of Ugarit', or is more detail (direction of the photo, archaeological square) needed? ACOR has largely employed simpler metadata, with the idea that users can research details about individual images; however, archive staff are happy to help when contacted. The balance of providing more items in lesser detail is an active decision given the practical limitations of resources (e.g. staff time). Additionally, minimal description (a widely accepted archival description practice) can always be improved upon later; numerous projects have utilized crowdsourcing to generate metadata. The important thing is that the content is available in a timely and efficient manner.

Transliteration of place names is a challenge for anyone creating metadata. While thesauruses (such as the Getty Thesaurus of Geographic Names)[16] have a standardized choice available for locations around the world, these are often not practical or user-friendly.[17] To help solve this issue and make our materials more readily searchable, ACOR has been providing multiple names for locations and sites in the collections. Two fields created that were beyond the scope of Simple Dublin Core were the 'Historic Period' field and the 'Site' field. As their names imply, the 'Historic Period' field allows users to see all images related to Roman, Byzantine, Ottoman, etc. images. The 'Site' field is a more detailed version of the place, including individual buildings and archaeological sites. Having this granular level of detail also allows for more precise mapping of images; for example, beyond just 'Palmyra', users can see the geographic relationship between the Temple of Baal and Fakhr-al-Din al-Ma'ani Castle.

While the majority of the metadata for the 2016 grant was created in English only, the 2020 grant matching has allowed for Arabic metadata to be created for every image. This will hopefully increase the utility and searchability for users whose native language is Arabic; they compose the greatest share of in-person visitors to ACOR's library. Considerable effort was invested to create a glossary of Arabic terms to be used to help improve consistency amongst different staff members. Additionally, adding Arabic metadata to half the images requires retroactively adding Arabic metadata to 2016–2020 materials, since without doing so we could give users the impression that the search results they see for عمان include all items with that keyword, when in fact it would include only materials that were part of the 2020–2024 grant. For subject terms and locations, this process is fairly straightforward; for titles, however, it will be a time-consuming process of translating existing English metadata.

The metadata is a challenge for audio-visual materials, particularly the digitized ACOR lectures. While all lectures have descriptive titles (e.g. 'Stone Age of Jordan, Lecture 6: Middle Paleolithic, Upper Paleolithic' by Gary Rollefson, 1982), is that detailed enough for researchers? Perhaps committed users will listen to the entire hour-long recording, but others may prefer being able to search a transcript of the lecture. A test of one automated transcription platform with one lecture was very disappointing, with virtually unusable results. Summarizing and/or transcribing the lectures is an option, but does that provide enough benefit to offset the resources consumed doing so? These are representative of the issues we must confront.

Use of the Archive

ACOR launched the Photo Archive in November 2018, and as of December 2021, it had received more than 10,500 distinct visitors. The United States and Jordan account for the majority of visitors, with about 30 per cent each; the United Kingdom is the only other country to exceed 5 per cent of the total visitors. Browser language settings for visitors were heavily skewed in the favour of English (73 per cent of total users), while only

---

[15] See: <https://www.dublincore.org/> [accessed 16 October 2022].

[16] See: <https://www.getty.edu/research/tools/vocabularies/tgn/index.html/> [accessed 16 October 2022].

[17] For Alexandria, Egypt, Getty recommends 'Al Iskandarīyah'. While technically accurate, few native English-language searchers (ACOR's primary audience) are likely to search with that spelling.

11 per cent had Arabic set as their language. This makes sense because the overwhelming majority of metadata is in English, but we are hopeful that the goal of creating equivalent Arabic metadata for each item with the 2020 grant will increase usage in Arabic (from anywhere) and usage in Jordan and the wider region.

Hosting archival collections online has also allowed ACOR to link and share content through Wikipedia (in both English and Arabic). Today, some 10 per cent of visitors to the online archive come from Wikipedia. Jordan and its rich history and archaeological sites are under-represented in both English and Arabic Wikipedia; to help remedy that, ACOR has hosted Wikipedia edit-a-thons that have both improved and increased the content about archaeology in Jordan as well as other topics while, when possible, linking to ACOR resources.[18] This has the benefit of increasing awareness of ACOR, its mission, and its resources, as well as the content available. Likewise, consistent promotion of the collection through sharing images on our social media accounts has increased traffic to the archive (13 per cent of visitors come from Facebook), as well as followers of ACOR accounts. In addition to increasing access points to ACOR holdings through Wikipedia, the opportunity exists to improve Wikidata's structured data for Jordanian archaeological sites, which can be used by archaeologists, the public, and other libraries and archives.

Dozens of researchers, students, librarians, and journalists have made use of ACOR archival images since 2018 in a variety of projects ranging from event posters at the Smithsonian to blog posts, student journals, newspapers, and academic publications. With the 2020–2024 grant focusing on outreach to teachers and academics, we are hopeful that use of our resources in studies and academic work will increase.

Having the archival images and data online has the potential to be used in a wide variety of digital humanities projects that can use the images in new ways. The contents of the 'Place Name' field have been mapped already; these can provide needed context for users unfamiliar with the geographical relationships amongst archaeological sites.[19] The collections can also be part of a chronological project on the history of various sites. A researcher interested in Palmyra may use the Harald Ingholt collection for early depictions of the site while utilizing ACOR's holdings for the 1970s to 1990s.

Still, while preserving access to archival materials is important, without sustained engagement to activate these resources digitization efforts fail to meet their goals of breaking down barriers to information. With intensified interest in the region, Middle Eastern studies researchers, students, faculty, and the public alike face bombardments of media commentary and require public education/coverage and outreach on controversial contemporary issues.[20] Added to these pressures in American higher education is a recent heightened focus on internationalizing course materials that address broad transnational themes, such as the environment or migration, rather than area-specific regions. Accordingly, there is a concurrent increase in the number of programmes specifically committed to delivering a global education, but at the present, there are insufficient educational resources to fully support such growth. The ACOR Archive serves as an access point for such content.[21]

Engagement with Community Colleges and Minority-Serving Institutions

While ACOR has been providing access to materials online since 2018, the 2020 grant aims to specifically increase usage among community colleges and minority-serving institutions (MSIs) in the United States. To do so, we will create open access curricular materials that draw from the archive. Each summer from 2022 to 2024, three Educator Fellowships will be awarded to faculty at community colleges or MSIs, who in turn will develop teaching materials utilizing ACOR's archival collections. These will then be hosted online for free dissemination and classroom use for any educator around the world.

In addition to the fellows, direct outreach to faculty at universities and research institutions around the world is also much easier and more productive with collections to link to. LibGuides[22] and databases of resources at U.S. and European universities, as well as Middle Eastern and archaeological groups, have helped increase awareness and usage of research collections.[23]

---

18 Salzinger 2020; Malko and Salzinger 2021.

19 See: <https://www.google.com/maps/d/edit?mid=1Df KCmmMw6UvUq7xXIf0whDNzNNr7DDSA&usp=sharing/> [accessed 16 October 2022].

20 Shami and Miller-Idriss 2018.

21 The preceding paragraph includes contributions of John D. M. Green, Jessica Holland, and Noreen Doyle, while on staff at ACOR, with thanks.

22 See: <https://springshare.com/libguides/> [accessed 16 October 2022].

23 For an example, see: <https://cmes.arizona.edu/outreach/lessons/> [accessed 16 October 2022].

Other Advantages

Providing access to digital collections has also provided opportunities (as well as challenges) for collaboration with other institutions in the region and around the world. Collaborative digital libraries are not new: both the World Digital Library[24] and Europeana[25] launched in 2009 and enabled institutions to share their materials and metadata in a centralized location. The Digital Library of the Middle East (DLME)[26] and Arabic Collections Online[27] each started a few years later with the goal of allowing users to search digital collections at institutions in the region and elsewhere. ACOR intends to join and have our collections linked to from the main DLME site. While not all potential users may be aware of ACOR, having our collections searchable in a centralized location alongside well-known institutions such as Stanford University and the Qatar National Library can only be beneficial in improving knowledge and use of our archive. Unfortunately, at this time technical challenges with our hosting platform have prevented our holdings from being ingested into the DLME, but we are looking forward to contributing soon.

The current Title VI grant has a justifiable emphasis on undergraduate instruction; digitized materials can be utilized by scholars and students in new ways, given the large amounts of data available. Projects such as Antiquity À-la-carte[28] can employ existing data innovatively, for instance, by using georeferencing to help provide spatial context that a location listed in a metadata field cannot.

Value to Archaeologists?

We argue that the primary value to archaeologists for the materials housed at ACOR and similar institutions lies in their potential. Much of their practical value, as records of changing sites and landscapes, has been discussed above, but there are other critical future uses. Organizations such as ACOR are the ones that can keep records organized, accessible, and alive across generations. Organizations such as ACOR can and often do serve as the *de facto* tenders of the legacies of individual scholars and the sites they work, assuming their records upon their retirement, death, or departure for other careers. Often, these events are not planned but triaged. More often than not, archaeological sites are worked on over the span of one person's career (e.g. the dig director's), or perhaps even just a small part of that person's career. As there has been in the past decades a proliferation of archaeological jobs and institutions that conduct archaeological work, there has also been a proliferation of site and record 'orphaning'.[29] It seems fewer and fewer universities and colleges are planning for and curating the personal archives of the scholars they support, even those who served for decades. When the lead investigator is done with a site, the project very often meets its end, published or not. That investigator has, it seems more often than not, failed to designate a clear successor to carry on the works or make plans for their notes and unpublished data. Institutions that take on these transitions and house such records and data are, today, the exception. It is the dedicated research centres, like ACOR (as opposed to the generalist university departments whose geographic and temporal interests change with each faculty member), who are in the best position to serve the field as archival repositories. With archaeology's inherently destructive nature, all of the potential knowledge acquired during a project is trapped in notebooks, archival records, photographs, and whatever samples/artefacts remain. If those categories of materials are splintered, it becomes even more difficult to actualize their value and release the knowledge of the past they contain. In these conditions, archives such as ACOR's have growing value every day.

What Is Next?

While ACOR has a rich photographic collection that is being preserved in archival digital storage, current and certainly future archaeological accessions are more and more born-digital. This is hardly surprising, given the rapid rise of digital photography, particularly with smartphones, but it does present new challenges and opportunities. While ACOR staff diligently digitizes twenty thousand of Barbara A. Porter's 35 mm slides, there are over fifty thousand born-digital photographs that are, content-wise, very similar to the slides, but they were created twenty

---

[24] See: <https://www.loc.gov/collections/world-digital-library/about-this-collection/> [accessed 16 October 2022].

[25] See: <https://www.europeana.eu/> [accessed 16 October 2022].

[26] See: <https://dlmenetwork.org/library/> [accessed 16 October 2022].

[27] See: <https://dlib.nyu.edu/aco/> [accessed 16 October 2022].

[28] See: <http://awmc.unc.edu/wordpress/alacarte/> [accessed 16 October 2022].

[29] For an example, see the Temple of Winged Lions in Petra (Piraud-Fournet and others 2021).

years later with a digital camera or smartphone. ACOR has recently undertaken its first major effort to attend to born-digital resources, making a further 4265 images available with English and Arabic finding aids.[30]

While digital preservation practices are already being applied to digitized images, descriptive metadata could require an adjustment. Rather than having a staff member create metadata (or use the donor's written description) for each individual slide, with the born-digital photographs perhaps the location and date will be applied to a thousand photographs within a single folder. Archivists and librarians are now experimenting with using artificial intelligence to generate metadata; our platform, Starchive, automatically generates tags for each image, although these are quite generic. Additionally, born-digital photographs may have usable exchangeable image file format (EXIF) data attached, such as geographic coordinates and the exact time the photograph was created (often missing from physical photos), that can be used to help better describe as well as map images.

Moreover, while current ACOR collections include audio and video cassettes that require digitization for long-term preservation of the content and ease of access, more and more donations will not include physical items but may instead link to lectures on YouTube or podcasts. While archiving YouTube videos is (currently) simple, podcasts or data in various applications may prove more difficult to extract and preserve.

Ironically, the present and immediate future of archival work involves preserving and providing access to older digital formats. The ACOR Archive contains hundreds of 3.5-inch floppy disks and compact disks (CDs), as well as unusual and hard-to-access physical formats. While these are largely back-ups of data that exist in either physical formats or on ACOR servers, that is not true of all the disks. Migrating data from floppy disks has been largely successful, although there have been setbacks that will require further investigation. Some disks are password protected or written in a code that is unreadable by a modern Windows-based system; even trying to forensically access the raw bits has proved impossible. Likewise, most of the CDs straightforwardly had their data migrated to our storage server, although CDs that require software (such as RealPlayer) from the mid-1990s to run properly are difficult to use as intended.

New collections will contain more legacy digital formats that will take more effort to migrate and preserve than paper records or photographs that exist as positives (prints, slides) or negatives. The software required to read them may no longer be commonly available. Luckily, the archival community has begun recognizing the issue of software preservation; the Software Preservation Network, UNESCO PERSIST, and the Internet Archive,[31] as well as others, are currently working to maintain legacy software that may be required to properly access data in the future.

Another considerable change in archival practices, with which we have engaged, is web archiving materials. Unfortunately, 404 errors are all too common when one is browsing the web, and academic projects are no exception; active institutional policies and archiving are necessary to preserve these data. Whereas previously to challenge findings archaeologists may have published a letter to the editor in their journal of choice, now there are Twitter threads and blog posts. In terms of content, this is the logical continuation of letters, but preserving and providing access to tweets and websites present new challenges. However, because ACOR's mission is advancing knowledge, it is imperative we preserve and provide access to relevant knowledge regardless of format. It is also necessary to document ACOR's own history, whether of the sort contained in the news announcements and press releases being online or 'in life' activities, such as interactions with the public.

The ACOR Digital Archive is an important resource for archaeology in Jordan and the region, particularly the numerous sites that are quite poorly documented in digital collections elsewhere. Beyond images of archaeological work itself, photographs documenting the daily life of staff and workers provide a more human view of archaeology. The collections also provide a valuable resource regarding at-risk cultural heritage in Syria and Yemen, and it is important that such content be made available to researchers and the public alike. We are excited for the Digital Archive to continue to grow as new collections are received and digitized, and new formats that will require new processes and ideas for the creation of effective metadata and access are added. No doubt the archival images within our collections will be employed in many ways and innovative projects will come from them. These collections, and those held elsewhere, also offer the potential for wider, collaborative initiatives amongst ACOR and similar institutions.

---

[30] Carter, Abu Aballi and Al Adarbeh 2020.

[31] See, respectively: <https://www.softwarepreservationnetwork.org/>; <https://unescopersist.org/>; <https://archive.org/> [all accessed 16 October 2022].

Works Cited

Beck, T. 2021. 'A New Perspective on Archaeological Fieldwork in Egypt: The Local Workmen of the Asyut Project', *Forum kritische Archäologie*, 10: 23–43.

Carter, S., S. Abu Aballi, and N. Al Adarbeh. 2020. 'USAID SCHEP Update', *ACOR Newsletter*, 32.2: 4–5.

Green, J. D. M. and J. Holland. 2021. 'Photo Archive Update – and toward the Digital Archive', *ACOR Newsletter*, 32.2: 13.

Holland, J. 2021. 'Announcing the ACOR Digital Archive: Developing a Multimedia Teaching and Learning Resource', American Center of Research, 29 April 2021 <https://photoarchive.acorjordan.org/announcing-the-acor-digital-archive-developing-a-multimedia-teaching-and-learning-resource/> [accessed 1 July 2022].

Hussein Moustafa, L. 2018. 'Research without Archives?: The Making and Remaking of Area Studies Knowledge of the Middle East in a Time of Chronic War', *Archivaria*, 85: 65–95.

Lumb, A. 2020. 'Unearthing the Past: ACOR from 1988 to 1991 through the Lens of Bert de Vries', American Center of Research, 28 January 2020 <https://photoarchive.acorjordan.org/unearthing-the-past-acor-from-1988-to-1991-through-the-lens-of-bert-de-vries/> [accessed 1 July 2022].

Malko, H. and J. Salzinger. 2021. 'Interns', *ACOR Newsletter*, 33.1: 12.

Piraud-Fournet, P., J. D. M. Green, N. Doyle, and P. P. Creasman. 2021. 'The Temple of the Winged Lions, Petra: Reassessing a Nabataean Ritual Complex', *Near Eastern Archaeology*, 84.4: 293–305.

Rowland, J. 2014. 'Documenting the Qufti Archaeological Workforce', *Egyptian Archaeology*, 44: 10–12.

Salzinger, J. 2020. 'Collaborative Wikipedia Editing: Digital Community Resources for an Online Era', *ACOR Newsletter*, 32.1: 13.

Shami, S. and C. Miller-Idriss (eds). 2018. *Middle Eastern Studies for the New Millennium: Infrastructures of Knowledge* (New York: New York University Press).

Zamora, K. 2000. 'The ACOR Library, Past and Present', *ACOR Newsletter*, 12.2: 11.

19. From Legacy Data to Urban Experiences: Reconstructing the Byzantine Athenian Agora

Fotini Kondyli

Department of Art, University of Virginia (fk8u@virginia.edu)

Introduction

New methods and technologies in recent decades have dramatically changed the study of the past and have led to both new discoveries and ways to analyse, share, and disseminate archaeological results.[1] At the same time, the high costs of archaeological projects, coupled with storage limitations and concerns about conservation, access, and sustainability of archaeological material introduce new challenges to the future of archaeological practice. Under these circumstances, it might increasingly become more difficult to justify new projects when older ones have not completed their analysis and published their results. This is especially true for long-lived excavations that have been going on for decades, constantly producing more data, but lacking the infrastructure, staff, and funding to fully study and publish their results. This situation not only creates a backlog of material that requires detailed study but also places limitations on the advancement of scholarship since new and potentially important discoveries remain hidden in excavation notebooks and old dusty boxes or forgotten in private databases and external drives. In making this claim, I am not suggesting that all new projects should cease; there is great value in starting anew and bringing new theoretical frameworks and technologies into the work we do. Nor am I suggesting that the old excavations and surveys hold the answer to all our questions and problems. I am arguing, however, that studying and publishing legacy data have ethical dimensions — it is simply the right thing to do. Furthermore, there are great benefits in working with legacy data both because of the variety and volume of information and the opportunities for collaboration, experimentation, and democratization of knowledge that they afford.

In this chapter, I am presenting some key challenges in dealing with legacy data in terms of organizing, analysing, and synthesizing heterogeneous data recorded in different media and with different degrees of accuracy and preservation. Equally, I discuss opportunities for reusing and enhancing legacy data to serve different projects and their diverse research agendas, and argue for legacy data's role in new discoveries and approaches to the past. In doing so, I introduce aspects of my project Inhabiting Byzantine Athens that relies on legacy data from the Athenian Agora Excavations and offers concrete examples of how archival material can be used to reconstruct excavated built environments and past urban experiences. Furthermore, I discuss how such archival material can shed new light on Byzantine spatial and social practices and contribute to large-scale questions about Byzantium's social, economic, and political life. I conclude this discussion by exploring how working with legacy data can contribute decisively towards a more sustainable, inclusive, and outward-facing archaeology.

Legacy Data = Bad Data?

Legacy data refers to archival data, both analogue and digital, from old archaeological projects that remain understudied and unpublished. These tend to be voluminous datasets, most often obsolete and non-machine-readable recording systems, and thus difficult to analyse, quantify, and study. Such material comes in the format of written reports in excavation notebooks, small notepads, card catalogues, loose pieces of paper, and even

---

[1] This research was supported by the American School of Classical Studies at Athens. I am deeply grateful to the Director of the Athenian Agora Excavations, Prof. John McK. Camp II, for allowing me to work on this material and for his continuous support. This work has greatly benefited from discussions with Bruce Hartzler who has offered invaluable encouragement and advice. Special thanks to the Agora staff — Sylvie Dumont, Maria Tziotziou, Pia Kvarnstrom, Aspa Efstathiou, and Georgios Verigakis for their continuous help, support, and friendship. The architectural plans in this chapter were created in collaboration with Laura Leddy and the 3D models in collaboration with UVA students Estelle Teske, Evan Bell, and Adrees Basharmal whose work was supported by the NEH Horace W. Goldsmith Distinguished Teaching Professor and the Interdisciplinary Archaeology Program at UVA.

cigarette cases with field notes on them that have found their way to the archives. Photographs taken in the field, architectural plans, drawings of individual features and finds, and, in most cases, the archaeological finds themselves are also part of such archives.[2] Despite the increasing efforts to protect, curate, and digitize such archives, their state varies tremendously in terms of access and preservation. Furthermore, much of this material is endangered as the spaces in which they are kept deteriorate, and there is a real danger of contextual information being lost, making their restoration and restudy urgent.[3]

While some scholars might be put off by legacy data's complexity, fragmentary nature, and even lack of easy access, others might also dismiss their value as 'old' ways of doing archaeology, not only in terms of methodology but also of theoretical approaches and research agendas — for example, privileging specific questions, social groups, and material that determine which 'past' is being discovered and worth publishing. For those who have worked in the eastern Mediterranean, 'chasing walls' and 'focus on the marble, leave the rest' should be familiar expressions that highlight the fascination with a specific version of the past and its archaeological recovery and the indifference or silence regarding anything else that does not fit grand narratives of elite material culture.

These archaeological archives, however, act as a 'means of translation' between the excavated material and the production of archaeological knowledge.[4] Understanding and making use of them requires a deep understanding of their internal logic, from what is recorded, where, and why, to how the records cross-reference each other, and how they make visible the archaeologists' thought process and decision-making about what is being recorded, how it is presented as 'objective', what is being discarded, and why.[5] Understanding 'archives as practice' is thus an invaluable window to the history and development of archaeological practice through time as well as to the impact of political and social trends of each 'present' on the study and narration of the past.[6] The dynamic nature of legacy data allows them to transform and evolve with different media, especially digital tools, while their large quantity offers new opportunities for 'big data' analysis.[7] Furthermore, their management and curation can also offer new insights into the curation and sustainability of born-digital data, encouraging a more reflexive analysis of archaeological practice and offering new insights on managing and integrating archaeological datasets from different sites and collected with different methodologies.[8] Equally, archival material's integration with digital tools invites further experimentation with publication in different formats, ranging from standard publications to online databases, open-linked data platforms, and websites.[9] At the same time, as the demand for more interactive and virtual environments increases, especially for archaeological sites that are major tourist attractions, the return to legacy data becomes the only way forward.[10]

The Athenian Agora Excavations' Legacy Data

The Athenian Agora Excavations have taken place from 1931 onwards, bringing to light vast amounts of archaeological finds and contributing substantially to the understanding of Athens's diachronic history.[11] The Athenian Agora's archives include excavation notebooks that record daily progress and include photos and sketches of structures and other archaeological features and finds, as well as annual reports that summarize and synthesize important excavation results. Finds are also recorded both in the excavation notebooks and in the finds' card catalogue organized by material (i.e. metal, ceramic, bone, etc.).[12] The Athenian Agora Excavations archives include extensive visual resources such as a rich photographic archive as well as numerous architectural

---

[2] For other definitions of legacy data, see Allison 2008; Aspöck 2020, 11.

[3] Aspöck 2020, 19–20; Zaina 2020, 89.

[4] Baird and McFadyen 2014, 15.

[5] Aspöck 2020, 20. See also Caraher 2016, 435.

[6] See the discussion in Baird and McFadyen (2014) on the importance of understanding how an archive is constructed and the implications in knowledge production. Roosevelt and others (2015, 325) also discuss biases in excavation and the interest in understanding archaeologists' engagement with archaeological complexities.

[7] Allison 2008; Baird and McFayden 2014; Zaina 2020, 73; Frey 2020, 28–29.

[8] For the benefits and challenges of data integration, see for example Merriman and Swain 1999; Kintigh 2006. See also discussion in Gordon, Averett, and Counts 2016.

[9] See for example the discussion on the digital publication of a mid-Republican House from Gabii in Opitz 2018.

[10] See for example Rome reborn: <https://www.romereborn.org/> [accessed 21 July 2022]; Visualizing Venice: <http://www.visualizingvenice.org/visu/> [accessed 21 July 2022]; Digital Giza: <http://giza.fas.harvard.edu/> [accessed 21 July 2022].

[11] <http://agathe.gr/overview/the_excavations.html> [accessed 21 July 2022].

[12] Mauzy 2006, 12–19. See also <http://agathe.gr/overview/the_card_catalog.html> [accessed 21 July 2022]; <http://agathe.gr/overview/the_notebooks.html> [accessed 21 July 2022].

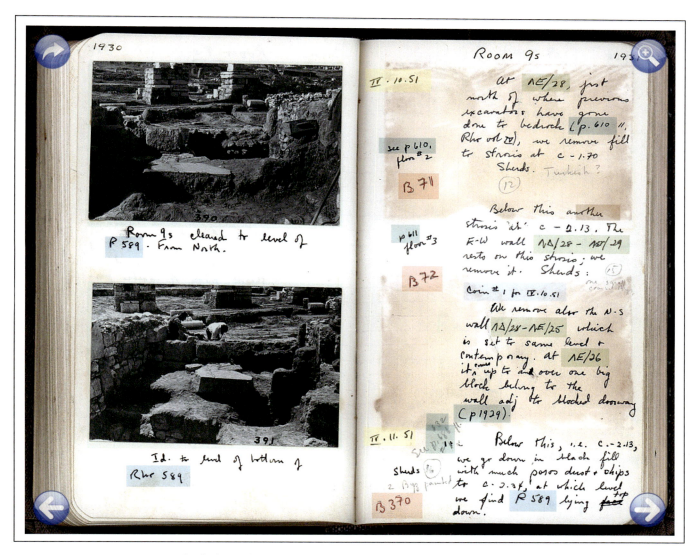

Figure 19.1. Example of a digitized notebook from the Agora. Highlighted areas function as links connecting the data on the page to other parts of the archives, including to other parts of the notebooks and corresponding coin and pottery lists (photo credit: American School of Classical Studies at Athens: Agora Excavations).

plans and artefact illustrations.[13] Kept artefacts such as pottery, coins, and a vast number of other objects made of stone, clay, bone, and metal as well as human and animal remains are also part of the Agora's legacy data. All these different elements of the archives are already interconnected thanks to Lucy Talcott, who is credited for establishing an elaborate cross-reference system of record-keeping at the Agora for finds and photographs that are repeated also in the notebooks and the card catalogue, thus making it easy to move between the different parts of the archive.[14]

In the last decade, the Athenian Agora Excavations have moved from analogue to born-digital recording systems, making substantial efforts to better organize their datasets, make their data more accessible and user-friendly, and invest in the archives' long-term preservation. For example, iDig designed by Bruce Hartzler is used in the current excavation and allows for real-time collection, organization, and visualization of excavation data.[15] In terms of the legacy data of the Athenian Agora Excavations, the entire archive has been digitized

---

[13] On the role of photographic archives of 'big digs': Baird 2011.

[14] Rotroff and Lamberton 2005, 46–47. Frey (2020, 26–27)

makes a similar claim for the interconnected records at Isthmia.

[15] Hartzler 2009. For an overview of the iDig platform, see also <http://idig.tips/> [accessed 21 July 2022]. For a review of the basic functions and capabilities of iDig: Uildriks 2016.

Figure 19.2. Central and west areas of the Agora in 1934 showing the extent of excavated Byzantine layers (photo credit: American School of Classical Studies at Athens: Agora Excavations).

and annotated and is now mostly accessible online. The digitization respects the pre-existing recording system and aims at enhancing and making it easier to use rather than replacing it. For example, the excavation notebooks have been scanned and annotated, and links have been created to connect information across notebooks and with different parts of the archive (Fig. 19.1). Photos included in the notebooks can now be expanded online, downloaded, and easily shared; finds mentioned in the notebooks are linked to their card catalogue entries as well as to other relevant parts of the archive, such as deposit lists and conservation reports; architectural plans have also been scanned and are in their majority available online.[16] The digitization process also led to the creation of a search engine to enhance the accessibility and visibility of the material and enable a direct and productive dialogue between old and new excavation data, thus providing a better understanding of the recording ecosystem and the archaeological practice at the Agora.

These innovations have revolutionized the study of the Agora's material in several ways, including navigating the archives easier and faster and most notably allowing access to this material anytime and from any place. However, while digitization is meant to provide the foundation for new research, it does not automatically get rid of the problems, gaps, and inconsistencies of the archives. Challenges persist even after the digitization and require further steps of data analysis and re-evaluation, which 'second-generation' projects can undertake, thus enhancing the archaeological record and producing new knowledge. For example, even if one wishes to see a complete list of all the Byzantine houses that have been excavated, that is not possible; the online database will only yield partial results, presenting only the entries labelled by the archaeologists as 'Byzantine house', omitting other structures that could have functioned as Byzantine houses and the finds and photos associated with them. This exemplifies both the fundamental need for accessibility to the archives and effective digital tools for further data analysis, as well as the fact that digitization should not be seen as the end goal; it still requires archaeologists who invest time and make critical use of this archival material to produce new knowledge.

---

[16] <https://ascsa.net/research?v=default> [accessed 21 July 2022].

Legacy Data's Second Life: The Inhabiting Byzantine Athens Project

While many archaeological projects — mainly rescue excavations in various parts of Athens — have dealt with the history of post-classical Athens, much of this work relates to Byzantine monumental architecture and religious life.[17] The Athenian Agora Excavations have brought to light a densely inhabited part of Byzantine and Frankish Athens (seventh to fifteenth centuries) with houses, production installations, roads, burials, etc., most of which remain understudied and unpublished (Fig. 19.2).[18] After being excavated, recorded, and photographed, all Byzantine and Frankish layers and structures were demolished so the excavation could continue down to earlier phases of the city's past.[19] As such, there is no possibility of on-site observation or re-analysis of the physical architectural remains previously excavated; the only way to reconstruct the Byzantine built environment and people's engagement with it is through the legacy data.

I have been working with the Athenian Agora Excavations' legacy data to explore the socio-economic and political conditions of Byzantine and Frankish Athens and study ordinary people's lives and urban experiences. As such, Inhabiting Byzantine Athens can be understood as a 'second-generation' project that exemplifies the reuse of an already digitized excavation archive to analyse and publish old data and produce new research. The project's main goals include the reconstruction of the city's biography in terms of its architecture and infrastructure, focusing on domestic architecture, industrial installations, water and waste management systems, as well as open spaces and road networks. I pay equal attention to archaeological and architectural evidence that speak specifically to non-elite inhabitants' socio-economic, religious, and political activities, and their participation in city-making processes.

Such reuse of legacy data is not a neutral act; we are not simply transcribing and reorganizing datasets but asking completely new and different questions of them, thus producing new information and new ways of thinking about the past. While the project relies on and respects the recording principles of the Athenian Agora Excavations, it also seeks to complement and enhance the existing records by reorganizing and reanalysing information and producing new visualizations to serve the project's research agenda and period-specific focus, thus offering a new perspective of Byzantine Athens and its inhabitants.[20] Besides standard publications, we are also building a digital publication using ArcGIS StoryMaps to present the project's objectives and methods and publish some of its results in more interactive and user-centred ways, using storytelling, interactive maps, and 3D visualizations. Remaining respectful of the guidelines and regulations of the Hellenic Ministry of Culture and the American School of Classical Studies at Athens, we also envision this as a platform for sharing newly created digital data, such as 3D models of structures and objects. Consequently, this project offers a blueprint for working with archaeological archives, focusing on workflows, data enhancement, and student involvement that can be useful to scholars who wish to use this or similar archives to create their own 'second-generation' project.

Main Challenges

Working with legacy data is a complex and time-consuming process.[21] The distance between the time and people who collected the data and their analysis and reinterpretation almost a hundred years later comes with challenges, while the heterogeneity of the material further complicates their digital integration and restudy. Even in cases of well-organized excavation archives such as those of the Agora, the usual challenges mentioned by other scholars working with similar data persist; for example the use of different terminology and periodization, changes in recording methods, missing data, and imbalanced records in terms of the level of detail and specificity.[22] Further questions pertain to how we can record with clarity and communicate our own interven-

---

[17] See for example the emphasis on religious and monumental architecture in Bouras's (2017) most recent publication on Middle Byzantine Athens.

[18] Publications are limited to the two important Agora volumes on the late antique period at the Agora (Frantz 1988) and on the Middle Byzantine Church of the Holy Apostles (Frantz 1971). Brief discussions of the Byzantine discoveries also appear sometimes in *Hesperia* as part of annual reports of the Agora's activities; see, for example, Shear 1997; Camp 2003; 2007.

[19] The only Byzantine monument still standing on-site is the Middle Byzantine Church of the Holy Apostles.

[20] For the challenges and value of preparing archaeological datasets for reuse, see Kansa, Kansa, and Arbuckle 2014.

[21] Allison 2008 also emphasizes the time and effort required to both digitize and study legacy data.

[22] Aspöck 2020, 16; Loy, Stocker, and Davis 2021. See also individual contributions in that volume.

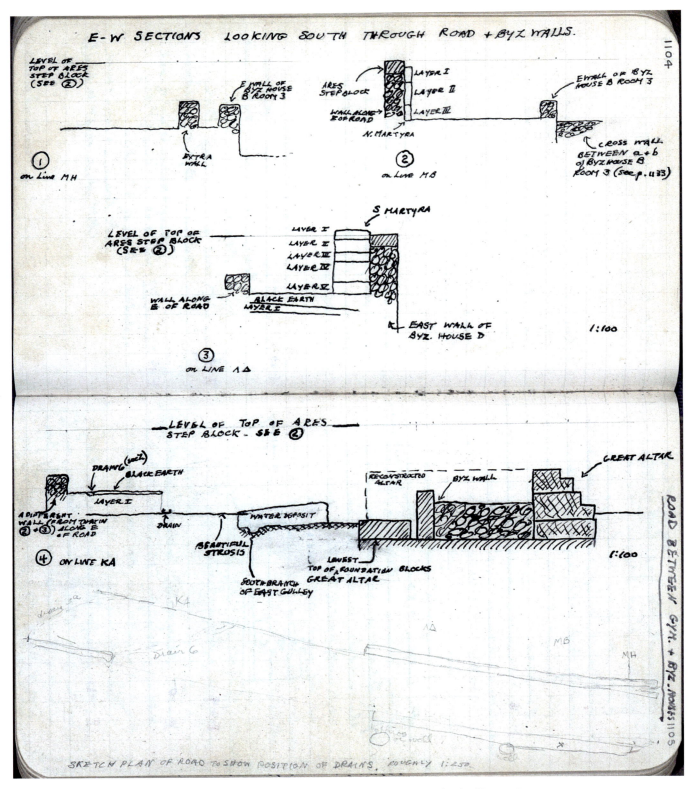

Figure 19.3. Example of a cross-section in an excavation notebook of Section E, noting the stratigraphic layers of various structures, measured in this case by the level of the top of the Temple of Ares step block (photo credit: American School of Classical Studies at Athens: Agora Excavations).

tions when we reinterpret old information, redate artefacts and assemblages, rename or correct mislabelled entries, and produce new data visualizations. Finally, as we incorporate old data into new narratives, how can we do so effectively, creatively, and for different audiences without flattening the data and without hiding the 'messy bits' but rather by making the data's complexity and fragmentation a starting point of exploration and engagement?[23]

Working without a Matrix

Dealing with a multiperiod site of the magnitude and importance of the Athenian Agora is a haunting task especially since structures, parts of the city's infrastructure, and building materials were constantly reused and modified. Thus, establishing a clear sequence of events and understanding the stratigraphic relations at the site are of paramount importance. For the earlier decades of the excavations, the exploration and discussion of such relationships are present, but in the absence of a matrix recording system, they are expressed in different ways and in different locations within the archive.[24] Methods for establishing spatial and temporal relationships at the Agora include measuring the depth of features from a fixed point, although in many cases that initial point of reference changes in different excavation seasons. For example, often the top of a modern wall visible from the entirety of a section could be used to measure main features' depth, but more localized features such as the top of a threshold would be used to measure the levels of consecutive floors within a room. Stratigraphic relationships are also described in terms of similarities in soil type and assemblages between neighbouring entities; for example, floors in adjacent rooms with the same soil composition and contemporary finds that are also found at approximately the same level would be labelled as contemporary and understood as part of the same event. Occasionally, such descriptions accompanied by section drawings to indicate spatial and temporal connections among features and layers, which are extremely helpful (Fig. 19.3). However, the lack of consistency combined with the plurality of information dispersed in the notebooks, drawings, and photos makes the reconstruction process complex, time-consuming, and not always straightforward,

especially since the architectural features and layers do not physically survive.[25] This situation creates a pressing need to read notebook descriptions together with the architectural plans and lists of artefacts and try to restore relations across space and time as accurately as possible.

Architectural Plans

The Agora archives contain around fourteen thousand architectural plans and drawings with a few exclusively dedicated to Byzantine remains. General architectural plans for each section struggle to find a balance between capturing key structures and the state of the excavation at the time that they were drawn; as a result, features and structures of different periods coexist in the same plans. For example, it is common for late Roman and Byzantine walls to be depicted together with foundations of both Roman and Ottoman buildings with no clear indication of what is what (Fig. 19.4). Even in cases where there are architectural plans dedicated to Byzantine remains, they are not detailed enough, since they can often present together features that never coexisted while omitting contemporary ones; this problem is augmented when the chronological relations between walls are also not clear in the notebooks, and the descriptions of spaces and features, their sizes, and their shape are not detailed enough.

The publication of these old plans without a re-evaluation and discussion about how they were produced and what they are perpetuates notions of chaotic and ad hoc Byzantine built environments. This situation creates serious obstacles in the study of the post-classical built environment and necessitates the creation of new, comprehensive, detailed, and geo-referenced architectural plans of Byzantine and Frankish built and open spaces that capture major changes in the architecture and spatial organization of the site.[26] Nevertheless, existing architec-

---

[23] Caraher 2016, 430; Kersel 2016, 490.

[24] On recording stratigraphic contexts in archaeology before the Harris matrix: McAnany and Hodder 2009, 4–6.

[25] Ellis and others (2008) provide a great example of how to combine on-site architectural analysis with the digitization and reintegration of legacy data within a GIS environment to reconstruct the stratigraphy and biography of a site, but in their case the standing architecture provides new opportunities of re-examination and 'ground-proofing' that are not possible at the Athenian Agora. See also Ellis and Poehler 2015. For a similar example on the integration between legacy data and GIS: Loy, Stocker, and Davis 2021.

[26] For example, the discoveries from the Agora are discussed by Bouras (2017, 66–83), both as very promising and difficult to understand. Even though he includes a lot of information from the Agora Excavations archives, he reproduces the architectural plans and sketches from the excavation notebooks without further

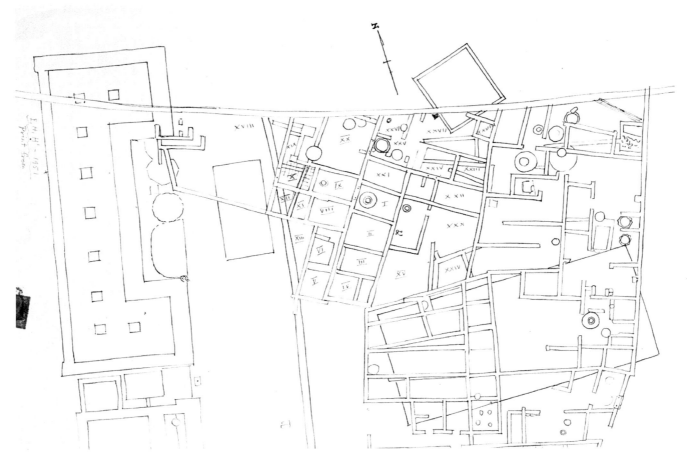

Figure 19.4. Architectural plan of Sections H and H' showing parts of classical, Roman, late Roman, and Byzantine structures (photo credit: American School of Classical Studies at Athens: Agora Excavations).

tural plans have a valuable role to play since they provide a foundation for redrawing more period-specific and detailed drawings and include important information that might not exist or be clear in the notebooks, such as the location and spatial proximity between important features or their measurements.

Dating

The vast amounts of Byzantine and Frankish artefacts kept in the Athenian Agora provide opportunities for completely new insights, especially for periods such as the seventh to eleventh centuries, which have only recently started being better understood materially. However, as with many legacy data projects, redating is inevitable since both our dating methods have become more refined and the way we think of artefacts and artefact assemblages as dating tools has changed. Inconsistencies in periodization and terminology require a deep understanding of how specific terms are used and when their chronological span changes. In the Agora archives, for example, the term 'Middle Byzantine' can sometimes describe eleventh-century assemblages and other times refer to mid-twelfth- to mid-thirteenth-century objects. Furthermore, the explicit and direct use of coins as dating tools, which is prominent in the early decades of excavation requires reconsideration. With so much reuse and rebuilding within the Agora, many coins were not found in their original place of deposition. Furthermore, a better understanding of coin circulation patterns is necessary since some coins seem to have enjoyed a longer life than previously understood, and need to be studied as part of larger assemblages and in combination with other categories of finds.[27] It is worth mentioning that

---

explanation of what is being depicted and how all these features relate to each other.

[27] For the implications of taking coins at face value, see for example Sanders's (2003) discussion on the chronology of the

such acts of redating come with their own challenges; for example, how to be transparent and clear about both the original and new dates and balance such discrepancies in a new narrative.

New Insights

New Discoveries in Old Data

With significant challenges and limitations inherent in legacy data, why bother dealing with such problematic datasets? Why not just turn our attention to new projects and make the best use of new technologies to record new data in more systematic ways, learning from the mistakes of the past? The obvious answer is, of course, that our job as archaeologists is not done until we publish and make our data available. Another important argument is that the restudy and careful publication of legacy data has the potential to enrich, challenge, and complicate the way we have come to understand past societies as well as lead to completely new avenues of research. For example, we can extract new information from old data with the help of new technologies and methodologies, recontextualize old data in new frameworks, or creatively reuse these older data in new experimental simulations about the past.[28] In the Athenian Agora Excavations, many Byzantine layers, houses, roads, and other archaeological features and artefacts were discovered already in the first decade of excavation. Yet it is not an exaggeration to suggest that the lack of timely publication has been detrimental to the understanding of Byzantine cities, including urban planning, architecture, and household archaeology, as well as to a deeper appreciation of the site's post-classical history and its place within the medieval Mediterranean. Consider, for example, that even in recent publications about Byzantine Athens, the area of the Agora continues to be presented as either an empty space or an incoherent labyrinth of walls.[29] I cannot help but wonder how

Figure 19.5. Middle Byzantine installation with vats and basins in Section MM, probably for winemaking (photo credit: American School of Classical Studies at Athens: Agora Excavations).

an earlier publication of urban sites such as the Athenian Agora would have impacted our view of the Byzantine Empire. Would we still insist on a Constantinopolitan-focused discussion on urbanism? Would we have the same view of non-elites and their role in the empire?

A close and careful reading of the Agora's legacy data reveals entire neighbourhoods with distinct phases of occupation as well as numerous major roads that organized the built environment in blocks and connected the Agora to other parts of Athens. Smaller alleys and open spaces further facilitated easy communication among houses and afforded different ways of moving within the city. Had this image of wide streets organizing movement in the Agora and forming building blocks become better known earlier, we might have been more sceptical about the lack of urban planning and the 'organic' character of Byzantine cities that is so prominent in scholarship.[30]

In terms of Byzantine houses, the legacy data from the Athenian Agora, even if incomplete, still offer a vast amount of information on domestic architecture; they record a wide range of features such as benches, staircases,

---

Byzantine layers at Corinth.

[28] Wylie 2017. Atici and others (2013) also show how the study of old datasets can lead both to new discoveries and multiple and different interpretations.

[29] Bouras 2017, 66–83, including the book's accompanying map of Byzantine Athens where only two roads are noted in the

Agora. This is not meant as a criticism of the author but as an illustration of the obstacles to the understanding of the Byzantine built environment at the Agora without a fully studied and published archive.

[30] Bouras 2013, 174; Kazanaki-Lappa 2002, 643. See also discussion in Kondyli 2022b, 200–01.

drains, cellars, and pithoi; and afford a better understanding of the cultural and socio-economic principles driving the design of Byzantine houses. Furthermore, the descriptions of building materials, techniques, and the variety of architectural solutions that are being recorded provide a foundation for rethinking the skill and time investment involved in domestic structures and their socio-economic implications. I briefly mention two examples to highlight the difference that such evidence can make in the study of Byzantine houses. Most information we have on multiple-storey houses, especially the presence and internal arrangements of the upper floors, comes primarily from textual sources since, in the archaeological record, the ground floor or just its foundation is often what survives. Yet, several Byzantine houses discovered in the Athenian Agora offer evidence for multiple floors, including built staircases leading to an upper floor, and vaulted cellars below ground indicating a basement. The presence of built basins, hearths, and subterranean storage spaces such as pithoi sunk in house floors, wells, and cesspits also allow us to imagine certain types of activities taking place on the ground floor and other activities reserved for the upper floors. Furthermore, the presence of an upper floor not only contributes to our understanding of domestic architecture but also invites new questions about privacy, surveillance, and spatial and social interaction between neighbouring buildings.

Another example relates to the role of courtyards in Byzantine houses. In the case of Athens, the Byzantine courtyard has been emphasized and presented as a 'natural' continuation from the ancient Greek classical house, thus creating a direct chronological and ideological link between the different 'pasts' of the city. As alluring as this imagined continuity in architectural design may be for some scholars, archaeologically we encounter far more complex and varied ways in which Byzantine Athenians dealt with the city's past and incorporated it into their built environment. The variety of attitudes towards ancient architecture, ranging from reuse to indifference and purposeful display, challenge the monotony of a single and unified approach and the idea of an unchanging and continuous architectural tradition. Returning to courtyards, the Athenian Agora Excavations archives include many courtyard biographies built in different parts of the house and with different materials; since many of these courtyards were located at the edge of houses and close to a street rather than centrally placed as in ancient Greek houses, we should expect that their role within the Byzantine house and its urban setting

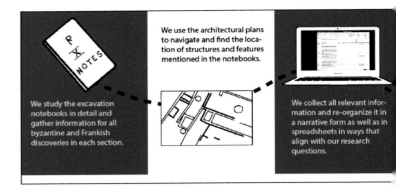

might vary significantly from that of its ancient predecessor. Such nuanced observations raise new questions about the interaction between built and open spaces within the city, the boundaries of public and private, as well as how identities and social norms were articulated through domestic architecture in Byzantium.

Finally, the abundance of evidence of economic activities within and around Byzantine houses at the Agora such as pottery and lime kilns, wine-making facilities, and purple-dying installations awaits further exploration (Fig. 19.5); their study and publication can significantly contribute to a deeper appreciation of the economic character of the city as well as the socio-economic identities of the city's inhabitants.[31]

These are only a few examples to argue that despite the imperfect datasets, there is still abundant information to explore a wide range of questions about the city's architecture and organization as well as to its inhabitants' activities and identities. A detailed restudy and publication of this legacy dataset holds the promise of many new discoveries that can both change and enrich our understanding of the Byzantine world, including making urban non-elite groups and their experiences more visible and allowing them more agency in city-making processes.

From Excavation Notebooks to Byzantine Urban Experiences

The Athenian Agora was divided up and excavated in sections designated by a series of Greek letters (Α–Ω) or by a combination of letters indicating initials or abbreviations of the names of the actual areas or buildings. The excavation records follow the same organization principle with several notebooks corresponding exclusively to

---

[31] Kondyli 2022a.

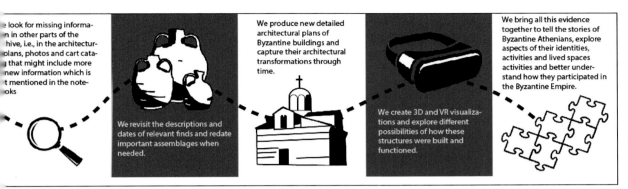

Figure 19.6. Project workflow highlighting the key steps in reanalysing and enhancing the Athenian Agora legacy data (image credit: Inhabiting Byzantine Athens (drawing by Dan Weiss)).

each of the sixty-four sections of the Agora.[32] This system also informs our project, studying and reconstructing each section separately and then trying to understand its spatial and chronological correlations with the sections around it. Within the study of each section, the starting point is always the annual reports and excavation notebooks. The annual reports summarize the main discoveries of one or multiple seasons in each section of the excavations and are thus a good starting point for locating areas of intense Byzantine activity at the site. For a more detailed understanding, we turn to the actual excavation notebooks, which include a narrative of daily progress, lists of finds, thumbnail photos, and occasionally drawings of key features as well as cross-sections of excavated areas. A first reading of the notebooks is a good way to become familiar with what was found and how much of it was found. Some notebooks also include a summary of the main phases of the Byzantine structures and provide an index of the most important finds associated with these structures. These summaries are useful because they offer a window into the excavators' methodologies, dating techniques, and modes of interpretation that might not be so apparent in the recording of daily progress. The next step is a deeper and slower re-reading of a section's notebooks to locate and record all the information about Byzantine and Frankish material and incorporate them into a more coherent narrative while also creating a more detailed index, listing all relevant architectural remains, features, and finds discovered.

This is also the right time to deal with discrepancies, mistakes, and problems in the data. For example, often features are labelled differently in different parts of the notebooks so it is important to identify each correctly and decide on consistent naming practices.[33] In this phase, we read the notebooks together with all relevant architectural plans. This joint reading of notebooks and plans is vital for understanding the location and spatial relation among features and identifying discrepancies in the data. For example, there are many features and parts of structures mentioned in the notebooks that do not appear in the architectural plans, while valuable information on spatial relations, size, and scale in the plans is missing from the notebooks. We do a similar parallel reading for the finds, cross-referencing their information on the notebooks with the corresponding records in the card catalogue, which occasionally provides additional information. Once we have a first index of all the Byzantine and Frankish material found in a section, we then proceed to a more detailed recording in separate spreadsheets allocated to specific categories such as walls, floors, surfaces, features, finds, and pithoi, which are recorded separately.[34] These spreadsheets are populated from the notebooks and enriched with additional information from the finds card catalogue and architectural plans. The spreadsheets become the foundation for a new narrative that emphasizes a better understanding of assemblages, relationships, and events. We start with well-defined entities such as a room or a road, and based on their associated features, layers, and finds, we try to reconstruct the sequence of events in that space, taking into consideration but also rectifying excavators' discussions of dates and relations between objects/features/spaces (Fig. 19.6).

We follow the same steps for every part of the section, and once that phase is completed, we then try to sync the

---

32 <https://agora.ascsa.net/research?v=default> [accessed 21 July 2022].

33 In the project's database, we always maintain the original name as recorded in the notebooks and have additional columns for alternative names. If there are mistakes in the records, they are discussed in detail in the notes' column.

34 Pithoi are recorded separately from other features due to their high number as well as their ability to provide information about floor levels, activities, and sequence of event within a structure.

biographies of all spaces and their features and finds in the same narrative, expanding our quest of what is contemporary with what, what remains the same, and what changes over time. In doing so, we are also very interested to detect both localized, minor events such as the blocking of a door or the remodelling of a house's courtyard, and major events that affect a bigger part of the site such as a widespread fire or extensive rebuilding episodes that are experienced across the site. These minor and major events are recorded separately, aggregating data from the rest of our database to describe the date, location, and type of event and discuss their archaeological signature.

This is a very structured way to examine the archival material, designed as a step-by-step process to help new team members familiarize themselves with the excavation and recording methods at the Agora and navigate the complexity and inconsistency of the data. Parallel to that section-focused approach, we also spend time browsing different types of data regardless of their location, such as studying photos and accompanying descriptions of Byzantine walls across the Agora to get a better sense of the different types of building materials and techniques that can help us better appreciate Byzantine building and spatial practices.[35] Similarly, we collect information and record groups of artefacts separately based on their material or primary function, such as Byzantine bread stamps or spindle-whorls so we can study and visualize their distribution and relation to other finds and further understand their chronology, use, and production patterns. These 'side projects' offer a different avenue of inquiry through which a focused study of minor objects can shed more light on economic and social behaviours in the city. Most such objects are found in wells and pits and thus also highlight clearing episodes and acts of deposition that impact the biography of the city and its houses.

While we utilize such approaches to reconstruct aspects of the Byzantine built environment at the Agora, narrate the biographies of specific buildings and objects, and trace minor and major events in the life of the city, we are fully cognizant that this is not our end goal. What we are creating is a foundation of knowledge — a starting point from where we and others can start asking more meaningful and complex questions about people, their lives and experiences, social norms, and beliefs. In other words, this methodology allows us to create diverse pathways from the archaeological archives to Byzantine society, which we intend to share in different ways and with different audiences.

Enhancing Legacy Data

One way to address issues of incomplete and missing data in the reconstruction of the built environment is to experiment with different scenarios and solutions and create multiple possible versions of the same buildings and spaces using 3D modelling and Virtual Reality. Thus, newly produced, detailed, and Byzantine-specific architectural plans provide a foundation for architectural 3D models where we can experiment, among other things, with different numbers of floors, entry points, and roofing solutions. Here we are not striving for historical accuracy but treat this phase as a thinking exercise to help us discern which scenario might be more plausible and prompt new discussions about issues of accessibility, visibility, privacy, etc. For example, in the study of two adjacent Middle Byzantine houses, we wanted to better understand how they interacted structurally and consider how architectural relations could inform social relations. One task involved finding a suitable place to add a hypothetical balcony where it would make sense architecturally and structurally while taking into consideration Byzantine laws on construction and privacy among neighbouring houses.[36] After planting balconies in different locations of the house, it became clear that some locations were more viable in terms of available space, sufficient support, and privacy.[37] For example in Figure 19.7, the balcony looks towards the house's internal courtyard, and since it shares a wall with the adjacent house, the balcony's location protects the privacy of both houses. However, from its side, the balcony would look directly out onto a major road, a decisive factor for its location, depending on the socio-economic activities and identities of the house's inhabitants.

Such experiments forced us to engage with these house spaces at a deeper level and allowed us to better grasp issues of scale and how the location and size of each structure informed its relationship with its surrounding built environment, including blocking sunlight and vistas.[38] These are important questions because they speak to Byzantine urban experiences and can help us explore perceptions of what Byzantines considered private, comfortable, and safe, as well as culturally and socially acceptable. These 3D models then show us what

---

[35] Baird 2011.

[36] Tourptsoglou Stephanidou 2014, 136–37, 142–44, 152.

[37] That does not mean that the house necessarily had a balcony or that it could not be located elsewhere.

[38] For Byzantine building regulations on vistas: Tourptsoglou-Stephanidou 2014, 127–70.

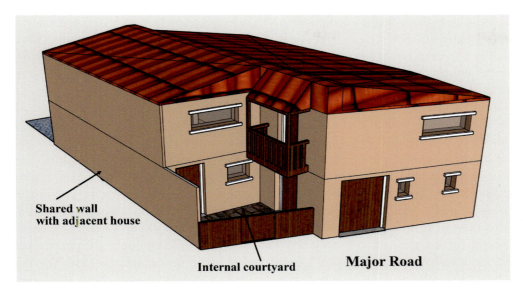

Figure 19.7. 3D model of a hypothetical balcony overlooking an internal courtyard in a Middle Byzantine house in Section E (image credit: Inhabiting Byzantine Athens).

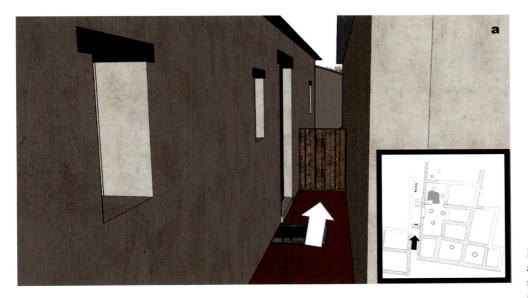

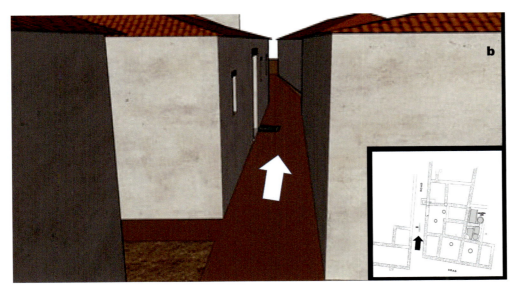

Figure 19.8. a) Virtual reality application of a Middle Byzantine street in Section MM blocked by a gate (photo credit: Inhabiting Byzantine Athens); b) without the gate (image credit: Inhabiting Byzantine Athens).

was possible, spatially and structurally, in terms of house and urban design, and further help us address even on a small scale the imperfections and the gaps of the archival material while also reinterpreting it and producing new data for these Byzantine structures.

Another interesting aspect of combining information from the Agora's legacy data and 3D modelling is the opportunity to challenge previous misconceptions and share new information about Byzantine architecture in direct and engaging ways. For example, people might not be aware of how Byzantine houses' façades looked. When visiting archaeological sites or seeing photos of excavated buildings, one encounters the inner cell of the walls, built usually with field stones, bricks, and occasionally spolia and with some type of mortar or mud as bonding material. However, wall surfaces were often plastered and, on some occasions, painted. In the Agora's archival material, there are records of yellow and red colour plaster found *in situ* in buildings' external façades. Such discoveries not only inform our 3D visualizations but open new questions about how architecture and the exterior façade of Byzantine houses could be used as nonverbal cues communicating aspects of the inhabitants' socio-economic identities.

Recently, we have also started experimenting with Virtual Reality (VR) and inserting some of our 3D models in Unity (a Virtual Reality development platform) to encourage a more experiential and sensorial approach to our data and further reflection on Byzantine urban experiences. The inspiration for a VR experience came from a Byzantine street on the north-west corner of the Agora where access seems to have been regulated through a door or gate in the Middle Byzantine period.[39] The foundation of this gate was running east–west along the street and rested on the external walls of two houses that flanked the road on the east and west sides. At some point in the twelfth century, a fire that spread to both houses and the street between them caused serious damages, and led to a series of alterations and rebuilding. It seems that the fire also destroyed the street gate which, in the post-fire phase, was not rebuilt, thus allowing free movement in the street. To explore people's experiences traversing the same street with (Fig. 19.8a) and without a gate (Fig. 19.8b), we decided to recreate that built environment in VR and walk down the same street ourselves. In doing so, all members of our research team noted how unwelcoming and narrow the street felt with the gate and how much more pleasant, safe, and welcoming it was without it. We also realized that the gate was blocking the vistas towards the south part of the Agora, thus concealing other buildings and parts of the site, which only became visible once the gate was destroyed.

While we noted that our experiences are connected to modern and western ideas that might not map onto Byzantine values and spatial practices, our small-scale VR experiment made us appreciate the stark difference between a road with and without the gate. It also opened new possibilities regarding how we engage the public with our research, for example by sharing the VR environment and asking users' input on the differences they experienced when walking down the street with and without a gate blocking their way — and inviting broader participation and discussion about the interpretation of the archaeological record. Finally, a deeper and more holistic understanding of such architectural alterations offers a starting point for discussions about what it meant to regulate traffic in the street in such a way, who might have been involved in such actions, and what were some of the political implications of regulating public spaces.[40] An important takeaway point here is that new technologies and tools cannot necessarily repair fragmented and missing data, nor can they always produce more accurate versions of the past. But they allow exploration and experimentation that pushes our data and our understanding of the past in new directions. Through some of these experiments, we have been able to establish that some scenarios are more plausible based on comparanda from other sites and from what we know about Byzantine spatial practices and societal norms through textural and material evidence. This is then a new pathway to both reinterpret old data and add new information, thus correcting and enhancing the Agora's archives.

Towards a More Inclusive and Sustainable Way of Doing Archaeology

'Studying legacy data makes us better archaeologists' is a claim made by many of my students who have spent hundreds of hours going through excavation notebooks; especially when their engagement with the notebooks is followed by fieldwork where they can put their experiences with legacy data to good use. Perhaps this sounds anecdotal, but in the Inhabiting Byzantine Athens pro-

---

[39] Kondyli 2022a; 2022b.

[40] Kondyli 2022a.

ject, the students' deep reading of the excavation notebooks gave them a language to describe and interpret what they excavate in the field. It also offered an awareness (if not fear) of possible biases, inconsistencies, and gaps in the archaeological record that in return made the students diligent note-takers in the field and more consistent in their record-keeping, creating references and links between different parts of the record.[41] Such a deep study of the archaeological archive demands time and focus but enhances our understanding of the archaeological record and practice, and as Frey notes, it often leads to unintended discoveries.[42] There is thus some common ground between the students' experiences, mentioned above, and Frey's emphasis on the benefits of deep and detailed reading of the archival material as well as Caraher's discussion of slow archaeology, who insists that regardless of how quickly and efficiently we record and analyse archaeological data, their interpretation requires time, deep thinking, and deep understanding of the material itself.[43]

Furthermore, the study of legacy data introduces the internal logic of the excavation, helping scholars and students to understand how the information was recorded, what was omitted or discarded, and how the excavators conveyed information about their discoveries and the relationships between finds, layers, and people. Such information speaks to the developments and changes in archaeological science, and as Frey notes 'have just as much to teach us about the effective long-term organization and maintenance of archaeological recording systems as they do about the ancient peoples and places documented therein'.[44] Legacy data is therefore a great avenue for such a reflective analysis and deeper familiarity with archaeological methods and discoveries.[45]

Besides different ways of learning and analysing archaeological information, as mentioned above, legacy data include new information and exciting discoveries. Their publication will thus not only make these discoveries more widely known but will also offer new comparanda and support new directions and narratives of the past, thus impacting current and future projects.[46] But what about rethinking the ways in which we have come to interpret the past? Much discussion in the last decades has emphasized how collecting methods, research agendas, and archaeological fieldwork in the previous centuries operated by and facilitated colonial and Eurocentric approaches of the past.[47] Legacy data can offer an opportunity to disentangle archaeological finds from their original political and philosophical frameworks while also making these processes of entanglement more visible and better understood. Furthermore, we can revisit these old data to highlight the voices and experiences of individuals and groups of the past that were overlooked or silenced when they did not promote dominant political and social agendas.

Returning to my students' involvement with the Athenian Agora archives, their experiences underscore the opportunities that legacy data afford for shaping the present and future archaeological practice and creating bigger, more diverse, and inclusive research teams. More specifically, student involvement in my project has been at the core of my work with legacy data, and I routinely involve undergraduate and graduate students both through paid internships and class assignments, allocating different roles and tasks from data entry to GIS mapping, 3D modelling, and working with ArcGIS storymaps. As such, my research project now also serves as a training ground for archaeological research, archival studies, and digital humanities, and provides opportunities, especially to students who cannot afford expensive field schools and conducting research abroad.

Increasing accessibility to material, research projects, and funding for *ALL* should be a priority in archaeologists' agenda. Yet, the need for extended periods of time in the field privileges tenure/tenure-track faculty with both institutional funding and a support system to take care of their family/personal responsibilities, making it harder for women and minorities and excluding scholars with more precarious positions and less or no funding. Furthermore, fieldwork without the right infrastructure and accommodations also privileges able-bodied scholars and can be challenging for archaeologists with disabilities who as Heat-Stout argues 'are silenced and overlooked by this culture of compulsory able-

---

[41] On the value of reading and keeping fieldwork notebooks for understanding archaeological processes: Mickel 2015; Caraher 2016, 435. Frey (2020, 31–31) also notes the value of archaeological archives as a teaching tool.

[42] Frey 2020, 27.

[43] Frey 2022; Caraher 2016.

[44] Frey 2020, 25.

[45] For the role of archaeological archives in understanding the history of archaeology: Schlanger 2004.

[46] Baird 2011.

[47] Baird and McFadyen 2014, 20. See also Baird 2011, 432–37 on archaeological photography as an active agent of colonial practices and narratives.

bodiedness and able-mindedness'.⁴⁸ Legacy data projects allow collaborations around the globe with fewer restrictions on time and costs. Digitized archives thus provide opportunities for new research projects in more inclusive, low-cost, and sustainable ways since people can conduct research remotely at their own pace and design projects on a scale that is right for them and match their available resources, skills, and needs.⁴⁹

Such an inclusive and participatory mode of research can also be expanded to include the wider public. Initiatives are already flourishing in sciences and in archaeology, which invite the public to help with data collection and analysis, including transcribing archaeological excavation notebooks and working with archival material.⁵⁰ A quick browse in platforms such as MicroPasts gives one a sense of the wide range of projects and tasks undertaken by citizen archaeologists and provides a model of public engagement with archaeological research and knowledge production about the past.⁵¹

I also wish to highlight here the exceptional projects of the New York Public Library (NYPL) that showcase more complex activities that can be done with public participation, including tagging, georeferencing, mapping, etc.⁵² Equally inspiring are the easy-to-follow training videos and advice that the NYPL provides, thus also enhancing public awareness of digital tools and overall promoting digital literacy.⁵³ Consider the implications of such a level of public participation in archaeological research. It is the foundation for democratizing knowledge since such participation helps people appreciate knowledge production processes and makes them more aware of gaps, biases, and uncertainties in scientific research. More importantly, participants become producers of knowledge, which can come with a sense of excitement, pride, and above all responsibility. One of the best ways to effectively address issues of fake news and distrust in scientific methods and results is to broaden scientific communities and invite more people to participate in research. Inviting wider participation in the study of archaeological archives is a step in that direction and can contribute to the way we, as a society, participate in knowledge production and engage with the past.

---

48 Heath-Stout 2022.

49 See also discussion in Aspöck 2020, 14. While I remain optimistic about such digitized archives coupled with different ways and media of sharing and publishing the data and their analysis and interpretation, I also share Kersel's (2016, 489) concerns about how born-digital data and digital platforms in archaeology might reinforce divisions instead of creating more inclusive working environments without a self-reflective and critical approach on how they are being used and who is producing and using them.

50 For a discussion on crowdsourcing in archaeology: Bonacchi 2017, 63–65; on citizen archaeology: Smith 2014, 749–62.

51 <https://crowdsourced.micropasts.org/> [accessed 21 July 2022].

---

52 Gan 2011.

53 See for example the NYPL Map Warper tool for digitally aligning/rectifying historical maps with present-day locations and its tutorial: <https://wayback.archive-it.org/13216/20210520171637/http://maps.nypl.org/warper/> [accessed 21 July 2022].

Works Cited

Allison, P. M. 2008. 'Dealing with Legacy Data: An Introduction', *Internet Archaeology*, 24 <https://doi.org/10.11141/ia.24.8>.

American School of Classical Studies at Athens, Digital Collections <https://ascsa.net/research?v=default> [accessed 21 July 2022].

Aspöck, E. 2020. 'Old Excavation Data: What Can We Do? An Introduction', in E. Aspöck, S. Štuhec, K. Kopetzky, and M. Kucera (eds), *Old Excavation Data: What Can We Do?* (Vienna: Austrian Academy of Sciences Press), pp. 11–24.

Athenian Agora Excavations: Card Catalog <http://agathe.gr/overview/the_card_catalog.html> [accessed 21 July 2022].

Athenian Agora Excavations Notebooks <http://agathe.gr/overview/the_notebooks.html> [accessed 21 July 2022].

Athenian Agora Excavations: Overview <http://agathe.gr/overview/the_excavations.html> [accessed 21 July 2022].

Athenian Agora Excavations: Research <https://agora.ascsa.net/research?v=default> [accessed 21 July 2022].

Atici, L., S. W. Kansa, J. Lev-Tov, and E. C. Kansa. 2013. 'Other People's Data: A Demonstration of the Imperative of Publishing Primary Data', *Journal of Archaeological Method and Theory*, 20.4: 663–81.

Baird, J. A. 2011. 'Photographing Dura-Europos, 1928–1937: An Archaeology of the Archive', *American Journal of Archaeology*, 115.3: 427–46.

Baird, J. A. and L. McFayden. 2014. 'Towards an Archaeology of Archaeological Archives', *Archaeological Review from Cambridge*, 29.2: 14–32.

Bonacchi, C. 2017. 'Digital Media in Public Archaeology', in G. Moshenska (ed.), *Key Concepts in Public Archaeology* (London: UCL Press), pp. 60–72.

Bouras, C. 2013. 'Byzantine Athens, 330–1453', in J. Albani and E. Chalkia (eds), *Heaven and Earth: Cities and Countryside in Byzantine Greece* (Athens: Hellenic Ministry of Culture and Sports), pp. 168–79.

—— 2017. *Byzantine Athens, 10th–12th Centuries* (London: Routledge).

Camp, J. McK. II. 2003. 'Excavations in the Athenian Agora: 1998–2001', *Hesperia*, 72.3: 241–80.

—— 2007. 'Excavations in the Athenian Agora: 2002–2007', *Hesperia*, 76.4: 627–63.

Caraher, W. 2016. 'Slow Archaeology: Technology, Efficiency, and Archaeological Work', in E. W. Averett, J. M. Gordon, and D. B. Counts (eds), *Mobilizing the Past for a Digital Future: The Potential of Digital Archaeology* (Grand Forks: Digital Press at the University of North Dakota), pp. 421–42.

Digital Giza <http://giza.fas.harvard.edu/> [accessed 21 July 2022].

Ellis, S. J., T. E. Gregory, E. E. Poehler, and K. R. Cole. 2008. 'Integrating Legacy Data into a New Method for Studying Architecture: A Case Study from Isthmia, Greece', *Internet Archaeology*, 24 <https://intarch.ac.uk/journal/issue24/ellisetal_toc.html>.

Ellis, S. J. and E. E. Poehler. 2015. 'The Roman Buildings East of the Temple of Poseidon on the Isthmus', in E. R. Gebhard and T. E. Gregory (eds), *Bridge of the Untiring Sea: The Corinthian Isthmus from Prehistory to Late Antiquity*, Hesperia, Supplement, 48 (Athens: American School of Classical Studies at Athens), pp. 271–87.

Frantz, A. 1971. *The Church of the Holy Apostles*, The Athenian Agora, 20 (Princeton: American School of Classical Studies at Athens).

—— 1988. *Late Antiquity, 267–700*, The Athenian Agora, 24 (Princeton: American School of Classical Studies at Athens).

Frey, J. M. 2020. 'The ARCS Project: A "Middle Range" Approach to Digitised Archaeological Record', in E. Aspöck, S. Štuhec, K. Kopetzky, and M. Kucera (eds), *Old Excavation Data: What Can We Do?* (Vienna: Austrian Academy of Sciences Press), pp. 65–78.

Gan, V. 2011. 'All Hands on Deck: NYPL Turns to the Crowd to Develop Digital Collections', New York Public Library blog <https://www.nypl.org/blog/2011/09/15/all-hands-deck-nypl-turns-crowd-develop-digital-collections> [accessed 21 July 2022].

Gordon, J. M., E. W. Averett, and D. B. Counts. 2016. 'Mobile Computing in Archaeology: Exploring and Interpreting Current Practices', in E. W. Averett, J. M. Gordon, and D. B. Counts (eds), *Mobilizing the Past for a Digital Future: The Potential of Digital Archaeology* (Grand Forks: Digital Press at the University of North Dakota), pp. 1–32.

Hartzler, B. 2009. 'Applying New Technologies', in J. McK. Camp II and C. Mauzy (eds), *The Athenian Agora: New Perspectives on an Ancient Site* (Mainz: Von Zabern), pp. 128–37.

Heath-Stout, L. E. 2022. 'The Invisibly Disabled Archaeologist', *International Journal of Historical Archaeology*, 2022: 1–16.

iDig <http://idig.tips/> [accessed 21 July 2022].

Kansa, E. C., S. W. Kansa, and B. Arbuckle. 2014. 'Publishing and Pushing: Mixing Models for Communicating Research Data in Archaeology', *International Journal of Digital Curation*, 9: 57–70.

Kazanaki-Lappa, M. 2002. 'Medieval Athens', in A. E. Laiou, C. Bouras, C. Morrison, N. Oikonomides, and C. Pitsakis (eds), *The Economic History of Byzantium: From the Seventh through the Fifteenth Century*, 3 vols (Washington, DC: Dumbarton Oaks Research Library and Collection), pp. 639–46.

Kersel, M. M. 2016. 'Response: Living a Semi-Digital Kinda Life', in E. W. Averett, J. M. Gordon, and D. B. Counts (eds), *Mobilizing the Past for a Digital Future: The Potential of Digital Archaeology* (Grand Forks: Digital Press at the University of North Dakota), pp. 475–92.

Kintigh, K. 2006. 'The Promise and Challenge of Archaeological Data Integration', *American Antiquity*, 71.3: 567–78.

Kondyli, F. 2022a. 'The View from Archaeology', in F. Kondyli and B. Anderson (eds), *The Byzantine Neighborhood: Urban Space and Political Action* (Abingdon: Routledge), pp. 44–68.

—— 2022b. 'Community-Building and Collective Identity in Middle Byzantine Athens', in Y. Stouraitis (ed.), *Identities and Ideologies in the Medieval East Roman World* (Edinburgh: Edinburgh University Press), pp. 200–28.

Loy, M. P. A, S. R. Stocker, and J. L. Davis. 2021. 'From Archive to GIS: Recovering Spatial Information for Tholos IV at the Palace of Nestor from the Notebooks of Lord William Taylour', *Internet Archaeology*, 56 <https://doi.org/10.11141/ia.56.5>.

Mauzy, C. A. 2006. *Agora Excavations, 1931–2006: A Pictorial History* (Athens: American School of Classical Studies at Athens).

McAnany, P. A. and I. Hodder. 2009. 'Thinking about Archaeological Excavation in Reflexive Terms', *Archaeological Dialogues*, 16.1: 1–22.

Merriman, N. and H. Swain. 1999. 'Archaeological Archives: Serving the Public Interest?', *European Journal of Archaeology*, 2.2: 249–67.

Mickel, A. 2015. 'Reasons for Redundancy in Reflexivity: The Role of Diaries in Archaeological Epistemology', *Journal of Field Archaeology*, 40: 300–09.

MicroPasts <https://crowdsourced.micropasts.org/> [accessed 21 July 2022].

New York Public Library: Map Warper <https://wayback.archive-it.org/13216/20210520171637/http://maps.nypl.org/warper/> [accessed 21 July 2022].

Opitz, R. 2018. 'Publishing Archaeological Excavations at the Digital Turn', *Journal of Field Archaeology*, 43, special issue: *Web-Based Infrastructure as a Collaborative Framework across Archaeological Fieldwork, Lab work, and Analysis*: S68–S82.

Rome Reborn <https://www.romereborn.org/> [accessed 21 July 2022].

Roosevelt, C. H., P. Cobb, E. Moss, B. R. Olson, and S. Ünlüsoy. 2015. 'Excavation Is Destruction Digitization: Advances in Archaeological Practice', *Journal of Field Archaeology*, 40.3: 325–46.

Rotroff S. I. and R. Lamberton. 2005. *Women at the Athenian Agora* (Athens: American School of Classical Studies at Athens).

Sanders, G. D. 2003. 'Recent Developments in the Chronology of Byzantine Corinth', in C. K. Williams and N. Boukidis (eds), *Corinth: Results of Excavations Conducted by the American School of Classical Studies at Athens*, xx: *The Centenary, 1896–1996* (Athens: American School of Classical Studies at Athens), pp. 385–99.

Schlanger, N. 2004. 'The Past Is in the Present: On the History and Archives of Archaeology', *Modernism/Modernity*, 11.1: 165–67.

Shear, T. L. 1997. 'The Athenian Agora: Excavations of 1989–1993', *Hesperia*, 66: 495–548.

Smith, M. L. 2014. 'Citizen Science in Archaeology', *American Antiquity*, 79.4: 749–62.

Tourptsoglou Stephanidou, V. 2014. 'The Roman-Byzantine Building Regulations', in B. S. Hakim (ed.), *Mediterranean Urbanism: Historic Urban/Building Rules and Processes* (Springer: Heidelberg), pp. 127–70.

Uildriks, M. 2016. 'iDig: Recording Archaeology: A Review', *Internet Archaeology*, 42 <https://doi.org/10.11141/ia.42.13>.

Visualizing Venice <http://www.visualizingvenice.org/visu/> [accessed 21 July 2022].

Wylie, A. 2017. 'How Archaeological Evidence Bites Back: Strategies for Putting Old Data to Work in New Ways', *Science, Technology, & Human Values*, 42.2: 203–25.

Zaina, F. 2020. 'Back to the Archive: The Challenge of Old Excavation Data from Ancient Mesopotamia', in E. Aspöck, S. Štuhec, K. Kopetzky, and M. Kucera (eds), *Old Excavation Data: What Can We Do?* (Vienna: Austrian Academy of Sciences Press), pp. 65–78.

20. The Future of Corinth's Archaeological Archive: Toward an Inclusive and Interactive Heritage

Ioulia Tzonou

American School of Classical Studies at Athens-Corinth Excavations (itzonou.corinth@ascsa.edu.gr)

Introduction: Corinth

People chose Corinth as a place to live already in the seventh millennium BC for a variety of reasons (Fig. 20.1). Paramount among them were the richness of the soils, the abundance of water and resources, the proximity to the sea, and the location, which made the site a natural hub of networks of trade and communication over land and sea towards east–west and north–south.[1]

Archaeologists of the American School of Classical Studies (ASCSA) came to explore Ancient Corinth already in 1896, and both excavations and related research projects continue to this day. Investigations have generated a massive multimedia archive, including excavation notebooks, drawings, and photographs, as well as a vast collection of objects. The paper and object archives created by American archaeologists are stored on the site where they were produced. They are housed in the Museum in Ancient Corinth under the auspices of the Greek Ministry of Culture and Sports protected by the Greek guards of the Museum and used by Greek and American archaeologists as well as others from around the world. The Corinth Excavations are therefore a rich resource for archaeologists working to understand the habitation history of the site.

During the last two decades, in which I have been working at the site, changes in recording techniques and technology have been rapid and exciting. The digitization of a major part of the paper and photograph archive starting in 2007 added a valuable tool for research, teaching, and outreach. But it has also exposed a number of problems that were invisible before. Our great effort is to tame the volume of data generated, to make the digital archive mistake-free, accessible, and user-friendly, while curating the objects and legacy records.

The digital archive has attracted two major groups of users. Academics use it as a source for reconstructing the history and urban landscape of Corinth. More recently, laypeople have discovered it, and their interest seems to get deeper every day. Their curiosity is very exciting for the public-facing part of the excavation team who, for the last fifteen years, have been spearheading outreach to people of all ages, locally and globally. These efforts are bearing fruit and expanding. But how can and should we share our rich digital holdings? Accessibility is a real issue. While the digital side is open to the world, its main language, English, is not ideal for communicating with the local Greek community. Our progress is both rewarding and instructive, as we look forward to developing our excavation practices, curation, information systems, and outreach programmes in sync.

Our day-to-day use of the archive as a whole only serves to emphasize that it is a creation of people before us and like us. We are actively involved in its formation as a source of information. Decisions we make now will shape the experience of users far in the future. In addition to careful planning and management of the archive, studies of the archive itself as a subject are needed. We aspire to involve a young generation of scholars to do that.[2] I am not an archivist myself and there is no posi-

---

[1] I am grateful to Rubina Raja and Amy Miranda for the invitation to present at the conference and for the opportunity to learn from the participants and reconsider with fresh eyes all the parameters involved in our effort to disseminate the knowledge we create, an issue that is very much in my thoughts. The presentations and the discussions made me reflect on our practices for the future. I would also like to thank my colleagues at Corinth Excavations and the ASCSA for our teamwork on the collections and the archive, the Ministry of Culture and Sports, and the Ephoreia of Antiquities of the Corinthia (EFAKOR) for our collaboration on-site for the last twenty years I have been working in Corinth. Our outreach collaborations include the Centre for Culture and Athletics of the Municipality of Corinth (KEPAP), the American College of Greece-Pierce, Homo Educandus, the elementary school of Ancient Corinth, and many other schools in the Corinthia. I would like to thank Betsey A. Robinson for reading through a draft and making valuable editing suggestions and James Herbst for the plans. The photographs and plans are part of the Corinth Excavations Archive and can be viewed online on ascsa.net. All errors that may remain are mine.

[2] Thompson (forthcoming); De Clercq (forthcoming).

Figure 20.1. View of Corinth with Peribolos of Apollo, Peirene Fountain, Carpenter's Folly, and Tselios's house in the foreground and with Acrocorinth in the background, from north-east, 1930, Corinth Excavations Archive, scan of bw 2624 black-and-white large format (24 × 30) glass negative.

Unless otherwise indicated, all images in this chapter are courtesy of the American School of Classical Studies at Athens — Corinth Excavations.

tion for an archivist in the excavations. The conference helped me realize the value — truly the necessity — of specifically studying our archives in the future; it helped me understand that, as Baird and McFadyen have said, 'the form of the archive itself, for example how it is organized, labelled, and accessed, is something that has a direct relationship to the creation, form and possibilities of archaeological knowledge'.[3] The structure we impose on the archive now will influence and shape the knowledge about Corinth's past that future generations of archaeologists will create.

I organize my considerations below around three themes. First, I discuss briefly the site with a view to familiarize readers with what I consider to be the universal value of Corinth for human history and patrimony, thus, why its archive is important for us to preserve for future generations. Second, I describe the structure and information included in our extensive archive, analogue and digital, as it reflects our physical collections. Third, I concentrate on the work of researchers in the site and the archive, the most essential aspect and the reason why we do all our research — indeed, the reason why the archive exists in the first place. I focus on users with a vested interest, the academics, but also the wider public where we want to incite interest. How do we structure our archive to best suit all of us, how do we interact with its users now, and what are our desiderata for the future in terms of sharing our archive for an inclusive and interactive heritage?

---

[3] Baird and McFadyen 2014, 16.

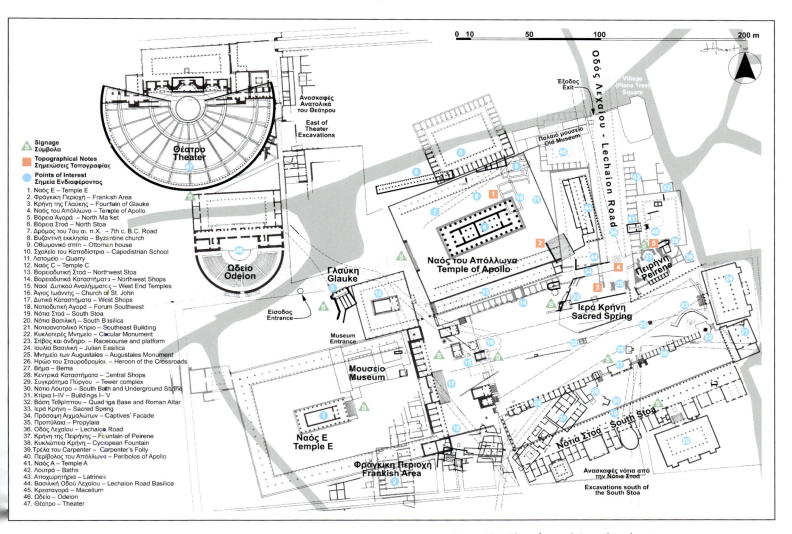

Figure 20.2. Plan of central Corinth with major monuments, mostly Roman, indicated in Greek and English, Corinth Excavations Archive, James Herbst.

Corinth Excavations: Research and Management of Cultural Heritage

Excavations conducted in Corinth for such a depth of time as a century and a quarter have resulted in uncovering the centre of habitation of the ancient city with its religious, political, economic, and administrative functions throughout time (Fig. 20.2). This centre, nestled within the modern village of Ancient Corinth, forms the fenced archaeological site visited by tourists today. The modern administrative function may mislead visitors into believing that this was all that existed in the past, but the reality is quite different. People inhabited the whole landscape from the protective mountain of Acrocorinth to the south, to habitation nuclei on multiple terraces overlooking the Corinthian Gulf to the north, and finally, one of four harbours of the city by the sea, the Lechaion harbour, its access protected by Long Walls (Fig. 20.3). Archaeologists explore this whole landscape as life continues throughout.

Corinth's long existence as a focus of human activity only serves to underline the outstanding value for all humanity that the site possesses. In Antiquity, Corinth's geology and favourable location contributed to the wealth of its inhabitants. Water and trade were two of the most substantive powers of the city through time. Pottery; the local, soft, poros limestone; bronze and agricultural products were widely exported. Corinth's location helped its merchants move goods by sea between the eastern and western Mediterranean. The city became the 'mother' of at least eleven other cities in Greece, Albania, and Sicily in the Archaic period. The Corinthians were experts in shipbuilding, shipping, trade, and the arts. Centuries later, a Roman army would destroy and depopulate the city in a victory that reduced the Greeks to Roman subjects. After refoundation in the mid-first century BC, the city and its ports came to be inhabited by a polyglot, multi-ethnic community. These qualities made Corinth attractive to St Paul who visited three times in the first century AD.[4] Through the centu-

---

[4] Sanders and others 2018.

ries it was a place where people met and exchanged ideas and technology. This amalgamation of the populations and the resulting resourcefulness of the human spirit were part of Corinth's success in the past. These ideas are very much in our minds nowadays with the movements of populations, ideas, and technology we are experiencing in our lives.

The coexistence of different people and the participation of all are evident on-site today in the polyglot, multi-ethnic tourist population. This everyday reality serves to underline for all of us working at the site that cultural heritage is a common good for all. The existence of the archaeological site in Corinth as an integral part of a living residential landscape forces us to assert that societies live in the immediate vicinity of creations of the people of the past without the ancient remains hindering the continuation of life. On the contrary, people and archaeological vestiges are directly involved and coexist. Through communication of the values of these remains, local inhabitants and global tourists recognize their ideals in their personal experience and contact with the past as they build the future.

Corinth affects the life of so many people on a day-to-day basis and, thus, an attempt to formulate a Management Plan for the site's cultural and natural heritage was initiated twenty years ago (Fig. 20.4).[5]

All stakeholders, from the local community to archaeologists, need to collaborate to manage the site in order to experience it in the most meaningful way for all. We are now in the process of formulating plans and deciding on best practices for the use of the spaces of the ancient site by a multitude of users with

---

[5] The Management Plan was initiated by Guy Sanders (Corinth Director 1997–2017). In 2015 James Wright (ASCSA Director 2013–2017) led the effort and the ASCSA organized a workshop in collaboration with the EFAKOR and the Ministry of Culture and Sports. The architectural office of Thymios Papayiannis and Ivi Nanopoulou and Associates (Παπαγιάννης and others 2015; 2016) was instrumental in producing, in collaboration with staff from EFAKOR and ASCSA, a volume containing a description and an analysis of the existing problematic conditions on-site and the parameters in need of improvement.

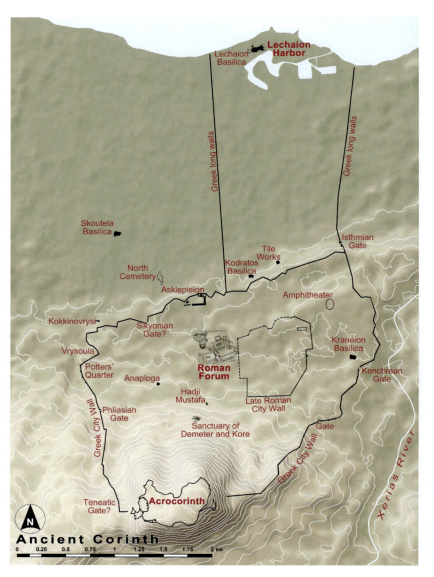

Figure 20.3. Map of the landscape around Corinth from Acrocorinth to the south to Lechaion harbour to the north, Corinth Excavations Archive, James Herbst.

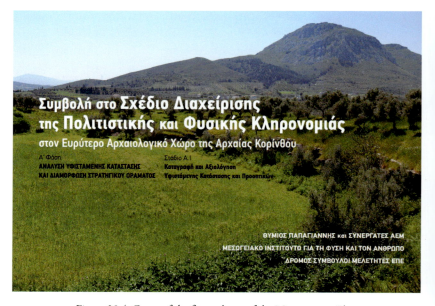

Figure 20.4. Cover of the first volume of the Management Plan for ancient Corinth, Corinth Excavations Archive.

Figure 20.5. Group of workmen at the Theatre, Corinth Excavations Archive, scan of bw 0011 black-and-white large format (155 × 21) glass negative, 1896.

Corinth Excavations: History of Collections and Archive

All these activities and their practitioners generated, and they still do today, an enormous paper and photographic archive recording remains left by actions during the life of inhabitants in Antiquity, as well as the life of archaeologists and their contemporaries. We follow the interests of archaeologists as they recorded the day's research in their field diaries. During the first half of the twentieth century they were primarily interested in the monumental landscape of the site.[7] Under their supervision large numbers of local workmen did the digging, and the amount of labour that went into these early explorations is evident both in the creation of a man-made hill from the dumped soils of the excavation and in the hard work of workmen shown in numerous photos, often covered in dirt or even in mud.[8] These early photos demonstrate that the effort was a communal endeavour that included archaeologists, but also the entire village as the workmen, the authorities, the priest, and the policeman, are depicted among the group (Fig. 20.5). While we do have a number of photos in the archive in which the photographer probably included people for scale, workmen are moreover depicted in action or plainly asked to pose for the photo, some almost heroized, such as the unnamed workman holding hands with a third-century AD male statue and in another instance, the foreman, George Kosmopoulos, in the company of Gaius Caesar (Figs 20.6–20.7).[9]

diverse interests.[6] Consequently, excavation, site and artefact conservation for study and display, collections research and storage, academic publication, public education and outreach, and heritage management activities are integrated into the objectives of the ASCSA's field project at Corinth and they all contribute to the vast archive of the excavations.

---

6 This new effort to move the Corinth Master Plan forward, in continuation of its initial phase, is headed by the EFAKOR and its director, Panagiota Kassimi, in collaboration with the ASCSA-Corinth Excavations. Significant collaborators and stakeholders in this process are the architectural office of Thymios Papayiannis and Ivi Nanopoulou and Associates, the mayor of Corinth, and the local council.

7 See, for example, Scranton 1951; Broneer 1954; Hill 1964.

8 For the mudmen, see Robinson 2011, 90–92. In general, Robinson discusses the time period and the work very eloquently in 2011, 65–119.

9 Robinson 2011, 93 refers to George Kosmopoulos. Another Kosmopoulos, Angelis, worked with the DAI in Olympia and other sites between 1879/1880 to 1938 (Brandt 2021, 11); Thompson (forthcoming) is working on our photo archive. Baird and McFadyen 2014, 19, discuss the absence of the identity of the workman in photos.

Figure 20.6. Unnamed workman resting his hand on the arm of a Roman life-sized male statue (S 47), Corinth Excavations Archive, scan of bw 0036 black-and-white large format (155 × 21) glass negative, 1898.

Figure 20.7. George Kosmopoulos with Gaius Caesar (S 1065) in the Julian Basilica, Corinth Excavations Archive, scan of bw 1280 black-and-white large format (13 × 18) glass negative, 1914.

Figure 20.8. 1974 excavation group (left to right): C. Koehler, K. Slane, J. Hurwit, L. Siegel, T. Martin, C. K. Williams, N. Bookidis, D. Mentin, M. Evans, S. Bouzaki, and J. Fisher at the time of discovery of the pier with archaistic relief figures (S 1974 27), Corinth Excavations Archive, scan of bw 1974 032 14 black-and-white medium format negative, 1974 (photographers: I. Ioannidou and L. Bartzioti).

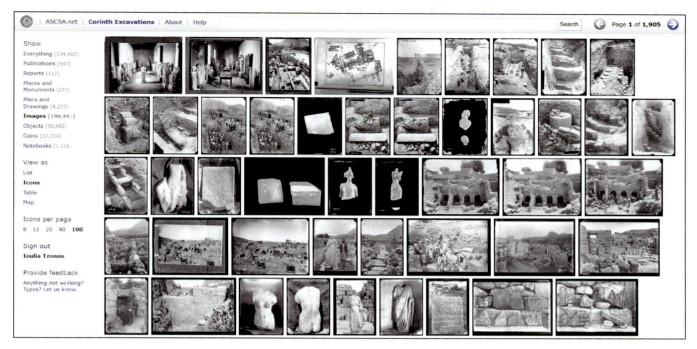

Figure 20.9. Screen capture of a search page at <http://ascsa.net> [accessed 2 June 2022].

In the 1960s, Charles K. Williams II as Corinth Director (between 1966–1997) inaugurated a training school of excavation where PhD candidates from US universities spending a year at the American School participated in the excavations (Fig. 20.8). With his group of excavators, Williams vowed to clarify unanswered questions by previous excavators and to gather and present the evidence that led past generations to produce certain interpretations about the monuments around the site.[10] Objects acquired a renewed significance.

Computerization was first attempted by Williams in 1977. Under the directorship of Guy Sanders (Corinth Director 1997–2017) in 2001, the contextual associations of objects became very significant, and a relational database in Microsoft Access was designed by James Herbst, architect and IT specialist of the excavations. With the new database, the focus of the excavations shifted from the object to the context. The digital age found Corinth well prepared in establishing a digital archive. Since the cataloguing of part of the objects existed in computer form, digitizing large parts of the archives such as images and notebooks in analogue format created a vast digital archive from the beginning. Bruce Hartzler (IT specialist of the Agora Excavations 1998–2021) was instrumental in designing ascsa.net, the research portal through which our catalogue database entries appear online after we create them in Microsoft Access.[11]

Digital Archive Use

The paper and object archive of the excavations includes, but is not limited to, 1116 excavation and artefact notebooks, 186,206 inventoried artefacts including coins, 4237 drawings, and 190,441 images. Large portions of the physical collections were digitized in 2007 including the excavation notebooks (over 223,200 pages) and the photographic collection (149,800 negatives).[12] This digitization formed the initial basis (over 373,000 records) on which the current digital archive has been accruing and has resulted now in a total of over half a million records (now 534,467).[13] Much of our archive remains

---

[10] Sanders and others 2018, 25–26; Williams 1968; 1969; 1970; 1978; 1979; 1980; 1981; Williams and Fisher 1971; 1972; 1973; Williams, MacIntosh, and Fisher 1974.

[11] <https://corinth.ascsa.net/research?v=list> [accessed 31 October 2022].

[12] The project was co-funded by the European Union and the Greek state under the programme Ανάπτυξη Υποδομής και Ψηφιοποίηση Εκδοτικών Συλλογών, Μουσειακών Εκθεμάτων και Βιβλιογραφιών της ΑΣΚΣΑ και Δημιουργία Ψηφιακών Εφαρμογών για τη Διάθεσή τους Μέσω του Διαδικτύου. Additional funding was provided by the Andrew W. Mellon Foundation and the Samuel H. Kress Foundation.

[13] <ascsa.net> [accessed 8 May 2022].

in analogue formats.[14] At the same time as we manage the digital archive, we continue to produce paper copies of our digital records. The digital resources are made available free of charge for teaching and research purposes. Password-protected material exists but is limited to specific projects. Unpublished material is largely open to the public.

The growing of the archive, over 161,467 records in fifteen years, is due to our continuing research both from staff on the ground who are excavating and doing research projects but also from numerous scholars and students from around the world, over a hundred each year before the COVID-19 pandemic, who excavate with us and have been assigned material to publish. The growth is astounding and exponentially high and serves to emphasize the need for organization so that use and dissemination can be streamlined.[15]

Structure of the Archive: Definition of Types

In the digital archive the records are organized into a schema that replicated the types that already existed in the physical collections (Fig. 20.9). During the process of organization, the division that existed in the archiving between structural (places and monuments) and artefactual (objects and coins) records was kept, as these components were formed archivally from the beginning of the excavations. Digital archiving is helping in their integration through linking of material culture into the structures in which it was deposited.[16] Types are also practical units based on functional criteria such as media, photographs, drawings, books, as well as how and where part of the archive is stored. In a way our types trace the whole excavation process from the field through notebooks and images to the museum with catalogue entries of artefacts to final published reports.

The targeted audience for these categories is mostly academics as the terminology is exceedingly complex for laypersons, even teachers, to familiarize themselves with and then proceed to using the data contained therein. Our outreach records, even though they are based on these types, do no reside online under the academic archive but are housed on the ASCSA general website. We need to integrate the use of professional archaeologists with the teaching and layperson interest. As the archive becomes a subject of study itself, in addition to a source for archaeological information, separate categories may indeed need to be created in the future.[17] We also need to include the personal papers of the archaeologists who worked on the site.[18]

A short description of each type as they appear on the public website follows.[19]

The first includes the **Publications** where our excavations appear, mainly *Corinth* monographs and *Hesperia* articles. This collection of publications is not exhaustive, and ideally, in the future, hyperlinks would be added to services like JSTOR, Google Books, and publishers. Link collection between bibliographic records and artefacts, coins, places, and monuments is ongoing but is a long effort and far from complete. The discussion in these publications, while it situates the reader in the wider context and meaning of the monuments or artefacts of the site, is intended for an academic audience.[20] Publications for the wider public exist but are limited and not available to download.[21] A digital interactive guide based on the Corinth site guide recently published is also desirable.[22]

---

[14] We have successfully secured a new grant titled, Αναδεικνύοντας το Πολιτιστικό Περιεχόμενο της Αμερικανικής Σχολής Κλασσικών Σπουδών στην Αθήνα με την Βοήθεια της Τεχνητής Νοημοσύνης, <ascsa.edu.gr/ascsa-espa-project> [accessed 31 October 2022], to finish digitizing the remainder of our records. The major part that is still in need of digitization is the inventory cards of the artefacts and coins, *c.* two hundred thousand scans.

[15] The need for a position of a data administrator to work in the excavations is grave.

[16] With the new grant we will work towards that integration using the new technologies to locate artefacts in space.

[17] See Baird and McFadyen 2014, 15–21, on archives as subject.

[18] The main archives of the ASCSA in Athens hold many of the personal papers of archaeologists who worked in Corinth. We will continue to work with the main archives, and we will need to catalogue additional papers that are still housed in Corinth.

[19] The types are shown as links on the sidebar to the left in Figure 20.9, and they can, thus, be used to filter the search results to the type of interest.

[20] A number of the Corinth volumes are downloadable from our webpage: <https://www.ascsa.edu.gr/publications/books/open-access-books/corinth-oa> [accessed 31 October 2022] as well as our excavation manual, Sanders, James, and Johnson 2017: <https://www.ascsa.edu.gr/excavations/ancient-corinth/research-publications/excavation-manual> [accessed 31 October 2022].

[21] Bookidis and Stroud 1987; Lang 1977. They should be translated into Greek, and additional booklets on diverse subjects similar to these would be embraced by the wider public with great enthusiasm, judging by how the existing ones are received.

[22] The site guide, Sanders and others 2018, was published in both Greek and English, and it is the seventh edition. Previous guides to the site and the museum were published between 1928 and 1972. A digital interactive guide exists for the Athenian Agora:

20. THE FUTURE OF CORINTH'S ARCHAEOLOGICAL ARCHIVE

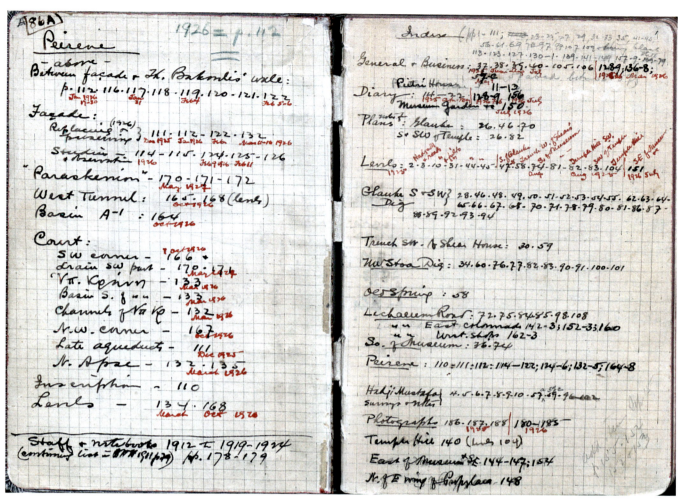

Figure 20.10. B. H. Hill notebook 86A, pp. 1–2, Corinth Excavations Archive, scan of notebook pages, Corinth Notebook Page: NB 86a, spread 5 (p. 1), 1926.

Figure 20.11. Drawing by Piet de Jong of C-1954-1, the so-called Pyrvias aryballos, Corinth Excavations Archive, 1954.

Figure 20.12. Nora Jenkins Shear documenting the wall paintings at the Theatre in 1925, Corinth Excavations Archive, scan of bw 9112 black-and-white large format (4 × 5) glass negative, 1925.

The second category is **Reports**, synthetic narratives of the excavation process produced by the area supervisors at the end of excavation sessions. As a training ground for members of the ASCSA, Corinth Excavations is offering the opportunity for both experienced and first-time excavators to supervise and document the work of trained workmen. At the end of their tenure, excavators submit summaries as part of their training. These reports contextualize the more detailed records of **Contexts**, **Images**, and **Objects**. They remain password-protected until the formal report on the excavation season is submitted to the Ministry of Culture and Sports in the autumn of each year. These reports are for in-house consumption mainly, as they serve as examples for future excavators producing their own and for archaeologists composing the final publications of the excavations described therein.

The third category includes the **Places** and **Monuments** around which excavation occurred. Early excavation journals commonly covered many places, as seen in B. H. Hill's notebook of 1925–1927 (Fig. 20.10).[23]

In these early days, a reference to a monument may be the best information available for the provenance of an artefact. Later, as excavations became more focused and standardized using an alphanumeric grid, excavators and their notebooks were restricted to a particular area and references exist to the specific grid squares excavated each time. Today, electronic total stations and GPS provide spatial control in excavation, linking locations to global map projections. Users of this category may range from researchers to parties interested in locating specific objects in space.

<http://www.agathe.gr/guide/Introduction.html> [accessed 31 October 2022].

[23] The Index pages include a number of headings, such as General Business, Diary, Plan, and notes for Glauke, Levels, Glauke Dig S &SW, Trench SW of Shear House, NW Stoa Dig, Old Spring, Lechaeum Road, S of Museum, Peirene, Hadji Mustafa, Temple Hill, E of Museum, N of E wing of Propylaia.

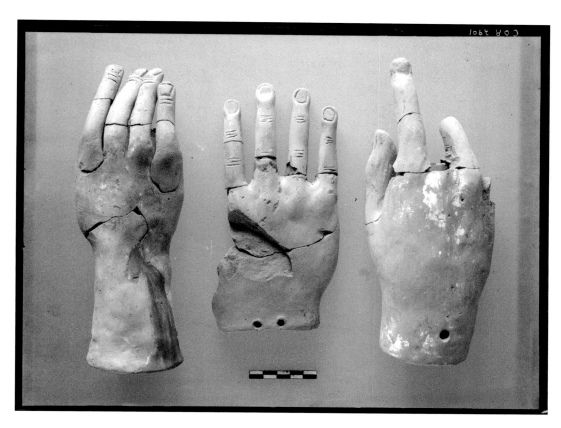

Figure 20.13. Terracotta votive hands from the Asklepieion (V 171, V 172, V 164), Corinth Excavations Archive, scan of bw 2901 black-and-white large format glass negative, 1931.

The fourth category is **Plans and Drawings** that document the spaces of the excavation in various formats: topographic maps, state plans of structures, restoration drawings, orthophotos, watercolours, as well as hand drawings of objects (Fig. 20.11). Multiple architects and draftspersons were employed throughout the life of the excavations to produce these (Fig. 20.12).[24]

The fifth category, **Images**, includes various categories of photographs in different formats. Since 1896, the excavations have been recorded in a wide range of photographic media: glass plates, cellulose nitrate based, acetate-based black-and-white negatives, colour slides, large-format colour positive, and digital. Object drawings born digital are also included here. Some of the first photographs were developed in chamber III of the fountain of Peirene in the 1910s.[25]

Numerous photographers worked for the excavations, and their names are not always recorded in our records.[26] The move towards digital photography has meant that our photographic archive has expanded manifold. While the photos we used to produce with a regular camera may have been up to 3600 within a year (one hundred films/year at most, with thirty-six shots per film), digital photography would produce seven–eight thousand photos/year, which means a huge amount of labour necessary in order to process all these photos and record their metadata. In addition to cameras, we now take photographs using iPads with the introduction of iDig in the excavation.

The sixth category is **Objects**, artefacts found during excavation, catalogued, and stored in the museum, selected because of their preservation and as representative examples of similar groups of objects (Fig. 20.13). Each object's provenance and physical characteristics are thoroughly documented and described, and museum

---

[24] Richard Stillwell, Charles K. Williams II, and James Herbst are among the architects. Piet de Jong, Mary Wyckoff, Nora Jenkins Shear, Karen Hutchinson-Sotiriou, Sally Rutter, Julia Pfaff, Yuki Furuya, and Christina Kolb are among the objects' draftspeople. Corinth's page on topographic maps run by James Herbst is very rich: <https://www.ascsa.edu.gr/excavations/ancient-corinth/digital-corinth/maps-gis-data-and-archaeological-data-for-corinth-and-greece> [accessed 31 October 2022].

[25] Robinson 2011, 96.

[26] Mme Hassia, Ino Ioannidou, and Lenio Bartzioti (1964–2004) are among them. Petros Dellatolas is our current photographer. Thompson's work (forthcoming) with our photographic archive is bringing attention to Hermann Wagner who was one of the photographers of the excavations in the first part of the twentieth century.

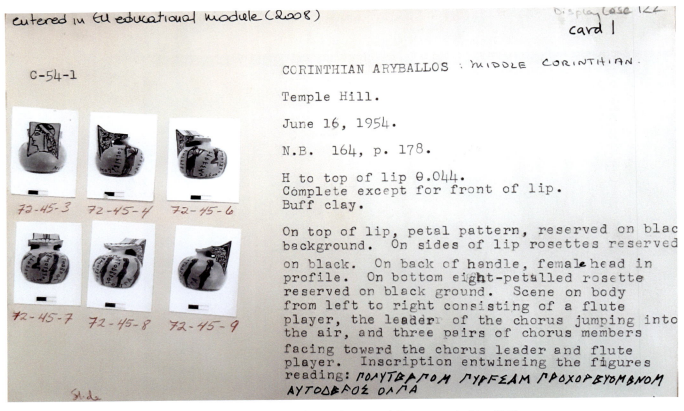

Figure 20.14. Inventory card of C-1954-1, Corinth Excavations Archive, 1954.

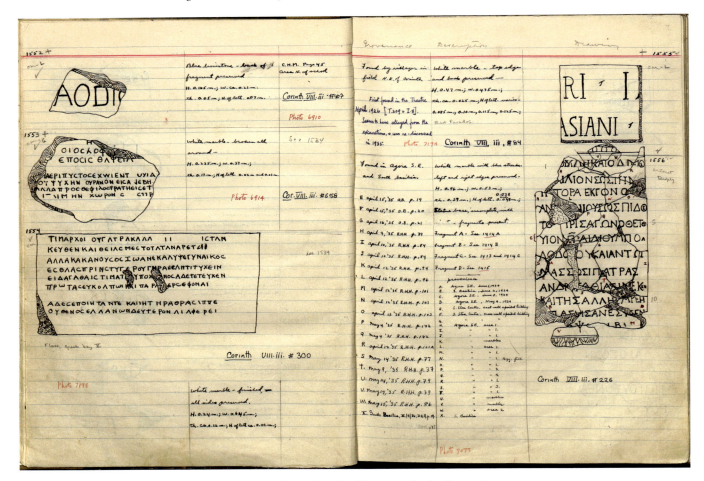

Figure 20.15. Scan of pages from Find Inventory Book of Inscriptions, I, inscription entries for I 1552–1556', Corinth Excavations Archive.

Figure 20.16. Coins from gold hoard of Manuel, Corinth Excavations Archive, scan of bw 4941 black-and-white large format glass negative, 1938.

staff supervise data entry into appropriate fields of the database. Ninety-two thousand and sixty-two have been created on the database, but only less than a third of the objects have been completely inventoried digitally.[27] Still, the majority of our artefact data records exists only on inventory cards (Fig. 20.14) or in older find inventory books (Fig. 20.15).

The seventh type is **Coins**, which are separated as a category from the rest of the artefacts because of their ubiquity, their use as dating devices, and the condensed historical information they contain (Fig. 20.16). Only 37,734 have catalogue entries created, but over ninety-five thousand coins exist in the collection (Fig. 20.17).[28]

Our coin study collection of 3282 is an invaluable tool put together by numismatist emeritus Orestes Zervos and is now available online (Fig. 20.18).[29]

The eighth type is **Notebooks**, excavation diaries that cover the period from 1896 to 2007. Early free-form day journals gave way to later excavation notebooks which were increasingly detailed and standardized as the excavation methodology became more complex and systematized (Figs 20.19–20.20). In 2007, Guy Sanders opted for loose leaf recording, while from 2017 on Chris Pfaff, Director of Corinth Excavations, adopted iDig, an excavation app designed by Bruce Hartzler, which makes recording of the process of excavation on iPads very easy. Additional categories include **Lots** and **Baskets**. These contain the material culture as excavated in stratigraphic

---

[27] Accessed 2 May 2022. Out of these, only 26,559 have complete entries.

[28] Accessed 9 May 2022: 95,302 coins registered until the end of the excavations of 2021.

[29] With funding from the Kress Foundation, we were able to digitize our study collection of coins.

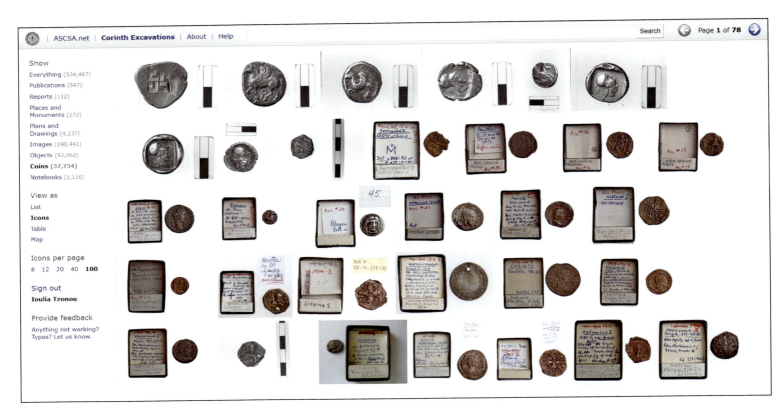

Figure 20.17. Screen capture of a search page at <http://ascsa.net> showing results of a coin search [accessed 2 June 2022].

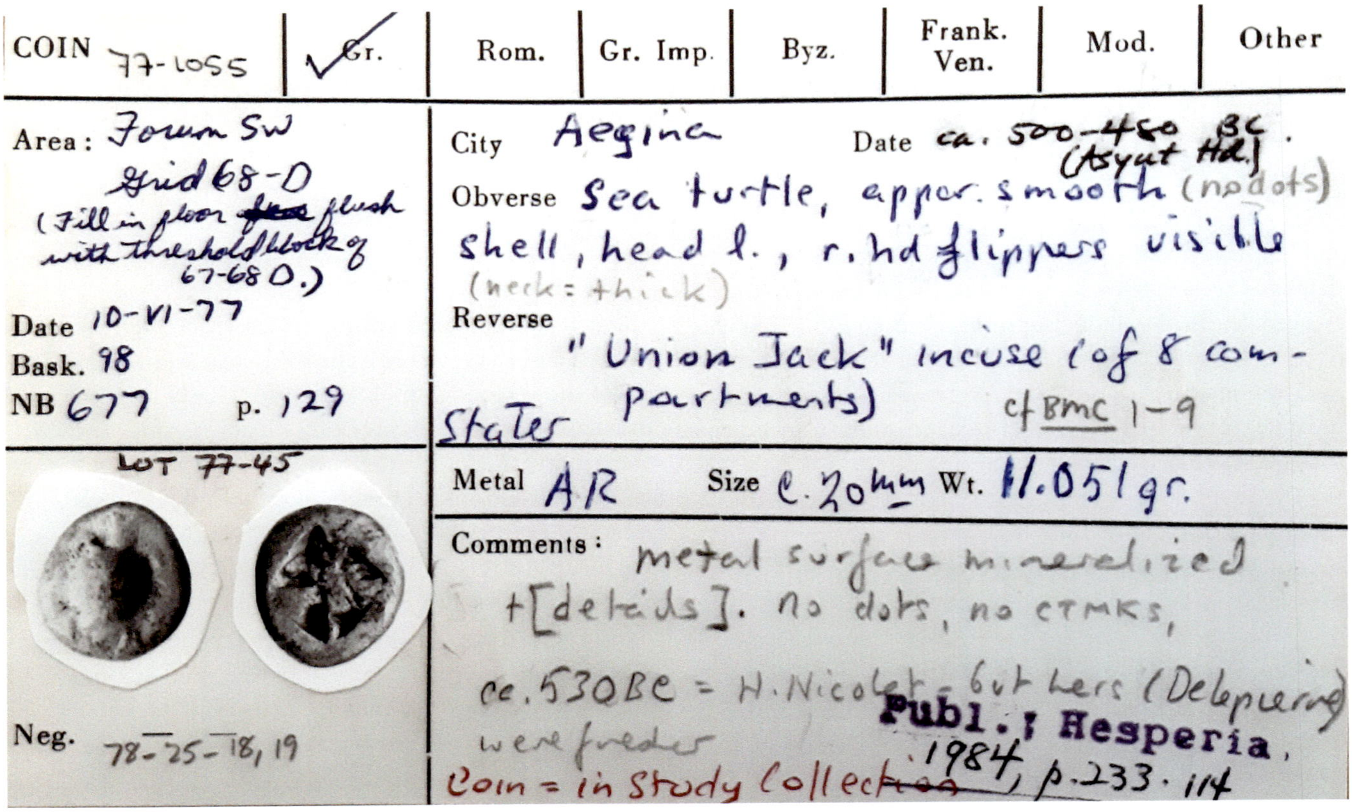

Figure 20.18. Scan of inventory card of Coin 1977–1055 in the Study Collection, Corinth Excavations Archive.

20. THE FUTURE OF CORINTH'S ARCHAEOLOGICAL ARCHIVE

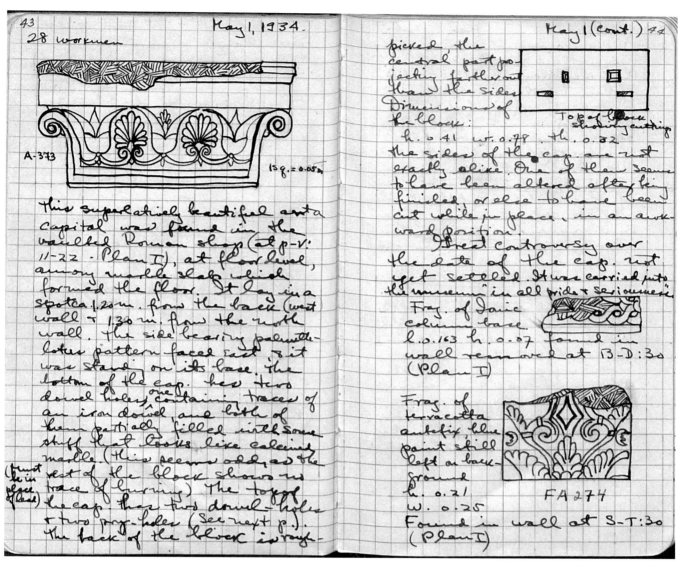

Figure 20.19. Scan of Notebook 143 by Gladys Davidson, pp. 43–44, Corinth Excavations Archive, 1934.

units (baskets), and stored in lots, storage groups formed based on our interpretation of the stratigraphic units that represent discrete human activities.

The Future of our Archive: Dissemination to Users

The immensity and complexity of the archive force us to consider on a daily basis ways to make this highly technical collection of data user-friendly to both archaeologists and the public. Our twofold dissemination, the academic use of the archive, and our outreach efforts to laypersons, encounters different sets of problems.

Regarding the first category, dissemination and accessibility by users in academia, we cater towards the needs of established scholars who have been using our analogue archive for decades as well as young researchers who are just beginning to delve into its richness. The use of the archive has been almost exclusively to derive information on the archaeology of the city. Exceptions, such as Betsey Robinson and the author, have used the archive additionally to get closer to the personalities and methodologies of past archaeologists as well as their relationships with the village.[30]

On the subject of its academic use, the archive must be accurate; it must be easily used by professors and PhD students to further their research; and it must be included by professors in teaching their students how to do research. I use examples of three professors involving their students in research and contributing towards the

---

[30] Robinson 2011; Tzonou-Herbst 2015.

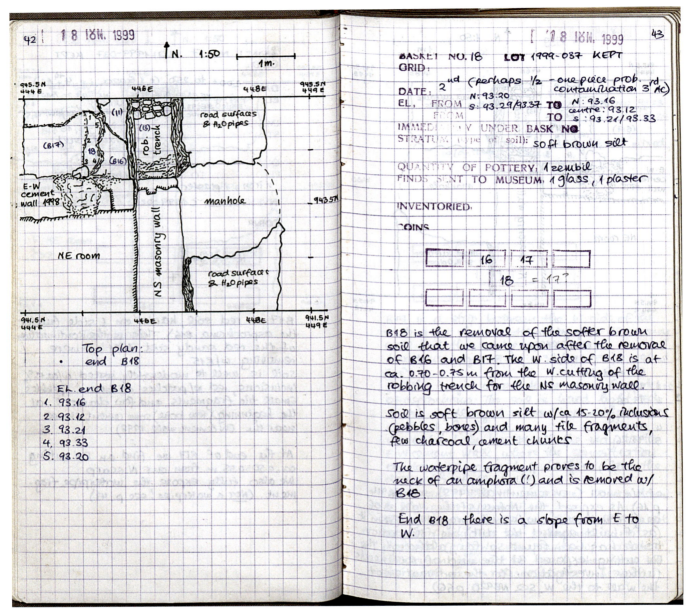

Figure 20.20. Scan of Notebook 922 by Leda Kostaki, pp. 42–43, Corinth Excavations Archive, 1999.

accuracy of the archive, along with a PhD candidate, in order to illustrate the different uses and various needs. It is mostly researchers from English-speaking countries that use our archive, along with scholars in Greece and other countries in Europe, for example Italy and Spain.[31] Our community of scholars is invaluable since they are the source of the knowledge we disseminate more widely. Finally, we need the archive to grow and be part of large online collaborations.

The digitization of the records has made numerous problems visible. For this reason, a button to provide feedback has been created on our webpage on ascsa.net for users to notify us of the inaccuracies they encounter. Kathleen Slane, professor emerita of Art and Archaeology at the University of Missouri, has been working at the site for the last forty years, on literally tons of Roman pottery, and, thus, she has deep knowledge of the site and the archive.[32] We can depend on her to bring problems to our attention.

---

[31] Current examples include Alexandropoulou (forthcoming); Amara (forthcoming); Romero 2021; Valente 2021.

[32] A selection of her publications includes Slane 1986; 1987; 1990; 1994; 2003; 2017; (forthcoming).

Staff and volunteers work on corrections and data entry. Given the fact that the paper archive took 126 years to form, it may take a long time to digitize and incorporate all the information. As an active excavation, we are always generating new data, and, thus, the archive is in a state of constant expansion and ongoing correction. Without a dedicated person for data management the process is slow. A dream for the future is to become a partner into the Linked Open Data (LOD) ecosystem so that our stand-alone digital database is integrated into larger schemata, giving scholars the ability to make corrections on ascsa.net online from anywhere in the world.[33] The questions of who may have the right to enter corrections, or if there should be an approval process for these corrections, are complicated issues to discuss and resolve.[34]

While the process of correcting mistakes will be ongoing for a long time, use of the data to extract meaningful information about phases of occupation of the past that have been removed in excavation or lie underneath later habitation layers is crucial as we create the history of the site. Betsey A. Robinson, associate professor of Roman Art and Architecture and Mediterranean Archaeology in Vanderbilt University, has said she takes great pleasure in losing herself in Corinth's archives. Following her publication of the Peirene Fountain and Bert Hodge Hill's prosopography, she inaugurated the Peirene Valley Project (PVP), a collaborative project which aspires to use our digital archive in an innovative way, while at the same time enriching it.[35] Working through the old notebooks, photographs, and plans, Robinson retrieves data, which are then amplified by new technologies such as drone photography and photogrammetry to re-establish chronological phases no longer visible. The landscape of the Peirene Valley is optimal for this investigation since it contains deep deposits preserving crucial information on formation processes in action at a very important area of Ancient Corinth. Collaboration is key in our research.[36]

We are fortunate to work with dedicated generations of Corinthian scholars, but equally imperative is to inspire and attract young researchers to carry the torch forward. My third example is Emily Hurt, a PhD candidate in the Department of History at Yale University and a novice in Corinthian matters. Hurt has started work on our coins with the questions of identity and self-presentation in Roman Corinth in mind.[37] Her work will augment the online catalogue of our coins and bring attention to this valuable resource, while enriching our knowledge of the city's identity. Partnerships, such as with nomisma.org, and incorporation in digital corpora would be essential for Corinth.[38]

My final example in academia is Simone Oppen and her initiative to help us join the forefront of digital epigraphy and include students in research dissemination.[39] Above all, Oppen is opening the door to online collaborations to expand the reach of our resources. As a visiting lecturer at the Department of Classics at Dartmouth, she secured funding to digitally publish vase inscriptions from the area of the forum. The inscriptions will be made easily accessible on a webpage as, for example, the inscriptions of Sicily are.[40] Oppen is collaborating with the US Epigraphy Project at Brown, which provides access to hundreds of Greek and Latin inscriptions from the classical Mediterranean.[41] Corinth needs to be part of such large online collaborations.

---

[33] Chen and Folsom 2021; Geser 2016.

[34] Ann Chen discussed the issue of LOD during the conference along the lines of what I consider to be a very constructive way for Corinth also to move our efforts forward.

[35] Robinson 2011; 2013.

[36] I have the pleasure of participating in the PVP along with others, such as James Herbst and Eric Pohler. Another collaborative undertaking which involves a number of researchers working on archival material and bringing new insights to it is the Potters' Quarter volume currently edited by Ward and Harrington (forthcoming).

[37] Hurt (forthcoming). Other PhD candidates working on Corinth materials at the moment include Banks (forthcoming); Bertram (forthcoming); Nastasi (forthcoming). Nancy Bookidis is heading a group of scholars as they publish material from the sanctuary of Demeter and Kore. In addition to herself these include Sonia Klinger (small finds), Sue Langdon (figurines), Geoffrey Schmaltz (iron finds), Anastassios Antonaras (glass objects), Elizabeth Milleker (sculpture), Mike Ierardi (coins). A final volume is planned to discuss the sanctuary as a whole after the individual categories of artefacts recovered have been studied in detail (Klinger 2021 includes bibliographic reference to the volumes that have appeared so far).

[38] In training young excavators in coin reading, a number of digital resources are implemented to help in the teaching and identification of coins, among them <nomisma.org>, but also <https://www.forumancientcoins.com/numiswiki/view.asp?key=monogram> [accessed 2 November 2022] and <https://www.tesorillo.com/aes/home.htm> [accessed 2 November 2022]. I would like to thank Guy Sanders for bringing the last two resources to my attention.

[39] Oppen and Romero (forthcoming); Oppen and Chang (forthcoming).

[40] <https://isicily.org/> [accessed 2 November 2022].

[41] <https://usepigraphy.brown.edu/projects/usep/about/>

The great divide between academia and the public is bridged by our outreach. Going hand-in-hand with the digitization and with continuing academic research and dissemination, outreach is a powerful route of making the archive known and accessible to teachers and students. The author's initial efforts were met with success in 2014 when the Steinmetz Family Foundation awarded Corinth Excavations a Museum Fellowship.[42] We have had two fellows so far, Katie Petrole (2014–2018) (Fig. 20.21) and Eleni Gizas (2019–2022) (Fig. 20.22).[43] The Steinmetz Fellows use the archive to teach about Corinth and its many facets of history to interested audiences, mostly K-12, but also adult laypersons.[44]

Corinth Excavations currently offers diverse educational online and on-site resources. The online resources are all free and in English, except for one lesson plan translated into Mandarin and one webinar in Greek. Our efforts in the future will centre on translating these resources into Greek for local teachers to be able to use more freely. The resources are based on our digital archive at ascsa.net. We would like to make our archive more user-friendly and will work towards that direction in the future.

Based on this archive, we have created K-12 lesson plans, downloadable from our website, and Gizas added Flipgrid lessons, which are much shorter.[45] Petrole and Gizas conducted live virtual field trips, and Gizas spearheaded a virtual international exchange programme for students (the Urkesh One-on-One project) in collaboration with Rania Sazakli and the Centre of Culture and Athletics of the Municipality of Corinth (KEPAP).[46] James Herbst uploads 3D models of artefacts and monuments.[47] Gizas and the

---

[accessed 2 November 2022].

[42] I would like to thank the Foundation and Mr Steinmetz personally for his continuing enthusiasm and support of our work to bring the knowledge of the past to young audiences over the last eight years.

[43] Petrole is currently Director of Education at the Parthenon in Nashville TN. Eleni Gizas is Program Coordinator in the Program in Hellenic Studies at the Classics Department of Columbia University.

[44] We will shortly be welcoming the next fellow.

[45] <https://www.ascsa.edu.gr/teachers/k-12-educational-resources/lesson-plans> [accessed 2 November 2022]; <https://admin.flipgrid.com/discovery/partners/ascsa-corinth-excavations> [accessed 2 November 2022].

[46] The Urkesh project won a European award, the Illucidare Special Prize for 2020. For the virtual field trips, see here: <https://www.ascsa.edu.gr/teachers/k-12-educational-resources> [accessed 2 November 2022].

[47] <https://www.ascsa.edu.gr/excavations/ancient-corinth/

Figure 20.21. Katie Petrole in action in the Corinth Museum during an educational programme on Sacred Prostitution and Aphrodite, the protecting goddess of the city, Corinth Excavations Archive, 2017.

Figure 20.22. Eleni Gizas in action during an Open Day session guiding a group of Ancient Corinthians at the excavation site NE of the Theatre, Corinth Excavations Archive, 2019.

Figure 20.23. A kindergarten student holding an aryballos during an educational session on the uses of olive oil in Antiquity in the Corinth Museum, Corinth Excavations Archive, 2019.

author hosted live webinars that are stored and retrievable on our website.[48]

Our on-site resources include general tours and thematic programmes for adult groups and for student classes, locals and international, K-12 but also undergraduate and graduate students, 'Open Day' programmes and international celebrations, and most recently our first exhibit in the Museum in Corinth.[49]

As the requests for dissemination may be overwhelming, a way to multiply the effect is to teach the teachers who will then share the knowledge with their students. We organize teacher workshops to introduce them to our digital resources, and we have been leading teacher groups around the site. The ASCSA awards fellowships to teachers to participate in our summer programmes.[50]

We collaborate with and educate local as well as international teachers. In 2014 in partnership with the EFAKOR and KEPAP we organized a teacher workshop titled Τα Μνημεία της Κορινθίας μας Απλώνουν το Χέρι [...] Σεμινάριο Μουσειακής Εκπαίδευσης για Εκπαιδευτικούς Π.Ε. Κορινθίας (The Monuments of the Corinthia Are Reaching out [...] Museum Education Seminar for Primary Education Teachers of the Corinthia), which included both presentations but also on-site workshops for teachers from schools in the Corinthia.[51] We continue our teamwork with local teachers. One of them is Lambros Psomas, an inspiring high-school teacher at the local school of Homo Educandus.[52] We envision having his students use our archive to learn about artefacts imported to Corinth from Sicily; in a next step they will communicate with their peers in Sicily, and we will share our common history and connect the two places by having the young generations learn about their common heritage.

An example of our international collaboration with teachers is the online seminar and on-site tour for the Teacher-Fellows of *The Examined Life*, an online programme and organization that promotes Greek culture, history, and legacy and impacts hundreds of educators and thousands of students in schools across the US.[53] Stephen Guerriero, who leads the group 'is a firm believer that students should learn not just what we know about the past, but how we know it'.[54] The interactive, hands-on learning experiences we prepared for the teachers on-site were met with enthusiasm.

Gizas was especially active in the digital dissemination.[55] She incorporated data from the Corinth archive into platforms such as Skype in the Classroom and Flipgrid used by over one hundred million teachers, students, and families. Between Petrole and Gizas, from October 2017 until June 2021, in three and a half years, 487 Skype lessons were organized for over twenty-one thousand students in fifty-seven countries from Australia to Argentina to India to Nigeria. The consensus among the evaluations is that students enjoy learning live from an expert in the field. At the same time Corinth Excavations was added to many distance-learning platforms: the Archaeology Channel, the National Art Education Association, the American Alliance of Museums' Museum Distance Learning Repository, UC Berkeley's How to Smile, Skype-a-Scientist, and the Archaeological Institute of America.[56]

Conclusions

Corinth, the polyglot, multi-ethnic site of Antiquity, lives on in the multitude of tourists visiting the site from everywhere in the world, to the researchers using our

---

digital-corinth/3d-models> [accessed 2 November 2022].

48 <https://vimeo.com/ascsathens> [accessed 2 November 2022]. The site contains, in addition to the webinars, recorded lectures on various subjects, some Corinthian, as for example the Conservation of Roman Frescoes in Corinth by Charles K. Williams II and Roberto Nardi, and Mycenaean Corinth by the author, among others.

49 In collaboration with EFAKOR and the financial support of the mayor of Corinth. Gizas and others 2022.

50 <https://www.ascsa.edu.gr/programs/summer-session-and-seminars/scholarships-for-educators> [accessed 2 November 2022].

51 The workshop was organized in collaboration with the Directorates of Primary and Secondary Elementary Education of the Corinthia as well as with the Folklore Museum of Corinth. In 2022, Gizas and the author gave two online workshops to local teacher groups, one for the teachers of the elementary schools of Ancient Corinth, Perigiali, and the sixth elementary school of Corinth, 11 March, and a second one for the schools of Vochaiko, Vrahati, and Kokkoni-Poulitsa, 1 April, organized in each case by the principals of the schools.

52 <https://www.hea.edu.gr/> [accessed 3 November 2022].

53 <https://teachgreece.org/> [accessed 3 November 2022].

54 <https://teachgreece.org/personnel/stephen-guerriero/> [accessed 3 November 2022].

55 Gizas (forthcoming).

56 In our question to local Greek teachers as to whether educational platforms such as the English-speaking ones mentioned above exist for Greek teachers, they mentioned the Μουσείο Σχολικής Ζωής και Εκπαίδευσης (School Life and Education Museum): <https://ekedisy.gr/category/mousio-scholikis-zois-ke-ekpedefsis/> [accessed 3 November 2022], which we will investigate in order to incorporate our resources there as well.

collections, and in the students learning about Corinth worldwide. The Corinth Excavations is fortunate in a number of ways as it leads its dissemination efforts into the future. The advantage of our research community cannot be stressed enough, and the examples of academic dissemination I included above are obviously very selective.[57] The digitization has enabled our researchers to have access to the archive while being away from Corinth. Lacunae, mistakes, and issues of rights of access to materials have been brought to the fore. We still have it in front of us to continue the digitization of the archive in a timely manner, and we need dedicated personnel both for data entry and corrections, as well as IT staff to work towards accommodating to our current data structures disparate legacy data generated by scholars over many decades.[58] We have to constantly upgrade our storage capacities to save the data. At the same time, we should look into the possibility of LOD and updating our data online by selected users, and into collaborating with online platforms and datasets that publish groups of artefacts, such as the inscriptions or the coins. In the spirit of collaboration, issues of rights of access are resolved. Even if the data is open access, we communicate who is working on what.

We have by now converted most of our analogue data into a digital format, and the data is for the most part available online.[59] What about international access to all of our legacy data? The data is discoverable mostly through us, that is, scholars affiliated with the ASCSA. However, researchers active in English-speaking countries, for example PhD candidates such as Laura Nastasi, and archaeometric researchers such as Agnese Benzonelli, have contacted us after discovering the materials online.[60] Greek researchers also communicate with us in order to include artefacts in their work.[61] Our online database does not necessarily make it as widely discoverable or as useful for sharing across projects, and more online collaborations would seem beneficial in that respect so that there is more communication across similar projects.[62]

Simultaneously as the archive was made widely accessible digitally to academics, there has been considerable interest from laypersons to learn and interact with it. We have a dedicated individual, the Steinmetz fellow, with a background both in archaeology and museum education. The Steinmetz fellow builds on our researchers and, thus, communicates research results as they come out of the ground, so to speak. Our aim is to be able to have in the future a tenure-track year-round person to manage our programmes and educate. The complexity of our digital resources is such that the presence of such a person is necessary to create a bridge between the data-driven aspect of archaeology and the interested public. We want to make the archive more user-friendly and create multimedia tools for teaching archaeology locally and globally.

Our purpose is to engage decisively with a global online community as well as with the local community. We encourage experiential learning, active participation, and collaboration. Our online educational resources and on-site programmes facilitate communication to active groups and tactile participation for the latter. The pandemic has forced the online dissemination on us, and this pressure has had many advantages. One of the most important ones is the increased global awareness, which I see as a huge gain.

The digital resources help us reach wider audiences. During the Flipgrid Live event led by Eleni Gizas in May 2021, Corinth Excavations reached twenty-seven US states, thirty-three countries, and 551 endpoints, which the organizers estimate amounts to up to 7500 people. The comment box was flooded with 720 questions during the half-hour presentation.[63] I see this as a blessing

---

[57] When Nancy Bookidis, excavator of the sanctuary of Demeter and Kore and author of multiple books discusses her research with teenage students of Pierce, our purpose is fulfilled. See 'Interpreting Ancient Mysteries of Demeter: A Collaboration between the ASCSA, a Corinthian School, the American College of Greece-PIERCE, Dr Nancy Bookidis, Diazoma, Olympia Odos, and the Greek Ministry of Culture': <https://www.ascsa.edu.gr/teachers/k-12-educational-resources/programs-on-site-off-site-online> [accessed 3 November 2022]. Our collaboration with Nektaria Glinou, psychologist of Pierce, is exceptional.

[58] We are currently working with two such archives, the archive of the excavations at the sanctuary of Demeter and Kore from the 1960s and 1970s, and the excavations to the East of the Theatre in the 1980s. James Herbst is leading the effort from the technical side and expertise, and we are collaborating with Nancy Bookidis and Kathleen Slane.

[59] Closed collections include groups of materials scholars are currently researching in order to produce definitive publications, such as groups of dedications from the Demeter and Kore sanctuary, the Gymnasium excavations, and the East of Theatre excavations.

[60] Nastasi (forthcoming) is a PhD candidate at the University of Manchester, and Benzonelli is a researcher and technician in archaeomaterials preparation and analysis at UCL Institute of Archaeology.

[61] For example, Alexandropoulou (forthcoming).

[62] Chen and Folsom 2021.

[63] Gizas (forthcoming).

and a curse. A thing that strikes me here is the humanly unmanageable situation. The educator can in no way answer seven hundred questions in the course of half an hour. Does it mean that this is superficial learning and not interaction as you would have with your actual students in a classroom or on-site?

This is part of a wider discussion of digital versus analogue that is ongoing. Digital atrophies our deepest layer of thinking.[64] It is a new way for humans to communicate, a speedy superficial first exposure to the complex world of the past which, however, as our world, requires steady focus to be understood and needs to be thought about and comprehended slowly. We want to use the digital to attract people to come to the site to experience it. The in-person knowledge is irreplaceable, since we all, as people, learn with all of our senses. The role of the digital archive and new digital strategies are to make the site accessible and open to the public, locally and globally. Our shared humanity viewed digitally and then in person can help us educate future generations for a world of empathy. We embrace local community collaborations as well as global interactions. We create an inclusive heritage where people act and are not passive recipients (Fig. 20.23).

---

[64] Hari 2022.

Works Cited

Alexandropoulou, A. (forthcoming). 'Epichysis: The Origin and Circulation of a Disputed Ceramic Type of the 4th Century B.C.', in G. Ackermann and V. Vlachou (eds), *Greek Pottery of the 4th Century B.C.: New Data from the Field*, International Workshop at the EFA, November 2021.

Amara, G. (forthcoming). 'Bridging the Gap: Producers and Consumers in Corinth and Syracuse', in A. Ward and K. Harrington (eds), *Potters' Quarter Revisited*, Hesperia Supplement.

Baird, J. A. and L. McFadyen. 2014. 'Towards an Archaeology of Archaeological Archives', *Archaeological Review from Cambridge*, 29.2: 14–32.

Banks, J. (forthcoming). 'Early Helladic Corinth' (unpublished doctoral thesis, University of Cincinnati).

Bertram, H. (forthcoming). 'Archaic Pottery Production and Consumption at Corinth' (unpublished doctoral thesis, University of Cincinnati).

Bookidis, N. and R. S. Stroud. 1987. *Demeter and Persephone in Ancient Corinth* (Princeton: American School of Classical Studies at Athens).

Brandt, K. 2021. 'Ἐπέτειος 2024–150 Χρόνια Γερμανικό Αρχαιολογικό Ινστιτούτο Αθηνών', in *DAI-AtheNea* (Athens: Τυπογραφείο Πλέτσας/Καρδάρη), pp. 8–11.

Broneer, O. 1954. *The South Stoa and its Roman Successors*, Corinth, 1.4 (Princeton: American School of Classical Studies at Athens).

Chen, A. H. and J. Folsom. 2021. 'Origins and Antidotes of Omission: Southeastern European Archaeology, Linked Open Data, and the Possibilities of Archaeological Integration', in S. E. Bond, P. Dilley, and R. Horne (eds), *Linked Open Data for the Ancient Mediterranean: Structures, Practices, Prospects*, ISAW Papers <http://hdl.handle.net/2333.1/xsj3v7j6> [accessed 12 February 2023].

De Clercq, N. (forthcoming). 'Considering a Woman in Greek "Big Dig" Archaeology: Mary Wyckoff (1906-1932) at the American School of Classical Studies at Athens,' *Cahiers François Viète*, III (15).

Geser, G. 2016. *ARIADNE WP15 Study: Towards a Web of Archaeological Linked Open Data* <http://legacy.ariadne-infrastructure.eu/wp-content/uploads/2019/01/ARIADNE_archaeological_LOD_study_10-2016-1.pdf> [accessed 12 February 2023].

Gizas, E. (forthcoming). 'From Ancient Corinth to Every Corner of the World: Teaching Archaeology through Virtual Field Trips and Flipgrid Topics', in S. Fonseca, B. Thomas, A. Basterrechea (eds.), *New Ways of Communicating Archaeology in a Digital World* (Berlin: Springer Nature).

Gizas, E., P. Kasimi, I. Tzonou, and M. Agrevi. 2022. *Corinth in the Years of the Revolution of 1821*, Ministry of Culture-EFAKOR and ASCSA-Corinth Excavations (Kiato: Katagramma).

Hari, J. 2022. 'Are Screens Robbing Us of our Capacity for Deep Reading?' <https://lithub.com/are-screens-robbing-us-of-our-capacity-for-deep-reading/#:~:text=There's%20broad%20scientific%20evidence%20for,year's%20growth%20in%20reading%20comprehension> [accessed 12 February 2023].

Hill, B. H. 1964. *The Springs: Peirene, Sacred Spring, Glauke*, Corinth, 1.6 (Princeton: American School of Classical Studies at Athens).

Hurt, E. (forthcoming). 'Palimpsest Cities of the Roman Empire' (unpublished doctoral thesis, Yale University).

Klinger, S. 2021. *The Sanctuary of Demeter and Kore: Miscellaneous Finds of Terracotta*, Corinth, 18.8 (Princeton: American School of Classical Studies at Athens).

Lang, M. 1977. *Cure and Cult in Ancient Corinth* (Princeton: American School of Classical Studies at Athens).

Nastasi, L. (forthcoming). 'Greek and Latin in Roman Corinth: Language Use and Language Contact in a Bilingual Commercial Centre' (unpublished doctoral thesis, Manchester University).

Oppen, S. and T. Chang (forthcoming). 'Beyond the Duumvirate: Freedmen, Local Civic Offices, and Social Status in Roman Corinth,' *Journal of Epigraphic Studies*.

Oppen, S. and A. Sáez Romero (forthcoming), 'Vase Inscriptions from the Punic Amphora Building'

Παπαγιάννης, Θ., Η. Νανοπούλου, Γ. Μελισσουργός, Δ. Πούλιος, Ε. Τσακιροπούλου, Δ. Μπάρτζης, Π. Καραμανέα, Κ. Ζέκκος, Β. Τριβυζά, Ν. Γιαννάκης, Σ. Μπηλιώνης, Α. Ἴκκος, Θ. Ανθοπούλου, Σ. Νικολαΐδου, Σ. Κουρσούμης, Ι. Τζώνου-Herbst, Α. Τσιτούρη, Α. Στρατής, Ι. Δαμανάκη, J. Herbst, Γ. Νίνος, and Ν. Αναστασάτου. 2015. *Σχέδιο Διαχείρισης της Πολιτιστικής και Φυσικής Κληρονομιάς στον Ευρύτερο Αρχαιολογικό Χώρο της Αρχαίας Κορίνθου*, I: *Ανάλυση Υφιστάμενης Κατάστασης και Διαμόρφωση Στρατηγικού Οράματος* (Athens).

Παπαγιάννης, Θ., Η. Νανοπούλου, Μ. Κουτουλάκης, Γ. Μελισσουργός, Ι. Δαμανάκη, Σ. Κουρσούμης, Α. Στρατής, Ι. Τζώνου-Herbst, Θ. Ανθοπούλου, Δ. Μπάρτζης, Σ. Νικολαΐδου, Δ. Πούλιος, and Β. Τριβυζά. 2016. *Σχέδιο Διαχείρισης της Πολιτιστικής και Φυσικής Κληρονομιάς στον Ευρύτερο Αρχαιολογικό Χώρο της Αρχαίας Κορίνθου*, II: *Στρατηγική-'Οραμα-Στόχοι για την Ολοκληρωμένη Αειφόρο Ανάπτυξη της Αρχαίας Κορίνθου* (Athens).

Robinson, B. A. 2011. *Histories of Peirene: A Corinthian Fountain in Three Millennia*, Ancient Art and Architecture in Context, 2 (Princeton: American School of Classical Studies at Athens).

—— 2013. 'Hydraulic Euergetism. American Archaeology and Waterworks in Early 20th Century Greece', in J. L. Davis and N. Vogeikoff-Brogan (eds), *Philhellenism, Philanthropy or Political Convenience? American Archaeology in Greece*, Hesperia, 82 (Princeton: American School of Classical Studies at Athens), pp. 101–30.

Romero, A. S. 2021. 'Just Wine and Fish? A Preliminary Report on the Punic Amphorae from a Specialized Tavern of the Classical Period at Corinth', in M. L. Lawall (ed.), *Assemblages of Transport Amphoras: From Chronology to Economics and Society*, Panel 6.6, Archaeology and Economy in the Ancient World, 36 (Heidelberg: Propylaeum), pp. 11–26.

Sanders, G. D. R., S. James, and A. Carter Johnson. 2017. *Corinth Excavations Archaeological Manual* (North Dakota: Digital Press at the University of North Dakota).

Sanders, G., J. Palinkas, I. Tzonou-Herbst, and J. Herbst. 2018. *Ancient Corinth Guide* (Princeton: American School of Classical Studies at Athens).

Scranton, R. L. 1951. *Monuments in the Lower Agora and North of the Archaic Temple*, Corinth, 1.3 (Princeton: American School of Classical Studies at Athens).

Slane, K. W. 1986. 'Two Deposits from the Early Roman Cellar Building, Corinth', *Hesperia*, 55.3: 271–318.

—— 1987. 'Roman Pottery from East of the Theater: Quantifying the Assemblages', *American Journal of Archaeology*, 91: 483–85.

—— 1990. *The Sanctuary of Demeter and Kore: The Roman Pottery and Lamps*, Corinth, 18.2 (Princeton: American School of Classical Studies at Athens).

—— 1994. 'Tetrarchic Recovery in Corinth: Pottery, Lamps, and Other Finds from the Peribolos of Apollo', *Hesperia*, 63: 127–68.

—— 2003. 'Corinth's Roman Pottery: Quantification and Meaning', in C. K. Williams II and N. Bookidis (eds), *Corinth: The Centenary, 1896–1996*, Corinth, 20 (Princeton: American School of Classical Studies at Athens), pp. 321–35.

—— 2017. *Tombs, Burials, and Commemoration in Corinth's Northern Cemetery*, Corinth, 21 (Princeton: American School of Classical Studies at Athens).

—— (forthcoming). *The Pottery from East of Theater Excavations (1981–1989)*.

Thompson, P. A. (forthcoming). 'Photocorinthia: The American Excavations at Ancient Corinth and the Role of Photography in the History of Archaeology', in J. M. Frey and R. Raja (eds), *Current Trends in Archival Archaeology* (Turnhout: Brepols).

Tzonou-Herbst, I. 2015. 'From the Mud of Peirene to Mastering Stratigraphy: Carl Blegen in the Corinthia and Argolid', in N. Vogeikoff-Brogan, J. L. Davis, and V. Florou (eds), *Carl W. Blegen: Personal and Archaeological Narratives* (Columbus: Lockwood), pp. 39–61.

Valente, R. 2021. 'The Archaeology of the Byzantine Peloponnese: New Research Perspectives', *Archaeological Reports*, 67: 155–70.

Ward, A. and K. Harrington (eds) (forthcoming). *Potters' Quarter Revisited*, Hesperia Supplement.

Williams, C. K. II. 1968. 'Excavations at Corinth, 1967', *Archaiologikon Deltion*, 23: 134–38.

—— 1969. 'Excavations at Corinth, 1968', *Hesperia*, 38: 36–63.

—— 1970. 'Corinth, 1969: Forum Area', *Hesperia*, 39: 1–39.

—— 1978. 'Pre-Roman Cults in the Area of the Forum of Ancient Corinth' (unpublished doctoral thesis, University of Pennsylvania).

—— 1979. 'Corinth, 1978: Forum Southwest', *Hesperia*, 48: 105–44.

—— 1980. 'Corinth Excavations, 1979', *Hesperia*, 49: 107–34.

—— 1981. 'Corinth: Excavations of 1980', *Hesperia*, 50: 1–44.

Williams, C. K. II and J. E. Fisher. 1971. 'Corinth, 1970: Forum Area', *Hesperia*, 40: 1–51.

—— 1972. 'Corinth, 1971: Forum Area', *Hesperia*, 41: 143–84.

—— 1973. 'Corinth, 1972: The Forum Area', *Hesperia*, 42: 1–44.

Williams, C. K. II, J. MacIntosh, and J. E. Fisher. 1974. 'Excavation at Corinth, 1973', *Hesperia*, 43: 1–76.

21. The Challenge of Spatial Ambiguity in Geographic Information Systems Using Legacy Archaeological Records

Jon M. Frey
Michigan State University (freyjona@msu.edu)

Introduction

With the increase in personal computing power and improved utility of software interfaces, Geographic Information Systems (GIS) have been almost universally recognized as an advantageous way to organize, analyse, and present the types of complex spatial data that are common in archaeological research.[1] The earliest and most effective uses of such software were projects that examined the material past on a regional scale.[2] Thus, landscape studies and systematic surveys took advantage of this new technology to assemble a host of ever more accessible digital maps and images into richly layered visual displays of large swaths of land that formed the background against which newly collected archaeological evidence could be studied. Moreover, because both the raw digital data and the resulting visualizations of diachronic artefact densities or lines of sight among archaeological features in the landscape could be shared quickly and easily, GIS enabled archaeologists to generate convincing, yet testable, visual arguments based on relatively large amounts of complex data.[3] As a result, the use of GIS has now spread to projects at many different scales and is now an essential part of any archaeologist's digital tool kit.

Arguably, the ready and often uncritical adoption of GIS has reshaped the ways in which archaeologists think about space and place.[4] At the very least, it has affected the way in which they collect spatial data. Now, in the interest of speed and efficiency, monuments are scanned or modelled from digital images, and the locations of artefacts are more likely to be recorded digitally than with pencil and paper, so that the often impressionistic work of representing and interpreting the physical components of the archaeological record is more likely to occur on a digital screen and at a distance (physically and chronologically) from the place and time of discovery.[5] While a host of introspective digital archaeologists have called attention to the ways in which this GIS-thinking has altered the archaeological process, one important aspect of this development that has been less discussed concerns the migration of the large quantities of legacy spatial data that was not collected with a digital analysis or output in mind.[6]

The transition from hand-drawn maps and plans to a GIS has been one issue among many at the Michigan State University Excavations at Isthmia, an archaeological project in Greece that has prioritized the study and open access dissemination of nearly a half century of records documenting the progress of excavation at the site (Fig. 21.1).[7] And while Isthmia, like all archaeological sites, is unique in its historical and geographic details, it is clear that the challenges that the research team faces as a project with one foot each in the analogue past and digital future, is quite common. Thus, it is expected that the lessons learned with respect to creating a site-wide interactive plan of catalogued artefacts will be of use to many archaeological projects as the archive archaeology movement gains momentum.

Digitalizing an Analogue Dig

Until recently, fieldwork at Isthmia was generally conducted without the benefit of an overarching grid system or even a consistent set of datum points. The reasons for this oversight must remain a matter of speculation. The

---

[1] Allen, Green, and Zubrow 1990; Lock and Stančič 1995; Kvamme 1999; Wheatley and Gillings 2002; Conolly and Lake 2006; Gillings, Hacıgüzeller, and Lock 2020.

[2] Biswell and others 1995; Maschner 1996; Harris and Lock 1995; Howey and Brouwer Burg 2017.

[3] McCoy and Ladefoged 2009; McCoy 2017.

[4] Ebert 2004; Hacıgüzeller 2012; Lock and Pouncett 2017.

[5] Kvamme 1999; Huggett 2015.

[6] For the influences of GIS on data collection practices, see Hacıgüzeller 2012; Brouwer Burg 2017; Lock and Pouncett 2017. For the intersection of archival research and GIS, see Allison 2008; Witcher 2008; Katsianis, Tsipidis, and Kalisperakis 2015; Wylie 2017; Landeschi and others 2019; Richards-Rissetto and Landau 2019.

[7] Frey n.d. (<https://www.msuisthmia.org> [accessed 28 September 2022]).

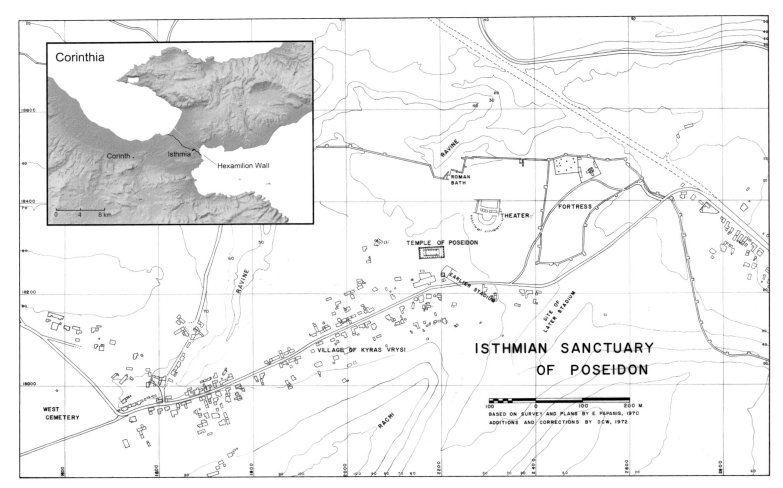

Figure 21.1. Overall plan showing location of site and monuments in relation to the modern village of Kyras Vrysi (MSU Excavations at Isthmia and the American School of Classical Studies at Athens).

first phase of systematic work at the site (1952–1960) was largely confined to the temenos of the Temple of Poseidon where the trench boundaries and the architectural elements remaining *in situ* must have been considered sufficient as spatial controls. Elevations appear to have been based on a single datum, set into one of the few undisturbed stylobate blocks of the temple. The other areas of the site that were explored at this time may have been too distant to warrant the effort required to impose an overall grid plan for the site. Thus, the publications from this period include carefully drawn plans of individual monuments and even an overall plan of the modern village of Kyras Vrysi and the surrounding terrain, but these illustrations are not at a sufficient resolution to be of use in a systematic study of the excavated features.

Records from the second phase of work at the site under a different director (1967–1987) contain evidence of an unsuccessful effort to establish a north–south grid line based on the first phase datum, but the locations of brass pins atop different monuments throughout the site do not fit into any grid system and must have been established only as benchmarks for elevations. But even these datum points must be referenced with caution, as the individual field journals from this time also contain numerous notes of warning about subsequent adjustments and corrections to the elevation data. An effort to measure these points by GPS produced inconsistent results, perhaps due to the use of a cartographic projection system that still cannot be identified. This suggests that the work of establishing a uniform system for spatial control was left to individuals with less experience than was required for the task. As a result, the earlier tradition of state plans for individual monuments and a less detailed plan of the overall site remained in place.

For the most part, this approach to representing spatial information was sufficient for publication of the results of these excavations in the customary reports in field-specific journals and volumes in the project's monograph series. Incidentally, this reveals a great deal about the standards and traditions of such publications, which were largely focused on studies of monumental architecture and typological catalogues of artefacts, intended solely for a small group of professionals.[8] In these cases, a

---

[8] Broneer 1971; 1973; 1977.

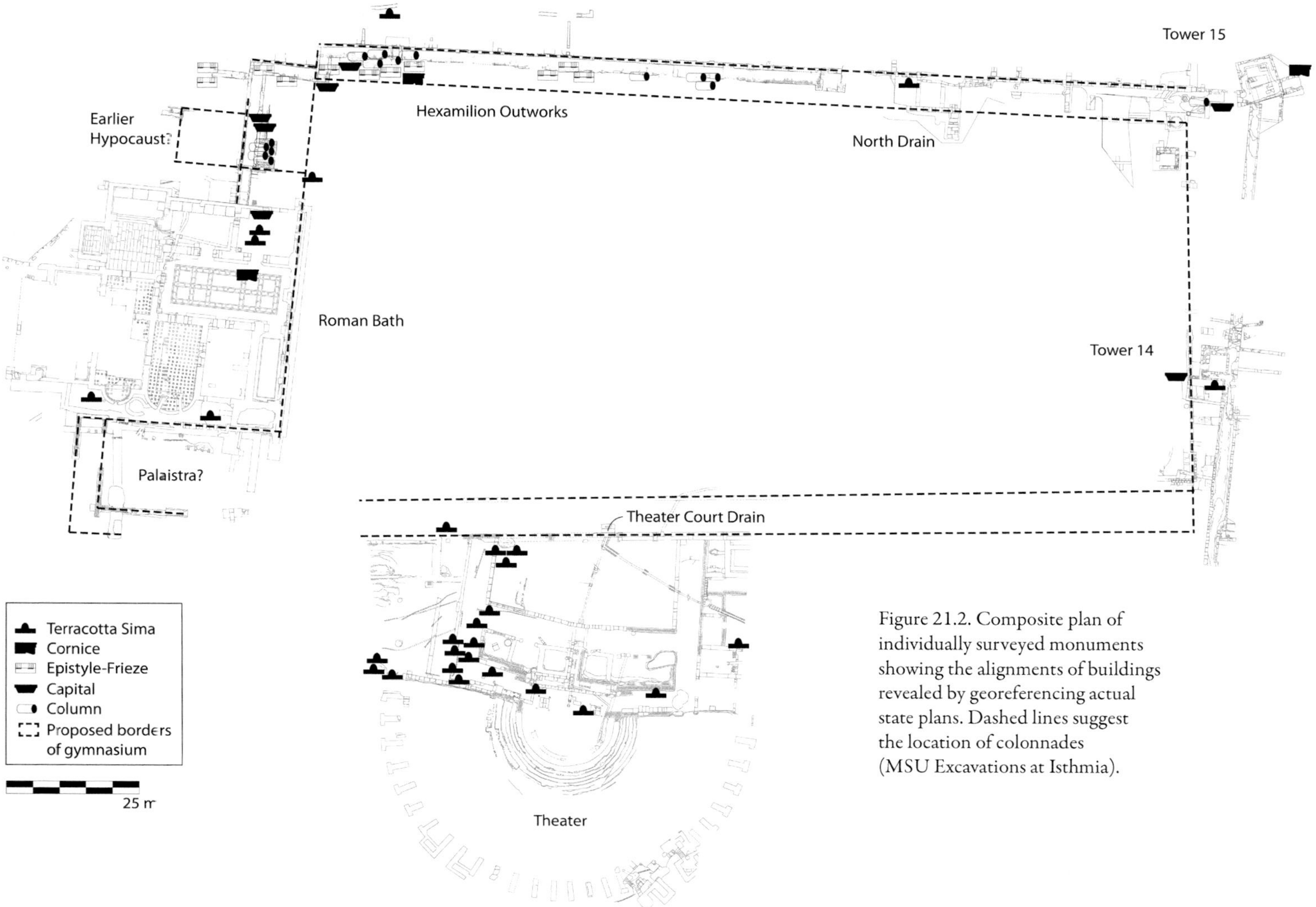

Figure 21.2. Composite plan of individually surveyed monuments showing the alignments of buildings revealed by georeferencing actual state plans. Dashed lines suggest the location of colonnades (MSU Excavations at Isthmia).

detailed understanding of archaeological context appears to have been either assumed and/or undervalued. Yet, more recently, as the goals of the project have shifted to consider different uses of the evidence as well as a wider range of audiences, such traditional methods of dissemination have become insufficient. Thus, like many other legacy projects in Greece, the Isthmia team was forced to consider the best way to migrate this spatial data from an analogue to a digital format. Of course, this process is not as simple as sharing digital copies of archival maps and plans online. Instead, the translation of the information contained in the archived documentation of fieldwork into geospatially accurate data suitable for GIS analysis involves several interpretive steps that must be given careful consideration, especially when the original documentation was more impressionistic than is usual in the digital era.[9]

---

[9] Richards-Rissetto and Landau (2019, 121) call this interpretive process 'datafication' while Loy, Stocker, and Davis (2021, sec. 1) introduce the term 'digitalisation'.

Migrating the Data

Initial attempts to integrate the various state plans into a single scalable site-wide plan relied on the collection of DGPS points at locations that could be identified in both the scanned plans and on the monuments. However, in spite of the excellent quality of the drafting work, approximations of features and other errors in hand-drawn plans made them incompatible with the geospatially accurate reference points and attempts to 'rubbersheet' or stretch the scanned plans to fit real world locations introduced significant distortions that negatively affected the accuracy of the resulting digital plan. A second, far more successful solution relied upon the use of a remote-controlled drone to gather images that could be stitched together to form an orthophoto mosaic of the entire site at a high degree of accuracy (2–7 cm per pixel). Due to the placement of targets that had been previously registered by GPS at various locations throughout the site prior to the aerial survey, the final image of the entire site could be georeferenced and consequently used as a base map to register the various

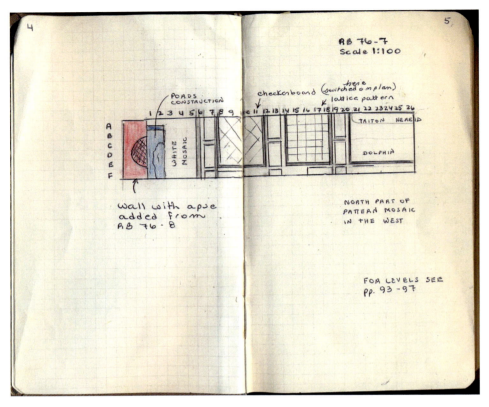

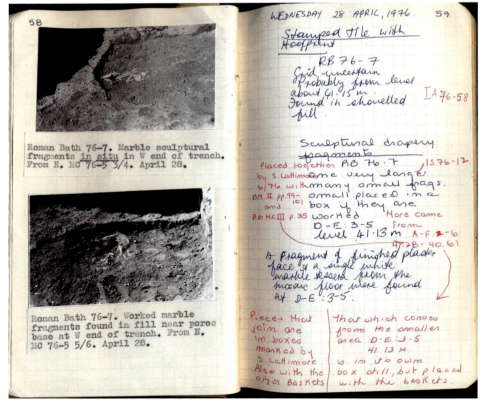

Figure 21.3. Notebook page providing specific coordinates next to a map from first pages of bound volume (MSU Excavations at Isthmia).

state plans and sketches contained in the excavation archives. The process was largely the same as before, but the orthophoto mosaic allowed for a larger number of points to be identified as similar between the image and the scanned plans. When combined into a scalable site plan using a GIS, the various actual state plans for individual areas immediately revealed alignments among various features that had not been recognized in the past and that hinted at a coordinated reorganization of the sanctuary in Antiquity (Fig. 21.2).

Success at the site-wide level suggested that this same method might be used to study the locations of other types of archaeological evidence in a GIS. In particular, several ongoing research projects could benefit from the ability to visualize and analyse collectively the find-spots for catalogued artefacts as well as stratigraphic units within the context of individual monuments or excavated trenches. At Isthmia in the past, in the absence of a systematic grid plan, such information was typically recorded by individual archaeologists as part of the descriptive narrative in their field notebooks. Each excavator established their own grid system for each trench, which was typically illustrated in the first pages of their field journal. Subsequent descriptions of spatially significant information typically relied upon references to these 'hyperlocal' grids. Thus, in order to develop a more holistic and uniformly formatted visualization of this data, it was necessary to digitize and georeference each hand-drawn plan that appears

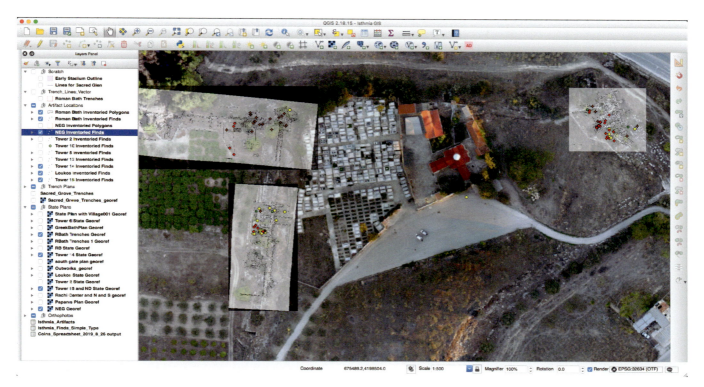

Figure 21.4. Orthophotomosaic of the area of the Byzantine Fortress at Isthmia showing individually georeferenced state plans with the find-spots of coins from different eras superimposed (Jon M. Frey).

in a field diary, then plot the locations of artefacts and other significant features using those imported plans.

The process of moving these individual plans into a GIS was generally straightforward, but with two important exceptions. First, because the accuracy of the sketch plans varied considerably among excavators and field diaries, it was often the case that the georeferencing procedure resulted in significant distortions to the drawing, which could make the identification of specific coordinate locations difficult. Second, the accuracy and level of detail concerning the locations of artefacts and features differed among excavators and even within a single archaeologist's field journal. Typically, in cases when the archaeologist has identified the artefact as significant at the time of discovery, specific coordinates and an elevation were provided (Fig. 21.3). Yet, when an artefact or feature was catalogued some time after its excavation, that item could only be associated with a stratigraphic unit or perhaps even the entire trench.

In order to address these problems, the following procedure was adopted: each plan from a field journal was printed on paper, and the stated locations of each artefact or relevant feature mentioned in the excavator's narrative was plotted by hand onto the printed plan. When grid coordinates were provided, this took the form of a point, but when the location was more ambiguous, a polygonal area was drawn instead. This 'marked up' printout was then scanned and imported into the GIS by georeferencing it to any existing project layers (orthophoto, state plans, other trench drawings) that helped to provide a best fit. Points and polygons indicated in this imported plan were then plotted into their respective layers in the site GIS by tracing over the georeferenced field journal plans.

While this process of translating points from paper to a GIS is time consuming — for example, the excavation of monuments like the Roman Bath at Isthmia resulted in no fewer than eighty-five individual trench plans that had to be added to the GIS, containing a total of 508 securely located artefacts — the results are relatively straightforward and immediately available for analysis. For example, in the area of the Byzantine Fortress, the study of find-spots for coins suggests that a gate through one part of the wall was used predominantly in the Frankish period while another gate saw more activity in the Venetian period and may reflect changes in traffic patterns through the site over time. At present, the only concern with this method has to do with the tendency of points to cluster along grid lines, which is clearly an effect of the literal translation of excavators' stated coor-

Table 21.1. Confidence scores for artefacts identified in field journals.

Score	Characteristics
1	Specific coordinates and elevation data are provided for the artefact and no errors are suspected.
2	An alternative form of location description is provided for the artefact (e.g. 'in the corner of the room') or an error is suspected in the coordinate reference.
3	The artefact can only be associated with an area (e.g. stratigraphic unit or area as defined by the excavator).
4	The artefact can only be associated with the trench.
5	The artefact can only be associated with the site.

Table 21.2. Roman Bath artefacts organized by 'confidence score'.

Type of Artefact	Score 1	Per cent of Total	Scores 2–5	Per cent of Total	Total
IA (Architecture)	237	59.2	163	40.8	400
IC (Coins)	20	80	5	20	25
IM (Miscellaneous)	40	44	51	56	91
IPB (Byzantine Pottery)	0	0	92	100	92
IPG (Greek Pottery)	6	66.7	3	33.3	9
IPL (Lamps)	136	38.4	218	61.6	354
IPR (Roman Pottery)	12	10.3	104	89.7	116
IS (Sculpture)	39	60.9	25	39.1	64
IΣ (Inscriptions)	18	60	12	40	30
Total	508	43	673	57	1181

dinates into the GIS and which may cause future problems depending on the level of resolution of analysis (Fig. 21.4).

Accounting for Inaccuracy

A far more difficult problem concerns the large amount of spatial information that was not recorded in the original legacy documents with the requisite level of accuracy to be plotted as points in a GIS.[10] These inaccuracies, which are common among excavations that also served as field schools in past decades, may be categorized as follows: first, in areas where fieldwork preceded the creation of sufficiently rigorous spatial controls, the locations of some artefacts are given in reference to natural or built features that have changed over time or simply cannot be identified today. Second, because of a lack of experience, those documenting the progress of an excavation often failed to recognize objects of archaeological significance at the time of discovery. When they are eventually identified at a later stage of analysis, such artefacts must be retroactively assigned to as specific an area as possible, which is often the stratigraphic unit being excavated at the time of discovery. Thirdly, there are moments when conflicting evidence concerning the location of an artefact cannot be resolved through the available documentation. Most often this takes the form of typographical errors or mistakes in transcription between different records. Finally, because archaeological projects and their associated museums often serve as repositories for objects recovered by members of the local community, there are a number of artefacts that have passed into the archives either as surface finds or as objects without a known location.

In order to address these various inaccuracies, all catalogue entries were scored according to the scale shown in Table 21.1. This score provides a readily accessible way to determine whether the location of any given artefact can be relied upon when making assertions concerning spatial patterns — an important consideration given the potential use of the resulting dataset by individuals who may not be directly familiar with the evidence.

Yet, these 'confidence scores' only offer a partial solution. As a digital tool that depends on very precise data in the form of vector primitives (points, lines, and polygons) to visualize and analyse spatial information at various scales, GIS are simply not intended to present this type of 'fuzzy' data.[11] This has long been understood among GIS specialists, and while some have developed ways to 'trick' the visual display of spatial data into indicating that datasets contain ambiguity, most discussions of this issue focus on methods for eliminating such inaccurate data prior to analysis. Where the topic of uncertainty in archaeological data has been addressed, the focus has been on outputs — that is, ways to assess the accuracy and reliability of more sophisticated uses of GIS for predictive modelling of ancient resources and human behaviours — rather than the basic inputs of observed

---

[10] Harris and Lock 1995; Miller 1995; Kvamme 1999; Boldrini 2007; Allison and others 2008 represent earlier discussions of this problem. Recent examples of the use of GIS to represent and study archival spatial data are Katsianis, Tsipidis, and Kalisperakis 2015 and Landeschi and others 2019 for excavation and Casarotto 2018 for survey.

[11] Beale 2011.

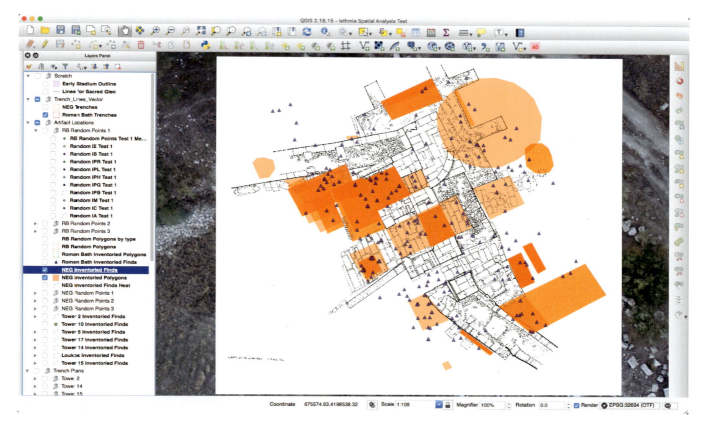

Figure 21.5. Orthophotomosaic of the area of the North-East Gate of the Byzantine Fortress at Isthmia showing objects with detailed find-spots plotted as points and those with more ambiguous find-spots (typically trenches or strata of excavated soil) represented as polygonal areas (Jon M. Frey).

features from the past.[12] This is because it is commonly understood that inaccurate data, the use of which has a clear negative impact on subsequent analysis, should be corrected, replaced, or eliminated altogether.[13] Yet, in the case of legacy projects like Isthmia, where context can only be reconstructed from the original documentation of excavation, this is not possible. More importantly, the complete elimination of uncertain data would represent a significant loss of potentially meaningful evidence. For example, in the case of the Roman Bath, close to 90 per cent of the catalogued Roman pottery and 100 per cent of Byzantine pottery can only be associated with a general area of excavation (see Table 21.2).

Incidentally, 80 per cent of coins, 60 per cent of inscriptions, and nearly 61 per cent of coins were identified at the trowel's edge and given clear locations. This perhaps says as much about our preconceptions concerning important archaeological information as it does about the ease with which these particular artefacts are identified. In essence then, a rejection of inaccurate location data would remove from consideration whole classes of objects and potentially entire periods of activity. Therefore, the question of how to represent or even analyse ambiguous spatial data is, for legacy projects at least, a critical issue.

When the spatial component of an artefact can only be plotted as a polygonal shape representing the total area in which it may have been discovered, the resulting display of artefact find-spots as a combination of points and polygons offers a visually confusing representation of the spatial data (Fig. 21.5). Moreover, the differently shaped areas within artefact polygons offer a potentially misleading representation of the relative significance of certain objects, especially when multiple unique artefacts are associated with an identical area, most commonly the entire trench. Not only do these issues complicate simple visual scans for spatial patterns, but the majority of spatial analysis tools in GIS do not operate across the different data types of points, lines, and polygons.

---

[12] De Runz, Piantoni, and Herbin 2011; Lawrence, Bradbury, and Dunford 2012; Fusco and De Runz 2020; Gupta 2020.

[13] Brouwer Burg 2017.

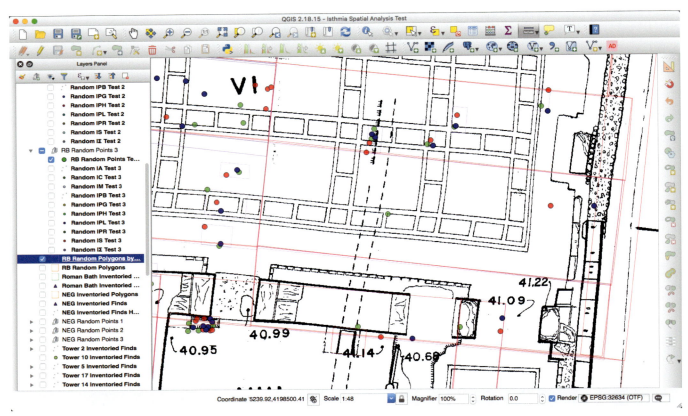

Figure 21.6. Detail view of trenches and stratigraphic units in the Roman Bath at Isthmia showing the results of three attempts to plot ambiguous find-spots for objects using the Random Points from Polygons function in QGIS (Jon M. Frey).

While there is no clear solution to this problem, a number of ways to accommodate the ambiguities outlined above exist, but each has its own drawbacks. For example, it is possible to represent polygon data as a centroid — that is the geometric centre point of an area.[14] This would allow all find-spots to be displayed as points. Yet, even if the observer understands that this is a geometric approximation of inaccurate data, there is a natural tendency to treat these centroids as the actual location where an artefact was uncovered, thus giving the false impression of accuracy. Moreover, in those cases where multiple artefacts are associated with a similarly bounded area, the centroids will overlap, thus masking the true number of artefacts in that location. While it is possible to offset the polygons slightly, and thereby display several coincident centroids as a cluster of points, this approach effectively introduces a second type of inaccuracy to remedy the first.

Another approach, which has been adopted in some legacy projects, is to make use of GIS utilities to create 'random points' in order to generate hypothetical find-spots equivalent to the number of inaccurately located artefacts within a defined area.[15] On one level, this is potentially a better solution, as it utilizes controlled randomness as a proxy for inaccuracy in the archaeological record. Arguably, such randomly generated points should not significantly affect any potential spatial patterns, especially in cases where very small areas have been defined as the possible location of an artefact. On the other hand, if the number of inaccurately located artefacts is relatively small and the area defined by the polygon is large (e.g. the entire trench), the possibility that a randomly generated point misrepresents the original location of an artefact increases. Again too, this approach gives the false impression of an accuracy that masks the true ambiguity of the evidence, but at certain scales may present a workable solution.

In order to test the efficacy of this approach at Isthmia, a 'random points from polygons' tool in QGIS was used to create three different sets of points based on

---

[14] Allison and others 2008.

[15] Loy, Stocker, and Davis 2021.

Figure 21.7. Comparison of heatmaps of random points representing three different attempts to plot ambiguous find-spots for objects using the Random Points from Polygons function in QGIS (Jon M. Frey).

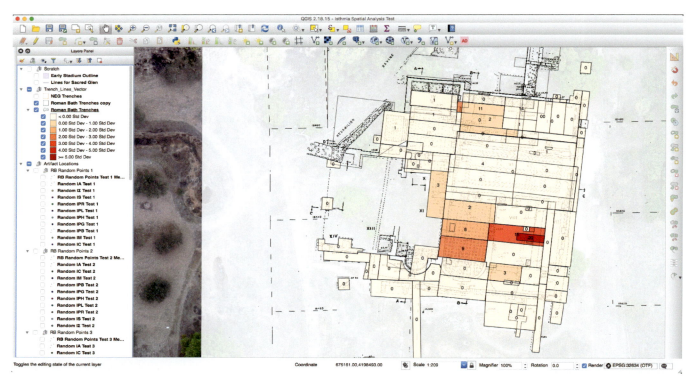

Figure 21.8. Plan of the Roman Bath at Isthmia showing individual trenches sorted by the number of examples of Byzantine pottery uncovered in excavation (Jon M. Frey).

the same set of polygons for inaccurately located artefacts found in the Roman Bath (Fig. 21.6). As a comparison of heat maps — a rough visual indicator of the existence of concentrated clusters of points — based on these tests shows, there is little difference between locations of artefact concentrations over the area of the entire monument (Fig. 21.7). This suggests that at least under certain circumstances and at larger scales, this approach may be an effective way to incorporate inaccurate spatial data into an otherwise accurate dataset.

A final, more promising approach actually moves in the opposite direction of the previous two by following the example of regional surface surveys. As some of the earliest adopters of GIS in archaeology, those conducting systematic surveys have consistently struggled with the representation of artefact scatters when such data comes as a total number of objects counted by individuals crossing a field along specific transects. Typically, studies of this sort 'zoom out' to a level of resolution at which a discrete area of land can be reasonably said to contain a specific artefact count.[16] The resulting 'mosaic' of polygons are coded, most often by colour, as a way to indicate the relative densities of artefacts over a larger area.

When applied to the inaccurate legacy data found in excavation records, this method represents artefacts as part of a total count of items within the most appropriate polygon — typically that associated with a stratigraphic unit — sorted by type. In this way, artefacts with lower 'confidence scores' can still contribute to a spatial analysis without the creation of potentially misleading centroids or random points. Visualizations of the resulting dataset can highlight the various polygons for stratigraphic units or trenches that contain artefacts by type. For example, at Isthmia, the display of trenches containing lamps draws our attention to the same general locations as the heatmaps of randomly generated points, yet avoids the practice of creating false point data (Fig. 21.8). Moreover, because GIS allow the visualization of spatial data as layer overlays, points for artefacts with specific location data can still be displayed atop the polygons. This in turn may provide additional nuance to a spatial pattern suggested by the polygon data.

At the same time, there are some drawbacks to this method. When displayed as two-dimensional data, stratigraphic units will inevitably 'stack up', potentially obscuring lower polygons with different artefact concentrations. Ideally, this can be remedied by making the layers semi-transparent or by adding information to the

---

16 Tartaron 2003; Tartaron and others 2006.

attribute table for each of the polygons, such as elevation or chronological data, then sorting polygons into layers by period. It should also be noted that, with advances in 2.5D and 3D GIS technology, it is quickly becoming possible to view the strata in an excavation as volumetric spaces or as cross-sections, perhaps eliminating this concern altogether. More importantly, with this method there is inevitably a loss of resolution to the data, which can now reveal patterns only at larger scales. Yet, far from being a drawback, this recognition invites a more careful consideration of what goals we may reasonably achieve through archaeological excavation and whether GIS-thinking is giving us too much confidence in our spatial data altogether.[17]

Regardless of which method is selected, the final presentation of digitalized legacy spatial data must follow a set of display protocols that will encourage the type of remote user that is imagined in archive archaeology to approach inaccurate data with caution.[18] For monuments and other permanent features, projects should make a visual distinction among those structures that remain *in situ*, those that no longer exist but that have been included on the evidence of legacy documentation, and those that offer any suggested reconstruction of features. In this case, standards have been a matter of discussion for some time now, and several options have been proposed (e.g. differences in the colour, thickness, or style for lines or surface pattern for volumetric spaces).[19] For less permanent features such as catalogued finds, the standards are less clear. At a basic level, the display of spatial data should distinguish between the find-spots of objects that have been provided in the documentation of excavation and those that have been artificially generated as centroids or random points. In the Isthmia dataset, artefacts with originally documented locations are indicated by points and labels containing the object's catalogue number, while artificially generated points are only identified by the artefact type (e.g. architectural fragment, pottery, or inscription). The advantage to this method is that objects with inaccurate location data cannot be accidentally assigned to a specific point on the site plan. Yet, this also means that objects with inaccurate location data cannot be searched or queried in the GIS individually and an explanation for a 'missing' object must be sought in a separate database. It is also recommended that layers intended to contain randomly generated points be shared as research data only in the form of the bounding polygonal shapes and not the artificially generated points. This will require a distance user to create the points for themselves, thus highlighting their manufactured and potentially unreliable nature. Lastly, any presentation of spatial data that combines reliable point locations with artificially generated point data should adopt a symbology that clearly indicates the character of each (e.g. triangular markers for reliable points and circles for centroids or randomly generated points).

Conclusion

Given the amount of time and effort involved in translating inaccurate or 'fuzzy' legacy data into a GIS, it might reasonably be asked whether it would be better simply to start over by collecting spatial data in 'born-digital' formats. However, it is clear that the digitalization of archival spatial data is not just advantageous, but potentially quite impactful. When excavation is involved, there is no way to re-excavate the various stratigraphic sequences and moments of discovery that are recorded in the documents held in excavation archives. Yet, this is not restricted to layers of earth alone. In the case of the monuments themselves, changes to the local environment often prohibit access to the physical remains (e.g. trenches have been backfilled, monuments have changed through conservation or decay, or the land has been given over to commercial development). Even in cases when an archaeological feature can be resurveyed, the original excavator's hand-drawn plans and elevations are an invitation to engage with another scholar in a conversation that we would be foolish to ignore.

More generally though, these records, and the difficulties we have in translating them into digital formats, have much to teach us about not only the ancient past, but about the traditions and assumptions that underpin our data collection methodologies more generally. Consider the issue of location data presented above. It is clear that in archaeology, the location of a discovery is just as important as the thing itself. For example, knowledge that an artefact was found beneath, atop, or beside the remains of a person in a grave can drastically change our understanding of its significance as part, or perhaps no part at all, of the mortuary process. At the same time though, it is worth asking what our inherited practices of recording measurements in the field are actually intended to accomplish, especially in the context of the final dissemination of the results of archaeological

---

[17] Miller and Richards 1995.
[18] Beale 2011.
[19] Schäfer 2018.

fieldwork.[20] Many have engaged in the time-consuming practice of studiously recording the locations and elevations of excavated features with the greatest accuracy possible only to discover at the end of a season that the opening elevations of most stratigraphic units are somehow higher than the closing elevations of the previous. Equally common is the experience of carefully noting the locations of important artefacts only to have an object of equal significance appear some time later after cleaning and sorting, rendering it unable to be located with equal accuracy. Such inaccuracies are not so much a result of observer error as they are simply the nature of the materials and processes that are part of field research.[21] Yet, by the time the final publications of fieldwork appear, these ambiguities and conflicts have been resolved through an interpretive process that sacrifices the accuracy of measurements in favour of a best fit for the majority of the evidence. Unfortunately, this 'black box' process finds little representation or discussion in the articles and monographs that appear in print. Boundaries between strata are crisply delineated in illustrations, elevations and dimensions are given in centimetres, and the locations of artefacts are plotted in maps and plans with a clarity that does not match the reality of fieldwork. This tradition has only been further enabled by the technological sophistication of digital recording tools. They impress and amaze not only because they speed and simplify recording procedures, but also because the data they produce suggest a type of scientific precision that masks the inherently incomplete nature of the evidence. In this context, archival documentation and the difficulties we encounter in attempting to reconfigure it to fit digital systems serves as a healthy reminder that archaeology is an inexact science, if it is a science at all.

As a widely adopted tool of the trade, GIS can be an important way of organizing, exploring, and sharing archaeological information, but should not be imagined as a 'fix all' for inaccurate legacy data. Instead, it is important to seek out ways to bridge the gap between the accuracy demanded by the vector-based interface of a GIS and the inherent inaccuracy of archival archaeological documentation. Three possible methods have been presented here — the first two attempt to accommodate the needs of the GIS system by giving inaccurate archival evidence a degree of accuracy that it does not possess, while the third downgrades certain data to a level of 'least common accuracy' in order to give equal status to the representation of all object periods and types. This last option seems most promising for three reasons. First, it relies on existing survey methods to prioritize the interests of the archaeologist for reliable data over the demands of a digital tool. Next, it acknowledges that in most cases, the presence or absence of artefacts in a stratigraphic layer is the level of accuracy that actually informs interpretations. Last, it reminds us that all spatial data — even that collected with the most advanced digital tools — are interpretations and approximations of real world features. To be sure, detailed and accurate observations are important, but there is an equally important place in our practice for the rough sketch, the shaded area, and the dotted line that together indicate ambiguity, uncertainty, and evolving interpretations.

---

[20] Gero 2007.

[21] Wylie 2017.

Works Cited

Allen, K. M. S., S. W. Green, and E. B. W. Zubrow (eds). 1990. *Interpreting Space: GIS and Archaeology* (Bristol: Taylor and Francis).

Allison, P. 2008. 'Dealing with Legacy Data: An Introduction', *Internet Archaeology*, 24 <http://dx.doi.org/10.11141/ia.24.8>.

Allison, P., P. Faulkner, A. Fairbairn, and S. Ellis. 2008. 'Procedures for Measuring Women's Influence: Data Translation and Manipulation and Related Problems', *Internet Archaeology*, 24 <http://dx.doi.org/10.11141/ia.24.6>.

Beale, G. 2011. 'Visualising Discourse: An Approach to Archaeological Uncertainty. Interpretation and Reconstruction of the Grandi Magazzini di Settimio Severo at Portus, Italy', in E. Jerem, F. Redő, and V. Szevérenyi (eds), *On the Road to Reconstructing the Past: Computer Applications and Quantitative Methods in Archaeology (CAA); Proceedings of the 36th International Conference, Budapest, April 2–6, 2008* (Budapest: Archaeolingua), pp. 46–52.

Biswell, S., L. Cropper, J. Evans, V. Gaffney, and P. Leach. 1995. 'GIS and Excavation: A Cautionary Tale from Shepton Mallet, Somerset, England', in G. R. Lock and Z. Stančič (eds), *Archaeology and Geographical Information Systems: A European Perspective* (Bristol: Taylor and Francis), pp. 269–85.

Boldrini, N. 2007. 'Planning Uncertainty: Creating an Artefact Density Index for North Yorkshire, England', *Internet Archaeology*, 21 <https://doi.org/10.11141/ia.21.1>.

Broneer, O. 1971. *Isthmia*, I: *Temple of Poseidon* (Princeton: American School of Classical Studies at Athens).

—— 1973. *Isthmia*, II: *Topography and Architecture* (Princeton: American School of Classical Studies at Athens).

—— 1977. *Isthmia*, III: *Terracotta Lamps* (Princeton: American School of Classical Studies at Athens).

Brouwer Burg, M. 2017. 'It Must Be Right, GIS Told Me So! Questioning the Infallibility of GIS as a Methodological Tool', *Journal of Archaeological Science*, 84: 115–20.

Casarotto, A. 2018. *Spatial Patterns in Landscape Archaeology: A GIS Procedure to Study Settlement Organization in Early Roman Colonial Territories* (Amsterdam: Amsterdam University Press).

Conolly, J. and M. Lake. 2006. *Geographical Information Systems in Archaeology* (Cambridge: Cambridge University Press).

De Runz, C., F. Piantoni, and M. Herbin. 2011. 'Towards Handling Uncertainty of Excavation Data into a GIS', in E. Jerem, F. Redő, and V. Szevérenyi (eds), *On the Road to Reconstructing the Past: Computer Applications and Quantitative Methods in Archaeology (CAA); Proceedings of the 36th International Conference, Budapest, April 2–6, 2008* (Budapest: Archaeolingua), pp. 187–91.

Ebert, D. 2004. 'Applications of Archaeological GIS', *Canadian Journal of Archaeology*, 282: 319–41.

Frey, J. M. n.d. *Michigan State University Excavations at Isthmia* <https://msuisthmia.org> [accessed 28 September 2022].

Fusco, J. and C. De Runz. 2020. 'Spatial Fuzzy Sets', in M. Gillings, P. Hacigüzeller, and G. Lock (eds), *Archaeological Spatial Analysis: A Methodological Guide* (London: Routledge), pp. 169–91.

Gero, J. M. 2007. 'Honoring Ambiguity/Problematizing Certitude', *Journal of Archaeological Method and Theory*, 143: 311–27.

Gillings, M., P. Hacigüzeller, and G. Lock. 2020. 'Archaeology and Spatial Analysis', in M. Gillings, P. Hacigüzeller, and G. Lock (eds), *Archaeological Spatial Analysis: A Methodological Guide* (London: Routledge), pp. 1–16.

Gupta, N. 2020. 'Preparing Archaeological Data for Spatial Analysis', in M. Gillings, P. Hacigüzeller, and G. Lock (eds), *Archaeological Spatial Analysis: A Methodological Guide* (London: Routledge), pp. 17–40.

Hacigüzeller, P. 2012. 'GIS, Critique, Representation and Beyond', *Journal of Social Archaeology*, 122: 245–63.

Harris, T. M. and G. R. Lock. 1995. 'Toward an Evaluation of GIS in European Archaeology: The Past, the Present and Future of Theory and Applications', in G. R. Lock and Z. Stančič (eds), *Archaeology and Geographical Information Systems: A European Perspective* (Bristol: Taylor and Francis), pp. 349–65.

Howey, M. C. L. and M. Brouwer Burg. 2017. 'Assessing the State of Archaeological GIS Research: Unbinding Analyses of Past Landscapes', *Journal of Archaeological Science*, 84: 1–9.

Huggett, J. 2015. 'A Manifesto for an Introspective Digital Archaeology', *Open Archaeology*, 1: 86–95.

Katsianis, M., S. Tsipidis, and I. Kalisperakis. 2015. 'Enhancing Excavation Archives Using 3D Spatial Technologies', in C. Papadopoulos, E. Paliou, A. Chrysanthi, E. Kotoula, and A. Sarris (eds), *Archaeological Research in the Digital Age: Proceedings of the 1st Conference on Computer Applications and Quantitative Methods in Archaeology Greek Chapter (CAA-GR) Rethymno, Crete, 6–8 March 2014* (Rethymno: Institute for Mediterranean Studies — Foundation of Research and Technology), pp. 46–54.

Kvamme, K. L. 1999. 'Recent Directions and Developments in Geographical Information Systems', *Journal of Archaeological Research*, 72: 153–201.

Landeschi, G., J. Apel, V. Lundström, J. Storå, S. Lindgren, and N. Dell'Unto. 2019. 'Re-enacting the Sequence: Combined Digital Methods to Study a Prehistoric Cave', *Archaeological and Anthropological Sciences*, 11: 2805–19.

Lawrence, D., J. Bradbury, and R. Dunford. 2012. 'Chronology, Uncertainty and GIS: A Methodology for Characterising and Understanding Landscapes of the Ancient Near East', *Journal for Ancient Studies*, special volume, 3: 1007–14.

Lock, G. and J. Pouncett. 2017. 'Spatial Thinking in Archaeology: Is GIS the Answer?', *Journal of Archaeological Science*, 84: 129–35.

Lock, G. R. and Z. Stančič (eds). 1995. *Archaeology and Geographical Information Systems: A European Perspective* (Bristol: Taylor and Francis).

Loy, M., S. R. Stocker, and J. L. Davis. 2021. 'From Archive to GIS: Recovering Spatial Information for Tholos IV at the Palace of Nestor from the Notebooks of Lord William Taylour', *Internet Archaeology*, 56 <https://doi.org/10.11141/ia.56.5>.

Maschner, H. D. G. 1996. *New Methods, Old Problems: Geographic Information Systems in Modern Archaeological Research* (Carbondale: Center for Archaeological Investigations).

McCoy, M. D. 2017. 'Geospatial Big Data and Archaeology: Prospects and Problems Too Great to Ignore', *Journal of Archaeological Science Journal of Archaeological Science*, 84: 74–94.

McCoy, M. D. and T. N. Ladefoged. 2009. 'New Developments in the Use of Spatial Technology in Archaeology', *Journal of Archaeological Research*, 173: 263–95.

Miller, P. 1995. 'How to Look Good and Influence People: Thoughts on the Design and Interpretation of an Archaeological GIS', in G. R. Lock and Z. Stančič (eds), *Archaeology and Geographical Information Systems: A European Perspective* (Bristol: Taylor and Francis), pp. 319–33.

Miller, P. and J. Richards. 1995. 'The Good, the Bad, and the Downright Misleading: Archaeological Adoption of Computer Visualisation', in J. Huggett and N. Ryan (eds), *Computer Applications and Quantitative Methods in Archaeology 1994: CAA94* (Oxford: Tempus Reparatum), pp. 19–22.

Richards-Rissetto, H. and K. Landau. 2019. 'Digitally-Mediated Practices of Geospatial Archaeological Data: Transformation, Integration, and Interpretation', *Journal of Computer Applications in Archaeology*, 21: 120–35.

Schäfer, U. U. 2018. 'Uncertainty Visualization and Digital 3D Modeling in Archaeology: A Brief Introduction', *International Journal for Digital Art History*, 3: 86–106.

Tartaron, T. F. 2003. 'The Archaeological Survey: Sampling Strategies and Field Methods', in J. Wiseman and K. Zachos (eds), *Landscape Archaeology in Southern Epirus, Greece*, I, Hesperia Supplement, 32 (Princeton: American School of Classical Studies at Athens), pp. 23–46.

Tartaron, T. F., T. E. Gregory, D. J. Pullen, J. S. Noller, R. M. Rothaus, J. L. Rife, L. Tzortzopoulou-Gregory, R. C. Schon, R. William, D. K. Pettegrew, and D. Nakassis. 2006. 'The Eastern Korinthia Archaeological Survey: Integrated Methods for a Dynamic Landscape', *Hesperia*, 75.4: 453–523.

Wheatley, D. and M. Gillings. 2002. *Spatial Technology and Archaeology* (New York: Routledge).

Witcher, R. 2008. 'Resurveying Mediterranean Rural Landscapes: GIS and Legacy Survey Data', *Internet Archaeology*, 24 <https://doi.org/10.11141/ia.24.2>.

Wylie, A. 2017. 'How Archaeological Evidence Bites Back: Strategies for Putting Old Data to Work in New Ways', *Science, Technology, and Human Values*, 422: 203–25.

22. Digitized Archives of Illicit Antiquities: Academic Research, Dissemination, and Impact

Christos Tsirogiannis

Aarhus Institute of Advanced Studies, Aarhus University (christos.tsirogiannis@cantab.net)

Introduction

Individual cases of previously recorded antiquities, which were subsequently stolen from archaeological sites and museums, later appearing on offer on the international market, were scarcely reaching wider audiences before the early 1990s.[1] Likewise, before this period, relatively few cases of antiquities looted from the ground, and thus archaeologically unrecorded, were known.[2] However, the vast majority of the antiquities on offer were (and remain) actually unprovenanced, as they were not identified as recorded antiquities illegally removed from archaeological sites, nor as unrecorded antiquities looted from the ground. At the same time, both categories were (and still are) lacking any kind of written documentation which could justify their legal discovery, export, and sale. The volume of such material on offer by the most 'reputable' auction houses and dealers' galleries, combined, at the same time, with large-scale looting evidenced in several countries, was making obvious that networks of organized criminals were operating in systematically supplying a market which was, at the very least, indifferent to the continuous destruction and criminal activities. Among the most affected countries was Italy, as Etruscan, Dunian, and Apulian antiquities, lacking complete and documented provenance, were being paraded in the glossy sales catalogues in London and New York. Although statistically almost all these antiquities came from the Italian Peninsula,[3] the relevant authorities were lacking proof of the antiquities' illicit origins, required by law for seizing the antiquities and prosecuting the individuals and companies involved.

The Main Raids and Discoveries of the Archives

Below I present, in chronological order, the main events that led to the discoveries of the biggest and most important photographic and documentary archives, which were confiscated from notorious and convicted illicit antiquities dealers. The course of events that changed the field of forensic archaeology regarding illicit antiquities was first presented in 2006,[4] but my account corrects certain dates, expands our knowledge with information not previously taken into account, and updates the narrative with some of the events that followed post-2007.

On 26 May 1986, several antiquities, including one sarcophagus and two Roman capitals were stolen from the villa De Marchi in San Felice Circeo, in the Latina province, south of Rome.[5] The owner of the villa, Alessandra De Marchi, contacted the Carabinieri and reported the theft and the stolen antiquities. At the Sotheby's antiquities auction 18 May 1987 in London, the stolen sarcophagus and the two capitals were consigned by 'Edition Service', a company belonging to the Italian antiquities dealer Giacomo Medici.

On 14 October 1994, following a request from the Greek police art squad to the German authorities, the German, Greek, and Italian authorities jointly raided the house of Antonio Savoca, an Italian-origin antiquities dealer, living in Pullach, a suburb of Munich. They discovered hundreds of looted antiquities and Savoca's meticulous archive of documents.[6] What is generally perceived to be Savoca's photographic archive in reality consists of the *c.* 240 images that the authorities took of the antiquities discovered during the raid. Savoca proved to be the recipient of eight magnificent ancient

---

[1] Meyer 1977, 29–33; Axarlis 2001, among others.
[2] e.g. Watson 1997, 188; Watson and Todeschini 2007, 215.
[3] Elia 2001.
[4] Watson and Todeschini 2006.
[5] Muntoni 2004, 11.
[6] Watson and Todeschini 2007, 6–10.

vases stolen from the Melfi Museum, east of Naples. All eight vases were found during the raid. The Melfi vases case led to the middleman Pasquale Camera and after his accidental death on 31 August 1995, based on evidence found at the site, the Italian authorities started to organize a raid in Rome, at an apartment familiar to Camera.

On 17 March 1995, the De Marchi sarcophagus and the two capitals were eventually identified by Paolo Del Pennino, son of Alessandra De Marchi, in the 1987 Sotheby's catalogue, as being three of the antiquities stolen from villa De Marchi in 1986. Further research on the case pointed to Medici's 'front man' Jacques Henri Albert, who was operating 'Edition Service' on behalf of Medici. Mr Jacques stated that that 'Edition Service' was a Panama-based company created on 24 September 1981 and purchased on 24 February 1986 by Giacomo Medici, who owned all the shares and was the beneficiary. The public prosecutor of the Latina province, Mr Riccardo Audino, requested permission from the Swiss authorities to search the company's warehouse in the Geneva Free Port, as antiquities stolen from the villa De Marchi could have been stored there. The case was further reinforced after the results from the research conducted by the London-based journalist Mr Peter Watson were published in 1997, further involving Giacomo Medici.[7] On 13 September 1995, the Italian authorities, together with their Swiss colleagues, raided Giacomo Medici's rented premises in the Free Port of Geneva and other premises in Italy, discovering thousands of antiquities and Medici's photographic and documentary archive.[8] The Medici archive consists of thirty albums of Polaroids, fifteen envelopes with photographs, and twelve envelopes with rolls of film. Additionally, about thirty-five thousand pages of documents were discovered.[9]

---

[7] Watson 1997, 186–93.

[8] This account of how the link to Medici was made therefore differs from that of Watson and Todeschini (2007, 19–20), who state that this major conceptual breakthrough came when the Italian authorities were investigating the case of another sarcophagus, stolen from the Church of San Saba in Rome, for sale at Sotheby's in London. According to Mashberg 2020, this first breakthrough was achieved because of the investigation of 'the theft of a statue from a villa in Rome and its sudden appearance at a Sotheby's auction in London'. It appears that Mashberg was probably referring to a different antiquity, a headless female statue stolen from villa Torlonia in Rome, on 31 December 1983. Even though this statue, as well, ended up with Medici (but also with Symes and Michaelides, through Sotheby's and Christie's), this case was not the one that led to the raid in the Free Port and the discovery of the Medici archive.

[9] Watson and Todeschini 2007, 66–67.

On 15 February 1996, in an apartment that Camera used to visit in the centre of Rome, the so-called 'organigram' was discovered (a one-page, handwritten document mapping the main Italian branch of the international illicit antiquities network).[10] It is believed that Pasquale Camera was the one who created the 'organigram'. From that point, this document was used as a map for the raids that followed. The first publication of the 'organigram' as well as the presentation of the relevant raids that followed and the archives discovered, was in the book *The Medici Conspiracy* (2006) by the journalists Peter Watson and Cecilia Todeschini.[11] In the updated (2007) edition, their Greek colleague Nikolas Zirganos contributed one chapter.

In 1997, following the suggestion of General Roberto Conforti (then head of the Italian Carabinieri art squad),[12] Dr Paolo Giorgio Ferri, a successful prosecutor with vast experience in researching other types of organized crimes, especially drug trafficking,[13] was appointed at Rome's prosecution office, to investigate the various webs that could emerge from the confiscated 'organigram'. In November 1997, Ferri received the file on the antiquities trafficking case from his colleague, Audino; Ferri then masterminded a detailed plan of police raids, legal assistance, and forensic archaeological research, which changed forever the antiquities world on an international level.

On 1 February 2001, following information from the 'organigram', the French and Italian authorities jointly raided the flat of Robert (Bob) Hecht Jr. in Paris. Under the bed, they discovered plastic shopping bags containing 'some ancient vases-Attic, Apulian, Corinthian-full of earth. Then they found a bronze helmet, and a bronze belt, both dusted in soil. Next, they came across a number of vase fragments, in the same dirty condition'.[14] In addition, several folders with *c.* 245 photographs packed inside were discovered, forming what has since been called the Hecht archive. Finally, letters and other documents, as well as Hecht's eighty-eight-page handwritten memoir were discovered and seized.[15]

---

[10] Watson and Todeschini 2007, 15–18.

[11] An incomplete transcription of the 'organigram' was made by Dr Neil Brodie (Brodie 2012).

[12] I am grateful to journalist and friend Mr Fabio Isman for clarifying this detail.

[13] Watson and Todeschini 2007, 23–24.

[14] Watson and Todeschini 2007, 158.

[15] Watson and Todeschini 2007, 161–81.

In October 2001, the Swiss and Italian authorities raided the apartment and laboratory of the Zurich-based restorer Fritz Bürki and his son Harry. They discovered and seized many antiquities pointing to Becchina, documents and other evidence pointing to Medici and Hecht,[16] as well as *c.* 660 images of antiquities, most of which had been already sold abroad. From the seized antiquities, about 450 remained in custody with the Bürkis, but when the authorities returned to collect them, these were missing; in 2009 the Swiss authorities rediscovered and sent to Italy 137 of them, while about three hundred are still missing.[17]

In May 2002, the Swiss and the Italians jointly raided Medici's rival in the antiquities business, Giovanni Franco (Gianfranco) Becchina, at his premises in Basel and Italy.[18] They discovered more than five thousand antiquities, but also an archive of more than eleven thousand images and documents.

In late December 2003, the Italian authorities raided the looter Giuseppe Evangelisti, a resident of Capo di Monte, situated north of Rome. They discovered 'hundreds of looted antiquities — still broken, still dirty with soil, all local, fragments in sacks and fruit boxes'.[19] Additionally, they discovered several agendas and diaries covering the years 1997–2002, as well as seven albums of photographs, containing *c.* 465 photographs in total. Included in the notes were, among other names, Giacomo Medici and the Lebanese-origin antiquities dealers Ali and Hitcham Aboutaam operating with galleries in New York and Geneva.

In April 2006, the Greek police art squad raided the premises of the Papadimitriou family (close relatives of the late illicit antiquities dealer Christos Michaelides, business and life partner of the illicit antiquities dealer Robin Symes), both in Athens and on the Schinousa island in the Cyclades. I participated in the raid as a forensic archaeologist, sent by the Greek Ministry of Culture. Dozens of antiquities were discovered and confiscated, as well as the Symes-Michaelides photographic archive (also known as the 'Schinousa Archive'), which contains *c.* 2200 images.[20] The case reached the courts in January 2018, and in July 2018 Despoina Papadimitriou (sister of Christos Michaelides) and her first-born son, Dimitris, were found guilty 'for the act of embezzlement of monuments and [each one] convicted [...] to suspended imprisonment of 4 years. The judge also ratified the seizure and ordered the confiscation of the seized items'.[21] Currently (March 2022) the case is at the Court of Appeals in Athens.

Apart from these, however, there have been more raids and archives, which have not been mentioned by Watson and Todeschini; in June 2000, a photographic archive was confiscated by the US Customs authorities, in collaboration with the Italian police, from David Holland Swingler, an individual described as a food importer. Additionally, the US authorities confiscated from Swingler's home in Laguna Hills, California, 230 antiquities originating from illicit excavations in Etruscan and Apulian sites. They were later returned to Italy, together with an additional 650 antiquities related to Swingler, recovered from the US and Europe.[22] As Dr Neil Brodie wrote:

> Swingler who, it emerged, was actively engaged in smuggling antiquities from Italy using a pasta import company as cover, was **sentenced by an Italian Court** (in absentia) to 4 years in jail, and fined 12 million lire, has not been prosecuted in the US.[23]

Edoardo Almagià, another antiquities dealer and a 1973 Princeton alumnus, was selling antiquities in New York from 1980 to 2006, when he was raided by the US federal agents at his East 78th Street apartment and later flew to Italy. During the raid, illicit antiquities were discovered,[24] as well as Almagià's archive, containing *c.* 6500 photographs and documents. Since 1996, Almagià was involved in several legal cases regarding illicit antiquities.[25]

Shaping the Confiscated Archives and their Fourfold Use

After their discovery, these photographic and documentary confiscated archives were digitized to enable the law enforcement authorities and the archaeologists who assisted them to work on this material,[26] which in its physical form remains secured by the Italian and Greek

---

16 Watson and Todeschini 2007, 185–88.
17 Independent Online 2010.
18 Watson and Todeschini 2007, 292–97.
19 Watson and Todeschini 2007, 266.
20 Watson and Todeschini 2007, 314–24.
21 Mödlinger 2018.
22 Ruiz 2000; Gill 2014.
23 Doole and Brodie 2000, 15, bold in original.
24 Mashberg 2021a.
25 Mashberg 2021a.
26 Watson and Todeschini 2007, 53–79 and 321–24.

state authorities (apart from the physical images from the Medici archive, which were returned to Giacomo Medici as a result of a separate trial, see below, 'Accessing the Archives'). It proved crucial for subsequent research, academic or other, that some of the confiscated archives were not digitized in the form in which they were discovered (e.g. the Symes–Michaelides one).[27] This unfortunate event irreversibly restricted us from accessing the thoughts of their creators regarding the reasons for giving a certain order to these archives, which, in cases of criminals dealing in illicit antiquities, would have been valuable, not only for archaeology but also for criminology, law, history of art, and finance, among other disciplines. In addition, in most of the cases, the digitization did not include all the seized documents, e.g. only about 140 of the thirty-five thousand documents seized from Giacomo Medici were digitized and shared for legal and archaeological research. The reverse sides of the vast majority of the printed images discovered (Polaroids, regular-print, and professional), were not digitized either: since the reverse can include serial numbers, dates, handwritten notes, and photographers' stamps with names and addresses, this omission has caused crucial information on the provenance of the objects and the trafficking paths that these followed, etc. to be lost or remain largely inaccessible.

The aim of the authorities regarding work on the digitized version of these archives was the identification of the depicted objects, in museums, private collections, auction houses, and dealers' galleries around the world, and the subsequent claim of the identified pieces from the various institutions and individuals. Indeed, based on this research, archaeologists, like the pioneers in this kind of forensic archaeological research, Dr Daniela Rizzo, Mr Maurizio Pellegrini, and myself, managed to identify more than five hundred antiquities by 2008. From these, about three hundred were

Figure 22.1. Polaroid image from the Medici archive, depicting a broken Attic black-figure kylix with a symposium scene, attributed to the style of the Lysippides Painter and to the potter Andocides, *c.* 520 BC.

Figure 22.2. Author's photograph of the same kylix, restored, on a loan exhibition at the New Acropolis Museum in 2008, after its repatriation to Italy from the Jean Paul Getty Museum, in Malibu, California, due to the identification by the archaeologists Mr Maurizio Pellegrini and Dr Daniela Rizzo (© Christos Tsirogiannis).

---

[27] Watson and Todeschini 2007, 53–79 and 317. After the Symes-Michaelides images were discovered and recorded on the spot, the police officers did not put them back in their folders in the order they were found.

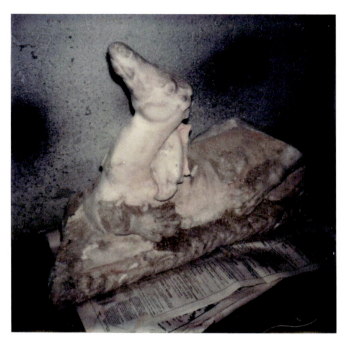

Figure 22.3. Polaroid image from the Medici archive, depicting the central part of a sculpture with two griffins attacking a hind, on an Italian newspaper, after the sculpture was broken by the Italian looters, who removed it from an Etruscan grave.

Figure 22.4. Author's photograph of the same part, incorporated in the restored sculpture, on a loan exhibition at the New Acropolis Museum in 2008, after its repatriation to Italy from the Jean Paul Getty Museum, in Malibu, California, due to the identification by the archaeologists Mr Maurizio Pellegrini and Dr Daniela Rizzo (© Christos Tsirogiannis).

repatriated mainly to Italy, and a few were repatriated to Greece. To date, having switched my career from a field archaeologist to a desk-based academic, I have managed to identify a total of 1586 antiquities depicted in these archives. About five hundred of them have already been repatriated to Italy, Greece, Syria, and Iraq, but many more identified cases are ongoing with various state authorities. Therefore, the first significant use of the photographs in the confiscated archives was as proof of post-1970 illicit activity, during negotiations — especially with museums (Figs 22.1–22.2) and private collectors — for the return of stolen archaeological material of significant cultural, artistic, and financial value.

Each forensic archaeologist followed a different path working with the archives; I chose to divide the digitized images into different categories, according to their shape, material, decoration, geographic origin, etc., making each photograph easily and quickly accessible, each time I needed to compare it with an image of a published antiquity. This system allows me also to correlate images depicting the same antiquities but found in different confiscated archives. It enables me to reconstruct antiquities' true collecting histories, parts of which frequently differ or are omitted from the 'provenance' offered by the museums, private collectors, and members of the market involved in these antiquities' sale and acquisition. This use of the images, in the ever-growing area of provenance research in antiquities within the discipline of archaeology, is a secure way of recontextualizing some, at least, looted antiquities.[28]

Additionally, these images were also used as valuable criminological evidence during the prosecution of most of these dealers and looters, in various countries. Being presented by experts in courts, the images of the identified antiquities (as well as of

---

[28] For the term 'recontextualization' in this context, see first Renfrew 2010, 101; he discusses in particular the recontextualization of the griffins statue (trapezophoros, Figs 22.3–22.4 above) over pp. 97–102.

Figure 22.5. Regular-print image from the Medici archive, depicting a rare marble prehistoric idol of a female deity, broken in pieces and missing part of its head (© Manhattan District Attorney's Office).

Figure 22.6. The same idol, restored, was identified by the author 21 November 2014, in the Christie's, New York, 11 December 2014 antiquities auction catalogue, as part of the Michael and Judy Steinhardt collection. The immediate publication of the image and the case in expert academic and university websites, before the sale, greatly contributed to the withdrawal of the idol from the auction. It was finally confiscated from the Steinhardt premises in Manhattan in January 2018 and repatriated to Italy in February 2022 (© Manhattan District Attorney's Office).

pieces not identified at the time, but presented in fragmented condition, encrusted and covered with soil, in a warehouse, stable, or in the countryside) became the basis of proving the guilt on the part of individuals involved. For example, the Polaroid images from the Medici archive, depicting a statue of griffins and hind (a trapezophoros), broken in pieces (Fig. 22.3) and in the boot of a car, were presented among other photographic material by the archaeologists Mr Maurizio Pellegrini and Dr Daniela Rizzo during their testimony at the trial against Giacomo Medici, vastly contributing to his conviction as well as the object's later repatriation (Fig. 22.4).

The fourth use of these images was (and still is) their publication once an identification has been made. Especially in time-sensitive cases, where an identification of one or more antiquities is made while their sale is imminent, the publication of the relevant images and the announcement of the identification in the press (newspapers and magazines with national and international circulation, expert blogs, TV, and radio programmes, etc.) is of great importance. This immediate publication informs simultaneously the authorities, the market, and the public and provides everyone access to the raw evidence, leaving no doubt regarding the true origin of the objects (Figs 22.5–22.6). Their immediate publication also highlights the particular issues that are being raised in each case and adds pressure to the seller and/or the owner (frequently not the same person), at least to withdraw the identified antiquities from the sale. This tactic has greatly contributed to the subsequent return of many identified antiquities to their country of origin, also in cases that are not time-sensitive (e.g. when an antiquity is identified in the permanent collection of a museum). In this way, the best result is achieved quickly, and lengthy legal procedures are avoided, as are significant legal and other costs for the parties involved in such a negotiation. After the finalization of each case and without the urgency imposed by a sale deadline, I produce an academic publication that contains all the evidence as well as detailed information on the development of the case. This publication thus becomes the complete record of the case at the time, correcting any subsequent news reports or market-supportive blogs that have contained inaccuracies or a misleading spin on the case.

Accessing the Archives

Contrary to the norm, these confiscated archives of illicit antiquities are not accessible in their physical (paper) form in a place which can be visited by appointment and with researchers consulting them 'in the flesh'. In fact, due to the legal status of the archives and the criminal and cultural value of their contents, only the confiscating authorities and authorized archaeologists have official access, even to their digitized versions. From 2006 until the present, Pellegrini, Rizzo, and myself are publishing only images of already identified antiquities, in order to enable the authorities to act as well as to inform the public to put pressure on the current owners to return the stolen property to its rightful owners. However, over the years, other groups of people, academics, journalists, and the public, either directly from the relevant authorities or indirectly, have gained complete or partial access to some of the confiscated archives, to both identified and unidentified material, and have published some of their contents. Some of the main examples include:

a. Photographs and documents were openly presented by expert archaeologists while they were testifying at the trials of convicted individuals (e.g. Maurizio Pellegrini and Daniela Rizzo presented many images during the trials of Medici, Hecht, and the former Getty curator of antiquities, Dr Marion True). Those images were reproduced by the press in various countries.

b. In 2000, about 30 per cent of the Medici archive (*c.* 1200 images) was made publicly available and downloadable at the website of the Carabinieri for almost eleven years.[29] The aim was to involve the public in the possible identification of the antiquities depicted in the published images and gain information on their trafficking. During the period that these images were available, many academics and members of the public accessed, researched, and downloaded these images (e.g. Dr Pieter Heesen, expert on Athenian black-figure cups, published: 'Italy, Website Carabinieri' in the index of museums and collections).[30] Nevertheless, very little extra information was received by the Carabinieri that contributed to the development of relevant cases (for a rare example, see Fig. 22.7). Although Giacomo Medici was convicted in Rome in three sequential trials from 2004 to 2011, he succeeded in a separate trial to re-obtain the images confiscated from him in their physical form and on 6 June 2011 the 1200 uploaded images were removed from the Carabinieri website.

c. From 1997 onwards, journalist Mr Peter Watson received copies of all the confiscated archives from the Italian public prosecutor Paolo Giorgio Ferri.[31]

d. In May 2006, journalist Mr Nikolas Zirganos published in a magazine article dozens of images from the confiscated Symes-Michaelides archive.[32] This and other publications also include images of already identified antiquities from the Medici and Becchina archives, contributing to their successful repatriation later on.

e. On the website 'Chasing Aphrodite', maintained by the US journalist Jason Felch (co-author of the *Chasing Aphrodite* book),[33] a separate section called 'Photos' includes images from the Medici archive, presumably originating from the material that was made available by the Carabinieri.

f. In January 2016, Dr Neil Brodie, on his website 'Market of Mass Destruction', reported on the work of Jason Felch and Professor David Gill regarding a ninth-century BC Villanovan hut urn (inventory number 4.021) in the collection of Fordham University Museum of Greek, Etruscan, and Roman Art.[34] Brodie accompanied his post with an image from the confiscated Evangelisti archive, thus demonstrating that he gained access to this archive. He had received a copy from Peter Watson while working together in the Illicit Antiquities Research Centre at the University of Cambridge.[35]

Apart from the above, the truth is that everyone without exception (including members of the market, their clients, the public, etc.) has the right to gain indirect access to the archives through the state authorities, especially the Italian authorities who seem to hold digital copies of the entirety of the archives mentioned. The Carabinieri will respond, albeit on equal terms i.e. only when they are

---

29 I am grateful to Dr Daniela Rizzo and Mr Maurizio Pellegrini for this information and that regarding Figure 22.7.

30 In Heesen 2011, 346; and Dr Pieter Heesen (pers. comm.), expert on Athenian black-figure cups, in March 2022.

31 Mr Peter Watson (pers. comm.) in March 2022.

32 Zirganos 2006.

33 Felch and Frammolino 2011.

34 Brodie 2016.

35 Dr Neil Brodie (pers. comm.) in March 2022.

Figure 22.7. Regular-print image from the Medici archive, depicting an Etruscan bronze statuette of a togatus, broken in pieces and lying on a white piece of paper with a tape measure next to it. It was returned to Italy from a private collection in France, after this image (no. 63265/549, 002) was noticed on the Carabinieri website.

told who is asking for which objects and where these are situated at the time of the request.[36] However, in reality, extremely few market members or clients seem to exercise this right,[37] to check with the authorities the legality and the provenance of the objects they own or intend to sell. Despite the repeated appearance of illicit archaeological material identified in auction houses and dealers' galleries every single year since 2006,[38] the appearance of these cases in newspapers of international circulation,[39] and the continuous repatriations of antiquities depicted in the confiscated archives,[40] the members of the antiquities market continue to offer (at least) unprovenanced material depicted in the same archives.

In addition, they continue to reproduce in public their false argument that since I am not sharing the confiscated archives with them, they do not have the ability to check their objects before their sales take place.[41]

---

36 Tsirogiannis 2015.

37 I am aware only of a single individual, a private collector, who followed my advice and is checking his antiquities collection with the Italian authorities. However, even he continues to acquire objects with no documented provenance, running the risk that at least some of them will later be proven to be illicit or even fakes.

38 e.g. Alberge 2020.

39 e.g. Alberge 2022.

40 e.g. Watson 2019.

41 e.g. Alberge 2019.

In an attempt to further mislead the public, they always avoid stating that they do not bother to check their stock with (at least) the Italian authorities months before they compile their sale catalogues, a step that has become the most basic one in provenance research of antiquities. Christie's are asking for the public release of the confiscated archives, but they themselves are not at all transparent when they are contacted and asked to provide access for academic research to information they hold.[42] Christie's stated: 'We have in the past sent individual queries to the Carabinieri but they have not responded. We are, of course, continuing actively to try to explore this route both with the Greek and Italian authorities as well as through other avenues.'[43] Therefore, the members of the market have the right of access — even indirectly, as everyone else does — to the confiscated archives, but in reality they do not use it or present bad excuses in order not to use it, while at the same time they complain about not having it; ultimately, not using their right of access serves their financial goals.

The market's continuing involvement with illicit antiquities puts its would-be clients in a difficult position. Buyers, too, should exercise due diligence when it comes to the provenance of objects in which they are interested. However, the market's assurances mean that, in practice, buyers (both individuals and institutions) very rarely check with the authorities beyond the information with which they are presented by the seller. The result is that they fall into similarly low ethical standards and run practical risks of losing their objects and the money they spent on them, and receiving negative publicity on an international level; see e.g. Mashberg on the Getty Museum, the San Antonio Museum of Art, the Cleveland Museum of Art and the Museum of Greek, Etruscan, and Roman Art at Fordham University cases,[44] and Mashberg on the Michael Steinhardt case.[45]

Use of the Archives and New Methodologies in Current and Future Academic Projects

Meanwhile, academic research based on the confiscated archives is thriving. Among other examples, the latest confiscation of hundreds of illicit antiquities at the Free

---

42 Tsirogiannis 2013.

43 Gerlis 2015.

44 Mashberg 2021a.

45 Mashberg 2021b.

Port of Geneva and their repatriation to Italy[46] allowed Dr Vinnie Nørskov, associate professor at Aarhus University, to secure a long-term loan of the fragmented Apulian vases included in this trove, once owned by Symes and Michaelides.[47] One of the project's aims is to discover the missing links in the provenance of these fragments, starting with examining the objects themselves and any related material, including newspapers and other paper material used in the 1980s and 1990s for wrapping the fragments. Through this work, the connection of part of this material to Giacomo Medici has been already established, while some of the fragments have been identified in the Becchina archive, verifying that Medici and Becchina were supplying Symes and Michaelides. Ultimately, by discovering further links of the trafficking chain, the project aims to recontextualize at least some of the material, possibly making connections with fragmented material that has been legally excavated in Apulia.[48]

However, since 2014 when I received from the Italian prosecutor Dr Paolo Giorgio Ferri the last digitized copy of the aforementioned archives, I was trying to find a way to help archaeologists and other academic researchers who do not have direct access to these archives, to conduct research in illicit antiquities that would lead to original results. Based on a case I identified in the Christie's 1 October 2015 antiquities auction in London,[49] I developed a new method of proving various issues on illicit antiquities without the use of the images in the confiscated archives.[50] With the help of thirteen volunteers from all over the world, about 63,500 images have been collected from the most 'reputable' auction houses and dealers' galleries with a record of previous involvement in cases of illicit antiquities. Based on provenance research exercised under the lens of the new method, dozens of new cases have been discovered, proving that we have been collectively and continually misled by the members of the antiquities market regarding the true origin of the objects they have sold during the last decade (2011–2020). I am currently preparing the complete publication of the results of this project, which was funded by a three-year fellowship at the Aarhus Institute of Advanced Studies.

The vast number of images collected during this project led to their painstaking manual allocation into different categories, which were created based on the successful way in which I categorized the images in the confiscated archives (see above). At the same time, a need for an automated categorization solution became obvious, and I am currently developing such a tool in collaboration with Dr Ross Deans Kristensen-McLachlan, assistant professor of Cognitive Science and Humanities Computing at Aarhus University and Ms Orla Mallon at the Center for Humanities Computing, also at Aarhus University. We are also developing a separate, but related, algorithmic program, which identifies a single object among numerous images within a database. The success of the categorization solution has reached, via machine learning, 50 per cent accuracy on the images given to it, while the second tool is currently identifying the requested object among the first five images that the program choses from the whole database. We have already identified the ways in which we can improve the performance and the results of both tools, and we will soon apply for funding to develop them further, after a detailed publication submitted by our team appears in a journal on cognitive science and/or humanities computing. These tools are proving valuable for forensic archaeology but also for other, seemingly unrelated or completely unrelated, disciplines where vast amounts of data (hundreds of thousands or even millions of images or other kinds of data) need to be processed quickly and accurately, producing valuable results. Our next goal is the implementation of these tools as a new methodological approach in forthcoming projects related to cultural heritage.

The academic value of the archives confiscated from convicted and notorious dealers is higher than one would have imagined on hearing that they began as products of a police investigation. It is unfortunate for the burgeoning field of archive archaeology that the false impression that their study involves 'mere' detective work continues among non-experts and is deliberately reproduced by those within the academic community who support the antiquities market and its practices. The work of reorganizing the archives and creating a database are just the necessary first step towards tracing and analysing international trafficking networks and patterns of involvement and identifying and pursuing particular themes and potential applications in new projects. A volume such as the present should help further to establish the value of archival archaeology and its manifold wider benefits.

---

[46] Tsirogiannis 2016.

[47] Nørskov 2018.

[48] Van de Ven 2021.

[49] Tsirogiannis 2015, 31–32; Mackenzie and others 2020, 144–46.

[50] Tsirogiannis 2020.

Acknowledgements

Christos Tsirogiannis would like to thank and credit the Aarhus Institute of Advanced Studies (AIAS), Aarhus University, DK-8000 Aarhus, the European Union's Horizon 2020 Research and Innovation Programme under the Marie Skłodowska-Curie grant agreement no. 754513 and the Aarhus University Research Foundation. I am, once again, extremely grateful to Mr Maurizio Pellegrini and Dr Daniela Rizzo for all the information with which they provided me, based on their first-hand experience and their participation in most of the events that led to the discovery of some of the archives. I am equally grateful to the Italian judge Mr Guglielmo Muntoni, for providing me with accurate information about the Giacomo Medici case, being the judge who first convicted Medici in 2004. I would like to thank Professor Rubina Raja and Dr Amy Miranda for inviting me to participate in the conference that resulted in the production of the present volume. I remain most grateful to Dr Helen Van Noorden for her constant copy-editing support and overall help.

Works Cited

Alberge, D. 2019. 'Christie's Urged to Pull Sale of Roman Statue "Linked to Illicit Dealers"', *The Guardian*, 24 November 2022 <https://www.theguardian.com/artanddesign/2019/nov/24/christies-urged-to-pull-sale-of-roman-statue-linked-to-illicit-dealers> [accessed 16 March 2022].

—— 2020. 'Christie's Withdraws "Looted" Greek and Roman Treasures', *The Guardian*, 14 June 2022 <https://www.theguardian.com/culture/2020/jun/14/christies-withdraws-allegedly-looted-greek-and-roman-treasures> [accessed 16 March 2022].

—— 2022. 'Fresco Fragment from Pompeii Reopens Row over "Looted" Artefacts', *The Observer*, 20 March 2022 <https://www.theguardian.com/science/2022/mar/20/getty-museum-fresco-fragment-pompeii-row-looted-artefacts> [accessed 24 March 2022].

Axarlis, N. 2001. 'Corinth Antiquities Returned', *Archaeology*, 6 February 2001 <http://archive.archaeology.org/online/features/corinth/index.html> [accessed 12 February 2023].

Brodie, N. 2012. 'Organigram', *Trafficking Culture*, 21 August 2012 <https://traffickingculture.org/encyclopedia/case-studies/organigram/> [accessed 1 March 2022].

—— 2016. 'The Fordham University Villanovan Hut Urn', *Market of Mass Destruction* website, 27 January 2016 <https://market-massdestruction.com/2016/01/> [accessed 15 March 2022].

Doole, J and N. Brodie. 2000. 'Recent Returns', *Culture without Context*, 7: 15 <https://traffickingculture.org/app/uploads/2012/07/CWC-7.pdf> [accessed 8 February 2022].

Elia, R. 2001. 'Analysis of the Looting, Selling, and Collecting of Apulian Red-Figure Vases: A Quantitative Approach', in N. Brodie, J. Doole, and C. Renfrew (eds), *Trade in Illicit Antiquities: The Destruction of the World's Archaeological Heritage* (Cambridge: McDonald Institute for Archaeological Research), pp. 145–53.

Felch, J. and R. Frammolino. 2011. *Chasing Aphrodite* (Boston: Houghton Mifflin Harcourt).

Gerlis, M. 2015. 'Calls to Open Looted-Art Archives Grow Louder', *The Art Newspaper*, 2 June 2015 <https://www.theartnewspaper.com/2015/06/02/calls-to-open-looted-art-archives-grow-louder> [accessed 16 March 2022].

Gill, D. W. J. 2014. 'Pasta, Swingler, Christie's and the Krater', *Looting Matters*, 5 December 2014 <https://lootingmatters.blogspot.com/2014/12/pasta-swingler-christies-and-krater.html> [accessed 8 February 2022].

Heesen, P. 2011. *Athenian Little-Master Cups* (Amsterdam: Chairebooks).

Independent Online. 2010. 'Italy Recovers €165 Million in Stolen Art, Relices' [sic], 15 January 2010 <https://www.iol.co.za/business-report/economy/italy-recovers-165-million-in-stolen-art-relices-824292> [accessed 8 February 2022].

Mackenzie, S., N. Brodie, D. Yates, and C. Tsirogiannis. 2020. *Trafficking Culture: New Directions in Researching the Global Market in Illicit Antiquities* (London: Routledge).

Mashberg, T. 2020. 'Paolo Giorgio Ferri, Hunter of Looted Antiquities, Dies at 72', *The New York Times*, 20 June 2020 <https://www.nytimes.com/2020/06/20/arts/paolo-giorgio-dead.html> [accessed 7 February 2022].

—— 2021a. 'A Trove of Artifacts Officials Call "Stolen" Are Returned to Italy', *The New York Times*, 15 December 2021 <https://www.nytimes.com/2021/12/15/arts/design/antiquities-repatriated-district-attroney.html> [accessed 8 February 2022].

—— 2021b. 'Michael Steinhardt, Billionaire, Surrenders $70 Million in Stolen Relics', *The New York Times*, 6 December 2021 <https://www.nytimes.com/2021/12/06/arts/design/steinhardt-billionaire-stolen-antiquities.html> [accessed 8 February 2022].

Meyer, K. 1977 [1974]. *The Plundered Past* (New York: Atheneum).

Mödlinger, M. 2018. 'GREECE: Verdict on the Schinoussa Case & Intimidation of Witness', *European Association of Archaeologists (Committee on the Illicit Trade in Cultural Material)*, 1 August 2018 <https://heritage-lost-eaa.com/2018/08/01/greece-verdict-on-the-schinousa-case-intimidation-of-witness/comment-page-1/> [accessed 8 February 2022].

Muntoni, G. 2004. *Sentenza* (Tribunale di Roma). 13 December.

Nørskov, V. 2018. 'Apulian Pottery from the Antiquities Market', *The Museum of Ancient Art, Aarhus University* website, 28 February 2022 <https://antikmuseet.au.dk/en/research/apulian-pottery-from-the-antiquities-market> [accessed 12 February 2023].

Renfrew, A. C. 2010. 'Combating the Illicit Antiquities Trade: Progress and Problems', in J. Papadopoulos and E. Proietti (eds), *International Meeting on Illicit Traffic of Cultural Property* (Rome: Ministero per I Beni a le Attivita Culturali Segretariato Generale), pp. 92–102.

Ruiz, C. 2000. 'Artefacts Smuggled in Spaghetti', *The Art Newspaper*, 1 June.

Tsirogiannis, C. 2013. 'Something Is Confidential in the State of Christie's', *The Journal of Art Crime*, 9: 3–19.

—— 2015. 'Due Diligence? Christie's Antiquities Auction, London, October 2015', *The Journal of Art Crime*, 14: 27–37.

—— 2016. 'Attitudes in Transit: Symes Material from Market to Source', *The Journal of Art Crime*, 15: 79–86.

—— 2020. 'Cultural Heritage Protection: Investigating the Illicit Trade of Antiquities', *Aarhus Institute of Advanced Studies (AIAS) Annual Report*, 2019–2020: 12–13.

Van de Ven, M. H. 2021. 'Research to Recontextualize Looted Antiquities: Red-Figured Pottery in a Genevan Warehouse', *Klinai*, 11 November 2021 <https://klinai.hypotheses.org/2053> [accessed 16 March 2022].

Watson, P. 1997. *Sotheby's: The Inside Story* (New York: Random House).

—— 2019. 'Auction Houses Are Too Careless about Looted Antiquities', *The Times*, 7 March 2019 <https://www.thetimes.co.uk/article/auction-houses-are-too-careless-about-looted-antiquities-g0568f6d9> [accessed 16 March 2022].

Watson, P. and C. Todeschini. 2006. *The Medici Conspiracy* (New York: Public Affairs).

—— 2007. *The Medici Conspiracy*, rev. edn (New York: Public Affairs).

Zirganos, N. 2006. 'Σκάνδαλο Γκετί: Έγκλημα και δικαίωση', *Epsilon*, 21 May.

INDICES

Index of Archives

Athenian Agora Excavations Archives: 354–56

Beazly Archive: 316

Dörner Archive: 5, 181, 184–91

Ingholt Archive: 4, 50, 53, 55, 58–63, 71–72, 75–81, 103, 106, 120–22
International (Digital) Dura-Europos Archive: 3, 33, 39–43

Samarra Archives: 5, 281, 283–98, 301
Sir Arthur Evans Archive: 143–44

Trendal Archive: 6, 312, 316

Index of Databases and Projects

ACOR Digital Archive: 344–51
Agorha (Accès global et organisé aux ressource en histoire de l'art): 317
Arabic Collections Online: 350
ARCHES: 305
ARIADNE Plus: 315, 320
ASCSA Digital Collections: 377–86
Digital Library of the Middle East: 350
FASTI: 315
Feminicon project: 317
International (Digital) Dura-Europos Archive: 19–23
Karanis Housing Project: 159, 173–76
Kerameikos Database: 316–17
LASIMOS project: 317
MédiHAL: 11–12
MOSYS–3D Project: 303–04
National Geoportal for Archaeology (GNA): 313
Palmyra Portrait Project: 49–50, 53–55, 58, 62, 66, 75, 99–100, 104
Peirene Valley Project: 387
Petra Church Project: 346
Pompeii Artistic Landscape Project: 4, 137–39, 152
Pompeii Bibliography and Mapping Project: 4, 127, 129, 137–39
Russian project/Palmyra 3D/ Palmyra GIS/ Palmyra in Time and Space: 14–16
URU Fayum Project: 171
US Epigraphy Project: 387
World Heritage Database: 2, 10, 12–16

Index of Names

Beazley, John Davidson: 311, 316
Bellinger, Alfred: 23
Bey, Halil Edhem: 283
Bonucci, Carlo: 131
von Bothmer, Dietrich: 337
Brödner, Erica: 189

Cassas, Louis-Francois: 49, 73
Christensen, Charles: 197–98
Crowfoot, Dorothy: 5, 213, 217–18, 225, 235, 239, 241
Crowfoot, Elizabeth: 213
Crowfoot, Grace Mary: 5, 213, 216, 218, 225, 235, 239, 241
Crowfoot, John Winter: 213, 216, 239
Cumont, Franz: 35

Dawkins, James: 15, 49, 73
De Santis, Agostino: 327, 329
Doll, Christian: 145
Dörner, Friedrich Karl: 5, 181–91

Erdmann, Kurt: 285–87
Evans, Arthur: 4, 143–50, 153–56
Evas, Joan: 143

Falconer, H.: 163
Fiorelli, Guiseppe: 128, 131, 133–35, 139, 326
Fisher, Clarence: 217
Freiin von Freytag-Löringhoff, Bettina: 189
Fugmann, Ejnar: 196, 200, 204, 209
Fyfe, Theodore: 145

Gaetano Gallo, Marquis: 325–26
Gute, Herbert: 241
Guy, Philip L. O.: 196
Guyer, Samuel: 295

Hamilton, Gavin: 73
Hamilton, William: 217, 311
Herzfeld: 282–89, 291, 293–94, 302–03, 305
Hill, Bert Hodge: 380, 387
Hopkins, Clark: 20, 27, 218
Hopkins, Susan: 216–17

Hornemann, Bodil: 196, 202
Horsfield, George: 213, 219
Husselman, Elinor M.: 163, 168

Ingholt, Harald: 3-4, 49-53, 55-66, 71-72, 74-82, 99-124, 194, 196-97, 198-204, 206-09, 349

Jacobsen, Carl: 47-48, 100
Jensen, Frode: 196, 198
Johnson, Jotham: 26-27, 30
Jones, Arnold H. M.: 217

Kelsey, Francis W: 170
Kenyon, Kathleen: 200, 217
Kosmopoulos, George: 375
Kühnel, Ernst: 287

Le Berre, Marc: 197
Lucius, E.: 186, 190

Mackenzie, Duncan: 143-45, 154
Mau, August: 135
Mazois, François: 131

Northedge, Alastair: 286-87
Nowothnig, W.: 184-87, 190

Østrup, Johannes Elith: 48, 73-74, 100

Perkins, Ann: 20-23
Peterson, Enoch: 161, 163, 166, 168, 173
Petrie, Flinders: 160
Pillet, Maurice: 27-31
Piranesi, Francesco: 131
Ploug, Gunhild: 58, 61, 76, 80
Porter, Barbara A.: 345, 350
Poulsen, Frederik: 51, 331

Reich, Ignaz: 217
Riis, Poul Jørgen: 194, 196, 205, 207, 209
Roesch, K.: 184-87
Rohweder, Jørgen: 197
Rostovtzeff, Mikhail: 20, 35

Saint-Non, Jean Claude Richard de: 131
Saladini, D. Abramo: 324
Santangelo, Nicola: 325
Sarre, Friedrich: 282-83, 285, 293
Schack Elo, Mathilius: 197
Schlumberger, Daniel: 11
Schwertheim, Elmar: 186
Seetzen, Japser Ulrich: 213
Serra, Luigi: 324
Spinelli, Domenica: 131
Stoop, Maria W.: 327, 331-33
Swain, George R.: 170

Talcott, Lucy: 355
Tchalenko, Georges: 197
Temple, William: 315
Terentieff, J.: 163, 197, 204
Trendall, Arthur Dale: 312, 316

Vincent, Père Loius-Hugues: 218
Viollet, Henri: 283

Wheeler, Mortimer: 200
Williams II, Charles K.: 377
Winkelmann, Wilhelm: 184-85, 189
Wisner Bacon, Benjamin: 213
Wood, Robert: 15, 49, 73

Yeivin, Shmuel: 163, 166

Zancani Montuoro, Paola: 327

Index of Places

Apulia: 311, 317-18, 411, 417
Area Rovitti: 326-27
Athens: 6, 143, 353-68, 411

Corinth: 6, 318, 371-91

Damascus: 13, 36
Dura-Europos: 3, 11, 19-31, 33-45, 190, 217, 241

Eski Kâhta: 5, 181-91
Eski Kale: 184, 189

Francavilla Marittima: 324-25, 335

Geneva: 311, 324, 410-11, 417
Gerash: 5, 213-78

Hama: 5, 50, 52, 75, 101, 193-209

Isthmia: 7, 128, 395-406

Jebel Bal'as: 11
Jericho: 200

Karanis: 159-78
Kerameikos: 317-18
Knossos: 4, 143-56

Megiddo: 196-97

Palmyra: 2-4, 9-16, 30, 47-66, 71-83, 99-124, 196-97, 343, 348-49
Petra: 343, 346
Pompeii: 4, 127-40, 152

Rome: 73, 80, 317-18

Samarra: 5, 281-99, 301-08
Soknopaiou Nesos: 169

Tell Sailun/Shiloh: 196
Tell Sukas: 196
Terenouthis: 169
Timpone della Motta: 6, 323-39

Verulamium: 200

Yeni Kale: 184

Index of Museums

Agricultural Museum, Cairo: 170
Archaeological Museum of Ancient Corinth, Corinth: 371
Arthur M. Sackler Gallery, Washington: 302
Ashmolean Museum, Oxford: 4, 53, 143-53, 156, 241
British Museum, London: 53, 151, 283, 288, 311, 315-16
Cairo Museum, Cairo: 163, 170, 283
Coptic Museum, Cairo: 170
Freer Art Gallery, Washington: 284
Freer Gallery of Art, Washington: 293, 302
Iraq Museum, Baghdad: 304-05
İstanbul Arkeoloji Müzeleri, Istanbul: 47, 57
J. P. Getty Museum, Los Angeles: 331
Kelsey Museum of Archaeology, Michigan: 163, 165, 169-70, 176-77
Michael C. Carlos Museum, Atlanta: 333, 337
Musée du Louvre, Paris: 47, 53, 283, 302, 315, 317
Musei Vaticani, Rome: 53
Museo Archeologico Nazionale di Napoli, Napoli: 325
Museo Archeologico Nazionale del Vulture e Melfese, Melfi: 410
Museo Civico Archeologico di Castrovillari, Castrovillari: 326, 329--30
Museo Civico di Foggia, Foggia: 316
Museo Civico die Bretti e degli Enotri di Cosenza, Cosenza: 326-27
Museo di Scultura Antica Giovanni Barracco, Rome: 53
Museum für Islamische Kunst, Berlin: 5, 281-82, 284-98, 301, 303
Metropolitan Museum of Art, New York: 53, 284, 288, 291, 296, 315, 337
National Museum of Athens, Athens: 170
National Museum of Denmark, Copenhagen: 5, 53, 193-94, 202, 205-09
Ny Carlsberg Glyptotek, Copenhagen: 4, 47, 49, 51, 53, 58, 61-63, 74-77, 79-80, 99, 101, 103-04, 205, 331
Princeton University Art Museum, Princeton: 333, 337
State Hermitage Museum, St Petersburg: 14
Victoria and Albert Museum, London: 288, 302, 305
Yale University Art Gallery, New Haven: 5, 19, 33, 40, 53, 190, 213, 218, 225
Zentralarchiv der Staatlichen Museen zu Berlin, Berlin: 285

General Index

3D digitization: 5, 302–08
3D documentation: 301
3D modelling: 13–14, 123, 152, 154–56, 318–20, 357, 364–68
3D replicas: 304, 308
3D scanning: 303

Absence: *see* Lacuna
Accessibility: 1–6, 10–16, 19, 25, 31, 33, 35–38, 50, 53, 55, 58, 72, 77, 79–83, 106, 130, 138, 145, 148, 156, 159, 161, 173, 177, 185, 193, 209, 290–91, 298, 306, 308, 312–16, 320, 345, 347, 350, 355–56, 364, 366, 371, 385–86, 388, 390, 395, 413, 415
Actor-Network-Theory: 82
Aerial photography: 6, 318, 399
Archaeological Data Management Systems (ADMS): 5, 305–07
Archaeological Information System (AIS): 318
Archaeological Resource Cataloging System: 174
Art Dealers: 7, 47–48, 54, 58, 311, 323–24, 330, 332, 409, 411–13, 416–17
Auction Houses: 47, 54, 58, 77, 317, 330, 409, 411, 416–17

Banqueting tesserae: 4, 79, 100, 103
Bias: 2, 9, 11–12, 33, 37, 159–60, 173, 207, 306–07, 367–68
Big data: 3, 25, 159, 178, 301, 305, 307, 315, 354
Blue prints: 287, 290–91, 293, 296, 298, 357
British Protectorate of Transjordan: 13
Bronze objects: 134, 323, 334, 336–37, 373, 410

Ceramics: *see* pottery
Churches: 213–50, 346
Clearing: 21, 28, 131, 159, 161, 213, 364
Coins: 7, 103, 129, 151, 169–71, 173, 175, 177, 181, 190–91, 217, 355, 360, 377–78, 383, 387, 390, 399, 401
Collectors: 54, 58, 74, 100–01, 216, 323, 413
Colonialism: 2–4, 9–16, 25–26, 31, 33, 35, 38, 40, 43, 45, 71–74, 77–81, 83, 101, 304–05, 312, 367
Community archaeology: *see* community engagement
Community engagement: 7, 16, 349–50, 371
Conflict zones: 2, 9–10, 71, 74, 81, 83, 344
Cultural Heritage: 2–4, 6–7, 9, 12, 15–16, 36, 38, 49, 58, 61, 72, 74, 78–81, 151, 159, 178, 206, 301–03, 305, 313, 316, 320, 343–44, 351, 373–74, 417
Cuneiform tablets: 207

Da'esh: 9, 16, 72, 74, 77, 80–81
Databases: *see* Index of Databases
Diaries: 144–45, 411. *See also* excavation diaries
Digital colonialism: 2–4, 10–11, 14, 71–72, 77, 80, 82, 304
Digital humanities: 1, 4, 127, 349, 367
Digitization: 1, 3, 5–7, 19, 23, 25, 35, 53, 77, 79, 81, 143–50, 153, 155–56, 178, 209, 281, 289–91, 298–99, 301–08, 311–13, 316, 319, 344–47, 349, 351, 356, 371, 377, 386, 388, 390, 412
Drawings: 4–5, 7, 11, 21, 37, 40, 49, 73, 78–79, 103, 124, 128, 143, 145–55, 161, 165, 181, 184, 187, 190, 194, 202, 204, 213, 216–39, 241–47, 249–50, 283–85, 288, 291, 293, 319, 332, 354, 359–60, 361, 371, 377–78, 381, 399
Drones: 10, 12, 15, 387, 397

Excavation diaries: 1, 4, 49, 62–66, 72, 75, 77, 79, 82, 99–124, 159, 171, 194, 201–02, 204–09, 283–84, 295, 343, 353–54, 356, 362–63, 366–68, 371, 375, 377, 383, 399
Excavation methodology/techniques/process/practices: 4, 66, 100, 124, 133, 159, 161, 173, 198, 290, 371, 378, 380, 383
Excavation notebooks: *See* excavation diaries

FAIR Principles: 316, 320
Field diaries: *see* excavation diaries
Fieldwork: *see* excavation
Figurines: 169, 323, 330, 335, 337–38
French Mandate: 3–4, 11, 20, 49, 74–75, 77–79, 99, 101

Geographic Information Systems (GIS): 7, 14–15, 153, 160–61, 174–75, 177, 179, 209, 312–13, 318, 367, 395–406
Glass negatives/ glass plates: 146, 285, 287, 289, 291, 293–95
Glass objects: 134, 173, 217, 239, 241, 282, 302, 335
Globalization: 80
GPS: 380, 396–97

Heritage Preservation: 61, 74, 77, 81, 343

Illicit antiquities: 6–7, 318, 409–17
Illicit excavations: 6, 103, 311, 319, 323, 327–32, 335, 337–39, 409
Illicit trade: 6, 77, 47, 77, 324
Inscriptions: 4, 11–12, 21, 23, 30–31, 43, 54–57, 61–62, 65, 71–72, 77–78, 80, 99, 102–03, 106, 112–14, 116, 118–19, 123–24, 131, 134, 183, 185, 195, 213, 219–20, 294–95, 387, 390, 401, 405
Ivory objects: 323, 335

Knowledge control: 10, 12, 16

Lacuna: 6–7, 26, 31, 50, 114, 128, 168, 187, 327, 338, 358, 390, 398, 406
Letters: 21, 30, 48, 54, 76, 106, 147, 148, 165, 181, 184–87, 189–91, 194, 198, 241, 285, 293, 324, 326, 410
Linked open data (LOD): 37–40, 45, 150–52, 156, 176, 305, 387, 390
Local communities/stakeholders: 7, 13, 35, 39, 43, 77, 79, 101, 103, 181, 191, 371, 374, 388–91, 390–91, 400
Local workers / Local labour: 23, 25–27, 31, 193, 198, 203, 298, 328, 375
Looting: 6–7, 47, 48–49, 62, 73–74, 77, 282, 284, 304, 311, 315, 318–21, 409, 411, 413. *See also* illicit excavations

Metadata: 12–13, 15, 19, 23, 33, 35–45, 140, 146, 160, 174–75, 177, 289, 290, 305, 347–51, 381
Mosaics: 5, 56, 134, 138, 154, 181, 183, 189–91, 213–50, 346

Natural Language Processing: 306

Object biographies: 6–7, 62, 66, 290
Object-Oriented Ontology: 82
Open access: 1, 3, 7, 33, 36, 50, 72, 77, 301–02, 313, 318, 343, 349, 390, 395
Ottoman Empire: 47–49, 77–79, 144, 282–83
Outreach: 298, 347, 349, 371, 375, 378, 385, 388

Papyri: 27, 160–61, 163, 165, 168–73, 176–77, 346
Photogrammetry: 15, 302, 387
Photography: 6, 11–12, 21, 23, 26–27, 30, 35, 37, 40, 43, 71, 76, 122, 147–48, 145, 190, 200, 235, 241, 283, 286, 290, 298, 318, 350–51, 371, 381, 387, 413
PostgreSQL: 159, 161
Pottery: 6, 128–29, 146, 161, 169–71, 175–76, 178, 181, 186, 190–91, 201, 204, 282, 302, 311–12, 315–21, 323, 326–27, 329, 332, 335–38, 354, 362, 373, 386, 401, 405
Provenance: 1, 6, 20, 35, 47, 71, 77, 140, 162, 290, 293, 298, 311–12, 315, 320, 323, 331, 337, 380–81, 409, 412–13, 416–17
Public engagement: 16, 308, 368, 374

QGIS: 402

Reconstruction: 2, 9–10, 13, 16, 110, 123, 145, 148, 150–52, 155, 197, 206, 282, 284, 303–04, 319–20, 332, 357, 359, 364, 405
Recontextualization: 6, 78, 291–93, 311, 319, 329, 331, 335–39, 361, 413, 417
Reparation: 2, 305
Repatriation: 5, 148, 156, 301, 304–05, 308, 324, 331–33, 335–39, 413–17
Replica: 12, 81, 148, 303–04, 308, 319

Sculpture: 48–51, 53–62, 66, 71–73, 75–81, 101, 103, 106, 114, 119, 121, 134, 138, 197, 203–06, 375, 414
Silver objects: 136, 335
Sketchbooks: 284–85, 293, 299
Slag: 184, 189
Standardization: 55, 191, 302, 306–07
Stratigraphy: 125, 128–29, 189, 200, 209, 326, 359, 383, 398–400, 404–06
Stucco: 282–84, 287, 289, 291, 293, 302–03

Tagging: 307–08, 368
Terracotta: 134, 202, 323, 325–26, 330, 335–38
Tesserae: 218–19, 221, 239
Tombs: 4, 15, 18, 51, 56, 58, 62–66, 72–73, 75, 77–78, 99–124, 135, 143, 166, 196, 282, 319–20, 405
Topography: 131, 136, 163, 318

UNESCO: 11, 13–14, 16, 77
UNESCO Convention: 7, 77
UNESCO World Heritage Site: 148, 282

Virtual Reality: 304, 364, 366
Visualization: 177, 303–04, 317, 355, 404
Votive objects: 321, 330–31, 333, 336–35, 338

Wall paintings: 56, 73, 100, 138, 241, 282–85, 291, 302
Watercolours: 209, 218, 284–85, 288, 291, 381
Wikidata: 3, 37, 39–45, 150, 349

Archive Archaeology

All volumes in this series are evaluated by an Editorial Board, strictly on academic grounds, based on reports prepared by referees who have been commissioned by virtue of their specialism in the appropriate field. The Board ensures that the screening is done independently and without conflicts of interest. The definitive texts supplied by authors are also subject to review by the Board before being approved for publication. Further, the volumes are copyedited to conform to the publisher's stylebook and to the best international academic standards in the field.

Titles in Series

Johannes Østrup, *Shifting Horizons: Observations from a Ride Through the Syrian Desert and Asia Minor. A Translation of Johannes Elith Østrup's 'Skiftende horizonter'*, trans. by Cisca Spencer (2022)

The Ingholt Archive: The Palmyrene Material, Transcribed with Commentary and Bibliography, ed. by Olympia Bobou, Amy C. Miranda, Rubina Raja, and Jean-Baptise Yon (4 vols) (2022)

Archival Historiographies: The Impact of Twentieth-Century Legacy Data on Archaeological Investigations, ed. by Olympia Bobou, Amy C. Miranda, and Rubina Raja (2022)